PROGRAM EVALUATION

PROGRAM EVALUATION

An Introduction

FOURTH EDITION

DAVID ROYSE
University of Kentucky

BRUCE A. THYER
Florida State University

DEBORAH K. PADGETT
New York University

TK LOGAN
University of Kentucky

BROOKS/COLE
CENGAGE Learning™

Australia • Brazil • Japan • Korea • Mexico • Singapore • Spain • United Kingdom • United States

BROOKS/COLE
CENGAGE Learning™

Program Evaluation:
An Introduction,
Fourth Edition
David Royse, Bruce A. Thyer,
Deborah K. Padgett,
TK Logan

Executive Editor: Lisa Gebo

Assistant Editor:
Alma Dea Michelena

Editorial Assistant:
Sheila Walsh

Technology Project Manager:
Barry Connolly

Executive Marketing
Manager: Carolina Concilla

Senior Marketing
Communications Manager:
Tami Strang

Project Manager, Editorial
Production: Rita Jaramillo

Art Director: Vernon Boes

Print Buyer: Lisa Claudeanos

Permissions Editor:
Sarah Harkrader

Production Service:
Sara Dovre Wudali, Buuji, Inc.

Copy Editor: Cheryl Hauser

Cover Designer: Lisa Berman

Cover Image: Artville

Compositor: International
Typesetting and Composition

For product information and
technology assistance, contact us at
Cengage Learning Customer & Sales Support,
1-800-354-9706

For permission to use material from this text or product,
submit all requests online at **cengage.com/permissions**
Further permissions questions can be e-mailed to
permissionrequest@cengage.com

Library of Congress Control Number: 2004116026

ISBN-13: 978-0-534-50827-2

ISBN-10: 0-534-50827-8

Brooks/Cole
10 Davis Drive
Belmont, CA 94002-3098
USA

Cengage Learning is a leading provider of customized
learning solutions with office locations around the globe,
including Singapore, the United Kingdom, Australia, Mexico,
Brazil, and Japan. Locate your local office at:
international.cengage.com/region

Cengage Learning products are represented in Canada by
Nelson Education, Ltd.

For your course and learning solutions, visit
academic.cengage.com

Purchase any of our products at your local college store or at
our preferred online store **www.ichapters.com**

Printed in the United States
4 5 6 7 8 11 10 09 08

CONTENTS

Preface   xi

CHAPTER 1
Introduction   1

The Importance of Program Evaluation   1
What Is a Program?   5
Characteristics of "Good" Programs   5
Program Evaluation Defined   11
Reasons Why Programs Are Evaluated   12
Motivations for Program Evaluation   13
Overcoming the Subjective Perspective   17
Philosophical Assumptions of Program Evaluation   21
More on Positivism   26
Chapter Recap   28

CHAPTER 2
Ethical Issues in Program Evaluation   33

Historical Background: Why IRBs Are Necessary   33
Ethical Guidelines   34

How Ethical Guidelines Get Operationalized   40

Research with Special Populations   43

Potential Problems in Conducting Ethical Research   44

The Practitioner's Ethical Responsibilities   47

Chapter Recap   50

CHAPTER 3

Needs Assessment   53

What Is Needs Assessment?   53

The Need for Needs Assessment   54

Definitions of Need   55

Planning a Needs Assessment   57

Selecting a Needs Assessment Approach   62

Convergent Analysis and Multimethod Approaches   72

Thinking Creatively about Needs Assessment   75

Community Readiness   80

CHAPTER 4

Qualitative Methods in Evaluation   87

Introduction   87

What Is "Qualitative Evaluation"?   88

When Is Qualitative Evaluation Useful?   89

Qualitative Methods and Single System Evaluation   91

Variants in Qualitative Evaluation   91

Methods of Qualitative Evaluation   94

Managing and Organizing Qualitative Data   102

Data Analysis   102

Quality Control   105

Writing the Report   106

An Important Final Step: Dissemination
    and Advocacy   108

Examples of Qualitative Evaluations   108

CHAPTER 5
Formative and Process Evaluation   116

Formative Evaluation   116
Conducting a Formative Evaluation   118
Other Uses of Formative Evaluation   122
Process Evaluation   124
Program Description   125
Program Monitoring   130
Becoming a Program Monitor   131
Mission Statements, Goals, and Objectives   133
Writing Program Objectives   138
Hierarchy of Goals, Objectives, and Activities   140
What Should Be Monitored?   141
Quality Assurance   147
Total Quality Management   150
Chapter Recap   153

CHAPTER 6
Single System Research Designs   161

What Are Single System Research Designs?   161
Selecting Outcome Measures   163
Assessing Measures over Time   165
Needs Assessments   166
Notation and General Principles   167
Formative Evaluations   169
Quality Assurance Studies   173
Summative Evaluation Designs   175
Experimental Designs   177
External Validity   184
Inferential Statistics   185
How to Prepare Graphs   187
Ethics of Single System Research Designs   188
Chapter Recap   190

CHAPTER 7
Goal Attainment Scaling   194

Introductory Scenario   194
What Is Goal Attainment Scaling?   195
Illustration of Goal Attainment Scaling   198
Goal Attainment Scaling and Program Evaluation   199
Variations of Goal Attainment Scaling   201
Problems with Goal Attainment Scaling   202

CHAPTER 8
Client Satisfaction   207

The Importance of Monitoring Consumer Satisfaction   207
The Problem with Client Satisfaction Studies   209
A Sampling of Recent Client Satisfaction Studies   212
Annotations about Client Satisfaction   212
Explanations for High Ratings   215
Recommendations for Client Satisfaction Studies   216
Determining Sample Size   222

CHAPTER 9
Group Research Designs   231

What Are Group Research Designs?   231
Starting an Outcome Evaluation   232
Outcome Evaluation Designs   234
General Principles of Group Research Designs   236
Pre-Experimental Research Designs   237
Quasi-Experimental Research Designs   248
Threats to the Internal Validity   254
Protection against Alternative Explanations   257
Experimental Designs   258
Efficacy and Effectiveness Studies   265
A Note on the Term *Experiment*   266
Chapter Recap   267

CHAPTER 10
Cost-Effectiveness and Cost Analysis Designs   274

Cost as an Evaluative Criterion   274
Example of a Cost-Effectiveness Evaluation   276
How to Do a Cost-Effectiveness Study   277
Whose Point of View?   279
Cost-Benefit Analysis   281
Chapter Recap   285

CHAPTER 11
Measurement Tools and Strategies   290

Importance of Measurement   290
Deciding What to Measure   292
Reliability   295
Validity   302
Locating Appropriate Instruments   306
Constructing "Good" Evaluation Instruments   308
Levels of Measurement   316

CHAPTER 12
Illustrations of Instruments   323

Child Abuse Potential Inventory   324
Clinical Anxiety Scale   327
CES-D Scale   329
The Hope Scale   331
Rosenberg Self-Esteem Scale   333
Adult-Adolescent Parenting Inventory   335

CHAPTER 13
Data Analysis   339

What Does It Mean to Analyze Data?   339
Data Analysis and the Computer   340

Univariate Analysis   341
Bivariate Analysis   348
Multivariate Analysis   358
Myths about Statistical Significance   359
Understanding Trends   361
Using Statistics in Reports   364
Type I and Type II Errors   365

CHAPTER 14
Pragmatic Issues   371

Treatment Fidelity   371
Fidelity Nightmares   373
Program Drift and the Transfer of Programs   377
Political Nature of Evaluation   378
"Threat" of Evaluation   381
Guidelines for Evaluation in Politically
   Charged Arenas   383
Culturally Sensitive Evaluation Practice   386

CHAPTER 15
**Writing Evaluation Proposals, Reports,
and Journal Articles   394**

Components of the Evaluation Proposal and Report   395
Mistakes to Avoid in Planning and Writing
   Evaluation Reports   404
Checklist for Writing and Assessing Evaluation Reports   409
The Utilization of Evaluation Reports   410
Writing for Professional Publication   412

Index   417

PREFACE

Program Evaluation: An Introduction is designed, first and foremost, as a primary textbook for graduate students in social work, sociology, psychology, public administration, counseling, education, and other related disciplines. It may also be used as a supplemental textbook in research methodology classes. Another targeted group consists of practitioners, administrators, and persons who have just acquired or are about to assume responsibility for overseeing or evaluating a specific program. Because our focus is on communicating the *essentials,* that is, providing the basic tools and knowledge necessary to understand the tasks associated with examining and appraising program performance, we believe that even those who have been out of the classroom a number of years will not be intimidated or threatened by our presentation. As educators, we have learned that sometimes a down-to-earth example is more valuable than too much explanation, that it is easier to grasp a concept if the reader is not inundated with all the author knows about a topic.

Further, we understand that most of our readers probably do not, at this moment, see themselves earning their living by becoming program evaluators. Many readers may not feel passionate about the topic or even perceive that research and evaluation can be interesting. If this describes you, be forewarned that we hope to change your mind. We feel strongly that conducting program evaluation can be very rewarding. On a personal level, it can be exciting, challenging, and intellectually stimulating. Program evaluation also benefits society and helps practitioners, whatever the problem or specialty, to practice more effectively. Best of all, it *is* possible to earn a living—to be reasonably well paid—for making these contributions.

In this era of greater and greater information flow and accountability, program evaluation skills are not only needed, but necessary. Even if you do not wish to be employed full time as an evaluator, we believe that a critical appreciation of the concepts and methods explained in this book will ultimately assist you in providing better services to clients and in becoming a good manager of the resources affiliated with those services.

The trend toward evidence-based practice (EBP) has emerged as a dominant theme in many areas of health and human services. Fueled by risk reduction concerns and limitations imposed by insurance carriers and other sources of reimbursement, there has been a drive toward identifying and providing only interventions that have been shown empirically to be successful. EBP requires careful data collection and a knowledge of research design and other topics covered in our book. This book supports the movement toward evidence-based practice and prepares human services staff to understand as well as to develop scientific evidence of effectiveness for their areas of practice.

In this fourth edition we have added new examples and illustrations to several chapters and slightly expanded others with new topics. The attempt has been not to dramatically make over, but rather to fine-tune and refine our explanations. The goal has been one of continued incremental improvement—to present the basic structure of program evaluation methodology in an interesting to read and digestible format for graduate students and professionals wanting a refresher or introduction to the subject. We hope you will enjoy this experience! And if you don't, please write to one of us with suggestions as to how we might improve the textbook in the next revision.

INTRODUCTION

CHAPTER I

THE IMPORTANCE OF PROGRAM EVALUATION

Welcome to the field of program evaluation, that aspect of professional training aimed at helping you to integrate research and practice skills, using the former to enhance the latter. We recognize that relatively few practitioners in the human services of social work, psychology, counseling, education, public administration, and nursing will have careers devoted to scientific research. However, everyone in those fields will be concerned with providing services to clients at some level (individuals, families, couples, small groups, organizations, or communities), and *every* human services practitioner will be intensely interested in learning whether the services provided really do help the clients they are intended to serve. Thus, even if research may not be your cup of tea, evaluating services and programs using scientifically credible research tools is a professional skill that you will find valuable. And apart from possibly being involved in the design and conduct of program evaluations yourself, you will read and critically analyze evaluation studies conducted by others and published in disciplinary journals and books. Your ability to judge the value of published and unpublished program evaluations is another valuable skill to enhance. Otherwise, how will you be able to decide what types of services are worth providing to clients?

In the human services field, scientific research can be broadly classified into having three main (often interrelated) purposes: to objectively describe things; to empirically evaluate the effectiveness of services; or to validly explain things. Descriptive research can be undertaken to better understand the characteristics or needs of clients of a particular agency. Evaluative research helps determine whether these needs are being met or clients' goals attained, while explanatory studies aim at uncovering the *causes* of psychosocial problems or the *processes* by which interventions work (thus contributing to what is known respectively as etiological or interventive theory).

Program evaluation can be seen as a subset of those activities labeled **research,** which itself has been simply defined as "systematic procedures used in seeking facts or principles" (Barker, 2003, p. 368). **Evaluation research** refers to "systematic investigation to determine the success of a specific program" (Barker, 2003, p. 149). **Program evaluation** is a practical endeavor, not an academic exercise, and is not primarily an attempt to build theory or necessarily to develop social science knowledge (although it is wonderful when that happens). Tripodi (1987) has noted, in the *Encyclopedia of Social Work,* that "the mission of program evaluation in social work is to provide information that can be used to improve social programs" (p. 366).

Curiously, although for many decades the singularly crucial importance of human services professionals designing and conducting program evaluations has been widely recognized, program evaluation research remains rarely undertaken. Rosen, Proctor, and Staudt (1999) reviewed all articles ($N = 1,849$) published in 13 major social work journals from 1993 to mid-1997. Of these, only 863 (47 percent) were research articles. Of these 863 research articles, 314 were descriptive studies, 423 were explanatory ones, and only 126 involved evaluation (e.g., outcome) studies of some type. Overall, program evaluation articles with replicable interventions represented only 3 percent of all published social work articles! Consider this fact in light of the quotations contained in Box 1.1.

Currently, we have the very odd situation that although many authorities consider program evaluation to be perhaps the most valuable type of research contribution one can make, such studies seem to be very rarely undertaken and published. Instead, most studies have a focus on descriptive and explanatory research work, which, at best, may have potential *implications* for practice in the human services, not the potential for direct *applications* that a well-crafted outcome study would possess.

Why is it necessary to evaluate established services? Because there are always alternative, and sometimes *better,* ways to solve problems. For instance, consider an article entitled "Time-Limited Therapy in University Counseling Centers: Do Time-Limited and Time-Unlimited Centers Differ?" (Gyorky, Royalty, & Johnson, 1994). The authors found that counseling centers with time limits had longer waiting lists and served a smaller percentage of the student body than did centers with no limits on counseling duration. Now, if you were in charge of a university counseling center, would you want to read this article? Would it be important to understand the authors' methodology and sample?

BOX I.I	OPINIONS ON THE IMPORTANCE OF EVALUATION RESEARCH

I appeal to you. . . . Measure, evaluate, estimate, appraise your results, in some form, in any terms that rest upon something beyond faith, assertion, and "illustrative case." State your objectives and how far you have reached them. . . . Out of such evaluations will come, I believe, better service to the client. (Cabot, 1931)

The third type of research, evaluative studies of welfare programs and the activities of practitioners, are the most important of all. (Angell, 1954, p. 169)

[S]ocial work is not a science whose aim is to derive knowledge; it is a technology whose aim is to apply knowledge for the purpose of control. Therefore, on the research continuum social work research falls nearer to the applied end, because its purpose of practical knowledge. (Greenwood, 1957, p. 315)

Evaluation and client feedback are not only necessary for effective service delivery, but are an ethical requirement of the profession. Systematic methods must be developed to assess whether social workers are helping, harming, or doing nothing for the people they serve. (Rosenberg & Brody, 1974, p. 349)

Social work has no more important use of research methods than assessment of the consequences of practice and policy choices. . . . [S]mall scale, agency based studies are worthwhile if they succeed in placing interest in effectiveness at the center of agency practice and when they create a critical alliance between practitioners and researchers. (Mullen, 1995, pp. 282–283)

Studies are needed on the effectiveness of psychosocial intervention, including interventions previously tested under ideal controlled conditions, in real-world health care systems. (Ell, 1996, p. 589)

Research on actual service interventions is the critical element in connecting research to the knowledge base used by professional practitioners. . . . [T]he issue now is one of developing investigations of social work intervention initiatives, studies that go beyond descriptions and explanatory research. (Austin, 1998, pp. 17, 43)

We need to establish a research agenda for social work. . . . And intervention studies must be high in priority to such an agenda. (Rosen, Proctor, & Staudt, 1999, p. 9).

As another example, take a study authored by several behavioral scientists and social workers (Lynam et al., 1999). These authors evaluated a widely used drug abuse prevention program (known as Project DARE) by following up (10 years later) with over 1,000 fifth graders who had received either Project DARE (in 23 different schools) or a less structured drug education program (provided in 8 different schools). The schools were randomly assigned to provide DARE (17 one-hour sessions over 17 weeks, taught by police officers) or health education training (weekly 30 to 45 minute sessions over 2 to 4 weeks, taught by health educators). Ten years after training, there were no differences, as assessed by marijuana use, variety of illicit drugs used, or self-esteem, between the kids who received Project DARE versus the comparison health education training.

Suppose you were a school counselor and assigned the task of choosing a drug abuse prevention program for your school to provide. Given the much higher costs of the DARE program, relative to the less expensive (in terms of time and money) health education training; the failure by Lynam et al. (1999) to find a superior long-term effect of DARE; and prior evaluation studies indicating that DARE has no long-term effect on drug use (e.g., Dukes, Ullman, & Stein, 1996), would you try to obtain Project DARE for your school? Common sense suggests no, until such time as DARE develops a stronger empirical research base. But should you make a decision without looking at the studies yourself? Probably not.

Suppose you are asked to help provide mental health counseling services to women who experience posttraumatic stress disorder (PTSD) following a sexual assault. What should you do to help these clients? An evaluation study of therapy provided by social workers and psychologists conducted by Foa, Rothbaum, Riggs, and Murdock (1992) would be relevant in helping you decide what services to offer. Forty-five female rape victims who suffered from PTSD as a consequence of being sexually assaulted were randomly assigned to receive cognitive-behavioral therapy, supportive counseling, or to a wait-list condition. At three and one-half months after treatment, the cognitive-behavioral therapies were considerably more beneficial in helping the women overcome PTSD symptoms than supportive counseling or the passage of time alone (wait-list condition). Moreover, a second study with a much larger sample size ($N = 96$) recently replicated the finding that cognitive-behavioral therapy was superior to no treatment (Foa et al., 1999).

Evaluation studies such as these should have a very important bearing on your decision about choosing therapeutic services for clients. Empirical research is certainly not the *only* consideration in adopting treatment models, but we do view it as an *essential* one. Here is one other compelling study (Weiss, Catron, Harris, & Phung, 1999). One hundred and sixty children referred for mental health treatment were randomly assigned to conventional child psychotherapy as provided in community mental health clinics by clinical social workers, psychologists, or nurses *or* to academic tutoring by graduate students or elementary school teachers. Psychotherapy lasted an average of 60 sessions, while the tutoring lasted about 53 sessions, each over about 2 years. A number of reliable and valid outcome measures assessed psychopathology, adaptive functioning, and behavioral problems. The children receiving professional psychotherapy significantly improved over the 2-year period. This is a desirable outcome, of course, but so did the kids receiving academic tutoring, at a much lower cost intervention. In effect, the authors concluded that traditional child psychotherapy had no positive effects beyond those obtainable by nonprofessional academic tutoring not focused on mental health issues. Now, suppose you are employed as an administrator at a local mental health clinic, and you are asked to choose interventions for children referred to your program. You can spend a lot of money on licensed mental health providers, or less money on graduate student tutors, and expect similar results. What will you do? Well, it would take a pretty confident administrator to announce the abandonment of agency efforts to conduct psychotherapy for children (illustrating the potential influence of *nonscientific* issues into the decision-making process). And, in fact, a well-informed administrator might wait to see if the findings are replicated by other studies—that they were not just a fluke.

Nonetheless, studies like this one should serve as a stimulus to search the mental health literature very carefully for effective alternatives to traditional child psychotherapy (e.g., Christophersen & Mortweet, 2001; Hibbs & Jensen, 1996) or perhaps to see whether other more positive studies better support the use of traditional interventions. Again, the implications are clear.

Previously published and credible evaluation studies should be a major source of input into the design of an agency's programs. Our hope is that through reading this book, you will acquire greater skills in locating and critically evaluating such studies, and in designing and conducting empirical evaluations of your own practice and of the outcomes of the agency where you may be employed.

When we improve our programs and interventions by making them more effective and efficient, all those involved with or touched by the social service delivery system are affected. Consumers and their families may recover faster when we discover that one approach works better than another. Armed with information from the program evaluation, workers and managers can better treat and advocate for their clients—possibly making their own jobs more enjoyable and less frustrating. Ultimately, even taxpayers benefit. But let us back up a bit and discuss what constitutes a program.

WHAT IS A PROGRAM?

A program is an organized collection of activities designed to reach certain objectives. Let's consider the two main elements of this definition in depth. Organized activities—programs—are not a random set of actions but a series of planned actions designed to solve some problem. If there is no problem, then there is no need for programmatic intervention. So, programs are interventions or services that are expected to have some kind of an impact on the program participants. Could a bereavement support group for school-aged children be considered a program? What about a telephone hotline for parents? Would it be stretching things too much to describe a residential drug treatment facility's efforts aimed at reducing client attrition as a program?

CHARACTERISTICS OF "GOOD" PROGRAMS

Programs tend to have certain characteristics that help us identify them. First of all, programs tend to require **staffing**. A residential drug treatment facility, for instance, is going to need a lot of staff. It may even have a separate staff who run an aftercare or outpatient drug treatment program. The personnel of both programs may occasionally be asked to speak to high school students and groups in the community as part of the facility's drug education program.

Staff may have their time allocated among several programs or dedicated to only one.

Second, programs usually have their own **budgets.** Because employing staff requires financial resources, programs sometimes can be identified by their budgets. However, some fine programs have minimal budgets because of heavy reliance on volunteers. **Stable funding** is important to the success of most programs. Morale and performance fall when employees do not get paid on a regular basis, or when they are asked to put aside normal duties and engage in last minute fund-raising or grant writing to get the program through several more months. Programs started with "soft money" (grants or nonrecurring funds) often experience high rates of staff turnover until the programs secure some continuity in funding.

Another characteristic of programs is that they have their own identity. In short, they are visible or recognizable by the public. Big Brothers/Big Sisters is an example of an organization with a national reputation for a single program. In some communities, a program may be recognized by the location where it has been housed for a number of years, or by its unique slogan, sign, letterhead, spokesperson, or public service announcements.

When an organization has multiple programs, differences are sometimes found in philosophy, policies or procedures, and mission, and perhaps even in the way their corresponding staffs dress and how they account for their time. Such contrasts make it easy to differentiate one program from another.

Within an agency, one outpatient counseling program may have the **service philosophy** that "no one is turned away," while another outpatient counseling program may have a different philosophy—providing service only for those who meet certain eligibility guidelines, such as having private insurance or being able to afford to pay. A service philosophy may also clearly communicate how the clientele is to be treated, for example, "We respect the dignity and worth of all those we serve in caring for their physical, spiritual, psychological, and social well-being" or "The customer is always right."

Unfortunately for program evaluators, programs can be vague and hard to distinguish and define. A former governor once made a public announcement that he was unveiling "a new program" to put state social workers in public schools. The program, he said, should help prevent dropouts and poor achievement among students who faced serious personal and family problems. However, the newspaper account said the program would require no additional staff or funding. In essence, some social services employees would be placed in schools that could supply them with office space and phones.

Did the governor's announcement create a program? Not in this instance. It never got off the ground. Why not? It had no name, no staff, no funding, no slogan, no visibility. Most schools did not have surplus office space. Further, the governor made no suggestion of any new activities or ways of tackling the problems children and their families faced.

On the other hand, starting a bereavement support group in an elementary school, even if volunteers contribute the leadership and the group has no budget to speak of, could be considered a program if it has an ongoing presence and a presumed impact that could be measured. For evaluation purposes, speaking to an assembly of high school students once or twice a year about drugs and alcoholism might also be considered a program.

In the best of all possible worlds, every human services program would be solidly established on the basis of scientifically credible evidence that had been previously published in peer-reviewed professional journals. That is, before the practitioners jumped into a social problem and started "helping," someone did serious review and appraisal of the relevant evaluation studies that tested the usefulness of various methods of potentially helping. If a careful search of the literature and critical review of the existing outcome studies found that one or more models of intervention had credible evidence of effectiveness, and these approaches were "teachable" to the existing service providers, cost effective, and ethical, contemporary standards of ethical practice would suggest that the service program be focused around these "evidence-based services" as opposed to interventions lacking a sufficient foundation in empirical research.

Now this poses a dilemma for practitioners and administrators, namely, "What if no evidence-based interventions are known to exist for a particular problem?" In that case, one would be justified in primarily relying on the more traditional sources of practice knowledge, namely, *theory, practice wisdom, common sense, tradition,* and *authority.* But (and this is a *big* but), practitioners should only claim that no evidence-based interventions exist after having made a thorough and up-to-date search of the relevant practice research literature. Fortunately, evidence-based interventions are now well established for a majority of the serious conditions described in the *Diagnostic and Statistical Manual of Mental Disorders* (DSM; American Psychiatric Association, 2000), and increasingly for conditions that do not lend themselves to the DSM system—problems such as unemployment, domestic violence, child abuse and neglect, and troubled youth. We believe that every human services agency should keep abreast of these developments by subscribing to relevant journals (e.g., *Journal of Consulting and Clinical Psychology, Archives of General Psychiatry, Research on Social Work Practice*) and acquiring the latest edition of professional books that summarize the latest studies on evidence-based practice (e.g., Ammerman, Hersen, & Last, 1993; Giles, 1993; Hibbs & Jensen, 1996; LeCroy, 1994; Mash & Barkley, 1998; Nathan & Gorman, 1998; Seligman, 1998; Thyer & Wodarski, 1998; Van Hasselt & Hersen, 1996; Wodarski & Thyer, 1998).

The question may legitimately arise, "How much evidence is enough evidence in order for a given intervention to be considered to have an adequate empirical foundation?" The Task Force on Promotion and Dissemination of Psychological Procedures (Chambless et al., 1996, p. 16) of Division 12 (Clinical Psychology) of the American Psychological Association has promulgated one set of minimal recommendations. In order for a psychosocial intervention to be considered for inclusion in their list of empirically validated treatments, it had to meet the following criteria:

THE TREATMENT MUST BE SUPPORTED BY:

1. At least two good between-group design experiments demonstrating efficacy in one or more of the following ways:
   a. Superior to pill or psychological placebo or to another treatment
   b. Equivalent to an already established treatment in experiments with adequate statistical power, or
2. A large series of single case designs ($N > 9$) demonstrating efficacy. These experiments must have:
   a. Used good experimental designs, and
   b. Compared the intervention to another treatment, as in 1a

Among the other criteria to be applied are that experiments must be conducted using treatment manuals (this enhances the ability to replicate interventions), the characteristics of the clients must be clearly specified, and effects must have been demonstrated by at least two different investigators or treatment teams. Although these standards may seem a bit stringent to students and practitioners unaccustomed to rigorous research, they are not unwarranted; and they serve as an initial starting place to begin classifying particular interventions as evidence based or not. Human services professionals can employ this set of standards when selecting types of treatment programs to provide. Over time, it is likely that these standards will be augmented by additional criteria (e.g., "The treatment has been evaluated in real-life clinical settings") that will enhance their usefulness.

The human services professions are slowly moving in the direction of evidence-based practice, which has been defined as "the conscientious, explicit, and judicious use of current best evidence in making decisions about the care of individuals" (Sackett, Richardson, Rosenberg, & Haynes, 1997, p. 2). Further, it is "the integration of best research evidence with clinical expertise and patient values" (Sackett, Strauss, Richardson, Rosenberg, & Haynes, 2000, p. 1). Gambrill (1999) concurs: "It involves integrating individual practice expertise with the best available external evidence from systematic research as well as considering the values and expectations of clients" (p. 346). Although this statement may seem like common sense, the fact is that at present no clear ethical or legal mandates require that human services professionals deliver evidence-based practices, where evidence-based practices are known to be established. This could change, however, in the very near future. Clearly, it is the direction in which the profession needs to be heading (see also Thyer, 2004).

In the best of all possible worlds, every program would also be based on a sound **theoretical model.** That is, before the helpers jumped into a social problem and started helping, they would develop a model that would have examined the problem—how and why it originated and what would work best to remedy the situation.

The theoretical model can be an organizing principle for each program that provides a consistency of effort by suggesting a standard approach derived from some well-articulated and comprehensive social or behavioral science theory.

Such a theory may serve as a guide in recommending certain activities or procedures from all those available to be used for the intervention.

Hyperactivity in children, for instance, may be addressed with behavior therapy. Drug treatment may be used alone or in combination with behavior therapy. Are these the only approaches for dealing with hyperactivity? Not too long ago, a student brought to class an article describing the use of chiropractic manipulation to treat the problem. Can you see how the choice of a conceptual model has major implications for what is dispensed as intervention?

Consider a different problem. Suppose you are hired to run a treatment program for men who batter. Do these men fit a single profile? Is one interventive strategy all that is needed? Saunders (1992) argues that there are three theoretically distinct types of men who batter: those who were severely abused as children; emotionally volatile men with rigid sex-role attitudes, who fear losing their partners and are depressed, suicidal, and angry; and family-only aggressors who tend to have relatively liberal attitudes about sex roles, the lowest rate of abuse in childhood, the most marital satisfaction, and who are generally nonassertive. Is there a possibility that some interventions may work better with one type of abuser than with another?

Theoretical models can be important to understanding how a program should work and where one should look for indications that a program is successful. (See Box 1.2.) But all too often what passes for theory in many social service agencies is a blend of past experience and tradition. Evaluators would have no problem with that if the program was often successful in rehabilitating, helping, fixing, or curing clients. But when a program is not successful much of the time, the possibility exists that even though the program was implemented as designed, the underlying theory is flawed. Such a situation calls for new thinking and a new approach to the problem. Theories may be able to tell us how to accomplish our goals (Conrad & Miller, 1987), but not in every case.

Program evaluation helps determine when theories work and when they do not. Conceptual models do, after all, sometimes turn out to be wrong. We no longer believe, for instance, that autistic children are produced by cold, aloof mothers, as the purported child expert Bruno Bettelheim once argued.

To a certain extent, program designers and implementers are protected from many of the problems that accompany misguided and erroneous theories

BOX 1.2	CHARACTERISTICS OF GOOD SOCIAL SERVICE PROGRAMS
• Staffing	• Conceptual or theoretical foundation
• Budgets	• A service philosophy
• Stable funding	• Systematic efforts at empirical evaluation of services
• Recognized identity	• Evidence-based research foundation

when they base programs not solely on theories alone but also on methods of practice that have been empirically supported by research and evaluation. The best programs, those on the "cutting edge," will be built on a firm foundation of the latest empirical research. These programs can provide a level of confidence and knowledge about what to expect in terms of success rates. These would be the programs we would choose for ourselves if we or our families needed intervention.

Theory and programs are linked in complex ways that we will discuss at various times throughout the book. In this chapter, we will consider the ways theory and empirical research can influence and shape a program.

If you want to see how evaluators and researchers present an intervention in terms of a theoretical model, review the study by Telch, Agras, Rossiter, Wilfley, and Kenardy (1990) that examines the use of group cognitive-behavioral treatment for nonpurging bulimia. Similarly, Jemmott and Jemmott (1991) have applied the theory of reasoned action in order to increase the use of condoms and prevent the spread of AIDS. Zambelli and Derosa (1992) have looked at specific group intervention techniques for bereaved school-aged children that were theoretically based and derived from four protective mechanisms identified by Rutter (1987).

You should realize, however, that many (perhaps most) human services programs are *not* based on any explicit theory of human behavior or any etiological social or behavioral social science theory explaining how particular problems arise, or even any particular interventive theory. Such "atheoretical" programs may be based on common sense, authority, or tradition. For example, we know of one governor who arranged for the state to provide the mother of every newborn baby a compact disc (CD) of classical music. These CDs were duly distributed to thousands of new mothers, costing the state hundreds of thousands of dollars in taxpayer money. This authoritative initiative was instigated by the governor's reading about something supposedly called the "Mozart effect," wherein listening to a particular Mozart sonata resulted in college students earning higher test scores. The (vain) hope was that mothers who were given CDs of classical music (which failed to contain a recording of the particular Mozart sonata in question!) would play these within hearing of their infants, who would grow up to be smarter. This human services program was not based on any etiological theory about intelligence, or even an interventive theory on how listening to classical music was supposed to improve intelligence. It was based on *authority,* the governor's mandate. Unfortunately, subsequent studies failed to demonstrate the Mozart effect in test taking, and *none* demonstrated any improvement in infant intelligence.

Numerous examples of such atheoretical programs can be found from policies removing the driver's licenses of high school dropouts to policies within child protective service programs, homeless shelters, soup kitchens, and so forth. Ask the practitioners providing such services about their program's social or behavioral theoretical orientation, and often you will be met with puzzled looks. To be sure, these programs can be prospectively designed in accord with some theory, but in many instances they are not. And it can be misleading to *retroactively* attempt to fit a theoretical approach to explain a particular program, because the same program could no doubt be similarly explained by perhaps dozens of rival theories, leaving you no closer to a valid understanding of how the program may be exerting its effects, if any. The relationship between formal theory and research on practice outcomes is a complex one, and Thyer (2001) addresses it more completely than is possible here.

Programs vary greatly. Some are sophisticated and others simplistic—even composed of a single activity. In scale they range from a small cooperative babysitting program for young mothers to the federal food stamp program that touches millions of lives. It is not always easy to determine whether certain activities should be considered a program or part of the collection of activities that comprise a larger single program. Either way, program evaluation can be undertaken as long as a desired objective or outcome can be stated. Although in some agencies *programs* are referred to as *services,* in this book the terms will be used interchangeably.

PROGRAM EVALUATION DEFINED

Program evaluation is applied research used as part of the managerial process. Evaluations are conducted to aid those who must make administrative decisions about human services programs. Unlike theoretical research, where scientists engage in science for its own sake, program evaluation systematically examines human services programs for pragmatic reasons. Decision makers may need to know if a program accomplished its objectives, if it is worth funding again next year, or if a less expensive program can accomplish the same results.

Program evaluation is like basic research in that both follow a logical, orderly sequence of investigation. Both begin with a problem, a question, or a hypothesis. Normally, there is some review of what is known about the problem, including prior efforts and theoretical approaches (this is known as reviewing the literature). A research or evaluation design (a blueprint to guide the data collection efforts) is developed, and data are gathered and then analyzed. When thought of this way, both research and evaluation are similar to the task-centered or problem-solving process known to many human services professionals.

Research and evaluation differ with regard to the expected use or utility of the data. There may be no anticipated need or demand for "pure" research, whereas an assemblage of individuals may anxiously await the results of a program evaluation. Also, the goal of research is to produce generalizable knowledge, while information from a program evaluation may be applicable to only a specific program. However, both are approached with some degree of rigor. Think of program evaluation as a tool—a management tool that you can use to make (and to help others make) better decisions about social and human services programs. Program evaluation helps us to make the best use of our resources as we labor to improve the quality of life of our clients.

Program evaluation involves making comparisons. In fact, Schalock and Thornton (1988) have defined program evaluation as "structured comparison." Few programs can be evaluated without comparing them to something. Programs in one agency may be compared to similar programs in other agencies, to past or prior efforts, or against a stated objective; but without some form of comparison, there can be no evaluation. A major thrust of this book is to help you find or create (to conceptualize) bases of comparison for your own program evaluation efforts.

REASONS WHY PROGRAMS ARE EVALUATED

Quite often social and human services programs are evaluated because of a need to be accountable to a sponsoring or funding agency, or because competition for scarce funds requires that only one program (normally, the most effective or efficient program) can be funded. Program evaluation is needed whenever new interventions are being tried and it is not known whether they will be as successful as former methods, or when there is a perception that a program could be improved—that it could become more productive or better in some way. We evaluate on those occasions when it is important to have some objective assessment or feedback about the worth of our social and human services programs. The following scenarios illustrate some of the occasions when program evaluations are encountered.

Scenario 1: The Required Evaluation   Your agency is applying for funding from the United Way in your community to begin a new program designed to provide counseling to men who have been prosecuted for domestic violence. You have been asked to prepare the program proposal. As you read the instructions for preparing the proposal, you notice that besides describing the project, listing its objectives, pointing out its uniqueness, and stating the amount of funding that will be required, the proposal also requires a project evaluation. At the end of the project year, data must be presented to show that the project had a successful outcome and an impact on the problem of domestic violence.

Scenario 2: Competition for Scarce Funds   Your innovative program for men who batter has been operating for a year. You have been able to obtain some data that you hope will favorably influence the committee deciding the continuation of funding for your program. As you prepare your presentation, you discover that a second domestic violence project from another agency will also be making a request to be funded. You further learn that there is only enough money to fund one program.

Scenario 3: Evaluation of New Interventions   Many more clients desire the services of your outpatient counseling agency than you have staff to serve. At a planning session, one of the newer staff members suggests that the agency move from a one-on-one counseling model to a group services model. The benefits are clear—instead of limiting each practitioner to seven or eight scheduled clients a day, each therapist could conduct three or four group sessions a day and have contact with 25 to 30 clients. In spite of being able to serve more clients, the staff is not very supportive of this proposal, because they believe that individual counseling is much more effective than group counseling.

Scenario 4: Evaluation for Accountability   You work in a large residential agency serving young children. Unfortunately, a child care aide was recently discovered molesting one of the children. The public is in an uproar. Community leaders are calling for the agency director and all key staff to resign. You feel that the agency is a good one—better than other residential programs within the community. Because the agency director knows that you are enrolled in a program evaluation course at the nearby university, she calls you into her office and asks you to find some way of objectively documenting the strengths of the agency. "Can you show," she asks, "that the great majority of our young people have a favorable experience here, a good impression of the agency, and that they go on to do well in school and in life after they leave the agency?"

MOTIVATIONS FOR PROGRAM EVALUATION

Why do we evaluate human services programs? Programs are evaluated basically because administrative decisions have to be made, and it is important to know (or to show) that our programs are "good" programs. Individual policy or decision makers may have a hypothesis about a program (e.g., the free clinic's counseling program is highly effective). At other times, questions may be raised (e.g., is the free clinic's counseling program effective?). Hypotheses or questions provide the motivation for a program evaluation. It makes no real difference whether a question or a hypothesis serves as the catalyst for an evaluation. This can be seen in Box 1.3.

The list in Box 1.3 could easily be made much longer. An interest in exploring one question may lead to other areas. The evaluator may start off wanting to know whether clients were being helped, but in the process of designing a methodology the initial question or problem becomes modified somewhat. The evaluator may want to know not only whether clients were helped but also whether one approach was cheaper (more cost-effective) than another. Other questions may concern whether improvement has been made in a certain staff's productivity since last year or whether the program has reached its intended target population. On some occasions, administrators may want to use evaluation data to help garner public support for human services programs. (The public is much more likely to support tax increases for those programs perceived to be "good" than those thought to be ineffective or poorly run.) Program evaluation can also be used in terms of marketing programs to the public. (As a program manager or agency director, having data showing that 92 percent of your clientele say that they would refer their friends or family members to your agency could be very useful information to have on hand.)

MOTIVATIONS FOR PROGRAM EVALUATION

WE WANT TO SHOW:	WE WANT TO KNOW:
1. That clients are being helped.	Are clients being helped?
2. That clients are satisfied with our services.	Are clients satisfied with the services received?
3. That the program has an impact on some social problem.	Has the program made any real difference?
4. That a program has worth.	Does the program deserve the amount of money spent on it?
5. That one program or approach is better than another.	Is the new intervention better than the old?
6. That the program needs additional staff or resources.	How do we improve this program?
7. That staff are well utilized.	Do staff make efficient use of their time?

Social and human services programs have evolved to combat such social problems as drug abuse. Think for a moment of other social problems in this country. We could begin listing such problems as:

Poverty	Substance abuse
Homelessness	Adolescent pregnancies
Unemployment	Mental illness
Child abuse	Illiteracy
Domestic violence	High infant mortality rates
Crime	Hunger
AIDS	

For each social problem, there are hundreds if not thousands of programs. Some of these programs work and need to be continued; others are ineffective. If it cannot be demonstrated that certain programs have any impact on these problems, then further evaluative research should be undertaken to discover why the programs were not successful. There may be very logical reasons; for example, the programs could be poorly managed, underfunded, or poorly conceptualized or designed. There are many other reasons. As human services professionals, we need to be just as interested in the outcomes of national programs as we are in our local programs. Program evaluation is not to be understood as having application only to the agency that employs us.

Although the examples used thus far have helped us to understand the need for program evaluation primarily at the local level, an immense need remains for program evaluation of national expenditures and programs. For instance, an article in *Brandweek* (April 1998) entitled "Drug Money" has noted that the Partnership for a Drug-Free America and the White House Office of National Drug Control Policy have embarked on an antidrug campaign costing almost $2 billion. The author of the article, Daniel Hill, says that this enormous expenditure of money is backed only by "flimsy" research. Two of the three studies supposedly showing the effectiveness of media antidrug messages had yet to be published, and the author of the third acknowledged that her respondents might have been saying what they thought the researchers wanted to hear.

Several experts have pointed out that no well-controlled studies show that media campaigns are effective in changing behavior. The deputy director of the Office of National Drug Control Policy was, according to the Hill article, unable to cite any research supporting the contention that antidrug advertising works. Although there is no doubt that a serious drug abuse problem exists in this country, should billions of dollars be spent on untested interventions? Shouldn't research support the effectiveness of interventions (even those perceived to be harmless) before vast sums of money are spent on them?

The example of the antidrug advertising campaign is not an out-of-the ordinary one. According to an article in the *New York Times,* in the 1960s and 1970s, the federal government invested billions of dollars on job training "without a clue about what worked and what did not" (Passell, 1993). As a society we need to test new ideas to combat old problems. For example, do monetary incentives to mothers on welfare for using Norplant contraceptives significantly affect the number of children they have? Is offering full college scholarships to low-income students who remain in school, pass their courses, remain drug-free, and do not become pregnant or get in trouble with the law a realistic way to combat poverty?

Evaluators, through carefully controlled studies, can determine whether spending money "up front"—for example, paying low-income, pregnant women to attend prenatal education and care classes—saves money in the long run. There is some indication that giving pregnant Medicaid recipients a $10 bill for each appointment they keep results in a considerable reduction in the amount of time newborn infants stay in intensive care units (Kolata, 1994).

Whether at the local, state, or national level, program evaluation often begins by identifying a problem. Decision makers want to distinguish programs that work from those that do not and to know if their money is well spent. They may have developed questions about a program because of some incident or problems brought to their attention. These problems can be visible and well-recognized or those known only to a handful of staff, administrators, or trustees.

A problem is any undesirable situation or condition. Sometimes program evaluations are undertaken in order to determine the extent or magnitude of a problem or to confirm a suspected problem. As you think about the agency where you are working or interning, what problems come to mind? (If you do not initially think of any problems, have you seen any recent data suggesting that the program is effective or efficient?)

SELECTED PROFESSIONAL
ASSOCIATION GUIDELINES
ON THE ETHICAL MANDATE
TO EVALUATE PROGRAMS
AND SERVICES

Social workers should monitor and evaluate policies, the implementation of programs, and practice interventions. Social workers should promote and facilitate evaluation and research to contribute to the development of knowledge. Social workers should . . . fully use evaluation and research evidence in their professional practice. (National Association of Social Workers, *Code of Ethics,* 1999, p. 20)

All school social work programs, new or long-standing, should be evaluated on an ongoing basis to determine their relevance, effectiveness, efficiency, and contributions to the process of educating children. (NASW, 1992, p. 16)

Clinical social workers shall have . . . knowledge about and skills in using research to evaluate the effectiveness of a service. (NASW, 1989, p. 7)

There are periodic, systematic, and effective evaluations of psychological services. . . . When the psychological service unit is a component of a larger organization, regular assessment of progress in achieving goals is provided in the service delivery plan. Such evaluation could include consideration of the effectiveness of psychological services. . . . (Board of Professional Affairs, 1987, p. 8)

Monitor effectiveness. Counselors continually monitor their effectiveness as professionals and take steps to improve when necessary. (American Counseling Association, *Code of Ethics,* 1999, p. 6)

There are probably as many reasons for conducting program evaluation as there are different programs. In addition to the reasons already given, those in the helping professions also conduct program evaluations because they have a responsibility to improve programs. For instance, the National Association of Social Workers' *Code of Ethics* (1999) states, under ethical standard 5.02(a), "Social workers should monitor and evaluate policies, the implementation of programs, and practice interventions." And social workers' ethical responsibility to the profession is also seen in standard 5.02(b), which states: "Social workers should promote and facilitate evaluation and research to contribute to the development of knowledge."

We all have an ethical obligation to evaluate our practice. (See Box 1.4.) All too often, we get caught up in service delivery as measured by billable hours, home visits, numbers of phone calls, and internal audits of agency and accreditation forms without systematically appraising whether all this effort produces beneficial outcomes for clients. We have an ethical mandate to determine whether our clients are being helped, whether they are any better off as a result of our interventions. Program evaluation is a major means by which we can fulfill this ethical responsibility.

OVERCOMING THE SUBJECTIVE PERSPECTIVE

Anytime we have a choice, we find ourselves in a position where a decision must be made between two or more alternatives. Often, informal (and perhaps even unconscious) criteria guide us in making choices. Although these criteria may be more the product of visceral reactions than of contemplation, they aid us in the making of choices. They help us to determine such things as "good" restaurants and "good" movies, and to rate the services of care providers (e.g., a "good" physician). In each of these instances, *good* is defined subjectively and somewhat arbitrarily. For example, my notion of the best restaurant in town may be one that specializes in Italian food. You, on the other hand, may intensely dislike Italian cooking. My notion of a good movie may be *Texas Chainsaw Massacre*, whereas your taste may run to less violence. My notion of a good physician may be one who, although known for a disheveled appearance, answers my every question, while your opinion of a good physician requires that the physician dress appropriately and look distinguished. Because appearance is important to you, you may have no confidence in a physician who does not look the role (whether or not your questions get answered).

What does this have to do with program evaluation? Just this: every day (sometimes many times a day) human services professionals must direct people to their programs or refer them to other programs based on their subjective impressions. When we make referrals, we want clients to go, not to programs that are not effective, but to the "good" programs. We want them to have the best possible chance of succeeding or doing well in that program. We have a professional responsibility to avoid making referrals to ineffective or deficient programs. We also want the programs we direct or that employ us to benefit our clients. But, how do we recognize a good program, or a poor program?

How do we know when our programs are effective? We like to believe that we help our clients, but what actual evidence do we have that the majority of our clients are helped by our programs? Most helping professionals have had clients who have made giant strides as a result of skilled intervention. We feel rewarded by these successful clients. They help us feel that we are competent and that we have chosen the right career. Unfortunately, there are also those clients with whom we are unsuccessful. These clients, despite our best efforts, drop out of programs, make a mess of their lives, or seem to have gained nothing from our interventions. Think of all the clients who have made their exits from your programs. What is the proportion of "successful" clients to "unsuccessful" clients? Are you more successful than unsuccessful with your clients? What evidence could you present of your success?

We have raised these questions to help you understand that program evaluation involves a different perspective than you may normally employ when thinking about your clients. Clinicians and practitioners tend to evaluate their practice subjectively and in terms of selected individual cases. They think of Mrs. Smith (with whom they were successful), Mr. Arthur (who was a model client and who now comes back to volunteer his services), or perhaps Kathy M., with whom they were not a success. However, this "case focus" does not facilitate the aggregation of data at a program level so that an overall determination can be made about the effectiveness of the program as a whole. Although one bad apple may spoil an entire bushel, one client who does not succeed does not mean that a whole program needs to be overhauled.

The difficulties with attempting evaluation using a "case focus" with a single client can be demonstrated easily. Consider Mrs. Smith. Although you felt that you were successful in helping Mrs. Smith to quit drinking, others may not be so quick to shower accolades on you. Those who are skeptical of your abilities as a clinician may point out that while Mrs. Smith may no longer drink, the rest of her family is in turmoil. Her husband left home; a teenage daughter ran away. Mrs. Smith is now living with another recovering alcoholic and working for minimum wage as a waitress, although she was previously employed as a registered nurse. You reply to these critics, "She's not drinking. She feels good about herself. I think she's shown great improvement." Although it may be possible to argue that any given case was or was not a success, a manager needs to look at the program as a whole. Are the clients (as an aggregate) better or worse off as a result of participating in the program?

Consider the case of Mr. Arthur. Everyone in the agency agrees that he has made significant changes in his life since becoming a client of your program. However, on closer inspection, it is revealed that you spent twice as much time with Mr. Arthur as you did with the average client. Was he a success because he got twice as much attention? Would he have been a success if he had received only as much time as the "average client" receives? (Did he get so much time because he was an "easy" client to work with?)

We have already admitted that the program was not successful with Kathy M. However, is Kathy the typical client or the unusual client? Perhaps Kathy was the most severely disturbed client that your program has ever admitted. Given her previous history of multiple hospitalizations, perhaps no one really expected her to make any significant gains.

We can see from these examples that our perspective as practitioners often involves subjective evaluations. That is, we believe that a client has improved or not improved. The problem with subjective evaluations is that others may not share them. While you think of Mrs. Smith as an example of a successful client, perhaps your best friend and coworker thinks of Mrs. Smith as something less than a success. Although you are quite pleased that Mr. Arthur has overcome a great many of his problems, perhaps your program director has sent you a strongly worded memorandum suggesting that the program's waiting list is such that you are not to spend as much time with the rest of your clients. Although Kathy M. made no progress in treatment, the same program director is not disappointed. "We learned something," she says. "We learned what won't work with clients like this. Next time, we'll try something a little different."

In conversation we can get away with saying things like "I did a good job with that family," "She's a good therapist," or "It's a good program, you'll like it there." However, a thesaurus lists nine different meanings for the word *good* as an adjective. (See Box 1.5.) Seldom does anyone ask how we define good.

DENOTATIONS OF THE WORD *GOOD*

USAGE	EXAMPLE
1. Pleasant, fine	I had a *good* meal.
2. Moral, virtuous	Mother Theresa was a *good* person.
3. Competent, skilled	She is a *good* worker.
4. Useful, adequate	It was *good* that I read the book before the quiz.
5. Reliable	Pat is a *good* source of information.
6. Kind, giving	My grandmother is so *good*.
7. Authentic, real	He makes a *good* point.
8. Well-behaved	Rachel is such a *good* child.
9. Considerable	There is a *good* deal more poverty now than 5 years ago.

What we are allowed to do as conversationalists we cannot do as program evaluators.

Evaluators are concerned with specificity and measurements. We want verifiable evidence, not someone's opinion. It matters whether a program produces changes in behavior, attitudes, or knowledge. Further, we might want to know how much change was experienced by the average client, how long it was sustained, and at what cost.

Subjective evaluations about the success of individual clients are very much like the initial examples of a "good" movie and a "good" restaurant. We can expect differences in opinion. Within most groups, if someone says, "That is not a good restaurant!" there are sure to be others within the crowd who will disagree. Someone else may say, "Well, it is my favorite restaurant!" or "That's interesting. We were just there on Wednesday and had a wonderful meal." The problem with subjective evaluations is that everyone is usually right. The person who had a bad experience with a restaurant probably got poor service or an improperly prepared meal. The person who ate there on Wednesday could have just as easily not had a wonderful meal. The individual who boldly proclaimed the restaurant to be his favorite restaurant might be quite willing to forget an occasional bad meal because he goes there for the atmosphere, he is personal friends with the proprietor, or his girlfriend works there. Another possibility is that he just does not have a discriminating palate.

To become evaluators, we need to adjust our perspectives so that we are able to see beyond a single meal or a single client. We need to see the larger picture. We need to go from a micro focus to a macro focus. What are the experiences that most of the restaurant patrons or clients have? In a sense, we need to forget the individual and broaden our perspective to focus on the most common or frequent experience. What percent of the patrons would not return? With what percent of our caseload are we successful? We need to look for corroborative evidence that might convince neutral observers.

(For instance, counting the number of patrons leaving meals unfinished or leaving in the middle of a movie might substantiate rather powerfully one's own subjective experience.)

As evaluators, we want to be able to objectively conclude that this program is a good one and that another is not—based not on personal opinion but on factual evidence. When we go beyond our own personal experience or opinions and collect information about the experiences that others have had, we have begun to develop an evaluative stance—we have moved from subjectivity to objectivity.

An objective stance tends to place faith in numbers and counting. As a rough rule of thumb, the more individuals we are able to interview, survey, or contact, the more confidence we can place in our evaluative findings. Numbers constitute objective data. When, for instance, 97 out of 100 clients indicate that they would recommend our services to their friends, this constitutes objective data. Anyone examining the responses of the 100 clients and sorting them into piles of "would recommend" and "would not recommend" services ought to arrive at the same conclusion.

Evaluators are, in some respects, applied scientists. Scientists seek to understand and explain the world around them. However, it is not just explanations that scientists seek, but *correct* explanations. Whether we think of ourselves as program evaluators or as applied scientists, our findings must stand independently, apart from our claims or persuasive oratory. Our findings should be replicable (reproducible); others must be able to independently arrive at the same conclusions. If someone did not like or agree with the findings from a particular program evaluation, then this person could repeat the evaluation using the same methodology. Assuming that no major changes occurred within the agency in the interim and that the original evaluation methodology was sound, findings from the second study should be the same or very similar to those of the first study.

Objectivity demands precision. Evaluators must be precise about the program they are evaluating, what they will be measuring, how they will collect and analyze their data, and who they will be interviewing or observing during a given time period. Such matters require specificity. Vagueness is rarely tolerated in research or evaluation. Note the lack of specificity in the following: "This evaluation will determine if specialized inservice training on the use of empathy helps nurses perform their jobs better." Do you find it too vague? The statement is unclear because we are left wondering: What nurses are being discussed? Has it been established that empathy is necessary to perform their jobs? What jobs are under consideration? What does it mean to perform better? How is empathy to be measured?

One way that evaluators become more specific and precise is by using **operational definitions.** An operational definition is the way a variable or concept (such as empathy) is to be defined and measured for the purposes of the evaluation. The evaluator may use a standardized scale to measure level of empathy. Or the evaluator may use some sort of behavioral measures, such as the number of times during a therapeutic session the counselor nods affirmatively or makes supportive statements such as "I understand." Counselors may be operationally defined as those holding certain degrees or as all persons who work in a certain program regardless of their educational background.

As one begins to operationally define the key concepts for a proposed evaluation or study, often the vagueness disappears. In the case of the vague statement, "This evaluation will determine if specialized inservice training on the use of empathy helps social workers perform their jobs better," operationally defining important concepts might change it to: "Do social workers with higher levels of empathy place more children in adoptive homes per year than social workers with lower levels of empathy?"

The effort to become more precise does not rule out the subjective experience in program evaluation. Although a single "bad" subjective experience cannot constitute a program evaluation, it may lead to a formal evaluation as a program manager, agency director, or members of the board of directors become concerned about whether an incident or experience reflects what is "really going on" with the program. The program evaluator seeks to understand the "reality" or "truth" about a program. In the process, the evaluator may collect a large number of subjective opinions about the program. Objective evaluations do not rely on the opinions of any one person (no matter how influential), but instead attempt to gain a comprehensive view from the opinions of the aggregate or group.

Because the reality about a program's performance can sometimes be painful and have far-reaching implications (e.g., loss of funds and the corresponding laying off of a number of an agency's employees), program evaluators often seek the best possible objective evidence that they can obtain (given such pragmatic constraints as budget, time, access to clients or their records, and cooperation of the staff). Having objective or "hard data" to guide decisions about programs is superior to decision making without program evaluation data. By way of analogy, if you were on trial for an offense that you did not commit, you would want your lawyer to present as much objective evidence on your behalf as possible to assist the jury in realizing your innocence. You probably would not feel comfortable in allowing your attorney to hinge the entire case on the subjective testimony of a single character witness who would testify that you were a "good" student or a "good" friend.

PHILOSOPHICAL ASSUMPTIONS
OF PROGRAM EVALUATION

As a specialized form of social and behavioral science research, program evaluation is predicated on certain philosophical assumptions pertaining to the nature of reality, and of the design and conduct of research inquiry. Although these philosophical assumptions are often confused with *theory,* you can differentiate them by recalling that social and behavioral science theories are *explanations* of problems or interventions, explanations amenable to investigation via scientific research, and that theories themselves are based on certain

SELECTED PHILOSOPHICAL
FOUNDATIONS OF
PROGRAM EVALUATION

ACCEPTANCE OF:

Realism—The point of view that the world has an independent or objective existence apart from the perceptions of the observer

Determinism—The assumption that all phenomena have physical causes that are potentially amenable to scientific investigation

Positivism—The belief that valid knowledge about the objective world can be arrived at through scientific research

Rationalism—The belief that reason and logic are useful tools for scientific inquiry, and that, ultimately, truthful explanations of human behavior will be rational

Empiricism—A preference to rely on evidence gathered systematically through observation or experiment, and capable of being replicated (that is, verified) by others, using satisfactory standards of evidence

Operationalism—The assertion that it is important to develop measures of phenomena (e.g., client problems, interventive procedures) that can be reliably replicated by others

Parsimony—A preference for the simpler of the available adequate explanations for behavioral phenomena

Pragmatism—The view that the meaning or truth of anything resides in its consequences in action

Scientific skepticism—The point of view that all claims should be considered of doubtful validity, until substantiated by credible scientific data

REJECTION OF:

Nihilism—A doctrine that all values are baseless and that nothing is knowable or can be communicated

Anecdotism—The belief that anecdotes prove something empirically

---

philosophical assumptions that are fundamentally untestable. Some of these philosophical foundations of program evaluation are listed in Box 1.6.

Each of these points of view has occupied central controversies within philosophy for hundreds of years, and in some cases, millennia. In offering them as characterizing the philosophy of science undergirding program evaluation, we make no pretense that any one of them can be considered irrefutably justified either by logic or by empirical data. Consider them, like Euclid's axioms, as undemonstrated propositions (although common sense would suggest that they are self-evident) that serve as intellectual pivot points around which program evaluation efforts revolve. No one, for example—certainly not the authors—is capable of providing a philosophically irrefutable proof that the world has a physical reality (as opposed to a subjective construction in one's mind). But in order to take action, some assumptions are necessary. Thus, for example, the distinguished social work educator Bertha Capen Reynolds claimed "A second characteristic of scientifically oriented social work is that it accepts the objective reality of forces outside itself with which it must cooperate" (Reynolds, 1942, p. 24). Can this assumption of an objective reality, known in philosophy as **realism,** be irrefutably shown to be true? No, but for the purposes of attempting to improve the condition of the world we live in, some such practical assumptions must be accepted.

We urge the reader to understand that the assumption of the validity of some of these philosophical beliefs does not preclude accepting others, even those apparently at odds with the former. For example, the assumption of realism does not disavow the importance of individual clients' perceptions of their world, or of the meaning they ascribe to their lives and relationships. Nor does it deny that to some extent individuals construct their own reality. But realism asserts that there *is* an element to the client's world that objectively exists, and that this is often a very important one, in fact often the *most* important to program evaluators. For example, evaluations of domestic violence interventions are more likely to be interested in ascertaining whether or not acts of violence *really* declined or ceased, as opposed to trying to understand a spouse's "meaning" of what it means to be beaten. Evaluating a neighborhood watch crime reduction program may look at community members' perceptions of crime rates, but the *actual* rates of various crimes before and after the implementation of the neighborhood watch program are usually seen as more important. Program evaluations usually focus on determining objective *changes* in the lives of clients, not on understanding subjective processes. Of course, it is a legitimate part of science to study such subjective processes, such as the meaning to clients of changes brought about by a program, but such is not usually the primary focus of program evaluation. Sometimes evaluation studies encompass both aspects of the impact of programs, objective and subjective, and that can be worthwhile.

To accept **determinism** does not deny that many other phenomena (e.g., psychosocial problems) exist and possess such a complex constellation of interlocking etiological factors that creates an appearance of chaos or randomness at times. And it may be that only a portion of a particular psychosocial phenomena is "determined" in a scientific sense. If so, then it is the task of scientific inquiry and of program evaluation to fully explore the limits of this determinism, even if it yields an understanding less than 100 percent complete. A "Program of Assertive Community Treatment" that helps reduce psychiatric rehospitalization by 30 percent among the chronically mentally ill is not a failure because it is not 100 percent effective. Clearly, a 30 percent reduction leaves much to be understood and plenty of room for additional improvements. But 30 percent is 30 percent better than where the clients were previously. To be a **positivist** is not to assert that certain knowledge in a particular area currently exists, but rather to claim that it is a good idea to strive for such knowledge

through scientific methods because this will result in ever closer approximations to truth. Although one may be an **empiricist,** this need not deny the role
of common sense, intuition, authority, and tradition as potentially valuable
sources of knowledge.

Rationalism contends that factual explanations for psychosocial phenomena can be arrived at via logic—armchair reasoning if you will. Unfortunately,
rationalism can also lead to errors. Thus, rationalism and logical thinking are
seen as components of ultimately truthful explanations (e.g., being able to
explain logically why a program works), but these conclusions *must* be evaluated using empirical tests, as these are the best means of sorting out truth from
fiction.

Parsimony in theory is nothing new. Clinicians are taught, for example, to
exclude organic factors as possible causes of a client's depression prior to
implementing an intervention based on a presumptive psychodynamic etiol-
ogy. Similarly, a theoretical explanation that uses fewer unverified factors is
generally preferred over one that invokes more complex accounts. Consider,
for instance, that for many years homosexuality was associated with severe
psychopathology. Why? Well, many homosexuals sought treatment from psy-
chiatrists and other mental health professionals. Thus, they appeared to have
greater pathology than the general population. Was the assumption correct?
One possibility was that homosexuality was associated with mental disorder.
The second possibility was that this conclusion was only a distortion caused
by a selection bias (those seeking treatment for mental and emotional problems were not representative of all gays and lesbians). Parsimony suggested
that careful attention be given to the latter explanation prior to accepting the
former; and indeed, studies have found that gays and lesbians are no more or
less mentally disordered than heterosexuals. Certainly not all parsimonious
explanations possess greater validity than more complex reasons. After all,
many psychosocial problems are *really* very complex. Parsimony simply cautions us to rule out or entertain potentially simpler accounts prior to accepting more involved ones.

Pragmatism, although commonly seen as synonymous with practicality,
has a more in-depth meaning involving the *consequences* of some program.
According to pragmatism, the "meaning" of a child abuse prevention program
resides in the numbers of children who are not exposed to abuse as a result of
that program. A job-finding program's real meaning is based on the number of
clients successfully placed in good jobs. A program or intervention that fails to
produce any changes can be said, in a pragmatic sense, to be a meaningless program. The meaning of a program is not how clients or service providers view
the service, but stems from the practical, positive results obtained because of
involvement with it. Pragmatism does not exclude other (perhaps more subjec-
tivist) interpretations of what a program may mean to individuals; but for the
purposes of program evaluation and practice in the human services, it refers to
the practical outcomes of an intervention. And that, after all, is what program
evaluation is aimed at finding out.

Scientific skepticism is the profession's shield against the premature adoption of unsupported claims. The burden of proof lays at the feet of the person making an unusual claim. "Facilitated communication helps kids with an autistic disorder communicate." "Neurolinguistic programming is an effective treatment for phobias." "Primal scream therapy helps people who are depressed." It is not difficult for the reader to encounter such claims every day. Scientific skepticism is the modest request that such assertions be supported with credible evidence prior to being accepted or widely adopted in practice. The burden of proof is not on the skeptic to show that these things do not work—it rests with the proponents to demonstrate that they do. Unlike the doctrine of **nihilism,** a point of view fatal to the spirit of scientific inquiry, skepticism is a tempered perspective. It does not deny the possibility that genuinely truthful explanations can be obtained; skepticism requires only that appropriate proofs be provided for positive assertions. Whenever a human services professional encounters a proposal to fund a new program, it is always a good idea (scientifically, if not politically) to ask "Where are the data to support this approach?"

We like the idea of using the national census to illustrate these principles. At a given point in time, *one* number represents how many persons live in the United States (realism). The census is designed to try and capture this mythic number as closely as possible (positivism). The scientific methods used by the Bureau of the Census attempt to use empirical and operationalized methods to obtain data from U.S. residents. This is certainly not a perfect approach to trying to gain an accurate census—minorities of color, undocumented aliens, and other marginalized persons (e.g., the homeless) are undercounted. However, no reasonable alternative methodologies outside of conventional scientific inquiry can be employed for this purpose. We cannot simply ask some noted authority, "Excuse me, Mr. President, how many people are there in the United States at this moment?" Our intuition or even personal practice experience cannot help, and it is extremely unlikely that divine revelation will lend a hand. Similarly, it can be assumed that certain outcomes follow clients' experiences with a particular human services program, and it is the task of the program evaluator to best ascertain what these outcomes may be. Cumbersome and imperfect though they may sometimes be, there is no substitute for systematic, empirically oriented efforts at evaluation guided by the methods and philosophy of mainstream science, which, parenthetically, can embrace both quantitative and qualitative research approaches.

Lastly, the notion of what might be called **anecdotism**—the belief that anecdotes prove something empirically—needs to be addressed. Personal experiences and accounts can create very powerful belief systems that may yield true conclusions in a situation or for a particular individual. Someone who is mugged by a bearded bandit may justifiably be afraid of this fellow the next time he is encountered; however, to generalize that fear to all bearded individuals would be unfortunate. The problem with anecdotes is that their "truth" may not generalize.

At the same time, the personal experiences of clients and staff with a program are important to the program evaluator. We want to know about the problems encountered and the good things that resulted. These experiences may become part of a qualitative evaluation or aggregated into more of a quantitative evaluation. However, we should not assume that an individual anecdote (or even several of them) constitutes a *philosophical foundation* for program evaluation. Although a single event (e.g., death of a client) may trigger an evaluation, that event does not provide a worldview guiding all inquiry as do the positions previously discussed (scientific skepticism, pragmatism, and so on). Science does not reject anecdotes as false, or claim that all are false, but merely asserts that as evidence they provide a low level of proof and that they are most meaningful when augmented by more robust standards of evidence. It has been justifiably said that the plural of anecdote is not data.

MORE ON POSITIVISM

Much discussion has been expended in the program evaluation literatures over the meaning of the term *positivism,* and of its value as a foundation for inquiry in the human services. Keep in mind that from its inception, professional social work accepted the doctrine of positivism, established in the early part of the 1800s by the French philosopher and scientist Auguste Comte. Comte is said to have established the discipline of sociology, which he originally called *social physics,* based on his contention that human behavior could be studied using the same tools and principles that science used to study natural phenomena.

> The word *positive* came from *ponere* and had been employed since the fourteenth century to mean *laid down*. In the sixteenth century, it began to refer to knowledge that was based on facts and was thus reasonably certain. Eighteenth century thinkers used the word *positive* to oppose the *metaphysical*. (Pickering, 1993, p. 65)

According to Comte, "Unlike theological beliefs, scientific truths could be proved if necessary. . . . [S]cientific *truths* were always provisional because they could be proved wrong at any time" (Pickering, 1993, p. 171). Despite its name, positivism took a provisional approach to the development of knowledge, with Comte noting in 1825 that "Scientific laws were only *hypotheses* constructed by man with *external materials* and confirmed by observation; they amounted to no more than approximations of a reality that could never be rigorously understood" (Pickering, 1993, p. 294).

From its inception, positivism was concerned not just with studying human phenomena, but also with improving the human condition. "Social science was not . . . just an intellectual mixture of history, the physical sciences, physiology, and political economy. It had a practical vocation: *to regenerate society.* . . . Although Comte admitted that we could never fully know external reality, he assumed that scientific theories were getting closer to representing it *exactly*" (Pickering, 1993, p. 294, 296, italics added). Positivism came to exert an enormous influence on science, on the emerging social sciences, and in social welfare particular. In the United States, the American Social Science Association (ASSA) was established in 1865, and set forth as its mandate:

> *Social science* was understood by (ASSA) members to refer to the whole realm of problematical relationships in human affairs. One became a social scientist "by contributing to the store of esoteric knowledge and practical expertise . . . a *new way to care for the insane or to administer charity*—all of these were equally valuable contributions to *social science.*" (Haskell, 1997, pp. 97–98, italics added)

> This Association proposes to afford to all persons interested in human improvement, an opportunity to consider social economics as a whole. . . . They are to collect all facts, diffuse all knowledge, and stimulate all inquiry, which have a bearing on *social welfare.* (Haskell, 1997, p. 102, italics added)

From the ASSA emerged, in 1879, the Conference on Charities, transformed in 1884 into the National Conference of Charities and Corrections (NCCC). In 1917 the NCCC became the National Conference on Social Work, transformed again into the National Conference on Social Welfare in 1957, which in turn dissolved in the mid-1980s. A paper presented at the 1889 meeting of the NCCC was titled "Scientific Charity" and an article appearing an 1894 issue of the influential journal *The Charities Review* was titled "A Scientific Basis for Charity." Such early works were a part of the movement called scientific charity (or scientific philanthropy), which had its own origins in the 1870s, again based on the fundamental assumptions of positivism.

The distinguished social work educator Frank Bruno (1964) provided this overview of a National Conference on Charities meeting of the late 1800s:

> Most of the leaders of the Conference accepted the implications of a scientific approach to social work problems. They acted on the tacit assumption that human ills—sickness, insanity, crime, poverty—could be subjected to study and methods of treatment, and that a theory of prevention could be formulated as well. . . . This attitude raised these problems out of the realm of mysticism into that of a science. . . . As a result of the adoption of this scientific attitude, Conference speakers and programs looked toward progress, not backward toward a golden age. They believed in the future; that it was possible, by patient, careful study and experimentation, to create a society much better than the one they lived in. (pp. 26–27)

And about 30 years earlier Bruno (1936) had provided his own congruent perspective on the integration of science and social work:

> Social work holds as its primary axiom that knowledge of human behavior can be acquired and interpreted by the senses and that inferences drawn from such knowledge can be tested by the principles of logic. The difference between the social work of the present and all of the preceding ages is the assumption that human behavior can be understood and is determined by causes which can be explained. We may not at present have a mastery of the methods of understanding behavior, but any scientific approach to behavior presupposed that it is not in its nature incomprehensible by sensory perceptions and inference therefrom. It follows from such a theory that understanding is the first step in the direction of control and that the various forms of human misery are susceptible not only of amelioration, which our predecessors attempted, but also of prevention or even of elimination, when once their nature is understood. (pp. 192–193)

Both of the above statements, dated though they may be, could be said to characterize the mainstream contemporary perspective adhered to by science in general, and by program evaluation in particular.

You will often encounter the term *positivism* in your academic studies, and in the program evaluation literature. Keep in mind the relatively simple premise behind it: "A paradigm introduced by Auguste Comte, which held that social behavior could be studied and understood in a rational, scientific manner—in contrast to explanations based on religion or superstition" (Rubin & Babbie, 1997, p. G-6). Positivism is an approach, not intended to represent accomplished facts about human behavior. Nor does positivism deny the potential utility of other nonscientific approaches to knowledge development in social work—tradition, values and ethics, religion, mysticism, all may have a valuable contributing role to our field. Asserting that one approach (called A) is useful, is not to say that B is valueless. Positivism does make strong claims regarding the value of scientific approaches to knowledge development in general and program evaluation in particular. Some may even claim it makes the strongest claims. What is important is the development of reliable and valid information, and this can be approached through many methods, including positivistic ones.

CHAPTER RECAP

Whether you are a direct service worker, program director, or an agency administrator, you want the agency that employs you to be well managed and responsive to the needs of clients and community. How does an agency become a well-managed agency? One essential way is the evaluation of its efforts, where problems are identified and corrective action taken (Sugarman, 1988).

What is essential to learn about program evaluation? Besides understanding the purpose of program evaluations and some of the various reasons why they are conducted, you need to know the difference between a subjectively held opinion and one that is derived from objective data. This book will help you develop ways of identifying, collecting, and using data that will allow you to be as objective as possible when evaluating programs in the social and human services. Objective data are seen as having greater credibility and as providing better information for the decisions that face program managers. Evaluators use operational definitions to obtain objective data that can be replicated if necessary. Theoretical models suggest not only what interventions might work, but also where to find the changes that have resulted.

Questions for Class Discussion

1. Make a list of five or six human services programs with which you or members of the class are familiar. In another column, list what is known about how well each program does its job. For example, what is its success rate? Other than subjective feelings about these programs, what is known about

how "good" these programs are? In a third column, make a list of questions that you would like to have answered about each program.

2. Evaluators must operationally define what will be recognized as "success" or a "successful outcome." Try your hand at operationally defining "success" for several of the programs you listed in question 1.

3. For the human services programs you listed in question 1, discuss your ideas about theoretical orientations on which the interventions might be based.

4. Discuss your experiences with program evaluation in your job or field practicum.

5. What are the characteristics of a "good" television program? Make a list of all the subjective opinions held by the class members about a "good" television program. How could you objectively determine if a television program is "good"?

6. Why is it necessary to develop operational definitions about such things as what constitutes recidivism or a successful client outcome? Use specific examples.

Mini-Projects: Experiencing Evaluation Firsthand

1. Choose a product (e.g., coffee makers, tape recorders, DVD player, televisions, microwave ovens), and develop a set of objective standards that could help consumers select a model of superior performance and avoid the inferior models. Once you have finished, consult back issues of *Consumer Reports* to see how the standards you used compare with those used by the Consumer Products Testing Union.

2. What would you request in the way of an evaluation if you were in a position to require evaluation of a national program? Select a national program, and identify what information would be needed in order for an unbiased panel of experts to conclude that the program was successful.

3. Find an example of a program evaluation study published in a professional journal. We suggest that you learn to use the online database called PsycINFO, which is likely available via your local university library (it is an electronic database usually available in university libraries), to locate such studies. Briefly describe how key variables were operationally defined in this study, how the program's success was measured, and whether or not the program explicitly made use of an explanatory theory—etiological or interventive, or both.

References and Resources

American Counseling Association. (1999). *Code of ethics.* Alexandria, VA: Author. www.counseling.org/resources/codeofethics. htm.

American Psychiatric Association. (2000). *Diagnostic and statistical manual for mental Disorders IV-TR.* Washington, DC: Author.

Ammerman, R. T., Hersen, M., & Last, C. G. (Eds.). (1999). Handbook of prescriptive treatments for children and adolescents (2nd ed.). Boston: Allyn & Bacon.

Angell, R. C. (1954). A research basis for welfare practice. *Social Work Journal, 35,* 145–148, 169–171.

Austin, D. M. (1998). *A report on progress in the development of research resources in social work.* Austin, TX: University of Texas School of Social Work.

Barker, R. (Ed.). (2003). *The social work dictionary* (5th ed.). Washington, DC: NASW Press. Board of Professional Affairs, Committee on Professional Standards. (1987). General guidelines for providers of psychological services. *American Psychologist, 42,* 1–12.

Board of Professional Affairs, Committee on Professional Standards. (1987). General guidelines for providers of psychological services. *American Psychologist, 42,* 1–12.

Bruno, F. (1936). *The theory of social work.* New York: Health.

Bruno, F. (1964). *Trends in social work: 1874–1956.* New York: Columbia University Press.

Cabot, R. (1931). Treatment in social casework and the need of criteria and of tests of its success or failure. *Proceedings of the National Conference of Social Work.*

Chambless, D., Sanderson, W., Shoham, V., Johnson, S., Pope, K., Crits-Cristoph, P., Baker, M., R:Johnson, B., Woody, S., Sue, S., Beutler, L., Williams, D., & McCurry, S. (1996). An update on empirically validated therapies. *The Clinical Psychologist, 49*(2), 5–18.

Conrad, K. J. & Miller, T. Q. (1987). Measuring and testing program philosophy. *New Directions for Program Evaluation, 33,* 19–42.

Christophersen, E. R., & Mortweet, S. L. (2001). Treatments that work with children: Empirically supported strategies for managing childhood problems. Washington, DC: American Psychological Association.

Dukes, P. L., Ullman, J. B., & Stein, J. A. (1996). A three-year follow-up of Drug Abuse Resistance Education. *Evaluation Review, 20,* 49–66.

Ell, K. (1996). Social work research and health care practice and policy: A psychosocial research agenda. *Social Work, 41,* 583–592.

Foa, E. B., Dancu, C. V., Hembree, E. A., Jaycox, L. H., Meadows, E. A., & Street, G. P. (1999). A comparison of exposure therapy, stress inoculation training, and their combination for reducing posttraumatic stress disorder in female assault victims. *Journal of Consulting and Clinical Psychology, 67,* 194–200.

Foa, E. B., Rothbaum, B. O., Riggs, D. S., & Murdock, T. B. (1992).Treatment of posttraumatic stress disorder in rape victims: A comparison between cognitive-behavioral procedures and counseling. *Journal of Consulting and Clinical Psychology, 59,* 715–723.

Gambrill, E. (1999). Evidence-based practice: An alternative to authority-based practice. *Families in Society, 80,* 341–350.

Giles, T. R. (Ed.). (1993). *Handbook of effective psychotherapy.* New York: Plenum.

Greenwood, E. (1957). Social work research: A decade of reappraisal. *Social Service Review, 31,* 311–320.

Gyorky, Z., Royalty, G. M., & Johnson, D. H. (1994).Time-limited therapy in university counseling centers: Do time-limited and time-unlimited centers differ? *Professional Psychology: Research and Practice, 25*(1), 50–54.

Haskell, T. L. (1997). *The emergence of professional social science: The American Social Science Association.* Urbana, IL: The University of Illinois Press.

Hibbs, E. D., & Jensen, P. S. (Eds.). (1996). *Psychosocial treatments for child and adolescent disorders: Empirically based strategies for clinical practice.*

Washington, DC: American Psychological Association Press.

Hill, D. (1998). *Drug money. Brandweek*, 39(17), 20–26.

Jemmott, L. S., & Jemmott, J. B. (1991). Applying the theory of reasoned action to AIDS risk behavior: Condom use among black women. *Nursing Research, 40*(4), 228–234.

Kolata, G. (1994, May 4). Clinic entices patients by paying them $10 a visit. *New York Times*, B8.

LeCroy, C. W. (1994). *Handbook of child and adolescent treatment manuals*. New York: Lexington.

Lynam, D., Milich, R., Zimmerman, R., Novak, S., Logan, T. K., Martin, C., Leukefeld, C., & Clayton, R. (1999). Project DARE: No effects at 10-year follow-up. *Journal of Consulting and Clinical Psychology, 67*, 590–593.

Mash, E. J. & Barkley, R.A. (Eds.). (1998). *Treatment of childhood disorders* (2nd ed.). New York: Guilford.

Mullen, E. (1995). A review of *Research utilization in the social services. Social Work, 40*, 282–283.

Nathan, P. E., & Gorman, J. M. (Eds.). (1998). *A guide to treatments that work*. New York: Oxford.

National Association of Social Workers. (1989). *NASW standards for the practice of clinical social work*. Silver Spring, MD: Author.

National Association of Social Workers. (1992). *NASW standards for school social work services*. Washington, DC: NASW Press.

National Association of Social Workers. (1999). *Code of ethics*. Washington, DC: NASW Press.

Passell, P. (1993, March 9). Like a new drug, social programs are put to the test. *New York Times*, B5.

Pickering, M. (1993). *Auguste Comte: An intellectual biography, vol. I*. New York: Cambridge University Press.

Proctor, E. K. (1998). Social work research and the quest for effective practice. *Social Work Research, 23*, 4–14.

Reynolds, B. C. (1942). Learning and teaching in the practice of social work. New York: Farrar & Rinehart.

Rosen, A., Proctor, E. K., & Staudt, M. M. (1999). Social work research and the quest for effective practice. *Social Work Research, 23*, 4–14.

Rosenberg, M. L. & Brody, R. (1974). The threat or challenge of accountability. *Social Work, 19*, 344–350.

Rubin, A. & Babbie, E. (1997). *Research Methods for Social Work* (3rd ed.). Pacific Grove, CA: Brooks/Cole.

Rutter, M. (1987). Psychosocial resilience and protective mechanisms. *American Journal of Orthopsychiatry, 57*, 316–331.

Sackett, D. L., Richardson, W. S., Rosenberg, W., & Haynes, R. R. (1997). *Evidence-based medicine: How to practice and teach E.M.* New York: Churchill-Livingston.

Sackett, D. L., Strauss, S. E. Richardson, W. S., Rosenberg, W., & Haynes, R. R. (2000). *Evidence-based medicine: How to practice and teach E.M.* (2nd ed.). New York: Churchill-Livingston.

Saunders, D. G. (1992). A typology of men who batter: Three types derived from cluster analysis. *American Journal or Orthopsychiatry, 62*, 264–275.

Schalock, R. L., & Thornton, C. V. D. (1988). *Program evaluation: A field guide for administrators*. New York: Plenum.

Seligman, L. (1998). *Selecting effective treatments: A comprehensive, systematic guide for treating mental disorders*. San Francisco: Jossey-Bass.

Sugarman, B. (1988).The well-managed human service organization: Criteria for a management audit. *Administration in Social Work, 12*(4), 12–27.

Telch, C. F., Agras, W. S., Rossiter, E. M., Wilfley, D., & Kenardy, J. (1990). Group cognitive-behavioral treatment for the nonpurging bulimic: An initial evaluation. *Journal of Consulting and Clinical Psychology, 58,* 629–635.

Thyer, B. A. (2001). What is the role of theory in research on social work practice? *Journal of Social Work Education, 37,* 9–25.

Thyer, B. A. (2004). What is evidence-based practice? *Brief Treatment and Crisis Intervention, 4,* 167–176.

Thyer, B. A., & Wodarski, J. S. (Eds.). (1998). *Handbook of empirical social work practice: Vol. 1. Mental disorders.* New York: Wiley.

Tripodi, T. (1987). Program evaluation. In A. Minahan (Ed.), *Encyclopedia of social work.* Silver Spring, MD: National Association of Social Workers.

Van Hasselt, V. B., & Hersen, M. (Eds.). (1996). A sourcebook of psychological treatment manuals for adult disorders. New York: Plenum.

Weiss, B., Catron, T., Harris, V., & Phung, T. M. (1999).The effectiveness of traditional child psychotherapy. *Journal of Consulting and Clinical Psychology, 67,* 82–94.

Wodarski, J. S., & Thyer, B. A. (Eds.). (1998). *Handbook of empirical social work practice: Vol. 2. Psychosocial problems and practice issues.* New York: Wiley.

Zambelli, G. C., & Derosa, A. P. (1992). Bereavement support groups for school-aged children: Theory, intervention, and case example. *American Journal of Orthopsychiatry, 62*(4), 484–493.

ETHICAL ISSUES IN PROGRAM EVALUATION

Ethical issues in program evaluation encompass a broad realm of concerns that become heightened when the subjects of a study are vulnerable in some way. Although often assumed to be most acute during medical experiments, threats to research participants in evaluation research can also be harmful, even if not life threatening. Often relegated solely to discussions of the vagaries of IRB review, ethical issues play a vital and ongoing role in program evaluation.

HISTORICAL BACKGROUND: WHY IRBs ARE NECESSARY

Revelations of the outrages of Nazi wartime experiments and the Tuskegee study in the United States created a climate of dramatic reform by the 1970s that resulted in 1974 in federal regulations for research involving human subjects. The legislation created institutional review boards (IRBs) in all organizations receiving federal funds (universities, hospitals, and other large public service organizations). IRBs were empowered to review the investigator's research objectives, methodology, and procedures (the research **protocol**), with special emphasis on plans for recruiting subjects and gaining their consent.

IRBs were created to protect human subjects from research that is risky, harmful, or does not respect the rights and dignity of human beings. These boards are usually comprised of professionals knowledgeable about research methods as well as lay citizens representing the community. It is the IRB's task to consider proposed research and to determine whether it follows ethical guidelines set forth by the federal government. Perhaps not surprisingly, IRBs vary in the strictness of their interpretation of these guidelines, although most tend to require detailed protocols submitted for review before giving approval.

Do we need IRBs? Are they a waste of time for the knowledgeable and ethical researcher? Despite widespread awareness of the Nazi atrocities by physicians and other professionals, serious and flagrant abuses of human subjects occurred in this country, the most notorious of these was the infamous Tuskegee study conducted by the U.S. Public Health Service. Beginning in 1932, 400 black males, mostly poor and illiterate, with tertiary-stage syphilis were informed that they would receive free treatment for their "bad blood." In actuality, these men received no treatment for syphilis even after penicillin became available. Instead, they received free physical exams, periodic blood testing, hot meals on examination days, free treatment for minor disorders, and a modest burial fee.

Although the Public Health Service officials reviewed the Tuskegee study, it continued uninterrupted until 1972, when a reporter exposed the study in the *New York Times*. Only afterward were the survivors and their infected wives given treatment for the disease (Jones, 1981). Indeed, the public outcry over the Tuskegee study led Congress to pass the National Research Act (Public Law 93–348) in 1974 mandating the formation of IRBs. The legacy of Tuskegee, and the profound distrust it engendered regarding research ethics, continues today in African American communities and elsewhere.

The National Commission for the Protection of Human Subjects in Biomedical and Behavioral Research (the Belmont Report) identified three ethical principles for research on humans: *beneficence*—maximizing good outcomes for humanity and research subjects while minimizing or avoiding risk or harm; *respect*—protecting the autonomy of all persons and treating them with courtesy and respect, including those who are most vulnerable; and *justice*—ensuring reasonable, nonexploitative, and well-considered procedures are administered fairly (the fair distribution of costs and benefits).These principles have been fashioned into the following ethical guidelines for researchers and evaluators to follow.

ETHICAL GUIDELINES

Guideline 1: Research Subjects Must Be Volunteers   All of those participating in a research or evaluation effort should freely decide to participate. No coercion of any kind can be used to secure participants for a study. Subjects must also be competent to understand their choices. If they are not considered able to fully comprehend (e.g., individuals under age 18 or impaired mentally), then their legal caretakers must give permission, and the subjects still must give assent. This means that even if parents give permission for their children to participate in a research project, these children may still refuse. Although very young children are generally asked to *orally* assent to research procedures in language they can understand, the older the minor, the more the informed consent should conform to a written document like adults would receive.

The subject's right to self-determination must be respected, and the research participant is free to withdraw from the study at any time. In most instances, IRBs require that written permission be obtained from subjects of the research. Consent forms usually provide general but brief information on the nature of the project and indicate that the subject is free to withdraw consent and to discontinue participation in the project at any time without any penalty or loss of benefits. (See Figure 2.1.)

When evaluating a social service program, it is vitally important that recipients of services fully understand their right to refuse participation in a study and that this will in no way affect delivery of services to them in the present or at any future time. Evaluators can use the checklist to ensure that all the necessary informational items are contained in the informed consent forms they write. (See Box 2.1.)

Consent forms are not typically employed with routine mail or telephone surveys unless the data being gathered are in some way sensitive (e.g., involve information about a client's past or present drug use or illegal activities). In such cases, consent forms may need to be mailed by the host social service organization and consent obtained before the researcher is given access to clients' names or addresses.

When questionnaires are used or interviews are conducted with adults who are not part of a vulnerable population, for example, a needs assessment survey, the principle of implied consent is often used—that is, the act of participation is

 BOX 2.1 | CHECKLIST FOR INFORMED CONSENT FORMS

Each informed consent form should contain explanation of the following points:

___ How the research subject was chosen/invited to participate and how many will be involved
___ Who is conducting the study
___ The purpose of the study
___ Where the study will take place and how long it will last
___ What is required of the research subject
___ Possible risks or discomforts
___ Possible benefits of participation
___ Alternatives associated with nonparticipation
___ Any costs of participation
___ Payment or incentives for taking part in the study
___ Stopping or ending participation
___ What happens if medical attention is needed
___ Who can answer questions about the project

FIGURE 2.1 | **CONSENT TO PARTICIPATE IN A RESEARCH STUDY**

Outpatient Drug Treatment Program Aftercare Study

Investigator:
Ellen Samovar, MSW, Principal Investigator, (231) 555–5760

I _____ have been asked to participate in an evaluation of the Outpatient Drug Treatment Program (ODTP) being conducted by Ms. Samovar.

Purpose:
I understand that the purpose of this study is to examine the success of the Outpatient Drug Treatment Program in which I am participating—to learn how approximately 300 clients have stopped using drugs and what factors may influence these decisions.

Duration and Location:
I understand the study will take place at the ODTP offices on 717 South First Street. Further, I understand that the study will take about 60 minutes of my time on two different occasions.

Procedures:
I will be asked to answer questions about my social and psychological well-being, relationships, employment, drug use, and illegal activities. In addition, I will be asked to provide a urine sample to test for evidence of drugs in my system and will be given a Breathalyzer to test for alcohol.

Risks/Discomforts:
It has been explained to me that some of the interview questions are very personal, involving drug and criminal behavior, and may cause some discomfort in answering them.

Benefits:
I understand that the benefits from participating in this study may be to help researchers and those involved in public policy better understand the factors that lead to the starting and stopping of drug use.

Confidentiality:
I understand that a research code number will be used to identify my responses from those of other clients and that my name, address, and other identifying information will not be directly associated with any information obtained from me. A master listing of persons participating in the study and their identifying information will be kept in a secure location under lock and key except when being used by select staff. Further, I understand that a certificate of confidentiality has been obtained from the Department of Health and Human Services (DHHS) that protects investigators from being forced to release any of my data, even under a court order or a subpoena. When results of this study are published, my name or other identifying information will not be used.

Payments:
I will be paid $20 for my time and cooperation for each scheduled testing episode. If I stop early, I understand that I will be paid an amount appropriate to the time I have spent.

Right to Withdraw:
I understand that I do not have to take part in this study, and my refusal to participate will involve no penalty or loss of rights to which I am entitled. I may withdraw from the study at any time without fear of losing any services or benefits to which I am entitled.

FIGURE 2.1 | CONTINUED

Signatures:
I have read this entire consent form and completely understand my rights as a potential research subject. I voluntarily consent to participate in this research. I have been informed that I will receive a copy of this consent should questions arise and I wish to contact Ms. Samovar or the University of Somewhere's Institutional Review Board (231-555-4949) to discuss my rights as a research subject.

_____	_____
Signature of Research Subject	Date
_____	_____
Signature of Witness	Date
_____	_____
Signature of Investigator	Date

seen as giving informed consent. In these instances, IRBs may not require written consent. However, a problem arises when potential subjects feel that they cannot refuse to participate. If these subjects are clients (for example, persons on probation or parole, or recipients of some form of public assistance), they may not feel free to refuse without putting themselves in some jeopardy. This is when consultation with an IRB can come in handy. The IRB may suggest alternative ways to collect data or to reduce any implied coercion by informing potential subjects of their rights in writing.

Human services professionals must be alert to the possibility that encouraging clients to participate in research can be perceived as coercion. Because professionals are "gatekeepers" of services, clients can feel pressured into participating in order to gain access to or continue receiving services.

Guideline 2: Potential Subjects Should Be Given Sufficient Information about the Study to Determine Any Possible Risks or Discomforts as Well as Benefits
Sufficient information includes an explanation of the purpose of the research, the expected duration of the subject's participation, the procedures to be followed, and the identification of any of procedures that might be experimental. The evaluator must be specific about any procedures that will involve the research subjects. Any potential risks must be identified. Subjects should be given the opportunity to raise and have answered any questions about the study or any procedures that will be used. Subjects must also be allowed to inquire at any time (and have their questions answered) about procedures that are used.

Consent forms should be written at a level of readability that the program participants can understand. A good rule of thumb is to try not to exceed a ninth- or tenth-grade reading level with adult populations. Further, the use of first person "I" seems to make the informed consent easier to understand than use of the second or third person.

Guideline 3: No Harm Shall Result as a Consequence of Participation in the Evaluation   Although there is much less possibility of harm resulting from an intervention in the social or human services than from biomedical research, this guideline suggests that *no* harm should result. This guideline would be violated, for instance, if an evaluator contacted battered women some months after they had returned to an abusive situation and if there was a risk that talking to the evaluators might trigger another episode of violent assault. Clients can also suffer emotional or psychological harm. Psychological risks could result from procedures that reduce subjects' self-esteem or give them a sense that they are not as smart as some others. Asking questions about past traumatic or abusive episodes could make certain subjects depressed and even potentially suicidal.

Other risks to consider are those associated with damage to reputations and one's employment if information about illegal behaviors—drug use, child abuse, stealing, and so on—became known. Although a rare event, subjects' confidentiality would surely be compromised if the evaluator receives a subpoena and is forced to reveal sensitive information. An employee's job could be jeopardized in an evaluation that asked for an honest appraisal of management if someone else in the agency was able to read or overhear responses that were critical of a supervisor.

More frequently confronted is the issue of mandated reporting in which confidentiality *must* be breached by a researcher who is a social worker or teacher legally bound to report incidents of child or elder abuse. Such a likelihood must be noted in the consent form signed in advance by research participants. In summary, the "rule" favoring confidentiality should be superseded only by legal requirements and the potential for inadvertent harm should concern every evaluator.

Guideline 4: Protection of Sensitive Information   The privacy of human subjects is protected by:

- Allowing subjects to respond anonymously, if at all possible. If the research design cannot accommodate anonymity, protection is provided by:
- Separating any personally identifying information from the research data through the use of numeric or other special codes. Where complete anonymity is not possible (a common occurrence in program evaluation), it is preferable to use code numbers to help guard against unauthorized persons accidentally recognizing or identifying program participants.

ANONYMITY AND CONFIDENTIALITY

Anonymity means that the research participant cannot be identified by any means or by any person. When anonymity is promised, not even the researcher should be able to associate a response with a particular individual. Researchers need to be sensitive to the issue that participants can sometimes be recognized not from their personal identifiers like addresses and social security numbers but from sociodemographic information. For instance, a small agency might employ only one female Asian American or only one Ph.D. who is 50 years of age. With small samples of research subjects, researchers might want to use broad categories for such variables as age, education, ethnic groupings, and years of experience in order to keep from identifying persons with unique characteristics.

   Confidentiality means that the potentially sensitive or private information is being supplied with the understanding that the research participant's identity, although known to the researcher, will be protected. Sometimes it is necessary to know a research participant's name, address, phone number, or social security number in order to match current information with medical records or prior offenses, or even when pre- and posttesting of an intervention are being done. Where it is necessary to know the identities of research subjects, investigators routinely use a coding scheme so that personally identifying information is not contained on clients' survey forms, assessment forms, and so on. The listing that links code numbers with individuals' names is always kept in a secure, locked area except when being used.

The privacy of human subjects is further protected by not capturing or reporting personal information unless it is necessary to the study. When sensitive data must be obtained, it should be kept in locked cabinets or files until no longer needed, and then destroyed. (Material to be protected includes master lists of codes, lists of respondents, mailing lists, completed questionnaires, and transcripts of interviews.) (See Box 2.2 for further discussion of anonymity and confidentiality.)

In health care, the federal government recently enacted legislation designed to protect the privacy of medical patients and their records. The Health Insurance Portability and Accountability Act of 1996 (HIPAA), which required compliance effective April 14, 2003, introduced sweeping changes in outside access to medical records even as it promoted streamlined electronic record keeping to reduce paperwork. Although a patient's experience of HIPAA typically involves reading and signing an information sheet about medical privacy rights, researchers in health care must meet the challenges of HIPAA-related restrictions and the additional permissions that are required. Because hospital and medical institutions tend to interpret HIPAA requirements with varying degrees of strictness, we recommend that researchers consult closely with the IRBs under whose jurisdiction the study is being conducted.

The choice of methodology can affect how vulnerable a research participant may feel. Compared to qualitative methods that depend on in-depth information and use of verbatim quotes, quantitative methods offer greater protection via research findings presented in the aggregate, for example, group means and totals. For qualitative evaluations, the challenge is to never report anything that could be traced back to a specific individual. For instance, it would be a serious mistake to use the following quotation to show the depth of employees' feelings about a new director in a study of job satisfaction at a county-run social service agency:

> I've been working abuse investigation longer than anyone else here—22 years—and I can say, without any doubt in my mind, that our new executive director is all fluff and no substance. He doesn't have a clue about how to do his job; I'm not sure he would even recognize an abused child if he saw one.

To protect privacy, many IRBs prefer that researchers recruit participants through flyers soliciting volunteers who contact them directly, but this mode of sampling may not conform to an evaluation's design requirements. Other means of gaining access to eligible participants can take a number of forms. For example, an outside researcher may request that the agency contact clients through a letter informing them of the study and requesting their participation. If they give permission, client names, addresses, or phone numbers would be released to the researcher. If such contact conveys even a perception of coercion by the agency (and consequent fear of loss of services), the outside researcher may wish to reach out to clients directly by having study staff approach them in a waiting room or by letter and follow-up telephone call.

HOW ETHICAL GUIDELINES GET OPERATIONALIZED

As we mentioned earlier, institutional review boards (IRBs) must approve of research involving human subjects when the investigators are affiliated with large research-conducting institutions like universities and hospitals that receive federal funds. (See Box 2.3.) Institutional review boards perform several levels of review. The most cursory of these (the "exemption certificate") requires a brief form where the investigator specifies the objectives, the characteristics of the subject population, how the subjects will be recruited, the research procedures, and any potential physical, psychological, social, or legal risks to the subjects.

Research and evaluation activities are considered exempt from the federal policy for the protection of human subjects when the only involvement of human subjects falls within one or more of the following categories:

(a) Research conducted in established or commonly accepted educational settings, involving normal educational practices, such as (i) research or regular and special educational instructional strategies, or (ii) research on the effectiveness of or the comparison among instructional techniques, curricula, or classroom management methods

(b) Research involving use of education tests (cognitive, diagnostic, aptitude, achievement), survey procedures, interview procedures or observation of public behavior, unless (i) information obtained is recorded in such a manner that human subjects can be identified, directly or through identifiers linked to

EVALUATION VERSUS RESEARCH: IRB RAMIFICATIONS

Although it is abundantly clear that university-based researchers who are planning on recruiting and using human subjects ought to seek approval from their IRB, program evaluators employed by a private nonprofit agency just across the street may not have the same mandate. First of all, as noted earlier, program evaluation activities are generally exempted from IRB review when they are confined to internal monitoring and program development. That is, agencies, departments, bureaus, programs, and the like are entitled to look at the benefit and effects of their interventions without viewing it as research as long as the goal is to improve service delivery. [See exemption category (e).] Data that are routinely collected on individual clients within agencies often can be aggregated to evaluate programs without any special effort or imposition on the clients.

The threshold of what is considered research can be fuzzy and revolves largely around intent. A study intended for wide dissemination and knowledge building is considered research even if it involves use of routine program monitoring data. Second, many agencies do not receive any federal funds and therefore are not legally required to maintain their own IRB. However, this does not mean that evaluators in public agencies or private nonprofits can violate and ignore the ethical guidelines presented in this chapter. One cannot cloak oneself in the mantle of "evaluator" and treat clients or staff disrespectfully or harmfully. Not only would that be unethical, it might also fatten the wallets of some attorneys at one's expense. Researchers and evaluators ought to observe the same safeguards and protections for their subjects.

Confusion about IRB review may arise in a number of ways in community-based research (Wolf, Croughan, & Lo, 2002). First, a program might involve independent practitioners (e.g., physicians providing HIV/AIDs education) who are not affiliated with any institution and thus fall under no IRB jurisdiction. Second, multisite evaluations can involve some sites with IRBs and some without. The coordination and timing of review can be time and resource consuming because contradictory requests may arise or even a standoff when one IRB makes its approval contingent on approval by another IRB and vice versa!

A third challenge comes from the recent federal requirement that all research funded by the National Institutes of Health demonstrate that "key personnel" have received training in human subjects protections and passed an exam either administered by a local IRB or on the NIH website. This requirement is vague in defining key roles on a research project but it could be interpreted conservatively, including not only principal investigators but the receptionist who hands out the recruitment flyer (Wolf, Croughan, & Lo, 2002). Program evaluations (not an NIH research priority) might seem immune to this requirement, but many institutional IRBs are requiring that researchers take such training and pass an exam as a matter of course.

Despite the daunting nature of these challenges, most have been and continue to be met by creative solutions that adhere to federal requirements (Wolf et al., 2002). The safest approach in such situations is to contact a university's IRB and ask for guidance.

the subjects; and (ii) any disclosure of the human subjects' responses outside the research could reasonably place the subjects at risk of criminal or civil liability or be damaging to the subjects' financial standing, employability, or reputation

(c) Research involving the use of educational tests (cognitive, diagnostic, aptitude, achievement), survey procedures, interview procedures, or observation of public behavior that is not exempt under category (b) of this section, if the human subjects are elected or appointed public officials or candidates for public office; or (ii) federal statute(s) require(s) without exception that the confidentiality of the personally identifiable information will be maintained throughout the research and thereafter

(d) Research involving the collection or study of existing data, documents, records, pathological specimens, or diagnostic specimens, if these sources are publicly available or if the information is recorded by the investigator in such a manner that subjects cannot be identified, directly or through identifiers linked to the subjects; **to qualify for this exemption the data, documents, records, or specimens must be in existence before the project begins—the principle behind this policy is that the rights of individuals should be respected; subjects must consent to participation in research**

(e) Research and demonstration projects which are conducted by or subject to the approval of department or agency heads, and which are designed to study, evaluate, or otherwise examine (i) public benefit or service programs; (ii) procedures for obtaining benefits or services under those programs; (iii) possible changes in or alternatives to those programs or procedures; or (iv) possible changes in methods or levels of payment for benefits or services under those programs

(f) Taste and food quality evaluation and consumer acceptance studies. Exemption certifications *cannot* be granted for projects that involve:

- Minors (except in studies of curriculum and pedagogy)
- Pregnant women
- Prisoners
- Patients
- Those who are mentally disabled
- Deception
- Techniques that expose the subject to discomfort or harassment beyond levels encountered in daily life

The "expedited" category is another level of review that involves *minimal risk* (defined as meaning that the probability and magnitude of harm or discomfort anticipated in the research is not greater than ordinarily encountered in daily life or during the performance of routine physical or psychological examinations or tests). For instance, a study could be classified as expedited if it involved moderate exercise of healthy volunteers or the collection of a blood sample or other biological specimens such as hair clippings, sputum, or skin swabs. Also, collecting routine data from X-rays, ultrasound, magnetic imaging, or other diagnostic procedures as well as voice, video, digital, and image recordings made for research purposes fall into the expedited category.

Research projects that do not qualify for the exempted or expedited categories must go for "full review." Generally full review involves completing an application and meeting with the committee members of the IRB. Full review projects involve either vulnerable populations (e.g., minors, or prisoners) or procedures that are more than "minimal risk."

Although the thought of preparing a research protocol and appearing before an institutional review board might be somewhat intimidating, another way to see the process is as a review by concerned peers—individuals who really want good research to be produced. Their suggestions and comments may well improve your project.

RESEARCH WITH SPECIAL POPULATIONS

Children

As mentioned earlier, minors cannot give informed consent, and permission from their parents or guardians must be obtained. In the past, it was often possible to obtain survey-type data from schoolchildren with the principal's approval by sending home a notice to parents stating that if they objected to their child's participation, they could send a note or return a form to the principal. This practice, known as "passive consent," usually worked well from the researcher's perspective because few parents objected and refused their child's participation. From the parents' perspective, however, this was not a good practice because they did not always receive notices from the school about the upcoming research. Children are not always a reliable conduit of information, and many forms get lost or thrown away before parents see them.

As a result, the Family Privacy Act now requires explicit written consent from parents before their children can participate in any research containing sensitive questions about sexual, illegal, antisocial, or self-incriminating behavior and psychological problems. Researchers are concerned that this law will make it difficult to obtain representative samples of students because typically 40 to 50 percent of parents fail to respond to mailed or student-delivered active consent forms. Further, minority students and those from single-parent households are underrepresented in samples requiring active parental consent (Dent, Sussman, & Stacy, 1997).

Other ethical dilemmas are associated with conducting research with children. Gensheimer, Ayers, and Roosa (1993) have pointed out that the very act of recruiting special children (e.g., the children of alcoholics or children who are very obese) places them in a situation where labeling from other children is "almost assured." Additionally, some at-risk children may fear being harmed by a parent if they ask or indicate they want to participate in special programming. In order to ensure that parents sign permission forms, evaluators have to struggle with the issue of how much coaching or prompting of children is ethical. On the other side of the issue, could children who were adverse to participation truly feel that they could refuse if parents and teachers are encouraging them?

People with Diminished Capacity

Individuals with mental retardation, dementia, and severe psychosis pose special challenges for the researcher. Although persons with these diagnoses are often capable and willing research participants, they are usually not considered legally competent to give permission to participate in research without additional consent from a family member or guardian. There is no well-accepted standard for determining when a person with serious mental illness is stable enough to give informed consent or when persons with Alzheimer's disease have lost the capacity to give consent. Even mildly cognitively impaired older subjects with Alzheimer's may experience difficulty in understanding consent information (High, 1992). However, assent from the subject should still be sought (High, Whitehouse, Post, & Berg, 1994).

POTENTIAL PROBLEMS IN CONDUCTING ETHICAL RESEARCH

Deception

Generally speaking, deception should not be employed unless there is no other way to study the phenomenon and the risk of participation is minimal. For example, deception might be acceptable if without it respondents would be too defensive or dishonest to respond truthfully.

At times, the informed consent that subjects must read and sign alerts them that some deception may be involved. At other times, the IRB can decide to waive the right of subjects to be fully informed but require a full debriefing after the data has been obtained from the subject(s). Because it is important that the deception does not cause subjects to lose confidence in science or the scientific process, IRBs also expect that subjects should be given ample opportunity to have their questions answered about the project at the time of the debriefing, and if they choose to do so, subjects should be allowed to withdraw their own data from the study.

Should you involve a deception? Clearly, you should not if someone could be harmed or could go away from the study with a feeling of having been degraded or exploited. For this reason, the decision to use deception should not be made without consultation with others. As part of this process, alternative methodologies for studying the problem should be considered.

Compensation

Is paying respondents or research subjects ever unethical? Although reimbursing subjects for costs incurred (such as babysitting, time away from work, transportation) might seem reasonable, questions are raised when there is a large financial incentive for participation. The guideline here is to avoid giving incentives that are so large or excessive that they constitute "undue inducement." When large financial rewards are offered for research subjects, there is also a risk that some individuals may fabricate information in order to become eligible for the payment.

Novice researchers should check with their more experienced colleagues to learn about the norms associated with research compensation because these can vary by time and place (Dickert & Gracy, 1999). Generally, the payment is greater if more time is being requested. Although participation in a one-hour interview might bring a $20 incentive, participation in a longitudinal study lasting several years could result in several hundred dollars in payouts.

For the typical program evaluation (which is budgeted on a shoestring), such research incentives can be prohibitive. There are alternatives, however. For example, lotteries have become popular as incentives because they enhance interest in participating without being as expensive as providing every participant with an inducement. Small incentives, such as a coupon for a meal at a fast-food restaurant or subway tokens, often can be valuable motivators and may even be more acceptable than handing out cash.

What is excessive compensation depends on the particular setting and group. For instance, Hornblum (1998), in discussing the experimentation that took place at Holmesburg Prison, cites a report describing prisoners who earned $100 a month, which is not a large amount of money by most standards. However, inside the prison it was a colossal sum that had a "disastrous effect upon the operations of Holmesburg Prison" and was a major contributor to low employee morale. What this compensation did was to create "disproportionate wealth and power in the hands of a few inmates" that led to "favoritism, bribery, and jealousy among the guards resulting in disrespect for supervisory authority and prison regulations" (p. 191).This "wealth" also contributed to sex-for-money schemes where research subjects were in a position to solicit young inmates by giving them "a steady stream of luxuries." Predatory inmates, after giving cigarettes, candy, and other items to these inmates for a few days, would demand repayment with sexual acts. Inmates who were not employed as research subjects earned 15 to 25 cents a day, and half of the inmates had no prison job at all (p. 190). To prevent this from occurring, some prisons refuse to allow inmates to be paid incentives and others require researchers to "bank" incentive payments until the inmate's release.

Denial of Treatment/Use of Control Groups

Sometimes professionals voice strong objections to evaluating social service programs because they are of the mistaken opinion that any clients who are assigned to a control group must be denied treatment. Although it is true that drug trials randomly assign participants to a control group where they receive a **placebo** (a neutral substance or activity that *appears* to be treatment but actually has no effect), no-treatment groups are extremely rare in evaluations conducted in social service agencies.

However, this does not mean that the concept of control groups is abandoned. Subjects in the control condition may be given "standard or usual care" or they may be administered an alternative form of the program or intervention (e.g., peer group versus individual counseling approaches to treating substance abuse). In agencies or programs where there is a long waiting list, evaluators have a natural quasi-experimental control group—those who are waiting for service. Pretest measures can be administered to the members of this group at the point of first contact, and then posttests can be administered immediately before they begin the intervention.

A third measure could also be taken at the point of completion of treatment. Thus, the evaluator can use a time series (longitudinal) evaluation design, as shown in the schematic in Figure 2.2. Because there is no treatment between O_1 and O_2, this period of waiting for services constitutes a baseline against which any improvement that occurs between O_2 and O_3 can be compared.

Although it is extremely unlikely that anyone would propose implementing an intervention that did not have at least some evidence that it worked in a pilot test, one problem with new interventions is that their effectiveness is not established. Clients or patients assigned to receive the new treatment could be worse off than those who received usual care. Thus, another approach is to allow those in the experimental condition to get the new intervention *plus* the old intervention and to compare those results with those who got just the usual intervention. Although this approach is more expensive and labor-intensive, it can establish that the intensive approach is superior to the standard intervention. Such a finding then provides grounds for another study to determine if the new intervention alone is just as good or better than the usual intervention.

A quasi-experimental approach to obtaining a control group is to compare the program participants in one agency with those in a similar program or agency. A *comparison* group is not the same as a randomly assigned control group because there may be obvious, or not so obvious, differences in the clientele of the two agencies. However, sometimes the clientele are very similar in their important characteristics—it is just that the clients live in different parts of the city or in different cities. If the management of the other program is willing to participate and contribute client data, it is possible to determine, with statistical tests, if the two different client groups are, in fact, similar in terms of age, income, gender, education, and other important characteristics.

FIGURE 2.2 | TIME SERIES (LONGITUDINAL) DESIGN

O_1	O_2	X	O_3
Initial contact	Assessment immediately before treatment	Treatment	Posttest

Natural comparison groups occur in most agencies and should not be overlooked as research subjects who can provide information about those who receive no or little treatment. That is, some portion of every agency's clients makes an initial contact, perhaps receiving an intake assessment, but then never follows up for a second appointment. So, dropouts, no-shows, and treatment refusers (some court-mandated clients opt to go to jail rather than to participate in counseling or psychoeducational services) can be utilized for a quasi-experimental type of evaluation design. Of course, the evaluator needs to be cautious and not assume that these clients are representative of the total agency caseload, because they are not.

Lastly, another possibility for evaluating a new program is to compare its success rate with that of clients who received services prior to the implementation of the new program. This entails digging into archival or historical (closed) cases or following up on former clients. Many agencies that routinely evaluate their services request clients to sign consent forms at intake in the event that a program evaluator might some day need to draw data from records or to contact clients. Accessing existing data is not generally viewed as having any real potential for harming subjects and, depending on the type of information desired, may even be a matter of public record.

THE PRACTITIONER'S ETHICAL RESPONSIBILITIES

As we learned in Chapter 1, psychologists, counselors, and social workers have an ethical responsibility to conduct program evaluations. Because we are in the "people business" and could easily harm our clients, every human services professional must be accountable for his or her interventions. This means that we really do not have an option *not* to engage in program evaluation and research activities. Social workers, for example, should be familiar with the National Association of Social Work's *Code of Ethics,* which requires that we evaluate our policies, programs, and interventions—that we develop professional knowledge while protecting our research participants. A relevant section of the code addressing ethics in research and evaluation is reproduced in Box 2.4.

What can you do when confronted with an ethical dilemma? Here is a process that may help you figure out the best solution:

- First, examine your options. What are the alternatives and ramifications of each decision? Write down the problem as you see it.
- Conduct a literature review for how other evaluators may have handled this problem.
- Check the *Code of Ethics* for guidance. (You might also want to look at the codes of ethics of the American Psychological Association, the American Evaluation Association, etc.). Apply appropriate ethical principles to the situation.
- Discuss the problem with colleagues and professionals whose opinions you respect. Ask for consultation from the nearest IRB. Share your plan with them, and ask for honest appraisal and feedback.

BOX 2.4 | NASW *CODE OF ETHICS*

5.02 EVALUATION AND RESEARCH

(a) Social workers should monitor and evaluate policies, the implementation of programs, and practice interventions.
(b) Social workers should promote and facilitate evaluation and research to contribute to the development of knowledge.
(c) Social workers should critically examine and keep current with emerging knowledge relevant to social work and fully use evaluation and research evidence in their professional practice.
(d) Social workers engaged in evaluation or research should carefully consider possible consequences and should follow guidelines developed for the protection of evaluation and research participants. Appropriate institutional review boards should be consulted.
(e) Social workers engaged in evaluation or research should obtain voluntary and written informed consent from participants, when appropriate, without any implied or actual deprivation or penalty for refusal to participate: without undue inducement to participate; and with the regard for participants' well-being, privacy, and dignity. Informed consent should include information about the nature, extent, and duration of the participation requested and disclosure of the risks and benefits of participation in the research.
(f) When evaluation or research participants are incapable of giving informed consent, social workers should provide an appropriate explanation to the participants, obtain the participants' assent to the extent they are able, and obtain written consent from an appropriate proxy.
(g) Social workers should never design or conduct evaluation or research that does not use consent procedures, such as certain forms of naturalistic observation and archival research, unless rigorous and responsible review of the research has

---

- Talk with your supervisor.
- Deliberate and decide.

Will you be confronted with ethical challenges in your practice as an evaluator? Morris and Cohn (1993) surveyed over 400 members of the American Evaluation Association. Two-thirds (65 percent) of the respondents said they had encountered ethical problems. Surprisingly, three of the four most frequently reported conflicts arose *after* the data had been collected.

As we discussed earlier in this book, administrators, staff, clients, and other stakeholders sometimes have a strong interest in seeing that evaluation data are presented in a favorable light—and what is considered favorable by one party may be anathema to another! A common dilemma for the external evaluator is often: Do I tell the truth about the program or obfuscate and gloss over the evidence that a program is substandard? What if the program seems

found it to be justified because of its prospective scientific, educational, or applied value and unless equally effective alternative procedures that do not involve waiver of consent are not feasible.

(h) Social workers should inform participants of their right to withdraw from evaluation and research at any time without penalty.

(i) Social workers should take appropriate steps to ensure that participants in evaluation and research have access to appropriate supportive services.

(j) Social workers engaged in evaluation or research should protect participants from unwarranted physical or mental distress, harm, danger, or deprivation.

(k) Social workers engaged in the evaluation of services should discuss collected information only for professional purposes and only with people professionally concerned with this information.

(l) Social workers engaged in evaluation or research should ensure the anonymity of confidentiality of participants and of the data obtained from them. Social workers should inform participants of any limits of confidentiality, the measures that will be taken to ensure confidentiality, and when any records containing research data will be destroyed.

(m) Social workers who report evaluation and research results should protect participants' confidentiality by omitting identifying information unless proper consent has been obtained authorizing disclosure.

(n) Social workers should report evaluation and research findings accurately. They should not fabricate or falsify results and should take steps to correct any errors later found in published data using standard publication methods.

(o) Social workers engaged in evaluation or research should be alert to and avoid conflicts of interest and dual relationships with participants, should inform participants when a real or potential conflict of interest arises, and should take steps to resolve the issue in a manner that makes participants' interests primary.

(p) Social workers should educate themselves, their students, and their colleagues about responsible research practices.

clearly worthwhile (e.g., health education in low-income housing) but shows modest outcomes or none at all?

Sometimes evaluation ideals collide with community needs and politics (Emshoff, 2003) and ethical choices surrounding the findings place the evaluator in a bind (Morris, 2002). Internal evaluators may also be caught in a dilemma where, because of loyalty to an employer, there is self-imposed pressure to compromise one's scientific objectivity.

Clearly, the ethical course of action would be to maintain one's professional objectivity and not be swayed by financial, political, or personal interests. But this position of neutrality can be exceedingly hard to maintain when one subscribes to an ethos of social justice and advocacy, especially when community advocates argue that even a modestly successful program is better than nothing at all. After all, measures of success can themselves be politically influenced; for example, cost benefits are generally harder to produce compared to improvements in quality of life or client satisfaction.

Evaluators would do well to anticipate that pressure may be exerted to try to influence the outcome of a final evaluation report. Giving some thought to how one might respond to such influence may prevent unnecessary stress. The evaluator might, for example, share interim findings with the study's intended users to lay the groundwork for future results that might prove controversial (Sengupta, 2002). It helps to remember that evaluators are hired because of their perceived ability to report fairly and accurately. If we lose our integrity, we have lost a great deal indeed.

CHAPTER RECAP

Many researchers have come to see IRB reviews as onerous and capricious, particularly because the biomedical thrust of federal regulations can seem a poor fit for the social sciences and human services. Even medical research is subject to delays due to IRB scrutiny. A recent study prepared for the National Institutes of Health found that few research proposals are rejected outright but that less than 20 percent are approved as submitted! (For further information, see http://www.aaup.org/statements/Redbook/repirb/htm American Association of University Professors, 2004.)

We have discussed a number of scenarios in this chapter that would give any program evaluator pause before deciding to cross the threshold from routine program monitoring to research. Yet research and dissemination are needed more than ever in an era of tight funding and competition for scarce resources. Studies of accountability and effectiveness need to be conducted as rigorously as possible and shared as widely as possible. In this context, the price of IRB review is worth the effort.

We do not need to apologize to clients for involving them in evaluation activities. They may well benefit—even show giant gains—from new therapeutic procedures. Even if that does not happen, subjects may feel that they have helped to make a contribution to our knowledge base that may improve treatment for others. They may feel honored that they were selected to participate in a research project. Most of us like to share our opinions about things and many evaluation efforts invite subjects to do that very thing (and those using qualitative methods elicit participants' opinions in their own words). These projects are often interesting—providing clients with new insights or learning into their illness or treatment. These are just some of the reasons why clients might want to participate in research.

We owe it to our research subjects not to waste their time or to engage in such frivolous pursuits that they become skeptical of participation in future research. But program evaluation research rarely entails more than minimal risks to participants. Furthermore, it offers direct benefits in terms of improved practices and policies.

Questions for Class Discussion

1. What are the arguments both for and against using prisoners for research?
2. If you were a member of an IRB, would you allow deception to be used in some instances? If so, give examples.
3. Discuss, without naming any names or providing identifying information, instances where you have observed or think you have observed unethical behavior.
4. Discuss your own experience (if any) with HIPAA regulations on medical privacy and how these might affect the evaluation of a cancer screening program.
5. List the agencies known to the class that have their own IRBs or human subjects committees.
6. Discuss, without naming any names or providing too much information, instances where you have observed or read about unethical behavior in a research-related activity.
7. Discuss the external evaluator's responsibilities on concluding that objectivity has been lost or that a program evaluation cannot be done well. Discuss whether the responsibilities would differ if an internal evaluator were involved.

Mini-Projects: Experiencing Evaluation Firsthand

1. Obtain a copy of the application forms used by an IRB at your university. Complete the form as if you were proposing a program evaluation at a local social service agency.
2. Draft consent forms to be signed by youths and their parents or guardians who will be interviewed in an evaluation study of foster care. Compare your product with an example or model of a informed consent form obtained from the IRB at your university.
3. Have there been incidents in which human subjects were abused in the name of research since the formation of IRBs? Using the resources of your library or the Web, write a paper that reports on suspected unethical research projects from recent years.

References and Resources

American Association of University Professors. *Protecting human beings: Institutional review boards and social science research.* Retrieved January, 29, 2004 from http://www.aaup.org/statements/Redbook/repirb/htm.

Annas, G. J., & Grodin, M. A. (1992). *The Nazi doctors and the Nuremberg Code.* New York: Oxford University Press.

Dent, C. W., Sussman, S. Y., & Stacy, A. W. (1997). The impact of a written parental consent policy on estimates from a school-based drug use survey. *Evaluation Review, 21,* 698–712.

Dickert, N., & Gracy, C. (1999). What's the price of a research subject? Approaches to payment for research participation. *New England Journal of Medicine, 341*(3), 198–203.

Emshoff, J. (2003). Commentary: Practical realities and ethical choices. *American Journal of Evaluation, 24,* 419–422.

Gensheimer, L. K., Ayers, T. S., & Roosa, M. W. (1993). School-based prevention interventions for at-risk populations. *Evaluation and Program Planning, 16,* 159–167.

High, D. M. (1992). Research with Alzheimer's disease subjects: Informed consent and proxy decision making. *Journal of the American Geriatrics Society, 40,* 950–957.

High, D. M., Whitehouse, P. J., Post, S. G., & Berg, L. (1994). Guidelines for addressing ethical and legal issues in Alzheimer's disease research: A position paper. *Alzheimer Disease and Associated Disorders, 8,* 66–74.

Hornblum, A .M. (1998). *Acres of skin: Human experiments at Holmesburg Prison.* New York: Routledge.

Jones, J. H. (1981). *Bad blood: The Tuskegee syphilis experiment.* New York: Free Press.

Lifton, R. J. (1986). *The Nazi doctors.* New York: Basic.

Morris, M. (2002). Ethical challenges: The potpourri. *American Journal of Evaluation, 23,* 101.

Morris, M., & Cohn, R. (1993). Program evaluators and ethical challenges. *Evaluation Review, 17*(6), 621–642.

National Association of Social Workers, Inc. (1999). NASW *Code of Ethics.* Washington DC.

Proctor, R. N. (1988). *Racial hygiene: Medicine under the Nazis.* Cambridge, MA: Harvard University Press.

Sengupta, S. (2002). Commentary: Begin with a good program theory: The case of the missing guiding principle. *American Journal of Evaluation, 23,* 103–106.

Wolf, L. E., Croughan, M., & Lo, B. (2002). The challenges of IRB review and human subjects protections in practice-based research. *Medical Care, 40,* 521–529.

NEEDS ASSESSMENT

CHAPTER 3

WHAT IS NEEDS ASSESSMENT?

Communities struggle with many social problems and social service needs. For example, the range of problems includes the following:

- Drug addiction
- STDs/HIV
- Teen pregnancy
- Fetal alcohol syndrome
- Homelessness
- Domestic violence
- Sexual assault
- Child abuse and neglect

However, especially in today's social, economic, and political environment, resources are limited. Thus, social service providers must answer several key questions before they can make a case about why a particular program deserves funding. The primary question is "What is the greatest area of need?" And, the secondary question is "How do we best or most efficiently target the primary identified problem areas?"

For example, let's say that drug abuse has been identified by Normal Town, USA, as a major problem. Key community leaders, parents, hospital staff, criminal justice officials, and school representatives all agree that drug abuse must be addressed in the community. So, the primary question about what problem area to target with resources has been identified. However, assume that it is not clear to this community how to best to direct resources within that problem area. In other words, should they address individuals involved in the criminal justice system who also have drug problems for drug treatment? Should they target kids in middle and high school with drug prevention? Or, should they focus on pregnant women who are abusing drugs and alcohol? These are the kinds of questions that should be examined with a needs assessment.

Needs assessments utilize multiple methods to answer questions such as those described above. McKillip (1998) defines needs assessments as "decision-aiding" tools used for "resource allocation, program planning, and program development" based on the "assumption that planned programming can alleviate distress and aid growth" (p. 262).

THE NEED FOR NEEDS ASSESSMENT

Although we, as professional helpers, may feel that we know the needs of our clients (or of certain neighborhoods and communities), this presumed knowledge is only subjective opinion until we obtain evidence of the extent of unmet needs in our communities. In order to properly plan programs, needs assessment and program planning should precede the development of programs. In other words, long before programs begin serving clients, **needs assessments** should be conducted to ensure that scarce resources are being utilized in the best way, as well as to determine further program planning issues. Needs assessment is also the measure against which program implementation and outcome will be compared.

Hornick and Burrows (1988) define needs assessment as the first type of program evaluation—using the logic that one needs to *evaluate* whether the proposed program is needed before it is begun. Needs assessments are also known as needs analyses, as feasibility studies, and even as "front-end analyses." In addition, needs assessments can provide valuable information for program planning, including what groups to target for services, the best ways to publicize or market services, estimates of the numbers of persons who could benefit from a specific program or service, information about the geographic distribution and sociodemographic characteristics of potential clients, and barriers that may be encountered by clients (see Box 3.1). For example, it may be important to ask questions like "How far will potential clients have to travel to reach the agency?" or "What hours would be most convenient for potential clients?"

In other cases, an agency may already have a specific program designed, but the target population may not be accessing the services. For example, perhaps at one point the waiting list was so long that potential clients no longer viewed that program as a real source of help. Thus, a needs assessment might also clarify questions: What do potential clients know about our services? How do they view our services—as being of top or inferior quality? In fact,

| BOX 3.1 | REASONS FOR CONDUCTING A NEEDS ASSESSMENT |

1. To document the existence of an ongoing/exacerbating social problem(s).
2. To prioritize the needs for services in communities.
3. To determine whether interventions and other resources to address the identified needs exist in a community as well as their strengths and weaknesses.
4. To determine whether existing interventions are known to or are acceptable to potential clients.
5. To determine the major barriers preventing clients from accessing existing services.
6. To determine whether there are enough clients with a particular problem to justify creating a new program.
7. To obtain information for tailoring a program to a specific target population.

in a perfect world, needs assessments would be conducted on a regular, ongoing basis to provide information to service providers and program planners. With this information, adjustments could be made as programs mature and evolve and target populations change.

DEFINITIONS OF NEED

Bradshaw (1977) conceptualized four types of need:

1. *Normative need*—a condition or situation defined by an expert. By looking at poverty figures for a given county and then the number of children enrolled in free lunch programs, an expert might recommend that additional steps be taken to inform families in a particular school district where too few children are receiving meals. Normative estimates of need are strongly affected by the expertise and knowledge of the expert. However, normative estimates of needs can also be biased and nonrepresentative. In other words, only asking "experts" about needs may not accurately reflect the full picture of program needs because the perspective is based on the opinions of only a few individuals.
2. *Felt need*—perceptions of need as ascertained by consulting actual clients. Felt need data is collected by surveying clients either in person or by mail or telephone. Each approach has drawbacks. Clients may not want to tell an investigator what their most personal or private needs are. Mailed surveys may yield unrepresentative samples and low response rates.
3. *Expressed need*—a demand for service. For example, clients who have applied for services or received services in a given time period and those clients on a waiting list for service represent the demand for a particular program. The problem with this approach to defining need is that many clients who *could* benefit from services may not be receiving them because they do not meet eligibility guidelines, they do not have transportation, or they do

not know where to apply for the services. Expressed need is always going to underestimate the true level of need in a community.

4. *Comparative need*—an inferred measure of need determined by examining the characteristics of those receiving services and then locating those characteristics in the population. For instance, a study of senior citizens living in one high-rise apartment building revealed that 12 percent needed transportation services. This information might provide a useful estimate to apply to other high-rise apartment buildings populated primarily by senior citizens. This approach to defining need is vulnerable to problems of nonrepresentativeness. Clients of a particular program or agency (as well as those living in a specific apartment building) are, by definition, a self-selected sample. Their needs may or may not resemble those of other persons who have similar demographics (for example, age and ethnic group) in common.

From these different ways of thinking about need it should be obvious that conflict and disagreement can arise when individuals do not share the same definition of need. To take a ludicrous example, we all know intuitively when we "need" something like a sandwich or a steaming hot cup of coffee. However, a neutral observer might take a look at us and conclude that, being 10 pounds overweight, we do not really need that fattening sandwich. The observer's recommendation might be that someone else needs it more. Our physician might also take a contrary position and be of the opinion that we should cut caffeine from our diets—that we would be better off without that additional cup of coffee that we so crave. Whose assessment of need is right? And who is the best judge of need?

Evaluators who are conducting needs assessments should strive to be sensitive to different perceptions about need. This is an inexact science at best. Here is one guideline that seems to make some logical sense: When trying to determine what a client population needs, always try to involve clients in the process—no matter whether secondary data, or experts, or surveys are used as a primary foundation.

Further, evaluators need to be mindful that there can be multiple **stakeholders** in a community. Stakeholders are all those who have an interest in a program and can include such groups as:

Funders

Administrators

Politicians

Community members

Staff and potential staff

Other programs and organizations that might be making or receiving referrals

Businesses

Unions

Current, past, and potential clients

As Mika (1996) notes, each group of stakeholders can have a different perspective on the program and may tend to interpret results from their own reference point. Various groups may use the same data to argue that a program is a waste of public funds or a dire necessity—depending on whether they favor or oppose the program.

Needs assessment efforts can range from the simple to the complex. There is no one standardized approach. In some communities, it might make sense to start with the local United Way's resource inventories to determine what is missing in the way of programs and services. In other communities where every imaginable service is available in some form, the task might be to examine issues of accessibility and availability. A program that is available only in one neighborhood or only operates during selected daytime hours may not be of any benefit to potential clients without child care or transportation or those who cannot leave their employment in order to access services with limited hours.

Needs assessments may also have indirect or direct targets. (See Box 3.2.) For example, in order to improve conditions for children at risk, one approach might be to consider which skills child protection workers need to perform their jobs in a manner that will keep as many children safe as possible and then to conduct a needs assessment of the skills they need to upgrade. Thus, the ultimate target might not be the worker, but children at risk.

A formal needs assessment weighs the accumulated data and makes a judgment about the severity of need that can result in the setting of priorities.

PLANNING A NEEDS ASSESSMENT

How would you go about evaluating whether there is sufficient need to justify the start of a new program?

Suppose you feel that there is a need for a latchkey program in your community. You are particularly concerned about elementary school-aged children who, because of working parents, are at home for several hours in the afternoon without adult supervision. You learn that a local foundation has expressed interest in funding a pilot latchkey program in your community during the next school year if it can be convinced of the need.

Before beginning a needs assessment, ask yourself, "What information sources are available?" As you think about the information sources that would be helpful and obtainable, it occurs to you that among your friends are three elementary school principals. You contact them and find that two are convinced that a latchkey program is needed, while the third is undecided. You do not feel that this is sufficient information to take to the foundation. What more could you do? You could ask all of your friends and neighbors if they thought that this program was needed. Unfortunately, as one friend indicates to you, these opinions do not constitute objective information. Asking only people you know about their opinions will give you *biased information*—even if the number of people you have talked to is now up to 25.

A MULTIMETHOD NEEDS
ASSESSMENT APPROACH
EXAMPLE

The purpose of this project was to conduct a statewide needs assessment in order to determine the counties in the State of Kentucky in which a drug court program is needed and feasible. The assessment was conducted in two phases.

Phase I Methodology and Results:

Phase I focused on collecting information for each of the 107 counties across the State of Kentucky that did not have a drug court program or in which a drug court program was not currently being planned. This phase took approximately 4 months to complete.

The following information was collected for each of the 107 counties: (1) population estimates from the 1990 census data; (2) number of nondrug arrests; (3) percentage of nondrug arrests by population; (4) number of drug arrests; (5) percentage of drug arrests by population; (6) number of DUI closings; (7) average time to disposition for nondrug arrests; (8) average time to disposition for drug arrests; and (9) average caseload of probation officers by district.

In addition to the social indicator data, a preliminary overview of various community resources was collected by county for three major categories—psychological/medical services, vocational/educational services, and social services. The sources included Kentucky Mental Health and Mental Retardation—Comprehensive Care Centers and related substance abuse programs; Kentucky Department of Vocational Rehabilitation; and Department of Social Services. For each agency listed by county, the following information was recorded: the number of locations for each office and whether the agency provided basic resources such as food, clothing, shelter; education/employment; counseling—family and/or individual; drug and alcohol programs; and group therapy/support group.

After collecting the criminal justice and community resource information for each county, the data was analyzed. First, percentages of nondrug arrests, drug arrests, and DUI arrests were computed based on population estimates. Then, frequencies were used to determine the counties that fell in to the 75th percentile or higher for each of the following measures: percentage of drug arrests, percentage of DUI arrests, times to disposition for drug charges, probation caseload, number of psychological resources, and number of other resources. Each time the county fell into the 75th percentile on one of the variables described above, it was given a 1. Each time the county did not fall into the 75th percentile on the variables above, it was given a 0. The counties' scores were summed across all the variables. Counties were then given a score of 1 to 6 depending on the number of times the specific county fell into the 75th percentile on any one of the six variables.

Next, another list of counties was produced; only those that fell into the 75th percentile in both psychological resources and percentage of drug arrests were included in this list. The two lists were then compared: counties with a score of 4–6 from the first list and the counties that fell into the 75th percentile, on both the percent of drug arrests and psychological resources, were selected. The counties that were on both of these lists were the 12 counties identified as needing a drug court program. These 12 counties represented 11 percent of the 107 counties.

Phase II Methodology and Results:

Phase II focused on the feasibility of, and community readiness for, implementing a drug court program in the counties identified as being most in need of a drug court program. Key informant surveys were then conducted with: judges; prosecutors; defense attorneys (including a representative from the public defenders office); jail staff; probation and parole officers; and police officers. Overall there was a 91 percent response rate between those contacted and those who completed a survey.

These surveys were conducted with the purpose of determining the level of support that each "representative" would be willing to give to a local drug court, potential barriers to a drug court program, and the overall feasibility of implementing a drug court program in their county. Specifically, surveys asked each representative about:

- Perceived strengths of a drug court program
- Benefits to their office of having a drug court program
- Perceived barriers to having a drug court program in their community
- Strategies suggested for overcoming those barriers

Community readiness ratings were assigned based on the degree of respondent cohesiveness and enthusiasm in the overall need for a Drug Court program in the specific county, the strengths, weaknesses, barriers, and strategies for overcoming the barriers in the county.

In addition, community resources were examined. Ratings were assigned to each county based on the number of community resources that were available. These included (1) the number of AA or NA meetings available; (2) the distance to comprehensive care from the courthouse; (3) the number of private and individual substance abuse counseling services; and, (4) the number of other services available in the community (e.g., YMCA program, battered women's program).

Counties with the greatest number of resources, and which had available and accessible substance abuse treatment (the comprehensive care facility was located close to the courthouse and/or other private and individual substance abuse counseling services were available), were given a higher rating than those with limited resources and a greater distance between the courthouse and comprehensive care.

Finally, socioeconomic and demographic characteristics that distinguished the county from the state averages and rankings relative to the other counties were examined. First, relative rankings were assigned for each indicator. If the county was in the top two or three rankings relative to the other counties, and if the county had higher or lower rates compared to the state averages or overall state rates, then the specific county indicator was noted as a distinguishing characteristic for that county and highlighted.

Overall Results

Results of Phase I indicated that of 107 counties included in the study (out of 120 counties in Kentucky) 12 were identified for further assessment. Results of Phase II indicated that, of the 12 counties identified for further assessment, four counties were ready to move toward an implementation of a drug court program by applying for a planning grant. Four counties were close to being ready to applying for a planning grant, but needed further information about drug court programs. Two counties indicated they could utilize extensive information about a drug court program and had judges that are supportive of the idea. About half of the counties in each category had

BOX 3.2 | CONTINUED

adequate community resources and half had more limited resources. Several county indicators suggested that a juvenile drug court program may be needed. Finally, two counties were not able to consider a drug court program at the time of this study.

Source: Logan, T., Williams, K., & Leukefeld, C. (2001). A statewide drug court needs assessment: Identifying target counties, assessing readiness. *Journal of Offender Rehabilitation, 33,* 3, 1–25.

What else could you do? If there is a "true" need for the latchkey program, it would be evidenced by parents who are interested in having their children participate in the program. Their interest could be documented (with the principals' support) by sending home a brief questionnaire to every parent with elementary-aged children explaining that a planning effort is being conducted to gauge interest in a latchkey program. When parents and guardians return the questionnaire, you will have objective information regarding the perceived need for a latchkey program. However, another information source could provide useful data. With the cooperation of the child protection agency, you could survey the child protection staff in your community in order to learn if they, too, perceive the need for a local latchkey program.

As this example shows, much of what constitutes needs assessment revolves around thinking about what sources of useful information you could obtain. The emphasis is on *useful*. In this day and age, information from hundreds of sources is available in libraries and may be as close as a computer screen. But before gathering information, focus on the necessary steps in conducting a needs assessment (Box 3.3). Although these steps may be similar for process and outcome evaluation as well as needs assessment, it is the focus on documenting needs that should be emphasized throughout each step.

Step 1 sets the parameters for the needs assessment. The more resources at your disposal, the larger your budget, and the more time you have, the more comprehensive and sophisticated your needs assessment can be. Keeping the purpose of the needs assessment constantly in mind will help you keep your efforts focused. In addition, you need to determine the level of your needs assessment: is it a statewide assessment, community, or neighborhood assessment? What stakeholders should be included in the needs assessment?

Step 2 requires identifying information needed for decision making. Many times key stakeholders or planning committees add specific questions or goals to the needs assessment that could provide interesting information. However, the test of whether these items should be included is whether they will provide information useful to program managers. If no direct use can be made of proposed information items, then they should not be added.

Step 3 requires a little exploratory work to avoid "reinventing the wheel" or "spinning your wheels." You might want to check with other social service

BOX 3.3	STEPS IN NEEDS ASSESSMENT

Step 1. Clearly understand:

    a. The purpose of the needs assessment

    b. The level of assessment: Statewide, community, neighborhood

    c. What stakeholders to include: Clients or potential clients, program staff, key community leaders, state officials, etc.

    d. Budget and available resources

    e. Time allotted for the project

Step 2. Identify the specific information you need to acquire.

Step 3. Determine whether the information already exists or can be obtained with your resources.

Step 4. Design the methodology and instrumentation (if necessary).

Step 5. Collect and analyze the data.

Step 6. Prepare the report.

Step 7. Disseminate preliminary results to key stakeholders to obtain their feedback.

Step 8. Formally disseminate results.

---

agencies, look through past reports, talk with staff about the information they collect, and perhaps conduct some literature searches in the library. Ultimately, you need to decide on a methodology for providing the best information given the constraints in your particular situation. As an example, Shearer (2003) described the development, reliability, and validity assessment of an instrument to assess the special needs of female offenders. An evaluator could read the article and contact the author for a copy of this instrument that has had extensive preliminary work. Using this instrument would save an evaluator a lot of time in assessing the service needs of female offenders.

In step 4, the needs assessment planner creates something akin to a blueprint—that is, a methodology that will structure the data-gathering efforts. The methodology is a description of the procedures, the research subjects, key variables, and objectives in the proposed study.

Once the methodology is approved, then the next phase (step 5) involves the actual collection of the needs assessment data and the analysis of that data. Depending on the design and scope of the effort, many different people could be involved with gathering or processing data at this stage. The planner or coordinator of the needs assessment becomes, on occasion, a supervisor of others to ensure that important tasks are completed well and on time. The coordinator may also be engaged in data entry or data editing in addition to "number crunching."

Step 6 probably should involve multiple drafts of the written report. The first rough draft simply gets the main ideas down. The second draft puts flesh to the bones. The third draft corrects spelling, grammar, and polishes the written document. The more that is riding on this needs assessment, the more important it is that you have someone else proofread the final report for clarity of expression, accuracy, and to protect you from any political blunders that it might contain.

Step 7 should include dissemination of the preliminary results to key stakeholders. Not including key stakeholders or the initial agency in the needs assessment process and in finalizing the results could be problematic for a number of reasons (Amodeo & Gal, 1997). First, it takes time to conduct a needs assessment and the stakeholders may forge ahead without the results if they don't see the needs assessment process and progress. Second, keeping key stakeholders involved in the process will keep the needs assessment a central focus, which is important when agencies are busy with other concerns. Third, it is important to involve key stakeholders in interpreting the results so that they have time to process and understand the results as well as have input into how the results are presented. For example, key stakeholders may have questions that are easily answered with a few additional analyses but the evaluator may not have initially considered these questions and left them out of the report. It is also important that recommendations generated from the report be conducted in collaboration with key stakeholders or with the key agency personnel to ensure utilization of the needs assessment results. More information about these issues and what can go wrong with needs assessment utilization can be found in an article by Amodeo and Gal (1997).

Step 8 is the formal dissemination of the results. There is more information about disseminating results in Chapter 15. However, it is probably important to write a report with an executive summary as well as to make a formal presentation of the final results to key stakeholders.

SELECTING A NEEDS ASSESSMENT APPROACH

There are a variety of ways to go about estimating the need for a human service program. And numerous questions and issues will affect the particular needs assessment strategy you select. Besides your budget, the resources available to you, and the amount of time you have to finish the project, you need to consider whether this assessment will be a one-time phenomenon or an effort that will be built on—perhaps even repeated each year. Is the purpose of the needs assessment to satisfy some bureaucrat in the state capital, or will the data really be used by the agency? Is it seen as "busywork" or as a useful activity? Is your supervisor or agency director anxious to see the needs assessment, or are your instructions to just put "something" on paper? Is it likely the needs assessment will be used by others in the community, or will it simply be typed, submitted to some government office, and promptly forgotten?

How much can be spent on the needs assessment? Can you afford consultants and paid interviewers for your community survey? What kind of technical expertise or staff resources will be available from your agency or cooperating agencies? If you are creative, low-budget approaches to needs assessment can be found. Stefl (1984), for instance, reported on a community survey that volunteers conducted. The way some of these volunteers were recruited is interesting. One of the agency's board members was a probation officer. He was able to offer community service to a select group of offenders as an alternative to incarceration. These persons were screened very closely, trained as interviewers, and were said to have performed very well. They obtained 822 telephone interviews in 21 days. The overall refusal rate was comparable to those reported by professional survey organizations.

Agency staff are also resources. Besides yourself, who else can be asked to assist with the needs assessment? What skills can they contribute?

Planning a community survey obviously takes more time than contacting a handful of key informants. If you are working against a rapidly approaching deadline, your choice of a needs assessment approach may be justifiably influenced by what can be accomplished in a short period of time.

Another issue is the amount of detail or information desired—whether the assessment has to be objective and data oriented or whether it can be more perception oriented. How "hard" does the data need to be? Will your audience be skeptical or supportive of your efforts? If you cannot directly assess need, what surrogate measures are available to you—what programs are most similar to the one you must assess? How was need for those programs determined? Deadlines for grants and sponsors sometimes have a way of boiling down the selection issues about what data can be obtained within a certain time period. Even then, you will have certain choices. The next section discusses different approaches available to you.

Secondary Data Analysis

Secondary data refers to existing information that comes from census data, public documents, and reports. Even data generated by other researchers or surveys can be reexamined for relevance to the new program. Census data, for instance, contains a wealth of information, and because it is readily available in machine-readable form and from the Internet (www.census.gov), it should be reviewed before collecting any other data. At a minimum, census data can provide you with estimates of the population likely to need or to benefit from the program you are proposing.

Census data are available for geographical units known as census tracts and census blocks. (Note that the block data are available only for large metropolitan areas.) By referring to census data, it is possible to learn how many school-aged children reside in a defined geographical area. You can learn the race and sex of these children and the number living in poverty. There is even a category that provides information on the number of females in the labor force with children under 6 and between 6 and 17 years of age.

To switch examples for a moment, census data can also be used to provide estimates of the number of persons 55 and older, the areas within the community where these older adults tend to reside, and the number of older adults living in poverty. Census data can also be used to provide such information as the general level of affluence in a community, the average level of educational attainment, the number of substandard dwellings, and the number of persons with work disabilities.

In order to protect the confidentiality of information supplied to it, the Census Bureau suppresses data that could be used to identify specific individuals or families. Census data *cannot* be used to gain personal information on a specific family or families. It *cannot* supply you with the names, addresses, or phone numbers of families having school-aged children or living in poverty. You can, however, use census data to plot a map of those areas in the community that have the highest concentrations of older adults or children or families living in poverty.

In addition to census data, every state maintains a wealth of useful data for planners and evaluators. It is possible to learn from the state health department information such as the number of births, marriages, deaths, and suicides that occurred in a county in a given year. If you were developing a prenatal program for teenage mothers, it would be possible to find both the number of babies born to teenage mothers and the number of infant deaths in the years prior to the start of the program. Persons interested in starting an alcoholism prevention or treatment program may want to document the number of persons who have died as a result of cirrhosis of the liver. Many times information is already published about how other evaluators have assessed needs. For example, McCarty, McGuire, Harwood, and Field (1998) published an article discussing the availability and challenges to accessing state data systems to estimate the organization, use, costs, and cost-effectiveness of their publicly funded substance abuse treatment services for three states.

Other studies have used drug and alcohol mortality rates, drug and alcohol-related arrests, drug and alcohol-related hospital discharges, drug and alcohol treatment admissions to estimate substance abuse treatment gaps for specific areas (McAuliffe, Woodworth, Zhang, & Dunn, 2002; McAuliffe, LaBrie, Woodworth, Zhang, & Dunn, 2003). Several studies used the above mentioned indicators along with social indicators identified in the literature as risk and protective factors for substance use such as poverty and social disorganization indicators, which have been identified as risk factors for substance abuse (e.g., percentage of rental units, population mobility, ethnic heterogeneity, Medicaid cases, unemployment rates, participants in the Women, Infants, and Children (WIC) program, participants in the early intervention program, indices of liquor sales) and indicators of protective factors (e.g., the diversity of activities conducted by local nonprofit organizations) (Crook & Oei, 1998; Kreiner et al., 2001). Kreiner et al. (2001) also included AIDS cases, fetal syndrome cases, and as well as activities of nonprofit organizations as protective factors. Nonprofit organizations are required to file program and activity reports with the Internal Revenue Service (IRS) for each area they serve; and Kreiner et al. (2001) argued that the resources available in the community, as estimated from nonprofit organization activities, were indicators of community resources to address social problems. These and many other categories of information are available through various local, state, and federal agencies.

(These variables and others that help gauge the extent of social problems are known as **social indicators.**)

From the state department of education you can find such information as the number of school dropouts, the number of ninth graders reading at grade level, and school enrollments. Other state departments keep records of such social indicators as the number of children receiving food stamps, medically indigent children, free or reduced-cost school breakfast recipients, child abuse allegations, substantiated abuse allegations, delinquency cases, unemployment, psychiatric admissions to public hospitals, and so on.

In addition to state-produced reports, a little library work may uncover national reports that provide detailed information on a state-by-state basis. For example, the Annie E. Casey Foundation annually publishes the *Kids Count Data Book,* which compares states on a number of variables, such as infant mortality rate, percentage of births to single teens, juvenile violent crime arrest rate, percentage graduating from high school, and percentage of children not living with a parent. It is also available online (www.aecf.org). Information from over 70 federal government agencies that produce statistics can be located at the website (www.fedstats.gov). A good many of these agencies provide their own search engines to make it easier for you to find the specific statistics you are seeking.

Administrative records, reports, and files within your own agency are a source of already existing data that should not be overlooked for needs assessment purposes. Such information, which comes directly from the agency itself, is called **patterns of use** or **client utilization data.** It may also be known as a **rates-under-treatment approach.**

Most human services agencies report annually on the characteristics of those who have been clients in the past year. These data can be reviewed to see what groups within the community are being served (and underserved). Table 3.1 shows how the data from one counseling agency could be used for needs assessment purposes.

From this table, we can identify potentially underserved segments of the community based on the numbers of clients who have received service. The table shows greater demand for the adult program than the children's program and more usage of it than the older-adult program. These figures could be used to understand **expressed need**—that is, official requests for service. We can also see that the drug abuse treatment program appears to need additional staff. In 2000, almost 25 percent of their current caseload was awaiting service and the need for services has grown about 5 percent over time. Clearly, this program is in need of additional staff or resources in order to reduce the number of clients waiting for service to an acceptable level. None of the other programs had so many clients awaiting service or had the increased need for services over time like this particular program.

Client data can also be used for such purposes as locating neighborhoods or streets with the highest prevalence rates of certain problems (e.g., drug abuse). Multicolored pins representing client families can be placed in maps to help staff focus their outreach and education activities.

TABLE 3.1 | CLIENT UTILIZATION DATA, PUBLIC
COUNSELING SERVICES, INC.

	2003	2004	2005
Children served	363	383	407
Number on waiting list	16	19	21
Adults served	785	791	818
Number on waiting list	14	12	15
Older adults served	63	72	84
Number on waiting list	0	3	9
Drug abusers served	302	414	545
Number on waiting list	75	124	183
Total clients served	1,513	1,660	1,854
Clients on waiting list	105	158	228

Secondary data sources are generally convenient to access and easy to understand and use. Anyone can rank counties or census tracts in terms of those having the most or least of some characteristic. Anyone can identify the county with the highest unemployment rate or determine what the unemployment rate has been in a selected county for the past 5 years. In metropolitan areas, census tracts or blocks may be ranked in terms of percentage of families living in poverty or number of older adults. An additional advantage of social indicator approaches is that they can be used in multivariate statistical analyses.

However, a few drawbacks are associated with secondary data. The data may be outdated, unreliable, incomplete, or from an agency that is not really similar (because it is in a different geographical region, serves a different population, or has different eligibility guidelines). Even with the best agency data, there is always the problem of counting those potential clients who qualify for services but who have never been referred and who do not self-refer. Anytime you rely solely on client utilization data, you are likely to be underestimating the problem to some extent.

Last, using social indicators to estimate the health or social conditions of persons living in a certain geographic area can, at times, result in a misinterpretation known as an **ecological fallacy**. The fact that a neighborhood with colossal rates of drug overdoses is also highly populated with a particular ethnic group does not mean that every member of that ethnic group is going to overdose, or even that the ethnic group has the highest rate of drug overdose. It is possible that the absolute number of overdoses in that neighborhood may be elevated because of the extremely high rates by other underrepresented populations, thus giving a misleading impression (Fiorentine, 1994).

Impressionistic Approaches

After you have consulted the census data or other secondary data and have a firm grasp on the extent of the problem (or of the population to be served), additional information can come from consulting with service providers and other **key informants.** Key informants are those persons who are informed about a given problem because of training or work experience—usually because they are involved in some sort of service with that population. In the latchkey example, key informants could be the principals, guidance counselors, social workers, and teachers. One person conducting a key informant needs assessment for the latchkey program could easily contact all of these personnel in a single elementary school. Key informants could also include child protection workers and their supervisors, or area ministers.

Impressionistic approaches have a subjective quality to them. That is, these approaches are not as accurate or scientific as large-scale community surveys. Why not? For one thing, the sample sizes are often too small to be representative of the larger population. Think about the situation where the needs assessment involved talking with three principals. Even if the needs assessment were expanded to include three teachers, three area ministers, and three parents, we still would not have a sample necessarily representative of the opinions of all the principals, teachers, ministers, and parents in the community. Our data would not be scientific—especially if we chose these individuals because we knew them. (We will discuss sample size and representativeness more fully in Chapter 8.) Although the opinions of these people may be well founded and based on a superb knowledge of the problem, they may also be based on nothing other than personal bias, beliefs, or values. Suppose, for example, that two of the principals you selected strongly believed that women should not be employed outside of the home. These principals may be less likely to acknowledge the need for a latchkey program than a principal with more egalitarian values.

A cynical view of a key informant type of needs assessment might caution against warmly embracing the perceptions of key informants without first examining what they stand to gain or lose by over- or understating a particular problem. Thus, a principal might be expected to be in favor of a latchkey program if it makes his or her life easier—even if there does not appear to be great need for such a program in the community. There could, for instance, be one or two "problem children" who must be watched after school because their parents are always late in picking up their children, which causes teachers to complain to the principal. The problem of dealing with subjective opinions is also present (and perhaps more visible) in another type of impressionistic needs assessment.

Public hearings and **community forums** are a type of needs assessment that are grassroots oriented. What is more democratic than acquiring a public meeting room and posting a notice or advertising that anyone concerned with the problem of (fill in the blank) is invited to attend and share their concerns? This approach has the advantage of being reasonably inexpensive, not requiring a lot of preplanning, and again, needing little research expertise to interpret or summarize the results.

There are also some serious difficulties with public hearings. For one, the "public" seldom seems to attend. Unless the issue is a controversial one, rarely would potential clients attend the public hearings that are supposed to generate planning data. Often, the only attendees are the planning staff and a few service providers from other agencies who have an interest in working with that specific population.

A second problem with community forums and public hearings is that even when citizens from the community attend, there is no guarantee that they represent the larger community. Sometimes certain interest groups can "pack" the meeting so that the opinions of others are not represented. Numerically small but vocal groups can dominate meetings. And persons most in need of the proposed service (e.g., families in poverty, juvenile delinquents, teenage parents) probably will not be in attendance at all.

A third problem that can result from impressionistic approaches such as public hearings is that because they are usually focused on a single issue, other major problems or needs in the community may not be addressed even though more lives or citizens might be affected.

Nominal Groups, the Delphi Technique, and Focus Groups

Several other impressionistic techniques provide good information from small groups. The nominal group technique (Delbecq, Van de Ven, & Gustafson, 1975) involves a small group of persons who, in response to a common problem or question, work independently at first, and then share their ideas. The group leader asks each person to offer one idea in round-robin fashion. These ideas are recorded in front of the group on a chalkboard or a large sheet of paper. This process continues until all new ideas are exhausted. A discussion period follows when participants can elaborate, eliminate, combine, and add new ideas to the list. Next, each participant privately ranks the five most important ideas from those remaining on the list. The group compiles the individual rankings in order to arrive at the most popular ideas or solutions to the question posed. The group then discusses the anonymous rankings to resolve any misunderstandings. After the discussion, group members are asked to give a final independent rating.

The Delphi technique (Delbecq et al., 1975) involves the use of a questionnaire that is distributed to a panel of key informants or experts. (They do not meet together in person and may remain anonymous.) Their ideas are solicited, and their replies are compiled. If there are areas of disagreement, a second questionnaire is developed based on the responses. This new questionnaire is sent to the panel, and their opinions solicited once again. This process continues until consensus is reached in all areas.

In an interesting application of the Delphi method, Raskin (1994) sent a questionnaire to 450 directors of field instruction in accredited undergraduate and graduate social work programs and asked them to list national experts in field instruction. From this list Raskin constructed a smaller list of those who received five or more votes. The resulting 12 experts were asked to participate in a three-round Delphi study that sought to learn the critical problems in the field and whether consensus could be reached on these problems.

Focus groups represent another perception-oriented approach to assessing needs. Although focus groups originally evolved from market research, their popularity has grown greatly in recent years to the point where it is not at all uncommon for social service agencies to make use of them for needs assessment, program evaluation, and so forth.

Focus groups usually involve six to eight individuals who participate in structured discussion (Krueger, 1993). For needs assessment, a moderator facilitates a dialogue with constituent members of a client or target group. The goal is not to have these persons arrive at consensus but to identify and delineate their particular needs—some of which will be common to all group members and others unique to one individual. The moderator obtains in-depth information by probing and asking clarifying questions.

Butterfoss, Houseman, Morrow, and Rosenthal (1997), for instance, have reported on the use of six focus groups involving 41 mothers drawn from a WIC clinic, Head Start program, homeless shelter, school for teenage mothers, and parents from a children's hospital volunteer group to inform a community immunization coalition attempting to identify barriers to the vaccination of young children. After identifying such barriers as a need for clear, simple information about when and where immunizations could be obtained and difficulties in accessing clinic hours and locations, strategies were developed to overcome the problems. (See Chapter 4 for additional discussion on focus groups.)

Although impressionistic approaches have much to recommend them (they can "involve" the community, are inexpensive, are relatively quick to implement, and require no special knowledge of needs assessment), it is difficult to assess the accuracy of the obtained data. Those who are invited or chosen, or who elect themselves, to participate may not be truly representative of the larger community. Their views may be atypical and not reflect those of the majority. If this is a major concern, a community survey would provide less biased and more accurate information. Perhaps the best use of impressionistic approaches is to add the "personal angle" to those approaches that have relied heavily on "hard data."

Surveys

Surveys are familiar to most of us. Businesses use surveys to learn why we choose the brand of toothpaste that we buy; politicians use them to identify who will vote for them in the next election. Social scientists use surveys to determine the prevalence of such social problems as elder abuse. Surveys are also used for program development purposes. For example, Rutz and Shemberg (1985) surveyed fifth and sixth graders' beliefs, feelings, and behavioral intentions toward mental health issues prior to the development of mental health education programs.

Surveys are exceptionally valuable tools to use for needs assessment. Although they require more planning and resources than the impressionistic approaches, they provide information that is much more objective and scientific. When a careful probability sampling design has been used to ensure a representative sample, it is possible to talk very precisely and confidently about the extent of a problem in a community. You could find, for instance, that only 42 percent of the respondents had heard or read anything about a mental health center in their community. Similarly, only 44 percent knew that counseling could be obtained in the community for children who were not doing well in school or getting along with their families. Because the sample of adults was derived from a probability sampling design, the researcher was 95 percent confident that the results were accurate within plus or minus 5.5 percent. That is the type of accuracy that the other needs assessment approaches cannot provide.

On the other hand, a large representative survey may not be possible or necessary. If you are interested in a specific population you may need to survey representatives from that population. For example, Acosta and Toro (2000) surveyed a sample of 301 homeless adults in New York two times over a period of 6 months. Their sample was recruited from homeless shelters, soup kitchens, inpatient hospitals, outpatient facilities, and homeless service agencies. These researchers found that although housing was rated as an important need, participants rated other needs as at least as important as housing, including safety, education, transportation, medical/dental care, and job training/placement. Many of these needs were also identified as difficult to obtain. They also found that needs for formal mental health and substance abuse services were rated as relatively unimportant and easy to obtain, although satisfaction with the services in these areas was low.

As another example, you may be interested in assessing training needs of staff for a particular agency or organization. One study surveyed a random sample of substance abuse treatment providers working in New England substance abuse treatment facilities (Hall, Amodeo, Shaffer, & Bilt, 2000). These researchers found that although participants reported limited previous training and barriers to current training opportunities, the respondents had high levels of knowledge and skills regarding substance abuse treatment. However, providers did identify a need for more training on assessment strategies, more advanced clinical techniques, and dual diagnosis and treatment.

Regardless of whether you use a probability sample of households or a targeted sampling strategy, the precise estimate of the community's needs, beliefs, values, or behavior can come about only when the survey methodology has been sound. This type of needs assessment requires knowledge of both research methodology and sampling procedure. And, you must consider trade-offs or strengths and limitations in whatever sampling strategy you choose.

Although it is possible to conduct surveys with persons who are near at hand and easy to access, those who are chosen merely because it is convenient may not adequately represent the community. For instance, one could choose to survey those in attendance at a meeting of the parents' organization regarding the need for a latchkey program in a specific elementary school. If the parents who attend this meeting are representative of all the parents in the community, they would be a good source of information. If, however, the parents' organization meeting was attended only by parents from upper-middle-class and two-parent households, then the organization may not represent the opinions of all the parents with children attending the school.

Why might we assume that the parents who attend the parents' organization meetings may not be representative of the larger community? First of all, parents from impoverished households may lack transportation to get to these meetings—they may not own cars. In rural areas and smaller cities, public transportation may not always be available (especially for evening meetings). Even if these parents do have transportation, impoverished households often have multiple problems associated with day-to-day existence. Attendance at a school meeting (which is not required) often has very low priority. Additionally, single parents have the inconvenience of having to arrange for babysitters—still another financial burden on households.

So, even if you were successful in surveying those in attendance at the monthly parents' organization meeting, your findings might be representative only of middle- or upper-middle-class households. The majority of these relatively affluent parents may have sufficient resources so that they may have no need, or perceive no need, for a latchkey program. This would be especially true in those affluent households where only one parent was employed outside the home.

In order to be representative of the whole community, every person in the population must have an opportunity to provide input. With small populations it may be necessary to contact everyone, or at least a majority, to have a representative sample of the population. With large populations, random sampling can be employed so that perhaps less than 10 percent of the population is contacted (but every person in the population still had an equal chance of being selected to provide their opinions). Although the method used to select the sample is important, the size of the sample chosen to represent the population is just as important.

Although we are going to spend more time discussing sampling in Chapter 8, you can understand the importance of representativeness if you think about a large metropolitan community of about one million persons. Suppose a friend of yours from another country is interested in the quality of life as perceived by persons in this country who live in large cities. Your friend (who knows nothing about sampling) asks you to send her the address of one person from your metropolitan community so that she can mail this person a questionnaire. Can any one person adequately reflect the diversity of opinions, experiences, and lifestyles that are found in large cities? "Do you think it would be possible," your friend later asks, "for you to send me the addresses of two more people?" Could a large metropolitan area be represented by the opinions of three persons? What if you sent 30 addresses? How many addresses would you have to send in order for this sample to be representative of the opinions held by the majority of persons living in your metropolitan area? The return or response rate is also important. A low response rate is the equivalent of inviting a large number of people to a party and only one or two show up.

The purpose of the previous illustration is to show that an evaluator needs to have a good grasp of sampling before beginning a community survey. There is nothing wrong with conducting small convenience surveys of 20, 40, or even 50 respondents as pilot studies to provide for some beginning estimates of need. However, remember that unless all the members of the population are contacted or have an opportunity to be selected, it will not be possible to assess the accuracy of the results. Even if you go to a fair amount of trouble to obtain a random sample, you still may end up with biased results. You may be particularly susceptible to this problem with a mailed survey.

For instance, Thompson, Ruma, Authier, and Bouska (1994) mailed a community needs assessment questionnaire to every household in an Iowa county ($n = 1,850$) and got a response rate of only 23 percent. They found that of those who returned completed surveys, college-educated people and those who were middle-aged and upper-income were overrepresented. Young adults and lower income groups were the most clearly underrepresented.

Epidemiologic surveys seek to learn the extent of problems (usually diseases and injuries) in a community and typically express these as rates within the population. Epidemiologic surveys must, by definition, be based on scientific, representative samples and for this reason tend to be much more expensive than smaller scale, more informal surveys.

Ciarlo, Tweed, Shern, Kirkpatrick, and Sachs-Ericsson, N. (1992), for instance, have reported that a comprehensive psychiatric survey in Colorado generating need estimates for just 6.4 percent of the population cost over $700,000, or approximately $150 per respondent. These costs did not include questionnaire design, computer editing, and data analysis costs. At this rate, it would have cost $ 11 million to survey the whole state.

Done properly, large-scale community surveys are more expensive, more time consuming, and tend to require more research expertise than secondary data analysis or impressionistic approaches. But they offer a level of precision and confidence not found with the other needs assessment approaches.

CONVERGENT ANALYSIS
AND MULTIMETHOD APPROACHES

In our initial example of assessing the need for a latchkey program, several sources of information could be tapped. We talked first about going to the school principals, key informants, and parents. Then, we discussed the use of census or secondary data, the use of public hearings, contacting the parents' organization, and doing a community survey. Because any one approach may provide a somewhat incomplete picture of the true need for a latchkey program, convergent analysis should be the focus of the needs assessment effort (Siegel, Attkisson, & Carson, 1978; Warheit, Bell, & Schwab, 1977).

Convergent analysis involves using multiple sources of information and attempting to confirm the need for the program by means of different assessment strategies and perspectives. For instance, Sung (1989) reported on a needs assessment that converged the views of 200 American residents living on a military base overseas and 30 professional officers and civilians engaged in the human services. Sung initially found noticeable differences in the way the two groups ranked problems and needed services. However, Sung was able to converge the needs data by computing an average for the two groups in terms of the seriousness of problems and desired services.

Because all needs assessment approaches have conceptual, empirical, and inferential problems (Fiorentine, 1994), experts often recommend a multimethod approach to needs assessment in order to reduce the underlying problems found with a single method. (See Box 3.2 for an example of a multimethod needs assessment approach.)

However, when needs assessment data are obtained from more than one source, areas of agreement may not always be immediately identifiable. For that reason, needs assessors attempt to converge the data by looking for patterns and areas of agreement. This strategy is similar to a process in navigation and surveying called triangulation where multiple reference points are used to locate an exact position. Information from various sources is integrated and synthesized to provide a "reasonably viable portrait" of the community's perceptions (Nguyen, Attkisson, & Bottino, 1983, p. 104). Including key stakeholders or key agency personnel to help interpret the results and to help make sense out of seemingly different results may also be important. What would this process look like if applied to our latchkey example?

A Convergent, Multimethod Illustration

Let us imagine that as a school social worker you first became convinced of the need for a latchkey program when you learned of an 8-year-old child who started a fire in his bedroom and barely escaped serious injury. Because both parents were at work and the child had been regularly without adult supervision from 3:00 P.M. until 5:30 P.M., legal and child protection authorities had become involved.

As you talk about your idea of a latchkey program with several elementary school teachers during lunch hour, they become excited and each names about four children who could benefit from such a program. The school principal agrees that a latchkey program is needed and suggests that you talk with the parents' organization scheduled to meet the next evening. The parents' organization wholeheartedly endorses the concept and asks the principal if a questionnaire can be sent to every child's home. The principal agrees. A small planning committee meets with you and designs a questionnaire that looks something like the one in Figure 3.1.

The needs assessment questionnaires are prepared and given to each child in the elementary school to take home. About 60 percent of the questionnaires are returned. The results are as follows:

FIGURE 3.1 | GLENOVER PARENTS' ORGANIZATION
            AFTER-SCHOOL CARE QUESTIONNAIRE

Dear Parent:
Because of the recent fire in our Glenover community and the narrowly averted
tragedy, we believe that there is a need for an after-school program. Our children
would be supervised at school by teachers. Tutoring, games, and special "fun"
classes could be arranged—if there is sufficient interest from the parents. The
school board may agree to pay several teachers for two hours each day after
school if sufficient need can be documented. Please take five minutes to complete
the following survey and have your child return it tomorrow to his or her homeroom
teacher.

1. If an after-school program were available January 15 and there were no
    charge for enrolling your child, would you enroll one or more of your children
    (kindergarten through sixth grade)?
    __ YES, I WOULD ENROLL __ (number of children)
    __ NO, I WOULD NOT ENROLL ANY OF MY CHILDREN
    __ UNDECIDED, I NEED MORE INFORMATION ABOUT THE PROGRAM

2. If the school board does not have sufficient funds and there is a charge of
    $25.00 per week for each child, would you still make use of an after-school
    program?
    __ YES, I WOULD ENROLL __ (number of children)
    __ NO, I WOULD NOT ENROLL ANY OF MY CHILDREN
    __ UNDECIDED, I NEED MORE INFORMATION ABOUT THE PROGRAM

3. If you want to make sure that we reserve a place for your children, please
    write your name and address below. However, please return the question-
    naire whether or not you want us to reserve a place at this time.

    _____ (Name) _____ (Phone)
    _____ (Address)

Q1: Twenty percent of the parents would enroll their children in an after-
school program if there were no charge. A total of 105 children would
be expected to participate if there were no charge for the after-school
program.

Q2: Ten percent of the parents would enroll their children in an after-school
program if there were a $25 a week charge per child. Approximately 50
children could be expected to participate if there were a $25 a week charge
per child.

Q1 AND Q2: Thirty percent of the parents were undecided about enrolling
their children and wanted additional information.

Each of the informational sources explored in this fictitious example leads
us to believe that there is a definite need for an after-school program. Visually,
we might demonstrate this convergence of the data as shown in Figure 3.2. The
need for a latchkey program could be further supported by including secondary data such as the number of calls to police or rescue squads by unsupervised

FIGURE 3.2 | CONVERGENCE OF DATA

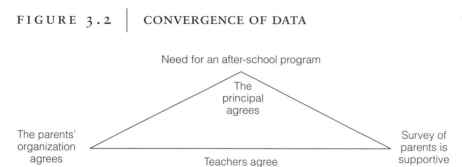

children. Such a needs assessment would make a strong and compelling argument for the proposed latchkey program. However, not every needs assessment could be expected to find such a high degree of convergence.

For instance, it is entirely possible that the parents' organization may not feel that a latchkey program is needed. Or, perhaps the principal, cognizant of the increased costs in utilities, janitorial services, and staff for the program, is not supportive because of an inadequate school budget.

There are no easy solutions as to what you should do if your sources of information do not converge. Sometimes you can explain away the lack of support from one sector (for example, the parents' organization is not representative of those parents who might make use of the latchkey program). On the other hand, the principal's concern must be addressed even if *everyone* else you contacted thought the project was viable.

Multimethod needs assessment is a model that strives to include many sources of data. These efforts are more comprehensive than other forms of needs assessment, and the many "reference points" give them more credibility. At the same time, they are more complex in the data collection phase as well as in the analysis. (See Box 3.4.)

THINKING CREATIVELY ABOUT NEEDS ASSESSMENT

Needs assessments do not have to be terribly complex. Sometimes the simplest of documentation procedures provides useful data for establishing that there is a need for a new program or facility. Once, after lecturing to a class about needs assessment, a student who believed that she did not know enough about needs assessment to do an assignment came to my office to talk to me (TK Logan). As she told me about where she worked (a diversion program for juveniles who had been arrested) and the kinds of problems she experienced in her work, she mentioned a desperate need that she encountered every day. There simply was not enough temporary shelter for status offenders (young people who were picked up by the police for running away, being out too late, or being in possession of alcohol). Because of the lack of suitable shelter, young people were placed in jail until beds became available elsewhere.

	A NEEDS ASSESSMENT
BOX 3.4	PRACTICE SAMPLER

I. A county health agency surveyed high school, middle school, and community youth ($n = 1,567$) to learn what these young people knew about HIV/AIDS and the sources of their information.

Seventy-five percent of the middle school sample but only 58 percent of the high school sample indicated they got information about HIV/AIDS from their families.

In response to the question, "If someone were to talk to you about AIDS, who would you be more likely to listen to?" 24 percent of the middle school youth but only 7 percent of high school youth chose the category "Parent." Both groups reported they would be more likely to listen to a person with AIDS than to anyone else.*

II. A needs assessment survey was mailed to school staff most likely to address health-related issues at junior and senior high schools in a large school district in Minnesota to inquire about programs to prevent weight-related disorders. This group included social workers, school nurses, as well as all science, home economics, and physical education teachers.

Respondents identified four potential difficulties in implementing school-based programs to prevent weight-related disorders. These were (1) structural issues such as scheduling difficulties, overworked staff, and lack of funds; (2) lack of administrative or staff support; (3) concern about stigmatizing students; and (4) low student interest (for example, apathy and low interest in nutrition).

Seventy percent of respondents indicated that they would be interested in participating in a staff training program to provide them with the tools to prevent weight-related disorders.**

III. Homeless mentally ill clients' perceptions of service needs were compared to those of their service providers. At the time of referral to case management services, outreach workers identified on the referral form which of 17 services they felt clients needed and then selected the three they thought were most important for that client. Clients were asked to identify which of the same 17 specific services they needed.

Seventy-four percent of the providers but only 44 percent of the consumers thought mental health services were most needed.

Twenty percent of the providers but only 8 percent of the clients thought substance abuse services were most needed.

More clients than providers thought job assistance was needed.***

*Source: Shields, G., & Adams, J. (1995). HIV/AIDS among youth: A community needs assessment study. *Child and Adolescent Social Work Journal, 72(5)*, 361–380.
**Source: Neumark-Sztainer, D., Story, M., & Coller, T. (1999). Perceptions of secondary school staff toward the implementation of school-based activities to prevent weight-related disorders: A needs assessment. *American Journal of Health Promotion, 73(3)*, 153–156.
***Source: Rosenheck, R., & Lam, J. A. (1997). Homeless mentally ill clients and providers' perceptions of service needs and clients' use of services. *Psychiatric Services, 48(3)*, 381–386.

I asked her how many times a month the jail was used inappropriately. She said about 18 to 20 times. I asked if she could document this, and she indicated that it would be easy to do because a special form had to be completed each time. In a few minutes, we outlined an approach she could use to show county and state officials the ongoing need for additional shelter care for juveniles. She not only met the requirements for a class project but also used a methodology that could produce documentation for local officials and the community to help them understand the need for additional temporary shelter for status offenders.

In another example, a community mental health agency was required by a state agency to conduct a needs assessment. However, practically no funds were available during the fiscal year. The agency improvised using data that was available from other counties. This is demonstrated in the next illustration.

A Needs Assessment Illustration

Warbler County (population 99,570) hired a consultant to conduct a community survey using a standardized instrument derived from earlier studies. This instrument contained scales from which could be inferred the extent of the population having either a possible or a probable need for mental health services. Various scales made up the instrument, but for the purposes of illustration, the relevant data from the needs assessment effort have been simplified in Table 3.2.

A short time later, Thrush County (population 90,831) also retained the consultant to conduct a needs assessment of their county. Once again, a probability sample was obtained, and the same instrument used. The agency executive

TABLE 3.2 | WARBLER COUNTY NEEDS ASSESSMENT DATA

Scale	Need for Counseling	Percent
Anxiety	Possible	6.2
	Probable	5.3
	Total	11.5
Depression	Possible	8.5
	Probable	4.5
	Total	13.0
Psychosocial	Possible	3.6
dysfunctioning	Probable	5.5
	Total	9.1

TABLE 3.3 | ESTIMATED NEEDS IN FRANKLIN COUNTY

Scale	Need	Warbler Co.	Thrush Co.	Franklin Co.
Population		99,570	90,831	85,422
Anxiety	Possible	6.2%	6.9%	6.5%
	Probable	5.3%	5.1%	5.2%
	Total	11.5%	12.0%	11.7%
Depression	Possible	8.5%	9.6%	9.0%
	Probable	4.5%	5.1%	4.8%
	Total	13.0%	14.7%	13.8%
Psychosocial	Possible	3.6%	4.5%	4.0%
dysfunction	Probable	5.5%	6.0%	5.8%
	Total	9.1%	10.5%	9.8%

in adjoining Franklin County wanted very much to have a needs assessment conducted in his county, but a severely limited budget could not be stretched to encompass a community survey. However, he contacted the agency directors in the neighboring counties, and both were cooperative and shared the data produced from their needs assessments. With this information, it was possible to estimate needs that a similar study might have found in Franklin County (Table 3.3).

Note how similar the percentages are between Warbler and Thrush counties. Although there are some minor variations, the percentages of persons in need of mental health services in both counties are almost equal. We can arrive at the estimated number of persons in Franklin County in need of services by averaging the Warbler and Thrush County data. Thus, Franklin County would expect a slightly larger proportion of depressed persons than Warbler County, but less than Thrush County.

This approach uses survey data, but in its methodology it is most akin to the use of secondary data. Of course, the problem with this approach is that the data did not come from Franklin County. In actuality, 17 percent of the population of Franklin County might be depressed and 20 percent might score above normal levels of anxiety. We would not know the "true" level of these dimensions without conducting a probability survey in Franklin County. However, if a convincing case of the similarities among these three counties can be built, then this type of estimation is as good as any of the other indirect approaches. How would we know if the counties were similar? We would begin by making comparisons on such variables as the average age of the population, average income per capita, the percentage of families in poverty, and the percentage of divorced and separated persons, and by looking at the racial and religious mix of the counties. Sometimes it is relatively easy to know if two counties are similar or dissimilar. If one county borders on a large metropolitan area and the other is rural and remote from any large city, then the two counties probably should not be compared. If two counties are primarily rural, in close proximity to each other, and compare well on demographic variables, then it is reasonable to use them to estimate needs in a third, similar county.

Even if you do not have access to needs assessment data from other counties, it may be possible to use social indicators or rates as developed by others. Ciarlo, Tweed, Shern, Kirkpatrick, and Sachs-Ericsson (1992) recommend that other states consider using percentage of persons in poverty and percentage of divorced males as indirect measures for estimating total need for alcohol, drug, and mental health services. However, it should be remembered that such methods are only estimates and that substantial variations across different geographical areas can be expected.

Needs assessments do not have to be financially burdensome to a human service agency. Some surveys (e.g., key informant studies) can be conducted without major expenditures of monetary or personnel resources. On occasions when a needs assessment will cost several thousand dollars, cooperative efforts among social service providers or funders (for example, United Way) should be explored. Partial funding may also be possible with creative planning. For instance, in a needs assessment of mental health services in one community, additional questions were incorporated that asked respondents about their favorite radio stations (during day, evening, and "drive" time). Because advertising is based on the number of listeners, radio stations were interested in this data and several purchased that portion of the results dealing with their listening audiences and thus underwrote part of the cost for the study.

If you are given the assignment of designing a needs assessment, think creatively. Shifman, Scott, Fawcett, and Orr (1986), for example, reported on the use of a game called "Family Few," modeled after the television program "Family Feud," to assess attitudes, beliefs, and knowledge about sexuality among female adolescents. In the process of obtaining a needs assessment profile on these adolescents, they were also able to provide didactic instruction!

Given the assignment of conducting a needs assessment, spend some time brainstorming all of the various ways one *could* go about examining the needs of the clientele. Make a list of these—whether they are feasible or not. When you run out of ideas, review the list and choose the best approach. Following is a list of several different types of needs assessments that one mental health agency conducted during a 6-year period. This list will give you some idea of the variety of ways in which needs assessment information can be obtained.

- *Community survey.* Over 300 questionnaires were mailed to elected officials, school principals, attorneys, and other "key informants." In addition, over 500 questionnaires were mailed to randomly selected community respondents.
- *Clergy survey.* Over 100 questionnaires were mailed to clergy to ascertain their knowledge and perceptions of the community mental health system.

- *Client utilization study.* The characteristics of present and past clients of the mental health system were examined. Potential groups who were not being adequately served (e.g., minorities, low-income families) were of special interest. This client utilization study was felt to be so useful that it was subsequently prepared in an annual report for several successive years.
- *Key informant study.* Representatives from 35 human service organizations were contacted by phone and letter about their perceptions of the community mental health system.
- *Community awareness survey.* Over 300 respondents were contacted by telephone to discover the extent of their knowledge about the availability of local mental health services.

COMMUNITY READINESS

When the needs assessment is finished and it suggests there is a need for a specific type of program, another consideration is the community's readiness to respond. For example, let's say that a needs assessment for a drug abuse prevention program examined such data as the number of teen drug users, teen pregnancies, and juvenile arrests. The community's rates of drug use and related problems were higher than national rates, and there is no drug use prevention program locally. Before a new program is designed and implemented, it can be very important to know if the community will be receptive. Resistance can make the implementation difficult or possibly even cause the program to fail.

Because communities differ in their resources, strengths, challenges, and political climates, what works in one may not be fully endorsed in another. Fortunately, the community readiness model is a method for assessing a community's willingness to support a new program.

The community readiness model identifies nine stages or levels of readiness (Oetting et al., 1995; Plested, Smitham, Thurman, Oetting, & Edwards, 1999). These stages are briefly described as follows.

1. *No awareness.* In this stage, community leadership tolerates the problem behavior in certain contexts. The community climate may overtly or covertly encourage the problem behavior. There are no formal or informal policies in place regarding the behavior.
2. *Denial.* In this stage, the community leadership recognizes that the behavior is or can be a problem but not as a local problem. Even if it is perceived as a local problem, there is a feeling that nothing can be done about it. The attitudes of community leaders are passive and apathetic.
3. *Vague awareness.* Community leaders in this stage generally recognize it as a local problem and that something ought to be done about it, but have no immediate motive to do anything. Ideas about who has the problem tend to be stereotyped and/or vague. Policies exist but may be inconsistently followed. The leadership lacks energy or motivation for dealing with the problem, and the community climate does not motivate the leaders.

4. *Preplanning.* At least some leaders clearly recognize that there is a local problem and that something should be done about it. There are some identifiable leaders, maybe even a committee, but efforts are not focused or detailed. Policies are known and generally followed. Community leaders discuss the problem but no real planning or actions address the problem. Community climate may or may not support leadership efforts to deal with the problem.

5. *Preparation.* Planning is going on and focuses on practical details. There is general information about local problems and about the pros and cons of prevention activities. Leadership is active and energetic. Decisions are being made about what will be done and who will do it. Policies are best known to those directly affected: offenders and victims. Resources are being actively sought or have been committed. Community climate may or may not support these efforts.

6. *Initiation.* Enough information is available to justify prevention activities, actions, or policies. An activity or action has been started and is underway, but is still viewed as a new effort. Staff are in training or have just finished training. Leaders may feel great enthusiasm because limitations and problems have not yet been experienced.

7. *Stabilization.* One or two programs or activities are running, supported by administrators or community decision makers. Programs, activities, or policies are viewed as permanent. Staff are usually trained and experienced. Policies are known to most community members. Limitations may be known, but there is no in-depth evaluation of effectiveness nor is there a sense that limitations suggest a need for change. There may be some criticism, but community climate generally supports what is occurring.

8. *Confirmation/expansion.* Standard programs, activities, and policies are in place; and authorities and community leaders support expanding or improving programs. Original efforts have been evaluated and modified, and new efforts are being planned or tried in order to reach more people, those more at risk, or different demographic groups. Resources for new efforts are being sought or committed. Policies are consistent and followed, with new policies being implemented as needed. Data are regularly obtained on the extent of local problems, and efforts are made to assess risk factors and causes of the problem. Community climate may challenge specific programs, but is fundamentally supportive. All groups may not support every activity.

9. *Professionalization.* Detailed and sophisticated knowledge of prevalence, risk factors, and causes of the problem exists. Some efforts may be aimed at general populations while others are targeted at specific risk factors and/or high-risk groups. Highly trained staff are running programs or activities; authorities are supportive; and community involvement is high. Effective evaluation is used to test and modify programs, policies, or activities. Community climate should challenge specific programs, but is fundamentally supportive and supports continued evaluation, seeking improvement.

Once the level of community readiness is assessed using scales the authors have developed for key informants, further planning can be undertaken. If the community is at a low stage of readiness, major educational activities should be undertaken. These activities may include training and media messages to inform both leaders and the community about the problem as well as to educate them regarding possible alternative solutions.

To bring about change in a community, key community leaders must be involved in the needs assessment planning (Kretzmann & McKnight, 1993; Thurman, Plested, Edwards, Foley, & Burnside, 2003). They must be both informed about the problem and concerned. Involving them in the planning process helps these leaders to feel ownership of the findings and prepares them for advocating for the program. (See Box 3.5.)

How would you go about conducting a citywide needs assessment in Saskatoon, Saskatchewan, a city with a population of 188,000? Could you do it for approximately $14,500 and issue a final report in 6 months?

Questions for Class Discussion

1. On the hypothetical questionnaire designed by the parents' organization, would better information have been obtained if either of the following questions were substituted? Why or why not?
    a. Do you ever leave your elementary school-aged children alone after school without adult supervision? If yes, how often?
    b. In an average week, how many days per week do you leave your children alone after school without adult supervision?
2. List on the board several social agencies familiar to most of those in the class. What information are these agencies likely to collect on a routine basis, and how could this information be used for needs assessment purposes?
3. Bring in census data for your community. Choose a social service program that has recently been in the news, and brainstorm ways the census data could be used to assess the need for that program.
4. Have the class identify a social service need in the community, and then discuss various ways in which this need could be documented.
5. Discuss why surveying only people you know is likely to generate biased information. Discuss what shared events or characteristics people who know each other are likely to have in common.
6. Discuss how opinions may not reflect true need. For instance, is the social problem of homelessness best attacked by constructing more overnight shelters? Would there be a difference in what the homeless say their needs are and what the average citizen might say are their needs? Which is the most important need of the homeless: vocational training, job opportunities, medical care, or shelter?
7. The management staff of a public housing project comes to you for assistance. They have been given a grant to train and empower resident leaders in an effort to build a sense of community and eliminate drug abuse problems.

WHAT IS IT REALLY LIKE TO DO A NEEDS ASSESSMENT? A CASE STUDY

Ervin (1997) describes the experience of having less than one month to construct a research design while finishing classes and exams at his university. The community needs assessment required participation in nearly 30 meetings with three student researchers and a consultative committee of United Way officials and representatives of local agencies. He met twice with all 28 executive directors of the United Way agencies. Some of these agencies were strongly opposed to the needs assessment, arguing that the money for the research was money taken away from direct services. They also feared that participation in the project would consume valuable staff time and that the report would create "major winners and losers." They grumbled that the needs assessment might focus too much on new, unmet needs and devalue programs already established and complained that United Way was not stimulating enough public interest in fund-raising.

Concerns were raised about too much attention to new, unmet needs (as opposed to the old, ongoing needs) and about nuances of labeling (do women's issues get categorized separately or within other categories like health and poverty?).

It was not possible to conduct a community-wide survey using a standardized questionnaire because of time and money constraints. Consequently, a multimethod approach was employed involving:

The examination of previous reports

The gathering of social indicator statistics

A Delphi procedure (using the 28 executive directors of United Way agencies)—*this* took 90 days and involved 16 separate substages including reminder letters and phone calls

Key informant interviews ($n = 135$) with non–United Way agencies

Focus groups ($n = 6$)

Public forums; notices were sent out to 200 organizations and were announced through the media

The final report was 209 single-spaced pages. In concluding the description of his experiences, Ervin (1997) notes, "What this experience again reinforces is the necessity to come to a fuller understanding of the context of public policy before proceeding with this kind of volatile research" (p. 386).

Source: Ervin, A. M. (1997). Trying the impossible: Relatively "rapid" methods in a citywide needs assessment. *Human Organization, 56*(4), 379–387.

The resident councils are new, and their meetings are not well attended. The management staff is convinced that the housing project should have a new playground. They ask you to help them design a needs assessment process that will show this. What would you do in this situation?

8. What would be the pros and cons of conducting a mall-intercept type (a convenience sample) for a community needs assessment?

Mini-Projects: Experiencing Evaluation Firsthand

1. Choose an article on needs assessment from the references list. Write a brief paper identifying:
    a. Useful information that you acquired
    b. Problems, bias, or limitations of the reported needs assessment
    c. Things you might have done differently if the needs assessment had been your responsibility
2. For a human service program with which you are familiar, design a needs assessment using exclusively secondary data. Be sure to describe:
    a. The program
    b. The purpose of the needs assessment
    c. The data collection procedure
    d. Estimates of the amount of time and money that will be required
    e. The advantages and disadvantages of the approach you will be using
3. For a human service program with which you are familiar, design a needs assessment using an impressionistic approach. Be sure to describe:
    a. The program
    b. The purpose of the needs assessment
    c. The data collection procedure
    d. Estimates of the amount of time and money that will be required
    e. The advantages and disadvantages of the approach you will be using
4. For a human service program with which you are familiar, design a needs assessment using a community survey. Be sure to describe:
    a. The program
    b. The purpose of the needs assessment
    c. The data collection procedure
    d. Estimates of the amount of time and money that will be required
    e. The advantages and disadvantages of the approach you will be using
5. For a human service program with which you are familiar, design a needs assessment that combines secondary data, impressionistic, and community survey approaches. Be sure to describe:
    a. The program
    b. The purpose of the needs assessment
    c. The data collection procedure
    d. Estimates of the amount of time and money that will be required
    e. The advantages and disadvantages of the approach you will be using

References and Resources

Acosta, O., & Toro, P. (2000). Let's ask the homeless people themselves: A needs assessment based on a probability sample of adults. *American Journal of Community Psychology, 28*, 3, 343–366.

Amodeo, M., & Gal, C. (1997). Strategies for ensuring use of needs assessment findings: Experiences of a community substance abuse prevention program. *Journal of Primary Prevention, 18*, 2, 227–242.

Bradshaw J. (1977). The concept of social need. In Neil Gilbert and Harry Specht (Eds.), *Planning for social welfare: Issues, models and tasks.* Englewood Cliffs, NJ: Prentice Hall.

Butterfoss, F. D., Houseman, C., Morrow, A. L., & Rosenthal, J. (1997). Use of focus group data for strategic planning by a community-based immunization coalition. *Family and Community Health, 20,* 49–59.

Ciarlo, J. A., & Tweed, D. L. (1992). Implementing indirect needs-assessment models for planning state mental health and substance abuse services. *Evaluation and Program Planning* 15(2), 195–210.

Ciarlo, J. A., Tweed, D. L., Shern, D. L., Kirkpatrick, L. A., & Sachs-Ericsson, N. (1992). The Colorado social health survey of mental health service needs: Sampling, instrumentation, and major findings. *Evaluation and Program Planning, 15(2),* 133–147.

Ciarlo, J. A., Tweed, D. L., Shern, D. L., Kirkpatrick, L. A., & Sachs-Ericsson, N. (1992). Validation of indirect methods to estimate need for mental health services. *Evaluation and Program Planning, 15,* 115–131.

Crook, G., & Oci, T. (1998). A review of systematic and quantifiable methods of estimating the needs of a community for alcohol treatment services. *Journal of Substance Abuse Treatment, 15(4),* 357–365.

Delbecq, A. L., Van de Ven, A. H., & Gustafson, H. (1975). *Group techniques for program planning: A guide to nominal group and Delphi processes.* Glenview, IL: Scott, Foresman.

Fiorentine, R. (1994). Assessing drug and alcohol treatment needs of general and special populations: Conceptual, empirical and inferential issues. *Journal of Drug Issues, 24,* 445–462.

Hall, M., Amodeo, M., Shaffer, H., & Bilt, J. (2000). Social workers employed in substance abuse treatment agencies: A training needs assessment. *Social Work, 45(2),* 141–154.

Harvard Medical School, Division on Addictions, Addiction Training Center of New England, Brown University. (1997). Measuring substance abuse treatment provider training needs: Developing an index of training need. *Journal of Substance Abuse Treatment, 14,* 593–606.

Hlady, W. G. et al. (1994). Use of a modified cluster sampling method to perform rapid needs assessment after Hurricane Andrew. *Annals of Emergency Medicine, 23,* 719–725.

Hornick, J. P., & Burrows, B. (1988). Program evaluation. In R. M. Grinnell Jr. (Ed.), *Social work research and evaluation.* Itasca, IL: Peacock.

Kreiner, P., Soldz, S., Berger, M., Elliott, E., Reynes, J., Williams, C., & Rodriguez-Howard, M. (2001). Social indicator-based measures of substance abuse consequences, risk, and protection at the town level. *Journal of Primary Prevention, 21(3),* 339–365.

Kretzmann, J., & McKnight, J. (1993). *Building communities from the inside out: A path toward finding and mobilizing a community's assets.* Chicago, IL: ACTA.

Krueger, R. A. (1993). *Focus groups: A practical guide for applied research.* Newbury Park, CA: Sage.

Logan, T., Williams, K., & Leukefeld, C. (2001). A statewide drug court needs assessment: Identifying target counties, assessing readiness. *Journal of Offender Rehabilitation, 33(3),* 1–25.

McAuliffe, W., LaBrie, R., Woodworth, R., Zhang, C., & Dunn, R. (2003). State substance abuse treatment gaps. *American Journal of Addictions, 12,* 101–121.

McAuliffe, W., Woodworth, R., Zhang, C., & Dunn, R. (2002). Identifying substance abuse treatment gaps in substate areas. *Journal of Substance Abuse Treatment, 23,* 199–208.

McCarty, D., McGuire, T., Harwood, H., & Field, T. (1998). Using state information systems for drug abuse services research. *American Behavioral Scientist, 41(8)*, 1090–1107.

McKillip, J. (1998). Needs analysis: Process and techniques. In L. Bickman & D. Rog (Eds.), *Handbook of applied social research methods*. Thousand Oaks, CA: Sage.

Mika, K. (1996). *Program outcome evaluation: A step-by-step handbook*. Milwaukee, WI: Families International.

Nguyen, T. D, Attkisson, C. C, & Bottino, M. J. (1983). The definition and identification of human service needs in a community. In R. A. Bell, M. Sundel, J.F. Aponte, S. A. Murrell, & E. Lin (Eds.), *Assessing health and human service needs: Concepts, methods, and applications*. New York: Human Sciences Press.

Oetting, E. R., Donnermeyer, J. F., Plested, B. A., Edwards, R. W., Kelly, K., & Beauvais, F. (1995). Assessing community readiness for prevention. *International Journal of Addictions, 30(6)*, 659–683.

Plested, B., Smitham, D. M., Thurman, P. J., Oetting, E. R., & Edwards, R. W. (1999). Readiness for drug use prevention in rural minority communities. *Substance Use and Misuse, 34*, 521–544.

Raskin, M. S. (1994). The Delphi study in field instruction revisited: Expert consensus on issues and research priorities. *Journal of Social Work Education, 30(1)*, 75–89.

Royse, D., & Drude, K. (1982). Mental health needs assessment: Beware of false promises. *Community Mental Health Journal, 18(2)*, 97–106.

Rutz, M., & Shemberg, K. M. (1985). Fifth and sixth graders' attitudes toward mental health issues. *Journal of Community Psychology, 13*, 393–401.

Shearer, R. (2003). Identifying the special needs of female offenders. *Federal Probation, 67(1)*, 46–52.

Shifman, L., Scott, C. S., Fawcett, N., & Orr, L. (1986). Utilizing a game for both needs assessment and learning in adolescent sexuality education. *Social Work with Groups, 9(2)*, 41–56.

Siegel, L. M., Attkisson, C. C., & Carson, L. G. (1978). Need identification and program planning in the community context. In C. C. Attkisson, W. A. Hargreaves, & M. J. Horowitz (Eds.), *Evaluation of human service programs*. New York: Academic Press.

Stefl, M. E. (1984). Community surveys in local needs assessment projects: Lessons from a case study. *Administration in Mental Health, 12(2)*, 110–122.

Sung, K. (1989). Converging perspectives of consumers and providers in assessing needs of families. *Journal of Social Service Research, 12(3/4)*, 1–29.

Thompson, R. W., Ruma, P. R., Authier, K. J., & Bouska, T. C. (1994). Application of a community needs assessment survey to decategorization of child welfare services. *Journal of Community Psychology, 22*, 33–42.

Thurman, P., Plested, B., Edwards, R., Foley, R., & Burnside, M. (2003). Community readiness: The journey to community healing. *Journal of Psychoactive Drugs, 35(1)*, 27–31.

Toomey, B. G., First, R. J., Greenlee, R., & Cummins, L. K. (1993). Counting the rural homeless population: Methodological dilemmas. *Social Work Research and Abstracts, 29(4)*, 23–27.

Warheit, G. J., Bell, R. A., & Schwab, J. J. (1977). *Planning for change: Needs assessment approaches*. Rockville, MD: National Institute of Mental Health.

QUALITATIVE METHODS IN EVALUATION

CHAPTER 4

INTRODUCTION

The following quote by Carol Weiss (1998), a leader in evaluation methodology, speaks volumes:

> The most striking development in recent years is the coming of age of qualitative methods. Where once they were viewed as aberrant and probably the refuge of those who had never studied statistics, now they are recognized as valuable additions to the evaluation repertoire. Qualitative methods accomplish evaluative tasks that were previously done poorly or entirely scanted. (p. 252)

We have come a long way toward embracing qualitative methods as applicable to program evaluation as well as the loftier goals of knowledge building and theory development (Greene, 2000; Padgett, 2004; Patton, 2002; Rist, 2000; Strauss & Corbin, 1990; Swanson & Chapman, 1994). Two notable examples of this growing popularity: qualitative methods interest groups are among the largest interest groups in both the Society for Social Work and Research and the American Evaluation Association despite the dominance of quantitative methods in these organizations' membership and conference proceedings.

The goals in this chapter are threefold. First, the chapter will give an overview of qualitative evaluation and its relevance within the larger context of evaluation research. Second, it will describe how qualitative evaluation proceeds, beginning with design and continuing through the iterative process of sampling, data collection, and analysis. Finally, it will offer some specific examples of qualitative evaluation.

WHAT IS "QUALITATIVE EVALUATION"?

Many different approaches fall loosely under the rubric of "qualitative"—ethnography, grounded theory, and narrative analysis, to name only a few. Their differences are rooted in a mix of different philosophical and disciplinary foundations, with some approaches more in tune with the anti- and post-positivist trend of the last two decades (Denzin & Lincoln, 2000) and others more pragmatic about accommodation with the quantitative methods that dominate scientific inquiry (Greene, 2000; Padgett, 2004; Patton, 2002). However, virtually all qualitative studies—regardless of their epistemological backdrop—share in common a few key ingredients: (1) a focus on naturalistic inquiry in situ; (2) a reliance on the researcher as the instrument of data collection; and (3) reports emphasizing narrative over numbers.

Contrary to a popular perception of qualitative research as little more than personal opinion masquerading as expertise, these methods are *empirical* and *systematic,* relying on careful documentation and analysis grounded in the data—just like their quantitative counterparts. To be sure, doubts about bias persist in some quarters. Sechrest and Figueredo (1993), for example, express concerns about the nonstandardized, ad hoc nature of qualitative evaluation and question whether it has yielded any exemplary findings. (This judgment is a bit unfair, because the findings of qualitative evaluation are often "buried" within process evaluations and lack the visibility and authority of quantitative evaluations of outcome.) Nevertheless, the voices of doubt have faded significantly in recent years, as evidenced by the earlier quote by Carol Weiss.

Interestingly, success in terms of wider acceptance has not produced consensus or unanimity among qualitative evaluation researchers. Just as qualitative inquiry in general has its epistemological factions, proponents of qualitative evaluation disagree in their stance vis-à-vis scientific research in general and quantitative methods in particular. Thus, critics of scientific post-positivism are often followers of Guba and Lincoln's "fourth generation evaluation" movement (1987) and take comfort in the strong postmodern positions throughout Denzin and Lincoln's *Handbook of Qualitative Research* (2000). Meanwhile, those of a more pragmatic orientation (including Deborah Padgett) carry on without subscribing to a postmodern ideology that entails rejection of quantitative or mixed methods designs (Fishman, 2003; Patton, 2002). Rather than engage in any further debate over the merits of the various epistemological positions, we wish to call for agreement on one point—all evaluations need to be empirically driven and adhere to some standards for rigor.

WHEN IS QUALITATIVE EVALUATION USEFUL?

As with all forms of research, evaluation research has been, and continues to be, heavily quantitative. Indeed, it might seem surprising that methods pioneered by anthropologists in exotic locales over a century ago have immediate application to the nitty-gritty world of program evaluation. But this link was made some time ago by social scientists working in the field of education—George and Louise Spindler, Harry Wolcott, and Jules Henry, to name just a few. Even a leading quantitative methodologist (Cronbach, 1982) has argued persuasively that context-rich observation and interviewing are keys to understanding a program's success or failure. In particular, the qualitative techniques of focus group interviews and participant observation have a long history in marketing research, political polling, and educational evaluation.

Of course, qualitative methods are not appropriate for every evaluation. The key is knowing when to deploy them alone, when to go the quantitative route, and when to consider using both methods conjointly. How do you make this decision? Your choice should be driven first and foremost by the goals of the evaluation. Given the basic distinction between process and outcome evaluation, qualitative methods are generally associated with the former, that is, the *hows* and *whys* of the program and its inner workings. Qualitative methods are also suitable for *formative* evaluation where the primary goal is improving the program prior to full implementation.

Certain facets of a program are difficult to capture and quantify—staff morale, executive decision making, cross-cultural misunderstandings, and client perceptions, for example. The advantage of a qualitative approach is that it allows us to examine these complex phenomena without relying on structured data collection necessitated by quantitative designs. By digging deeper and more sensitively, we can increase our chances of discovering unanticipated but meaningful insights into a program's inner workings.

One important by-product of qualitative evaluation makes it especially attractive—its interpersonal nature. When done well, qualitative methods have immediate benefits for participants—an especially liberating experience for a low-level staffer or a disaffected client. Though this by-product is not reason enough to go the qualitative route, it generally makes stakeholders feel more engaged and appreciated (which is not a bad legacy to leave behind after the evaluation is completed).

The strengths of qualitative methods can also be liabilities. First, there is the trade-off of choosing depth over breadth. Qualitative methods are not well suited to evaluations requiring data from large numbers of respondents. Second, qualitative methods are time- and labor-intensive in their implementation. Lengthy in-depth interviewing and in situ observation, labor-intensive transcription of audiotapes, and the iterative process of data analysis and re-interviewing all combine to make traditional qualitative studies a challenge to carry out in the pressured environment of program evaluation. (There are, however, strategies for focusing qualitative methods to fit the needs of evaluators—a topic to which we will return later in this chapter.)

Finally, qualitative methods are less useful when we need to report on program outcomes with precision. It is usually more authoritative to offer statistical analyses of program outcomes—analyses that can control for confounding variables and support conclusions with a known degree of confidence (Weiss, 1998). Although there are occasions where a qualitative approach is sufficient to establish a program's effectiveness, the world of program evaluation (as in the larger world) remains firmly entrenched in the scientific, quantitative paradigm.

Does this mean that qualitative methods have no place in outcome evaluation? Not at all. Qualitative findings are frequently presented along with the quantitative findings. Let's assume that you are interested in a jail diversion program for violent adolescent boys. Your evaluation found that 67 percent of boys randomly assigned to an anger management program improved compared with 42 percent of boys who were given "standard" behavioral treatment. In this instance, "improvement" was measured by scores on an anger control scale and by reports from parents and teachers. We can see how exact percentages (and statistical significance tests) offer more than a qualitative finding citing "most" or "some" of the boys improved.

Yet qualitative evaluation can supply something the numbers cannot—vivid descriptions of how individual boys responded to the different programs. Thus, although numbers and statistical analyses tell us that one program worked better, case studies of individual successes and failures give an understanding of *how* these results came to pass.

To take this hypothetical program a step further in demonstrating the utility of qualitative evaluation, we can argue that qualitative approaches could have been useful in the *formative* phases of the program, for example, in identifying ways to shape the anger management classes so that they could overcome the resistance of adolescents in crisis. Similarly, a *process* evaluation could examine how well the program instructors were communicating the anger management message to their students, whether the boys were completing their take-home exercises, and so on.

This concern with the pitfalls of program implementation is critical. Even manualized treatments can drift away from their protocols when well-meaning program staff decide the manual is not working or that it takes too much time to follow (Mullen & Iverson, 1986). Qualitative methods are capable of capturing the subtle nuances of program drift that quantitative measures cannot.

We are left with little doubt that qualitative methods have a place in the evaluation researcher's repertoire. Of course, they cannot address every question evaluators need to ask. Nor can they provide the precision and finality that living in a quantitative world renders so important (yet so elusive). But it is difficult to imagine any type of evaluation that could not benefit from the qualitative perspective if time and resources permit.

QUALITATIVE METHODS AND SINGLE SYSTEM EVALUATION

A bit of discussion is needed here regarding single system (SS) evaluation and qualitative methods. Single system designs emerged from a quantitative (or measurement-oriented) approach to evaluating intervention with a single client system. For reasons that will be explained shortly, the focus in this chapter is on qualitative evaluation at the program or community level rather than at the level of the individual.

Qualitative techniques of observation and interviewing have gained increasing popularity among social work practitioners in the United States (Franklin & Jordan, 1995; Sherman & Reid, 1994) and abroad (Fook, 2001; Shaw & Lishman, 1999; Whitmore, 2001). But their usefulness for research and evaluation during treatment is quite limited. Of course, one could conduct a qualitative evaluation of a single system by observing the practitioner–client treatment encounter, by interviewing both parties, and by examining case records.

However, such an activity is rarely done, because a quantitative SS approach already exists that enables the practitioner to carry out the evaluation and the treatment simultaneously. By contrast, a practitioner who seeks to self-evaluate using qualitative methods does so at some risk. The role confusion inherent in trying to qualitatively understand one's own words and actions in situ threatens the integrity of the treatment as well as the evaluation of the treatment. It is a wiser course to leave evaluation of single systems to the extant methodology and to carry out qualitative evaluation of, but not in, practice (Padgett, 1999; 2003).

There are other reasons that qualitative methods match up better with program- and community-level evaluation. One practical reason is the labor intensiveness of qualitative methodologies and the poor cost-benefit payoff of using them to study one-on-one encounters. Another, more substantive reason comes from the holistic and contextualizing nature of qualitative inquiry. When individual treatment encounters are the exclusive focus, they risk becoming decontextualized, thereby robbing qualitative inquiry of one of its greatest strengths.

Qualitative evaluators are most comfortable when they have access to a variety of arenas of human activity within an agency or program rather than in only one. The natural ebb and flow of agency activities—clients entering a program, staff grappling with training and morale issues, community advocates arguing for a greater voice in agency policies—these are the natural habitat of the qualitative evaluator.

VARIANTS IN QUALITATIVE EVALUATION

The methods and techniques used in qualitative evaluation do not differ from those used in any other type of qualitative research—the difference lies in how they are put to use and to what end. Program evaluation methods are directed to pragmatic concerns such as decision making, problem solving, policy analysis, and community and organizational development (Patton, 2002). Because there are many how-to texts on qualitative methods (see the list of Suggested Readings at the end of this chapter), you are advised to consult these for more details than we can provide here.

There are a few different approaches to qualitative evaluation. While much of the description in this chapter is consistent with what are considered *mainstream* qualitative evaluation methods, variants might include time-pressured *focused* methods, mixed methods, and action/participatory evaluations.

Focused Qualitative Evaluation (FQE)

There are few published guidelines for designing and implementing time-sensitive, or focused qualitative, evaluation. Most of the information available on this topic comes from public health projects in developing countries where anthropologists, epidemiologists, and health care organizations must make quick assessments of needs or program efficacy related to nutrition, sanitation, family planning, and infectious diseases such as HIV/AIDS (Scrimshaw, Carballo, Ramos, & Blair, 1991). Rapid assessment procedures (RAPs) and rapid ethnographic assessments (REAs) typically have timelines measured in days or weeks rather than in months or years (Manderson & Aaby, 1992). Their application in urban settings remains largely unaddressed.

Real-world constraints have always impinged on evaluation, but an evaluator's use of methods rooted in prolonged engagement and in capturing an insider perspective raises special challenges. In FQE, extensive ethnographic observation and interviewing may not be possible, but time-efficient options such as focus group interviewing and rapid ethnographic assessment can often be substituted (and, in many cases, may be more appropriate for the problem at hand).

Although shortcuts in qualitative methods make some purists wince (and admittedly entail compromises), FQE strategies are often the only way an evaluation can be done if done at all. Later in this chapter, we will offer specific examples of FQE that were used in an all-qualitative study of congregate care for youths in New York City in 2002. The Youth in Congregate Care (YCC) evaluation was conducted on a tight timeline of 18 months and involved over 70 interviews with youths, judges, child advocates, social workers, and law guardians (Padgett & Freundlich, 2004).

Mixed Methods in Evaluation

The type of problem under study may lead you to forego a fully qualitative design in favor of **mixed methods.** Mixing quantitative and qualitative methods can provide the best of both worlds if carried out effectively (Cook & Reichardt, 1979; Kidder & Fine, 1987; Patton, 2002; Tashakkori & Teddlie, 2003). By offering a form of *triangulation of method,* we can take advantage of the strengths and offset the weaknesses of each.

A number of mixed methods designs are available, including temporal sequencing—for example, using qualitative methods during the formative phase and quantitative methods during the outcome phase of the evaluation. You can also use both methods concurrently. For example, an evaluator might follow a quantitative design but also collect qualitative data from a subsample of the total population being studied.

Robert Drake and his colleagues (1993) conducted qualitative interviews with a subsample of clients in their mixed methods evaluation of a treatment program for dually diagnosed homeless persons in Washington, DC. In addition to measuring number and length of case manager–client encounters and degree of satisfaction with the case manager–client relationship, evaluation staff interviewed participants to understand how and why the relationship succeeded or failed. By integrating the qualitative and quantitative findings, Drake et al. were able to understand how clients could rate their relationships with case managers highly and yet express ambivalence and even resentment toward their case managers' authority and control over their access to resources (housing, medical care, etc.). The structured questionnaires were not able to capture clients' fear of retribution if they rated their case managers negatively. Ultimately, these attitudes were associated with dropout from the program (Drake et al., 1993).

During data analysis, qualitative data may be analyzed using qualitative techniques such as coding—or it may be reduced to numbers. Similarly, during the write-up of the evaluation's findings, numbers *and* narratives may be presented to enhance the quantitative findings with richness and depth.

Mixed methods are relatively rare in the literature on evaluation, probably reflecting the scarcity of resources needed to accommodate the additional tasks linked to the dual approaches. When and if such resources can be marshaled, mixed methods can lend an evaluation a unique strength—the capacity for breadth *and* depth. Agency-based programs are complex, multidimensional organisms. Their internal functioning and productivity are subject to a myriad factors not easily captured by one method alone.

Action (Participatory) Evaluation

The preceding discussion has been based on a rather apolitical (and naive) premise—that qualitative evaluation is a neutral enterprise showing no alliance with any particular group of stakeholders. Although the political context of evaluation is dealt with elsewhere in this book, we should note that some qualitative evaluators adopt an overtly activist agenda known as **action**, or **participatory, research** (Weiss, 1972; Stringer, 1999). Action research, rooted in community activism, feminism, and Third World liberation movements, places a commitment to social justice at the forefront of its goals (Cancian, 1990; Reinharz, 1992) but it may also be pursued in a local community as a coalition-building strategy less inclined to conflict than consensus (Stringer, 1999).

The design of a participatory evaluation centers on enlisting the cooperation of the least powerful stakeholders in the evaluation from start to finish.

There are no standard procedures to follow, but the study's success is defined by its ability to empower communities and clients to achieve greater self-determination and control over programs that affect them. In a sense, the *process* of carrying out an action evaluation is part of the *product*.

Brunner and Guzman (1989) describe a participatory evaluation of a literacy program for women in rural Mexico. Portrayed as an educational and interactive process, local volunteers were asked to form an evaluation team that was at first coached by professional evaluators but eventually was encouraged to act independently in carrying out the evaluation's goals as defined by the indigenous community. All phases of the evaluation, from design to dissemination, depended on active involvement by members of the team working collaboratively with their communities.

It is difficult to find fault with a praxis-oriented approach that promotes social justice and empowerment. However, as noted by Brunner and Guzman (1989), the real-world application of these valued principles is problematic for a number of reasons. First, most sponsoring institutions—private or public—are not enamored of disrupting the status quo to organize grassroots change. Second, such projects often become bogged down when differences in goals and values emerge between the participating parties. Disagreements can pit members of the professional evaluation team against members of the local group, or they can arise when factions within the local group vie for control. Third, professional evaluators who embrace the values of action research may find themselves in a painful quandary when they feel the evaluation is going awry or even contributing to the formation of a new oppressive elite. Thus, the evaluation itself may lead to unintended, but nonetheless harmful, outcomes. Finally, the expenditures of time and effort that must accompany the lengthy process of consensus building among disparate groups make action research exceedingly difficult to carry out.

Despite these caveats, the core values of participatory action research can be brought into play during the design and execution phases of an evaluation. Indeed, they should be guiding principles for all evaluators who seek maximal involvement of stakeholders, especially those least powerful and (often) most affected by an evaluative study.

METHODS OF QUALITATIVE EVALUATION

In the following pages, we will focus on qualitative methods specifically as they apply to program evaluation, starting with design, then proceeding to sampling, data collection, and data analysis. As we review these, please remember a fundamental of qualitative research—these procedures do not follow a linear "cookbook" sequence, as do quantitative research procedures, but instead tend to unfold in an iterative fashion, going back and forth between steps. While describing these methods, we will on occasion introduce strategies for focused qualitative evaluation (FQE) and offer examples drawn from our recent experience in carrying out an evaluation of youth in congregate care in New York City.

Designing a Qualitative Evaluation

The meaning of the word *design* in qualitative research bears almost no resemblance to its use in quantitative studies where randomized experiments reign as the gold standard. Yet qualitative studies are not haphazard. For the sake of convenience, we will use the term *qualitative research design* knowing that it refers more to flexibility in making choices than to some overarching plan that must be adhered to at all costs.

We begin with the decision that qualitative methods are appropriate (a decision to be made carefully based on the evaluation's goals and the availability of time and resources).The next steps are much the same as the quantitative evaluator's—decide on your unit(s) of analysis, sampling strategies, types of data collection and analysis, and strategies for rigor (Padgett, 1998; Patton, 2002).

For qualitative evaluators, **units of analysis** typically refer to individuals (staff, clients, etc.). But they may also include agencies, group homes, hospital units, or any other settings that are arenas of human activity organized around a particular program (or programs). Such settings provide a naturalistic laboratory for the ethnographic observer seeking a holistic picture of the program and its key actors.

Another design consideration is whether comparisons will be made. This consideration may seem unusual for a qualitative design because controlled comparisons are the heart and soul of quantitative designs. Comparisons in qualitative research lack artificial or statistical controls but are nonetheless plausible and even useful. For example, imagine that you are carrying out an observational study of a residential treatment program for mentally ill persons who are also substance abusers that promotes "harm reduction" rather than detoxification and abstinence from drug use. Under this somewhat controversial policy, clients are urged to reduce their drug dependency, but their treatment is not contingent on compliance with this policy.

It might be instructive to design your study to include interviewing staff at a program where the harm reduction approach was rejected as sending a message of agency endorsement of illicit drug use. You may also want to exert some control by choosing a comparison program that is alike in most other ways, for example, in client population, neighborhood location, and so on. In this manner, you can make comparisons that illuminate what is working (or not working) in the less traditional harm reduction approach.

Given the inherent flexibility of the qualitative approach, qualitative evaluators do not follow a preconceived design, opting instead for a straightforward description of what they plan to do (with the obvious caveat that the plan can change during the course of the study). In the write-up phase of the evaluation, a detailed documentation of what was actually done is provided. To be sure, there is an element of unpredictability to this process—a degree of faith in the "researcher as instrument" is required.

The strictures and structure of an experimental design are a far cry from the eyes, ears, and insights of even an experienced qualitative researcher. This distinction is what makes qualitative research somewhat more risky but also more likely to produce serendipitous findings.

Gaining Access to the Site

Even when a researcher has a commitment from financial backers and from the program's chief administrator to carry out the evaluation, the evaluator must gain the trust of all of the shareholders and enter the site with the least amount of disruption and miscommunication. This step requires careful groundwork on the part of the evaluator, including gaining the permission of **gatekeepers**—individuals up and down the organizational hierarchy whose involvement is needed to make the study happen.

Qualitative researchers depend on the goodwill engendered by their willingness to listen without judgment and to seek input from everyone regardless of his or her status within the organization. On the other hand, the role of evaluator places him or her in a sometimes precarious position of an outsider with the potential to cast the program in a negative light. Although no evaluator can promise a rosy picture, the qualitative evaluator must somehow maintain a position of neutrality even as he or she seeks to make stakeholders feel comfortable enough to participate in interviews and to be observed over a period of time.

One path to easing entry into the organizational culture is to rely on **key informants,** that is, individuals who are especially knowledgeable and willing to share their knowledge. With or without key informants, the success of the qualitative evaluator depends on a degree of sensitivity, a tough hide that can withstand rejection and even hostility, and a sense of humor to carry the evaluator through the awkward initial phase of getting acquainted.

Reciprocity, Payback, and Feedback

Various forms of reciprocity are appropriate and even commendable during an evaluation. At the outset, the evaluative researcher communicates what the study will entail (there are no good reasons to deceive or mislead participants about what you will be doing). Types of payback can range from monetary incentives for formal interviews to an informal presentation for staff. Payback in the form of sharing the final results—a common practice in research—is a delicate issue given the potential for distortion (or suppression) of unflattering findings by the powers that be.

At the start of the project, the astute evaluator should negotiate how—with an eye to maximizing the involvement of diverse stakeholders—findings will be presented. Of course, evaluators need a degree of sensitivity as well as consideration of levels of disclosure. The main findings may be summarized for mass consumption, and the more sensitive problem areas may be discussed with the affected parties (a feedback mechanism that will be discussed further in the following text).

As the evaluation proceeds, there are other ways to reciprocate that emerge naturally from the level of engagement the qualitative evaluator experiences. Offering *on-site feedback* can be particularly helpful during formative evaluation or when a system problem emerges that is relatively easy to remedy. For example, say that you are evaluating a breast cancer screening program and you learn from patients that the clinic's letters notifying them of abnormal mammogram results are confusing (or only in English despite a large Spanish-speaking clientele). Your immediate feedback can ameliorate this system problem; you may even wish to assist in rewording and/or translating the letters—a situation where feedback leads to payback.

However, offering on-site feedback changes the evaluator's role in a number of ways and should be done with caution (Patton, 2002). First and foremost, the qualitative evaluator drops all pretense of detachment and becomes an intervener—stakeholders are now put on notice and may welcome your suggestions or bristle with resentment. If you prefer to maintain a more detached stance, feedback may need to be postponed until the final evaluation report. Another caveat relates to the timing of the feedback—avoiding premature conclusions before the evaluation is complete. Qualitative evaluators should resist the temptation to offer suggestions gratuitously when they are better left to a more comprehensive final report.

Sampling

Patton (2002) uses the term *purposeful* to describe the various sampling strategies qualitative evaluators favor. All of these strategies sacrifice breadth for depth—the choice depends in large part on what types of data are needed and who is best able to supply it. Among these choices are *deviant case sampling, typical case sampling, maximum variation sampling, snowball sampling, convenience sampling, negative case sampling,* and *politically powerful sampling* (Patton, 2002).To Patton's lexicon we would add the *sampling of experts or key informants.* In describing each of these in the following text, we will assume individuals are the sampling units.

Deviant case sampling is driven by the need to learn about the *outliers*—persons who exemplify unusual successes or failures of the program. If you are evaluating a teen pregnancy prevention program, you may want to interview the problem graduate who ultimately had three children before the age of 21. By contrast, **typical case sampling** would focus on the program graduates who most closely typify the norm.

Maximum variation sampling is the choice when you seek representativeness—cases that cut across wide variations in program processes and/or outcomes. **Snowball sampling** is an essential when the population of interest is isolated, hard-to-reach, or suspicious of outsiders. For example, if you were evaluating a respite program designed for Korean-American women taking care of elderly relatives, you may want to speak with women in the Korean-American community who did not respond to the outreach initiative—women who are isolated or in some other way unable or unwilling to take advantage of the program. The best approach could be to start with some caregivers known to outreach workers, gain their trust, and ask for names of additional women they know who are in the same situation. In this way, a sample snowballs, or expands, by tapping into existing social networks.

Convenience sampling is undoubtedly the easiest approach, because it implies doing little more than taking advantage of cases at hand. Any number of constraints may steer the evaluation toward convenience sampling. But the evaluator should beware—this method is least purposeful and least likely to yield rich information.

Data Collection

Qualitative designs and qualitative data collection need not necessarily go hand in hand (each can be paired with a quantitative counterpart), but they are a natural fit. There are three basic forms of data in qualitative research and evaluation: (1) field notes generated by *on-site observation,* (2) transcriptions and other documentation generated by *in-depth interviewing,* and (3) *use of documents* and other sources of existing data. The evaluator's choice of data collection mode should be driven by the goals of the evaluation and the availability of resources. Whenever possible, more than one source of data should be pursued. In any case, the evaluator should make it clear what types of data are needed and what evaluation questions they can address.

On-site observation is known by a number of terms—ethnography, fieldwork, participant observation, and so forth (Fetterman, 1984). What is central to all of these methods is the pivotal role of the "researcher as instrument"— his or her ability to enter the program setting, gain rapport with the participants, and unobtrusively observe the "natives" as they go about their daily activities. Detailed observations are recorded in *field notes,* a key form of qualitative data. Most qualitative evaluators develop ways to take notes either in real time (if done unobtrusively) or to retreat to a quiet space as soon as possible while the memories are still fresh.

A good deal of variation exists in how much the field-worker participates in the ongoing activities. At one end of the continuum, the evaluator stays at a distance, acting as a fly on the wall. **Participant observers,** on the other hand, actively take part and become engaged with their surroundings.

While in the field, the degree of participation often shifts, depending on the situation. During a period of observation at an agency, staff may naturally turn to you and ask your opinion or your help. If the request is relatively innocuous (e.g., helping set up chairs for a meeting or assisting a staff person with some new computer software), your participation is sensible and even enhances rapport.

But a line needs to be drawn if the request (or even the perceived need) to intervene tugs you too far away from a position of studied neutrality. For example, let's say that you are evaluating a zero-tolerance domestic violence arrest program in the local police department and you begin by adopting an outsider stance by observing morning roll call and the special training sessions. You are pleased when you are invited to accompany two officers to observe an arrest, but the abuser is violent and you have an irresistible urge to help out as the officers struggle with him. Although there are no doubt times when good conscience and professional ethics demand action, these should be rare occasions. After all, sometimes good intentions turn out to have bad (though unanticipated) consequences.

Because we cannot hope to capture everything we see, we aim for unbiased observation of the physical setting, actors' behaviors and interactions, and both verbal and nonverbal communication. The importance of the physical setting—the spatial layout and visual decor of the agency, clinic, school, nursing home, and so on—cannot be overstated. Too often overlooked in favor of human activity, the setting can itself play a powerful role in shaping or influencing behavior. A spacious, light-filled mental health clinic decorated with colorful artwork is a different stage for program activities than a dingy, crowded clinic with peeling plaster and dilapidated furniture. Similarly, if the program director occupies a huge luxurious office while staff are confined to cramped cubicles, a notation on this discrepancy may come in handy later when you are evaluating staff morale. A good place to start is by drawing a floor plan and layout of the agency, followed by a detailed description of the setting.

The tricky part in recording observational data is knowing how to separate minutiae from meaning. Because you are attempting to get behind the scenes—to capture the mundane as well as the unusual—you need to cast a very wide net. Yet you do not want to overburden yourself with trivia. (Of course, trivia at one point may later turn out to be a critical part of the puzzle.) One way to separate the wheat from the chaff is to zero in on what the evaluation is supposed to accomplish and focus your observations accordingly. For example, you have been asked to conduct a process evaluation of an adolescent mental health program in Chinatown designed to increase mental health referrals from the school system. Although the program appears to be successful in increasing the number of referrals, it has been plagued by a high dropout rate.

As the number of no-shows and cancellations increased, the program director asked you to evaluate this problem and to come up with recommendations. You begin holistically—observing all phases of the program, including the outreach workers as they give presentations to teachers, parents, and students; the clinic waiting area; staff meetings, and so on. You may also seek the requisite permission to observe individual and group therapy sessions where newly referred teens are being seen.

Although you will most certainly want to use interviews to collect data, we will focus here on observation. As you begin to take field notes, the main purpose behind your efforts—to identify why adolescents terminate treatment early—puts some parameters around what you are looking for. You may notice any number of potential problem areas—the outreach workers are ad-libbing too much and promising teens that they will feel better soon after beginning treatment. Or, the clinic hours happen to conflict with an after-school tutoring program. Maybe the therapists are poorly trained and do not understand the dilemmas faced by these youngsters whose parents emigrated from China and cannot adjust to their teenagers' American ways.

Regardless of whether your summary recommendations focus on improved training, changing the clinic hours, or both, your initial observations would follow a path consonant with a qualitative approach—flexible and holistic, yet sensitive enough to capture subtle problems that can lead to premature termination by adolescent clients.

The importance of skilled observation in qualitative evaluation is difficult to overstate. The previous example illustrates how using interview data alone almost certainly would have missed nonverbal phenomena that were key to understanding what was going wrong. Stakeholders—staff and clients alike— are often least able (or willing) to talk about what is happening around them when they are in the midst of it.

Of course, the optimal approach is to combine observation with *in-depth interviewing* and *use of documents*. The qualitative interviewer observes the setting of the interview and the nonverbal cues emanating from the respondent and records these observations. Whenever possible, the qualitative evaluator also seeks to observe him or herself using **reflexivity**. This process of self-monitoring helps the researcher identify personal biases that may arise during the evaluation.

We now turn to the whats and hows of qualitative interviewing in evaluation. Qualitative interviewing is distinguished by its skillful but sensitive style of probing, balancing the need to cover relevant areas with the need to remain open to new avenues of information (Padgett, 1998; Weiss, 1994).The essential goal is to allow respondents to express themselves freely and in their own words.

Because time is invariably limited, it is best to compile an **interview guide** in advance for each type of respondent you plan to interview—administrators, staff, clients, community advocates, and so forth. This guide consists of key questions or domains of the inquiry. Serving more as a checklist than a straitjacket, it sets the stage for a comprehensive but flexible discussion with plenty of latitude for additional topics to emerge.

Types of interview questions span the usual areas of inquiry: attitudes, feelings/ emotions, knowledge, and behaviors. *Attitude questions* inquire about opinions ("What do you think about the _____ policy in this agency?" "What is your opinion of the caseworker who assisted you during your last visit?"), and *feelings questions* elicit emotional reactions ("How did you feel when your supervisor reprimanded you in front of the others?"). *Knowledge questions* are asked to test the informant about how much he or she knows about certain facts or verifiable information. For example, you may ask, "What are the criteria for discharging patients from the inpatient unit?" or "How often are Quality Assurance reports filed by the agency?" *Behavior questions* focus on actions taken (or not taken) by the informant, for example, "What did you do when the client threatened you?" or "Did you attend the in-service workshop on staff burnout?"

Focus group interviews represent a productive and time-efficient variant of in-depth interviewing; they multiply dramatically the number of respondents and create a new synergy in disclosure not available from one-on-one interviews. However, practitioners should understand that focus group interviewing is not group therapy nor even group discussion—the focus group is conducted by an interviewer who maintains the central goal of obtaining information valuable for program evaluation (Krueger, 1994; Patton, 2002).

Ideally, focus groups consist of no more than 10 individuals of more or less the same status; that is, supervisors are not grouped with subordinates, and caseworkers are not grouped with clients. Lasting an hour or more, the group is convened by a facilitator who skillfully leads the group through a series of questions designed to make participants feel at ease in sharing their views. Data are recorded either by audiotape or by a note taker (someone other than the leader). Although focus group interviews are clearly not as confidential as one-on-one interviews, the group leader should take pains to ensure sensitivity and respect for diverse points of view expressed without fear of exposure.

It is difficult to overstate the value of focus groups in a variety of evaluation scenarios, especially because group interviews are accessible and even enjoyable for most participants. Focus groups especially come in handy during the needs assessment and formative phases when program planners are beginning to formulate program goals and objectives. Similarly, they can be convened during a process evaluation to discover the strengths and weaknesses of a program or intervention from the standpoints of key stakeholders.

Documents are a final and essential source of data in qualitative evaluation (as well as in quantitative evaluation). Use of documents is also a data collection technique that is least **reactive** (i.e., distorted by the presence of the evaluator). From the standpoint of the qualitative evaluator, documents are the natural by-products of agency activity and a vital source of information on the inner workings of agency life. They can include minutes, memos, correspondence, by-laws, mission statements, financial records, regulatory guidelines, fund-raising proposals, and any other printed materials related to the program and its functioning.

As with so many aspects of an evaluation, we recommend that the evaluator negotiate access to documents at the outset of the study to forestall any difficulties later on. As with other forms of data collection, the evaluator should provide assurances of strict confidentiality to ease this process of negotiation. Although the politically sensitive nature of some documents makes sharing them a tough sell for some program administrators, it also renders them a critical part of the evaluation.

When to Stop Data Collection?

Unlike quantitative studies where there is a built-in stopping point (i.e., the instruments have been administered), qualitative data collection has no inherent endpoint beyond what is known as **saturation**. Saturation occurs when the data analyses begin to reveal repetition and redundancy, when new data tend to confirm the existing findings rather than expand on them.

Given the overlap between data collection and analysis in qualitative research, the researcher must make a decision about when to recognize saturation during the analyses and cease further data collection. Even when it is time to depart, qualitative researchers prefer to leave a few doors open to revisit respondents for feedback, clarification, or additional questions.

Nevertheless, the end must come, and in program evaluation it is usually sooner rather than later. In FQE, short-term deadlines require the most efficient means possible of collecting the data and beginning analysis right away. In the YCC project, this meant recruiting and hiring graduate students with experience in interviewing and/or working with adolescents through ads placed on a website for nonprofit programs (www.Idealist.org). It also meant putting a relatively large team of 6–7 interviewers in the field and simultaneously interviewing multiple stakeholder groups—for example, judges, counselors, and youths.

MANAGING AND ORGANIZING QUALITATIVE DATA

It is incumbent on the qualitative evaluator to begin organizing and analyzing the data as soon as possible. The sheer volume of raw data generated by qualitative research—audiotapes, transcripts, interview protocols, consent forms, analytic memos, field notes, documents, coded excerpts—makes some system of organization imperative. **Data management** refers to developing a system for filing and retrieval that will provide a solid foundation for analysis. There are no right or wrong ways to do this—you need only develop a style of organization that works for you. What is of absolute importance is the need to have extra copies of everything. This means backing up all computer files early and often and photocopying all handwritten notes and hard-copy documents for safe storage.

Using QDA Software

Whether you use qualitative data analysis (QDA) software (such as ATLAS/ti, NUDIST, or HyperQUAL) is a personal decision. (For more details on qualitative data analysis and types of computer software, consult the list of qualitative methods books at the end of this chapter.) QDA programs, designed to ease the burden of the manual cut-and-paste system of working with mass quantities of paper, allow the researcher to store and analyze qualitative data as well as to record analytic decisions in memos. Some qualitative researchers prefer to stick with their favorite word processing programs rather than learn a new, somewhat demanding, software program. Others insist that QDA software has saved a great deal of time and enabled them to manipulate data more efficiently.

DATA ANALYSIS

Occurring simultaneously with data collection and management, **data analysis** is when the cerebral functions really kick in—that elusive but critical ability to find "meaning units" in the data and develop a conceptual scheme that is empirically grounded and richly descriptive. The task is both creative and reductionistic. Without data reduction, we would be overwhelmed by raw data devoid of meaning. Without creativity and insight, we could not unearth the meaning in the data.

Because many how-to books on qualitative data analysis contain specific guidance (see Suggested Readings at the end of this chapter), we will focus here on general aspects that are most relevant to evaluation. You will want to begin by addressing the original goals of the evaluation and how the data help answer key questions. At the same time, you will remain open to new insights that emerge during the analysis. Despite a plethora of epistemological traditions in qualitative research ranging from traditional positivist science to interpretivism, qualitative data analysis most often comes down to two different tasks (which may be performed together or alone). The first of these involves generating **codes,** or conceptual themes, from the data and using these to guide additional analysis (with the proviso that new or refined codes may be added later).

The second approach does not fracture texts to extract meaning across cases but instead focuses on rich description of individual cases. Qualitative evaluators make generous use of **case studies** in their final reports, presenting in-depth portrayals of individuals, an agency, or even a whole program (Stake, 1994). The implications of these two approaches for data analysis are fairly clear—case studies organize the data analysis around the individual case and coding analyses sweep back and forth across cases to generate crosscutting themes and overarching narratives.

Qualitative evaluators may draw on both **emic** and **etic** codes, the former referring to indigenous categories of meaning and the latter to researcher-constructed categories. Examples of emic codes often emerge from interviews when participants reveal their own classificatory terms. For example, staff in a mental health agency may have insider names for problem clients (or problem supervisors). Or you may be interviewing adolescents in an experimental school and learn that they share special (perhaps unprintable) names for teachers, classroom aides, and other school staff.

In contrast, etic codes are outsider interpretations that draw on insight and an ability to conceptualize (see, for example, the hypothetical typology of leadership styles in Figure 4.1). Although the etic perspective reflects a view from the outside, it is still grounded in the subjective meanings of respondents even as it achieves levels of abstraction and meaning that allow higher-level interpretation and, ultimately, development of theory (Padgett, 1998).

Time-Saving Strategies for Data Management and Analysis

Surely the most labor-intensive aspects of qualitative research are data collection and analysis, specifically: (1) the conduct of minimally structured interviews (and re-interviews as needed); (2) verbatim transcription of audiotaped interview data; and (3) open coding of the data followed by development of themes. In our experience with the YCC project, all of these aspects presented obstacles to completing the report in the time frame demanded by funders and stakeholders.

While taking the time-saving step of one-time-only interviews was a straightforward (and oft-used) option, our decisions about focusing interview content, cutting down dramatically on transcription time and truncating data analysis

FIGURE 4.1 | A TYPOLOGY OF LEADERSHIP STYLES

Decision-Making Approach

Leadership
Philosophy

Democratic/Inclusive ◄————————————► Autocratic/Exclusive

Proactive

"Hands-On"	"Firm Hand"
"Hand-Wringing"	"Underhanded"

Reactive/
Avoidant

required creative compromises that would maintain the study's integrity without too much loss of texture and depth. The strategies we employed included:

- Using consensually developed domains to structure the interviews, analyses, and findings
- Substituting note taking for verbatim transcription
- Identifying themes based on the domains rather than indirectly via open coding

The six domains that structured the study from start to finish were the product of intensive discussions with stakeholders involved in foster care for adolescents in New York City. The most relevant issues in congregate care were: *placements, services, safety, permanency planning, youth involvement* in decision making, and *transitioning* from foster care. These six domains formed the skeletal structure for the interview protocols and the data analyses.

This template approach, which stands in sharp contrast to the fully inductive approach that is the hallmark of qualitative inquiry, is hardly new in qualitative research (Crabtree & Miller, 1999) but it receives little attention despite its obvious applicability to evaluation. Even less attention is given to transcription, a task that strains the resources of qualitative studies and causes consternation among the most seasoned of researchers. Finding and training good transcribers, paying them the going rate, and waiting out the lengthy transcriptions—all of these tasks combine to create enormous pressures on a time-sensitive evaluation plan.

To cut back on the many hours required to transcribe even one interview in the YCC project (and we had a total of 70 interviews!), we developed a system where a research assistant listened to the audiotape and took notes on responses to each of the six question domains. She was also trained to write down quotes that appeared especially descriptive or insightful. To guard against bias as much as possible, a second research assistant independently listened to the tape, read the notes and documented any discrepancies or additional information overlooked by the first note taker.

Though by no means quick and easy, our note-taking compromise cut back considerably on the amount of time required for transcription and line coding. For example, every hour of interview time takes roughly 2 to 3 hours to transcribe and produces a 20–30 page transcript. Open (line-by-line) coding of a single transcript can take 2 hours and up depending on the density of the material and the skills of the coder. Re-coding, clustering codes, and identifying themes takes many more hours. The domain-focused interviews fit this truncated model of analysis—less structured interviews would have undoubtedly introduced more variation (and discrepancies) in documenting themes.

By pre-structuring our conceptual framework, we cut to the chase in terms of zeroing in on the areas stakeholders identified as most important. At the same time, we tried to remain vigilant about unexpected findings and to include those even if and when they did not fit into our schema.

QUALITY CONTROL

Attention to quality control in qualitative evaluation begins early on and starts with the importance of adequate training and experience. Field data are only as good as the researcher's powers of observation and insight. Without sufficient training and practice, the observer will be unfocused at best, and intrusive and disruptive at worst. Such expertise comes only from experience.

During data collection and analysis, the researcher must resist the inevitable temptation to let personal bias or outside pressure influence the study. Qualitative inquiry is vulnerable to concerns about such bias—particularly because the researcher is the instrument of data collection and interpretation. Most qualitative researchers avoid using terms such as *reliability* and *validity* (preferring *credibility* or *trustworthiness*) but are nonetheless concerned about minimizing and properly identifying investigator bias. Because the techniques available to enhance the rigor of a qualitative study are the same for program evaluation as for other qualitative studies, they will be reviewed only briefly here—you may wish to consult additional readings for greater detail.

Six strategies for rigor emerge from the diverse literature on qualitative methods (Padgett, 1998). These are prolonged engagement, triangulation, peer debriefing, member checking, negative case analysis, and audit trails. Some of these strategies may already sound familiar, for example, staying engaged in the field long enough to develop trust and a nonsuperficial degree of understanding about what is happening. **Triangulation** of data collection refers to relying on more than one type of data to corroborate findings and enhance the accuracy of our interpretations.

Peer debriefing may be difficult for the qualitative evaluator, because it requires having knowledgeable and vigilant peers available to monitor potential sources of bias as they creep into data collection and analysis. When feasible, peer debriefing can give the researcher both instrumental and emotional support. **Member checking,** returning to respondents with preliminary findings to seek verification or clarification, helps keep the researcher grounded in the subjective meanings of respondents. It also enhances the participatory nature of the study.

Negative case analysis refers to the obligation to search for cases that refute, rather than affirm, the emerging findings as the data analyses proceed. This step clearly requires discipline and integrity, because it is difficult to play devil's advocate with oneself. But only by deliberately pursuing rival explanations within the data can we say with some confidence that our conclusions are credible.

The final strategy—**leaving an audit trail**—refers to thorough documentation of the steps taken and the decisions made during the analyses. If carefully done, a knowledgeable outsider could follow the trail and understand how the data were collected and analyzed and how bias was addressed each step of the way.

In the rough-and-tumble arena of program evaluation, the ability to implement these strategies is always open to question. Member checking can be a time-consuming (and possibly disruptive) task, and it is the fortunate few evaluators who have peers available for debriefing. And yet, qualitative evaluators almost always pursue triangulation, because interviews, observation, and documents are so essential to understanding a program. Time spent maintaining an audit trail is a solid investment for the evaluator to establish his or her credibility.

WRITING THE REPORT

Given the importance of rich description and depth of insight, qualitative reports are usually quite lengthy and difficult to truncate. (The final report of the YCC project, for example, ran 140 pages!) Yet the realities of program evaluation demand that you get to the point fairly quickly or risk losing your audience. At a minimum, the evaluation's sponsor receives the full report, and participants are provided a customized, briefer version (usually referred to as an Executive Summary).

Although there is no standardized outline to follow in writing a qualitative evaluation report, it is always a good idea to address the evaluation's goals at the very beginning. In the body of the full report, you will want to describe the program (its history, goals, staffing, clientele, etc.) and the background to the evaluation. The report should also include an overview of the evaluation's methods, including sampling techniques, modes of data collection and analysis, and strategies for enhancing the rigor of the study. (You may want to give a more detailed account of your methods in an appendix.)

The Results section of the report is where you present the codes, or themes, that emerged from the analyses and interpretation of the data. You may also present case studies of exemplary individuals or agencies to illustrate key points in the findings.

You need not avoid using numbers in a qualitative evaluative report. Though never the center of attention, numbers such as frequencies, percentages, and averages can convey important descriptions of the program and its constituents.

Graphic presentations of the findings in tables, charts, and diagrams offer a refreshing (and efficient) visual display for word-weary readers. *Typologies* and matrices are a favorite way of summarizing qualitative findings. For example, let's say that your observations during a multiagency evaluation have led you to classify administrative leadership styles along two axes—personal leadership philosophy (proactive vs. reactive/avoidant) and approach to organizational decision making (democratic/inclusive vs. autocratic/exclusive). As shown in a cross-tabulation (Figure 4.1), we have a typology of four leadership styles to which we may give titles for shorthand reference—Hands-On (proactive and inclusive), Firm Hand (proactive and autocratic), Hand-Wringing (avoidant and inclusive), and Underhanded (avoidant and autocratic).

We can flesh out these types by giving profiles of hypothetical leaders and their potential influence on staff morale and the organization's ability to function smoothly. Some leadership types work well in some organizations and poorly in others (although the Underhanded leader is probably dysfunctional everywhere and the Hands-On leader a blessing to behold). Nevertheless, we need to establish a program context for understanding the impact of these various styles.

The final section of the report—Conclusions and Recommendations—is all too often the only section closely read by your intended audience (some get no further than the Executive Summary). Therefore, it is the place to put your most concise and insightful summary. If time and space permit, you may link your findings to other evaluations of similar programs to contextualize them for your audience. In any case, this section is also where you are candid about the limitations (and strengths) of the study.

You will also want to provide formal acknowledgments in the report. Aside from a valuable means of expressing gratitude to gatekeepers and others who helped you (and who are willing to be named), it is vitally important to name those who funded the report. When the sponsor has an apparent conflict of interest, this clouds the credibility of the report and of the evaluator. For example, it is important to know if the evaluation of a teen pregnancy prevention program was sponsored by a contraceptive manufacturer or by a conservative religious foundation.

Financial sponsors of the evaluation have a vested interest in the outcome; otherwise, they would not be committing funds to it. Of course, interest need not translate into interference. This issue underscores the importance of the delicate process of negotiating with the sponsor to ensure that the integrity of the study and its findings is not compromised.

A Note on Writing Style

The absence of a standard format for qualitative reports offers room for creativity seldom found in quantitative writing. Indeed, an elegantly written qualitative report has intrinsic appeal to a wide variety of audiences.

However, the risk in this scenario is quite simple—a poorly written qualitative report can nullify all the work that came before it. This is not so for quantitative reports where the numbers (and tables) do most of the talking. A good rule of thumb in adopting a writing style is to be straightforward and richly descriptive but avoid jargon and technical terminology. Qualitative evaluation reports, even those intended for academic audiences, need to be accessible and readable. To pursue this end, remember two points: (1) Write early and often, and (2) read as many qualitative reports as you can and absorb through osmosis their format and style.

AN IMPORTANT FINAL STEP: DISSEMINATION AND ADVOCACY

There are a variety of audiences for evaluative reports—practitioners, policy makers, community and client advocacy groups, and the general public If a program valuation has far-reaching consequences and powerful backers, the results might be disseminated through the print and broadcast media. This was a critical objective of the YCC project because advocacy for change depended on wide dissemination to increase public pressure on the city's Administration for Children's Services to reform their foster care system. Indeed, a press release was distributed, a press conference held (with volunteer youths testifying to problems in congregate care) and news reports filtered through the city's local media during November 2003.

Of course, releasing evaluation findings does not mean that they will be picked up by media; much depends on timing and other factors outside the evaluator's control. More troubling is what can happen to the report as it *does* make its way out into the world. Much has been written about the need to negotiate control over the report amid competing stakeholders and powerful interests seeking to shape findings to fit their own agenda. However, beyond this challenge is one far less negotiable, that is, controlling the message. Study participants may honor their agreement not to tamper with the report, and it still becomes distorted by media portrayals dependent on sensational excerpts plucked out of context.

Qualitative reports—with their emphasis on complexity and narrative—do not lend themselves to sound bites or quick summaries. Academic researchers are often naïvely surprised to see their carefully worded and balanced results end up distorted by forces both sympathetic and unsympathetic to what change they hope the findings will instigate.

Beyond advocacy and local applicability, an evaluation may also contribute to knowledge building and even replication in other venues. As with any research, dissemination of findings in peer-reviewed journals is an important avenue contributing to the growth in knowledge for program and practice evaluation.

EXAMPLES OF QUALITATIVE EVALUATIONS

It is almost impossible to capture in a few case examples the myriad ways that a qualitative evaluation can unfold. There are many qualitative approaches, many topics to be evaluated, and many types of human services programs. In addition to earlier descriptions of the YCC project, here are some other examples of qualitative evaluation.

<table>
<tr><td>CASE STUDY 1</td><td>PHENOMENOLOGICAL AND PARTICIPATORY RESEARCH</td></tr>
</table>

CASE STUDY 1

PHENOMENOLOGICAL AND PARTICIPATORY RESEARCH

Turning Program Failure Around During a Process Evaluation of a Program for the Seriously Mentally Ill

Larry Davidson and his colleagues (1997) began their study with a compelling problem—to understand why a program designed to reduce inpatient admissions among persons with schizophrenia failed miserably. Despite the best of intentions and the latest in psychoeducational treatment, all 36 hospitalized patients who took part in a "relapse recognition" and early intervention program failed to return to the group meetings after discharge and continued to be readmitted as if they had never participated in the program.

Rather than blame the patients for their lack of insight or mental incapacity, Davidson et al. decided to turn the tables and see if the problem was located in how the program was conceived and implemented. Employing a phenomenological and participatory approach, they tracked down 12 of the recidivists and sought to understand their experiences of relapse, hospitalization, and the program itself. Using open-ended interviews, they elicited from the respondents a world poorly understood by many mental health professionals. Moreover, they actively involved the respondents in the analyses to identify important findings and design a new intervention more closely tailored to the needs of the seriously mentally ill.

Analyses of the interviews yielded themes that are sadly resonant for this population—the relative safety and privacy of a hospital room (compared to life on the streets), few social ties to nourish a sense of belonging, and alienation from a mental health services system that treats them like recalcitrant students rather than human beings with unfulfilled dreams for the future. It seems that prevention of rehospitalization was an agenda embraced more by clinicians (and cost-conscious hospital administrators) than by the patients themselves. Looming over this narrow perspective was the much larger and more vital issue of their quality of life—or the absence thereof.

Based on these findings, Davidson and colleagues recommended a revamped approach focused on community integration rather than individual or group education. Some changes were logistical, for example, group meetings were moved from the mental health center to a convenient community location to convey a less stigmatizing, more integrative message. Additionally, transportation was provided.

Other changes centered on the program's philosophy, replacing the educational component with consumer decision making and peer support. Not surprisingly, participants preferred meetings focused less on illness and more on daily living—how to help one another during times of crisis, to enjoy social events together, and to get on with their lives.

Interestingly, the initial goal of the program—to reduce hospital readmissions—was achieved under the new approach. According to Davidson et al., 15 participants who were in the program for 6 months were compared to a similar matched group of nonparticipants and were found to have 70 percent fewer admissions and 90 percent fewer days spent in the hospital.

| CASE STUDY 2 | COMBINING PROCESS AND OUTCOME EVALUATION IN A MIXED METHODS STUDY *"Unpacking" Home-Based Family Treatment* |

An evaluative study conducted by Mark Fraser and David Haapala (1987) exemplifies how qualitative and quantitative methods can be combined to unpack and examine the components of a family preservation program. Family preservation has been embraced by many child welfare advocates as the best way to prevent foster care placement, but evaluations have focused almost exclusively on whether these programs work rather than what is happening within them. Fraser and Haapala addressed this gap and took us a step further by examining process *and* outcome simultaneously.

Their qualitative design included adopting a critical incident approach in open-ended interviews with members of 41 families participating in a state-sponsored program for high-risk families. The interviews with mothers, children, and their therapists were designed to elicit concordant (or discordant) accounts of discrete events that occurred during in-home family therapy sessions and whether these events were considered helpful.

Based on coding of the data, Fraser and Haapala identified eight types of treatment incidents ranging from outside interruptions to the therapist's teaching and support. Quantitative data included the total number and frequency of events, respondent ratings of helpfulness (on a 1 to 7 scale), and a dichotomous variable measuring treatment outcome—failure (child is placed out of home) or success (child remains in home).

Quantitative analyses of categorical variables (including those generated by the qualitative coding) revealed several interesting findings about the relationship between treatment process and outcome. Among the eight treatment incident types, only two differentiated successful cases from failed cases—"successful" mothers reported more concrete service provision by their therapists and more interruptions during therapy. Although it is not difficult to see the value of assistance with basic needs such as finances, housing, and health, the finding of more interruptions among the successful cases seemed counterintuitive and required some additional attention to the process aspects of the intervention. Specifically, therapists were trained to take advantage of the inevitable interruptions by neighbors, phone calls, and so on by demonstrating problem solving related to these events. Although additional research is needed to determine if interruptions (and therapeutic responses) actually have positive effects, the data suggest that such studies would be a logical next step.

CASE STUDY 3

HEY GIRLFRIEND . . .
A MIXED METHODS
EVALUATION OF AN AIDS
PREVENTION PROGRAM
AMONG WOMEN IN THE
SEX INDUSTRY

Just as the usual methods of health education have been altered dramatically to combat AIDS, methods of program evaluation have been tailored to fit programs that reach out to at-risk street populations such as prostitutes. With this in mind, Lori Dorfman and her colleagues included a strong qualitative component to their evaluation of an AIDS prevention outreach program among prostitutes (Dorfman, Derish, & Cohen, 1992).

AIDS outreach workers and the evaluators worked closely together in the field, renting a nearby motel room or using a mobile van to remain close to the streets where the women worked. Choosing to triangulate their sources of data, Dorfman et al. collected quantitative data (on health status, number of sex partners, frequency of condom use, etc.), open-ended interview data (to explore sense of vulnerability to AIDS), and field notes describing encounters with the prostitutes and other daily activities. Rapport was enhanced by distributing free condoms and providing a comfortable space nearby for refreshments and casual conversation.

Process evaluation findings revealed that field staff who were indigenous to the community became role models for positive behavior change for the sex workers. They also demonstrated that the women were generally well aware of how AIDS is transmitted and were concerned enough to use condoms with customers, but less vigilant with their steady partners. Thus, the evaluators were able to make recommendations regarding staff recruitment and a more fine-tuned educational message. Without qualitative data (and the rapport that attends this type of inquiry), it is doubtful that they could have arrived at these conclusions.

In closing, the examples provided here illustrate that qualitative evaluation has indeed "come of age" (Weiss, 1998). Whether used alone or in conjunction with quantitative methods, qualitative methods offer an in-depth and holistic portrait of how and why programs succeed or fail.

Questions for Class Discussion

1. Discuss some ethical issues that might arise when conducting the "up close and personal" style of qualitative evaluation.
2. Think of a program or agency in which a participatory, or action, evaluation could be conducted using qualitative methods. How might service recipients/clients be involved? Discuss some of the barriers to participatory evaluation and how these might be overcome.

3. Students in the class should identify an agency or program they know about (perhaps their field placement). Consider how to conduct a process evaluation of the program using qualitative methods. What are the goals of the process evaluation, that is, how can you determine if the program is being implemented as it should be? Once the goals have been identified, design a qualitative evaluation. What is the unit of analysis? How will you go about sampling? Collecting data? Analyzing the data? How might your findings assist in an outcome evaluation?

4. Discuss the difference between emic and etic perspectives during a qualitative evaluation. Give examples of each.

5. Consider how mixed methods could be used to collect and analyze data for a program evaluation. Think of a specific program and give some examples of both qualitative and quantitative modes of data collection. Discuss how these might complement each other.

Mini-Projects: Experiencing Evaluation Firsthand

1. Take some time (about 30 minutes) during a lunch break and carry out an ethnographic observation of your agency. Try to set aside all preconceptions and be an ethnographic researcher in the "field." Take field notes simultaneously (or if necessary a few hours later), and consider the following:

    a. What is the physical setting like? Could it influence behavior? How?

    b. What are the actors doing in this setting?

    c. What time of day/week/year is it? Does this affect the setting or the behavior you are observing?

    d. Does anyone notice you? If so, what happens?

    Your field notes should be as detailed as you can make them. Try to distinguish "pure" observation (unfiltered description) from your own interpretations and biases. Bring your field notes to class for discussion and sharing. In particular, discuss how ethnographic observation might assist in evaluating an agency's programs and services.

2. The class can break into focus groups of five to seven students. Each group should identify a facilitator and choose another member to take notes. The focus groups will then choose an evaluative question about the school (e.g., the curriculum) and discuss their feelings and concerns. After about 30 minutes, the groups should reconvene and share their reports.

3. Students in the class should identify a key informant in an agency or program and conduct a qualitative interview with that person about the agency's goals and performance. Before the interview, be sure to develop an interview guide with two or three open-ended questions. (Note: If this presents political or ethical problems, students can use one another as key informants and inquire about their field placements.)

References and Resources

Broadhead, R. S. (1989). Qualitative analysis in evaluation research: Problems and promises of an interactionist approach. *Symbolic Interaction, 3*, 23–40.

Brunner, I., & Guzman, A. (1989). Participatory evaluation: A tool to assess projects and empower people. In R. F. Conner & M. Hendricks (Eds.), *International innovations in evaluation methodology* (pp. 9–18). San Francisco: Jossey-Bass.

Cancian, F. M. (1990). Conflicts between activist research and academic success: Participatory research and alternative strategies. *The American Sociologist, 81*, 92–106.

Cook, T. D., & Reichardt, C. S. (Eds.). (1979). *Qualitative and quantitative methods in evaluation research*. Beverly Hills, CA: Sage.

Crabtree, B., & Miller, W.L. (1999). Doing qualitative research (2nd ed.). Thousand Oaks, CA: Sage.

Cronbach, L. J. (1982). *Designing evaluations of educational and social programs*. San Francisco: Jossey-Bass.

Davidson, L., Stayner, D. A., Lambert, S., Smith, P., & Sledge, W. H. (1997). Phenomenological and participatory research on schizophrenia: Recovering the person in theory and practice. *Journal of Social Issues, 53*(4), 767–784.

Denzin, N. K., & Lincoln, Y. S. (Eds.). (2000). *Handbook of qualitative research*. Thousand Oaks, CA: Sage.

Dorfman, L. E., Derish, P. A., & Cohen, J. B. (1992). Hey girlfriend: An evaluation of AIDS prevention among women in the sex industry. *Health Education Quarterly, 19*(1), 25–40.

Drake, R. E., Bebout, R. R., Quimby, E., Teague, G. B., Harris, M., & Roach, J. P. (1993). Process evaluation in the Washington, DC, dual diagnosis project. *Alcoholism Treatment Quarterly, 10*(3/4), 113–124.

Dreher, M. (1995). Qualitative research methods from the reviewer's perspective. In J. M. Morse (Ed.), *Critical issues in qualitative research methods* (pp. 281–297). Thousand Oaks, CA: Sage.

Fetterman, D. M. (1984). *Ethnography in educational evaluation*. Beverly Hills, CA: Sage.

Fishman, D. B., (2003). Postmodernism comes to program evaluation: A review of Denzin and Lincoln's Handbook of qualitative research (2nd ed.). *Evaluation and Program Planning, 26*, 415–420.

Fook, J. (2001). Identifying expert social work: Qualitative practitioner research. In I. Shaw and N. Gould (Eds). *Qualitative research in social work* (pp. 116–132). London: Sage.

Franklin, C., & Jordan, C. (1995, May). Qualitative assessment: A methodological review. *Families in Society: The Journal of Contemporary Human Services*, 281–295.

Fraser, M., & Haapala, D. (1987). Home-based family treatment: A quantitative qualitative assessment. *Journal of Applied Social Sciences, 12*(1), 1–3.

Goetz, J. P., & LeCompte, M. D. (1984). *Ethnography and qualitative design in educational research*. New York: Academic Press.

Greene, J. C. (2000). Qualitative program evaluation: Practice and promise. In N. K. Denzin & Y. S. Lincoln (Eds.), *Handbook of qualitative research* (pp. 530–544). Thousand Oaks, CA: Sage.

Guba, E. G., & Lincoln, Y. S. (1987). *Fourth generation evaluation*. Newbury Park, CA: Sage.

Kidder, L. H., & Fine, M. (1987). Qualitative and quantitative methods: When stories converge. In M. M. Mark & R. L. Shotland (Eds.), *Multiple methods in program evaluation* (pp. 57–76). San Francisco: Jossey-Bass.

Krueger, R. A. (1994). *Focus groups: A practical guide for applied research* (2nd ed.). Thousand Oaks, CA: Sage.

Manderson, L., & Aaby, P. (1992). An epidemic in the field? Rapid assessment procedures and health research. *Social Science and Medicine, 35*, 839–850.

Mullen, P. D., & Iverson, D. C. (1986). Qualitative methods. In L. W. Green & F. M. Lewis (Eds.), *Measurement and evaluation in health education and health promotion* (pp. 149–170). Palo Alto, CA: Mayfield.

Padgett, D. K. (1998). *Qualitative methods in social work research.* Thousand Oaks, CA: Sage.

Padgett, D. K. (1999). The practice-research debate from a qualitative perspective. *Social Work, 44,* 280–282.

Padgett, D. K. (2003). Cross-national context and qualitative social work research: Working the boundaries. *Qualitative Social Work, 2*(3), 347–357.

Padgett, D. K. (Ed.). (2004). *The qualitative research experience.* Belmont, CA: Wadsworth.

Padgett, D. K., & Freundlich, M. (2004). Doing focused qualitative evaluation: The YCC project. Workshop presented at the annual meeting of the Society for Social Work and Research, New Orleans.

Patton, M. Q. (2002). *Qualitative evaluation and research methods* (3rd ed.). Newbury Park, CA: Sage.

Pitman, M. A., & Maxwell, J. A. (1992). Qualitative approaches to evaluation: Models and methods. In M. D. LeCompte, W. L., Millroy, & J. Preissle (Eds.), *The handbook of qualitative research in education* (pp. 729–770). New York: Academic Press.

Reinharz, S. (1992). *Feminist methods in social research.* New York: Oxford University Press.

Rist, R. C. (2000). Influencing the policy process with qualitative research. In N. K. Denzin & Y. S. Lincoln (Eds.), *Handbook of qualitative research* (pp. 545–557). Thousand Oaks, CA: Sage.

Scrimshaw, S. C., Carballo, M., Ramos, L., & Blair, B. A. (1991). The AIDS rapid anthropological assessment procedures: A tool for health education planning and evaluation. *Health Education Quarterly, 18*(1), 111–123.

Sechrest, L., & Figueredo, A. J. (1993). Program evaluation. *Annual Review of Psychology, 44,* 645–675.

Shaw, I. F., & Gould, N. (2002). Qualitative research in social work (pp. 116–132). London: Sage.

Shaw, I., & Lishman, J. (Eds.). (1999). Evaluation and social work practice. London: Sage.

Sherman, E., & Reid, W. J. (Eds.). (1994). *Qualitative research in social work.* New York: Columbia University Press.

Stake, R. E. (1994). Case studies. In N. K. Denzin & Y. S. Lincoln (Eds.), *Handbook of qualitative research* (pp. 236–247). Thousand Oaks, CA: Sage.

Steckler, A., McLeroy, K. R., Goodman, R. M., Bird, S. T., & McCormick, L. (1992). Toward integrating qualitative and quantitative methods: An introduction. *Health Education Quarterly, 19,* 1–8.

Strauss, A., & Corbin, J. (1990). *Basics of qualitative research: Grounded theory procedures and techniques.* Newbury Park, CA: Sage.

Stringer, E. (1999). *Action research: A handbook for practitioners* (2nd ed.). Thousand Oaks, CA: Sage.

Swanson, J. M., & Chapman, L. (1994). Inside the black box: Theoretical and methodological issues in conducting evaluation research using a qualitative approach. In J. Morse (Ed.), *Critical issues in qualitative research methods* (pp. 66–93). Thousand Oaks, CA: Sage.

Tashakkori, A., & Teddlie, C. (2003). *Mixed methodology: Combining qualitative and quantitative approaches.* Thousand Oaks, CA: Sage.

Weiss, C. H. (Ed.). (1972). *Evaluating action programs: Readings in social action and education*. Boston: Allyn & Bacon.

Weiss, C. H. (1998). *Evaluation* (2nd ed.). Upper Saddle River, NJ: Prentice-Hall.

Weiss, R. S. (1994). *Learning from strangers: The art and method of qualitative interview studies*. New York: Free Press.

Whitmore, E. (2001). "People listened to what we had to say": Reflections on an emancipatory evaluation. In I. Shaw and N. Gould (Eds). *Qualitative research in social work* (pp. 83–99). London: Sage.

Woodhouse, L. D., & Livingood, W. C. (1991). Exploring the versatility of qualitative design for evaluating community substance abuse prevention projects. *Qualitative Health Research, 1*, 434–445.

Suggested Readings

In addition to the above citations, here are a few suggested sources on the basics of qualitative methods. Please keep in mind that this is only a partial (and selected) listing of what has become a growth industry in published books on qualitative methods.

Bogdan, R. C., & Taylor, S. J. (1975). *Introduction to qualitative research*. New York: John Wiley.

Boyatzis, R. E. (1998). *Transforming qualitative information*. Thousand Oaks, CA: Sage.

Glaser, B. (1992). *Basics of grounded theory analysis*. Mill Valley, CA: Sociology Press.

Lofland, J., & Lofland, L. (1995). *Analyzing social settings: A guide to qualitative observation and analysis* (3rd ed.). Belmont, CA: Wadsworth.

Marshall, C., & Rossman, G. B. (1999). *Designing qualitative research* (3rd ed.). Thousand Oaks, CA: Sage.

Miles, M. B., & Huberman, A. (1994). *Qualitative data analysis: An expanded sourcebook*. Thousand Oaks, CA: Sage.

Silverman, D. (2000). *Doing qualitative research: A practical handbook*. London: Sage.

Tesch, R. (1990). *Qualitative research: Analysis types and software tools*. London: Falmer.

5 CHAPTER | FORMATIVE AND PROCESS EVALUATION

Let's assume that the needs assessment and planning for the new program you wanted to start have been completed. The program has been implemented and has now been in operation about 3 months. If we were to talk to the staff, they probably would acknowledge that there are still some "rough edges" to the program due to its newness. Perhaps a few disgruntled clients have made complaints, and the agency director wants to initiate some sort of program review or evaluation. You are called into the director's office to design a procedure for obtaining constructive feedback on the program. The agency director is committed to making the program successful and wants a program that the community will be proud of. Because the concern is not whether to continue or discontinue the program, but how to improve the program, what type of evaluation will you recommend to the agency director? How would you go about designing an evaluation that is concerned solely with program improvement?

FORMATIVE EVALUATION

Formative evaluation ought to be your recommendation to the agency director. Formative evaluations are employed to adjust and enhance interventions. They are not used to prove whether a program is worth the funding it receives but serve more to guide and direct programs—particularly new programs. In other words, formative evaluation is used to "form" the program. For this reason, formative evaluations are not as threatening and are often better received by agency staff than other forms of evaluation.

A good analogy for formative evaluation would be an experienced driving instructor sitting beside a beginning driver. If you have taught anyone to drive recently (or can objectively remember your own initial experiences), you may recall the beginning driver's jerky steering movements and sudden accelerations and decelerations. The driving instructor helps the beginner become a more skillful driver by observing the process of driving and making constructive suggestions. The instructor is more concerned with the process than with any particular destination. Once driving skills have been acquired, it is assumed that the driver will be more likely to reach his or her destination.

The formative evaluator might look at interactions between clients and practitioners, management strategies and philosophies, and the costs associated with a program (Chelimsky, 1985). This type of evaluation can also be used to determine whether a new or pilot program has been implemented as planned. Formative evaluations reveal "what services were provided, to whom, when, how often, and in what settings" (Moskowitz, 1989). Such evaluations are often considered "internal" agency business. Both strengths and weaknesses of an initial program may be identified.

Formative evaluation does not rely on a specific methodology or set of procedures. Instead, its focus is on acquiring information that would be useful for program improvement—whatever that would be. This information may come from interviewing staff or clients, reviewing records and progress notes, or participant observation. One could expect formative evaluators to look for glitches, breakdowns, lengthy delays, and departures from program design. They may find such problems as communication difficulties among staff, communication difficulties between the administration and staff, poor client participation in a program, or a need for additional inservice training to standardize what is provided as an intervention.

There is no single recipe for formative evaluation. How you would go about conducting one depends somewhat on the program, your preferences, the agency, and the context of the request for a formative evaluation. Let's see what options are available in the following example.

Assume the manager of a program for children of substance abusers asked you to understand why they were having some problems "getting the program off the ground." The program is called the Strengthening Families Program (SFP), and this manager implemented the program approximately 3 months ago. Attendance was a major problem as well as getting the children in the session to pay attention during the class. In addition, the parents complained they did not like the program. A formative evaluation would be an excellent strategy, in this case, to examine these issues and provide some meaningful information for "fine-tuning" the program.

One of the first things you might want to do is to examine the nature and development of the program. In fact, in this case, the local program director conducted a search for model parenting and family programs using multiple criteria derived from a list of family risk factors formulated by the Office of

Juvenile Justice and Delinquency Prevention. The conclusion was that there is no single best family intervention program (Kumpfer, Molgaard, & Spoth, 1996). However, several principles for best practices in family programs were identified. These principles included selecting programs that are (1) comprehensive, (2) family focused, (3) long term, (4) of sufficient dosage to affect risk or protective factors, (5) tailored to target populations' needs and cultural traditions, (6) developmentally appropriate, (7) beginning as early in the family life cycle as possible, and (8) delivered by well-trained, effective trainers.

Consistent with the review conclusions as well as requests from parents in a methadone treatment program, Kumpfer and other researchers at the University of Utah developed the Strengthening Families Program (SFP) (Kumpfer, 1994). The National Institute on Drug Abuse (NIDA) included the SFP as an exemplary example of a selective prevention intervention in a resource manual entitled "Drug Abuse Prevention for At Risk Groups" (1997). NIDA indicated this program was selected because (1) it is a selective prevention program that has been successfully implemented in a variety of settings with diverse populations; (2) it has been demonstrated to be effective in reducing family environmental risk factors as well as behavioral and psychological problems associated with substance abuse; (3) it includes many of the key features characteristic of selective prevention programs; and (4) the effectiveness of the program has been established from extensive research and long-term evaluation.

Thus, the program itself seems to be well developed and tested. Knowing that the goal of formative evaluation is not to provide any sort of "final" or summative evaluation but to organize information needed for program improvement, where would you start a formative evaluation of this program?

CONDUCTING A FORMATIVE EVALUATION

At least three different ways to approach this formative evaluation come to mind. Faced with such a scenario, an evaluator could recommend any one or a combination of approaches.

Approach 1: Locate Model Standards

If standards for similar programs have been developed or proposed by national accrediting or advocacy groups, then the local program could be compared against these standards and any discrepancies identified. This approach is frequently used by governmental units that fund, license, or oversee human services. When there are written standards, they are often put into the form of a checklist, and evaluators can monitor compliance with the standards and identify any areas of deficiency. This approach appears to work best when the expectations are easily defined (a window in each bedroom, a fire escape from the second floor, and fire extinguishers every 50 feet). Standards are not so helpful when they are vague or difficult to operationalize (as when they state that a program should provide "adequate recreational opportunities").

Go back to the earlier example. The program principles that were identified from the literature search of programs (1 through 8) may be one specific place to begin. For example, one step would be to examine the original program content and the content actually being delivered. Is the program being delivered as recommended? Does it include the appropriate family members? Is it the recommended number and length of sessions? Do the program clients differ from the originally intended audience in any way? Are the facilitators trained appropriately? Do the facilitators understand the content of the material they are presenting? These types of questions can be generated simply by looking at the standards for a family-based prevention program such as the SFP.

We wish we could tell you that standards exist for every type of human service program that you might need to evaluate. Unfortunately, it is more likely that you will find the situation is somewhat "hit-or-miss." Some human service fields have well-developed and substantive standards. Other areas have minimal or no standards. However, you may find that standards developed for one human service program can be utilized for a similar program.

For instance, the overlap between substance abuse and crime is significant and has increased over time. Prisons and jails are filled with substance abusers. In response to the rising rate of incarceration and the overlap of substance abuse and crime, drug court programs were established. Drug court programs combine substance abuse treatment with intensive judicial oversight, or intensive case management of offenders. However, because there are numerous ways to combine both treatment and judicial oversight, some standards needed to be created. In other words, to ensure a treatment orientation combined with a judicial oversight process, the National Association of Drug Court Professionals created a Drug Court Standards Committee, which came up with a set of 10 key components and benchmarks that drug court programs must adhere to in order to be considered bona fide drug courts (USDJ, 1997). Adherence to the key components and benchmarks distinguish treatment-based, multidisciplinary, full-range drug court programs from other programs. However, any treatment program that provides services to criminal justice populations could adapt these key components and benchmarks as well. With a little bit of luck, an evaluator may be able to find a set of standards that can be adopted or slightly modified to fit the local program of interest.

Box 5.1 presents another example of how standards might be used to improve performance.

If several phone calls to state or national organizations fail to produce worthwhile standards, try university libraries or search the Internet for sources of information. You might come on a program evaluation in a journal article that provides useful "standards" that you can use to gauge a local program. For instance, an article reviewing the literature on inpatient alcoholism treatment may have found that the average relapse rate in five separate programs across the country was 48 percent during the first 6 months after discharge. If your local inpatient program was experiencing a 78 percent relapse rate within the first 6 months, this may be a strong indication of the need for a more in-depth formative evaluation.

BOX 5.1 | AN EXAMPLE OF USING STANDARDS TO ASSESS PERFORMANCE MEASUREMENT OF HEALTH CARE

How would you measure the performance of your doctor? Have you ever had a bad experience with a doctor? How do you think a doctor's performance should be measured? Should all doctors be held to the same set of standards for performance? Some think so.

An article in the *Journal of the American Medical Association,* Skolnick (1998) described an effort to examine doctor performance by establishing standards and measuring their performance against the standards. The nation's three leading health care accrediting organizations—Joint Commission on Accreditation of Health Care Organizations (JCAHO), the National Committee for Quality Assurance (NCQA), and the American Medical Accreditation Program (AMAP)—have established a council to ensure a more efficient collection of health care performance measures across all levels of the U.S. health care system.

There are several goals of this new council: (1) to reduce data duplication, which will reduce costs; and (2) to establish standards for individual physical quality accreditation. Accreditation procedures have been available as a quality standard for hospitals and managed care organizations; however, those accreditation procedures did not provide for individual physician accreditation.

The goal is to set a national "gold standard" for physical quality that will be accepted by all key stakeholders. At this time, there is a voluntary process to evaluate physicians, and the evaluation of individual physicians will be against national standards, criteria, and peer performance in the following five areas:

1. Credentials, including academic, training, and work histories of physicians
2. Personal qualifications such as ethical behavior and documented participation in continuing medical education, peer reviews, and self-assessment of performance
3. Environment of care, which reviews the clinical, operational, and management systems in a physician's office
4. Clinical performance, which measures key patient care processes
5. Patient care results, which measures clinical results and patients' satisfaction and health status

Source: Skolnick, A. (1998). JCAHO, NCQA, and AMAP establish council to coordinate health care performance measurement. (Medical News & Perspectives). *Journal of the American Medical Association,* 279(22), 1769–1771.

Professional literature is always a source of potentially useful standards or benchmarks. However, even if no standards are directly mentioned, a journal article might discuss how one agency dealt with problems such as lack of attendance or client dissatisfaction with certain features of a program. Even marginally relevant articles may contain the name of an agency or an "expert" who could be contacted to provide consultation for your program.

Approach 2: Get Expert Consultation

With this approach you might seek out consultation from a recognized expert or from a similar program with a solid reputation. A person of some authority—the director or program director—from the program could be asked to conduct a site visit of your program. The consultant could review operating policies and procedures; interview residents, staff, and board members; and make suggestions for improvement by making comparisons with his or her own program or some other "model" program. (The standards in this instance may be more informal than formal if they are drawn from the consultant's experience.) If money to pay the consultant is problematic, a low-cost alternative would be free consultation from the appropriate state officials who have an interest in the success of your program (e.g., the state department for mental health). It is not unusual for small agencies to have virtually no money for expert consultation. Because the perceived quality of the free consultation may be expected to vary considerably from community to community, some evaluators with no funds for consultation may be interested in still a third approach.

Approach 3: Form an Ad Hoc Evaluation Committee

This committee could be composed of substance abuse treatment staff, board members, professionals from the community, service consumers, and other concerned persons. The committee might begin by interviewing staff and then move to participating families and children, and then selected professionals outside the agency. Some or all of the committee members could visit similar programs. If this is not economically feasible, the committee could write to other programs asking for copies of their policies and operating procedures. From reviewing these, new policies or procedures may be developed as the evaluation committee devises their own set of standards for the program. The committee may identify a number of areas or discrepancies that, in their opinion, need to be addressed so that the program can conform to local expectations.

It is impossible to predict what might come from a formative evaluation using one of these three approaches. The ad hoc evaluation committee may find that the program needs additional staff training and recommend procedures for more closely monitoring it. The same committee might find that the program lacks learning activities and recommend increased activities in order to engage participants. Some formative evaluation recommendations may come from examining the operation of different programs, while others may be based on the opinions of a single "expert."

Because the staff who work day to day on a program are so close to it, it is not unusual for staff to be blind to certain areas where their program could benefit from improvement. (This may be particularly true in those environments where staff are tremendously overworked.) Formative evaluations often bring in experts or outsiders in order to obtain fresh perspectives so that the existing program can be seen in a new or different light.

It is not always necessary to bring in expensive experts to provide formative evaluation. Sometimes, other concerned professionals in the community can provide useful insights. Occasionally, students have told me (TK Logan) "horror stories" about program administration. Two instances where common sense should have prevailed come readily to mind. One former student was interning at a shelter for battered women. The shelter had a telephone, but because of concern that expensive long-distance phone calls would be charged to it, the phone was programmed to make only local calls. Whenever a long-distance call had to be placed, these women had to go to a pay phone at a gas station down the block. This procedure placed women who were attempting to avoid men who had assaulted them in jeopardy. It does not take a nationally prominent domestic violence expert to recognize that procedures that place sheltered women at risk needed revision.

In a second example, another graduate student told me of a residential program for children that had such an intricate and detailed admissions process that 3 to 4 weeks were often required to complete it. This certainly worked to the agency's disadvantage when, one summer, the agency had about 20 percent of its beds vacant at one time. Meanwhile, children in need of admission remained at risk in dangerous settings and without treatment because of the bottleneck in the admissions process. Again, it does not take a very high-powered expert to realize that the admissions process needed to be streamlined. Where cost is a major concern, it may be possible to ask friends who are social workers or other human service professionals to spend a day or two with your program in order to get some inexpensive, but potentially sound, commonsense feedback that could be called a formative evaluation.

OTHER USES OF FORMATIVE EVALUATION

Formative evaluation is also used to help ground interventions in theoretical underpinnings and to adapt interventions to specific target groups. For example, one research study used formative evaluation to identify appropriate strategies and barriers to providing ongoing dietary guidance to pregnant teens (Janis & Hymans, 1997). These authors used two phases to complete their formative evaluation. In phase one, 14 health and social service professionals participated in a focus group about nutrition services for pregnant teens. Respondents identified school nurses as potential providers of early and continuous counseling to pregnant adolescents regarding nutrition. In phase two, school nurses completed surveys designed to assess their interest in providing nutrition education to pregnant teenagers as well as barriers they perceived in doing so. Results from the formative evaluation were used to guide program development.

In the SFP example, perhaps a problem was that the program was not tailored to the target population's needs and traditions. In such a case, a focus group with clients and a staff survey could help adapt the program by producing ideas about useful changes and attitudes toward potential modifications.

As another example, a research team conducted a formative evaluation to guide HIV prevention efforts, specifically with regard to intervention development (Higgins et al., 1996). Formative evaluation was defined in this specific research article as "the process by which researchers or public health practitioners define the community of interest, ways to access that community, and attributes of the community relevant to the specific public health issue" (p. 29). The overall formative evaluation took 6 months to conduct and consisted of eight main steps: (1) defining the populations at risk for HIV. This included writing specific definitions for populations of each intervention group targeted (e.g., injecting drug users not involved with drug treatment programs, female sex partners of injecting drug users). Definitions were based on personal or professional knowledge and experiences shared by the research team; (2) conducting a search of the literature and identifying gaps in knowledge about the target population using the definitions developed in step 1; (3) surveying individuals who had knowledge of the target community (i.e., individuals from the health department working in the HIV early intervention clinic); (4) surveying "integrators." Integrators were defined as persons who had informal contact with the target community, but who were not themselves members of that population (e.g., shopkeepers—such as a clerk at a Laundromat or neighborhood convenience store, taxi drivers, motel clerks, and bartenders); (5) defining and prioritizing target populations; (6) interviewing and conducting focus groups with members of the target groups; (7) reducing and integrating the information from all of the interviews; and (8) interpreting data from all of the steps. The authors suggested this approach should be used in developing interventions that are culturally appropriate and meaningful to their respective target populations. On one hand, this formative evaluation could be characterized as a needs assessment because it did not tinker with program components in early stages of implementation, which is how formative evaluations are usually characterized. On the other hand, the in-depth focus on collecting information to develop or "form" a program rather than documenting program need exemplifies the formative evaluation nature of this example.

A third example in the literature used a formative research evaluation to develop an intervention to address primary barriers to immunization in a rural Head Start program (Mayer, Housemann, & Piepenbrok, 1999). Interviews were conducted with a purposeful sample of Head Start parents—parents with children who had up-to-date immunizations and parents whose children did not have up-to-date immunizations. The Health Belief Model was used to construct categories that were then used to analyze the interview data, identify barriers, and guide program development.

The formative evaluation design, as stated earlier, is employed to shape programs in their early stages. Once the program has been established, it is important to conduct a process evaluation. A process evaluation is defined as "a comprehensive description and analysis of how . . . programs are conceptualized, planned, implemented, modified, and terminated. Process evaluation attempts to assess the quality and purpose of program activities relative to the desired outcome or results of these programs" (Krisberg, 1980, p. 217). It is to this topic that we will next turn our attention.

PROCESS EVALUATION

Formative evaluations are sometimes referred to as process evaluations when the focus is not the final product but the intervention. Figure 5.1 shows where formative and process evaluation fit into the overall evaluation picture. One major difference between formative evaluation and process evaluation is that while a formative evaluation seeks to influence the initial development of a program, a process evaluation can be conducted anytime during a project—even at its end.

Why would anyone want to conduct a process evaluation at the end of a project? Process evaluations are typically required for research and demonstration projects because sponsors want to know what was learned during the implementation of the project. Such information could be valuable to other communities considering whether to start such a program. In addition, process evaluation can help determine whether the "failure" of a program was due to a poor program or poor intervention, or if it was because implementation of the program was problematic (Harachi et al., 1999; Orwin, 2000).

Specifically, a process evaluation may have the following overarching purposes or goals:

1. Program description
2. Program monitoring
3. Quality assurance

Each of these main purposes may have subgoals or objectives. In addition, a process evaluation may include one or some combination of all three of these goals.

To take an actual example of process evaluation used for program description, in one community an agency developed a proposal to recruit African American men to serve as mentors for minority teenagers. In the original proposal,

FIGURE 5.1 | WHERE DOES FORMATIVE AND PROCESS EVALUATION FIT INTO THE OVERALL EVALUATION PICTURE?

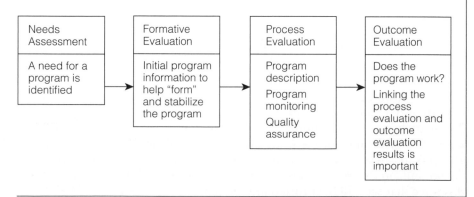

the agency specified that 80 mentors would be recruited and trained, and each would be matched with an adolescent. This proved to be a lot tougher than the agency expected. By the project's end, less than half the desired number of mentors had been obtained.

In this instance, process evaluators would look at the activities used to recruit mentors (e.g., public service announcements, speaking with ministers of black churches)—what the project staff found that had worked and what was a waste of time. Process evaluation might also look at other problems encountered, such as difficulties in presenting the project to teenagers or their parents, or in securing referrals from school counselors and other human service professionals in the community. Process evaluation informs others about what they might expect if they were to launch a similar program.

Another purpose of process evaluation is to assist in explaining why a program did or did not achieve expected outcomes. For example, a large statewide agency wanted to test whether the use of peer volunteers was more effective in reducing subsequent hospitalizations than a new procedure where clients with severe mental illness were assisted in developing a crisis support plan. Three different sites were selected from across the state, and staff received all necessary training. Four years later, at the project's end, a process evaluation revealed that (1) some staff did not complete crisis plans with their clients—evidently because they were not aware of the necessity to do so; (2) there had been no additional training of staff after the first year; and (3) monitoring of clinical records for clients without crisis support plans also was lacking.

Further, while most clients reported good experiences with their volunteers, the use of volunteers was not a standardized intervention. That is, there was tremendous variation in the volunteers' activities, responsibilities, and the amount of contact they had with assigned clients. Clients may have had daily, weekly, monthly, or only twice a year contact with a volunteer.

Obviously, even these brief observations would be important to other agencies contemplating similar projects with volunteers and crisis support plans. They surely would want to ensure greater use of crisis support plans by providing ongoing training and closer monitoring of staff's completion of these plans. Additionally, to make the interventions of volunteers more uniform, they would need to specify minimum requirements—for example, each volunteer meeting 30 minutes each week face to face with his or her assigned client. And, like the other recommendation, the amount of time volunteers spend with their clients should be carefully recorded and monitored.

PROGRAM DESCRIPTION

One goal of process evaluation is to describe the program. Program descriptions document the operations of a program, which is essential to those who want to replicate or transfer the knowledge/technology from the program. Process evaluations provide the data necessary to judge the intensity and reliability with which services were delivered; they rely heavily on data normally captured by agencies.

TYPES OF DATA USEFUL IN PROCESS EVALUATION

1. Client sociodemographic characteristics
2. Client service usage (type and amount of services received)
3. Referral sources (referral and coordinating agency perspectives of program strengths and weaknesses)
4. Staff characteristics:

   Professional degrees

   Length of experience

   Sociodemographics

   Staff perceptions of program strengths/weaknesses

5. Program activities:

   Special events and meetings

   Staff meetings

   Training provided

   Written program protocols, procedures, and training manuals

   Any information to answer the questions: "What happens to clients?" "What is the program?"

   Observation of program activities. Is the program being implemented as it is supposed to be?

6. Minutes of board, staff, and committee meetings
7. Correspondence and internal memos concerning the project
8. Client satisfaction data, client reports of program strengths, weaknesses, and barriers
9. Financial data; program costs and expenditures

To provide further detail, examples of information that a process evaluator might want to examine are contained in Boxes 5.2 and 5.3. Their contents draw on Scarpitti, Inciardi, and Pottieger (1993) and the *Evaluation Guidebook,* prepared by the U.S. Department of Health and Human Services, Office of Community Services (1992). Box 5.2 provides a quick overview of types of data that may be useful in a process evaluation, while Box 5.3 lists questions that might be asked and links these questions to possible data sources.

As indicated in column 2 of Box 5.3, there are numerous ways to collect process evaluation information about a program. These methods include face-to-face and telephone interviews, surveys, key informant interviews, focus groups, organization record analysis, program documentation analysis, observations, and case studies. Each of these data collection techniques is described in other chapters throughout this book.

In addition, specific strategies can be utilized to collect data. Some data collection strategies, such as focus groups and observations, are qualitative data

QUESTIONS AND DATA SOURCES USEFUL IN PROCESS EVALUATION

General Questions	Examples of Potential Data Collection Sources or Techniques
Why was the program introduced into the community or organization? What need did the program fill? What were the political mechanisms by which the program was initiated and/or maintained?	Literature reviews; local and national legislation review, existing local, state and national data; legislator interviews; administrative interviews; board member interviews; key community leader interviews
What people and organizations were involved with the implementation? What organizations are involved? What are future plans for involving other organizations? Why? What is being done to ensure the organization will be involved with the program?	Administrative interviews: board member interviews: key community leader interviews; program documentation
What collaborative efforts are utilized with this program? How have the collaboration relationships changed over time?	Administrative interviews; staff interviews; board member interviews; program documentation; interviews with collaborating agencies
What are the norms, assumptions, customs, traditions, and traits of the program? In other words, what is the culture of the program? What principles is the program based on?	Administrative interviews; staff interviews; client interviews; board member interviews; program documentation; interviews with collaborating agencies; focus groups; observations
What is the program? What are the components? What changes were incorporated into the program since inception? Why? What changes are planned for the future? Why?	Staff interviews; client interviews; administrative interviews; program documentation; observations; focus groups
What is the sociodemographic makeup of the program population? Is the program actually serving the population it was intended to serve? If not, why not? What changes are planned to reach the intended target population? How are clients recruited? How satisfied are clients with the program?	Case records; program documentation; client interviews or surveys; staff and administrative interviews

BOX 5.3

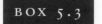 CONTINUED

	Examples of Potential Data Collection Sources or Techniques
General Questions	
Who are the staff? How effective are the staff members? How are staff trained? How are they evaluated? How satisfied are the staff? How often do staff attend meetings? What are the roles and responsibilities of the staff?	Administrative interviews; staff surveys; program documentation; client interviews
What design changes may be necessary to expand the program or offer it to other sites for replication?	Administrative interviews; board member interviews
What outcome evaluation activities are planned? What would the main outcome variables of interest be?	Administrative interviews; board member interviews; key community leader interviews; collaborating agency interviews
What are the program costs and expenditures? Have there been changes in funding since the inception? What about the future funding plans?	Administrative interviews; board member interviews

collection methods; and some, like surveys, are typically quantitative data collection techniques. When doing process evaluation, it is probably wise to use some combination of qualitative and quantitative data collection procedures to best capture what is happening with the program. It is also helpful to include representatives from multiple agencies in the interview process to get a picture of the program that is as accurate as possible. For example, one of the authors conducted a process evaluation of a local drug court program. This process evaluation used eight main steps. *Step 1* was clarifying with the program administrators what information they were actually interested in. A process evaluation provides a certain kind of information, and it is critical that all key stakeholders are clear about what information different kinds of evaluations produce. If administration is under the impression they are going find out whether or not the program is successful, process evaluation is not appropriate for providing that information.

Step 2 was developing a data collection plan to guide the process evaluation. Some of the questions listed in Box 5.3 guided the instrument development as well as an extensive literature review. The literature review included an extensive search of published literature about process evaluations, literature about drug court programs, and literature about evaluation of drug court programs as well as unpublished drug court evaluation reports.

Step 3 was to identify who would be interviewed about the program. This included key program stakeholders. Identifying the key stakeholders to interview for the process evaluation was negotiated with the program administration.

Program administrators are frequently in the best position to discuss what kinds of people come into contact with the program. In this case, judges, clients, staff, police officers, jail personnel, attorneys, and treatment personnel were all important stakeholders; and their perceptions of the program were important to include. Clients were also key stakeholders to talk with; however, there were approximately 100 active clients at the time. Due to funding and time constraints, it was impossible to contact all of the clients. Thus, a few (approximately 20 percent) were randomly selected for interviews.

Step 4 was to develop process evaluation instruments. Based on the information collected in step 3, eight different instruments were developed: (a) administrative interview; (b) judge interview; (c) law enforcement and corrections surveys; (d) treatment provider surveys; (e) prosecutor surveys; (f) defense attorney surveys; (g) client surveys; and (h) staff surveys. Instruments developed combined both quantitative and qualitative questions, and also provided flexibility to probe or write any comments made from quantitative questions.

Step 5 was to conduct the interviews. The process evaluation included a 6-hour interview with administrative personnel of the drug court program; 1-hour interviews with each of 5 judges involved in the drug court program; surveys and face-to-face interviews with 22 randomly selected active clients; and surveys of all drug court staff $(n = 7)$, 19 community treatment providers, 6 randomly selected defense attorney representatives, 4 prosecuting attorney representatives, 1 representative from the local probation and parole office, 1 representative from the local jail, and 2 local police department representatives. In all, 69 different individuals representing 10 different agency perspectives provided information about the drug court program for this process evaluation.

Step 6 was to examine program documentation and records.

Step 7 was to analyze and integrate the information. Responses were integrated and reported in specific sections guided by themes such as those in Box 5.2. Qualitative responses were integrated with main themes, and specific interviewee wording was used to highlight comments throughout the report. Quantitative responses were reported as indicated (e.g., client characteristic data) or were analyzed using means (e.g., client satisfaction data). A conclusion and summary section integrated the main findings across all of the respondents.

Step 8 was to complete the report. This step included several iterations of the report to include edits and comments by key program administrators. It is important to involve program administrators in the draft stages of the final report. For example, some of the information about the program was not explained initially in full detail, and program administration wanted specific information explained very clearly. Interestingly, although the overwhelming majority of the comments were positive, there were some negative comments about the drug court program. The program evaluator was, understandably, a little nervous during presentation of the first draft of the report. Evaluators want their results to be as accurate as possible, and there was some concern that the program administration might apply pressure to change the results. However, the administration accepted even the negative findings and felt that the results were portrayed accurately and fairly. Thus, the process evaluation findings were consistent with the program administrators' impressions about the program and what they expected the report would show. This process evaluation procedure worked well for the drug court program in this community and is being used in other drug court programs across the state. However, this overall procedure can be adapted to a variety of program process evaluations.

PROGRAM MONITORING

Program monitoring is the second overarching purpose of process evaluation. Program monitoring can be valuable to the process evaluator who is trying to understand what happened in a program and to whom. The novice evaluator should not develop the opinion that program monitoring is conducted *only* when a process evaluation has been requested. Ongoing program monitoring is essential to the sound management of all programs.

Like formative evaluation, program monitoring is a basic form of program evaluation. Why is it so elemental? Because a program that is not reaching its intended population is misdirected—perhaps duplicating services to a population already well served. Further, it makes no sense to conduct a more sophisticated evaluation to determine if the intervention worked when it was not applied to the population in need.

Program monitoring does not require elaborate research designs, nor does it usually require an advanced understanding of statistics. Often program monitoring starts with examining a program's specific goals and objectives and comparing these with the kind of data that most human service agencies routinely collect—what we previously discussed as patterns of use and client utilization data (Chapter 3). These data are "monitored" to ensure that the program is serving those for whom it was designed. It is entirely possible that with the passage of time a program may somehow get diverted and not serve the population originally targeted. (See the discussion on "program drift" in Chapter 14.)

Changes occur in practically all programs. Once the initial excitement of starting a new program has worn away, staff and agency resources may be siphoned off or redirected as newer, more urgent problems come along. As the original staff take other jobs, retire, become promoted, or move to other programs, incoming staff may have different notions as to what the program should accomplish or to whom it should be directed. Subtle, almost imperceptible changes in staff, the program philosophy, the composition of the clientele, or the orientation of new employees can result in programs departing significantly from what was first proposed.

It is crucial that conscientious program managers, administrators, and agency boards of directors continuously monitor the progress of programs. Only poor management would benevolently ignore a new program for 10 or 11 months, and then at the end of the funding period attempt to hold the program staff and its manager accountable. To ensure that a program serves the target population and obtains program goals and objectives in the manner expected by the funding source, regular program monitoring is required. Unlike formative evaluations, which tend to be single-episode evaluations, and others that we will discuss later, program monitoring ought to be ongoing. Program monitoring should be thought of as a routine activity where a program director reviews patterns of use data on a regular basis (more often than once a year). Routine monitoring can reveal problems before they become overwhelming and track progress toward meeting the sponsor's or agency's expectations.

BECOMING A PROGRAM MONITOR

Human service programs exist to provide either goods or services to clientele. Some programs provide tangible goods: food (soup kitchens), beds (emergency shelter), or clothing. Other programs provide services where the products are more intangible (counseling, mental health education or prevention services, self-esteem groups).

Regardless of whether the client/consumer receives a tangible or intangible product, there is always something that can be counted. For instance, a child protection agency may provide homemaker services to 189 families during the course of a year. This same agency may complete 42 adoptions, approve 64 foster homes, and provide 1,195 hours of individual or group therapy. Each of these program products can be used to provide some measure of accountability. The agency director may be unhappy with the provision of homemaker services to only 189 families because she had hoped that 200 families would receive homemaker services. On the other hand, the director may be pleased (since there had been major staff turnover in the program) that 64 foster homes were approved. (At one point it looked as if only 50 foster homes might be inspected and approved.)

The first step in program monitoring consists of deciding what program products, events, or activities are important enough to count. Not every activity associated with a program is important enough to monitor. For example, we have never seen an annual report that listed the number of times that the stapler was used. It may not be important to count the number of times that calls are placed. However, if you are the manager of a telephone crisis hotline or a telephone information and referral service, it may be important to keep records on the number of telephone contacts categorized by problem (e.g., suicidal ideation, drug use, or unexpected pregnancies). Box 5.4 provides an example of a possible monthly report a drug court program might use to monitor whether they are "on track" with the key components and benchmarks.

Just because something can be counted does not mean that it *ought* to be counted. Once we came across a report of a telephone counseling service that recorded daily (by shift) the number of telephone calls received by problem area. Even though they used 20 or so categories to log the type of call, about 15 percent of the calls fell into the miscellaneous category. We found this strange, since in our opinion they already had too many categories. As we investigated a little more, we learned that they were counting incoming phone calls that might be best described as "personal." A mechanic might call to report that a staff member's car had been repaired, or a child would call a parent at work on arriving home from school. Although these calls may have been important to the people receiving them, counting such calls in the monthly service report gave

DRUG COURT PROGRAM
MONITORING MONTHLY
REPORT EXAMPLE

1. Number of clients currently active:
2. Number of new clients accepted into the program:
3. Number of participants graduated to next phase:
   a. From phase I to phase II:
   b. From phase II to phase III:
   c. Graduated from phase III:
4. Number of court sessions:
5. Number of drug screens:
6. Number of participants identified as using based on drug screens:
7. Number of individual counseling sessions:
8. Number of group sessions:
9. Number of family support sessions:
10. Number of participants referred to outside agencies:
11. Number of participants referred to outside agencies for residential services:
12. Number of participants employed:
    a. Part time:
    b. Full time:
    c. Disabled:
    d. Homemaker:
13. Number of participants in educational pursuit:
    a. High school/GED:
    b. College:
    c. Vocational training/rehabilitation:
    d. Adult education:
14. Number of employment/education verifications:
15. Number of housing verifications:
16. Total amount paid toward court obligations:
17. Total number of sanctions:
18. Total number of participants rearrested for new charges:
19. Total number of terminations:

the appearance that the telephone hotline was actually a lot busier than it was. Counting these calls could not tell us anything important about whether the program was providing the type of service originally planned. So, while there was accountability, counting for the sake of counting led to some inane results.

Program monitoring can involve more than tallying the frequency of events. Program managers may wish to examine the length of time that clients receive service or the amount of time between events—such as from the point of initial contact until service delivery. Also, it is not unusual for administrators to be interested in how staff use their time—the proportion of it that is direct service (sometimes known as billable time in mental health centers) and that part that is supportive ("desk work," traveling, committee meetings).

MISSION STATEMENTS, GOALS, AND OBJECTIVES

In deciding what is important to count or monitor, it is helpful to become familiar with the agency's mission statement. **Mission statements** are statements of purpose—they explain what the agency is all about. Mission statements provide a common vision for the organization, a point of reference for all major planning decisions; they answer the question, "Why do we exist?" Mission statements not only provide clarity of purpose to persons within an organization, but also help gain understanding and support from those people outside the organization who are important to its success (Below, Morrisey, & Acomb, 1987). If you are in an agency that does not have a formal mission statement, or if you find it necessary to draft one, start by looking at the agency's charter, constitution, or bylaws. These documents describe the purpose behind the creation of an agency. Five examples of agency mission statements follow.

> The mission of the Northern County Victims' Assistance Program is to provide assistance to individuals who have been victims of felony crimes in Northern County. This assistance will be directed at the devastating emotional and psychological consequences that victims of crime and their families experience.

> Our mission calls us to live out the interdependent values of love and justice, to lift oppression, and heal brokenness of individuals and families, of groups, and of society itself. [Excerpt from the Mission Statement of a Catholic Social Service Bureau]

> The mission of the Western County Mental Health Board is to improve the quality of life in our community by promoting mental health, by preventing and reducing mental and emotional problems, substance abuse problems, and by minimizing their residual effects.

> It is the purpose of KET, a unique communications resource linking all Kentuckians by television, to be an institution of learning for children and adults of every age and need, a statewide town hall through which interested citizens can together explore issues of mutual significance, a performance stage for the outstanding talent of Kentucky and the great artists of the world, and a catalyst for uniting the citizens of the Commonwealth in common purpose to solve common problems and to stimulate growth and progress for all.

> The mission of the Drug Court program is "to stop the abuse of alcohol and other drugs and related criminal activity." (USDJ, 1997, p. 7)

As can be seen from these examples, mission statements are not going to tell you exactly how the agency will go about its business or when it expects to complete its missions. But, they do inform as to the nature of the organization. One can readily deduce the religious orientation of the agency in the second example. Mission statements are useful in that they communicate the agency's purpose and they express values, suggesting what is important for the agency to address with its resources. Mission statements are usually stated in somewhat vague terms. They are not specific as to what types of services will be provided or how the client will get those services. How important are mission statements? Sugarman (1988), in listing six major criteria that define a well-managed human service organization, noted that the first characteristic is "a clearly defined mission or purpose, well-understood by its members, and it has goals and plans based thereon" (p. 19).

Occasionally it becomes necessary for an agency to change its mission. Perhaps the best example of this is the March of Dimes. This agency was created because of the problem of polio (an infantile paralysis caused by a virus). With advances in research, vaccines were discovered, and the disease has now been virtually eliminated. The March of Dimes continues to exist, however, but its mission is now to fight birth defects. Whenever there is a change of mission, there must be a corresponding change of program goals and objectives.

Goals follow from mission statements and also tend to be general and global with regard to activities and products. Patton (1982) noted that a goal statement should specify a program direction based on values, ideals, political mandates, and program purpose. Goals are not specific as to when or how something will be accomplished but speak instead to aspirations.

Goals provide the focus, orientation, and direction needed to harness the combined energy and activities of a staff so that chaos and confusion are minimized and clients' needs are served by the program. Imagine a team of horses hitched to a wagon. Then picture that same wagon with a team of horses attached to each of the four sides. Which wagon is likely to move, and which will go nowhere?

Many people make the mistake of thinking that goals have to be accomplished within a short period of time (perhaps even within one's lifetime). However, there is no such requirement. Many human service agencies have goals that will likely never be accomplished because they involve continuing needs. How many of the following goals do you feel it will be possible to attain?

1. The agency will eliminate *all* poverty.
2. The program will *prevent* child abuse and neglect.
3. The hospital will *rehabilitate* persons who have problems with alcohol.
4. The university will *strengthen* its commitment to scholarship and academic excellence.

These sound more like mission statements from which specific goals should be derived. However, it is perfectly acceptable for an institution to have broad goals that they may never reach. An agency (or a program for that matter) has not failed when a goal is not achieved; the reason is that the goals that human service agencies typically set are not easy to achieve.

Unlike mission statements and goals, **objectives** are specific and precise. Objectives allow us to measure progress being made toward the achievement of a goal. They declare what will be accomplished by a certain date. Objectives should have a single aim and an end product or result that is easily verifiable. Drucker (1980) notes that program objectives such as "to aid the disadvantaged" or "to provide health care" are sentiments (and vague ones at that) explaining why a program was initiated rather than what it was meant to accomplish. He continues:

> To have a chance at performance, a program needs clear targets, the attainment of which can be measured, appraised, or at least judged. . . . Even "the best medical care for the sick," the objective of many hospitals in the British National Health Service, is not operational. Rather, it is meaningful to say: "It is our aim to make sure that no patient coming into emergency will go for more than three minutes without being seen by a qualified triage nurse." (p. 231)

Patton (1982) makes the distinction of separating the concept (the goal) from the measurement of it (the objective). We find this a useful way to think about the differences between the two. If you are still unclear, look carefully at Table 5.1.

TABLE 5.1	CONDUCTING A PROCESS EVALUATION THROUGH PROGRAM MONITORING
1. Examine the agency mission statement	Examine the history of the agency mission statement. What were the changes over time? Does the mission statement accurately reflect the agency activities today?
2. Examine or develop agency goals	Goals should be examined or developed in collaboration with key agency personnel. Goals should be related to the mission, more specific than the mission, and related to current agency activities. Goals answer the question "What does the agency hope to accomplish?"
3. Examine or develop objectives based on each agency goal	Objectives should be examined or developed in collaboration with key agency personnel. Objectives should be specific, definable, and measurable. Objectives answer the question "How do we know whether the agency is accomplishing its goals or not?"

BOX 5.5

EXAMPLE OF A KENTUCKY
DRUG COURT AGENCY
MISSION STATEMENT,
GOALS, AND OBJECTIVES

Mission:
The overall mission of Drug Courts is to stop the abuse of alcohol and other drugs
and related criminal activity.

Goals:

1. Promote client abstinence
2. Decrease client recidivism
3. Increase community safety
4. Increase client life skills
5. Increase community awareness about the program as well as about substance abuse
6. Expand and maintain resource base

Objective indicators for 1999 compared to 1998

1. Promote client abstinence
   a. To increase the number of drug-free babies born
   b. To increase the number of clean urines
   c. To increase the number of meetings attended for each client (AA/NA,
      treatment groups, education, case specialist meetings)
2. Decrease recidivism
   a. To decrease the percentage of clients re-arrested while in the program
3. Increase community safety
   a. To lower community drug arrests for FY 1999 compared to FY 1998
   b. To lower community property crime for FY 1999 compared to FY 1998
4. Increase life skills
   a. To increase the percentage of clients living in court-approved housing
   b. To increase the percentage of clients in court-approved employment
   c. To increase the percentage of clients obtaining a GED or in college
   d. To increase the percentage of clients gaining or keeping custody of children
5. Increase community awareness about the program as well as about substance abuse
   a. To increase the number of staff media contacts
   b. To increase the number of media stories on the program or program clients
   c. To increase program funding

When objectives are properly developed, they leave little doubt about
what will be done, the date when its accomplishment can be expected, as
well as a clear measure of whether the objective was achieved. To be useful,
objectives must specify events or activities that can be independently determined. As an example see Box 5.5. The objectives listed in this example can
be used to monitor the program over time or can be used more specifically
to target areas in need of improvement by making them even more specific.

    d. To increase the number of staff requests for speaking engagements

    e. To increase the number of client referrals to the program

6.   Expand and maintain resource base

    a. To increase the number of agencies for Drug Court client referrals

    b. To increase the number of agencies that will work with the Drug Court program

These goals and objectives would be used to develop a process evaluation and process evaluation indicators. However, there are two types of outcomes to consider. One type is the process indicator outcomes also called **proximal** outcomes. These outcomes are typically monitoring data collected during the program or as indicators of program functioning.

The other type of outcome is called **distal** or outcome evaluation. These are indicators that are typically measured after program completion. For example, one outcome evaluation of three drug court programs used all clients who graduated ($n = 222$), dropped out ($n = 371$), or who did not enter the program after being assessed for entry ($n = 152$) between 1995 and 1998 (i.e., the comparison group) for each of the three drug court programs for a total sample of 745 individuals. The program graduates, dropouts, and comparison groups were compared on a number of indicators during a 12-month period after the graduation date, after the dropout date, or after the assessment date. The comparison group included individuals who were assessed for the drug court program but who did not enter it because they did not want to do so or because they did not meet eligibility requirements (e.g., were not using illicit drugs, were not facing extended incarceration time). Specifically the outcome indicators included:

1.   Indicators of criminal justice involvement (e.g., new criminal charges, convictions, and incarceration)

2.   Social adjustment indicators (e.g., protective orders, mental health service utilization, traffic accidents, and child support payments)

3.   In-depth follow-up interviews were used with a random sample of drug court graduates and dropouts to supplement the information conducted with the secondary data sources.

Results indicated that, particularly for graduates, drug court involvement was associated with pronounced post-program reductions in criminal justice involvement, higher annual earnings, and reduced outpatient mental health service utilization. In addition, self-reported interview data also showed increased stability and productivity among the graduates. Finally, a cost-benefit analysis was also done and results indicated that there was a $3.83 in economic benefit generated for every dollar spent on a drug court graduate using all of the data collected to estimate costs and benefits.

Source: Logan, T., Williams, K., Leukefeld, C., & Minton, L. (2000). A Process Evaluation of a Drug Court: Methodology and Results. *International Journal of Offender Therapy and Comparative Criminology, 44,* 3, 369–394. Logan, T., Hiller, M., Leukefeld, C., & Minton, L. (in press). Drug Court Program Outcomes: Secondary Data Analysis and Interviews. *Journal of Offender Rehabilitation.* Logan, T., Hoyt, W., McCollister, K., French, M., Leukefeld, C., & Minton, L. (2004). Economic evaluation of drug court: Methodology, results, and policy implications. *Evaluation and Program Planning, 27,* 4, 381–396.

For example, objective number 2a listed in Box 5.5 could become: "To lower percentage of clients re-arrested in program from 10% of clients indicated in 1998 to 5% or less of clients in 1999." As indicated in Box 5.5, two types of outcomes must be distinguished.

One type of outcome is typically the focus of program monitoring—program indicators or proximal outcomes (often used in process evaluations). The other type of outcome includes indicators used to determine program outcomes—often called distal outcomes (often used in outcome evaluations). The difference between process and outcome evaluation indicators has to do with (1) the timing of the indicators; (2) whether or not control or comparison groups are used; and (3) what kinds of questions can be addressed with the indicator information. Outcome indicators are generally collected from participants after program completion while process indicators are generally collected during program participation. In addition, process indicators generally only include information from clients or program participants while outcome indicators include information from control or comparison groups as well as program participants. Finally, outcome indicators answer the question "Does the program work?" while process indicators answer questions like "What happens during the program?" "Is the program implemented according to how it is supposed to run?" "What is the program?" "Is the program meeting its annual goals?" Objectives help to identify what process indicators should be included in the process evaluation.

WRITING PROGRAM OBJECTIVES

To write an objective that provides some measure of accountability (so that it can be determined whether or not the objective was met), think in terms of activities that can be counted or observed. The objective should state what will be accomplished and when it can be expected. A model for writing specific objectives is as follows:

To *increase*	*admissions 10 percent*	*by June 30, 2007*
(verb)	(specific target)	(date)

Some examples of verbs that are useful when writing objectives are:

To increase, add, develop, expand, enlarge

To decrease, reduce, lessen

To promote, advertise, publicize

To start, create, initiate, begin, establish

However, the choice of the verb may not be as critical as ensuring that the reader can visualize a measurable result. The use of vague terms can make it difficult to determine whether the results were obtained. Avoid language such as that contained in the following program objectives:

To help clients discover healthier relationships with others.

To help clients develop an appreciation of etiquette.

To help students become better citizens.

To assist clients in getting their lives back together.

To increase the community's support of . . .

To improve clients' understanding of themselves.

To help families learn about alcohol and alcoholism.

All of these objectives share the same problem—they lack specificity. In other words, it is difficult to measure or to know if these objectives were ever obtained. They do not inform as to how much has to be learned, developed, or understood. (How would we know if clients had improved their understanding of themselves?) Also, they do not provide any indication of dates when these events will be accomplished. There is also no way of knowing exactly when the objective should be accomplished—the target event that should allow independent verification is too vague or absent.

Sometimes agency directors and program managers, in an effort to make their programs look good, write objectives that will be too easily achieved. Monitoring bodies can contribute to this situation. We once saw an evaluation form that contained these two questions: "Did the project achieve its objectives?" and "How many of the project's objectives were realized?" Every program manager would like to say that he or she accomplished 100 percent of the program's objectives. If the quality of these objectives is not assessed, program managers may write only objectives that they know they can meet. Setting objectives too low results only in pointless "busywork." If a program provided 2,200 units of individual counseling one year, then it should be expected to exceed that number in the next year. One exception to this rule might be when the program expects to lose a significant amount of staff, funding, or other resources. Another exception might be if the quality of those sessions were sacrificed. It is also important to balance quality with quantity, as we will see in the next section. Objectives should be set high enough to challenge the staff. They should not be impossible to obtain, but they ought to encourage staff to stretch a bit and perhaps to think a bit "out of the box" about how to meet objectives.

Once program objectives have been developed, monitoring for managerial purposes is possible. When objectives are being developed for new programs, there may be a natural tendency to make conservative estimates of what can be accomplished. Rather than overestimate the number of clients who can be served in a year, program managers may be more likely to underestimate what can be done. These objectives can be tempered by reality if data exist for the start-up phase of other formerly "new" programs. In the absence of such data, educated guesses are appropriate.

However, program monitoring really comes into play when programs have begun to generate service data. In the example from a counseling agency given in Table 5.2, it is possible to identify groups that are not getting their "fair share" of the agency's resources.

As can be seen from the table, widowed persons, those over the age of 60, and minorities are not represented in the agency clientele to the extent that

TABLE 5.2 | CLIENT UTILIZATION DATA, ACCEPT ALL COUNSELING SERVICES, INC.

Variable	2003	2004	2005	2006	2000 Census
Widowed	3%	3.6%	2.5%	2.3%	4.95%
Over 60 years old	4%	4.5%	5.5%	5.2%	24.75%
African Americans	5%	5.5%	6.3%	6.5%	13.25%

would be expected from their proportions in the population. With just this much information, a program manager could develop the following objectives:

OBJECTIVE 1. To increase the percentage of widowed persons served by the program to 5 percent of the total clientele by December 31, 2006.

OBJECTIVE 2. Through special outreach efforts, to increase the number of older adults served by the program until 15 percent of the program's clients are 60 or older. This objective to be reached by July 1, 2005.

OBJECTIVE 3. By January 1, 2007, to double the number of African American clients served by the program in 2004.

With these objectives in place, the program manager and the program's staff now have a clear set of expectations for their future efforts. Once these objectives are met, new ones can be developed. If they are not met, corrective actions may be needed (providing there were no extenuating factors to explain the nonperformance). The setting of objectives provides a basis against which the program's accomplishments can be examined.

HIERARCHY OF GOALS, OBJECTIVES, AND ACTIVITIES

Process objectives spell out the milestones necessary to achieve the intermediate outcome objectives. It is possible to envision a hierarchy that flows from the very general (the goal) to the very specific activities that must be completed before process objectives can be accomplished (Kettner, Moroney, & Martin, 1999).

A schematic way to portray the relationship between objectives and outcomes is known as a **program logic model.** According to the W. K. Kellogg Foundation's Web-based Evaluation Handbook (http://www.wkkf.org/Pubs/Tools/Evaluation/Pub770.pdf), program logic models have gained popularity in recent years for a number of reasons. First, their development helps program planners, staff, and other stakeholders to clarify and make manifest program goals and objectives. Second, a program logic model is a template, a handy visual device for charting program operations as they progress. Finally, by distinguishing between proximal and distal outcomes, these models make evaluation—both process and outcome evaluation—a realistic and integral part of program operations.

The generic program logic model below illustrates the flow from problem to outcome:

Problem ➝ Goals ➝ Objectives ➝ Program Inputs
Program Activities ➝ Proximal Outcomes ➝ Distal Outcomes

Program inputs refer to resource availability (staff, facilities, computer equipment) and **program activities** refer to the actual events that need to take place to make the program run (advertising and outreach, training of staff, intervention sessions). As an example of how this might work, let's look at Figure 5.2. Say that your program's primary goal is to increase safe sex practices among college students. Your program team used a needs assessment that utilized a probability sample of all college students on campus during one fall semester to develop the goal. Also, the college health clinic reported on the number of sexually transmitted infections and re-infections that they treated the preceding year.

During the initial program development the following objectives were developed: (1) to increase student knowledge about safe sex; (2) to decrease the average number of sex partners; and (3) to increase condom use. You conducted a literature review and used focus groups to determine what kind of intervention students thought might be successful in targeting these objectives. Based on the literature review and focus group findings, the program was initially selected and developed to include "3 one-hour safe-sex educational and experiential intervention led by trained peers." You then selected specific program activities and development, and then implemented the program. After the initial implementation, you used more focus groups to conduct a formative evaluation to work out any "kinks" in the program. Perhaps you discovered an awkward activity or some information students did not understand but they didn't want to ask the question during the intervention period. The focus groups could help identify needed improvements.

After the program has been implemented and stabilized you could conduct a process evaluation. In other words, after working out the program "kinks" and after several months of program operation, it would be time to conduct a process evaluation. Your proximal outcomes might include the number of student participants, participant knowledge levels immediately before and after the intervention, and participant satisfaction.

Then, the next year you could conduct another campuswide survey to compare to the previous survey to see if there were any changes in knowledge, average number of sex partners, and condom use.

Each of these components is included in the program development logic model in Figure 5.2. By listing these specific dimensions of the program in a schematic diagram, you provide all stakeholders with an efficient display of program components and how they are interrelated.

WHAT SHOULD BE MONITORED?

Program monitoring can be used to check a program's progress in meeting certain objectives (e.g., increasing the number of minority admissions). In this sense, it is analogous to being told by your physician what kinds of things to monitor

FIGURE 5.2 | LOGIC MODEL OF PROGRAM DEVELOPMENT FOR THE
"COLLEGE SAFE SEX" PROGRAM

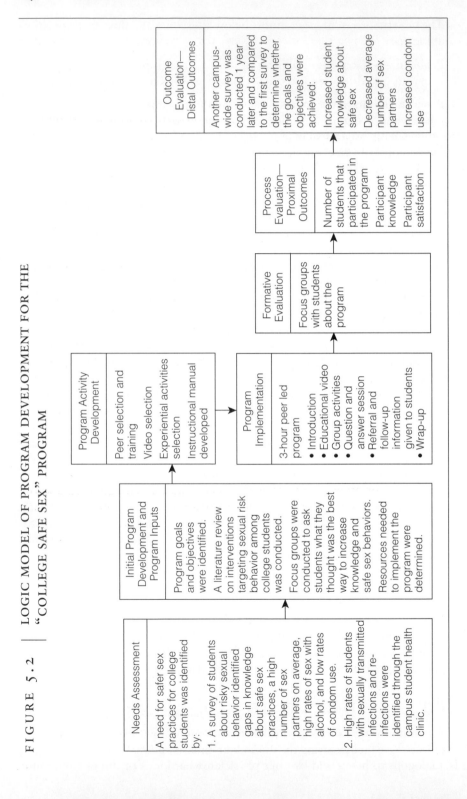

to maintain health. For instance, persons with a diagnosis of diabetes must monitor the amount of sugars and carbohydrates they consume. Persons with hypertension are told to monitor their salt intake. However, managers need not wait for their programs to become "ill" before employing program monitoring.

Program monitoring can be used most effectively in a diagnostic sense. Managers can use program monitoring to look for "symptoms" that would help them diagnose potential problems. The kinds of problems to look for are difficult to state succinctly because of the enormous diversity in human service programs.

They range from small, one-person programs to programs that employ hundreds of staff. Programs administered by the same agency in different locations may bear only a faint resemblance to one another. Every program can be expected to have a somewhat unique set of problems. Even similar programs are likely to have different problems. This is due to differences in staff composition, local (and often informal) policies and procedures, relationships with other professionals and agencies within the community, the guidance and leadership of the agency administrator, the amount of financial support, and such factors as the interest and involvement of the board of directors.

Veney and Kaluzny (1984) have summarized the data appropriate for monitoring as inputs, process, and outputs. They describe inputs as consisting of the resources by which the program is carried out. Resources include such categories as project staff, office space, and office equipment and supplies. With regard to inputs, the important thing to monitor is the amount budgeted for a program against what is actually used or allocated. For process, it is important to monitor the activities that were intended to be carried out during program implementation. Outputs are the results of the program—what the program actually produces.

Using this scheme, a manager might check to make sure that a program is not overspending its budget (or that it is getting all that it is entitled to); that planned activities are being conducted on a timely basis; and that regular accounting is being made of the number of service units produced (such as meals provided or other quantifiable products). Thus, a manager would know there were problems if the agency spent 75 percent of its budget by the half-year mark, if scheduled program activities were not being performed, or if the program started off providing 300 service units during the first month but fell off to only 125 service units during the second month.

Monitoring inputs, process, and outputs gives the program manager basic information needed to manage programs. However, this information may not be complete enough to allow a manager to "fine-tune" a program. A program could be meeting expectations in terms of its budget expenditures, its activities, and the number of products that were expected and still not be doing the job it was designed to do in terms of serving all facets of the population or community. This could come about because too little time was devoted to planning prior to program implementation, because of lack of management, or because of other reasons.

What other informational items might be helpful to monitor? One would be referral sources. The conscientious manager should monitor where referrals are coming from and in what proportion. It may be perfectly acceptable for a private counseling agency to have 92 percent of its clients self-referred. On the other hand, public agencies may want to see referrals coming from a broad spectrum of the community. The program manager in a public agency who notes that over a 3-month period no referrals have come from the criminal justice system may want to undertake some special efforts to ensure that professionals in that system, who are in a position to refer, know whom to contact and how to make a referral. Similarly, the program manager might be concerned if physicians, clergy, or other human service agencies are not referring to the program—or are not referring in the proportion that he or she expected.

A more refined level of program monitoring would examine the number of clients who drop out of the program. How many clients complete only one or two sessions? What proportion drop out by the third session? How many clients notify the program staff that they will not be returning? It is also important to know such things as how long it takes for clients to receive service from the time of their initial contact or application. Managers should know how many clients are on their waiting lists so that scheduling and programming can be planned accordingly.

Besides using program monitoring to determine whether the obvious segments of the population are being served (older adults, low-income persons, minorities), program managers can determine whether clients from remote geographical areas and those with special needs (such as persons with mental retardation or physical disabilities) are being served. Additionally, program monitoring can inform as to whether there is an increase of clients with certain types of problems or diagnoses. A significant increase in the number of clients reporting sexual abuse may necessitate training staff or require some other modification in the program. (Perhaps a support group for survivors of sexual trauma should be started.) The discovery of a substantial number of clients addicted to crack cocaine may require either program modification or at least closer working ties with other agencies in the community. Examining client data by area of residence may indicate the need for a new satellite office.

As management's use of program information increases, additional items, such as productivity of individual members of the staff, can be added to the items being monitored. As program managers make greater use of program information, often it becomes necessary to develop (or purchase) more sophisticated ways of managing data. Although the term **management information systems** can be applied to simple manual tabulations of service data, it has generally come to be associated with computerized systems.

Management information systems depend on source documents (sometimes called service tickets) that record transactions such as the service a client received, the number of hours of service received or service units provided, the staff member involved, the location, the date, and so on (see Figure 5.3). This information is useful for billing purposes as well as for understanding staff and program productivity.

Service tickets can be linked to a client's file containing the initial application data (sometimes called a "face sheet") or other forms containing the diagnosis and other pertinent information. Computerized information systems allow for the most sophisticated monitoring of service utilization because of the ease

FIGURE 5.3 | EXAMPLE OF A SERVICE TICKET

McDowell Counseling Center
Therapist # _____   Today's Date: ____ ____ ____   Client # _____-_____
Time spent with client: hours _____ minutes _____

Program (Circle one)

- Individual and family counseling
- Group counseling
- Crisis counseling (hotline only)
- Diagnostic assessment
- Case management
- Case consultation
- Community education
- Psychiatric consultation
- Client cancellation/no-show

---

with which the computer can process large quantities of data. (See Box 5.6.) Examples of program monitoring questions that a management information system could answer are:

1. How many service units, on average, did clients with the disorder receive? (Or, what was the average length of stay for patients with bipolar disorder?)
2. Which unit produced the most counseling during the last quarter? (Alternatively, which worker was the least productive last pay period?)
3. What percent of the clients were able to pay the full fee?
4. Of those clients referred for services last month, how many were referred by the criminal justice system?
5. How many cancellations (or no-shows) were there last month? What were the characteristics of those who canceled and gave no notification? (Were they single mothers with small children or unemployed persons with no transportation?)

Outside evaluators may not be familiar with the various facets of, and therefore, all of the data available from, an agency's management information system. There are several ways to approach this problem: one is to ask to see any routine monthly, quarterly, or yearly reports that are produced. These will likely provide a good overview of key variables such as the number of clients who applied for and received service and so forth. However, these reports are usually very selective and will not display *all* of the variables available for analysis.

Another approach is to systematically collect all of the forms used by the agency. Start at the intake department as if you were a client and gather all of the forms that initially must be completed. Then, move on to other departments where clients might be referred to receive service. Finally, ask for copies of forms that are used when clients terminate and cases are closed. All of the forms collectively compose the agency's management information system (MIS). What you are likely to find is that not every form is entered into the

AN EXAMPLE OF A LARGE,
NATIONAL AGENCY
MONITORING SYSTEM

How would you develop a monitoring system of a large national program such as the services of the Department of Veterans Affairs?

Rosenheck and Cicchetti (1998) described a national mental health program performance assessment developed and implemented in the Department of Veterans Affairs (VA). There were 68 key performance indicators in four major areas (population coverage, inpatient care, outpatient care, and economic performance) to assess how well the organization was meeting its goals and objectives. The overall goals developed that guided the selection of the program monitoring indicators were:

1. Quality of life, clinical improvement, and patient satisfaction with services should be maximized.
2. The availability and accessibility of VA mental health services should be similar throughout the nation and, in view of the growing number of Americans without health insurance, should increase.
3. Reliance on inpatient treatment should be reduced without compromising quality or outcomes of care.
4. Delivery of outpatient and community-based care should be expanded and strengthened.
5. Equity should be sought between the accessibility of mental health and other health service care services.
6. The cost of services should be minimized, without compromising quality or outcomes.

Examples of specific indicators developed from the overall goals include:

1. Percent of veterans in the general veteran population who used any VA mental health services each year.
2. Average length of stay of an index episode of care; average bed days of care.
3. The proportion of discharged inpatients who had an outpatient visit at the appropriate specialty clinic during the first 30 days of discharge.
4. The proportion of all VA health care funds allocated to inpatient, outpatient, and all mental health treatment.
5. The ratio of per capita mental health costs to per capita non-mental health costs.

Source: Rosenheck, R., & Cicchetti, D. (1998). A mental health program report card: A multi-dimensional approach to performance monitoring in public sector programs. *Community Mental Health Journal*, 34(1), 85–106.

MIS—many forms are filed or kept even though no one accesses the data from them. These forms may yield rich data for analysis or, on the other hand, they may contain repetitious information already accessible from other forms.

It should be noted that program monitoring data, while useful for some management purposes, does not necessarily inform as to the *quality* of care provided to the various groups of clients using the agency's services. Although you may be pleased with a program because poor or minority clients were well represented in the clientele, this does not guarantee that the services they received actually helped them. Your program could be serving a large number of persons inadequately or inappropriately. By examining only the characteristics of those clients being served, you still have very little idea about how "good" the program is. When you want to know if the clients are better off as a result of being served by the program, then you need to shift from program monitoring to program evaluation models. However, before considering program outcome evaluation, you might want to examine the quality assurance system.

QUALITY ASSURANCE

Quality assurance is another basic form of evaluation that usually involves determining compliance with some set of standards. The term is often associated with ongoing reviews of medical or clinical care records, although more may be involved than this. Quality assurance aims to identify and correct deficiencies occurring in the process of providing care to consumers of services.

Certain services have well-established federal and state regulations. Medicare, for instance, has specific requirements for certified home health care. Agencies providing this service may also wish to meet the accreditation standards of organizations such as the National League for Nursing, the National Homecaring Council, and the Joint Commission on Accreditation of Healthcare Organizations (Eustis, Kane, & Fischer, 1993).

Accreditation standards exist for many, if not most, human services. By way of example, since April 1987, all psychiatric hospitals in the United States must meet the standards developed by the Joint Commission of Accreditation of Health Organizations (JCAHO, 1988, 1990, 1991). Some residential treatment agencies also seek to meet JCAHO's standards as well as those of other accrediting organizations such as the Commission on the Accreditation of Rehabilitation Facilities.

Typically, quality assurance standards require agencies to document for all their clients such information as:

Presenting problem/diagnosis

Treatment plan

Frequency and length of treatment episodes

Service modality/provider

Drug prescriptions

Discharge plans

Staff qualifications

From this information, reviewers can determine if admissions were appropriate, treatment was consistent with generally accepted practice, the least expensive alternative resources were used, and continuity of care and reasonable treatment follow-up were provided. Known in some agencies as "utilization review," these efforts are increasingly concerned with such issues as length of stay (in treatment) and ensuring that resource usage is fiscally justified.

Unfortunately, many social and human service organizations have considered this "medical model" of quality assurance to be synonymous with program evaluation. All too often, quality assurance has been conceptualized as and limited to checking whether a sampling of reviewed cases was essentially in conformity with accepted standards of care. Such efforts, however, do not indicate the extent to which a program is successful—whether clients improve as a result of intervention—or whether a program is worth funding again next year. Quality assurance efforts, by and large, focus almost exclusively on the process of treatment rather than on treatment outcome.

Because of the confusion that exists, it is necessary to briefly highlight the differences between quality assurance and program outcome evaluation as presented in the remainder of this book. First, quality assurance efforts often stem from legislative mandate. In 1972, amendments to the Social Security Act (PL 92-603) established Professional Standards Review Organizations (PSROs). The intent of this legislation was to establish peer review systems to ensure that federal and state expenditures of Medicare, Medicaid, and the Maternal and Child Health Programs were spent on "medically necessary and high quality care" (Tash & Stahler, 1984). Second, clinicians tend to be involved in quality assurance efforts (peer reviews), whereas program evaluators are usually not a provider of the care that is being evaluated. Third, in quality assurance, recommendations are customarily relayed back to clinicians in order to improve the record-keeping process, whereas evaluation findings may or may not be given as feedback to the clinical staff and are more often used at the administrative level. Fourth, quality assurance often relies on the expert opinion of peer reviewers and consensus that a sample of records met expected standards. Program evaluation methodologies tend to rely much less on peer review and more on quantitative data, research designs, the formal testing of hypotheses, and statistical analysis (Tash, Stahler, & Rappaport, 1982).

Having gone to all this trouble to convince you that quality assurance is not the same as program outcome evaluation, we would not want to leave you with the impression that quality assurance is a waste of time—it is not. It provides a degree of consistency and uniformity by promoting adherence to clinical guidelines. When quality assurance standards are well established and interventions relatively dependable and constant, the program evaluator has an easier time understanding the positive and negative effects of an intervention and such problems as clients who recidivate or relapse.

Even if quality assurance is not required within an agency, the conscientious manager may want to implement these activities in some form. Coulton (1987) has noted, "A successful organization continually looks for, finds, and solves problems. In this context, quality assurance—with its cycle of monitoring, in-depth problem analysis, and corrective action—serves as a self-correcting function within an organization" (p. 443).

Some businesses have been aware that quality of service is what gives them a competitive edge. In fact, something called the International Standards

Organization (ISO) 9000 has been established for business, and refers to the set of standards established for quality management and assurance. Any type of company can apply for certification, from a staffing business to pharmaceutical companies. Businesses can also apply for ISO 14000 certification, which is designed for operations directly impacting the environment, while the QS 9000 sets the standards for the automotive industry. All three of these certification procedures have been adopted by more than 98 countries and businesses worldwide. More specifically, the international quality standard ISO 9000 is a widely accepted definition of the basic features of an effective quality-management system. The ISO 9000, as it is usually known, consists of 20 clauses that cover in minute detail all of the supposed requisites for a certified quality system (Wilson, 1998). These clauses cover the procedures of a well-run business, including detailed descriptions of management responsibility, the quality system, and purchasing, to mention only three. The certification comes after inspection by an outside body that examines any organization wishing to be ISO 9000 accredited to determine whether that organization is fit for registration. After registration has been granted, the organization will be reinspected at regular intervals to ensure that it is still fit to carry the standard.

In social service programs, quality assurance is critically important as well. For example, the quality of medical care is increasingly being analyzed as managed care takes over the health care market. It is important for every agency providing services to clients to be able to identify and monitor quality.

Some human service professionals resent the amount of time it takes to document what they have already done. Especially when caseloads are large, paperwork is an anathema. Workers may feel that time spent on paperwork is time taken away from needy clients. However, viewed from a manager's perspective, this "paperwork" is needed for a variety of reasons:

1. To protect clients from unethical or inappropriate treatment. Consider these "horror stories" of two consulting physicians whose contracts were canceled by different mental health agencies. At one center, the utilization review picked up a pattern of a physician overmedicating clients and using strange combinations of drugs that did not seem to provide any benefit. Staff at the other center found that their consulting psychiatrist was diagnosing an inordinate number of clients as multiple personalities. In a more positive sense, quality assurance activities help to demonstrate that the organization cares about the services provided.
2. To protect staff from charges of inappropriate treatment or incompetence. (In this litigious society, the documentation of services rendered is some protection against unfair or untruthful claims.) Quality assurance data also can be used to identify reasons for patient dissatisfaction with services. Satisfied clients always help to improve the marketability of programs and services.
3. To recover reimbursements from insurance companies and other third parties. (As noted earlier, quality assurance activities are required by Medicare, Medicaid, and other third-party payers.)

4. To better plan for effective and efficient utilization of staff and agency resources. (Having such information as the average length of stay or the numbers of patients with certain diagnoses can help program managers evaluate special and unmet needs as well as better supervise staff whose cases exceed the average.)

Quality assurance efforts in an agency may be elaborate or fairly elementary. Figure 5.4 provides a short checklist employed by the quality assurance office of a state social services department. Routinely, this office randomly selects cases from each of its district offices, reviews them, and where necessary asks for the records to be amended or corrected. Cases with deficiencies are clearly noted and returned to the caseworker's supervisor. Supervisors must then see that problems are corrected and report to the quality assurance office.

Once data such as this are collected on a regular basis, program evaluators and researchers can use it to explore various hypotheses—for instance, that employees in one division (for example, adoptions) obtain higher quality assurance ratings than those in another (such as adult protective services). We even went a step further and utilized this data and other information available to us to investigate whether those with social work degrees made better employees for the department than those without (Dhooper, Royse, & Wolfe, 1990).

Box 5.7 provides another example of quality assurance using a unique methodology to assess quality of a children's health program.

Another important advantage of quality assurance is accountability. When the National Committee for Quality Assurance (NCQA) released its "State of Managed Care Quality" report, which evaluates the quality of managed care plans, there were some very interesting results. For example, the NCQA found that health plans that submitted data for public release performed substantially better on clinical measures and attained significantly greater member satisfaction than plans that submitted data on the condition they not be identified. Health plans that submitted data for two consecutive years reported higher scores and higher overall improvement on 8 out of 10 performance measures. Also, NCQA-accredited plans outperformed nonaccredited plans on all clinical and satisfaction measures. Thus, quality assurance efforts do make differences in overall program quality—even service programs.

TOTAL QUALITY MANAGEMENT

Green and Attkisson noted as early as 1984 that while program evaluation and quality assurance were distinctly different approaches, they were converging. They observed that quality assurance had embraced the criteria of efficiency or cost effectiveness of services (cost containment in the medical field) and adequacy of services relative to the needs present in the population. At the same time, program evaluators were becoming more comfortable with incorporating features of quality methods into their evaluations.

In the last few years there has been a resurgence of interest in the quality of goods and services available to American consumers. Japanese industries,

FIGURE 5.4 | CASEWORK EVALUATION FORM

CASEWORK EVALUATION FORM

	Yes	No
1. Was a thorough, family-based assessment completed that reflects the family's needs for ongoing services?	_____	_____
2. Is a current, family-based treatment plan in the case record that is specific enough to be utilized in providing services?	_____	_____
3. Does service delivery follow the treatment plan?	_____	_____
4. Are types, frequency, and location of professional/family contacts appropriate?	_____	_____
5. Are problem-solving strategies used during family contacts that indicate good casework skills and knowledge?	_____	_____
6. Does the professional use identified resources through collateral contacts with service providers?	_____	_____
7. Does the running record clearly document casework activity and case progress?	_____	_____
8. Is the case being managed according to present policies and procedures?	_____	_____
9. Has the professional assured the safety of the adults/child(ren) in their current living arrangement?	_____	_____
10. Are the family's perceptions and preferences included in the provision of social services when possible?	_____	_____
11. Are services directed toward strengthening the family and preventing out-of-home placements?	_____	_____

(This form is scored as follows: 1 point is awarded for each "Yes" and a 0 is given for each "No." The quality of the casework is rated "Excellent" if there are 11 points; "Good" if there are 7 to 10 points; "Fair" if there are 3 to 6 points; and "Poor" if there are only 1 or 2 points.)

particularly automobile manufacturers, have popularized and demonstrated enormous success with a concept known as "total quality management." The same concern with quality is increasingly being discussed in the human services (see, for instance, Fountain, 1992; Janes, 1993; Mawhinney, 1992; O'Hair & Meissner, 1993; Rago & Reid, 1991).

Total quality management is based on a series of principles developed by William Deming. One major aim is to reduce variation from every process so that greater consistency of effort is obtained. Quality is defined by the customer, and improvement focuses on what customers want and need. However, total quality management is not a one-shot effort and must come from top management's commitment to improvement. It often requires a change in thinking that encourages participation in the planning process by all staff members. Deming

EXAMPLE OF A STATEWIDE QUALITY ASSURANCE APPROACH

Shenkman et al. (1997) assessed a school enrollment based health insurance program entitled the "Florida Healthy Kids Program." Specifically, the authors compared children's actual health care use across five different sites to the health care use that is expected based on a child with that profile.

In order to conduct the assessment, only children enrolled 6 months or longer were included. This was because children enrolled in a health plan less than 6 months do not have an adequate diagnostic profile in the claims databases to yield valid results. Thus, the final sample resulted in 14,688 children. Health observations were measured for a 1-year time period because the amount of health care use is partially related to the time frame considered—the longer the period of observation, the more visits to the doctor. Thus, controlling the time frame so that everyone will have the same exposure period makes the results more comparable across participants. In order to examine health, each HMO provided child-specific health care use data including Physician's Current Procedural Terminology codes and International Classification of Diseases, 9th Revision Clinical Modification codes. These are specific codes that identify what diagnosis the physician made for each child visit to the doctor. Health care use data from August 1994 through July 1995 were also used in the analysis.

The authors used some special software to compare the children's actual health care use to the expected health care use at each site. The software incorporates age, gender, and diagnoses as classified during health care visits. Thus, this study compared the expected number of health care visits based on the child's health condition, gender, and age to the actual number of health care visits the children made. This is one way to measure health care quality. Results indicated that for three of the five sites, children were receiving the health care that is expected based on their diagnoses. Two sites potentially had some underuse.

The authors ended their report with the following paragraph:

> In summary, health care system reform must focus on both the cost and the quality of health care for children and must include strategies to evaluate the quality of care enrollees receive in diverse settings. The Florida Healthy Kids Program is one mechanism for providing health insurance to previously uninsured children through private sector HMOs and their provider networks. The program represents an opportunity to understand the unique health care experiences of children within managed care environments. Using a method for risk adjustment, children in this program generally are receiving the appropriate amount of health care based on their needs. As legislators contemplate future health care reform initiatives for one of the nation's most vulnerable groups, the school enrollment based concept of coverage for children represents a promising approach.

Source: Shenkman, E., Pendergast, J., Wegener, D., Hartzel, T., Naff, R., Freedman, S., Bucciarelli, R. (1997). Children's health care use in the Healthy Kids Program. *Pediatrics*, 700(6), 947–953.

suggests that employees must be given freedom to dissent and stresses the importance of eliminating all barriers to communication. The organization must create an environment that fosters disclosure without penalty by all members of an organization (Maiden, 1993).

Sometimes known as continuous quality improvement, total quality management emphasizes client satisfaction surveys and uses feedback to make refinements. Although we will talk much more about such methods in a later chapter, it should be pointed out that much of the material we have covered so far (needs assessment, mission statements, goals and objectives, process evaluation, and program monitoring) is consistent with a total quality management orientation. We will be hearing more about total quality management in the coming years as the concept sweeps through social and human services.

Martin (1993) has identified 14 different dimensions associated with program quality (see Box 5.8). Although it probably is impossible for a program manager to target all 14 simultaneously for improvement, it does make sense for management to consider how a specific program may fare on selected criteria. For instance, under accessibility: Is the agency open at times convenient for clients who are employed (e.g., evening or Saturday hours)? Is the agency located on a bus line or close to other public transportation? Is it handicapped accessible? Once it is felt that a program is sufficiently accessible, management might then want to target another dimension, such as performance (effectiveness). These dimensions will have to be operationally defined by each program. What is acceptable performance by one might not be as satisfactory for another.

Box 5.9 describes how quality assurance procedures can help save lives. Of course, most program quality control procedures are not life and death, but if the overall goal or mission of the program is to help people or to contribute to the quality of life for clients, quality assurance procedures can help make sure that happens.

It is beyond the scope of this book to outline a quality assurance program to fit your agency. Rather, the purpose of this discussion has been to help you understand how quality assurance can be used for program improvement (e.g., to identify employees who tend to make inappropriate diagnoses or treatment plans, or whose interventions are not consistent with expectations or accepted practice; to identify the need for inservice or continuing education; and to provide other useful data for management decisions).

CHAPTER RECAP

Formative and process evaluation have in common a focus on improving programs. Because of their shared concern, it should be an obligation of every practitioner and every manager to learn more about and support these qualitative forms of evaluation within their agencies or practices. To improve a program's quality, we cannot focus on only one portion of the process, such as the product at exit. We must examine *every* aspect of the program—perhaps

 | ASPECTS OF QUALITY
PROGRAMMING

- Accessibility (few problems are encountered in gaining entrance to the program)
- Assurance (staff are facilitative)
- Communication (clientele and potential clientele are kept informed about the program)
- Competence (staff are skilled and knowledgeable)
- Conformity (meets generally accepted standards for best practice)
- Deficiency (not lacking anything needed to make it a quality program)
- Durability (the impact or change produced by the program lasts)
- Empathy (therapists and staff are understanding)
- Humaneness (clients are treated with respect and dignity)
- Performance (interventions work as intended)
- Reliability (the interventions are consistent and predictable)
- Responsiveness (the time from request of assistance to delivery of program is short)
- Security (there is no danger associated with accessing or receiving the intervention)
- Tangibles (the physical environment is acceptable—for example, the facility is clean and the furniture is not worn out)

Source: Adapted from Martin (1993).

beginning with goals for the program and the mix of appropriate and inappropriate admissions.

Depending on the age, complexity, and sophistication of the agency whose program you have been asked to evaluate, you may not find mission statements or statements of program goals and objectives. In fact, your first act as an evaluator may be to assist the agency to develop mission statements and program goals. You may find yourself writing goals and objectives simply because that has never been done and no one else has any experience with writing them.

Keep in mind that a program can have more than one goal, and each goal can have multiple objectives. For instance, I once heard of a mental health agency that had purchased a fast-food restaurant. This purchase enabled the agency to employ their clients with chronic mental illness while providing them with necessary training and income to become employable in a competitive job market. The restaurant also brought in needed operational income to the agency. Each of these goals would be evaluated independently (with different criteria).

Patton (1982) has made several astute observations about management information systems. He noted that "if there is nothing you are trying to find out, there is nothing you will find out" (p. 229). He suggested that a management information system is not an "endpoint" but a beginning point for raising issues for additional study. Management information systems only provide data—they do not make decisions. An evaluation does not occur until someone uses data to answer some questions.

| BOX 5.9 | ANALYSIS OF QUALITY ASSURANCE FOR HIV SCREENING IN BLOOD TRANSFUSION PROCEDURES IN DELHI |

Although HIV transmission through blood transfusion accounts for only a small proportion of new infections, it is a very efficient way to get HIV. The risk of obtaining HIV through a blood transfusion can be minimized in two main ways: (1) by selecting donors at low risk for HIV infection; and (2) by carefully screening the donated blood for HIV antibodies. It is also important to handle the blood and blood products appropriately. In other words, it is essential to introduce an effective quality assurance program covering inspection of specimens, maintenance of equipment, choice of assay, keeping of records, and verification of results. Quality assurance in testing blood from donors for HIV also minimizes the waste of blood units based on false-positive results.

Dhingra-Kumar, Sharma, & Madan (1997) reported on the level of quality implementation by blood transfusion centers in India. They essentially conducted a spot check of working conditions in the HIV laboratories. Results indicated that of the 11 labs evaluated, none had a total score for all the parameters examined qualifying as excellent; five labs had scores indicating procedures were satisfactory, and six were unsatisfactory.

Examples of results for individual indicators are:

- Standardization of sample collection and handling needed to be improved in eight labs along with more emphasis on adherence to recommended technical procedures. For example, several of the labs had no restriction on eating, drinking, smoking, and applying cosmetics in the laboratory, while in others staff did not regularly wear gloves while working in the lab.
- The labeling procedures needed to be improved in nine of the labs. For example, blood was not always labeled clearly; not all the labs disposed of HIV-positive blood units immediately; and not all the labs practiced the most satisfactory disposal method for infected waste and blood, that is, incineration.
- The removal and destruction of HIV-positive blood units needed to be improved in five labs.
- The availability and review of standard operating procedures needed to be improved in eight labs.
- Equipment quality control and staff training needed to be improved in eight of the labs.
- Record keeping needed to be improved in six of the labs. For example, only *two* labs had a computerized record-keeping system. As another example, some of the laboratory worksheets did not uniformly mention the type, the batch and lot numbers, and the expiration date of the blood test kit used.

Source: Dhingra-Kumar, N., Sharma, A., & Madan, N. (1997). Analysis of quality assurance programmes for HIV screening in blood transfusion centres in Delhi. *Bulletin of the World Health Organization*, 75(3), 223–228.

In summary, formative evaluation is used in the beginning stages of a program to help form the program. The specific goals of process evaluation, however, are less clear. It is important to clarify what the goals of the process evaluation are. The goals may include one or some combination of all three main goals of process evaluation—describing a program, program monitoring, and quality assurance.

Finally, much of what Deming has taught about how organizations continuously improve can be summarized in four words: Plan, Do, Check, Act. In the PDCA or Deming cycle, *plan* means study a program or process by collecting data and deciding what would improve it. In the *do* step, the plan is implemented (sometimes on a small scale). In the third phase, staff *check* the results obtained so that they can make the necessary changes *(act)* in the program or process. Whenever we are in a position to provide formative or process evaluation, program monitoring, or quality assurance, we would do well to remember these four simple guides.

Questions for Class Discussion

1. What is wrong with the following objectives?
   a. To improve statewide planning capacity and capability
   b. To maximize collections from first- and third-party payers
   c. To improve the skills of current staff through appropriate inservice training
   d. To improve staff–patient ratios in state psychiatric hospitals
   e. To participate more actively in economic development activities
2. Rewrite the following objectives to improve them.
   a. The Free Clinic will facilitate early initiation of prenatal care by maintaining relations with local physicians and other agencies to facilitate referrals to the clinic.
   b. The Free Clinic will distribute brochures and posters describing the need for early prenatal care and the location of these services.
   c. For high-risk patients, the Free Clinic will perform follow-up counseling as needed.
   d. The chronically mentally ill population will be served by a new "clubhouse" aftercare program to reduce inpatient hospitalizations.
   e. By the end of 8 weeks, all group members will have developed tools to help with panic attacks and flashbacks.
3. Discuss how a board of directors would know when a program is in need of a formative evaluation.
4. Tell what you know about the various ways in which social and human service agencies in your community conduct quality assurance and program monitoring activities.
5. Discuss the extent that social and human service agencies with which your class is familiar utilize computerized management information systems. What are their advantages and disadvantages?

6. Briefly describe a local social or human service program to the class. Discuss information that would be useful for program monitoring.
7. Refer to Table 5.2. What possible explanations could there be for certain populations utilizing services less than might be expected? Could it be argued that some populations have a greater need for services than their proportion in a community's total population?
8. Discuss your experience with quality assurance programs. Viewed from a management perspective, what do you believe to be the benefits of quality assurance?

Mini-Projects: Experiencing Evaluation Firsthand

1. Choose a human service program with which you are familiar and then do the following:
   a. Briefly describe the program.
   b. Write at least one program goal.
   c. Write three specific program objectives.
2. Write a mission statement for a fictitious agency of your choosing.
3. Imagine that a friend asks you to conduct a formative evaluation of the agency where you now work or intern as a practicum student. What sort of recommendations would you expect? List at least six realistic recommendations that could apply to this agency.
4. Outline a strategy you would use to conduct a process evaluation of the same program for which you conducted the formative evaluation in exercise 3, a year after program inception.
5. Briefly describe the quality assurance procedures of a social or human service agency with which you are familiar. Draft a short paper outlining how these procedures could be improved.
6. Obtain a monthly, quarterly, or yearly report from a social or human services agency. What additional information would be useful if you were a program monitor for that program? What information is missing and should be incorporated in future reports? Draft a set of recommendations based on your reading of the reports.
7. Read one of the articles from the References and Resources section and write a short reaction paper.

References and Resources

Below, P. J., Morrisey, G. L., & Acomb, B. L. (1987). *The executive guide to strategic planning*. San Francisco: Jossey-Bass.

Chelimsky, E. (1985). *Program evaluation: Patterns and directions*. Washington, DC: American Society for Public Administration.

Commission on Accreditation of Rehabilitation Facilities. (1990). *Standards manual for organizations serving people with disabilities*. Tucson, AZ: Author.

Coulton, C. J. (1987). Quality assurance. In S. M. Rosen, D. Fanshel, and M. E.

Lutz (Eds.), *Encyclopedia of social work.* Silver Spring, MD: National Association of Social Workers.

Dehar, M., Casswell, S., & Duignan, P. (1993). Formative and process evaluation of health promotion and disease prevention programs. *Evaluation Review, 17*(2), 204–220.

Dhooper, S. S., Royse, D., & Wolfe, L. C. (1990). Does social work education make a difference? *Social Work, 35*(1), 57–61.

Drucker, P. (1980).The deadly sins in public administration. *Public Administration Review, 40*(2), 103–106.

Dyme, B. S., Blaine, J. N., Bank, J. M., & Clark, W. L. (1993).Total quality management in contracted EAPs: A vendor's perspective. *Employee Assistance Quarterly, 8*(4), 121–140.

Eustis, N. N., Kane, R. A., & Fischer, L. R. (1993). Home care quality and the home care worker: Beyond quality assurance as usual. *Gerontologist, 33*(1), 64–73.

Finnegan, J. R., Rooney, B., Viswanath, K., Elmer, P., Graves, K., Baxter, J., Hertog, J., Mullis, R., & Potter, J. (1992). Process evaluation of a home based program to reduce diet-related cancer risk: The "Win at Home" series. *Health Education Quarterly, 19*(2), 233–248.

Fountain, D. L. (1992). Avoiding the quality assurance boondoggle in drug treatment programs through total quality management. *Journal of Substance Abuse Treatment, 9,* 355–364.

Green, R. S., & Attkisson, C. C. (1984). Quality assurance and program evaluation: Similarities and differences. *American Behavioral Scientist, 27*(5), 552–582.

Harachi, T., Abbott, R., Catalano, R., Haggerty, K., & Fleming, C. (1999). Opening the black box: Using process evaluation measures to assess implementation and theory building. *American Journal of Community Psychology, 27*(5), 711–731.

Higgins, D., O'Reilly, K., Tashima, N., Crain, C., Beeker, C., Goldbaum, G.,

Elifson, C., Galavotti, C., & Guenther-Grey, C. (1996). Using formative research to lay the foundation for community level HIV prevention paper outlining how these procedures could be improved: An example from the AIDS community demonstration projects. *Public Health Reports, 111* (Suppl.), 28–35.

Janas, B. G., & Hymans, J. K. (1997). New Jersey school nurses' perceptions of school-based, prenatal nutrition education. *Journal of School Health, 67, 2,* 62–67.

Janes, R. W. (1993).Total quality management: Can it work in federal probation? *Federal Probation, 57*(4), 28–33.

Joint Commission on Accreditation of Healthcare Organizations (JCAHO). (1988). *The Joint Commission guide to quality assurance.* Chicago: Author.

Joint Commission on Accreditation of Healthcare Organizations (JCAHO). (1990). *Accreditation manual for hospitals.* Chicago: Author.

Joint Commission on Accreditation of Healthcare Organizations (JCAHO) (1991). *An introduction to quality improvement in health care: The transition from quality assurance to continuous quality improvement.* Chicago: Author.

Kaskutas, L., Morgan, P., & Vaeth, P. (1992). Structural impediments in the development of a community-based drug prevention program for youth: Preliminary analysis from a qualitative formative evaluation study. *International Quarterly of Community Health Education, 12*(3), 169–182.

Kettner, P. M., Moroney, R. M., & Martin, L. L. (1999). *Designing and managing programs: An effectiveness-based approach.* Thousand Oaks, CA: Sage.

Krisberg, B. (1980). Utility of process evaluation: Crime and delinquency programs. In M. Klein & K. Teilmann (Eds.), *Handbook of criminal justice evaluation* (pp. 217–236). Beverly Hills, CA: Sage.

Kuechler, C. F., Velasquez, J. S., & White, M. S. (1988). An assessment of human services program outcome measures: Are they credible, feasible, useful? *Administration in Social Work, 12*(3), 71–89.

Kumpfer, K. (1994). *Strengthening America's families: Promising parenting and family strategies for delinquency prevention: Users guide.* Office of Juvenile Justice and Delinquency Prevention (U.S. Department of Justice Grant No. 87-JSCS-K495). Silver Spring, MD: Aspen Systems.

Kumpfer, K., Molgaard, V., & Spoth, R. (1996). Family interventions for the prevention of delinquency and drug use in special populations. In R. Peters & R. McMahon (Eds.), *Preventing childhood disorders, substance abuse, and delinquency.* Thousand Oaks, CA: Sage.

Logan, T., Hiller, M., Leukefeld, C., & Minton, L. (in press). Drug Court Program Outcomes: Secondary Data Analysis and Interviews. *Journal of Offender Rehabilitation.*

Logan, T., Hoyt, W., McCollister, K., French, M., Leukefeld, C., & Minton, L. (2004). Economic Evaluation of Drug Court: Methodology, Results, and Policy Implications. *Evaluation and Program Planning, 27,* 4, 381–396.

Logan, T., Williams, K., Leukefeld, C., & Minton, L. (2000). A Process Evaluation of a Drug Court: Methodology and Results. *International Journal of Offender Therapy and Comparative Criminology, 44*(3), 369–394.

Maiden, R. P. (1993). Principles of total quality management and their application to employee assistance programs: A critical analysis. *Employee Assistance Quarterly, 8*(4), 11–40.

Martin, L. (1993). *Total quality management in human service organizations.* Newbury Park, CA: Sage.

Mawhinney, T. C. (1992). Total quality management and organizational behavior management: An integration for continual improvement. *Journal of Applied Behavior Analysis, 25*(3), 525–543.

Mayer, J. P., Blakely, C. H., & Johnson, C. D. (1990). Formative evaluation of a community-based maternity services program for the uninsured. *Family Community Health, 13*(3), 18–26.

Mayer, J., Housemann, R., & Piepenbrok, B. (1999). Evaluation of a campaign to improve immunization in a rural Head Start program. *Journal of Community Health, 24*(1), 13–23.

Moskowitz, J. M. (1989). Preliminary guidelines for reporting outcome evaluation studies of health promotion and disease prevention programs. *Evaluating health prevention programs* (New Directions for Program Evaluation, No. 43). San Francisco: Jossey-Bass.

National Institute on Drug Abuse. (1997). *Drug abuse prevention: What works.* (NIH Publication No. 97-4110). Rockville, MD.

O'Hair, J. R., & Meissner, P. Y. (1993). Employee assistance program total quality management in government regulated industries: The Westinghouse experience. *Employee Assistance Quarterly, 8*(4), 77–100.

Orwin, R. (2000). Assessing program fidelity in substance abuse health services research. *Addiction, 95,* Suppl. 3, S309–S327.

Patton, M. Q. (1982). *Practical evaluation.* Beverly Hills, CA: Sage.

Rago, W. V., & Reid, W. H. (1991).Total quality management strategies in mental health systems. *Journal of Mental Health Administration, 18*(3), 253–263.

Rosenheck, R., & Cicchetti, D. (1998). A mental health program report card: A multidimensional approach to performance monitoring in public sector programs. *Community Mental Health Journal, 34(*1), 85–106.

Scarpitti, F., Inciardi, J., & Pottieger, A. (1993). Process evaluation techniques for corrections-based drug treatment programs.

Journal of Offender Rehabilitation, 19(3/4), 71–79.

Segal, S. P., & Hwang, S. (1994). Licensure of sheltered-care facilities: Does it assure quality? *Social Work, 39*(1), 124–131.

Sugarman, B. (1988).The well-managed human service organization: Criteria for a management audit. *Administration in Social Work, 12*(4), 17–27.

Tash, W. R., & Stahler, G. J. (1984). Current status of quality assurance in mental health. *American Behavioral Scientist, 27*(5), 608–630.

Tash, W. R., Stahler, G. J., & Rappaport, H. (1982). Evaluating quality assurance programs. In G. J. Stahler & W. R. Tash (Eds.), *Innovative approaches to mental health evaluation.* New York: Academic Press.

U.S. Department of Health and Human Services, Administration for Children and Families, Office of Community Services. *Evaluation guidebook: Demonstration partnership program projects.* (1992). Washington, DC: U.S. Government Printing Office.

U.S. Department of Justice. (1997, January). *Defining drug courts: The key components.* Office of Justice Programs, Drug Courts Programs Office.

Veney, J. E., & Kaluzny, A. D. (1984). *Evaluation and decision making for health services programs.* Englewood Cliffs, NJ: Prentice-Hall.

Wilson, H. (1998). *Do the right things right.* (Quality assurance using ISO 9000 standards.) Quality Progress, December 27–30.

SINGLE SYSTEM
RESEARCH DESIGNS

CHAPTER 6

WHAT ARE SINGLE SYSTEM
RESEARCH DESIGNS?

Single system research designs (SSRDs) have been used by social workers for clinical and program evaluation purposes for over three decades (see Thyer & Thyer, 1992). The topic made its debut in the professional social work literature through a seminal article in the *Encyclopedia of Social* Work, authored by Richard Stuart (1971). The early social work evaluation book by Michael Austin and his colleagues (1982) contains a whole chapter on the use of single case evaluation methods; an article by Elizabeth Mutschler (1979) described their use in a family service agency. This trend has continued through to the present, witness this present work as well as recent social work books dealing with the topic of evidence-based practice, which also include positive presentations on this approach to evaluation (e.g., Cournoyer, 2004; Gibbs, 2003; Jordan & Franklin, 2003). Several hundred research articles using single system research designs have appeared in all major social work journals, and there are enough textbooks on the topic to fill a small bookshelf.

These designs are a versatile methodology that may fruitfully be employed for most of the program evaluation purposes presented in this book, including needs assessments, formative program evaluations, quality assurance studies, and summative program evaluations.

Although we may tend of think of SSRDs having their greatest applicability to the evaluation of practice with individuals, the reality is that they also have considerable relevance to evaluate group work, organizational (see Daniels, 1989), and community practice (see Thyer, 1998), as well as a role in the evaluation of welfare and other forms of public policy (see Greene et al., 1987). Indeed, in many contexts, SSRDs may be the research method of choice, offering significant advantages over group designs or other forms of structured scientific inquiry.

Single system research designs are not easy to categorize as primarily a quantitative or a qualitative method. With their insistence on the use of outcome measures with documented reliability and validity, they are consistent with quantitative approaches. But the widespread practice of presenting all SSRD data in the form of simple line graphs, to make inferences primarily using the qualitative method of visual inference, and to not use inferential statistics for this purpose, is of course congruent with the traditions of qualitative methods. Although the outcome measures used in SSRDs usually take the form of some type of quantitative measurement (as in how much), this not always need be the case. For example, some outcome measures are simple dichotomous variables—was something present or absent?—without measuring the quantity involved. This could be something literal, like school attendance on the part of a given child, or the weekly results of a urine test for illegal drugs, for example, positive or negative, for a given client. Did the agency meet its goal for number of clients this week? Yes or no. This can be plotted on a graph over time, and if the numbers of "yes" responses is seen to obviously increase over some months (without being quantified or subjected to inferential tests), can this be most properly considered to be primarily a quantitative or qualitative research method? The answer is not obvious.

The phrase *single system research designs* has a number of synonyms, including interrupted time series research designs, single case experimental designs, and idiographic research designs. We have chosen single *system* research designs, as this term best reflects the fact that the unit of analysis can cover many different types of client systems—micro, meso, and macro. The prerequisites for conducting an SSRD are few and easy to understand (although they may be difficult to carry out in real life!). They are:

1. Select a practical and valid outcome measure that can be repeatedly assessed over time.
2. Assess this outcome measure over time.
3. Display the results on a graph, with time on the horizontal axis, and the outcome measure on the vertical axis.
4. Make any inferences that are *reasonable*. Ask yourself the following questions:
   a. Are the data showing client improvement?
   b. Are the data demonstrating client deterioration?
   c. Do the data depict no change?
   d. Are the data unclear?

These four steps can be seen as an attempt to deal with the recommendation made by Mary Richmond over 80 years ago (Richmond, 1935/1917):

> Special efforts should be made to ascertain whether abnormal manifestations are *increasing* or *decreasing* in number and intensity, as this often has a practical bearing on the management of the case. (p. 435)

SELECTING OUTCOME MEASURES

Outcome measures useful for single system research must possess several features. Among these features are the properties of reliability, validity, and sensitivity to change. Reliability has several dimensions. First is consistency. If multiple measures are taken of a program when nothing about the program has *really* changed, then the measure should yield the same information on each application. Second, the measure should be fairly easy to gather. Agency records and other archival material can be useful sources of data applicable for SSRDs. Alternatively, program evaluators can make prospective plans to gather additional, nonservice-related information specifically intended for evaluation purposes. If two people independently extract data from records, or prospectively gather or score the same data, their figures should agree. Data lacking good inter-rater agreement are suspect.

If standardized instruments are used, they should be relatively brief, easy to score, and understandable, and they should clearly pertain to the agency's mission. The Minnesota Multiphasic Personality Inventory (MMPI) is one measure that violates these principles. It consists of over 400 questions and is awkward to hand score (but can be machine scored for a considerable fee). Few agencies are in the business of personality change per se, and with repeated administrations, clients' MMPI scores tend to drift for reasons unrelated to program efficacy (Kelley, Jacobs, & Farr, 1994). Thus, the MMPI does not lend itself to most forms of program evaluation.

It may not be necessary, however, to seek a standardized measure to evaluate your practice using a SSRD.

The most direct approach to selecting an outcome measure is to ask, "What is the agency's mission?" As we discussed in Chapter 5, most agencies have a mission statement, charter, or charge. If not, ask the agency director and other professional staff this question. Usually the response allows you to identify the agency's mission. For example, an agency charged with providing child protective services may have several goals. One goal may be to *prevent* child abuse from occurring; a second may be to intervene so that child abuse does not recur after initially being brought to the attention of the agency. A foster care and adoption agency may have as its goal the placement of children in suitable foster homes or with adoptive families. A psychiatric service would be interested in working with clients to ameliorate behavioral, cognitive, and affective symptoms. A voter registration drive would aim to sign up unregistered voters and help them get to the polls. In intensive family preservation programs, the goal is to avert imminent family breakup, usually because of the risk of abuse or neglect.

In each of these examples, outcome measures seem to be clear. Official reports of child abuse or domestic violence may be useful outcome measures for child protective service agencies, whereas the numbers of children placed in foster care or with adoptive families each month or year by year are natural outcome indicators for those providing foster care and adoption services (see Briggs,1994, for one such example). Measures of psychiatric symptomatology that can be repeatedly administered are useful for evaluating change in clients at a mental health agency; the numbers of new voters registered and the numbers of these new registrants who actually cast ballots would be good indicators of the efficacy of a voter registration drive. In general, the closer you can keep your choice of outcome measure to the *real* issue being addressed by the agency, the better.

For example, suppose an agency serves women who have a history of abusing their children. Drawing on research that shows that abusive mothers tend to be more socially insular—they are alone with their children a great deal of the time with little adult contact, or they lack a social support network—an agency may devise an intervention that is aimed at expanding the social networks of these mothers in the hope that this will reduce the potential for abuse. A program evaluation could be undertaken of this approach, using a standardized measure of social insularity as an outcome measure. Note, however, that the concept of reducing social insularity is somewhat removed from the core mission of the agency—preventing child abuse. A program evaluation that shows reductions in social insularity but lacks data on incidents of child abuse could be faulted for not having *direct* evidence that the agency was accomplishing its mission. If indirect indicators are used, it is best to complement them with more direct ones. For a program outcome measure to be valid, it should provide an *accurate* indicator of what it is supposed to be measuring. For example, a written client self-report measure of drug abuse is not as direct (or as valid) an outcome measure as are periodic random urine tests for illicit substances.

Often we must acknowledge from the outset that outcome measures are flawed. *Reports* of domestic violence do not capture all occurrences of violent episodes. This is also true for child abuse and neglect reports, allegations of rape, and so on. Brief mental status examinations provide a measure of cognitive functioning of persons with chronic mental illness but are not a measure of their actual *thinking*. So, for practical purposes, we must do the best that we can with the available range of measures. Of course, this means choosing the *best* available indicators. It is professionally irresponsible to not make use of the best measures that are currently supported by empirical research, which are also practical, low-cost, reliable, and valid. Attempting to choose "best-supported" measures needs to be properly tempered with pragmatic considerations. (More information on how to locate and evaluate instruments for program evaluation is contained in Chapter 11.)

If the "best" measure is too expensive, then it is reasonable to consider the next best, and so on. This should not be grounds for rationalizing the use of poor measures, however. Frankly, if your outcome measure(s) is not reliable and valid, you should not waste time in attempting to evaluate practice or programs.

The well-known Michigan Alcoholism Screening Test (MAST) is a valid tool to help assess clients, but it is a poor measure for program evaluation. Why?

Consider the following items taken from the MAST:

8. *Have you ever attended a meeting of Alcoholics Anonymous (AA)?* (Yes or No)

17. *Have you ever been told you have liver trouble?* (Yes or No)

Although good initial screening questions, these MAST items are not useful for program evaluation because they are not sensitive to *change*. Even a recovering alcoholic who had not touched a drop of booze in 10 years would not show improvement (change in a positive direction) by answering such questions (and there are many like these on the MAST), because they will not change. To undertake a program evaluation using SSRDs requires that you familiarize yourself with the state-of-the-art outcome measures applicable to your agency, have the skills to choose the best ones (or seek skilled consultation in making such selections), and make use of them appropriately.

ASSESSING MEASURES OVER TIME

The repeated administration of a scientifically credible outcome measure can follow several strategies, depending on the purpose of the evaluation study itself. These strategies comprise the various *designs* used to construct an SSRD. The four variations are to:

1. Take repeated assessments of some measure *without* any intervention. This would occur, for example, when using a SSRD in the context of a needs assessment. This type of study can tell you (with *data,* as opposed to guessing or by intuition) if a problem is getting better, worse, or staying pretty much the same, over time.
2. Take repeated assessments of some measure *at the same time you begin* intervention. This approach would be used when it is inappropriate to delay intervention and generally results in a research design of lower internal validity. This measure can tell you if a client or system improved, got worse, or stayed the same during the course of intervention.
3. Take repeated assessments of some measure *before you begin* intervention. This is called taking a *baseline* and may be useful when you have existing or archival data that can serve as your baseline, or when delaying intervention so that a baseline may be developed. This can tell you if a client or system improved, got worse, or stayed the same after intervention was introduced, *compared to* functioning prior to treatment.
4. Take repeated assessments of some measure *before and after* intervention. This measurement may result in the most internally valid form of SSRD. It may tell you if any changes were *caused* by a program or other intervention.

We will now describe how SSRDs can be used for various program evaluation purposes, including needs assessments, formative evaluations, quality assurance studies, and summative evaluations.

TABLE 6.1	BURGLARIES WITHIN THE ROCKSPRINGS NEIGHBORHOOD DURING THE PAST TWO YEARS

Year	Month	Number of Burglaries
2003	January	9
	February	10
	March	8
	April	10
	May	8
	June	10
	July	11
	August	10
	September	12
	October	11
	November	13
	December	12
2004	January	8
	February	11
	March	9
	April	14
	May	9
	June	10
	July	13
	August	10
	September	14
	October	13
	November	14
	December	14

NEEDS ASSESSMENTS

Single system research designs can make invaluable contributions to a needs assessment process. If, for instance, members of a local community were concerned with an apparently growing number of burglaries in their neighborhood, they could petition or lobby the city government to provide greater police protection through increased patrols and decreased response time.

FIGURE 6.1 | BURGLARIES IN THE ROCKSPRINGS NEIGHBORHOOD

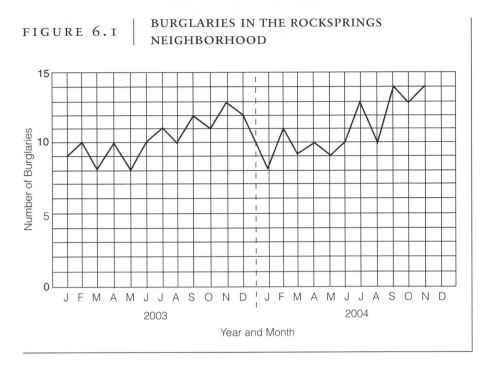

Depending on political influence and available resources, such increased police protection may or may not be forthcoming.

One way to increase the likelihood of community complaints being responded to by leaders or administrators is to systematically gather data *over time* that will corroborate (or refute) perceptions of an increase in burglaries. The police department has records of burglaries going back for several years. Citizens can compile these reports and plot on a graph the numbers of burglaries occurring within a given neighborhood on a month-by-month basis. The visual portrayal of data is a more powerful method of illustrating an increase in burglaries than a column of numbers. Compare Table 6.1 with Figure 6.1, and imagine presenting these illustrations at a city council meeting. Which do you think makes a more compelling argument for increasing police protection?

NOTATION AND GENERAL PRINCIPLES

Single system research designs have their own schematic code to describe their features. An **A** refers to a baseline phase, a period where reliable and valid data are gathered in a systematic manner that extends over some time frame *in the absence of a particular intervention*. A **B** refers to a design phase when the same reliable and valid data are gathered in a manner similar to that used in an **A** phase *during or after a particular intervention is implemented*. A **C** could refer to a still different phase. Thus, using these symbols, assessing a problem or situation over time is called an **A** design (baseline only); an **A-B** design consists of a baseline phase followed by a period of intervention; an **A-B-A** study examines what happens when an intervention follows a baseline period, and then that intervention is removed, followed by a second baseline phase. Similarly, an **A-B-A-B** design consists of alternating baseline-intervention-baseline-intervention phases; and a **B-A-B** design involves recording data while an intervention is in place, again after it has been removed, and yet again after its reinstatement. An **A-B-A-C** design allows for a possible comparison of the efficacy of intervention **B** versus intervention **C**; and so forth. The numbers of possible permutations are lengthy, but in practice most SSRDs used in program evaluation are relatively simple.

A common question is "How many data points do I need for each phase?" The answer is "The more the better." Two are better than one; three better than two; and so forth. Any two points can be connected to depict a line, but it takes a minimum of three data points to infer a trend, and more are better. One well-respected journal that publishes research using SSRDs almost exclusively (*Journal of Applied Behavior Analysis*) found that the modal (most common) number of data points in the individual phases of SSRDs published in *JABA* was only four. As a general standard, ask yourself, "Can I visually infer any changes occurring in the data, either within or between phases? If so, can I be confident that my inferences are accurate?" If the answers to those questions are "yes," then you have enough data.

The exception is that some methods of statistical analysis require relatively larger numbers of data points. For example, the inferential tool called "time series analysis" (a sophisticated statistical tool sometimes accompanying the use of SSRDs) may require over 50 data points in order to calculate statistics. However, most forms of program evaluation discussed in this chapter do not make use of inferential statistics.

Figure 6.1 could be said to represent the **A** design, data gathered during a period of time without any special intervention being applied. You can see that an **A** design lends itself quite naturally to the purposes of a needs assessment "to verify that a problem either currently ignored or being treated unsuccessfully exists in sufficient degree to warrant a new or additional intervention" (Rossi & Freeman, 1985, p. 107).

Some have contended that initial baseline phases are an essential feature of SSRDs, but such is not the case (witness the design **B-A-B**). Also, note that the term *baseline* applies to single system research designs, not to group designs. A baseline is quite literally that, a *line* or *series* of data points connected on a graph. It does not refer to the single-point-in-time measures associated with the pretreatment assessments characteristic of group designs, such as the **O-X-O** design that we will discuss later. Data for group designs are typically gathered on single occasions, reported descriptively and inferentially using statistics, and presented in tables reporting numbers like means and percentages, not graphs of connected data points. Data gathered before intervention and investigated using group designs are best referred to as the "pretest." Data gathered before intervention and evaluated using SSRDs are called the "baseline."

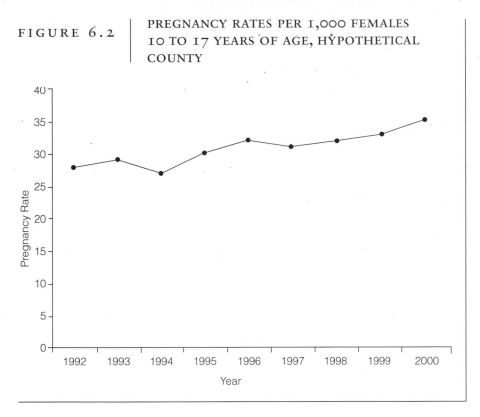

FIGURE 6.2 | PREGNANCY RATES PER 1,000 FEMALES
10 TO 17 YEARS OF AGE, HYPOTHETICAL
COUNTY

Adolescent pregnancy is said to be a growing problem, but is it? Where are the data? Are adolescents getting pregnant more often than they were 10 years ago? Take a look at Figure 6.2, which plots teenage pregnancy rates from 1992 to 2000 in a hypothetical county. Just by looking at the data it seems that the numbers of pregnancies occurring among females aged 10 to 17 years old increased from about 30 to 37 or 38 per 1,000. Another way to portray this is to note that pregnancies increased from about 3 percent to near 3.8 percent over this 9-year period. You do not need the statistical expertise of a rocket scientist to look at Figure 6.2 and determine that there were more pregnancies in the later years. Human service workers and community activists armed with graphic data like these are in a good position to argue for a need for pregnancy prevention programs in schools and related services.

FORMATIVE EVALUATIONS

Recall from Chapter 5 that formative evaluations are used to adjust and enhance existing interventions or programs. Single system research designs can be used for this purpose, as illustrated by a study conducted by J. Timothy Stocks when he was an MSW intern at a group home operated by Goodwill

Industries for persons with physical and mental disabilities (see Stocks, Thyer, & Kearsley, 1987).When Tim arrived at the group home to begin his internship, he found a point system in place, a program whereby residents earned points for performing daily living tasks (laundry, washing dishes, housekeeping, personal grooming). These points could be redeemed for extra consumable items (snacks and drinks) and privileges above and beyond what were noncontingently available to all group home residents. This point system had been in place for over 10 years, and no systematic evaluation of its usefulness had been undertaken during that time. Would the residents do their chores without contingent points being awarded by the staff? Maybe the point program could be dropped entirely, or maybe it should be improved. Tim approached the group home manager about conducting such a study and received permission.

Tim and the group home staff kept careful daily records for a week, tabulating the chores done by residents in exchange for points redeemable for privileges. This corresponded to a **B** phase, data gathered on an existing intervention. Thus, he had seven data points (total numbers of points earned per day by group home residents). During week 2, the group home manager informed the residents that they no longer needed to perform chores to earn points for extra privileges. The extras would be provided irrespective of how much they helped out in the running of the group home, chores, and personal care. Tim and the staff continued to monitor the residents' performance of such tasks. They recorded data daily for another 7 days, in the same manner as in the first week. This second week can be viewed as an **A** phase, gathering data in the absence of an intervention (in this case, the contingent point system). Finally, during the third week the program manager announced the restoration of the traditional point system. Privileges would once again be contingent on earning points through the performance of chores. This can be construed as a return to the initial **B** phase. When graphed, the data appeared as in Figure 6.3. We can see that the residents' performance of chores (as reflected by daily points accrued) underwent a significant dip during the week the point system was discontinued. Moreover, when the point system was restored, the performance of chores went back up. There appears to be a clear functional relationship between the point program and the performance of chores. As a result of this and other elements of Tim's evaluation, the point system was altered to make it even more effective.

Another example of using an SSRD for the purposes of conducting a formative evaluation is provided by Nugent, Bruley, and Allen (1999).The practice setting was a runaway shelter that served adolescents. The problem was antisocial behavior (e.g., stealing, aggression, or vandalism) committed by the clients while they stayed at the shelter. Careful records were kept of the weekly frequency of antisocial behavior, retrospectively for over 300 days prior to an intervention intended to reduce antisocial behavior, and prospectively for over 200 days after the intervention. The psychosocial intervention was a well-proceduralized program called Aggression Replacement Therapy (ART) provided to the adolescents while they stayed at the shelter. The results for the female adolescents are depicted in Figure 6.4 (a separate graph in the original report presents the male data, which were very similar). A mean line plotted

FIGURE 6.3 | AVERAGE NUMBER OF POINTS EARNED PER DAY BY 12 DISABLED ADULT HALFWAY HOUSE RESIDENTS

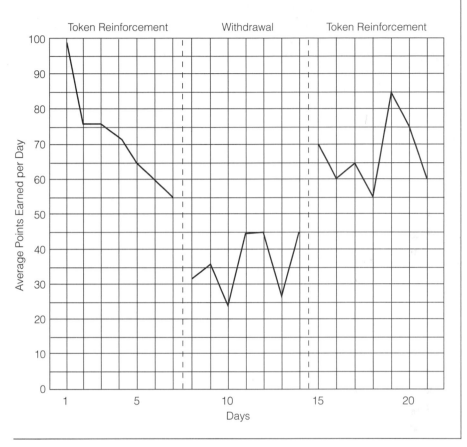

Source: Stocks, J. T., Thyer, B. A., & Kearsley, M. A. (1987). Using a token economy in a community-based residential program for disabled adults: An empirical evaluation leads to program modification. *Behavioral Residential Treatment, 1*, 173–185. Used with permission of John Wiley & Sons.

through the average of the data in each phase helps in the visual interpretation of the results. Inferential statistics calculated by Nugent et al. showed that the introduction of ART was followed by about a 30 percent reduction in anti-social behavior. This is a clear benefit and resulted in the permanent incorporation of ART into the psychosocial services provided by the runaway shelter staff. The fact that these results were used to help improve an existing program's services is one of the characteristics that defines this example as one of a formative evaluation. But this study did not address the helpfulness of the runaway shelter's services themselves.

A final example of using SSRDs in formative evaluation is presented in Engelman, Altus, Mosier, and Mathews (2003). The practice setting was a nursing home, which provided care for individuals with dementia. The problem was

FIGURE 6.4 | WEEKLY FREQUENCY OF FEMALE ANTISOCIAL BEHAVIOR

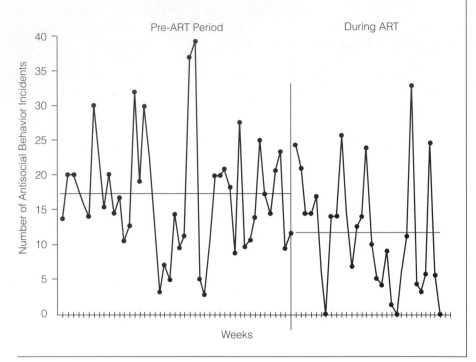

Note: Weekly number of female antisocial behavior incidents as a function of study phase. Horizontal lines indicate phase means.

Source: Nugent et al., *Research on Social Work Practice*, 9, p. 466–507, copyright © 1999 by Sage Publication. Reprinted by permission of the publisher.

the way in which direct care staff (Certified Nursing Assistants, or CNAs) undertook dressing the patients. Initially they approached dressing the patients as if they (the patients) were completely passive, treating them, in effect, like mannequins. Arms would be grabbed and thrust into sleeves, buttons would be fastened, zippers zipped, and voila, dressing was completed. From the nursing home and patient care perspective, it is instead desirable that patients be provided with maximum opportunities to participate in their own care, and prompted to provide as much self-initiated care as possible. Staff use of prompts while dressing patients was baselined and found to very rarely occur. Then, the CNAs were provided with individualized training in the "system of least prompts," a well-established training program aimed at helping patients to become more independent in dressing. When CNA #1 was provided training, that person's use of prompts marked increased, whereas CNA #2's use of prompts remained minimal. The effect was replicated over several different patients, and provided compelling evidence that the training program really did have a positive effect on the CNAs use of prompts when dressing patients. Again, the program evaluation was formative in nature, trying to improve the quality of existing services provided by staff, without looking to see if clients' lives themselves have been improved.

QUALITY ASSURANCE STUDIES

Another use of the versatile SSRD is for the purpose of conducting quality assurance (QA) studies. Quality assurance is most often construed as a checklist approach, reviewing paper records to determine compliance with various regulations. However, SSRD data are useful for the purposes of continued-stay utilization reviews, systematic audits of clinical records necessary to justify extended hospital stays, and outpatient treatments. Neuhring and Pascone (1986) contend that SSRDs are "capable of contributing to peer review questions, utilization reviews, clinical care evaluation studies, and profile analysis" (p. 359) and provide several examples of using SSRDs in peer review.

Neuhring and Pascone (1986, p. 364) show a graph depicting average length of stays on three different hospital units. Baseline phases for each unit depict the average length of stay (in months) for patients being treated at that unit. One unit had zero social workers, the second had one social worker, and the third unit had two social workers. When units one and two each added one social worker to their staff, length of stays declined. When units one and two then added discharge planning on admission as a part of the treatment plan, length of stays declined further still. When unit three added the element of discharge planning beginning at admission to its social work program (which already had two social workers), average patient length of stays declined again. Average length of stay data were plotted on a simple graph, one for each unit, with monthly data tabulated for a 2-year period. This is a fine example of making use of SSRDs, and these authors concluded that "several of the customary quality-assurance methodologies—peer review, continued stay utilization review, retrospective chart audits, clinical care evaluation studies, and profile analysis—may readily be operationalized using single-case designs" (Neuhring & Pascone, 1986, p. 364).

Johnson and Fawcett (1994) used a multiple baseline across individuals design to evaluation the effectiveness of a staff training program provided to employees of an antipoverty agency funded by the United Way. The agency provided free used clothing, food, information and referral services, and other forms of support to over 400 poor families each year. The agency's receptionists—those who had the most contact with clients—were the focus of the study. Courteous service and interactions (e.g., active listening, politely asking questions) were operationally defined and baselined for each of the three receptionists. Unobtrusive observations by independent raters obtained very high inter-rater reliabilities. Then, specific training in treating clients courteously was provided to one receptionist, Ann, but not to the others. Then it was provided to Sue, but not to Connie, who finally received it after the other two. Thus, a staggered baseline was developed.

Each receptionist's courtesy immediately and dramatically improved following the introduction of training, but not before (see Figure 6.5). After a peak of near 100 percent courtesy following the initial training, it began to

FIGURE 6.5 | PERCENTAGES OF RECEPTIONISTS'
APPROPRIATE COURTESY BEHAVIORS

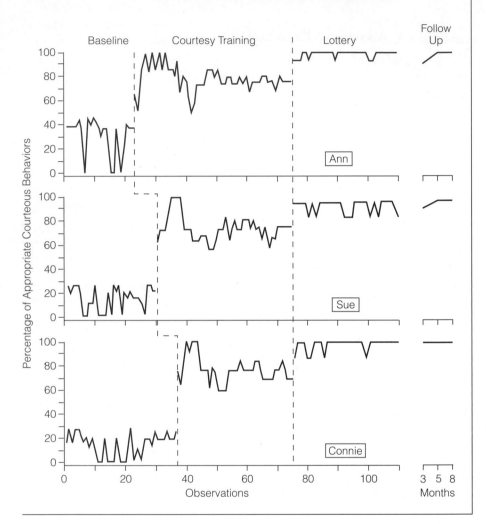

Note: The percentage of appropriate courtesy behaviors for each of the participants during each observation session. Baseline data were collected during February, courtesy training data were collected during March and April, lottery data were collected during May and June, and follow-up data were collected during July, September, and December.

Source: From Johnson & Fawcett (1994). Courtesy service: Its assessment and modification in a human service organization. *Journal of Applied Behavior Analysis, 27,* p. 145–152.

decline, prompting the trainers to introduce a further element, a lottery. The three receptionists were entered into the lottery based on the numbers of courteous client and staff interactions that were observed—the more polite they were with clients, the more entries each had placed in the lottery. The prize, based on a random drawing, was a $10 weekly cash award. At follow-up, 3, 5, and 8 months later, courteous behavior remained at very high levels. The initial training of the receptionists in interacting courteously with clients was fairly brief and low cost, and combined with the lottery seemed remarkably effective. This study can be construed as a form of quality assurance study, in that it was evaluating a program intended to assure greater quality (i.e., courteous service) of the services provided by the antipoverty agency. It was not, however, an evaluation of the effectiveness of the antipoverty program's services themselves.

SUMMATIVE EVALUATION DESIGNS

Summative program evaluation studies are those that provide an empirically based appraisal of the results, or final outcomes, of an innovative program. In order to do this, a more robust type of SSRD is needed. Before jumping to those designs, however, we need to learn about the B design and the very serviceable A-B design.

In Chapter 9, we describe the application of several simple group summative evaluation designs. The purpose of studies using summative evaluation designs is to answer the general question "Did our clients get better?" This can be paraphrased: "Did our program achieve its goals?" "Are things getting better?" "Did things improve after a new policy was implemented?" Often, program evaluators want to know only if meaningful changes have occurred within a given program—*not* to prove that a program *is responsible for* observed improvements. The question "Did clients improve *because of* their participation in a given program?" requires considerably more complex designs. It is much more difficult to prove that a particular program's services were causally responsible for observed changes than to show that changes occurred. Yet, most programs do not have adequate information to answer the question "Did our clients get better?" and it is immensely useful to obtain such data. SSRD counterparts to simple group designs can be used in evaluating program outcomes, and two of these will be reviewed next.

When using the B design, one gathers data (outcome measures) that occur coincident with the implementation of a new program, service, or policy. There is no preceding baseline or no-treatment phase. Thus, one cannot compare data from a time when the program was in effect and when it was not in effect. However, the B design does allow one to answer the question "Did things get better when this program was implemented?" or to test the predictive hypothesis "Implementation of Program X will be accompanied by an improvement in outcome measure Y." However, causal inference is not possible.

It is not legitimate in most cases, even with the most positive of improvements, to claim that the improvements were *caused* by Program X, because the B design does not allow one to rule out alternative explanations and threats to internal validity (more on these threats in Chapter 9). For instance, maybe the outcome measure was improving before Program X began, and the graphed results simply reflect a previous trend in the data. Or, maybe something happened in the community coincident with the implementation of Program X, and it was this concurrent historical variable that *really* caused the observed improvements. Maybe the process of being evaluated in some way affected the outcome measure, causing it to drift in the direction of improvement. Rival explanations such as these typically remain to plague the program evaluator attempting to study various programs using the B design. Nevertheless, this simple approach is *very useful* when programs have *no data at all* to show that things are getting better (much less data permitting causal inferences). It is also the design of choice if it is not logistically feasible or ethically appropriate to delay implementation of a new program in order to gather baseline data. So, go ahead and use the B design, but be modest about your conclusions.

The next logical improvement to the B design is the A-B design, which was used to evaluate a new public policy regarding the use of safety belts. Impressive statistics illustrate the immense carnage on our nation's highways because of motor vehicle accidents. Equally good data have shown that one's risk of being seriously injured or killed can be cut in half if one is wearing a safety belt when an accident occurs. Hoping to reduce injuries and deaths, a large number of states have enacted mandatory safety belt use laws (MUL) requiring drivers (and sometimes passengers) to wear a safety belt. In September 1988, the State of Georgia implemented a rather weak MUL: Drivers could be cited for not being belted only if they were stopped for an unrelated offense (e.g., speeding), and the fines were small (maximum of $25). Margaret Robertson, an MSW student at the University of Georgia, obtained monthly statistics on the numbers of injuries and fatalities per month and the death rate per 100 million miles driven for the 12 months before and after the implementation of the Georgia MUL. Robertson hypothesized that if the MUL were effective, injuries, fatalities, and the death rate would decline in the year after the MUL was in effect. The data are presented in Figures 6.6 and 6.7, which illustrate the numbers of persons seriously injured during the 12 months before and after the MUL and the death rate per 100 million miles driven (a statistic that adjusts for the possibility that more or less driving occurred within Georgia during the 2 years). These data are taken from Thyer and Robertson (1993).

Visual inspection does not suggest that injuries or the death rate appreciably declined, and statistical analysis supports the conclusion of no post-law reduction occurring in these two variables (or in the numbers killed each year). The authors' interpretation of these data was that the Georgia MUL provided for ineffective contingencies. They suggested ways in which the law could be improved so that it could become more effective, as has been demonstrated in other states with stiffer laws mandating safety-belt use. The benefits of empirically examining the effects of public policies like this one are obvious. How will we know which laws need improving if they are not regularly subjected to some form of evaluation?

The A-B design helps to eliminate the threat that a pretreatment trend may have been present, as the baseline data can be used for comparison purposes to rule out that possibility. It also helps exclude the rival hypothesis that the very act of evaluating (measuring) somehow affected the situation, because such measurement effects would likely also occur when gathering the baseline data. The threat of some concurrent historical variable accounting for any observed improvements is not usually ruled out by the A-B design, hence its designation as an evaluation design, not an experimental design. If circumstances permit,

FIGURE 6.6 | NUMBER OF PERSONS INJURED IN MOTOR VEHICLE ACCIDENTS IN GEORGIA FOR THE 12 MONTHS PRIOR TO AND FOLLOWING PASSAGE OF THE GEORGIA MANDATORY SAFETY BELT USE LAW

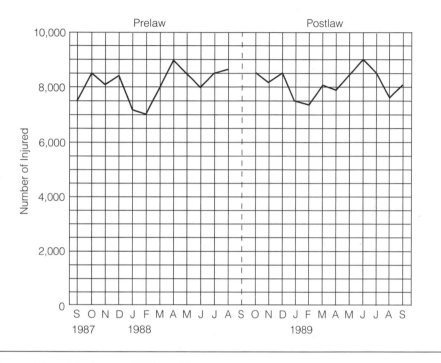

Source: Thyer & Robertson (1993), p. 510.

use the **A-B** in lieu of the **B** design. Archival or retrospective data may be useful for developing baselines and help you evaluate many programs.

EXPERIMENTAL DESIGNS

For program evaluation purposes, an **experimental SSRD** can be considered a research design that permits a reasonable degree of *causal inference*. An experimental design allows the program evaluator to be relatively confident that the *program* was responsible for any observed improvements rather than some extraneous variables (threats to internal validity). In SSRDs, threats to internal validity are removed by repeatedly demonstrating a functional relationship between the introduction or the removal of an intervention and some corresponding change in the outcome measure. By definition this is not feasible in the **B** design. It is also possible that things may have been improving at the same time program X was implemented. In the **A-B** design, the skeptic who is faced with improvements that began immediately after a new program was

FIGURE 6.7 | DEATH RATE PER 100 MILLION MILES DRIVEN IN GEORGIA FOR THE 12 MONTHS PRIOR TO AND FOLLOWING PASSAGE OF THE GEORGIA MANDATORY SAFETY BELT USE LAW

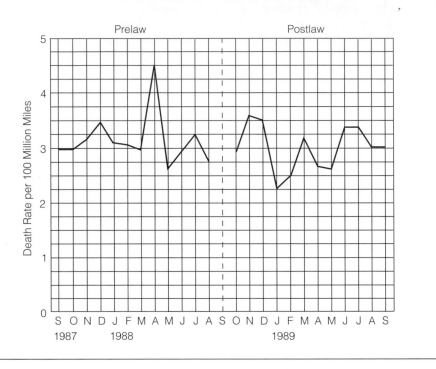

Source: Thyer & Robertson (1993), p. 510.

initiated could contend, "Well, maybe it was just a coincidence that improvements occurred right after the program began." In many cases this criticism is justified. Things occur in the natural environment, and lacking control over them means that clients in a program can be affected unbeknownst to the evaluator. Hence, the **A-B** design permits an evaluation of change (Did it improve?) but not causal inference (Did it improve *because* of the new program?).

Causal inference typically requires some type of experimental design. Experimental SSRDs are, of course, more rigorous than the simple **A-B** designs but do not meet one very important criterion said to characterize "true" experiments—that is, *random* assignment to a control or intervention condition. Partly for this reason Bloom, Fischer, and Orme (1995) refer to experimental single system designs as *experimental removal designs* (because the intervention is stopped or removed)—which helps us to remember that these are distinct from the experimental group research designs that will be discussed in Chapter 9. They state that inferring causal inference with single system designs requires "persistent concomitant variation" (p. 312) between the application of the intervention and changes that occur in the targeted behavior.

For instance, changes in behavior should be observed only after and not before the intervention is applied (this is called temporal arrangement).

The simplest of these experimental SSRD designs is called the **A-B-A** design, where a baseline phase is followed by intervention, which is then deliberately or inadvertently removed, and data continues to be collected following removal of the intervention. The idea behind the **A-B-A** design is that if two consecutive meaningful changes in outcome measures can be produced, one of improvement when the program is begun and the second of deterioration when it is removed, then it is much less likely that some coincidental happening unrelated to the program was responsible for these changes. The **A-B-A** design can also be seen as having a built-in effort to monitor or follow-up with clients postintervention. It allows practitioners the ability to assess whether intervention effects are maintained long term. Following is a simple example taken from Thyer, Thyer, and Massa (1991).

A social worker was consulting at a local senior citizens' center where a program provided a free hot lunch to local seniors. It was noted that many of the seniors who ate lunch at the center did not wear their automobile safety belts. The center director agreed that it would be useful to help promote safety belt usage among these elderly drivers. For 7 days an observer parked in the street and unobtrusively recorded safety-belt use of drivers leaving the senior center between noon and 1:00 P.M. The outcome measure was the *percentage* of drivers exiting each day who were buckled up. Data were gathered for 7 consecutive days.

The independent variable (intervention) was a female graduate social work student standing at the parking lot exit and displaying a sign to the exiting drivers. The sign read "Please Buckle Up—I Care" on one side (see Geller, Bruff, & Nimmor, 1985, for a description of this sign and its use). If drivers were wearing seat belts, the student flipped the sign over as they drove by, displaying the message "Thank You for Buckling Up." The sign was displayed from noon to 1:00 P.M., and observations of safety-belt use continued as before. This 14-day period constituted the **B** phase of the study. Finally, the display of the sign was discontinued, and baseline conditions were reinstated for 6 consecutive days, constituting the second **A** phase and completing the **A-B-A** design.

To establish reliability, an observer (an MSW student) independently rated over-the-shoulder safety-belt use on half of the days of the study. A very high inter-rater agreement was obtained between the two observers, suggesting that the recording methods were reliable. The data are depicted in Figure 6.8.

During the first A phase, only 42 percent of the drivers were buckled up; during the B phase (display of the sign), safety-belt use increased to 60 percent; use declined to 48 percent during the second A phase. It seems clear that safety-belt use improved during the prompting condition, relative to the first baseline, and declined after the prompt was removed. It is implausible (but not impossible) to argue that these changes occurred by coincidence, hence internal validity is relatively high in this simple design.

Obviously, **A-B-A** designs have shortcomings, but this should not deter beginning program evaluators from undertaking them. They can produce useful data, and your evaluation skills will be enhanced by completing them.

FIGURE 6.8 | DAILY PERCENTAGES OF OBSERVED SAFETY BELT USE AMONG DRIVERS EXITING THE SENIOR CITIZENS' CENTER

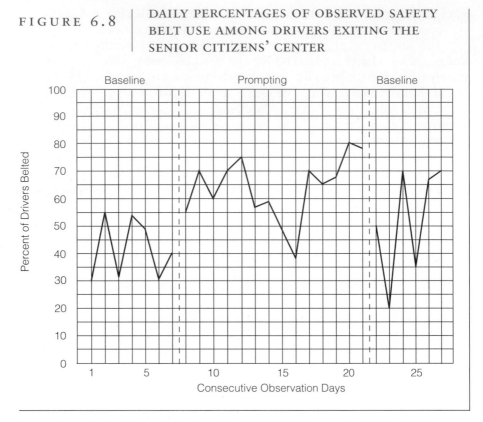

Source: Reproduced with permission from Kim, P.K.H. (Ed.). *Serving the Elderly: Skills for Practice* (New York: Aldine de Gruyter). Copyright 1991 Walter de Gruyter, Inc., New York.

Do not wait until you can undertake a "perfect" program evaluation before attempting such projects. You will never begin if you wait for the perfect program. Rather, think small, think simple, and gradually hone your program evaluation skills by undertaking successively more complicated studies. This study conducted at the senior citizens' center helped another social worker to design and complete an evaluation of an immensely more complex project.

A doctoral student in social work, Karen Sowers-Hoag (1986), was interested in child welfare—particularly in promoting safety-belt use among young children. Karen arranged to provide a safety-belt use training curriculum at a local private school to children ranging in age from 4.8 to 7.1 years of age (average age = 5 years). She monitored the safety-belt use of all children as they were picked up and driven away from school at the end of the day for a period and found 16 who *never* buckled up. She formally baselined these 16 after dividing them into two groups of 8 children. Then, she trained the ones in Group 1 in her safety-belt curriculum, continuing to gather safety-belt use data on all children in both groups. After a week had passed, children in Group 2 were trained. In effect, each group received an **A-B** design, but the

FIGURE 6.9 | INCREASING SAFETY-BELT USE AT A PRESCHOOL

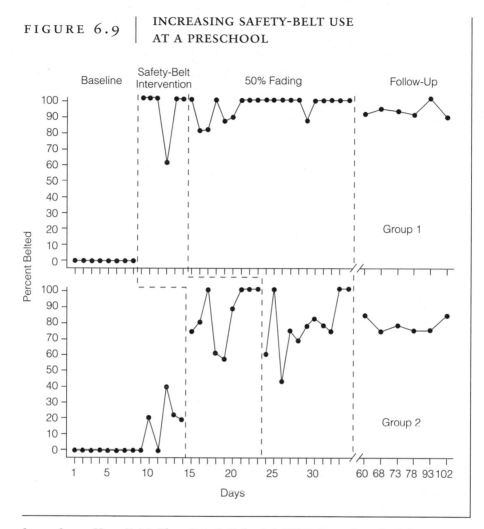

Source: Sowers-Hoag, K. M., Thyer, B. A. & Bailey, J. S. (1987). Promoting safety belt use among young children. *Journal of Applied Behavior Analysis*, 20, 133–138. Used with permission.

baselines were staggered and of differing length. The outcome measure was the percent of children in each group who buckled up as they were driven away from school each day. Highly reliable but unobtrusive observations were made of the outcome measure. The educational program was discontinued for both groups 34 days into the study, and follow-up observations were made over the next several months. The data Karen obtained are depicted in Figure 6.9. Following a stable (and low) baseline, those in Group 1 immediately began buckling up on a consistent basis after the program began. Regular safety-belt use was maintained while the program was faded, then discontinued entirely. Group 2's baseline, initially stable, went up a bit after Group 1 (but not Group 2) received training. It was later found out that this was because a brother and sister with different last names were randomly assigned to the two different groups. There was evidently "contamination" in Group 2's baseline—the child in Group 1 influenced his sister in Group 2. Nevertheless, a clear functional relationship between training and safety-belt use appeared to occur for Group 2 as well.

This design is called a **multiple baseline design**; like the **A-B-A** design, it may permit causal inference. It is not plausible to argue that Group 1 and Group 2 both changed following the implementation of the program because of some coincidental happenings in the natural environment. That is possible, yes, but not very likely. *All* 158 children attending the school received safety-belt training. It can be reasonably argued that a program found effective with children who did not initially use their safety belts at all would likely be effective with the children who initially used their belt sometimes. However, it is likely that a program found to be effective in getting small children who already buckled up *sometimes* to use their safety belts *consistently* would not prove equally efficacious with children who initially never buckled up at all. (Details on the study can be found in Sowers-Hoag, Thyer, and Bailey, 1987, and in Karen Sowers-Hoag's doctoral dissertation, 1986.)

Working in a psychiatric emergency room setting, Jones, Morris, and Barnard (1986) applied an intervention program intended to increase the staff's timely completion of required civil commitment forms. These researchers also used a multiple baseline design to evaluate the intervention's effectiveness. There were three required forms, and the outcome measure was the percentage of charts that contained properly completed forms. Baselines were initiated on all three forms separately, and intervention was sequentially applied for each form in a staggered manner. After baseline, intervention was applied to the first required form (notices of rights), while baselines were continued on the other two forms. Then intervention was applied to the use of the second form (imminent harm applications), while the baseline was continued on the third form. Finally, intervention was begun for the third form (witness list). In each instance, the percentage of charts containing correctly completed forms dramatically improved but only after the intervention was applied. At the end of the study, with 6-month follow-up, virtually 100 percent of the charts contained properly completed forms. This study involved 34 staff members and high inter-rater agreement pertaining to assessing the outcome measures. The quality of the data permitted clear causal inferences that it was the intervention program (involving simple instructions and feedback) that was responsible for the improvements and not some extraneous variables. This example may be considered a form of quality assurance study, in that the SSRD was used to improve the quality of the services provided in the emergency room setting, and was not an attempt to evaluate the usefulness or outcomes of the ER services themselves.

The problem of school violence provides the context for the next example of using an experimental SSRD to conduct a summative evaluation of a psychosocial intervention. Murphy, Hutchison, and Bailey (1983) developed operational definitions of child-to-child aggression as it was observed on the playground at an elementary school. Unobtrusive observations of the children during free time play yielded very reliable inter-rater agreements (mean of 87 percent agreement)

FIGURE 6.10 | FREQUENCY OF VIOLENT BEHAVIORS DURING UNSTRUCTURED PLAY TIME

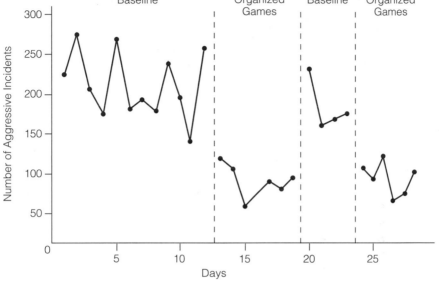

Note: Frequency of incidents recorded during the 20-minute morning observation periods on the playground.

Source: Murphy, Hutchison, and Bailey (1983). Behavioral school psychology goes outdoors: The effect of organized games on playground aggression. *Journal of Applied Behavior Analysis*, 16, p. 29–35.

for acts such as aggression (e.g., striking, slapping, tripping, kicking, pushing, or pulling others), property abuse (e.g., taking another person's property without permission, throwing objects at cars, or breaking pencils), and other forms of rule violations.

Baseline measures were taken of the frequency of violent behaviors for a 12-day period, during 20-minute sessions of unstructured free play time. The intervention consisted of organized games (jumping rope and foot racing) provided by a teacher's aide, introduced on the 13th day. Structured games were continued days 13 through 19, were then discontinued on day 20, and reinstated yet again on days 24 through 29.The results of this $A_1 B_1 A_2 B_2$ design are depicted in Figure 6.10. Aggressive incidents were very frequent during the first baseline phase (A_1), averaging 212 per day. These declined dramatically during the first intervention (B_1) phase, to an average of 91 per day. During the second baseline phase (A_2), aggression leapt up to a mean of 191 daily incidents, only to decline back down to 97 a day on average during the second intervention phase (B_2). School social workers and other human service professionals concerned with reducing school violence can similarly use experimental SSRDs like this **A-B-A-B** design to examine the effectiveness of any innovative programs introduced into the school setting in an effort to curb child-to-child aggression. Not only do the authors believe that this is a recommended practice, we would argue that to *not* systematically evaluate innovative programs in this manner borders on the unethical.

EXTERNAL VALIDITY

A criticism sometimes levied against SSRDs, with the implication that this renders them less than satisfactory for use as a program evaluation design, is their limited external validity. It is highly desirable for research findings to be generalizable *beyond* the particular participants in a research study. The extent to which a finding may be generalizable (also known as a study's external validity) is conventionally seen as a function of how *representative* one's study participants are with respect to a larger population of individuals with a similar problem. In many areas of scientific inquiry, efforts are made to enhance generalizability by using well-established statistical tools pertaining to selecting a representative sample of study participants, individuals whose characteristics mirror those of the larger group (population) from which they were drawn.

However, while sounding good in theory, in actuality, research on practices in human services in general, and in program evaluation in particular, is almost *never* able to use the tools of randomly sampling from a larger population of interest, due to practical limitations. Try to figure out how to gain access to the *population* of all male batterers, of all women who abuse children, or of all welfare recipients. Simply put, it cannot be done. Moreover, even if it could in theory, how could you really obtain a random sample of these folks? The difficulties are extreme. What program evaluation research most commonly does is make use of a *convenience* sample of individuals chosen primarily on the basis of their *availability*. And this is most often related to the willingness of particular social service agencies, schools, hospitals, and other facilities to serve as a host for evaluation research.

How is the problem of external validity overcome with single system research designs? The answer is a process called *replication*. Replication can be defined as:

> In research, the process of duplicating an experiment—in which the same hypotheses, variables, sampling procedure, testing instruments, and techniques for analysis are used—with a different sample of the same population. (Barker, 1999, p. 409)

The logic goes something like this: If Lynam et al. (1999) obtain a certain finding about the effects of DARE, and then another set of researchers find the same results in widely different contexts, then each time the original findings are replicated, confidence is strengthened that those findings are generalizable. As Thomas (1975) noted:

> The results of replication may be essentially positive, in which case confidence in the reliability of the procedures used is greatly increased. Indeed, each successive, positive replication increases plausibility multiplicatively, because the chance occurrence of such results becomes much more improbable with each additional replication. The same may be said, of course, for replicated failures. (p. 278)

Although Thomas was specifically addressing replicating SSRDs, the same principle holds with the generalizability of findings obtained from group designs. In other words, most forms of research on practice attempt to establish external validity/generalizability via the mechanism of replication, not random sampling. This is a crucial difference between evaluation studies (which attempt to develop valid knowledge about particular programs) and conventional behavioral and social science research (which is aimed at producing generalizable knowledge leading to the development of theory).

In short, the external validity of a single example of research using an SSRD may indeed be weak, but sometimes that is hard to say. The very first single subject study evaluating the effects of antibiotics on bacterial infections found that they cured the individual in question. Was this a generalizable finding, based, as it was, on a N of 1? Not yet. But was it a *valid* conclusion? Yes, indeed.

Concerns about external validity are legitimate in program evaluation. However, this weakness is shared by group research designs using convenience samples as well. The mechanism for overcoming this problem and establishing the generalizability of a finding is the same for both single system and group research designs, namely, *replication*. Indeed, the need for replicating findings is not something to apologize about: "The results of repetitions of the same experiments are fundamental to the creation of any body of knowledge" (Ziman, 1978, p. 56).

INFERENTIAL STATISTICS

Sometimes research textbooks advocate using various types of inferential statistical tests to make inferences from SSRD data. We do not recommend this for several reasons. First, the added dimension of using inferential statistics, if seen as essential to analyze SSRD data, will deter those who are unfamiliar with specialized statistical knowledge from attempting evaluation studies using SSRDs. A second reason is that many of the recommended statistical tests are based on the usual assumptions of parametric analysis (e.g., equality of variances, normally distributed data, independent data). Using SSRDs, often the data points, which determine the degrees of freedom for parametric analysis, are small in number, particularly if the design has several different phases. The small number of data points (i.e., the degrees of freedom) makes statistical inference problematic because the data points have low sensitivity (i.e., low statistical power) to detect differences. Imagine an **A-B** SSRD, with five data points in the A phase and five in the B phase. Assume that the data are level in each phase and you wish to test the hypothesis that the B phase data are statistically significantly (i.e., reliably) lower than the A phase data, using a *t*-test on the mean of the data from each of the A and B phases (we will assume that the data are not serially dependent, which is another complicating issue altogether). In terms of statistical power, that is equivalent to doing a pretest–posttest group design (i.e., **O-X-O**) with one group of five subjects tested at two points in time. No statistician would claim this to be an appropriate use of the *t*-test, rightly insisting that you would need 15 to 20 subjects to ensure that the statistical possessed adequate power to detect any difference between the means.

A third reason is that SSRDs by their very nature contradict the most crucial assumption of parametric tests, the independence of the data. For example, in a group design that compares the incidence of substance abuse among adolescents in Miami versus those in Anchorage, Alaska, the data are truly independent. The data from one group are in no reasonable way connected with or influenced by the data from the other group. Single system research designs only have data from one system (an individual client, a small group, a couple, family, organization, community, state, or even country) that is assessed repeatedly. Therefore, the data are not "independent" in a statistical sense, and may be serially dependent (i.e., autocorrelated). This means that one data point can be used to predict the location of another. If significant autocorrelation exists, then the parametric inferential statistical test is compromised.

A fourth reason to rely solely on visual inspection of data formatted in an SSRD is that this practice *reduces* the likelihood that small but statistically reliable differences will be detected. This is called a "Type 2" error, missing a "true" difference when one exists. The opposite is a "Type 1" error, claiming that a difference exists when it really does not. In practice research evaluating interventions, researchers and clinicians are not usually interested in statistically reliable changes that are practically unimportant. Program evaluators typically want to find interventions that make a big, practical difference. Visual inspection of data alone increases Type 2 errors (missing some valid but small effects), and decreases Type 1 errors (making exaggerated claims about effects). In essence, using visual inspection alone results in a *more* conservative analysis of one's data. This is good, and partially corrects for the tendency in evaluation research to overemphasize statistically significant but practically unimportant changes in the data.

You likely make use of visual analysis of graphically presented data all the time, and believe it to be a useful, practical way to interpret time series data. For instance, you look at a graph depicting the rise and fall of the stock market. Political candidates show graphs of crime or prosperity statistics to make a point during a debate. It is not usually difficult to figure out such trends using your own eyes. In fact, many agency directors and advisory board members' eyes will glaze over when you start talking about *t*-tests and chi-squares in the analysis of evaluation data, but they will quickly perk up at the sight of a crisp, clean graph showing things clearly going up or down.

Some specialized methods of statistical inference may be validly applied to SSRD data. For example, John Shields completed his Ph.D. in social work at the University of Georgia. His doctoral dissertation involved an analysis of the potential effects of statewide legislation enacted in 1994 that was intended to reduce the amount of use of inpatient psychiatric beds in public institutions. He obtained archival data on monthly psychiatric bed use from the state for several years prior to the 1994 legislation, and for several years thereafter. In effect, he had a naturally occurring **A-B** SSRD. Given the large numbers of data points, John elected to augment his visual interpretation of the data (which visually showed a clear and substantial decrease in psychiatric hospitalization following the legislation) with an inferential statistic called time series analysis (TSA). The TSA provided more of a detailed quantitative analysis, demonstrating not only that psychiatric bed use did decline statistically significantly following the legislation, but that the decline accelerated from about –1 day per month during the baseline to about –22 days per month after the legislation was enacted. Shields's dissertation represents the appropriate integration of SSRD and inferential statistics such as TSA. The drawback with TSA is that this approach may require a very large number of data points per phase (perhaps 50 or more) to properly run the test, and evaluation researchers rarely have access to data with such a high number of repeated measures, or have the requisite computer and statistical expertise needed to run such tests. The nonparametric inferential statistical tests suffer the same drawback as do the parametric ones, in terms of the number of data points (usually few) determining the degrees of freedom and resultant statistical power of a particular test.

On balance we recommend that program evaluators (particularly beginning ones) rely primarily on the visual inspection of SSRD, a recommendation that really has not changed much in 25 years:

> [T]he main criteria of change should be whether or not a *practical* difference has resulted from the intervention. Inspection of the data, without statistical tests, will ordinarily be enough to enable one to judge whether practically useful changes have occurred. After all, it doesn't matter that an outcome is statistically significant if it is practically meaningless (Thomas, 1975, p. 279, italics in original).

Some nonparametric statistical tests may lend themselves more readily to the analysis of data from single systems, but many graduate programs do not provide instruction in these techniques. Bloom, Fischer, and Orme (2002) provide a good overview of the topic of using inferential statistical tests in single system research for those who wish to pursue the topic.

HOW TO PREPARE GRAPHS

For the evaluation of one's own practice, using readily available graph paper and pencils or pens is the simplest way to prepare a graph. For class projects the instructor may require a more polished presentation, and professional-looking graphs would certainly be used if you were preparing a report for an agency, a paper for presentation at a conference, or submitting a paper for possible publication to a scholarly journal.

An alternative is for you to learn to prepare professional-looking graphs using a personal computer and software suitable to the task. For example, many statistical analysis programs (e.g., the Statistical Package for the Social Sciences) can be used to prepare graphs. The textbook *Evaluating Practice: Guidelines for the Helping Professional* (Bloom, Fischer, & Orme, 2002) is accompanied by specialized computer software developed by Walter Hudson that is intended, among other purposes, to help you prepare computer-generated graphs of SSRDs; and Arlene Conboy and her colleagues at Yeshiva University have also prepared a low-cost commercially available software program to enable you to graph SSRDs (see Conboy et al., 2000).

One of the best and most widely available options is to use the common software program, Microsoft Excel. Follow the simple instructions provided by Carr and Burkholder (1998). Both simple and complex (withdrawal designs, multiple baseline designs) can be created using this software. Following are some general guidelines to follow in preparing SSRD graphs.

THINGS TO DO

1. Use somewhat larger (i.e., thicker) lines to form the vertical and horizontal axes than those lines used to connect data points.
2. Use black ink only.
3. Use actual data points (e.g., solid black circles, open black circles, etc.), as opposed to a jerky line lacking data points.
4. Separate phases using a dashed vertical line.
5. Label each phase with an intelligible title (e.g., Baseline, Intervention, etc.).
6. Use abbreviations sparingly, or not at all. Spell things out if space permits.
7. If the vertical axis has a "zero" point, elevate this slightly above the horizontal axis so that the data points do not rest on it.
8. Make the graph big enough to be read easily.

THINGS NOT TO DO

1. Never use colored ink, and try not to use shades of gray, as colors and shadings reproduce poorly when photocopied.
2. Do not format your graph using a computer's three-dimensional features. Although these may look prettier, they do this at the expense of being able to clearly tell where data falls along an axis.
3. If you are submitting your report for publication in a journal, do not include a figure caption on the figure itself. Use a separate figure caption page, as required by the style set forth in the *Publication Manual of the American Psychological Association* (i.e., APA style).
4. Do not have a top or right border on the graph.
5. Do not use horizontal lines running from the vertical axis across the graph.
6. Do not connect data points *between* phases. Instead, have a break in the data.

The *Journal of Applied Behavior Analysis* periodically publishes guidelines for the preparation of SSRD graphs (e.g., see their Spring 1998 issue), and can be consulted for further instruction in this regard.

You can enhance the reliability of conclusions based on the visual inspection of graphically presented data with a few simple steps (see, for example, Fisher, Kelly & Lomas, 2003). Indeed, there is a relatively large literature on this topic.

ETHICS OF SINGLE SYSTEM RESEARCH DESIGNS

Human service professionals are of course guided by disciplinary codes of ethics that govern their actions with clients. Issues pertaining to client confidentiality, for example, would be important to take into account when preparing a study using an SSRD, in the same manner that you would if your research methodology involved a nomothetic group design or a qualitative case study (like those written by Freud). Our codes of ethics may also contain standards addressing the client's right to valid informed consent to participate in practice or in research. However, the evaluation of one's own practice is a gray area. For example, we are told in one's discipline's code of ethics that:

> Social workers should contribute to the knowledge base of social work and share with colleagues their knowledge related to practice, research, and ethics. Social workers should seek to contribute to the profession's literature. . . . [Standard 5.01(d)] . . . Social workers should monitor and evaluate policies, the implementation of programs, and practice interventions. [Standard 5.02(a)] . . . Social workers should promote and facilitate evaluation and research to contribute to the development of knowledge. [Standard 5.02(b)] . . . Social workers engaged in evaluation or research should obtain voluntary and written informed from participants, *when appropriate*. . . . [Standard 5.02(e)] (National Association of Social Workers, 1999)

Although written informed consent would seem to be indicated for clients participating in experimental investigations of novel interventions, perhaps involving potential assignment to a delayed treatment or no-treatment condition, for example, what about the everyday practitioner evaluating the outcomes of his or her work with a depressed client, using a **B** single system design (assessment and intervention occur at the same time) and the Beck Depression Inventory as an outcome measure? Or the practitioner conducting a retrospective chart review of pre- and postservice functioning of clients, seen several years ago and terminated, using measures already in the charts? Is this "practice," "evaluation," or "research"? Is written, informed consent necessary, beyond that required for practice? These issues are not always clear.

However, research can generally be identified by the researcher's interest in disseminating findings and increasing knowledge in the field; researchers typically want to publish their findings. Evaluators may or may not publish their findings. What is distinct for them is the underlying motivation to feed back information to the practitioner—to improve a *particular* program. Evaluators often are *not* concerned with the issue of the generalization of their findings.

In many states, the legal definition of social work practice includes conducting evaluation studies, so using SSRDs could be construed simply as good practice, fulfilling the ethical mandate to systematically evaluate the outcomes of our service programs and should not be construed as "research." The *National Association of Social Workers Standards for the Practice of Clinical Social Work* (1989) clearly states that social workers shall have "Knowledge about and skills in using research to evaluate the effectiveness of a service" (p. 7), which again indicates that evaluation efforts are part and parcel of good practice.

Human service professionals routinely take data in the form of case notes, observations, standardized measures, rapid assessment instruments of the programs, and work with clients. Sometimes these measures are repeated during the course of individual treatment, family therapy, or at the beginning and end of a group work program. This is a part of regular practice, and a part of practice consists of sharing this information with supervisors and sometimes colleagues. We do not believe that an agency's efforts to conduct program evaluation studies of its own routinely provided services falls under the designation of "research" as defined by our professions' codes of ethics. We do believe that practitioners engaging in such evaluation studies *should be* guided by one's discipline's general ethical guidelines pertaining to informed consent and those dealing with engagement into a treatment relationship, confidentiality issues, and client protection. Of course, students conducting evaluation projects in fulfillment of course or program of study requirements (e.g., a thesis or dissertation), should always follow the guidance provided by their university's institutional review board. Bloom and Orme (1993) provide a more extensive discussion of this topic.

CHAPTER RECAP

Single system research designs can be a useful tool in the methodological armamentarium of the program evaluator. Like group (nomothetic) research designs, which we will cover in Chapter 9, SSRDs can be viewed as falling along a hierarchy of sophistication, ranging from simple designs, useful in evaluating the occurrence of change, to relatively complex designs, used to determine whether or not a given program caused any observed effects. The unit of analysis in SSRDs is called a "system." In *clinical practice* the system can be a client, a family, a couple, or a small group. In *program evaluation,* the system can be conceptualized as a single program, an agency, a network of agencies, another type of organization, a city, a state, or even a nation. The key to using SSRDs is having a reliable and valid outcome measure that can be repeatedly assessed over time, plotting such data on a simple line graph, and interpreting the outcomes using visual inspection. In some cases, inferential statistics can be applied to SSRD data, but this is not usually necessary.

Conceptually, the reasoning behind SSRDs is not difficult, although the usual evils attendant on doing research in field settings (see Wodarski and Feldman, 1974) often complicate the otherwise elegant simplicity of these methods. Conclusions drawn from program evaluations using SSRDs usually possess limited external validity (generalizability), because almost by definition program evaluations make use of convenience samples, not randomly selected ones. This limitation, however, needs to be tempered with the recognition that program evaluations using group designs and other research methodologies are also likely to be compromised in this manner; hence, this limitation is in actuality not particularly salient. Most program evaluators are concerned with learning about a *particular program,* not with making generalizations to all programs, and SSRDs are a great tool for this purpose.

This chapter has illustrated the usefulness of SSRDs in a variety of program evaluation activities, including needs assessments, formative evaluation studies, quality assurance studies, and for conducting summative evaluations. A wide range of research designs have been illustrated, including the **A** design (assessment only, in the absence of intervention); the **B** design (assessment and intervention occur concurrently); and the **A-B-A, B-A-B, A-B-A-B,** and multiple baseline designs. Every human services worker involved in the design, conduct, and reporting of program evaluation studies should be familiar with the principles of SSRDs, as these are now an accepted and essential tool for evaluating practice in the human services.

Questions for Class Discussion

1. Make a list of problems in your community or on your campus. Discuss how an SSRD could be used for needs assessment with one of the problems. What data would need to be gathered? How long would the baseline need to be? How convincing would evidence from an SSRD be?
2. In relation to the social service agencies known to students in your community, brainstorm how an SSRD could be used for either formative evaluation or quality assurance. Start with a specific problem and then move to a discussion of possible interventions. What would be the outcome measure(s)? How long would the study take?
3. Could SSRDs be used in conjunction with consumer satisfaction studies? How?
4. Locate an example of a single system design published in a professional journal during the past 5 years. Identify the type of design, the outcome measure, and how well the intervention is described. Judge for yourself whether the author's conclusions are justified by the data.
5. Distinguish between the functions of needs assessments, formative evaluations, quality assurance studies, and summative evaluations.

Mini-Projects: Experiencing Evaluation Firsthand

1. For a client population with which you have worked or are working (or a fictitious population), select an outcome measure that follows from some problem they have in common. Construct a graph that could monitor their progress over time. In the accompanying paper, be sure to address the target behavior, the baseline, the type of design you would use, and any efforts you would make to improve or check the reliability of the data you obtain.
2. If you are not familiar with single system research designs, browse though back issues of the *Journal of Applied Behavior Analysis* until you find an article that interests you and describes the use of an SSRD. Summarize the findings of this article relative to the usefulness and limitations of the SSRD employed. How could the study have been improved?

References and Resources

Austin, M. J., Cox, G., Gottlieb, N., Hawkins, J. D., Kruzich, J. M. & Rauch, R. (1982). *Evaluating your agency's programs*. Newbury Park, CA: Sage.

Barker, R. (1999). *The social work dictionary* (4th ed.).Washington, DC: NASW Press.

Bloom, M., Fischer, J., & Orme, J. G. (2002). *Evaluating practice: Guidelines for the helping professional* (2nd ed.). Boston: Pearson Allyn & Bacon.

Bloom, M., & Orme, J. (1993). Ethics and single-system design. *Journal of Social Service Research, 18*(1/2), 301–310.

Briggs, H. E. (1994). Promoting adoptions by foster-parents through an inner city organization. *Research on Social Work Practice, 4*, 497–509.

Carr, J. E., & Burkholder, E. O. (1998). Creating single-subject design graphs with Microsoft Excel. *Journal of Applied Behavior Analysis, 31*, 245–251.

Conboy, A., Auerbach, C., Beckerman, A., Schnall, D., & LaPorte, H. H. (2000). M. S. W. student satisfaction with using single system designs computer software to evaluate social work practice. *Research on Social Work Practice, 10*, 127–138.

Cournoyer, B. R. (2004). *The evidence-based social work skills book*. New York: Allyn & Bacon.

Daniels, A. C. (1989). *Performance management: Improving quality productivity through positive reinforcement*. Tucker, GA: Performance Management Publications.

Engelman, K. K., Altus, D. E., Mosier, M. C., Mathews, R. M. (2003). Brief training to promote the use of less intrusive prompts by nursing assistants in a dementia care unit. *Journal of Applied Behavior Analysis, 36*, 129–132.

Fisher, W. W., Kelley, M. D., & Lomas, J. E. (2003). Visual aids and structured criteria for improving visual inspection and interpretation of single-case designs. *Journal of Applied Behavior Analysis, 36*, 387–406.

Geller, E. S., Bruff, C. D. & Nimmor, J. G. (1985). "Flash for life": Community-based prompting for safety belt promotion. *Journal of Applied Behavior Analysis, 18*, 309–314.

Gibbs, L. E. (2003). *Evidence-based practice for the helping professions*. Pacific Grove, CA: Brooks/Cole.

Greene, B. F., Winett, R. A., Van Houten, R., Geller, E. S., & Iwata, B. A. (Eds.). (1987). *Behavior analysis in the community*. Lawrence, KS: Society for the Experimental Analysis of Behavior.

Johnson, M. D., & Fawcett, S. B. (1994). Courteous service: Its assessment and modification in a human service organization. *Journal of Applied Behavior Analysis, 27*, 145–152.

Jones, H. H., Morris, E. K., & Barnard, J. D. (1986). Increasing staff completion of civil commitment forms through instructions and graphed group performance feedback. *Journal of Organizational Behavior Management, 7*(3/4), 29–43.

Jordan, C. & Franklin, C. (2003). *Clinical assessment for social workers: Quantitative and qualitative methods,* (2nd ed.). Chicago: Lyceum.

Kelley, P. L., Jacobs, R. R., & Farr, J. L. (1994). Effects of multiple administrations of the MMPI for employee screening. *Personnel Psychology, 47*, 575–591.

Lynam, D. R., Milich, R., Zimmerman, R., Novak, S. P., Logan, T. K., Martin, C., Leukefeld, C., & Clayton, R. (1999). Project DARE: No effects at 10-year follow-up. *Journal of Consulting and Clinical Psychology, 67*, 590–593.

Murphy, H. A., Hutchison, J. M., & Bailey, J. S. (1983). Behavioral school psychology goes outdoors: The effect of organized games on playground aggression. *Journal of Applied Behavior Analysis, 16*, 29–35.

Mutschler, E. (1979). Using single-case evaluation procedures in a family and children's service agency: Integration of research and practice. *Journal of Social Service Research, 2,* 115–134.

National Association of Social Workers. (1989). *NASW standards for the practice of clinical social work.* Silver Spring, MD: Author.

National Association of Social Workers. (1999). *Code of ethics.* Washington, DC: Author.

Neuhring, E. M., & Pascone, A. B. (1986). Single-subject evaluation: A tool for quality assurance. *Social Work, 31,* 359–365.

Nugent, W. R., Bruley, C., & Allen, P. (1999).The effects of aggression replacement training on male and female antisocial behavior in a runaway shelter. *Research on Social Work Practice, 9,* 466–482.

Richmond, M. (1935/1917). *Social diagnosis.* New York: Sage.

Rossi, P. H., & Freeman, H. E. (1985). *Evaluation: A systematic approach.* Thousand Oaks, CA: Sage.

Sowers-Hoag, K. M. (1986). *Promoting safety belt use among young children: An experimental analysis.* Ph.D. diss., Florida State University School of Social Work.

Sowers-Hoag, K. M., Thyer, B. A., & Bailey, J. S. (1987). Promoting safety belt use among young children: an experimental analysis. *Journal of Applied Behavior Analysis, 20,* 133–138.

Stocks, J. T., Thyer, B. A., & Kearsley, M. A. (1987). Using a token economy in a community-based residential program for disabled adults: An empirical evaluations leads to program modification. *Behavioral Residential Treatment, 1,* 173–185.

Stuart, R. B. (1971). Research in social work: Social casework and social groupwork.

In R. Morris (Ed.). *Encyclopedia of social work* (Vol. 2, pp. 1106–1122). Washington, DC: National Association of Social Workers.

Thomas, E. J. (1975). Research methods in interpersonal practice. In N. A. Polansky (Ed.), *Social work research* (pp. 254–283). Chicago: University of Chicago Press.

Thyer, B. A. (1998). Promoting research on community practice: Using single system research designs. In R. H. MacNair (Ed.), *Research strategies for community practice* (pp. 47–61). Binghamton, NY: Haworth.

Thyer, B. A., & Robertson, M. (1993). An initial evaluation of the Georgia safety belt use law: A null MUL? *Environment and Behavior, 25,* 506–513.

Thyer, B. A., & Thyer, K. (1992). Single-system research designs in social work practice: A bibliography from 1965 to 1990. *Research on Social Work Practice, 2,* 99–116.

Thyer, B. A., Thyer, K. E., & Massa, S. (1991). Behavioral analysis and therapy in the field of gerontology. In Paul K. H. Kim (Ed.), *Serving the elderly: Skills for practice* (pp. 117–135). New York: Aldine.

Wodarski, J. S., & Feldman, R. (1974). Practical aspects of field research. *Clinical Social Work Journal, 2,* 182–193.

Wodarski, J. S., & Lindsey, E. W. (1987). Training social work administrators to use evaluation in daily practice. In N. Gottlieb (Ed.), *Perspectives on direct practice evaluation* (pp. 123–133). Seattle: University of Washington School of Social Work.

Ziman, J. (1978). *Reliable knowledge: An exploration of the grounds for belief in science.* Cambridge: Cambridge University Press.

7

GOAL ATTAINMENT SCALING

INTRODUCTORY SCENARIO

A phone call came in from a frantic former student who had taken a position in a rural area. The executive director of his agency asked him to design a process by which a community mental health agency with numerous employees in several counties could begin evaluating its services.

"What do I do?" he said. "Where do I begin?"

"Can you start with a single program and then slowly bring in other programs?"

"I don't think so," he said. "The director wants something to use across the whole agency . . . and as soon as possible. I'm scheduled to make a presentation to staff in 2 weeks."

As we talked, it became clear that few resources were available to him. The agency did not use standardized instruments like the Brief Symptom Inventory or the CES-D for outcome measures, and their quality assurance process consisted of checking to see that agency forms were completed, signed, and dated. Because he had to implement something quickly, we recommended that he consider goal attainment scaling (GAS). The GAS approach would not have been our first choice for evaluation (for reasons we will explain later), but it seemed ideal for his situation.

WHAT IS GOAL ATTAINMENT SCALING?

Goal attainment scaling involves quantifying individualized goal set with clients during assessment and treatment using a five-point normative scale. A guide that identifies levels of progress is developed for each client. The **follow-up guide** lists the client's goals in one column along with the scale for evaluating each level of goal achievement. (See the examples in Tables 7.1 and 7.2 and note the variation in outcome levels from "Much better than expected" to "Much less than expected.")

Because clients' outcome levels can be converted into standard scores, the GAS approach allows comparison of "success" levels across a program or agency even when no common intervention is used. Thus, it has the capacity to monitor or evaluate clients' longitudinal change even when they have different kinds of problems.

Goal attainment scaling originated in the field of mental health during the 1960s but has been used with many different populations such as brain-injured patients in rehabilitation hospitals, geriatric patients, and infants with motor delays. Although GAS is not used all that frequently in most social service agencies, the concept is still alive and well, as can be seen in articles discussing its use examining the effectiveness of consultation versus direct intervention with preschool children with mild motor delays (Dreiling & Bundy, 2003), measuring

TABLE 7.1 | EXAMPLE OF GAS OUTCOMES FOR AN AUTISTIC CHILD

Level	Expected Outcome	Goal 1: Social Play
−2	Most unfavorable outcome	Isolated play—would not separate from parent, would not enter playroom, total dependence on parent
−1	Present level of performance	Parallel play—plays in group but does not interact with adult or children
0	Expected level of success	Interactive play—plays in group but interacts with child or adult less than 50 percent of time
+1	More than expected level of success	Interacts through adult structuring with other children 80 percent of the time
+2	Most favorable expected level of success	Interacts with peers cooperatively—imitates activities

From Oren & Ogletree, 2000.

TABLE 7.2	EXAMPLE OF GAS OUTCOMES FOR HOME HEALTH CARE CLIENTS

Level of Attainment	Expected Outcome	Goal 1: Mobility
−2	Much less than expected	Good bed mobility; two-person transfer
−1	Somewhat less than expected	One person transfer. Walks with walker up to 5 meters indoors. Uses wheelchair outdoors
0	Expected level	Independent transfer. Walks up to 10 meters with walker
+1	Somewhat better than expected	Walks up to 15 meters with cane
+2	Much better than expected	No aid, no distance limitation

From Forbes, 1998.

motivation to change in sexual offenders (Barrett et al., 2003), and rehabilitating patients with lower-extremity amputations (Ruston & Miller, 2002) and chronic pain (Fisher & Hardie, 2002). Rockwood et al. (2003) found that GAS was more responsive than such instruments as the Barthel Index, the Physical Self-Maintenance Scale, Instrumental Activities of Daily Living, and a modified Spitzer Quality of Life Index for detecting clinically important changes associated with rural, frail, older adults.

Forbes (1998) has listed the direct practice benefits and advantages of using GAS. The process:

clarifies the focus of treatment for clients and professionals alike by identifying the expectations of therapy in realistic, achievable terms

facilitates clients' problem-solving efforts

could potentially increase clients' participation in treatment

allows for interdisciplinary treatment planning and assists in team conferences

Steps in Goal Attainment Scaling

Goal attainment scaling requires the following steps:

1. **Selection of Goals**   In this step the client's problems are considered. Any number of problem areas and goals can be determined. Kiresuk, Smith, and Cardillo (1994) recommend at least three goals; more than five goals may become too cumbersome. Certainly, the number of problems clients bring

TABLE 7.3 | EXAMPLE OF VAGUE GOAL STATEMENTS

Outcome Level	Self-Esteem Level
Much less than expected (−2)	Feels totally worthless
Somewhat less than expected (−1)	Views self as having more deficits than assets
Expected outcome (0)	Views self as having strengths and weaknesses in balance
Somewhat more than expected outcome (+1)	Views self as having more assets than deficits
Much more than expected (+2)	Feels generally positive about self

differ greatly. Problems chosen for GAS should be those most significant to the client and those that intervention is most likely to change. The chosen goals are discussed and negotiated with the client.

It is vitally important that the goals be well defined, behavioral, and measurable so that it will be easy to determine whether they have been accomplished. Vaguely written goals that are not objective will make the evaluation of success difficult and debatable. An illustration of imprecise client goals is shown in Table 7.3. Do you see how these are lacking in measurement precision?

2. **Weighting Goals**   A nonobligatory step is to assign subjective weights to the goal areas to establish their relative importance when there is more than one goal. Thus, a problem that is the most important to the client or one that has persisted longer might receive more of a weight than a problem that is more minor. If all goals are equally important, each would receive a weight of 1.

3. **Follow-up Time Selection**   In this step the researcher or therapist decides when to obtain data at the end of the intervention (or at a specified *post-intervention* period for determining if the client's gains or changes have been maintained).

4. **Scaling Each Goal from −2 to +2**   Each goal must be operationalized in observable, behavioral terms. This step requires specifying a range of potential outcomes in an ordinal scale of five levels, where a +2 outcome represents achieving much more than expected and +1 somewhat more than expected. The 0 position represents an achievement of an expected outcome, −1 portrays achieving somewhat less than expected, and −2 much less than expected. A brief title is given to each goal.

5. **Specifying Other Scale Levels**   After developing the most realistic or expected outcome statement, it is necessary to create indicators of both less and more desirable possible outcomes. Once again, these should be objective

and observable gradients that identify less than expected progress and achievement of more than expected.

6. **Assessing the Client**   The client is assessed at the beginning of treatment and again at the stated follow-up interval.

It is important to the GAS process is that the therapist and client frequently refer to the operationalized goals. Progress toward meeting the desired goals should be monitored continuously during intervention, especially as the client nears termination.

ILLUSTRATION OF GOAL ATTAINMENT SCALING

To demonstrate how GAS could be used with a client, imagine that a 26-year-old woman, whom we will name Roberta, schedules an appointment with you at a counseling center. The first thing you notice about Roberta is that she is morbidly obese. She explains that she is unhappy and does not like herself. She believes that part of her problem is that she lives at home with overbearing parents who keep her from having friends and meeting people.

Roberta has lost 150 pounds or more on several occasions but cannot keep the weight off because she stays home and eats when she is unhappy. She wants very much to get her own apartment but has no job. She has never worked and has only a high school diploma. You determine that she has few marketable job skills. However, a retail store in her neighborhood has been advertising for counter help. Roberta has almost applied on several occasions, but chickened out each time.

Even though several other issues may need to be explored, Roberta wants to work on the two problems distressing her the most. Her goals are (1) to secure the means to live independently and (2) to lose weight. She appears to be motivated and capable of achieving her desired outcomes.

During the second session, the two of you create the follow-up guide shown in Table 7.4. Note how her two goals, "Financial independence" and "Weight loss" have been operationalized with outcomes that vary along a continuum that reflects both the best case and worst case scenarios.

Six months later, Roberta has achieved her first goal of financial independence by obtaining full-time employment. This was the anticipated or expected outcome. This job allows her to live in her own apartment. Additionally, she has enrolled in a weight loss program and has shed 65 pounds. Roberta reports being much happier, and she is thinking about a new goal of enrolling in college.

From an evaluator's standpoint, the identified goal statements must be concrete and observable or measurable. They should not be subjective. The documentation and determination of progress or lack of progress should be easy to judge even if the case file were read by various professionals uninvolved with the intervention. With these criteria in mind, is Roberta's progress easy to determine?

The benefits of utilizing GAS with individual clients are numerous. Its use should help set realistic expectations for treatment, facilitate clients' efforts at

TABLE 7.4 | GOAL ATTAINMENT FOLLOW-UP GUIDE

Problem: Lack of Self-Esteem

Level	Goal 1: Financial Independence	Goal 2: Weight Loss
Most unfavorable outcome (−2)	Not working, continuing to live with parents	Gains weight
Less than expected outcome (−1)	Obtains part-time job	Loses less than 34 lbs
Expected outcome (0)	Obtains a full-time job paying minimum wage	Loses 35–75 lbs
More than expected outcome (+1)	Obtains a full-time job paying slightly better than minimum wage	Loses 76–100 lbs
Most favorable treatment outcome (+2)	Obtains a full-time job with fringe benefits that pays much more than minimum wage	Loses 101–150 lbs

problem solving, increase goal direction in therapy, and perhaps even increase clients' motivation to work toward improvement.

GOAL ATTAINMENT SCALING
AND PROGRAM EVALUATION

If you wish to adopt GAS as a program evaluation technique in an agency, the first thing you must do is to train staff to write relevant, realistic, and measurable goals. Kiresuk and Lund (1994) estimate that staff may require 4 to 14 hours of training and another 45 to 70 minutes per client is needed to develop the follow-up guide and to provide quality control of the effort. About 3 staff hours per client are needed if in-home follow-up interviews are conducted.

Once staff are able to write measurable goal statements, an evaluator can compute composite or summary scores across clients. Creating composite scores can be handled in several ways. The first way, deriving an average scale score for each client, involves adding the outcome scores for each goal and dividing this amount by the number of goals or scales developed for that client. For example, Roberta would have obtained an outcome score of 0 on her financial independence goal and 0 on her weight loss goal. Adding the two 0s and dividing the answer by 2 (the number of goals) produces an average of 0, indicating that the expected goal was obtained. Box 7.1 provides an example of GAS goal statements from an article on nursing home patients.

 EXAMPLE OF GOAL ATTAINMENT
SCALING IN THE LITERATURE

Nursing home patients in long-term care often have multiple functional and medical problems. Problems such as dementia in this population often make the use of standard measurement tools, such as the Mini-Mental State Exam or the Katz Index of Activities of Daily Living, inappropriate.

Goals in this study were in response to a physician's consultation request and were set with the consensus of at least two geriatricians with contributions from nurses. Goal attainment scaling with an 84-year-old man with advanced Alzheimer's disease and metastatic prostate cancer included this goal:

Goal: Reduction of Aggressiveness

Level	Behavior
Much less than expected (–2)	Injures a staff member
Somewhat less than expected (–1)	Physically aggressive with care; nurses able to complete care only 50 percent of the time
Program Goal (0)	Nurses able to complete care 75 percent of the time; patient verbally but not physically aggressive
Somewhat better than expected (+1)	Nurses able to complete care 100 percent of the time
Much better than expected (+2)	No verbal aggression

The assessment process identified 463 problems in 53 patients, and goals were set for 89 problems. The mean number of goals per patient was 1.7 with a range of 1 to 5.

Source: Gordon, J. E., Powell, C. L., & Rockwood, K. (1999). Goal attainment scaling as a measure of clinically important change in nursing-home patients. *Age and Ageing, 28,* 275–281.

Suppose that Roberta had achieved a negative average scale score. This would suggest that her progress was less than expected. A positive value would indicate greater achievement than expected.

Alternatively, Kiresuk and Sherman (1968) created a formula to produce a standard score (*t*-score) of 50 and a standard deviation of 10. As a first step, the outcome scores for each goal for a client are summed. To this value, 50 is added; that value is multiplied by k where:

$$k = \frac{10}{\sqrt{n - np + n^2 p}}$$

where

$p = .30$

n = number of scales for client

Obtaining a T-score of 50 means that the average outcome level was scored as 0 (expected outcome). Higher scores than 50 indicate somewhat greater success, and lower scores suggest less success.

T-scores can also be computed by adding up the individual scales, multiplying that sum by one of the following values:

10.00 when there is one scale

6.2   when there are two scales

4.56   when there are three scales

3.63   when there are four scales

3.01   when there are five scales

and then adding 50. When prediction of client outcomes is perfect, the GAS would be 50, assuming each goal is scored using the –2 to +2 scale.

VARIATIONS OF GOAL ATTAINMENT SCALING

Let's return to the discussion with our frantic former student. As an alternative to the +2 to –2 scaling originally recommended for GAS, we suggested that he use a continuum of 100 points to evaluate goal attainment in his agency. In this scheme, a value of 100 would be awarded when the hoped-for outcome was achieved. Obtaining a less than desired outcome might be assigned a value of 80, 60, or some other number depending on the percentage of the goal achieved. Using this method, average goal attainment for each client and for all the clients of all caseworkers in an agency could easily be computed. It would not be necessary to operationalize "more than expected" or "less than expected" outcomes, although these and other levels of outcome could be stated. A variation of GAS called family goal recording (Fleuridas, Rosenthal, Leigh, & Leigh, 1990) assigns weights to goals, which allows for some goals to have higher priorities than others, and uses levels of achievement that add up to 100 percent.

Table 7.5 illustrates how the concept of GAS can be modified. One may make still other refinements—perhaps by inserting the category "Slight improvement" between "Less than expected" and "Major improvement." With this scheme, one can multiply the importance attached to achieving the first goal (.75) and the goal outcome obtained (.75) to arrive at a figure of .56. To this amount is added the value obtained by multiplying the second goal's importance and the outcome obtained (.25 × .75 = .1875). This amount is added to .56, and the resulting value of .7475 (.56 + .1875) can be interpreted as the client achieved 75 percent of her desired goals. This scoring system seems easier to understand and explain than the GAS scheme.

| TABLE 7.5 | MODIFIED GOAL ATTAINMENT FOLLOW-UP GUIDE | | |

Achievement	Goal 1: Financial Independence Priority (.75)	Goal 2: Weight Loss Priority (.25)
Optimal improvement Level = 1.0	Obtains full-time job paying better than minimum wage and with fringe benefits	Loses 76+ lbs
Major improvement Level = .75	Obtains full-time job paying minimum wage	Loses 35–75 lbs
Less than expected improvement Level = .50	Obtains part-time job	Loses less than 34 lbs
No progress outcome Level = .00	Does not acquire any job; continues living with parents	Gains weight

PROBLEMS WITH GOAL ATTAINMENT SCALING

Goal attainment scaling has been critiqued in the past (Cytrynbaum, Ginath, Birdwell, & Brandt, 1979; Seaberg & Gillespie, 1977) and had its shortcomings discussed more recently (MacKay et al., 1996; MacKay & Lundie, 1998). Some evaluators think that GAS permits too much subjectivity in the choice of goals selected. In considering the case of Roberta, for example, we might have developed goals centering on improving her self-esteem, reducing her depression, or helping her to become more assertive with her parents. Therapists have a great deal of latitude in their *choice* of goals. Even when clients have similar problems, two therapists may emphasize completely different goals—with varying levels of success. What if every therapist decided to work only on the problems easily solved and ignored the difficult ones because an evaluation was being conducted in an agency? Even with no system-wide bias, some therapists might be tempted to set (or encourage a client to set) easily obtained goals because they want to look good in their supervisor's eyes.

Along this line, some therapists or case managers might confuse goals with activities and list activities, which—although tangentially related—were not *directly or substantially* contributing to the problem. For instance, it one could set the following easily obtainable goals for Roberta:

- Attend at least three therapy sessions.
- Read the "Help Wanted" ads in the newspaper every day.
- Prepare a resume.
- Eliminate one candy bar from weekly grocery purchases.

TABLE 7.6 | MEAN GAS SCORES BY STAGE OF TREATMENT

	Group 1	Group 2
Pretreatment	−13.85	−12.89
Posttreatment	−3.80	5.07
Community follow-up	−5.70	8.12

The validity of the GAS depends highly on those who identify or negotiate goals and what they envision as varying levels of success.

A related problem with GAS is that a client's ability to achieve certain goals could be overestimated as well as underestimated—which poses an interesting question: Would overly optimistic clinicians obtain lower success rates than pessimistic clinicians? Obviously, if some kind of goal attainment scaling is to be used as part of an agency evaluation, therapists and program staff need training on goal setting and a supervision or quality assurance process should be constructed to review the goals. Ottenbacher and Cusick (1990) have suggested that one way to deal with this problem is to have one therapist set the goals and another provide the treatment.

A slight disadvantage may also be that average GAS scores can run into negative figures. At first glance, the numerical scores reported in the partial table (see Table 7.6) from a study of sex offenders (Stirpe, Wilson & Long, 2001) appear, if you ignore the minus signs, to show that the clients didn't improve at all. However, Group 2 showed steady upward progress while Group 1 made some progress but then lost ground during the community follow-up period.

Finally, when we use the goal attainment scaling as originally developed, a T-score of 50 may arise from offsetting successes and failures. However, depending on the nature of the goals, failure in one area may have many more ramifications than success in two or three minor areas. The weighing of goals—for instance, deciding that achieving financial independence is twice as important for a client as losing 50 pounds—creates real difficulties when summary T-scores are computed. Further, scores consistently higher than 50 could indicate that the goals were trivial or too easy to achieve (Zara, Stolee, & Prkachin, 1999).

On the plus side, there is evidence that GAS has therapeutic utility in increasing clients' self-awareness and goal orientation (Malec, Smigielski, & DePompolo, 1991). Stolee et al. (1992) found that two geriatricians working independently had an 82 percent agreement on the goals pertinent to their clients and identified the same primary goal 93 percent of the time. They found that the GAS has high inter-rater reliability, adequate content validity, and high correlations with a standardized outcome measure. Smith and Cardillo (1994) conclude that the GAS score

> is a credible but unimpressive measure of an undifferentiated concept of outcome. Its modest but statistically significant relationship with other criteria of outcome indicates that it is measuring some of the same features that are assessed by the other procedures; however, like most other measures, it has no special merit when considered as a general measure of outcome. (p. 272)

We do not routinely recommend goal attainment scaling or some modification of it to agencies for program evaluation. Program directors generally want to know if, at the point of exit, clients are leaving with the same basic competencies, skills, or have achieved a similar level of reduction in symptoms. Because GAS allows for each client to have unique and individualized goals, it is difficult to attribute, conclusively, the benefits of participation in a program. Used systematically agency-wide, GAS is better than not doing *any* monitoring of what clients are achieving. At best it gives you information about what percentage of clients achieved their expected outcome or did better or worse. Program managers will find that this level of information is not as valuable as employing a standardized instrument and an experimental research design or cost-effectiveness design as discussed in later chapters. In settings where it may be important to identify *both* goals that are of specific value to clients while at the same time monitoring the achievement of program goals, GAS may be employed along without other objective measures. Malec (1999), for instance, discusses the use of the Mayo-Portland Adaptability Inventory to assess level of impairment, disability, and handicap along with GAS in a rehabilitation setting for patients with acute brain injury.

Questions for Class Discussion

1. How is goal attainment scaling affected by subjectivity?
2. Discuss the advantages and disadvantages of using GAS or some modification of it to evaluate programs.
3. As a class, brainstorm potential follow-up guides for various types of clients (e.g., a 15-year-old high school dropout, a 73-year-old alcoholic). After developing a guide, go back and identify which statements are too vague.

Mini-Projects: Experiencing Evaluation Firsthand

1. Devise a goal attainment follow-up guide for a client (either real or fictitious). Provide basic information on the client (age, sex, employment history, etc.), and identify at least two problems and the associated achievement levels for each.
2. Read a journal article about a study that employed GAS, and then write a brief critique (approximately 500 words) of that study.

References and Resources

Barrett, M, Wilson, R. J., & Long, C. (2003). Measuring motivation to change in sexual offenders from institutional intake to community treatment. *Sexual Abuse, 15*(4), 269–283.

Cytrynbaum, S., Ginath, Y., Birdwell, J., & Brandt, L. (1979). Goal attainment scaling: A critical review. *Evaluation Quarterly, 3,* 5–40.

Dreiling, D. S., & Bundy, A. C. (2003). A comparison of consultative model and direct-indirect intervention with preschoolers. *American Journal of Occupational Therapy, 57*(5), 566–569.

Fisher, K., & Hardie, R. J. (2002). Goal attainment scaling in evaluating a multidisciplinary pain management programme. *Clinical Rehabilitation, 16*(8), 871–877.

Fleuridas, C., Rosenthal, D. M., Leigh, G. K., & Leigh, T. E. (1990). Family goal recording: An adaptation of goal attainment scaling for enhancing family therapy and assessment. *Journal of Marital and Family Therapy, 16*(4), 389–406.

Forbes, D. A. (1998). Goal attainment scaling: A responsive measure of client outcomes. *Journal of Gerontological Nursing, 12*(2), 34–40.

Gordon, J. E., Powell, C. L., & Rockwood, K. (1999). Goal attainment scaling as a measure of clinically important change in nursing-home patients. *Age and Ageing, 28,* 275–281.

Kiresuk, T. J., & Lund, S. H. (1994). Implementing goal attainment scaling. In T. J. Kiresuk, A. Smith, & J. E. Cardillo (Eds.), *Goal attainment scaling: Applications, theory, and measurement.* Hillsdale, NJ: Erlbaum.

Kiresuk, T. J., & Sherman, R. E. (1968). Goal attainment scaling: A general method for evaluating community mental health programs. *Community Mental Health Journal, 4,* 443–453.

Kiresuk, T. J., Smith, A., & Cardillo, J. E. (1994). *Goal attainment scaling: Applications, theory, and measurement.* Hillsdale, NJ: Erlbaum.

MacKay, G., & Lundie, J. (1998). GAS released again: Proposals for the development of goal attainment scaling. *International Journal of Disability, Development & Education, 45*(2), 217–231.

MacKay, G., Somerville, W., & Lundie, J. (1996). Reflections on goal attainment scaling: Cautionary notes and proposals for development. *Educational Research, 38,* 161–172.

Malec, J. F. (1999). Goal attainment scaling in rehabilitation. *Neuropsychological Rehabilitation, 9*(3/4), 253–275.

Malec, J. F., Smigielski, J. S., & DePompolo, R. W. (1991). Goal attainment scaling and outcome measurement in postacute brain injury rehabilitation. *Archives of Physical Medicine Rehabilitation, 72,* 138–143.

Oren, T., & Ogletree, B. T. (2000). Program evaluation in classrooms for students with autism: Student outcomes and program processes. *Focus on Autism and Other Developmental Disabilities, 15*(3), 170–175.

Ottenbacher, K. J., & Cusick, A. (1990). Goal attainment scaling as a method of clinical service evaluation. *American Journal of Occupational Therapy, 44,* 519–525.

Rockwood, K., Howlett, S., Stadnyk, K, Carver, D., Powell, C. & Stolee, P. (2003). Responsiveness of goal attainment scaling in a randomized controlled trial of comprehensive geriatric assessment. *Journal of Clinical Epidemiology, 56*(8), 736–743.

Ruston, P.W., & Miller, W. C. (2002). Goal attainment scaling in the rehabilitation of patients with lower-extremity amputations: a pilot study. *Archives of Physical Medicine and Rehabilitation, 83*(6), 771–775.

Seaberg, J. R., & Gillespie, D. F. (1977). Goal attainment scaling: A critique. *Social Work Research and Abstracts, 13,* 4–11.

Smith, A., & Cardillo, J. E. (1994). Perspectives on validity. In T. J. Kiresuk, A. Smith, & J. E. Cardillo (Eds.), *Goal attainment scaling: Applications, theory, and measurement*. Hillsdale, NJ: Erlbaum.

Stirpe, T. S., Wilson, R., & Long, C. (2001). Goal attainment scaling with sexual offenders: A measure of clinical impact at post-treatment and at community follow-up. *Sexual Abuse: A Journal of Research and Treatment, 13*(2), 65–77.

Stolee, P., Rockwood, K., Fox, R. A., & Streiner, D. L. (1992). The use of goal attainment scaling in a geriatric care setting. *Journal of the American Geriatrics Society, 40,* 574–578.

Zara, C., Stolee, P. & Prkachin, K. (1999). The application of Goal Attainment Scaling in chronic pain settings. *Journal of Pain and Symptom Management, 17*(1), 55–63.

CLIENT SATISFACTION

THE IMPORTANCE OF MONITORING
CONSUMER SATISFACTION

Client satisfaction studies can trace their roots back to the consumer movement of the late 1960s and early 1970s (Williams, 1994) as western society became enamored with the rights of the consumer and the concept of accountability. Consumers do not wanted to be "talked down to," patronized, or treated with disrespect. They want, if at all possible, to engage in a partnership with the service deliverer (Rada, 1986). English (2000) has noted that those who market health care services must increasingly be attuned to the "four Rs" of **Relevance** of service, **Response** (delivering on expectations), **Relationship** with the consumer, and **Results** (i.e., does the volume of clients increase?). He states that consumers are more assertive in seeking "value" in the services provided to them.

Most consumers not only desire to get "their money's worth" but are righteously indignant when they are charged for goods or services that are judged to be of less than acceptable quality. With the advent of the Internet, consumers are much more powerful than ever because of an ability to link with one another as well as to virtually unlimited storehouses of knowledge, literature, and statistics.

Like it or not, we live in a competitive world. Whether we are involved with home health care, mental health services, or simply selling hot dogs on the corner, if our clients do not like the way they are treated, they may not return. While one or two clients who go somewhere else will not be missed, what if 25 or 30 percent of consumers were disgruntled? What kind of serious problem might this indicate? What effect could that have on future referrals, funding, or on an agency's reputation in the community? In marketing terms, discontented clients mean a loss of business or market share. A large loss of consumers could translate into a reduction of staff, or could result in the termination of a program. Routine client satisfaction studies allow managers to keep a "finger on the pulse" of an agency and to detect problems before they get too out of control. Only after problem areas are identified can remedies be proposed and implemented.

If consumers are unhappy, they will tell others. Writing to an audience of physicians and hospital administrators about patient loyalty, Fisk et al. (1990) conducted research that found when patient loyalty was judged to be 95 percent, positive testimonials per 100 patients were almost three times more numerous than negative reports. When patient loyalty was 90 percent, there were only slightly more positive reports than negative ones. And when patient loyalty dropped to 80 percent, there were many more negative than positive comments. In other words, "negative word of mouth of unhappy patients occurs much more frequently than the positive testimonials of loyal ones" (p. 44). This conclusion is supported by a technical report by the Consumer Affairs Council of the U.S. Office of Consumer Affairs (TARP, 1986) that stated that a satisfied consumer gives a positive testimonial for a product or service to an average of 3 friends, whereas a dissatisfied consumer criticizes a product or service to an average of about 20 friends.

Client satisfaction alone is not sufficient as a measure of quality, but it is universally accepted as one of several necessary measures (Ingram & Chung, 1997). The importance of consumer feedback is seen in its requirement by many regulatory and certification agencies, such as the Joint Commission on the Accreditation of Healthcare Organizations. The 1997–1998 *Comprehensive Accreditation Manual for Behavioral Health Care* contains this standard under the goal of "Improving Organizational Performance": "The organization collects data about the needs, expectations, and satisfaction of individuals served" (p. 335). Clearly, the Joint Commission maintains that systematic improvement can come about only when data on the needs, expectations, and satisfaction of individuals are regularly and consistently sought.

Most professionals in the human services, if told to design a program evaluation, would likely begin thinking about surveying clients to determine what they thought of the services received. Such an approach is among the simplest and most frequently used measures of program evaluation and is variously known as soliciting consumer feedback, conducting a client satisfaction study, or exploring service acceptability.

Those who provide services need to understand the client's perspective— how clients are treated when they request and receive services. Service providers ought to be concerned about how long consumers have to sit in the waiting room, if they are treated rudely by a receptionist or staff person, if the clients' restrooms are dirty, if the phone lines are always busy when they try to call.

Clients have enough stresses and problems in their lives without service providers adding complications. Asking for feedback about their experiences gives professional staff and management the opportunity to remove obstacles that prevent clients from having satisfying encounters with programs.

There is much to commend the use of client satisfaction as a form of evaluation. Such approaches tend to be relatively inexpensive and easy to interpret, and they can be implemented on short notice without a great deal of planning. Furthermore, they indicate to clients that their experiences and observations are important. Whether we inquire about the *accessibility* or the *acceptability* of our services, these approaches are a "client-oriented," democratic form of evaluation (e.g., everyone gets a vote). They stem from the assumption and belief that clients are the best source of information on the quality and delivery of our services, if not also the best judges of impact and effectiveness. Agency executives, program managers, and staff desire high client satisfaction levels and find such evaluative information useful not only from a managerial perspective, but also for public relations and marketing efforts.

Some organizations may overuse client satisfaction studies because they are relatively simple and easy to conduct. Keep in mind, however, that these studies do not answer questions about outcome in human services—that is, they don't tell us whether clients actually improved as a result of the services provided to them. Critics of these studies note that they frequently fail to provide objective information about the real reason clients approach an agency for help—because they have a crisis or problem that is troubling them.

THE PROBLEM WITH CLIENT SATISFACTION STUDIES

There is only one problem with client satisfaction studies. In practically every instance, the vast majority of respondents indicate satisfaction with services received. For instance, a review of over 50 surveys by Lebow (1983) found that the average percentage of satisfied patients was about 78 percent. More recently, Ingram and Chung (1997) found, in a study of a large, national mental health managed care organization with a database of 8,522 clients, that the average satisfaction rating was 77 percent using four items from the CSQ-4, "a validated abbreviated form of the widely used and well-respected Client Satisfaction Questionnaire (CSQ-8)" (p. 42). Regarding the problem of client satisfaction studies having a predictable positive skew, Ingram and Chung say this:

> The preponderance of positive responses on consumer satisfaction surveys in all sectors of business . . . is even more apparent in the responses of health care recipients . . . whether caused by gratitude or fear of alienating their caregivers. This positive response set creates an obstacle for decision makers who want their plans to be based on unbiased data. (p. 43)

High levels of satisfaction are not found just in the United States. A study of patient satisfaction with government health services in Bangladesh found that only 8 percent of users were not satisfied with the length of the consultation time they received; however, on average it was only 2.33 minutes!

Politeness of the health provider was the most powerful predictor of client satisfaction (Aldana, Piechulek, & Al-Sabir, 2001).

Similarly, using the CSQ (a standardized 8-item client satisfaction scale developed by Nguyen, Attkisson, and Stegner [1983] and shown in Figure 8.1), Gaston and Sabourin (1992) found no differences in client satisfaction among Canadian patients receiving dynamic, eclectic, or cognitive-behavioral treatment in private psychotherapy. The mean CSQ they reported was 28.7. Compare that to a study conducted by Perreault and Leichner (1993) of French-speaking psychiatric outpatients in Montreal. The mean CSQ in that survey was 28.4.

Back in the United States, Locke and McCollum (2001) have reported on an evaluation of clients of a university-based training clinic for marriage and family therapists. Supervisors used one-way mirrors to observe interns' therapy sessions and phones to call in and consult with the interns. Occasionally, supervisors even came into the room and joined the therapeutic effort more directly. All sessions were videotaped. Despite what might be viewed as intrusions into the treatment process with the real-time supervision, the mean score on the CSQ-8 for the 108 clients was 28.4.

As Lebow (1982) noted, high satisfaction rates tend to be obtained even when clients have little choice of facility, type of treatment, or practitioner. Knowing that client satisfaction studies almost always yield positive, if not impressively high, ratings, it is logical to ask the question "Why bother to conduct consumer feedback studies?"

The answer depends, largely, on the particular program, its agency, and community context; but several generalizations can be made. First, if consumer feedback studies are not conducted, then there is no organized or systematic means for learning about clients' experiences with programs. Second, even if the ratings do tend to come back relatively high, that is a good thing—reassuring everyone (clients, staff, and management) that there are no hidden or obscure problems lurking just below the surface. If ratings come back with clients reporting below 75 percent satisfaction, then there is at least a suggestion that further investigation ought to probe for the source of dissatisfaction.

Client satisfaction studies are like weather vanes indicating current consumer sentiments. Opinions and views are changeable as clients bump into better or worse experiences—perhaps as a result of changes in agency policy or staff. Although these studies do not *prove* that a program is doing a good job in rehabilitating or assisting clients, administrators with no funds or expertise to conduct outcome studies often view high ratings as surrogate measures of treatment effectiveness. Should they make these assumptions? No, they should not, but they do and probably will continue to do so.

Although most consumer satisfaction studies focus simply on a single intervention or treatment process, Donovan et al. (2002) examined client satisfaction with three therapies for alcohol dependence (cognitive-behavioral, motivational enhancement, and 12-step facilitation). They found that outpatient clients receiving motivational enhancement therapy were significantly less satisfied than outpatients who received cognitive-behavioral therapy. Those in 12-step facilitation therapy did not differ from the other two groups. This well-designed

FIGURE 8.1 | **THE CLIENT SATISFACTION QUESTIONNAIRE (CSQ-8)**

Please help us improve our program by answering some questions about the services you have received. We are interested in your honest opinion, whether they are positive or negative. *Please answer all of the questions.* We also welcome your comments and suggestions. Thank you very much, we really appreciate your help.

CIRCLE YOUR ANSWER

1. How would you rate the quality of service you have received?

4	3	2	1
Excellent	Good	Fair	Poor

2. Did you get the kind of service you wanted?

1	2	3	4
No, definitely not	No, not really	Yes, generally	Yes, definitely

3. To what extent has our program met your needs?

4	3	2	1
Almost all of my needs have been met	Most of my needs have been met	Only a few of my needs have been met	None of my needs have been met

4. If a friend were in need of similar help, would you recommend our program to him or her?

1	2	3	4
No, definitely not	No, I don't think so	Yes, I think so	Yes, definitely

5. How satisfied are you with the amount of help you have received?

1	2	3	4
Quite dissatisfied	Indifferent or mildly dissatisfied	Mostly satisfied	Very satisfied

6. Have the services you received helped you to deal more effectively with your problems?

4	3	2	1
Yes, they helped a great deal	Yes, they helped somewhat	No, they really didn't help	No, they seemed to make things worse

7. In an overall, general sense, how satisfied are you with the service you have received?

4	3	2	1
Very satisfied	Mostly satisfied	Indifferent or mildly dissatisfied	Quite dissatisfied

8. If you were to seek help again, would you come back to our program?

1	2	3	4
No, definitely not	No, I don't think so	Yes, I think so	Yes, definitely

Source: Reprinted from Pascoe, G. C., & Attkisson, C. C. (1983). The Evaluation Ranking Scale: A new methodology for assessing satisfaction. *Evaluation and Program Planning, 6,* 335–347. Used with permission from Elsevier Science.

study reports that client satisfaction can differ by type of therapy, the degree of engagement in therapy (as shown by attendance and changes in drinking behavior), and clinical outcome status. Thus, Donovan et al.'s investigation demonstrates that client satisfaction studies can yield significantly more information than merely whether clients liked or disliked a program. Along this line, Mitchell (1998) found that mental health clients who participated in time-limited standardized group therapy were just as satisfied as those receiving individual treatment.

A SAMPLING OF RECENT CLIENT SATISFACTION STUDIES

Tables 8.1 and 8.2 furnish a quick summary of a small sampling of recent client satisfaction studies found in the literature. There are a great number of these studies—some that involved a very small number of respondents and others that involved hundreds and thousands of consumers. One of the first things that we noticed about Table 8.1 is that the half of the studies (which were more or less randomly selected) utilized the CSQ-8 or a condensed version of it (the CSQ-4). This may reflect a growing awareness of the necessity for using standardized items and instruments in order to have a uniform understanding of "satisfaction" with services.

Another thing we observed is that the response rate ranged from a low of 28 percent to a high of 93 percent and possibly even 100 percent (two studies did not report a response rate). The two studies with 93 percent response rates had captive audiences, so to speak—inpatients were asked to complete survey forms before they were discharged home. The studies with the 28 percent, 42 percent, and 51 percent response rates obtained these results from mailed surveys.

Table 8.2 confirms, once again, that most client satisfaction studies result in positive ratings. The satisfaction reported is often very high (88 and 90 percent). Additionally, we can see the advantage of using the CSQ-8 (or other standardized instrument) because of the ability to make comparisons across studies. For example, Greenwood et al. (1999) and Mitchell (1998) had very similar means on the CSQ-8, while the Pollack et al. (1997) investigation yielded a somewhat higher mean. The mean CSQ-8 score from those shown in Table 8.2 is approximately 24. This is the average most commonly reported (although they do range above and below the mean) when this instrument is used (Larsen et al., 1979).

ANNOTATIONS ABOUT CLIENT SATISFACTION

Here are some more observations on client satisfaction:

• Satisfaction is not a measure of whether clients' needs were met. Rather, positive ratings seem to be related to whether clients' pretreatment expectations are met (Holcomb et al., 1998). Clients can be satisfied with ineffective programs that are not meeting their goals (Sanders et al., 1998) or that may not provide high quality care (Aldana, Piechulek, & Al-Sabir, 2001).

TABLE 8.1 | RECENT CLIENT SATISFACTION STUDIES: TYPE OF PROGRAM, RESPONSE RATE, AND INSTRUMENT USED

Author	Program	Response Rate	Instrument
Gerber & Prince (1999)	Assertive Community Treatment	51% ($n = 88$)	From Hansson (1989) (35 items)
Ingram & Chung (1997)	Managed Health Care	28% ($n = 8522$)	CSQ-4 (4 items)
Tucker et al. (1997)	Vocational Rehabilitation	42% ($n = 253$)	VR Client Evaluation of Service Inventory (27 items)
Martin, Petr, & Kapp (2003)	Children's MH Services	44% of parents; 29% of youth	Kansas Family Satisfaction Survey (53 items for youth 12 yrs +)
Holcomb et al. (1998)	VA Psychiatric Inpatients	93% ($n = 81$)	Treatment Outcome Profile (27 items)
Greenwood et al. (1999)	Inpatient Psychiatric Services	93% ($n = 464$)	CSQ-8 (8 items)
Pollack et al. (1997)	Addiction Education Group	($n = 50$)	CSQ-8 (8 items)
Mitchell (1998)	Managed Behavioral Health Care	($n = 230$)	CSQ-8 (8 items)
McNeill et al. (1998)	Counseling-Ped. Acute Care Hospital	38% ($n = 83$)	Questionnaire constructed for this study
Constantine (2002)	Campus Counseling Centers ($n = 5$)	98% ($n = 112$)	CSQ-8 (8 items) plus 3 other instruments
Tang (2001)	Anger Management	36% ($n = 23$)	Questionnaire constructed for this study

- Consumers' evaluations of their service experiences can be influenced by the provider's preestablished reputation for reliability—consumers may discount a failure by a high-image provider as an aberration but focus on a minor problem experienced with a lower-image provider (Fisk et al., 1990). Clients can be satisfied with treatment staff but not with the environment in which the treatment was provided (Holcomb et al., 1998).

| TABLE 8.2 | RECENT CLIENT SATISFACTION STUDIES: METHODOLOGY AND FINDINGS |

Author	Methodology	Findings
Gerber & Prince (1999)	Mailed survey	Most (88%) felt satisfied with the help they received.
Ingram & Chung (1997)	Mailed survey	Those "very" or "mostly" satisfied ranged from 81.5 to 90.4% on the CSQ-4 items.
Tucker et al. (1997)	Mailed survey	Although 62% of VR clients did not achieve job placement (rehab failures), they gave high ratings of VR services and counselors.
Martin, Petr, & Kapp (2003)	Telephone survey	88% of parents satisfied with services, 89% would refer family & friends; of hospitalized youth, 70.5% were satisfied with their treatment.
Holcomb et al. (1998)	Self-administered	Self-reported improvement is an excellent at facility predictor of satisfaction. Those with fewer symptoms and higher level of functioning tended to be more satisfied.
Greenwood et al. (1999)	Personal interview	Younger patients less likely to be satisfied than older patients. The mean CSQ-8 score was 22.5; 73% described themselves as "very" or "fairly" satisfied.
Pollack et al. (1997)	Self-administered	The mean CSQ-8 score was 27.47 at facility (computed from their Table 1); 90% described themselves as "very" or "mostly" satisfied.
Mitchell (1998)	Self-administered	Mean CSQ-8 scores were 22.75 (individual treatment) and 21.71 for clients of standardized group therapy; no significant differences in satisfaction.
McNeill et al. (1998)	Mailed survey	87.5% rated the service they received as good or outstanding; 83.7% reported some or a lot of improvement.
Constantine (2002)	Self-administered	Mean CSQ-8 score was 25.04.
Tang (2001)	Self-administered	90% of clients found the program definitely helpful; 96% would recommend it to others.

- Quantitative assessments tend to yield high levels of satisfaction, while qualitative reports tend to reveal lower satisfaction (Williams, 1994).
- Satisfaction with services has shown to be positively related to age (reported in Williams, 1994); this is also a finding of Sanders et al. (1998) and Greenwood et al. (1999). However, Martin, Petr, & Kapp (2003) found that neither age nor ethnicity were related to overall satisfaction.
- Those who are not happy with services tend to drop out. Satisfaction is correlated with clients' length of stay in treatment (Sanders et al., 1998). Donovan et al. (2002) report that for outpatients being treated for alcohol dependence, the total number of weeks in treatment, the number of sessions attended, and the percent of sessions attended were all significantly related to overall client satisfaction. This relationship was not significant for clients in aftercare.
- Client satisfaction has been shown to be associated with symptom relief and improvement in a sample of outpatient psychotherapy clients (Ankuta & Abeles, 1993).
- Open-ended questions can provide "illuminating information" about the client's perspective that may not be discovered through using objective instruments (Sanders et al., 1998).
- Telephone surveys yield higher response rates than mailed surveys (LaSala, 1997).
- Low response rates should be expected. The average response rate for mailed client satisfaction questionnaires is usually between 38 and 46 percent (Lebow, 1982, 1983 as cited in Gerber and Prince, 1999) and at times may be more on the order of 15 to 20 percent, depending on the length of time since the client's exit from the program, the complexity of the form and information requested, and so on.
- Clients who return mailed surveys tend to have higher levels of educational attainment than those who do not respond.
- Families told to obtain services by the court, or school were significantly less satisfied (Martin, Petr, & Kapp, 2003); volunteers were more satisfied than those court-ordered to attend divorce education (Buttell & Carney, 2002).

EXPLANATIONS FOR HIGH RATINGS

There are numerous reasons why client satisfaction studies tend to yield highly positive evaluations. Here is a sampling of some of the methodological issues and other factors found in a recent review of client satisfaction literature.

- More satisfied and higher functioning clients complete the questionnaire (Gerber & Prince, 1999).
- Clients may not know what to expect from counselors, and thus perception of services received may not be credible (Parloff, 1983 cited in Tucker et al., 1997).
- Threats to the validity and reliability of satisfaction studies include recall bias, interviewer bias, nonneutral setting bias, social desirability, and perception by

the client that answers are not anonymous. Client satisfaction studies have used different definitions and instruments, making it difficult to compare findings across studies (Sanders et al., 1998). Clark et al. (1999) reported that outpatient mental health clients gave significantly more extremely negative responses to client interviewers than to staff interviewers. The results did not change when chronicity was added as a covariate in the analysis.

- Respondents were taking medication. Seventy percent of those in the Mitchell (1998) study were taking prescribed medication in conjunction with group or individual therapy.
- Selection bias can come from clients choosing their program or therapist.
- Clients may feel gratitude or fear of alienating treatment providers (Ingram & Chung, 1997).
- Instruments with unknown psychometrics may be used (see, for example, LaSala, 1997). Often client feedback studies rely on "homemade" instruments with unknown reliability and validity.
- Respondents tend to be in treatment longer than nonresponders (LaSala, 1997). Those receiving the least amount of service tend to be overrepresented in the nonresponse group. Clients who are having bad experiences drop out of treatment—leaving those having better experiences to evaluate the program. Unrepresentative samples can also be caused by either low response rates or unscientific sampling procedures.
- Clients who have "invested" a considerable amount of time, energy, and hope into their involvement with a human services program may rate their satisfaction more favorably as a means of reducing what has been called "cognitive dissonance." To provide low satisfaction ratings would be to, in effect, acknowledge that one's participation in a treatment or service program has *really* been a waste of time. Higher than legitimately justifiable satisfaction ratings may be a psychological mechanism by which consumers help convince themselves that the services they received were worthwhile.

RECOMMENDATIONS FOR CLIENT SATISFACTION STUDIES

1. *Use a scale that has good reliability and that has been used successfully in other studies.* Look in the literature for how programs similar to yours have evaluated their efforts. If necessary, write the authors of those studies to inquire about using the previously tested instrument. By all means, avoid the use of any hastily created questionnaires for which there is no psychometric information. (See Figure 8.1.)

Where do you find good instruments? Some scales like the 25-item Client Satisfaction Inventory can be purchased directly (see McMurtry & Hudson, 2000). An article on the Spanish language version has been prepared by McMurtry & Torres (2002). Other instruments are in the public domain and available for use free of charge. For example, the Mental Health Statistics Improvement Program's instruments can be found at www.mhsip.org/surveylink.htm. The adult version of the outpatient mental health consumer survey is composed of 28 items.

FIGURE 8.2 | CLIENT SATISFACTION RATINGS

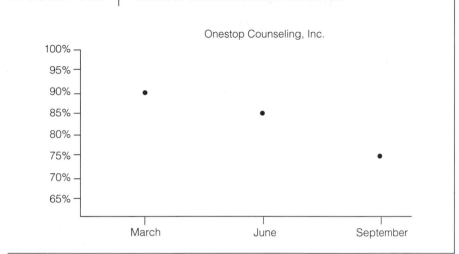

Onestop Counseling, Inc.

The standardized portion of the Youth Services Survey consists of 21 items as does the Youth Services Survey for Families. There's also a 35-item Inpatient Consumer Survey (7 items are demographic) that may be used without charge. Translations into Spanish and a number of other languages are also available for the adult survey. The longer instruments allow evaluators to move beyond overall, global satisfaction and to assess specific aspects of care (i.e., "Staff returned my call in 24 hours" and "Staff were sensitive to my cultural background").

2. *Use the same instrument on repeated occasions, and develop a local baseline of data so that departures from the norm can be observed.* Conduct client satisfaction studies regularly. Compare your findings with results from prior efforts. The advantage of planned, periodic consumer feedback studies is demonstrated in Figure 8.2. In this example, it can be seen that the level of client satisfaction with services is dropping. Such a trend could be discovered only by doing more than one study. Had the evaluator conducted just one study, say in March or June, then this pattern of decreasing satisfaction with services would not have been detected. Would it provide some level of confidence in a program if client satisfaction ratings did not vacillate wildly? (For an example of a study where satisfaction with a divorce education program did not differ across 5 years, see Buttell & Carney, 2002.)

3. *Employ at least one and possibly two open-ended questions so that the consumers of your services can alert you to any problems that you did not suspect and could not anticipate.* For instance, you might want to ask, "If you could make any improvements to this program, what one thing would you change?" or "What do you like best about this program? What do you like least?"

Open-ended questions are important to build in because there is no way to know all of the terrible or uncomfortable situations clients encounter. (See Figure 8.3.) A student once told us of a social service that prepared a

FIGURE 8.3 | EXAMPLES OF CLIENT SATISFACTION
POSTCARDS EMPLOYING
OPEN-ENDED QUESTIONS

We are interested in what you think of Greene County's Head Start Program. Please
share your experiences.

Services are:

Good because _____
_____

Fair or ordinary because _____
_____

Poor because _____
_____

We are interested in what you think of Greene County's Clothing Bank. Please share
your thoughts with us.

Services are *good* because:

Services are *not* good because:

We are interested in what you think of Project Success. Your experiences are
important to us.

Services are:

Good because _____
_____

Fair or ordinary because _____
_____

Poor because _____
_____

We are interested in what you think of Specialized Employment Services. Please tell
us what you like and dislike.

This is *good* agency because:

This is *not* a good agency because:

standardized exit evaluation form for children and adolescents who were exiting foster care. As a 16-year-old filled out the form, she checked that the food had been fine, that she got along well with the foster parents, that she had never been harmed, that there had been no major incidents, and that she would rate the home as "good." However, on the back of the form, a question asked: "If you could change anything about this foster home, what would you change?" At that point the teen began detailing how uncomfortable she felt when the foster father came into her bedroom at night and sat on her bed as she was changing into her pajamas. Clearly, he had no business doing that, but the foster care staff would have had no way of knowing about his misbehavior had they not asked an open-ended question.

4. *In order to avoid the problem of surveying only the clients who remain in a program (and therefore would be more likely to have positive experiences than those who drop out), use a "ballot box" approach where one week is set aside when every client entering the agency is given a brief questionnaire while waiting for his or her appointment.* To improve a program, it is necessary to know about clients' experiences in every phase, from intake to ongoing services to termination. The in-agency ballot box solves the problem of locating clients who move frequently and do not have stable addresses and often yields high response rates. Nebeker (1992, as cited in Attkisson & Greenfield, 1994) obtained response rates of 91 percent and 97 percent in two on-site waiting room studies using the ballot box approach.

Another advantage of this approach is that nontreatment personnel (e.g., the waiting room receptionist or other assigned staff) can be trained to observe and assist clients who appear to need help reading the questionnaire or writing a response. At the same time, it is important not to give the impression that clients are being forced or coerced to participate in the consumer feedback study. If a staff person is watching the client fill out the form, the consumer may feel that his or her anonymity is jeopardized. Although it is permissible to *encourage* clients to fill out surveys, instructions to all parties must clearly state that this is a *voluntary* activity and that clients cannot and will not be affected adversely in any way by anything that they report about their experiences. Consulting with a focus group of clients about the procedures to be used with the client satisfaction study could provide helpful advice about how the effort could be interpreted and how it should be presented.

Another variation of the ballot box approach would be to set up a computer in a vacant room where clients could register their satisfaction or dissatisfaction with services. Alternatively, in some locations (i.e., a college campus), a website could be created and clients could be given a slip of paper with the URL of the website feedback center.

5. *Do not focus only on solving the problems of the dissatisfied consumers, assuming that you will be able to convert them into satisfied customers.* Ingram and Chung (1997) recommend working toward a goal, for instance, of 90 percent "maximally satisfied." They cite studies where customer relations experts agree that most consumers who "report themselves strongly dissatisfied will never give up their misgivings, despite the efforts made to please them" (p. 44).

6. *If you conduct a mailed survey, do what you can to get a response rate over 50 percent.* Because clients of social service organizations often have a lot of chaos in their lives and may be battling every day for survival (e.g., because of drug addiction, domestic violence, terminal illness, homelessness, mental illness), it is understandable that completing your questionnaire may not be a high priority. In order to improve the response rate, you may need to offer small incentives such as coupons at a fast-food restaurant. See Box 8.1 to see how response might vary.

7. *Target specific dimensions.* Instead of thinking about client satisfaction as an all-or-nothing phenomenon, try to identify an area where you suspect there may be problems. For instance, you might aim to improve satisfaction

---

RESPONSE RATES AND CLIENT SATISFACTION: AN INTERESTING EXCERPT FROM THE LITERATURE

Baker, Zucker, and Gross (1998) conducted a client satisfaction study of five inpatient treatment facilities for adults with serious and persistent mental illnesses. Three facilities were locked, one was open, and one was a combined (locked unit and unlocked bed unit) facility.

The authors rejected the CSQ-8 because it provided only a global measure of client satisfaction and devised a new one spanning eight areas of service (nursing, counseling, groups and rehab activities, family services, social services/case management, the facility, food services, and treatment philosophy). Surveys were administered in group settings with a staff member available to answer questions. It was decided at the beginning of the study that the two lowest areas of satisfaction would be targeted for improvement.

The average response rate varied considerably across facilities and over time. (There were three survey administrations: May, 1995; March 1, 1996; and May 30, 1996.) The highest response rate was 88 percent and the lowest 46 percent. Within three facilities, response rates varied as much as 30 percent over the survey administrations.

The two highest rates of response came from facilities with the lowest and highest functioning clients. The authors concluded that much of the difference in response rates could be attributed to survey administration techniques. At the second administration there was little or no encouragement or introductory remarks and no group time allotted for completing the surveys. Before the third data collection, each facility was visited and the importance of obtaining a high response rate was emphasized. The third administration then saw a rise in overall response rates to an average of 75 percent.

The authors also concluded that the survey process had two important and unexpected benefits: (1) it allowed tracking and documentation of the successes in program improvement over time, which seemed to increase staff morale and pride; and (2) it increased client participation and involvement.

Source: Baker, L., Zucker, P. J., & Gross, M. J. (1998). Using client satisfaction surveys to evaluate and improve services in locked and unlocked adult inpatient facilities. *The Journal of Behavioral Health Services & Research, 25,* 51–63.

with availability of services, accessibility of facility or staff, competence of staff, helpfulness of staff, continuity of service provision (e.g., continuation with same therapist), or satisfaction with service outcome. Talk with your staff to obtain anecdotal information about what might be causing clients difficulty. Is it too much paperwork initially? A long waiting period before delivery of services? Cost of services? Use this information to gather client input that can be your baseline for improving.

8. *Keep your expectations realistic.* Do not overgeneralize from a small sample of clients. It is not always comforting to know that 90 percent of clients find services helpful if only 36 percent of clients respond to your survey. Favorable data do not mean that your program is achieving the results it was planned to produce—that requires a different kind of evaluation effort.

9. *Look for behavioral indicators (i.e., attendance) to supplement the client satisfaction data.* In a weekly treatment group, for example, 35 percent attendance rates might suggest either that the group is held at an inopportune time of day or that reported high levels of satisfaction are not credible. On the other hand, 90 percent attendance, 85 percent response rates, and 90 percent satisfaction with services is much more convincing because of the strong consistent pattern. Alternatively, you may want to consider a qualitative approach and look for themes (see Box 8.2).

| BOX 8.2 | QUALITATIVE INVESTIGATIONS OF CLIENT SATISFACTION |

You may have noticed that there has been little content, thus far, on qualitative research efforts examining client satisfaction. This is due to the fact that the vast majority of the literature on client satisfaction is quantitative in nature. You may wish, however, to examine the two studies highlighted here to get a flavor of qualitative investigations.

One qualitative effort involved eight focus groups of parents with children in foster care. The purpose was to help design an ongoing system for collecting client satisfaction data. However, along the way the parents provided extensive information (347 pages of transcribed text) about their treatment as consumers of a privatized foster care system.

Six general themes emerged from the focus groups: communication difficulties, problems associated with worker turnover and work load, perceived lack of respect from the child welfare professionals, failure to involve caregivers in decision making, lack of information about rights of parents, and comments about best ways to gather consumer data.

Kapp and Propp (2002) report that "Many felt that a mailed survey was unable to capture their sentiments about what it was like to have a child in the foster care system. Other participants were insulted by the use of a 1-page form asking about their experiences" (p. 240). More details can be gleaned from reading the full article.

Source: Kapp, S. A. & Propp, J. (2002). Client satisfaction methods: Input from parents with children in foster care. *Child and Adolescent Social Work Journal, 19*(3), 227–245. Another qualitative investigation that employed focus groups can be found in Conners, N. A., & Franklin, K. K. (2000). Using focus groups to evaluate client satisfaction in an alcohol and drug treatment program. *Journal of Substance Abuse Treatment, 18*(4), 313–320.

DETERMINING SAMPLE SIZE

An issue concerning many of those planning client satisfa[...] and need assessments is related to the question: "How many cli[...] nple?" or "How many interviews are enough?" Although this pro[...] thodological one, it can at times become somewhat of a politica[...] nen stakeholders who do not have a good understanding of random sampling or the concept of representativeness try to influence sample size by insisting on some kind of a quota (e.g., "The study must include *at least* 100 left-handed individuals"). Unfortunately, setting quotas for certain types of respondents is not an accepted procedure for producing samples that are representative of the population being studied. Quota samples are nonprobability samples and share the same problems as convenience samples, which are described later.

There is no single, quick response to questions about how large the sample should be. Before discussing sample size, let's talk a bit about concerns related to *how* a sample is selected.

In the simplest of client satisfaction studies, random sampling may not be an issue. If your agency only has 25 clients in a selected program, then the study ought to involve all of the clients. However, if you wanted to potentially draw from a list of every client who completed the program in the last 10 years, then it would make sense to think about using a random sampling design that would allow you to get a representation from a smaller group than the entire pool of clients. Suppose staff in the program get together and start listing the clients that they can remember with the idea that those clients would be mailed a client satisfaction form. Stop for a moment and think what might be wrong with that sampling plan. Would the clients who are remembered be the staff favorites (the compliant, successful clients), or would they be the troublemakers, the pains-in-the-neck who called in bomb threats or threatened suicide every holiday? Either way, there is an element of selection bias being introduced with such a sample.

Similarly, if the evaluator chose to contact just *active* consumers, then those who dropped out because they were dissatisfied with the program would be missed. Might that lead to biased findings? Just choosing the active consumers because they are the easiest to contact or reach is known as a **convenience sample.** With samples of this type, there is always a strong possibility of biased results.

Samples of convenience are just what they sound like—a group of persons easily obtained because they are close at hand and accessible. An example of a sample of convenience would be interviewing the first 15 clients who walked past your office on a Monday morning, the first day of the month. Such a procedure might appear on the surface to generate a random sample, but what if all 15 were new clients who had just been sent over by their probation officers?

Because a convenience sample of clients is not randomly selected from a larger population, it is impossible to know how well the sample represents the "true" population. For that reason, convenience samples are known as nonprobability samples and are generally not viewed as being scientific. Does that mean you cannot learn from them? No, but the results are likely to be regarded as more preliminary or exploratory than definitive.

Think for a moment what might result if you offer a new, experimental intervention for a certain problem, and you advertise in the newspaper for volunteers. Those who contact you are likely to be more severely affected by the problem (they are highly motivated) than those who also have the problem but who *do not* contact you. What might you conclude about the intervention? If it works with highly motivated volunteers, will be successful with those who are less motivated? If it does not work, there is the possibility that it may be beneficial to those who did not volunteer and whose problem is less chronic or milder in some way. A strong selection bias (because respondents selected themselves) prevents you from knowing as much as you might have known if a random sample from all those with the problem had been chosen.

Given a choice of contacting the program dropouts in the past 30 days or random sampling *all* the dropouts in the past year, you obtain a stronger evaluation from a random sampling of *all* those who dropped out. If the program has undergone a major change in the recent past, you may want to begin your study that point. Sometimes it may be more informative to contact program dropouts than active program participants—particularly if there is a perception that dropouts have been increasing recently.

In a situation where a program is relatively new (i.e., 100 or fewer clients have completed the program) gather evaluation data from all of the clients. You will never obtain a 100 percent response rate. Clients move and do not leave forwarding addresses; they may choose not to respond; they may be hospitalized or locked up; and some may have died. Even if you get addresses and mail surveys to all 100 clients, it is very likely that less than half of them will respond. So, if you randomly draw 50 names, as few as 15 and maybe no more than 25 may respond. The number of respondents you are likely to obtain is a major consideration when deciding on a sampling strategy. As a rule, the more recent a client's involvement and the more favorable his or her experience, the more likely the client will respond. Also, a telephone survey will likely yield a higher response rate than a mailed survey.

A common assumption when trying to decide how many persons to sample is that 10 percent of a client population makes an adequate sample. Yet, this rule of thumb could provide too small a sample (in the case of small populations) and is too unwieldy when there is a large population. To understand what sample size is appropriate, we need to consider the terms margin of error and confidence levels.

Margin of error (sometimes known as confidence intervals) refers to the precision of the findings. A margin of error of 5 percent means that the actual findings could vary by as much as 5 points either positively or negatively. A consumer satisfaction survey, for instance, with a 5 percent margin of error associated with a finding of 65 percent of clients "highly satisfied" with services would mean that the true value in the population could be as low as 60 percent ($65 - 5 = 60$) or as high as 70 percent ($65 + 5 = 70$). This 5 percent margin of error is a reasonable and accepted standard. If, however, you require greater precision (e.g., plus or minus 2 points), then you will need to increase your sample size.

The other term that is important to understand is confidence level. The **confidence level** is a statement of how often you could expect to find similar results if the survey were to be repeated. Because every survey varies slightly (depending on who is selected to be in the sample), the confidence level informs about how often the findings will fall outside the margin of error. For instance, in a sample developed to have a 95 percent confidence level with a 5 percent margin of error, the results would miss the actual values in the population by more than 5 percent only 1 time in 20 samples. In 95 out of 100 samples, the results would fall within the 5 percent margin of error.

You have three options for determining the appropriate sample size for your evaluation effort. One approach (as demonstrated in Table 8.3) is to find reference

TABLE 8.3 | APPROPRIATE SIZES OF SIMPLE RANDOM SAMPLES WITH A 5% MARGIN OF ERROR AND 95% CONFIDENCE LEVEL, ASSUMING A POPULATION PROPORTION OF 50%

Population Size	Sample Size
25	24
50	44
75	63
100	80
150	108
200	132
250	152
300	169
400	196
500	217
750	254
1,000	278
2,000	322
4,000	351
5,000	357
10,000	370
15,000	375
20,000	377
25,000	378
50,000	381
100,000	384
1,000,000	384

books or texts that contain tables to aid in determining necessary sample sizes. Prepared tables will allow you to determine sample size based on levels of confidence (99 to 90 percent) and margins of error (1 to 5 percent) when the absolute proportion of the traits, characteristics, or attitude in the population is not known. (When the level of the expected attitude, trait, or characteristic is unknown, a conservative estimate of 50 percent is used. Somewhat smaller samples can be developed when the known proportion in the population is less than 50 percent.)

A second approach is to manually calculate the sample size and adjust for the desired margin of error, confidence level, and population proportion. The following formula (found in Krejcie and Morgan, 1970) can be used if you want to make these calculations yourself:

$$\text{Sample size} = X^2 NP(1 - P) \div d^2(N - 1) + X^2 P(1 - P)$$

where

X^2 = 3.841 (the table value of chi-square for 1 degree of freedom at the 95 percent confidence level)

N = the population size

P = the population proportion (without other evidence, this is assumed to be .50)

d = the margin of error or degree of accuracy needed (e.g., .05)

From this formula, sample sizes for the populations in Table 8.3 can be calculated. Note that when the population is small, sample sizes constitute a larger proportion than when the population is very large. For example, 24 clients would be needed to make the necessary sample when the client population is 25 (a proportion of 96 percent), while only 357 would be needed when the population was 5,000 (a proportion of 7 percent). As the population size increases, the sample size increases at a slower or diminishing rate. Sample size remains relatively constant as it approaches 380, so that a sample of 384 is needed whether the population is 100,000 or 1,000,000 (given a 5 percent margin of error and 95 percent confidence level).

The 5 percent margin of error and 95 percent confidence level are regarded as providing all the precision needed for most research and evaluation purposes in the social sciences. However, there may be occasions when greater or less precision is required. If, for instance, you would be comfortable with a 90 percent confidence level and a 5 percent margin of error, smaller samples could be used. By substituting 2.71 for the chi-square value of 3.841, you can determine that for a population of 500, the 90 percent confidence level requires a sample size of 176, and with a population of 1,000 a sample of 213 is needed. Compare these with the sample sizes in Table 8.3.

Although it is seldom necessary to have more confidence than 95 percent or to decrease the margin of error below 5 percent, when greater precision and confidence is necessary, the formula can similarly be adjusted. To compute a sample size that would provide a 99 percent level of confidence and a margin of error of 3 percent, you would substitute 6.64 for the chi-square value of

EXAMPLES OF SAMPLE SIZE
CALCULATORS AVAILABLE
ON THE INTERNET

Easy-to-use interactive sample size calculators can be found below. Generally they only require that you choose the margin of error and confidence level and then type in the population size. A response will immediately appear showing the exact sample size needed.

> http://www.surveyguy.com/SGcalc.htm
>
> http://www.surveysystem.com/sscalc.htm (this one will also let you find the specific confidence interval [the margin of error] if you state the sample size and population)
>
> http://www.researchinfo.com/docs/calculators/samplesize.cfm

3.841 in the formula and .03 for d (the margin of error). For populations of 500 and 1,000, this would result in samples of 394 and 649, respectively.

A third approach to calculating sample size is to go to the Internet and use a sample size calculator. Several examples of these can be found in Box 8.3. These interactive tools are quick, precise, and easy to use.

No matter how you arrive at the sample size recommended for the confidence level and margin of error that you desire, it is understood that a random selection process will be used to select the sample. Note that random selection is not applicable when the population is very small. For instance, although Table 8.3 indicates that with a population of 25 you need to contact only 24 participants, you would probably want to interview all 25 anyway. If these 25 individuals were staff of some agency being asked about their job satisfaction, it is easy to imagine how the one who did not get asked for his or her opinions could feel devalued, angry, or even paranoid. Besides, by the time you figure out a fair and equitable random assignment process, you could have interviewed or contacted the lone individual.

Keep in mind that 20 to 30 percent response rates are not uncommon with mail surveys. If you had 1,000 clients in your program and you randomly selected 278 to receive a mailed questionnaire, you might plan on getting 55 to 85 responses. It is also possible that you might receive as few as 30. Could this pose a problem with interpretation of the data? You bet! Do not assume that a handful of responders have the same experiences or opinions as those who did not respond. Because less than a majority of the sample responded, you have a self-selected group that is very likely biased.

To give your consumer study credibility, one of the most important things you can do, besides drawing an adequately sized random sample, is to get a response rate greater than 50 percent. There are several ways to go about this—sending postcard reminders, mailing a second questionnaire, and so forth. Response rates are important to the evaluator, and low response rates are always suspect.

In order to be able to speak about your data in terms of the confidence level and margin of error reflected in Table 8.3, it is necessary to obtain the number of *responses* indicated under the "Sample Size" column. In other words, if you note that for a population of 500 a sample of 217 is needed and you mail to exactly 217 randomly selected clients, you cannot claim 5 percent margin of error and 95 percent confidence level *if* you obtain fewer than 217 completed questionnaires. So, in order to get 217 usable questionnaires, you may have to contact 300 or 400 of those in the population. A small pilot test with a sample of 30 to 50 clients can give you some idea of the kind of response rate you can expect.

Remember, if you are working with a *convenience* sample, there will not be any statistical or logical grounds to help you infer that your sample is truly representative of all those with a particular problem. Studies that make use of convenience samples will always suffer from limited external validity.

The most robust method for obtaining a truly representative sample is the random sampling procedure. When this method is used, you may infer or generalize findings from the sample to the larger population. Anything less than a randomly selected sample chosen from a population of interest compromises the researcher's ability to make inferences from that sample back to the population, *no matter how large the sample size.*

Although this chapter has focused exclusively on *clients'* satisfaction, the techniques described here are by no means limited to only consumers of services. In a competitive environment where referrals can be made to a variety of other agencies or programs, social service and health care providers may wish to conduct a survey of their referral sources (i.e., mental health practitioners, physicians, clergy, child protective service workers, officers of the court) to understand how satisfied these persons are with the changes produced in those whom they have referred. These surveys can use very general questions (i.e., "How would you rate the services we have provided?") or, with the client's permission, very specific ones (i.e., "How would you rate the services we have provided to Mrs. *Gomer Pyle* over the past 6 months?").

Similarly, evaluators can use this chapter's discussion of client satisfaction in planning studies of employee job satisfaction. Those interested in this topic might wish to review Bednar's (2003) literature review on research regarding job satisfaction in child welfare agencies and factors influencing workers to leave or remain on their jobs.

Questions for Class Discussion

1. Can the problem of positive bias with client satisfaction studies be "fixed"? What could be done to minimize this form of bias in a consumer feedback study?
2. How would you tackle the problem of variability in response rates within the same agency (as discussed by Baker, Zucker, and Gross, 1998)?
3. What variables could affect response rates of a client satisfaction study besides the survey administration procedures?

4. Although it is known that client satisfaction studies typically are positively biased, discuss why this form of evaluation is used so often in evaluating university faculty.

5. Knowing what you now know about client satisfaction studies, argue for and against their place in a comprehensive program evaluation.

6. What open-ended questions would you want to ask consumers participating in a client satisfaction study of a community mental health psychoeducational intervention? Would you think it would be best to use mailed questionnaires or telephone interviews?

7. What are the arguments for and against using standardized instruments to measure client satisfaction?

8. What are the pros and cons of using a convenience sample of clients for program evaluation activities?

Mini-Projects: Experiencing Evaluation Firsthand

1. Collect as many client satisfaction forms as you can from school, work, fast-food restaurants, or other sources. Examine them and determine how many questionnaires have similar or identical items. After you review several questionnaires, construct one of your own. Be sure to identify the program and audience that it is designed to target.

2. Ask the agency where you are working, interning, or volunteering if any client satisfaction studies have been conducted in the past 7 years. If so, review the instrument used, the data collection procedures, and the findings. What would you have changed or done differently? Write a brief paper on your observations and recommendations for a future client satisfaction study.

3. Design a client satisfaction study for a program of your choosing. Locate or create a suitable instrument, develop the data collection procedures, and draw up a budget and projected time line. Be sure to identify the program and the group from whom you will be drawing data.

4. For some program with which you are familiar, find the number of program recipients in the last 3 years. Then determine the sample size needed for a probability sample with a confidence interval of 95 percent and a 5 percent margin of error.

References and Resources

Aldana, J. M., Piechulek, H., & Al-Sabir, A. (2001). Client satisfaction and quality of health care in rural Bangladesh. *Bulletin of the World Health Organization, 79*(6), 512–517.

Ankuta, G. Y., & Abeles, N. (1993). Client satisfaction, clinical significance, and meaningful change in psychotherapy. *Professional Psychology: Research and Practice, 24*(1), 70–74.

Attkisson, C. C., & Greenfield, T. K. (1994). Client Satisfaction Questionnaire-8 and Service Satisfaction Scale-30. In M. E. Maruish (Ed.), *The use of psychological testing for treatment planning and outcome assessment.* Hillsdale, NJ: Erlbaum.

Baker, L., Zucker, P. J., & Gross, M. J. (1998). Using client satisfaction surveys to evaluate and improve services in locked and unlocked adult inpatient facilities. *The Journal of Behavioral Health Services & Research, 25,* 51–63.

Bednar, S. G. (2003). Elements of satisfying organizational climates in child welfare agencies. *Families in Society, 84*(1), 7–12.

Buttell, F. P., & Carney, M. M. (2002). Client satisfaction among parents attending a mandatory divorce education program: Results from a five-year study. *Arete, 26*(1), 12–20.

Clark, C. C., Scott, E. A., Boydell, K. M., & Goering, P. (1999). Effects of client interviewers on client-reported satisfaction with mental health services. *Psychiatric Services, 50*(7), 961–963.

Constantine, M. G. (2002). Predictors of satisfaction with counseling: Racial and ethnic minority clients' attitudes toward counseling and ratings of their counselors' general and multicultural counseling competence. *Journal of Counseling Psychology, 49*(2), 255–264.

Donovan, D. M., Kadden, R. M., DiClemente, C. C., & Carroll, K. M. (2002). Client satisfaction with three therapies in the treatment of alcohol dependence: Results from Project MATCH. *American Journal on Addictions, 11,* 291–307.

English, J. (2000). The four P's of marketing are dead. *Marketing Health Services, 20*(2), 20–23.

Fisk, T. A., Brown, C. J., Cannizzaro, C., & Naftal, B. (1990). Creating patient satisfaction and loyalty. *Journal of Health Care Marketing, 10*(2), 5–15.

Gaston, L., & Sabourin, S. (1992). Client satisfaction and social desirability in psychotherapy. *Evaluation and Program Planning, 15,* 227–231.

Gerber, G. J., & Prince, P. N. (1999). Measuring client satisfaction with assertive community treatment. *Psychiatric Services, 50,* 546–550.

Geron, S. M. (1998). Assessing the satisfaction of older adults with long-term care services: Measurement and design challenges for social work. *Research on Social Work Practice, 8*(1), 103–119.

Greenwood, N., Key, A., Burns, T., Bristow, M., & Sedgwick, P. (1999). Satisfaction with inpatient psychiatric services: Relationship to patient and treatment factors. *Journal of Psychiatry, 174,* 159–163.

Holcomb, W. R., Parker, J. C., Leong, G. B., Thiele, J., & Higdon, J. (1998). Customer satisfaction and self-reported treatment outcomes among psychiatric inpatients. *Psychiatric Services, 49,* 929–934.

Ingram, B. L., & Chung, R. S. (1997). Client satisfaction data and quality improvement in managed mental health care organizations. *Health Care Management Review, 22,* 40–52.

Krejcie, R. V., & Morgan, D. W. (1970). Determining sample size for research activities. *Educational and Psychological Measurement, 30,* 607–610.

Larsen, D. L., Attkisson, C. C., Hargreaves, W. A., & Nguyen, T. D. (1979). Assessment of patient satisfaction: Development and refinement of a service evaluation questionnaire. *Evaluation and Program Planning, 2,* 197–207.

LaSala, M. C. (1997). Client satisfaction: Consideration of correlates and response bias. *Families in Society, 78*(1), 54–64.

Lebow, J. L. (1982). Consumer satisfaction with mental health treatment. *Psychological Bulletin, 91*(2), 244–259.

Lebow, J. L. (1983). Research assessing consumer satisfaction with mental health treatment: A review of findings. *Evaluation and Program Planning, 6,* 211–236.

Locke, L. D., & McCollum, E. E. (2001). Clients' views of live supervision and satisfaction with therapy. *Journal of Marital and Family Therapy, 27*(1), 129–133.

Martin, J. S., Petr, C. G., & Kapp, S. A. (2003). Consumer satisfaction with children's mental health services. *Child &*

Adolescent Social Work Journal, 20(3), 211–226.

McMurtry, S. L., & Hudson, W. W. (2000). The Client Satisfaction Instrument: Results of an initial validation study. *Research on Social Work Practice, 10*(5), 644–663.

McMurtry, S. L., & Torres, J. B. (2002). Initial validation of a Spanish language version of the Client Satisfaction Inventory. *Research on Social Work Practice, 12*(1), 124–142.

McNeill, T., Nicholas, D., Szechy, K., & Lach, L. (1998). Perceived outcome of social work intervention: Beyond consumer satisfaction. *Social Work in Health Care, 26*(3), 1–18.

Mitchell, C. G. (1998). Perceptions of empathy and client satisfaction with managed behavioral health care. *Social Work, 43*, 404–411.

Nguyen, T. D., Attkisson, C. C., & Stegner, B. L. (1983). Assessment of patient satisfaction: Development and refinement of a service evaluation questionnaire. *Evaluation and Program Planning, 6*, 299–314.

Perreault, M., & Leichner, P. (1993). Patient satisfaction with outpatient psychiatric services. Qualitative and quantitative assessments. *Evaluation and Program Planning, 16*, 109–118.

Pollack, L., Stuebben, G., & Sobhan, T. (1997). Dually diagnosed inpatients' satisfaction with addiction groups. *Journal of Psychosocial Nursing, 35*, 18–23.

Rada, R. T. (1986). The health care revolution: From patient to client to consumer. *Psychosomatics, 27*, 276–279, 283–284.

Sanders, L. M., Trinh, C., Sherman, B. R., & Banks, S. M. (1998). Assessment of client satisfaction in a peer counseling substance abuse treatment program for pregnant and postpartum women. *Evaluation and Program Planning, 21*, 287–296.

Tang, M. (2001). Clinical outcome and client satisfaction of an anger management group program. *Canadian Journal of Occupational Therapy, 68*(4), 228–236.

TARP (Technical Assistance Research Programs Institute). (1986). *Consumer complaint handling in America: An update study*. Washington, DC: Consumer Affairs Council of the U.S. Office of Consumer Affairs, U.S. Department of Commerce.

Tucker, C. M., Abrams, J. M., Chennault, S. A., Stanger, T., & Herman, K. C. (1997).The relationship between client satisfaction and rehabilitation success as measures of VR counselor performance. *Journal of Rehabilitation, 63*, 49–53.

Williams, B. (1994). Patient satisfaction: A valid concept? *Social Science and Medicine, 38*, 509–516.

GROUP RESEARCH DESIGNS

WHAT ARE GROUP RESEARCH DESIGNS?

The most powerful research tools available for evaluators to use in rigorously examining program *outcomes* are the methodologies collectively known as **group research designs** (GRDs). As was the case with the single system research designs (SSRDs) described in Chapter 6, properly designed and conducted group research designs incorporate the fundamental principles of reliable and valid measurement, the introduction of an intervention, and an appraisal of outcomes. The more sophisticated GRDs allow for an evaluation of the effects of an intervention by comparing the results obtained from a group of clients who received a given treatment, with those from a similar group of clients who *did not* receive a given treatment or who received an alternative intervention.

As with SSRDs, GRDs may be arranged in a *hierarchy* of complexity, with successive variations in design intended to answer increasingly precise questions. At the lower end of scale, the pre-experimental group research designs may be capable of answering simple evaluative questions such as "Did the group of clients get better?" or "Were the consumers satisfied with the social services they received?" In order to provide credible answers to more complex questions such as "Did the clients get better *because* of the intervention?" or "Is Intervention X superior to Intervention Y?" or "Are the apparent effects of Intervention X due to the passage of time alone?" the program evaluator must use correspondingly more complex designs with the potential to provide valid answers. These more complex (and difficult to undertake) GRDs are labeled quasi-experimental and experimental research designs. Each of these three categories of GRDs— pre-experimental, quasi-experimental, and experimental—will be described and then illustrated. But first we will begin with some general principles before moving into a discussion of the specifics of the different types of GRDs.

STARTING AN OUTCOME EVALUATION

Your agency director wants you to conduct an evaluation for the agency. The agency currently does some program monitoring and has made use of consultants for formative evaluations in previous years. Now, however, the agency director wants an outcome evaluation and wants you to coordinate this effort. Where do you begin? Although the director may strongly urge you to do an evaluation of the whole agency (or examine all of the agency's programs simultaneously), it is not recommended that the novice evaluator attempt a multi-program evaluation. Instead, a single program should be chosen as the object or target of the evaluation. The wisdom of this recommendation can be seen if we look at the programs contained in a single "yellow pages" phone listing for one moderate-sized mental health center, shown in Figure 9.1.

It is hard not to notice the rich variety of programs that this agency provides. This assortment of programs prevents an evaluator from using any one tool or instrument to measure the same outcome for every program. One would expect the Day Treatment Unit to have a different set of outcomes than the Employee Assistance Program or the Chemical Dependency Outpatient Counseling Center. Thus, the evaluator may wish to begin an evaluation effort by selecting a single program to be the focus of the evaluation. (Later on, as you know more about evaluation, you may find the same evaluation procedure or the same instrument can be used with several programs simultaneously, but for now keep in mind that we are to evaluate one program at a time.)

Once a single program has been selected, it is possible to begin to think about criteria that would help differentiate a "good" program from a poor program. Start by thinking in terms of single indicators. For instance, with programs designed to employ the "hard-core" unemployed, success could be measured by the percentage who actually become employed. A program designed to help agoraphobics could be evaluated based on the percentage who, after treatment, are able to leave their homes without symptoms in order to shop, work, volunteer, or play. Bereavement counseling programs should help participants become less depressed. Treatment programs for impotence should determine the percent who are still impotent after intervention.

These examples provide illustrations of the kind of indicators needed for outcome evaluation. Evaluators do not always have to come up with these indicators on their own. If the agency already has developed goal statements and objectives for the program, outcome indicators can often be obtained from reviewing this information.

FIGURE 9.1 | YELLOW PAGES PHONE BOOK LISTING FOR THE COMPREHENSIVE MENTAL HEALTH SERVICES AGENCY

Main Office:	
234 W. Burton Street	885-4000
Adult Counseling Clinic	885-4001
Chemical Dependency Services	885-4911
Detoxification Center	885-4999
Inpatient Treatment Center	885-4949
Outpatient Counseling Center	885-4989
Child Guidance Program	885-4363
Community Support Services	885-4888
West Side Personal Care Home	885-4212
Campbell House	885-4175
Employee Assistance Program	885-4222
Forensic Services	885-4333
Lifestyles	885-4545
Parent's Place	885-4721
Partial Hospitalization Services	885-4110
Our Place	885-4166
Day Treatment Unit	885-4699
Passages	885-4677
Teen Help	885-4444

It is always a good idea to ask agency staff and administrators what *they* consider to be the goals or aims of the program, and to solicit their feedback about what are potentially suitable outcome measures. It is also a good principle to select measures that are as close as possible to the real problem that is the focus of intervention. Think of random urine tests as an outcome measure of the success of a substance abuse treatment program, versus asking clients to complete a pencil-and-paper measure of attitudes toward drugs or asking them if they have used drugs recently. Which measure would seem to provide stronger evidence as to the "true" outcomes of services? Or take a high school program aimed to enhance the academic performance of adolescents at high risk for dropping out of school. Clearly measures of drop out graduation rates and earned GPAs would usually be seen as more valid mirrors of the program's success than pencil-and-paper measures of self-esteem completed by the youth or of the teachers' impressions of how the kids are doing. This is not to assert that indirect or surrogate measures have no place in program evaluation. They clearly do, and in some instances are the best available indicators of outcome, but whenever possible they should supplement, not supplant, more direct indices.

Once the evaluator has chosen a useful outcome indicator (sometimes called a dependent variable), he or she can formulate a research question or hypothesis to further focus the program evaluation. For example, the evaluator might ask of a job-training program, "What percentage of clients completing the program secure full-time employment within 6 months of graduation from the program?" Sometimes a program director or the evaluator might propose a hypothesis instead of a research question. An example of a hypothesis might be: "The Teen Help outpatient counseling program is more effective in combating adolescent chemical dependency than the Life Adventure program." Another example might be "A greater percentage of the clients of Chrysalis House will be drug-free one year after completion of the program than those who complete residential treatment at Pilot House." No matter whether you tend to think in terms of hypotheses or of questions, both provide the necessary focal point with which to begin planning an evaluation.

Once a question or hypothesis has been selected to guide the outcome study, the next step is to choose an appropriate design. If the question is simply "Did clients improve?" the evaluator does not need to be concerned with control groups and random assignment. Random assignment can be difficult, if not impossible, to impose in a social service agency. Often, intact groups already exist, and involving these individuals in an evaluation effort makes a good deal of sense. Selection of a design is affected by multiple considerations, including the type of questions you need to answer, access to data, cooperation you expect from staff, the importance of controlling for variables that might contaminate the validity of the findings, the amount of time you have, and your technical analytical skills.

OUTCOME EVALUATION DESIGNS

Fitz-Gibbon and Morris (1987) have defined an **evaluation design** as "a plan which dictates when and from whom measurements will be gathered during the course of an evaluation" (p. 9). Evaluation designs are roughly analogous to blueprints in that they suggest a plan or model to be followed. Even though you may know nothing about building a new house, you can appreciate the carpenters' frustration if the only instructions they were given were "Build a house." Without more elaboration, the carpenters do not know whether to begin framing for a six-room house or a house with eight bedrooms. Should there be one bath or a bath adjacent to each bedroom? Will the house be brick or frame? Beyond even the basic features, there are still important details that must be worked out, such as the number of windows to be used, and their placement. To guide the carpenters as they work on the house, detailed sketches or blueprints are used. These diagrams provide guidance and direction to the carpenters in their construction.

Evaluation designs describe the key features and procedures to be followed in conducting an evaluation. They make it possible to estimate the cost of the evaluation, the length of time that will be required, and the rigorousness of the evaluation.

Just as a carpenter could take a set of blueprints to another site and build a house identical to the one that had just been constructed, an evaluation design contains the necessary information to allow other evaluators to replicate or reproduce the original evaluation.

There are plenty of designs and evaluative criteria to choose from. More than 30 years ago, Suchman (1967) discussed the focus of evaluation in terms of effort, performance, adequacy, efficiency, and process. Attkisson and Broskowski (1978) defined program evaluations as having a special focus on accessibility, acceptability, comprehensiveness, integration of services, awareness, availability, continuity, and cost of services. Shipman (1989), an employee of the U.S. General Accounting Agency, described general criteria that were developed to ensure fair comparisons and comprehensive reviews of federal programs for children. Three criteria assess the need for the program: problem magnitude, problem seriousness, and duplication of services. Three criteria relate to program implementation: program fidelity, administrative efficiency, and interrelationships between the program and other programs. The last set of criteria relate to the effects of the program: achievement of intended objectives, targeting success in reaching intended clients, cost-effectiveness, and other effects (e.g., unforeseen or unintended effects).

Michael Patton, the author of several books on evaluation, demonstrated his creativeness by listing 100 different types of evaluation in his 1987 book. However, unless you are particularly interested in the absolute number of variations that can be made of a small set of evaluation designs, there is little reason to contemplate, name, or enumerate all of the evaluation designs available to us. You will find it more useful to learn how to conceptualize ways of evaluating programs. Any program can be viewed from numerous perspectives and can be evaluated for various purposes.

How do you go about selecting a program evaluation design? The design follows from the research question or hypothesis and the purpose of the evaluation. Evaluation designs are selected based on what information is needed about the program. What do you want to know about the program? Often it is useful to make a list of all the relevant questions. (If this list becomes too long, it will have to be pared down to those questions that are crucial and that realistically can be addressed.)

Once it is clear what information is needed from the evaluation, the evaluator must consider the resources available and the constraints in the agency. In our experience, the selection of an evaluation design is made a great deal easier if some of the realistic constraints under which the evaluation must operate are considered. Students and agency personnel often complain: "We can't evaluate our services. We don't have any money."

Sometimes this is expressed another way: "The director is very supportive, but we don't have a computer and can't afford a consultant." Besides the problem of the cost of the evaluation, there occasionally are constraints on the type of data that the evaluator can access: "I don't know what kind of evaluation to do—the director says that we cannot recontact any of our former clients."

The amount of time allowed or available for completion of the evaluation can be another constraint. Because of the press of other concerns, an evaluation may need to be conducted and a final report prepared within 3 or 4 weeks. This constraint has a way of ruling out a number of evaluation designs.

Another consideration is the evaluation audience. On some occasions, the evaluator anticipates that the findings will be warmly received, with small likelihood of a hostile reception or attacks on the evaluation methodology. On other occasions, the evaluator may expect a hostile reaction to the evaluation results. Where the evaluation is expected to be strongly criticized, the evaluator will want to provide the best possible information from the most rigorous methodology that can be applied in that setting. Fitz-Gibbon and Morris (1987) have noted, "Your task as an evaluator is to find the design that provides the most credible information in the situation you have at hand" (p. 10).

When these and other constraints have been identified, the evaluator can effectively eliminate some evaluation designs from consideration and begin to develop a plan for selection of the sample, the timing of the evaluation, and the data collection procedures. The evaluation design will dictate when and from whom measurements will be gathered during the course of an evaluation. Your task as an evaluator is to find the design that provides the most objective and convincing information that can be produced in that particular setting.

In order to reduce the confusion associated with choosing among the plethora of evaluation designs available, the designs in this chapter have been arranged in terms of the simplest (pre-experimental) designs, followed by the quasi-experimental, and then the more rigorous (experimental). Generally, the simpler designs tend to require less effort and are therefore the least expensive. Although this is not a perfect categorization scheme, thinking about designs in this way may be of benefit to beginning evaluators. Because these designs are generally covered in introductory research methods courses, they will not be presented here in great detail.

GENERAL PRINCIPLES OF GROUP RESEARCH DESIGNS

You will recall the shorthand used in the previous chapter to describe the features of single system research designs: **A** means a baseline phase, **B** means an intervention phase, and so on. Group research designs have their own distinct terminology and shorthand. In GRDs, the letter **O** means an observation or assessment period, and the letter **X** means when an intervention is applied or begun. As in all scientific research, careful attention needs to be given to how to operationalize the variables in a research study. In program evaluation, the dependent variables are construed as the study's *outcome measures,* and the study's independent variables are seen as the human service *intervention.*

The choice of outcome measures is just as important in GRDs as in single system research designs, needs assessment, and other forms of evaluative research, if not more so. The ideal outcome measure is reliable and valid, easy to administer, low cost, understandable, and capable of being used by clients representing diverse groups. Whenever you need to select a potential outcome measure for a GRD, refresh yourself by rereading Chapter 11 in this book. The entire credibility of any given GRD depends on the study's having used a reliable and valid outcome measure(s). Even the most rigorous designs can be hopelessly compromised if you choose a poor outcome measure, so *pick a good one!*

Generally speaking, GRDs can be conceptualized along the three following features:

1. Whether or not pretest assessments are made of the outcome measures *before* intervention occurs
2. Whether or not the groups are constructed using *random assignment*
3. Whether or not various types of *control groups* are used.

The weaker designs lack these features (no pretests, no random assignment, no control groups), whereas the stronger ones possess them to varying degrees. We begin our review of the major designs by considering those group research designs that lack pretests, random assignment, or control groups. Collectively these are known as the pre-experimental group designs.

PRE-EXPERIMENTAL RESEARCH DESIGNS

Do not let the name throw you off—the pre-experimental research designs can be *very* useful at providing the answers to important questions, *if* the questions themselves are simple. For instance, evaluation questions of concern to agency staff and administrators such as "Are the clients satisfied with services?" or "What is the status of clients after they participated in our program?" are appropriate for pre-experimental designs because they are uncomplicated, general questions that may not require a great deal of scientific rigor. Pre-experimental designs can do an excellent job of providing the answers to these questions, and they are often very important questions to answer.

Although these designs cannot be considered rigorous when held up to the unblinking standards of idealized science, they are well suited and very satisfactory to many agencies with few resources that need to demonstrate some type of an effectiveness evaluation annually or biannually to funders such as the local United Way. In our experience, these designs are often undervalued and correspondingly underutilized. Replication of the findings is a way of gaining more confidence in the findings. We will review a few examples of these designs that will illustrate their utility for program evaluation purposes.

The One-Group Posttest-Only Design

Although it may sound impressive, this evaluation design is one of the most elementary. This design involves providing an intervention or program to a group of clients and then determining the clients' status after intervention. For example, suppose you are running a smoking cessation program. The goal of the program is for participants to be completely free of all smoking by the end of the intervention. Assuming this intervention was provided over a number of weeks, the evaluator could determine how many of the workshop participants had stopped smoking by the time of the last session. If you started the group with 18 participants and 9 stopped smoking by the time of the last session, then your program would have experienced a 50 percent success rate. Schematically, we can represent this design:

$$X \qquad O$$

where

X is the intervention for some smokers, and

O represents the observation or measurement of the clients' status after the intervention.

This design is most suited to situations where clients' preprogram status can be ascertained without formal assessment. Note that cost, staff support, research expertise, and the amount of time required to complete the evaluation could be minimal. Because so little is involved here, the evaluator could even get the results from prior workshops and compute an average success rate for the past year (or even the past 3 years). This evaluative data could be displayed rather handily in a single table, as shown in Table 9.1.

Of course, the problem with this design (as any smoker would know) is that "success" could be better determined if the participants were surveyed 6 months or a year after completion of the intervention. Often smokers quit for a brief period of time, only to start up again. However, tracking down former participants to learn if they are free of their smoking habit would involve some expenditure of possibly scarce funds. Postage would not be a large expense unless hundreds of questionnaires are to be mailed. Phone calls are not usually expensive (unless they involve long-distance tolls), but they do require staff time to place the calls. (However, these might be made by clerical staff in between other assignments.)

A problem with this design is that it is not rigorous. It tells us very little about the differential effectiveness of the intervention. We do not know if just

TABLE 9.1	NUMBER OF PARTICIPANTS NOT SMOKING BY LAST SESSION				
	Calendar Year 2005				Average Success Rate
	Feb.	April	July	Oct.	
Number of Participants	24	21	25	18	
Number Not Smoking	9	9	12	9	
Success Rate	38%	43%	48%	50%	44%

as many smokers were successful by quitting on their own, or how many would have quite simply over the course of an equivalent period of time. This is also a weak evaluation design because the workshop participants were not randomly selected to receive treatment. Without randomly selecting a sample of clients from all possible candidates for the service, there is the potential for a client self-selection bias (e.g., those who came to or volunteered for treatment may not resemble those who did not). Perhaps those who have enrolled in this program were encouraged to participate by their physicians because of smoking-related health problems. These smokers may be more willing to quit smoking than other (healthier) smokers because further smoking will be injurious to them. Your program may show better results with such "motivated" smokers than with those who do not currently have health problems related to smoking. Similarly, your program might be more effective with those who have quit previously than with those who have never been able to quit on their own. Because there was no control group, there is little "hard" evidence that it was your program and not some other influence that was responsible for the participants' success. (Perhaps physicians' stern warnings played a greater role than your program in any smoking cessation.) These limitations associated with the one-group posttest only design are most salient when you are dealing with highly labile problems, those subject to considerable change over time, or if you have outcome measures that are particularly weak. If, on the other hand, you are conducting a program evaluation of services provided to persons with really intractable problems, this design is less vulnerable to such criticisms. Take for instance, a psychosocial intervention aimed at improving the functioning of persons who are HIV-positive, and the one-group posttest-only design assesses their health status some 10 years postintervention. Imagine that it was found after 10 years that blood chemistries were all normal, no one had contracted AIDS, no one had died, and that 100 percent of the clients were all doing well! Such a study, despite its limitations, would certainly grab your attention, and could be well worth doing.

The one-group posttest-only design (this design has also been called the "one-shot case study," which is a less descriptive phrase than the one we employ) can be especially useful in consumer satisfaction studies. By definition, consumer satisfaction can only be assessed after an agency's clients have received a service. Therefore, any type of pretest assessment is inherently not possible. Ligon and Thyer (2000) used this design in their assessment of consumer satisfaction at the DeKalb Community Service Board, a public agency located in a suburb of Atlanta, providing mental health and substance abuse services. All clients who received services at the agency were invited to complete the Client Satisfaction Questionnaire (CSQ; Larsen et al., 1979), a standardized widely used rapid assessment instrument that (for better or worse) is the "gold coin" of consumer satisfaction measures in the human services field.

A total of 54 clients and 29 family members of these clients completed the CSQ, and mean scores were compared across the types of services provided (e.g., mobile crisis services, substance abuse services alone, or mental health services alone). It was also possible to compare the scores from *these* clients ($M = 27.6$,

$SD = 3.9$) to normative data available on the CSQ. In general the services were very favorably rated, and comparable in satisfaction ratings to previous studies using this measure. Thus, this "simple" pre-experimental study that made use of the supposedly inelegant X-O design did a fine job at answering the question "How satisfied are the clients we served?" Ligon (1995) provides another illustration of using this design in a consumer satisfaction study, this time in the context of employee assistance services.

The one-group posttest-only design is also useful in follow-up studies of various types, wherein formal preassessments were not obtained or otherwise possible. Take the case of a telephone hotline for reporting domestic violence, rape, or child abuse. It might be of great utility to recontact clients who made use of these services a month or two after the initial contact to assess their views on how helpful the hot line was in resolving their issues.

This X-O design was also the approach used by Glisson, Thyer, and Fischer (2001) in their appraisal of the effectiveness of a homeless shelter located in Athens, Georgia. Apart from merely providing a temporary bed and meals, the shelter employed a social worker whose job it was to try and place homeless individuals staying at the shelter into safe, affordable, and hopefully long-term housing. All clients receiving services at the homeless shelter during a given 4-month period one year earlier were divided into two groups—those who were clearly transient ($N = 24$ households), and those with a history of living in Athens (100 households). This latter group consisted of individuals or families forced into homelessness by personal catastrophe (e.g., home destroyed by fire), domestic violence, jail release, unemployment, mental illness, or substance abuse, and so on.

Diligent efforts were made to contact a representative of these 100 households with a history of living in Athens, to ascertain their family living circumstances about 10 months following their receipt of homeless shelter services, which included efforts at finding them a stable home. A total of 71 of the 100 households were successfully contacted (i.e., a 71 percent follow-up rate). Of these, 41 (58 percent) held leases in their own names, indicated that they occupied relatively stable homes, and they had lived in their present home for over 4 months, on average. Additional information was obtained about the former client's income and rent, and perceptions of how safe their present home was.

This "simple" X-O study was a excellent mechanism to evaluate the homeless shelter's outcomes. Although causal inferences could not be legitimately made (i.e., we could not conclude that the homeless shelter services *caused* these clients to obtain better housing conditions), this program evaluation was a good, practical approach to answering the question "What happens, in terms of housing, to the clients who received services at the Athens homeless shelter?" The answer was "Most of those we contacted were in relatively stable, safe, and affordable homes." Our experience is that very few homeless shelters can answer this question with any sort of credible data. We believe that this type of elementary program evaluation is needed on a much more widespread basis.

Social work student Wendy Pabian completed her MSW internship at a center providing diagnostic evaluations and recommendations for care for children with presumptive developmental disabilities. The major purpose of the center was to help parents and caregivers get linked to community-based care providers who could help them meet the needs of their child. Day in and day out the center conducted its business, arriving at specialized diagnoses and laying out a pattern of recommended programs and the agencies who could provide them, to the families they served. Oddly, though, no one had ever followed up with previously served families to determine the extent to which they had really followed up on the center's recommendations. Pabian chose to investigate this issue, using a one-group post-test only design. After obtaining permission from her university's and from the center's institutional review board, she was able to contact 36 of 51 eligible families who had received center services during a 6-month window. Not all families could be reached, and not all who were contacted agreed to participate (this introduces a confound, of course, since only 70 percent of her potential sample actually provided follow-up information! Perhaps the missing 30 percent differed in some meaningful ways from those who participated?). In brief, it was found out that responding families had obtained 84 percent of educational services, 89 percent of medical services, but only 49 percent of the social services recommended by the center's team. Overall, the families obtained about 79 percent of recommended services. Fully 4 of 11 types of recommended social services had a 0 percent success rate! This was very useful follow-up information for the center staff. It enabled them to make useful changes in their pattern of recommended services and to take steps to enhance the likelihood that social services in particular were obtained. Details of this program evaluation can be found in Pabian et al. (2000).

This type of pre-experimental design was also used by social worker Laura Myers in her innovative study of orphanage care. During the mid-1990s, welfare reform proposals were being widely debated, and when the question was asked of one politician about what would happen to the children of families whose welfare benefits met their lifetime cap, he said something like "Well, there are always the orphanages." This created a groundswell of protest, because it is an article of faith within the child welfare community that institutional or residential care is intrinsically inferior to community-based placements with families. Myers looked into the scientific literature on the effects of being raised in a traditional orphanage and found to her surprise that there was actually very little empirical literature on the topic. She was able to collaboratively work with a traditional, church-affiliated orphanage located in central Florida, and get their list of "alumni," individuals who had spend an appreciable portion of their youth living at the orphanage and who had "graduated" and were now living as independent adults. Some of these alumni had lived in the orphanage during the 1930s and were in their 80s! After obtaining institutional review board approval from her university, Myers developed, working closely with the orphanage staff, a brief survey, and selected three previously published measures of adult functioning to include with it. This survey was mailed out under the signature of the orphanage director with an explanatory letter and a request to participate in the study by completing the survey and instruments, and returning them to the director. He, in turn, provided them to Myers. The tabulated results were most interesting. The large majority of the respondents were doing well in life, in terms of socioeconomic factors, interpersonal relationships, family life, and career. Most provided strong positive appraisals about their experiences in living in the orphanage and of the quality of care they received. This suggests that certain forms of institutional care need not be automatically considered a "bad" care, and may well be appropriate for youth who are unable to be placed with community-based families. The orphanage itself was very pleased with this program evaluation, which was low cost and made practical use of the one-group post-test only research design. More details can be found in Myers and Rittner (1999, 2001).

The Posttest-Only Design with Nonequivalent Groups

This design is a modest improvement over the prior design because it uses some form of a control group, a set of individuals who it is hoped are comparable to the group receiving treatment, yet who themselves to not receive treatment. In the example of a smoking cessation program, the group of program participants is known as the experimental or treatment group. With the present posttest-only design with nonequivalent groups, another group of smokers could be located for comparison purposes. Ideally, this should be a similar group of smokers who are different only because they are trying to quit on their own. The evaluator compares the success rate of the workshop participants against the success rate of those smokers in the control group who were trying to quit on their own. This design might be diagrammed:

$$\underline{X \quad\!\!\! - - - \underline{O_1}}$$
$$O_2$$

where

> X is the intervention
>
> O_1 is the observation or measurement made of the group after they received the intervention
>
> O_2 is the measurement or observation made of the comparison group, taken at about the same time as the measurements made for O_1.
>
> The broken line between groups indicates the absence of nonrandom assignment.

The weaknesses of this design is evident. For one, it may not be easy to identify a group of smokers trying to quit on their own; and even if you learn that those attending the smoking cessation program have a much higher success rate than the control group, you do not know that the control group was a fair comparison. The two groups may have differed greatly in the average number of cigarettes smoked daily. Perhaps the majority of those in your smoking cessation program were young employees of a factory in town where they expected a cash bonus at the end of the year if they could quit smoking.

Although you had not intended the control group to be dissimilar from the intervention group, you discover later that the control group is much older and that they have been smoking, on the average, for 37 years. It could have been more difficult for this group to stop smoking than it was for young adults who had been smoking for 5 years or less. If the control and treatment groups are not equivalent, an "apple and orange" type of comparison is being made. Although it may be possible for you to find a control group that is more like the intervention group than the one mentioned here, the burden of trying to demonstrate the rough equivalence of the two groups is still yours.

A real example of the posttest-only design with nonequivalent groups can be found in Carrillo and Thyer's (1994) examination of the level of interviewing skills displayed by MSW students. Two groups of students were evaluated. The first group consisted of 23 two-year-program MSW students, who were assessed at the beginning of their second year in their MSW program, while the second group consisted of 15 advanced-standing MSW students (individuals who had completed a BSW degree and were exempted from the first year of coursework and internship of the MSW program). Both groups were enrolled in the same social work methods class taught in the fall at the University of Georgia. The outcome measure consisted of reliable judgments made of the students' videotaped performances during interviews with simulated clients. The authors went to great lengths to operationalize "interviewing skills" and to develop a very reliable way to assess these using two independent raters. The independent variable (intervention) consisted of the academic background of the two groups of students, two-year MSW program status versus advanced-standing MSW program status. The design could be drawn as follows:

$$\frac{X \ O}{Y \ O}$$

The absence of an **R** before each group indicates the *nonrandom* assignment to the two conditions (the dashed line also indicates this); the **X** stands for having completed the foundation (first year) of the MSW program, and the **Y** stands for having completed a BSW degree in lieu of the foundation year. This study was to test the hypothesis that advanced-standing students are equivalently prepared with respect to interviewing skills to students who completed the MSW program's foundation year. It was not possible to conduct pretests on interviewing skills, nor was random assignment to "earn the BSW versus earn the MSW via the two-year program" a feasible option. So the authors took advantage of the naturally occurring sorting of MSW students into these two groups based on their educational backgrounds. The two groups were indeed equivalently skilled with respect to interviewing skills, a finding that supported the practice of making an advanced-standing option available to holders of a BSW degree.

Another innovative use of this design was undertaken by social work student Emily Gary-McCormick and her MSW field instructor Thelma Patton. Emily was placed for her internship at a prenatal clinic that focused on providing prenatal care services in rural communities in Georgia, primarily to low-income women deemed to be at high risk for problem pregnancies. Briefly, the prenatal care teams would travel about the countryside in a van, holding prenatal care clinics in rural health departments. Over the course of time, a good many women received such care. Some questions arise quite naturally, such as "What are the results of this expensive program? Are problem pregnancies averted to any extent?"

Obviously it would be neither ethical nor practical to randomly assign women at high risk for problem pregnancies to not receive prenatal care. But over the course of the program's existence, it rather naturally happened that some women kept a large number of their prenatal care appointments, and some women missed a whole lot of them. Given that data were available on the outcomes of the pregnancy, it was possible to empirically examine possible disparities in birth outcomes among these naturally occurring groups of women, those who made a lot versus those who made very few prenatal care visits. The program, of course, hypothesized that those women who made more visits would have more favorable pregnancy outcomes than those who made few. About 119 patients had received services in this program, and drawing on patient records (again after obtaining university institutional review board approval), the top and bottom 25 percent (in terms of keeping appointments) of the patients were selected, yielding 27 women who had made 13 or more clinic appointments, and 28 who kept 4 or fewer appointments.

After analysis, lo and behold, those women who made more appointments had babies with significantly higher birth weights and older gestational ages (these are very good things to observe) compared to the women who made fewer visits! This suggests, but does not prove, that these prenatal visits do indeed help produce more favorable birth outcomes and can be seen to justify the continuing provision of this expensive mode of care. Imagine if no such difference had been found. This would be fairly strong evidence that the program did not "work," but as it happened it survived this particular test with flying colors.

Can we claim that the program is unambiguously effective? No, because of potentially confounding factors. Perhaps some variables rendered women particularly liable for high-risk pregnancies liable to miss appointments (e.g., being particularly poor and lacking reliable transportation)? The inability of this design to control for such rival hypotheses makes it less than ideal—but still a very serviceable—approach to program evaluation under conditions when more robust designs are not practical to implement. More details on this study can be found in Gary-McCormick et al. (2000).

The One-Group Pretest–Posttest Design

Obviously it is not always possible to recruit some form of a control or comparison group, and you may have only the one group of clients receiving agency services to work with. If you can measure client problems (or strengths, or both) before the intervention (this is called the **pretest**) and also get a measurement after the intervention (the **posttest**), you can construe this as what has been labeled the one-group pretest–posttest design. This design can be diagrammed:

$$O_1 \quad X \quad O_2$$

where

the first observation (the pretest) is represented by the O preceding treatment (the X), and the second observation period is the O following treatment.

Let's say that you are going to begin a support group for women who have recently gone through a divorce. Knowing that such women are often depressed, you decide on an intervention that is designed to reduce depression. In theory, these women should be less depressed after the 10-week support group than they were when they started. After some library work, you decide to use the 20-item depression scale (the CES-D) developed by the National Institute of Mental Health's Center for Epidemiologic Studies (Radloff, 1977) for both the pre- and posttest measures of depression.

When the group comes in for their first meeting, you explain the purpose of the pretest, respond to any questions, and then distribute the instrument. At the final meeting of the group, you administer the same depression scale a second time. Having both the pretest and posttest data, it is possible to determine what percentage of the support group showed an improvement by the end of the tenth week.

Because two measurements were obtained with a standardized instrument, success could be measured in terms of (1) any decrease in the percentage of support group members who were depressed or (2) improvements in the group's average score from pretest to posttest. This information would be valuable in terms of helping future consumers or policy makers decide whether the support group is effective. This evaluation design would meet many agencies' needs for evaluation.

However, this design is inadequate on those occasions when it becomes important to establish that it was the intervention—and the intervention only—that produced the improvement. For instance, perhaps you have observed that most persons who are depressed immediately after a divorce tend to improve with the passage of time—whether or not they get professional help. In other words, this design does not eliminate other explanations that might actually be responsible for the improvement. In many situations, it may not be necessary to rule out these alternative explanations. One therapist might say, "So what if it really was the passage of time and not the intervention? The vast majority of my clients improved in the past 10 weeks and that, after all, is the reason they came here."

Because this evaluation design is not very rigorous, it cannot rule out alternative explanations, such as changes due to greater maturity (a potential explanation to be especially considered when children are involved), or the effect of repeated use of the instrument (testing), or several others. On those occasions when there is a need to rule out alternative explanations (for instance, you may want to market the intervention), you can employ more rigorous (experimental) evaluation designs. Weiss (1972) advocated the use of experimental evaluation designs in those situations where

> it is for purposes outside the immediate program that experimental design is best suited. Decisions on the order of continuation or abandonment of the program, decisions on whether to advocate nation-wide use of the program model—these require great confidence in the validity of the research, and therefore experimental design. Other types of decisions may not need such rigor, at least initially. (pp. 66–67)

A real example of using a one-group pretest–posttest design can be found in Capp, Thyer, and Bordnick (1997). Holly Capp was a second year MSW student from the University of Georgia, completing her internship at the psychiatric unit at Georgia Baptist Hospital in Atlanta. Holly was able to arrange for all newly admitted patients to be asked to complete the Symptom Checklist-90 (revised) (SCL-90), a widely used, reliable, and valid measure of psychopathology. Apart from several global indices, the SCL-90 provided scores on several subscales, including depression, anxiety, and psychoticism. Then, a day or two prior to the patient's being discharged, Holly asked them to complete the SCL-90 again. If the inpatient psychiatric services were truly effective, one would predict that the patients' scores would improve, as assessed by the SCL-90. Over the course of some $4\frac{1}{2}$ months, this procedure was followed for most new admissions, with a final response rate of 78 out of 105 patients agreeing to participate (or 71 percent, a fairly high proportion of the patients treated during this time frame). The mean SCL-90 scores on admission constituted the group's *pretreatment* data, and their scores at discharge comprised the *posttreatment assessment;* thus, this procedure conformed to a one-group pretest–posttest design.

The average length of stay was 17 days, and fairly complete demographic information is reported for the patients. It was found that substantial declines in patient psychopathology, as assessed by the SCL-90, were obtained. This simple O-X-O design, coupled with the use of a valid outcome measure and a large (and presumably representative, but we cannot be sure) client sample, provided Capp, her supervisor, and the hospital staff with an answer to the question "Do clients improve while they are treated on our psychiatric ward?" The answer was "Yes!" (on average). Now the alert reader will no doubt be pounding the desk at this point, exclaiming, "But maybe the patients got better simply due to the passage of time!" or "Maybe they got better simply by virtue of taking the test a second time!" or "Maybe they faked their answers in order to please Holly Capp, the pleasant MSW intern!"

As sober, responsible textbook authors, we must agree with you. You are absolutely correct to raise these issues. But we would point out that these are substantially more complex and sophisticated issues than those raised by Capp et al. All the authors of the Capp study were trying to do was answer the question put to them by the staff at the psychiatric unit, namely, "Are our patients getting better?" They were not asked to answer *your* questions, which may be paraphrased something like:

"Do patients treated at the Georgia Baptist Hospital inpatient psychiatric unit improve to a greater extent than they would simply by the simple passage of time?"

"Does being treated on our psychiatric unit produce greater improvements than those attributable to completing the SCL-90 for a second time?"

"Does being treated on our unit produce greater improvements than those attributable by patients answering more positively in order to please the MSW intern?"

Worthy though these questions are, and important though they may be in general, they are *not* relevant in the context of the original question asked. The original question *was* answered satisfactorily. To answer *your* questions requires considerably more methodological rigor, rigor that *may* be provided by using the experimental designs described later in this chapter. The fact that such issues occurred to you is a good sign—it indicates that you are thinking *critically and scientifically,* always questioning a given finding, and posing rival explanations that need to be controlled for or otherwise taken into account. How can these alternative explanations be controlled for? One way is to subject a finding to a more rigorous test, via a more sophisticated group research design such as the quasi-experimental and experimental types of studies described in the next sections. But first, here are another couple of examples of the O-X-O design.

Social work student Wendy Schwartz did her MSW internship on the psychiatric unit of a large hospital in Atlanta. She worked with the partial-hospitalization program, whereby clients with presumptive mental disorders were provided care and recreation, in the context of a coordinated, comprehensive, and multidisciplinary program, more intensive than that afforded by usual outpatient therapy. The program operated from 9 AM to 3 PM, Monday through Friday. Less expensive than inpatient treatment, but more costly than outpatient, a clear objective of the partial-hospitalization program was to help bring about a decrease in clinical symptoms. Was it doing this? Who knew?

After consulting the (virtually nonexistent) program evaluation literature on partial-hospitalization treatment, Schwartz decided to try and find out how her program was doing. After obtaining university institutional review board approval and the cooperation of the other hospital staff, Schwartz arranged for all patients newly admitted to the program during a 2-month time frame to complete a standardized measure of depression on admission, and planned for this to be retaken at discharge. Twenty patients did complete the pretest, but only 9 the subsequent posttest (thus fully 55 percent of her potential sample were not available). The average length of stay was 8 weekdays. Of the 9 patients she did have pretest–posttest data on, their depression scores statistically significantly improved, with a very large effect size. Nevertheless, Schwartz was able to publish her results (Schwartz & Thyer, 2000), as her findings, limited though they were, added to the existing meager literature about partial-hospitalization effectiveness.

Please make no mistake, although the O-X-O possesses significant limitations because its results, no matter how promising, cannot usually be used to justify causal inferences, it is nevertheless an exceptionally useful design and is routinely published in top-ranked journals, *providing* the conclusions are conservatively expressed, and the findings actually add to an undeveloped literature. For example, Spinelli (1997) published (in a very good journal, the *American Journal of Psychiatry*), an O-X-O study involving 13 pregnant women being treated for antenatal depression using a novel form of treatment called interpersonal psychotherapy. The outcome measures were several previously published self-report scales assessing depression. The results were positive, in that depression scores significantly improved. This initially positive study, even though it involved such a small sample size, in turn, could be seen to justify the vastly more expensive investment of conducting a randomized controlled trial of IP by Spinelli (described later in this chapter). The one-group pretest–posttest design is too often unfairly disparaged as unworthy of being conducted. However, when viewed as a preliminary study in the ongoing development of new treatments, it can be very useful.

QUASI-EXPERIMENTAL RESEARCH DESIGNS

The evaluation designs described so far can be thought of as elementary or beginning designs. Campbell and Stanley (1963) call them pre-experimental designs. Methodologically, they are weak because they cannot rule out alternative explanations for any observed changes. Although the pre-experimental designs may provide information that satisfies friendly supporters of programs, they cannot provide conclusive evidence that the intervention alone was responsible for changes. Fortunately, other, more rigorous evaluation designs are available. Because the next group of designs tends to require more planning and more extensive involvement with control groups, and may result in more data to analyze, they are more expensive and may require more resources than the pre-experimental designs.

Program evaluation approaches can be thought of as a series of steps beginning with the simplest: formative, process, and program monitoring. The discussion of pre-experimental designs we just completed brings us another step closer to the strongest of quantitative methodologies. Quasi-experimental designs are better than the pre-experimental designs but not so good as the experimental designs for providing "hard evidence" that the intervention was responsible for the observed changes. Because they do not use randomization and may not always involve a control group, **quasi-experimental designs** draw their name from not quite being experiments.

Nonequivalent Control Group Design

The nonequivalent control group design is one of the most commonly used evaluation designs. In this design, a group of persons who are similar in composition to the group receiving the intervention is used as a comparison group, persons who received similar pretest and posttest observations, *but no treatment*. This design can be diagrammed:

$$\frac{O_1 \; X \; O_2}{O_3 \quad O_4}$$

where

O$_1$ and O$_3$ are pretests for the intervention and control groups, respectively, and

O$_2$ and O$_4$ are posttests for the intervention and control groups.

The broken line between groups indicates nonrandom assignment.

Suppose you are an evaluation consultant to a school principal who wants to implement a drug education program with all seventh, eighth, and ninth graders. If the principal, the parents, or the school board has determined that all of the students will receive the intervention, then it may not be possible to develop a control group from within the same school. It may be necessary to locate a control group in a different school or community.

With this design, the control group can be used to help eliminate alternative explanations. It is quite possible, for instance, that any increase in the intervention group's knowledge about drugs at the time of posttest could have occurred merely from interaction with older students or their own firsthand experience with drugs. Perhaps as seventh, eighth, and ninth graders mature, they read the newspapers to a greater extent and thus "educate" themselves about the dangers of drugs. These explanations and the effectiveness of the intervention can be understood by making comparisons to the control group. If those receiving the intervention are more knowledgeable at the time of the posttest than those in the control group, then the intervention appears to have been a success. If, however, the control group shows the same gains in knowledge about drugs as the experimental group, then you would know that it was not the intervention that was responsible but some other factor or combination of factors.

The problem with this design is that while you could establish that the seventh, eighth, and ninth graders in the control group were equivalent to those receiving the intervention in terms of knowledge about drugs at the time of pretest, students receiving the drug awareness program could simultaneously be exposed to other influences or have access to resources that were not available in the comparison school. For example, suppose that the principal in the intervention school has been especially active in getting local businesses to contribute computers to the school. Further suppose that although the great availability of computers in this school has nothing directly to do with the drug awareness program, use of the computers by a large majority of the student body serves to increase their reading skills. Even though you were concerned only about their scores on the instrument that measured their drug awareness, as the children in the intervention school learned to read better, they learned more on their own about the dangers of drugs. So, it may not have been the intervention program alone that was responsible for the improvement in test scores, but the double whammy of greater access to computers in addition to the drug awareness program. Conversely, if the control group showed greater improvement, it may have been the influence of factors not known to the evaluator (such as pairing every student with a volunteer reading tutor) that had the effect (as students began reading more on their own, they learned about the dangers of experimenting with illicit drugs).

It is easy to see the importance of obtaining groups that are similar not only in the skill, behavior, or characteristic being observed, but also in other major variables. What kinds of variables are important? (This question becomes especially critical if we have to go to another school to obtain a control group.) Would it be fair to compare a suburban school with an inner-city school? If one school was situated in a low-income, high-dropout area, would both schools need to be? How essential is it for the teachers to be similar with respect to commitment to teaching or years of experience?

Although finding a comparison group that is as alike as possible to the intervention group may be a problem at times; in other situations it presents no problem at all. For instance, the military attempts to produce companies of soldiers that are pretty similar to one another. There is a presumed equivalence in the comparison of one company of soldiers to another company. Majchrzak (1986) has reported an example. Evaluating a program designed to reduce unauthorized absenteeism in the Marine Corps, she used the nonequivalent control group design because complete random assignment could not be employed. Majchrzak first matched available infantry and artillery battalions on the variables of deployment schedule, mission, regiment, and tenure of commander and then randomly assigned battalions either to a control condition or to participation in the unauthorized absenteeism prevention program. All subordinate companies were then asked to participate in the experiment. This procedure yielded 20 treatment companies and 20 control companies of Marines.

Betsy Vonk (see Vonk & Thyer, 1999) used a quasi-experimental evaluation design to test the hypothesis that students who received counseling services at a university's student counseling center would be helped, and she also tried to show that these improvements (if they occurred at all) could be attributed to the center, and not to other factors such as the passage of time, or the retaking of some type of assessment procedure.

The agency setting was the student counseling center at Emory University in Atlanta, where Betsy was employed as a licensed clinical social worker. She arranged for all new clients seeking counseling services to be given the Symptom Checklist-90 (SCL-90), the reliable and valid measure of psychiatric symptoms mentioned earlier. As a part of the counseling center's normal operation, some students were enrolled in counseling *immediately,* whereas others had to be placed on a *wait list* because no counselor had an opening. Those assigned to the wait list completed the SCL-90 right away, and then were asked to complete it again when they were called off of the wait list and began counseling (about a month later). The quasi-experimental design can be depicted as follows:

Immediate treatment group ($N = 41$)   O X O

Delayed treatment group ($N = 14$)   O   O X O

You should be able to interpret this design as follows: students in both groups received an assessment, and some began treatment right away while others had to wait a brief period (on average it was about a month-long wait). When the immediate treatment group completed counseling (no less than 4 and no more than 20 sessions), they completed the SCL-90 again. The wait-list students completed the SCL-90 a second time just before beginning counseling, and a third time when they completed counseling (again after no less than 4 and no more than 20 sessions).

At the first assessment, both groups reported equivalent levels of disturbance. After counseling, the students treated immediately and assessed a second time reported substantial declines in psychiatric symptoms (yeah!), which is what one would hope for. When the wait-listed students were assessed a second time (not having received any counseling), their initially high levels of disturbance had not improved. But after counseling, they displayed substantial improvements comparable to those enjoyed by the students who were treated immediately. This design provides tentative answers to three questions:

1. Do students receiving counseling services at this agency get better? (Yes!)
2. Can these improvements plausibly be attributed to the mere passage of time? (No!)
3. Can these improvements plausibly be attributed to taking the SCL-90 a second time? (No!)

Thus, this particular quasi-experimental design takes us forward and allows us to be more confident in asserting that the counseling center is providing truly helpful services. Of course, important issues remain unresolved—such as the possible role of *placebo influences* (simply being in *any* type of treatment), or *social desirability factors* (simply answering more positively after treatment in order to please the therapist, or perhaps even to convince *oneself* that the whole experience had not been a waste of time).

Time Series Design

Another quasi-experimental design is called the time series or the interrupted time series design. The advantage of this design over some of the others is that it allows the evaluator to detect trends. If there is a trend in the data (maybe children in remedial math classes begin to do better simply as a result of growing older), this gradual process would become apparent. It could be observed prior to the start of an intervention and monitored afterward. We can use the following notation to represent this design:

$$O_1 \quad O_2 \quad O_3 \quad X \quad O_4 \quad O_5 \quad O_6$$

where

$O_1 - O_3$ are pretreatment measurements,

X represents the intervention, and

$O_4 - O_6$ represents the posttreatment measurements.

Often this design is depicted as having three equally spaced observations before the intervention and three (separated by the same time intervals) afterward. However, as with other designs, this may be modified according to the needs of the evaluator. There would be nothing wrong with having four or more observations prior to the intervention and the same number (or perhaps fewer) after the intervention. The time intervals between measurements might be days, weeks, or even months. The evaluator determines the length and number of these intervals. This type of design relies on **longitudinal data**. Longitudinal data are collected at several different times during the course of the study.

The time series designs are especially useful when finding nonequivalent control groups is a problem. These designs are often the design of choice when evaluating the impact of new legislation or policies. For instance, Shore and Maguin (1988) used a time series design to determine that the passage of a new law in Kansas that prohibited plea bargaining in driving under the influence (DUI) arrests resulted in a decrease of eight fatal accidents per month during the 18-month postintervention period. This translated to a 20 percent reduction in the number of fatal accidents. Of course, the revision of the law alone was not responsible for the decrease. Accompanying the change in the law were widespread publicity, media coverage, and an increase in DUI arrests. Still, the authors concluded that:

> The Kansas experience supports deterrence theory in that the increase in certainty and severity of punishment provided by the change in the state's Driving Under the Influence law was associated with a reduction in those accidents which are more frequently linked with the combination of drinking and driving. (p. 253)

Another interesting use of a time series design was reported by Ross and White (1987), who explored the effect that seeing one's name in the newspaper had on persons convicted of shoplifting, impaired driving, or failing to take the Breathalyzer test. They concluded that publishing the court results of persons arrested for shoplifting in the newspaper resulted in a decrease in the number of shoplifting incidents. However, publishing the names of impaired drivers and persons refusing the Breathalyzer did not reduce their numbers.

Thyer and Robertson (1993) also made use of this time series evaluation design methodology to examine the possible effects of a mandatory safety belt use law newly introduced into Georgia in 1988. State-provided archival data was obtained on the monthly incidence of the *numbers killed*, the *numbers injured*, and the *death rate per 100 million miles driven*, for the 12 months *prior* to the passage of the Georgia law, and for the 12 months *after* the law was passed. These were the outcome measures or *dependent variables* in the study. Thus, there were 12 data points before and 12 data points after the introduction of the independent variable (the treatment, or as in this case, the new law). Regrettably, both visual inspection of the graphed data and statistical analysis indicated that none of the outcome measures declined significantly. The authors speculated that this was due to the law's weak sanctions and infrequent enforcement. A stronger mandatory safety-belt use law has been introduced into Georgia, but an analysis of its potential effects has not yet been undertaken.

Multiple Time Series Design

Although the time series design seemed to work well tracing the benefits of legislation within Kansas, at least one alternative explanation cannot be ruled out. The number of DUI arrests may be decreasing across the nation not as a result of local legislation but due to such factors as increased awareness of health risks and decreased drinking among Americans. One might argue that the time series design suffers from tunnel vision—its scope does not encompass what may be going on in the larger world. Adding a control group eliminates the problems with this design:

$$\begin{array}{ccccccc} O_1 & O_3 & O_5 & X & O_7 & O_9 & O_{11} \\ \hline O_2 & O_4 & O_6 & & O_8 & O_{10} & O_{12} \end{array}$$

where

O_1 O_3 and O_5 are pre-intervention measurements of the intervention group;

X refers to providing an intervention to the top group;

O_7, O_9 and O_{11} are postintervention measurements of the intervention group; and

$O_2 - O_{12}$ are measures taken from a control group who do not get the intervention.

And the broken line between groups indicates nonrandom assignment

With this design, an evaluator could identify a control state (in terms of rural–urban mixture, the rate of DUIs per 100,000 population, etc.) or use several states as controls. If there were national trends (such as for a decreased number of arrests for drinking while driving), this should be picked up among the control state(s), and the evaluator would not be so quick to conclude that it was the new legislation that brought about fewer DUIs.

Time series designs are very similar in construction and logic to the single system research designs presented in Chapter 6, so do not be perplexed if you cannot clearly discriminate between the two. One notable difference: SSRDs use the A and B symbols for baseline and intervention conditions, and time series designs use the X and O notation system associated with other types of group research designs. Perhaps more importantly, SSRDs were developed for a specific purpose: to evaluate treatment outcomes for single clients (or single client systems) in direct practice settings. Another source of possible confusion is the distinction between time series *designs* (TSD) and time series *analysis* (TSA). The former is a research design, while the latter is a specialized form of inferential statistic analysis, one that has been developed to analyze data obtained from time series designs. Many forms of time series designs make use of time series analyses, just as other group evaluation designs may make use of, say, a *t*-test to examine a change within a group. But do keep clear the difference between TSD as a design versus TSA as a statistical tool. These are different things.

Eliminating Alternative Explanations

The designs that have been presented to this point are subject to problems with internal validity. That is, evaluators using these designs cannot conclude that it was the intervention alone that accounted for any observed changes. The pre-experimental and quasi-experimental designs do not rule out many (or most) of the alternative explanations that skeptics of a program's success might be quick to identify. The strongest and most credible information about the effectiveness of an intervention comes from experimental designs. Efforts to eliminate the alternative explanations result in the most rigorous designs but also tend to increase the costs of evaluation.

Before we begin discussing experimental designs, let's look at alternative explanations that sometimes make researchers (or critics) question evaluation results.

THREATS TO THE INTERNAL VALIDITY
History

The role of history can be understood if we consider significant events occurring at the local, state, or national level. For instance, in August 1987, 27 children were killed outside of Cincinnati when a drunk driver crashed into a bus returning from a weekend outing. Assume that prior to this you had been asked to evaluate a public education program designed to reduce the number of DUIs and planned on using a relatively weak evaluation design (for instance, the one-group time series design) to monitor the number of arrests for driving under the influence. Some months after the accident, you conclude that the decrease in DUI arrests was due to the intervention, when it probably was the tragedy that resulted in fewer drivers driving while intoxicated.

Without a control group, you might not detect the influence this tragedy had on drivers' attitudes and behavior. Such an event could also be responsible for a greater number of DUI arrests as a consequence of the public becoming less tolerant and more often reporting drunk drivers to law enforcement officials. Law enforcement officials themselves might decide to be more vigilant and to make more arrests for DUI. The comparison between the intervention and the control communities (or states) would help the evaluator to understand any national trends in DUIs.

Within agencies and organizations, changes in policies (e.g., eligibility standards) and procedures can present a historical threat in the sense that the clientele may change over time. Because of scarce resources, an outpatient counseling program may begin to limit itself to only those who are suicidal or who have already been hospitalized on at least one other occasion. How would such a change dilute the power of an intervention to show improvement?

Maturation

Sometimes problems improve as a result of the passage of time. An evaluator might conclude that an intervention was effective when actually the subjects receiving the intervention matured or the passing of time served to make the problem less acute. For instance, persons suffering from the loss of a loved one normally grieve less and are less depressed as time passes. Although the program staff may wish to think that it was the support group that made all of the difference, unless there is a control group, it is difficult to rule out the role that the passage of time alone may have played.

Testing

If you are using a design (e.g., the times series design) where the same test is administered sequentially a number of times, the persons receiving the intervention may show improvement in their scores as a result of figuring out "correct" responses on the test. On the other hand, their scores could also decrease as a result of becoming careless and bored with repeated use of the same test. Without a comparison group, it is difficult to rule out possible testing effects.

Instrumentation

Just as those enrolled in a program can become bored by taking the same test on numerous occasions, the evaluator or other persons making observations might subtly or unconsciously modify the procedures. Instead of counting every time a hyperactive child got out of his seat in the classroom, the weary observer by the end of the study may be counting only the incidents when the child got out of his seat and was corrected by the teacher. Observations ought to be made in the same way throughout the course of the evaluation. Tests should be administered the same way (e.g., in the same setting, at the same time of day, using the same rules or set of instructions) each time. The effect of this threat to the internal validity of a study can be quickly understood in a situation where, for example, a teacher gave more than the allowed time to a class to finish the posttest and less to the control group. Merely because they had more time, the intervention group might score higher than the control group.

Selection

This alternative explanation plays a potential role whenever control groups are used without random assignment. Suppose you were to start a new intervention and invite former clients (who may still be having problems) to attend. If there is improvement among these clients, will it be due to the recent intervention? Or did the improvement come about because it built on their prior involvement? Taking another example, suppose you want to start a new support group, and you want to open it up to anyone in the community. To announce the beginning of the support group, you run an invitation in the local newspaper. If this group later shows improvement, it may have been due to the fact that the individuals who participated were unlike others in the community with the same problem. Maybe those who answered the newspaper article were more literate (they read the ad in the newspaper), better educated, more assertive, or more intelligent. One would be left with the nagging thought that maybe the intervention was effective only with the kind of people who would answer an ad. This group may not be representative of the rest of the people in the community with the same problem who failed to respond to the invitation.

Mortality

Mortality refers to the loss of subjects from the evaluation. This threat to the internal validity is a problem for those evaluations that stretch over a long period of time. Professionals in the human services frequently find that their clients move (sometimes without leaving forwarding addresses), drop out of treatment, get locked up, become sick, and sometimes become rehospitalized. For various reasons, it is not at all uncommon to have fewer participants in a program at its conclusion than when it started. A problem exists when too many of the participants drop out. Any commonality among those who drop out could bias the study. For instance, suppose you were running a program for parents of adolescents. Twelve parents sign up to learn how to better communicate with their adolescents. A few parents drop out during the 9-week program, but this does not concern you because you can objectively show that the program is working—that communication is improving among those parents who remain. However, as you begin to examine your data, you realize that the parents who remained in the program were all college graduates. The parents who dropped out were high school graduates. Although the intervention may have worked, it did so only for parents who were college graduates.

PROTECTION AGAINST ALTERNATIVE EXPLANATIONS

The best protection against alternative explanations for the results you note in an evaluation is to control them. Control is made possible by anticipating the kinds of problems that may be encountered. For example, if you expect that you may have mortality problems, build in an incentive. With children, there could be some sort of a party on the last session or after the posttest data have been obtained. With adults, money is an incentive that works reasonably well. But when funds are not available, the evaluator can be creative in other ways, perhaps by issuing "certificates of completion" for the intervention group and "certificates of appreciation" for the control group. If you expect that repeated testing may present some problems, explore whether there are different or alternate forms of the same test.

If you suspect that critics of the evaluation may say things like, "Well, no wonder! The comparison groups weren't even similar!" then you need to ensure that the groups in the study are as similar as possible. Where random assignment is not possible, you can gain credibility by matching group participants with their controls on important variables (e.g., years of education, income, sex) and then using a statistical test to determine whether the groups are comparable. (See Chapter 11 for information on the appropriate statistical test to use.) The t-test tells you whether differences between the two groups are statistically significant. If there are no significant differences between the control and intervention groups on important variables, then the groups are similar for those variables. However, differences could still exist on variables that are not measured. Showing that groups are similar statistically on certain measures is a help in documenting comparability, but does not provide certainty that they are equivalent. Concern yourself with *plausible* rival hypotheses, and do not worry about every potential variable that could come into play. You need to try to control for as many plausible rival hypotheses as possible—not every one that a fertile mind could create.

Another way to produce a credible evaluation is to use a rigorous evaluation design known as an experimental design. These designs eliminate alternative explanations through the use of random selection and assignment; persons are assigned to either the intervention or control groups without any form of bias. Unexpected improvement within a control group developed with randomized procedures allows you to suspect that some alternative explanation (such as history, maturation, or testing) was having an influence.

Before we leave our discussion of alternative explanations, note that there are many more threats to the internal validity of a study than have been identified in this brief explanation. As an evaluator, you need to develop a sensitivity or an appreciation for factors that can influence the results of the evaluation. For instance, those involved in an evaluation may be keenly aware that they are being tested and may work harder than they normally would to make a good impression. Any "over cooperation" will confound the evaluator's data and make it more difficult to understand the true impact of any intervention. If you would like to read more about additional threats to the internal validity of a study, consult Campbell and Stanley (1963), Cook and Campbell (1979), or Campbell, Shadish, and Cook (2001).

EXPERIMENTAL DESIGNS

"Classic" Experimental Design

The "classic" experimental design is the standard against which other designs are compared. Experimental research designs are the most rigorous and represent the ideal for inferring that an intervention either did or did not have an effect. In an **experimental design,** participants are randomly assigned to either the intervention group or to the control group. The notation for the classical experiment in the social and behavioral sciences is:

$$R \quad O_1 \quad X \quad O_2$$
$$R \quad O_3 \quad\quad O_4$$

where

> R stands for subjects who have been randomly assigned to either the intervention or control groups
>
> O_1 is a pretest or first observation of the intervention group;
>
> O_2 is a posttest of the intervention group;
>
> O_3 is a pretest of the control group; and
>
> O_4 is the posttest or second observation of the control group

The experimental design allows the evaluator to assume that the groups are equivalent at the start of the study and thus inoculates the study against many of the threats to its internal validity. Can you see how with this design the evaluator would be able to determine if there were selection bias or effects from maturation or history? However, it should be noted that there is no *guarantee* of equivalence between the two groups. Comparability or similarity of the groups is much more likely to occur if the population is large and the size of each group reaches or exceeds 25 to 30 persons. If the population or the samples are small, then even random assignment may not produce equivalence. Many possible distributions *could* occur such as an outlier distribution. A strong advantage of this design is that it affords the evaluator the ability to check at the time of the pretest to confirm that the groups are roughly equivalent.

As an example of this design, consider the program evaluation of a 40-bed residential treatment program that provides milieu therapy (a structured therapeutic community). Velasquez and McCubbin (1980) evaluated such a program using an experimental design where applicants were randomly assigned to either the residential program or informed that they would not be able to enter the program for 6 months; for the latter group, alternative forms of health services were available (inpatient hospitalization in a different program, day treatment, or another residential facility not providing milieu therapy).

Nine different instruments were used to collect data about potential applicants. The program director gave ratings for such dimensions as degree of psychiatric impairment and social adjustment. The applicants completed other measures (the Tennessee Self-Concept Scale and the Problem Solving Scale). Analysis revealed strong evidence that the residential treatment program increased the participants' responsibility for self, social participation, and continuation in employment; improved their self-concept; and reduced the probability of hospitalization 6 months later. The authors concluded, "The consistency of findings from this experimental investigation present a clear and fairly convincing picture of the effectiveness of this residential program" (p. 357).

School social worker Rufus Larkin (Larkin & Thyer, 1999) conducted a true experimental evaluation of group work services provided to behaviorally disruptive elementary school children. A total of 52 children were referred to him at two elementary schools. Larkin provided the group work services himself, but could not see all the children at the same time, so he *randomly* assigned half the kids to immediate treatment and half to delayed treatment. He used four outcome measures as pre- and posttests: a reliable and valid measure of self-esteem, a reliable and valid measure of self-control, and "behavior grades" provided independently by the teacher and the teacher aides. His research design could be graphed as follows:

Immediate treatment group ($N = 31$)   R   O   X   O   O
Delayed treatment group ($N = 21$)   R   O   O   X   O

As could be expected with a true random assignment and with this sample size, the two groups were roughly equivalent in terms of the demographics and outcome measures, pretreatment. After the 8-week standardized group work intervention, the immediate treatment group improved statistically and clinically, whereas the delayed treatment group (who did not receive group work services during the same period of time) did not improve. Then, after the delayed treatment group completed the same program, they evidenced comparable improvements. Plus, at the follow-up assessment of the children assigned to the immediate treatment, some 5 months after they completed the group program, their gains had been maintained. This study possesses a number of the *desired* features of a true experiment: random assignment to conditions, the use of valid and reliable outcome measures, pretests, posttests, and a fairly lengthy follow-up period. It provided credible answers to the following questions:

1.   Did kids who received group work evidence improvements in self-esteem, self-control, and behavior? (Yes!)
2.   Were these improvements due to simply being assessed? (No!)
3.   Were these improvements *caused by* the group work? (Yes!)
4.   Were these improvements maintained over a fairly long period of time, after the intervention was completed? (Yes!)

Now, this is still not a perfect study. (Such a study will probably never be conducted.) For example, the role of placebo influences or of the kids simply wishing to please the school social worker cannot be excluded. Ideally, one would like to have included some measures from the *parents'* perspective on possible improvements in their children's comportment and to assess the students' *academic* grades as well. These issues give Larkin something to do now that he has left the school system for a career in university teaching, following the completion of his Ph.D., earned in part by conducting this study.

Social work doctoral student Patrick Bordnick used a randomized controlled study to examine the differential effectiveness of several different aversion therapies compared to a relaxation control group in reducing reported subjective craving for drugs among a convenience sample of cocaine abusers. Sixty-nine inpatients at a veteran's hospital volunteered for this study, which was approved by the university and VA institutional review boards. The patients were randomly assigned four groups—chemical aversion therapy ($N = 16$), electrical aversion therapy ($N = 17$), a treatment called covert sensitization (CS, $N = 16$), or to a relaxation control condition ($N = 20$). Aversion therapy in general was found to reduce reported craving, with chemical aversion therapy being more effective than electrical or CS, while relaxation therapy had few effects on craving.

Interestingly, pretreatment craving ratings were *not* statistically equivalent across the groups, suggesting that the random assignment process was not effective in producing equivalency on this variable, even though they were equivalent on the demographic variables tested. This illustrates the importance of pretests, and of actually determining if randomly assigned groups are equivalent on important measures, rather than simply assuming that this happened. Again, this is particularly important with groups containing fewer than 25 participants. Bordnick used various statistical procedures to take into account the pretreatment differences existing at the beginning of treatment on the dimension of craving, which is an acceptable procedure, but still not as desirable as obtaining legitimately equivalent groups on the basis of randomization. More details can be found in Bordnick et al. (2004).

Do you recall Spinelli's (1997) O-X-O design, evaluating interpersonal psychotherapy (IP) for depressed pregnant women? It is important to develop effective psychosocial treatments for depressed pregnant women because it is problematic to provide them with strong antidepressant medications, which can affect their baby. With the promising results of her pilot study, she (see Spinelli & Endicott, 2003) went on to design a controlled study, assigning 38 depressed women to IP ($N = 21$) or to parenting education classes ($N = 17$). Both interventions lasted about 16 weeks and were provided by a social worker and a psychiatrist. Women receiving IP improved significantly more than those getting parenting education. In fact, fully 60 percent of the IP group no longer met the diagnostic criteria for clinical depression at the end of the study! This study could be diagrammed as follows:

$$R \quad O_1 \quad X \quad O_2$$
$$R \quad O_3 \quad Y \quad O_4$$

If X refers to 16 weeks of IP, and Y refers to 16 weeks of parenting education, can you confidently describe what the other symbols stand for?

Posttest-Only Control Group Design

Another experimental design, the posttest-only control group design, is an elegant modification of the basic experimental design. Even without the initial pretests, it is a useful experimental design, ideal for those situations where it was not or is not possible to conduct a pretest or where a pretest could conceivably effect the posttest results. This design is also advantageous on those occasions when matching pretests with posttests is not possible or desired.

Random assignment of subjects establishes equivalence between the control and experimental groups. Measurement of the control group (O_2) serves as a pretest measure for comparison with the experimental group's posttest (O_1). This design can be diagrammed:

$$R \quad X \quad O_1$$
$$R \qquad\quad O_2$$

where

R indicates that participants were randomly assigned to either the control or intervention groups,

O_1 is an assessment made of the group who received treatment, after they received treatment, and

O_2 is an assessment made of the group that did not receive treatment, obtained about the same time as O_1 was measured.

As an example of this design, imagine that you work in a forensic program. Your boss, who is the county's prosecuting attorney, asked you to start an intervention program for persons who have been arrested for shoplifting. Careful screening eliminates any persons who have been previously arrested so that all of your clientele will be first-time offenders. If these first-time offenders complete a 4-week intervention program on consecutive Saturday mornings, the record of their arrest will be erased. Because the prosecuting attorney will be running for reelection in about 2 years, she asks that you design a sound evaluation component so that she can point to the program's success in her election campaign.

Assume that there will be more first-time offenders eligible for participation in the intervention program than can be initially served. Given this situation, the only fair procedure would be a random selection where some first-time offenders are chosen to participate in the program and others either are not invited to participate or are informed that they can participate at a later date.

In this example, there is no need to conduct a pretest because all of the persons eligible for participation in the program have already been arrested for shoplifting, and it has been determined that they are first-time offenders.

Vitally important is the measure that will be used to gauge the success of the intervention program. Let's say that you and the prosecuting attorney agree that the best indicator of success would be whether the first-time offenders are arrested again for shoplifting. For simplicity's sake, suppose that the posttest data consists of the number of arrests of those who received the intervention during the period beginning 1 month following their arrest and concluding 6 months later. The longest wait for the start of the intervention group would be 1 month; this means that if the intervention is effective, there should be no shoplifting arrests among these program participants in the 5-month period following the intervention. Similarly, arrest data will be examined for the control group beginning 1 month from the time of their arrest and will conclude 6 months later. During this time, they will receive no intervention.

If the shoplifters cannot be randomly assigned to the treatment or to the control conditions, or if the intervention cannot be postponed for those selected to be in the control group, the evaluator could not use this design. The evaluator must rely on a less rigorous design such as the nonequivalent control group design. With the quasi-experimental design, there is more flexibility, and several options present themselves.

Because not all shoplifters will agree to participating in an intervention program (some will refuse to attend, some will attend once and never return, some would rather pay a fine), those who choose not to participate constitute a "natural" comparison group for the nonequivalent control group design. If the intervention is successful, fewer of those receiving the intervention should be rearrested than those who were in the comparison group.

Another option would be to use historical or archival data for the comparison. In this instance, the control group would be those first-time shoplifting offenders who received no intervention (simply because it was not available). The evaluator could select a sample of shoplifters who were arrested during some interval of time (e.g., the year prior to the start of the intervention program) and then examine arrest data for each of these first-time offenders for a period of time comparable to that of the intervention group. If the intervention is effective, the intervention group should have fewer repeat shoplifters during a 12-month (or similar) time interval.

A real-life example using the posttest-only control group design can be found in Canady and Thyer (1990). The problem was the relatively low rate of voter participation in elections, especially among low-income and minority voters. In the fall of 1988, when the presidential election was in full swing, Kelly Canady obtained a printout of the names and addresses of all registered voters who lived in the poorest voting precinct in Dublin, Georgia. It listed about 2,500 voters, mostly (90 percent) African American, low-income, and living in public housing. Kelly randomly picked 400 names off of this list, and randomly assigned these to one of four groups. Group 1 received a bipartisan letter signed by the local chairs of the Democratic and Republican parties, urging them to vote in the forthcoming election. These letters were mailed to arrive a couple of days before the election. Group 2 received the same letter a week before, and a second one a few days before, the election. Group 3 received the same letter two weeks, one week, and a few days before the election. Group 4 got no letter. The posttest-only control group design could be depicted as follows:

Group 1 (1 letter)	R	W	O
Group 2 (2 letters)	R	X	O
Group 3 (3 letters)	R	Y	O
Group 4 (no letter)	R		O

The outcome measure was whether or not the registered voter actually voted in the election. This bit of information is a matter of public record, and after the election Canady went to the voter registrar's office and found out whether his participants voted (not *how* they voted, but simply *if* they voted). It was hypothesized that those voters who received a reminder letter would be more likely to vote than those who did not get the letter, and that those who received more than one letter would be more likely to vote than those who received one letter only.

Sadly, the letters seemed to have no effect. The null hypotheses could not be rejected, as voting was equally likely across the four experimental conditions. This counterintuitive finding both surprised and disappointed Canady, but it does illustrate the fact that you cannot always predict your outcomes when you conduct an experiment. As an honest program evaluator, Canady reported his findings as they emerged, not as he would have wished for them to turn out.

Solomon Four-Group Design

The Solomon four-group design is another elaboration of the basic experimental design. As can be seen from the following diagram, this design requires that two groups receive the intervention and that two groups do not. Only two groups are given a pretest, but all four groups are administered the posttest. This design is very rigorous because it allows the evaluator a great deal of control over testing and concurrent history and thus increases the confidence that can be placed in the findings. However, this design also requires more planning and coordination and, as a result, not many evaluators will have the opportunity to utilize it.

$$
\begin{array}{cccc}
R & O_1 & X & O_2 \\
R & O_3 & & O_4 \\
R & & X & O_5 \\
R & & & O_6
\end{array}
$$

where

R represents random assignment to one of the four conditions (two with treatment)

O_1 and O_3 are pretests, given about the same point in time.

O_2, O_4, and O_5 are posttests, also given about the same point in time.

O_6 can be considered a control for historical events perhaps effecting all participants.

As an example of this design, imagine you are the director of a summer camp for children who have come from poor homes. Many of the children have been victims of abuse or neglect. You feel that the summer camp experience significantly increases their self-esteem and improves their outlook on life. You know that if you demonstrate such results to funding sources, they will be interested in helping with the expense of the summer camp. You are anxious to conduct an evaluation that is as strong and rigorous as possible. In this example, you would randomly assign eligible children to one of the four conditions specified in the design: two groups would attend summer camp and two groups would not.

Although a simple experimental design could be used, you are concerned that the children, being anxious to please and to show that camp was meaningful to them, might infer the nature of the self-esteem instrument and by their responses indicate improved self-esteem, when this may not reflect reality. The more times a test is given to a group, the greater the likelihood that the subjects can understand or anticipate the purpose of the test. One of the advantages of the Solomon four-group design is that any influence of testing can be identified, because two of the four groups are tested only once.

A major problem with this design may come from the fact that you may not believe that children eligible should be denied the experience of summer camp. Depending on the length of the camp experience and the timing of the posttest, it may be possible for all of the children in the control groups to also participate in summer camp—they attend after they have finished serving in control groups. This would be possible in those situations where the duration of summer camp is only 1 or 2 weeks for each group of campers. The issue here is whether a 1- or 2-week camp experience increases self-esteem—not whether any improvements to self-esteem are maintained throughout the summer or the subsequent years. If you were concerned about whether the gains in self-esteem were maintained, the posttests would be planned for 6 months or a year after the completion of the intervention—which would prevent those in the control group from attending camp in the same summer as those in the intervention group.

Although the Solomon four-group design is rarely used in program evaluation because of its complexity, one good example can be found in the report by social workers Steven Schinke, Betty Blythe, and Lewayne Gilchrist (1981). The problem was unwanted pregnancies occurring among adolescents in high school. Thirty-six sophomores (19 women and 17 men) were randomly assigned to the four groups comprising a Solomon four-group design, as outlined earlier. The intervention was a well-proceduralized cognitive-behavioral training program conducted in small groups. Topics included reproductive biology, contraception, problem solving, assertiveness training, and so on. The outcome measures involved standardized role-plays requiring interacting with the opposite sex in a series of vignettes (e.g., being asked to spend the night with a date), and a number of reliable and valid pencil-and-paper measures related to contraceptive knowledge and problem-solving skills.

Posttests found that the adolescents receiving the intervention had enhanced knowledge, attitudes, and social skills related to contraception and problem solving, but there were no changes in the students assigned to the no treatment group—exactly what the researchers wanted to find. Gains were maintained at 6 months. This design controlled for the passage of time and for the effects of testing. But again, it was not perfect. It would have been wonderful if the investigators could have shown that the actual occurrence of *pregnancy* was smaller among the treated students, compared to no treatment. But this would likely have required a much greater sample size and follow-up period than was feasible. And the issue of denying some students any intervention at all raises the specter of unwanted pregnancies happening for the purposes of experimental rigor! Such a design would have difficulties in being approved by contemporary institutional review boards, who would likely insist on some form of "alternative treatment" condition as opposed to "no treatment."

EFFICACY AND EFFECTIVENESS STUDIES

In recent years, group experimental designs have been critiqued as not reflecting the real-life vicissitudes of practice. For example, some tightly controlled studies are conducted at university research centers, with extremely well-trained and supervised therapists, providing services to carefully selected clients, who may, for example, have been extensively prescreened to rule out multiple problems or concurrent diagnoses. The findings of such studies, it has been contended, cannot be generalized to apply to real life practice contexts that may employ less than well-trained therapists, provide poor supervision, and try to help clients presenting with myriad difficulties. We believe that such critiques are misguided, because they fail to recognize the development and incremental nature of intervention research. One of the ways to best initially test the effectiveness of a program is to make the study as "clean" as possible, reducing "noise" and "confusion," via the careful selection of clients who ideally are troubled only by the particular problem for which the intervention was designed. A test of an intervention for schizophrenia, for example, will be a fairer test if it is initially applied only to persons who meet criteria for schizophrenia, and for nothing else (e.g., drug abuse, bipolar disorder, epilepsy, spousal battering, etc.). In this way it is more likely that the true usefulness of the intervention for schizophrenia will be revealed. If it is initially shown to be helpful, and the results are replicated by independent researchers, then, and only then, is it useful to begin introducing variables into the equation, so to speak, so as to more closely approximate real-life practice with real-life clients. In this way a series of studies can measure whether this intervention helpful for persons meeting criteria for schizophrenia is equally helpful for this who meet criteria for schizophrenia *and* bipolar disorder, drug abuse, and so forth. Or, if the intervention is helpful when provided by doctorally trained therapists, see if it proves equally helpful when provided by master's-level therapists, and so forth.

These very tightly controlled studies have been called efficacy studies, whereas efforts at replicating treatments shown to be useful (via preliminary efficacy studies) in circumstances possessing greater verisimilitude to real-life practice have been called effectiveness studies. Scientific investigators are keenly aware that the findings of efficacy studies may not generalize to real-life practice, and initially promising efficacy studies need to be replicated in actual real-life clinical settings, via effectiveness research investigations, before they should be adopted on a widespread scale. And indeed this is exactly how science works (Clarke, 1995; Nathan, Stuart & Dolan, 2000). For example, Gail Steketee has been at the forefront of testing the approach called exposure therapy and response prevention (ETRP) as a psychosocial treatment for clients meeting the criteria for the disabling condition called obsessive-compulsive disorder (OCD). In a series of tightly controlled efficacy studies, ETRP has been shown to be helpful when applied with clients meeting the criteria for OCD (Cohen & Steketee, 1998). Steketee then went on to develop a self-help book based on the principles of ETRP, and when this was tested (by other researchers) in the context of a real-life mental health clinic, her self-help book was found to be very helpful in reducing the symptoms of OCD (see Fritzler, Hecker, & Losee, 1997). Again, this is *exactly* how science usually works—incremental progress approximating ever more closely real-life practice. The literature is replete with examples of practical effectiveness studies demonstrating that selected psychosocial treatments initially found useful in efficacy studies have effects that hold up in the messy real world of everyday programs (Friedman et al., 2003; Hickling and Blanchard, 1997; Johnson & Remien, 2003; Kirk, 1983; Krone, Himle & Nesse, 1991; Lincoln et al., 2003; McClellan & Werry, 2003; Shadish et al., 1997; Vinokur, Price & Caplan, 1991).

A NOTE ABOUT THE TERM *EXPERIMENT*

In the social and behavioral sciences, the term *experiment* has become virtually synonymous with studies characterized by features of what are known as randomized controlled trials—with the use of valid measures obtained pre- and postinterventions; large number of subjects who are randomly assigned to treatment, no treatment, or to some sort of comparison group condition; posttests; an independent variable (treatment) that can be reliably introduced, withheld, or sometimes removed; and the use of (perhaps) complex inferential statistics. It is important to keep in mind that this form of experiment is necessary in many program evaluation contexts due to the large amount of "noise" in the data—the use of less than perfect outcome measures; treatments applied with varying degrees of fidelity to the actual models they are derived from; clients who report with less than complete accuracy; clerical mistakes; labile problems; extraneous influences; and so forth. Because of the great variability and complexity of our subject matter—human behavior—considerable methodological efforts are required to sort out the legitimate influences of the treatments from other sources of variation in the data. However, a great many legitimate fields of scientific inquiry make little use of this type of experiment, and use nonexperimental methods that are nonetheless capable of discovering findings with a great degree of certainty (provisionally of course, always amenable to gathering further data). Astronomy and meteorology use primarily observational methods and can almost never manipulate their independent variables. Other sciences manipulate independent variables, but do not find it necessary to control for so many rival influences. A chemist mixing a compound in a beaker of distilled water need not go to great lengths to ensure that his or her sample of the compound is somehow "representative" of all of that material existing on the earth, or that the water is similarly representative. But a novel demonstration of a new chemical reaction, if repeatable, achieves the status of an accepted finding in science, even in the absence of a randomized controlled trial. Will a new airplane fly? Aerospace engineers and test pilots actually try and fly it. It does or it does not fly. No classical experiments in a behavioral or social science sense are necessary to prove a point. In the earlier years of science, such proofs of a new finding were called an "exact demonstration" and it is in that sense that the poet Walt Whitman wrote, in *Leaves of Grass,* "Hurrah for positive science! Long live exact demonstration!" So while we often turn our noses up at nonexperimental studies, let's keep in mind that you only need as much methodological rigor as is necessary to answer the question being asked. Science uses many methods, and randomized controlled studies, although being a very rigorous method indeed, are sometimes not necessary to convincingly gather enough evidence to prove a point.

CHAPTER RECAP

The aim of this chapter has been to present a range of designs, from the not very rigorous to the experimental. Although the "standard" may be the experimental design, it is not always feasible to implement it. The choice of an evaluation design is often the evaluator's alone, although this is clearly not always the case. The design should follow logically from the questions or hypotheses that need to be explored, the resources available, the constraints within the agency, as well as what is pragmatic.

Evaluation designs are tailored to a specific situation or program. For pedagogic reasons, the choice of a design has been presented here as being selected after an evaluation question has been formulated. But the choice of design and of the evaluation question may not be separate and distinct steps. Cronbach et al. (1980) noted, "We reject the view that 'design' begins *after* a research question is chosen, as a mere technical process to sharpen the inquiry. Choice of questions and choice of investigative tactics are inseparable" (pp. 213–214). Cronbach also referred to the choice of design as a "spiral process," where the evaluator lays out a rough plan and considers what will be left unsettled. The process may not be straightforward as concerns about information yield, costs, and political importance are considered and balanced (p. 261).

Beginning evaluators are sometimes too critical of their own efforts when they are prevented from using an experimental design. They may think that any design short of the "ideal" experiment will yield worthless data. This simply is not true. Something can be learned from just about any evaluation. Even highly competent evaluators often have to settle for designs much less stringent than the Solomon four-group design. Depending on your audience, nonexperimental designs may, in some instances, be desired, as they are less complex and more understandable.

For example, we know of a county prosecutor who was extremely pleased with the results of an evaluation that used the one-group posttest-only design. He had been instrumental in getting a drug treatment program started for felons that combined systematic urine sampling and a structured counseling program. At the end of the first 9 months, only 12 percent of over 4,500 urine samples from 176 felons indicated alcohol or drug use. Among those with "clean" urine samples, only 22 percent had been rearrested, while 66 percent of those with three or more "dirty" urine samples had been rearrested. Even though 48 percent of those in the program had been rearrested for some offense and there was no randomization or control group, the county attorney was making plans to speak to the state legislature about additional funding so that similar programs could be started in other communities in the state. In this example, the results of the study were perceived as being so powerful that even the relatively weak evaluation design seemed to be inconsequential.

Does the choice of a design make a difference? Yes, it does. It is not often that one can expect the same degree of success as reported in the previous example. We often see frustration and disenchantment with program evaluation when practitioners in the field and students realize much too late how any observed changes in clients after intervention could have been due to alternative explanations.

In our eagerness to evaluate programs, we would do well to remember that there are circumstances that do not warrant evaluation. Carol Weiss (1972, pp. 10–11), in her now classic book, noted that evaluation is not worth doing in four kinds of circumstances:

1. When there are no questions about the program. . . . Decisions about its future either do not come up or have already been made.
2. When the program has no clear orientation. . . . The program shifts and changes, wanders around and seeks direction.
3. When people who should know cannot agree on what the program is trying to achieve. If there are vast discrepancies in perceived goals, evaluation has no ground to stand on.
4. When there is not enough money or staff sufficiently qualified to conduct the evaluation. Evaluation is a demanding business, calling for time, money, imagination, tenacity, and skill.

Caution should be used though, against invoking any of the above factors simply as plausible excuses for not undertaking evaluations which are in actuality needed and feasible. It should also be noted that in any evaluation you may use more than one design. You may use multiple approaches (remember the triangulation discussion in the chapter on needs assessment?), you may use several different instruments, or you may even employ a different design with each instrument.

Suchman (1967) made some important observations regarding the choice of evaluation design. He observed that ultimately the best design is the one most suitable for the purpose of the study, and because designs often reflect compromises dictated by practical considerations, there is no such thing as a single correct design. Questions and hypotheses can be explored using different methods or approaches.

To help you have a comprehensive overview of the major research designs outlined in this chapter, we have prepared a summary of them in Table 9.2, listing them by name and with an illustration of the design itself. Keep in mind that these general designs are capable of being modified in various ways, limited

TABLE 9.2 | SELECTED TYPES OF GROUP RESEARCH DESIGNS COMMONLY USED IN PROGRAM EVALUATION STUDIES

Name of Design	Notation
Pre-experimental Designs	
1. One-group posttest-only	X O
2. One-group pretest–posttest	O X O
Quasi-experimental Designs	
3. Nonequivalent control group	O X O
	O O
4. Interrupted time series	O O O O X O O O O
5. Multiple time series	O O O O X O O O O
	O O O O O O O O O
Experimental Designs	
6. Pretest–posttest control group	R O X O
	R O O
7. Posttest-only control group	R X O
	R O
8. Solomon four-group	R O X O
	R O O
	R X O
	R O

Note: O = Observation or assessment period
  X = Intervention
  R = Randomly assigned

only by your own creativity. None of them can be considered as a "perfect" study—each possesses various strengths and limitations. It is not appropriate to assert that any particular design is better than or superior to any other. Each particular design's suitability needs to be appraised with respect to the availability of the numbers of potential research participants, the feasibility of completing pretests and follow-up assessments, the ethical appropriateness of random assignment, and so forth. Sometimes the very *best* design in a given circumstance may be the posttest-only design, or the one group pretest–posttest design. If one of these is your best option, it is certainly better to use it than to *not* conduct any form of outcome evaluation at all. These more limited (in terms of potential internal validity) designs may well be the option of choice if you are contemplating program evaluation efforts in a relatively new area of practice, or if it is your first effort at conducting an outcome study.

Questions for Class Discussion

1. Discuss conducting program evaluations in various community agencies. Do some of the designs in this chapter seem to "fit" some programs better than others? Why?
2. Discuss the advantages and disadvantages of an evaluator monitoring similar programs in different agencies using these four questions:
   a. Did this program have objectives derived from the goals for the program?
      ____ YES ____ NO ____ Cannot be determined
   b. Did the program serve as many clients as projected?
      ____ YES ____ NO ____ Cannot be determined
   c. Did the agency conduct an outcome evaluation of this program?
      ____ YES ____ NO ____ Cannot be determined
   d. Did the agency staff seem committed to evaluating the outcome of their program?
      ____ YES ____ NO____ Cannot be determined
3. Discuss the problems of using a self-report questionnaire with smokers in a smoking cessation clinic. What percentage might be motivated to indicate that they had stopped when in fact they were still smoking? What would constitute "hard evidence"?
4. Have the class identify a local program that would be interesting to evaluate using one of the designs in this chapter. What evaluation design would be used? What would be the primary outcome variable? What would be the threats to the internal validity? How would you control for these? What would be the data collection procedures? Who would need to assist with the evaluation? Who would be the subjects?
5. Discuss for any specific program the various outcome indicators that might be chosen in a program evaluation. Are some more valuable than others for showing the impact the program is having on the lives of clients?

Mini-Projects: Experiencing Evaluation Firsthand

1. Browse through professional journals in a field of your choice to find the report of an evaluation using a nonequivalent control group design. Read the article and critique it.
2. A program has recently been funded to provide intensive services to the homeless. The mission of the program is to identify those who, with the necessary supportive services, can realistically be expected to be employed and self-sustaining within 3 years. Design a program evaluation for this project. Be sure to identify your evaluation design and other necessary details.

References and Resources

Attkisson, C. C., & Broskowski, A. (1978). Evaluation and the emerging human service concept. In C. C. Attkisson, W. A. Hargreaves, M. J. Horowitz, & J. E. Sorensen (Eds.), *Evaluation of human service programs.* New York: Academic Press.

Bordnick, P. S., Elkins, R. L., Orr, T. E., Walters, P., & Thyer, B. A. (2004). Evaluating the relative effectiveness of three aversion therapies designed to reduce craving among cocaine abusers. *Behavioral Interventions, 19,* 1–24.

Campbell, D. T., & Stanley, J. C. (1963). *Experimental and quasi-experimental designs for research.* Chicago: Rand McNally.

Campbell, D. T., Shadish, W. R., & Cook, T. D. (2001). *Experimental and quasi-experimental designs for generalized causal inference.* New York: Houghton-Mifflin.

Canady, W. K., & Thyer, B. A. (1990). Promoting voting behavior among low income black voters using reminder letters: An experimental investigation. *Journal of Sociology and Social Welfare, 17*(4), 109–116.

Capp, H. B., Thyer, B. A., & Bordnick, P. S. (1997). Evaluating improvement over the course of adult psychiatric hospitalization. *Social Work in Health Care, 25*(4), 55–66.

Carrillo, D. F., & Thyer, B. A. (1994). Advanced standing and two-year program students: An empirical investigation of foundation interviewing skills. *Journal of Social Work Education, 30,* 377–387.

Clarke, G. N. (1995). Improving the transition from basic efficacy research to effectiveness studies: Methodological issues and procedures. *Journal of Consulting and Clinical Psychology, 63,* 718–725.

Cohen, I. & Steketee, G. S. (1998). Obsessive-compulsive disorder. In B. A. Thyer & J. S. Wodarski (Eds.). *Handbook of empirical social work practice* (Vol. 1, pp. 343–363). New York: Wiley.

Cook, T. D., & Campbell, D. T. (1979). *Quasi-experimentation: Design and analysis issues for field settings.* Chicago: Rand McNally.

Cronbach, L. J., Ambron, S. R., Dornbusch, S. M., Hess, R. D., Hornik, R. C., Phillips, D. C., Walker, D. F., & Weiner, S. S. (1980). *Toward reform of program evaluation.* San Francisco: Jossey-Bass.

Fitz-Gibbon, C. T., & Morris, L. L. (1987). *How to design a program evaluation.* Beverly Hills, CA: Sage.

Friedman, S., Smith, L. C., Halpern, B. & Levine, C. (2003). Obsessive-compulsive disorder in a multi-ethnic urban outpatient clinic: Initial presentation and treatment outcome with exposure and ritual prevention. *Behavior Therapy, 34,* 397–410.

Fritzler, B. K., Hecker, J. E., & Losee, M. C. (1997). Self-directed treatment with minimal therapist contact: Preliminary findings for obsessive-compulsive disorder. *Behaviour Research and Therapy, 35,* 627–631.

Gary-McCormick, E., Thyer, B. A., Panton, T. M., & Myers, L. L. (2000). The association between appointment-keeping and birth outcome in a prenatal care program for high-risk women. *Journal of Family Social Work, 4*(1), 47–58.

Glisson, G., Thyer, B. A., & Fischer, R. (2001). Serving the homeless: Evaluating the effectiveness of homeless shelter services. *Journal of Sociology and Social Welfare, 28(4),* 89–97.

Grossman, J., & Tierney, J. P. (1993).The fallibility of comparison groups. *Evaluation Review, 17*(5), 556–571.

Hickling, E. J., & Blanchard, E. (1997). The private practice psychologist and manual-based treatments: Post-traumatic stress disorder secondary to motor vehicle accidents. *Behaviour Research and Therapy, 35,* 191–203.

Johnson, M. O., & Remien, R. H. (2003). Adherence to research protocols in a clinical context: Challenges and recommendations from behavioral intervention trials. *American Journal of Psychotherapy, 57*(3), 348–360.

Kirk, J. W. (1983). Behavioural treatment of obsessional-compulsive patients in routine clinical practice. *Behaviour Research and Therapy, 21,* 57–62.

Krone, K. P., Himle, J. A., & Nesse, R. M. (1991). A standardized behavioral group treament program for obsessive-compulsive disorder: Preliminary outcomes. *Behaviour Research and Therapy, 29*(6), 627–631.

Larkin, R., & Thyer, B. A. (1999). Evaluating cognitive-behavioral group counseling to improve elementary school students' self-esteem, self-control, and classroom behavior. *Behavioral Interventions, 14,* 147–161.

Larsen, D. L., Attkisson, C. C., Hargreaves, W. A., & Nguyen, T. D. (1979). Assessment of client/patient satisfaction: Development of a general scale. *Evaluation and Program Planning, 2,* 197–207.

Ligon, J. (1995). Client satisfaction with brief therapy. *EAP Digest, 16,* 30–31.

Ligon, J., & Thyer, B. A. (2000). Client and family satisfaction with brief community mental health, substance abuse, and mobile crisis services in an urban setting. *Crisis Intervention, 6,* 93–99.

Lincoln, T., Rief, W., Hahlweg, K., & Frank, M. (2003). Effectiveness of an empirically supported treatment for social phobia in the field. *Behaviour Research and Therapy, 41,* 1251–1269.

Majchrzak, A. (1986). Keeping Marines in the field: Results of a field experiment. *Evaluation and Program Planning, 9*(3), 253–265.

McClellan. J. M., & Werry, J. S. (2003). Evidence-based treatments in child and adolescent psychiatry: An inventory. *Journal of the American Academy of Child and Adolescent Psychiatry, 42,* 1388–1400.

Myers, L. L., & Rittner, B. (1999). Family function and satisfaction of former residents of a non-therapeutic residential care facility. *Journal of Family Social Work, 3*(3), 53–68.

Myers, L. L., & Rittner, B. (2001). Adult psychosocial functioning of children raised in an orphanage. *Residential Treatment for Children and Youth, 18*(4), 3–21.

Nathan, P. E., Stuart, S. P., & Dolan, S. L. (2000). Research on psychotherapy efficacy and effectiveness: Between Scylla and Charybdis? *Psychological Bulletin, 126,* 964–981.

Pabian, W. E., Thyer, B. A., Straka, E., & Boyle, D. P. (2000). Do the families of children with developmental disabilities obtain recommended services? A follow-up study. *Journal of Human Behavior in the Social Environment, 3,* 45–58.

Patton, M. Q. (1987). *Creative evaluation.* Beverly Hills, CA: Sage.

Radloff, L. S. (1977).The CES-D Scale: A self-report depression scale for research in the general population. *Applied Psychological Measurement, 3*(1), 385–401.

Ross, A. S., & White, S. (1987). Shoplifting, impaired driving, and refusing the

Breathalyzer. *Evaluation Review, 11*(2), 254–269.

Schinke, S. P., Blythe, B. J., & Gilchrist, L. D. (1981). Cognitive-behavioral prevention of adolescent pregnancy. *Journal of Counseling Psychology, 28,* 451–454.

Schwartz, W. L., & Thyer, B. A. (2000). Partial hospitalization treatment for clinical depression: A pilot evaluation. *Journal of Human Behavior in the Social Environment, 3*(2), 13–21.

Shadish, W. R., Matt, G. E., Navarro, A. M., Siegle, G., Crits-Christoph, P., Hazelrigg, M. D., Jorm, A. F., Lyons, L. C., Nietzel, M. T., Prout, H. T., Robinson, L., Smith, M. L., Svartberg, M., & Weiss, B. (1997). Evidence that therapy works in clinically representative conditions. *ournal of Consulting and Clinical Psychology, 65,* 355–365.

Shipman, S. (1989). General criteria for evaluating social programs. *Evaluation Practice, 10*(1), 20–26.

Shore, E. R., & Maguin, E. (1988). Deterrence of drinking-driving: The effect of changes in the Kansas driving under the influence law. *Evaluation and Program Planning, 11*(3), 245–254.

Spinelli, M. G. (1997). Interpersonal psychotherapy for depressed antepartum women: A pilot study. *American Journal of Psychiatry, 154,* 1028–1030.

Spinelli, M. G., & Endicott, J. (2003). Controlled clinical trial of interpersonal psychotheraphy versus parenting education program for depressed pregnant women. *American Journal of Psychiatry, 160,* 555–562.

Suchman, E. A. (1967). *Evaluating research: Principles and practice in public service and social action programs.* New York: Russell Sage Foundation.

Thyer, B. A., & Robertson, M. (1993). An initial evaluation of the Georgia safety belt use law: A null MUL? *Environment and Behavior, 25,* 506–513.

Toseland, R. W., Kabat, D., & Kemp, K. (1983). Evaluation of a smoking cessation group treatment program. *Social Work Research and Abstracts, 19*(1), 12–19.

Velasquez, J. S., & Lyle, C. G. (1985). Day versus residential treatment for juvenile offenders: The impact of program evaluation. *Child Welfare, 64*(2), 145–156.

Velasquez, J. S., & McCubbin, H. I. (1980). Toward establishing the effectiveness of community-based residential treatment: Program evaluation by experimental research. *Journal of Social Service Research, 3*(4), 337–359.

Vinokur, A. D., Price, R. D., & Caplan, R. D. (1991). From field experiments to program implementation: Assessing the potential outcomes of an experimental intervention program for unemployed persons. *American Journal of Community Psychology, 19,* 543–562.

Vonk, E. M., & Thyer, B. A. (1999). Evaluating the effectiveness of short-term treatment at a university counseling center. *Journal of Clinical Psychology, 55,* 1095–1106.

Weiss, C. H. (1972). *Evaluation research: Methods of assessing program effectiveness.* Englewood Cliffs, NJ: Prentice-Hall.

IO

COST-EFFECTIVENESS AND COST ANALYSIS DESIGNS

COST AS AN EVALUATIVE CRITERION

In the last chapter, we were concerned more with examining a program's effectiveness than with its cost. Realistically, however, we know that most social service and public agencies have severely restricted budgets. Costs are *always* important considerations—whether or not fiscal emergencies or severe belt-tightening episodes are encountered.

Besides effectiveness, agency directors and managers must also weigh which intervention provides the *most affordable,* favorable outcome. In an ideal program planning scenario, both costs and program effectiveness would be considered before a green light was given for program implementation. It would make no sense to launch, for instance, a program that was inexpensive but that also possessed a lower success rate than another program of comparable cost.

More expensive therapy is not necessarily better treatment (Yates, 1994). To make his point, Yates cites a classic study Bandura and colleagues (1969) conducted in which they found that for clients with a snake phobia, systematic desensitization required on average 4 hours and 33 minutes to achieve the same results that a participant modeling procedure was able to accomplish in 2 hours and 10 minutes on average. And not only do some interventions get results faster, but cost data should be considered in terms of diminishing returns. At some point, it may be necessary to determine whether an intervention will produce any additional gains. If the client's progress has stopped, investing more in additional "doses" may not be a sound idea. Instead, a change of interventions may be required.

Although a relatively small percentage of treatment outcome studies in the literature has focused on the comparison of costs of competing interventions, the advent of managed care has certainly made most helping professionals keenly aware of the economic decisions involved in weighing various treatment options.

Economic decisions surround us. Whether we are planning on purchasing a new van, linens for the crisis nursery, or food for the residential group home, dollars have to be stretched as far as possible. Private funding groups, federal, state, and local agencies, consumers—everyone wants to get as much as possible for their expenditures and investments. In order to understand how outcomes and potential benefits relate to dollars spent, program managers may decide to conduct cost-effectiveness and cost-benefit analyses—a topic that some experts refer to as measuring **efficiency** (Rossi, Freeman, & Lipsey, 1999).

The notion is simple: those programs that provide the best results for the least cost are the most efficient. However, the process by which the most efficient program is determined can be somewhat technical. That is not to say that such determinations should not be attempted, just that for reasons that will become apparent later, they are still fairly rare in the literature. For instance, Plotnick and Deppman (1999) reported that a survey of the child welfare literature of the period 1990 to 1995 uncovered no benefit-cost analyses of child abuse prevention or intervention programs. (Note: One of the things that is somewhat troubling about this line of evaluation is that there is little standardization of vocabulary; what Plotnick and Deppman call benefit-cost analysis, others refer to as cost-benefit.)

Some authors avoid the problem of terminology by placing the term *costs* in their title and then making no reference to their approach (e.g., cost effectiveness) in their abstract. For example, Schoenwald et al. (1996), in an article entitled "Multisystemic Therapy Treatment of Substance Abusing or Dependent Adolescent Offenders: Costs of Reducing Incarceration, Inpatient, and Residential Placement," found that for a 1-year period multisystemic therapy (MST) was 50 percent more costly ($1,695 per youth) than usual services for juvenile offenders. However, the additional cost of MST was associated with 46 percent fewer days of incarceration and 64 percent fewer days in residential and psychiatric facilities relative to the youth receiving usual services. The decrease in incarceration savings resulted in $48,200 savings to the state and lowered the cost of MST to $877 per youth. Youths associated with the MST program spent less time in psychiatric inpatient care and less time in substance abuse residential and inpatient treatment, as well as fewer days in incarceration. In other words, the program was substantially more effective than the treatment these juvenile offenders usually received. The authors concluded that it is likely that the superior results obtained with MST will continue as the follow-up period extends beyond a year and that the costs of MST over the usual services will continue to drop as savings in incarceration accrue over time. Whether or not the authors refer to their own project as a cost-effectiveness study, there are good grounds for our considering it to be one.

Lombard et al. (1998) note that a cost-effective analysis is designed to answer one question: Given a host of treatment possibilities, which one should be offered to the patient? The authors go on to observe, "The obvious choice is the treatment or treatments that offer the most health benefit for the patient while using the lowest cost in dollars or resources" (p. 102). Clearly, this is what Schoenwald et al. (1996) were attempting to do in their study when they compared the usual approach taken with adolescent offenders with the MST approach although the authors were looking at benefits more generally defined than just health benefits and the perspective was a societal one, not an individual client point of view.

Later we will look at cost-benefit studies as a type of economic assessment, but for now let us try to understand cost effectiveness by working through a simple example.

EXAMPLE OF A COST-EFFECTIVENESS EVALUATION

Let's compare two programs with the same mission—to assist the "hard-core" unemployed to obtain employment. The first program is called JOBPREP (for Job Preparedness) and the second, WORK NOW. Both are located within large metropolitan areas and were developed to help adults who have never experienced full-time employment. The clientele is composed of about equal proportions of persons who dropped out of school and who are functionally illiterate. Many are recovering drug addicts and persons with criminal records. Both programs begin with teaching work preparedness skills (being prompt, proper attitude, appropriate dress) and progress to teaching marketable job skills. As a final step, "interns" are placed with potential employers for actual on-the-job training. Table 10.1 presents evaluative information on the two programs. We can tell at a glance that JOB PREP is a more expensive program than WORK NOW. In fact, JOB PREP requires 20 percent more budget than WORK NOW. We also note that the less expensive program has a higher graduation rate than JOB PREP. This is partly explained by the fact that WORK NOW is a less intense program and can be completed a month quicker than JOB PREP.

TABLE 10.1	COST-EFFECTIVENESS COMPARISON OF TWO JOB TRAINING PROGRAMS	
	WORK NOW, Inc.	JOB PREP, Inc.
Total program costs	$275,000	$345,000
Graduation rate	64%	40%
Persons employed full-time for one year	48	73
Cost per employed client	$5,729	$4,726

If we were to stop at just this point in comparing these two programs, WORK NOW would appear to be the better program. However, if we consider that the mission of the two programs is to help the hard-core unemployed to become *employed,* then we need to go a bit further. Contacting the employers with whom the "interns" of both programs were placed and locating former trainees who were no longer with those employers allows us to establish the number of trainees who are employed in a full-time capacity 1 year after completion of the program.

By dividing the total program cost by the number of employed graduates of the program, we can develop a cost-effectiveness comparison. We learn that it cost an average of $5,729 to produce an employed graduate of WORK NOW, but only $4,726 to produce a graduate from the JOB PREP program. Even though JOB PREP is a somewhat more expensive program overall, it is more successful than the less expensive program in doing what it was designed to do. The sophisticated comparison looks not only at the budgets and graduation rates, but also at the programs' outcomes in relation to their expenditures.

HOW TO DO A COST-EFFECTIVENESS STUDY

Six basic steps are necessary for a cost-effectiveness study.

STEP 1: DEFINE THE PROGRAM AND ITS OUTCOME INDICATORS

It is vitally important that the evaluator fully understand all components and features of the program, what it is designed to produce, and the target population. Accordingly, the evaluator should learn the history of the program, when it began, how it has been modified over time, how the clientele may have changed over the years, and what client data are available. When programs are compared, it is crucial that the same operational definition for successful outcome is used, one that is uniform, quantifiable, and relatively easy to measure. For instance, in evaluating a program for men who have been convicted of domestic violence, it might be logical to look at subsequent rearrests. However, the evaluator needs to define which future arrests "count." Would a disorderly conduct citation resulting from a brawl with another man suggest that intervention had failed? What about an arrest for selling cocaine? Also, the evaluator must be alert to the possibility that charges for more serious offenses often get reduced through plea bargaining. Using recidivism as an outcome indicator requires that comparable time periods be employed across agencies or programs.

STEP 2: COMPUTE COSTS

The evaluator must compute the total costs for operating the program. Although these will vary from program to program, the evaluator should identify such costs as the following.

a. Personnel This category includes the salaries and fringe benefits for all program employees. The value of efforts contributed by volunteers should also be included. This can be estimated on the basis of the number of hours worked and the type of assistance being provided. (An hourly wage for someone volunteering to help mail out a newsletter would be estimated at a lower rate than a physician donating free physicals.)

b. Facilities Programs must be housed, and this category includes rent for physical space and related costs of its share of the agency's insurance, electricity, heating, air conditioning, and so on. When these costs are not available by program, they can be crudely estimated by using a proportion derived from a ratio of the program's personnel budget over the agency's budget for all personnel. For example, if the drug education program's staff constituted 10 percent of the agency's personnel expenditures, then 10 percent of the agency's utility costs, rent, and so forth could be used as an estimate.

Where a building is owned by an agency, the cost for renting a similar space can be estimated by contacting a knowledgeable real estate agent or by following a set of procedures outlined by Levin (1983), which includes such steps as determining the replacement value of the facility, the life of the facility, the cost of depreciation, and the interest on its undepreciated value.

c. Equipment This category includes expenses for new computers and printers, office supplies, any audiovisual tapes, brochures, and any commercial tests or special instructional materials or books used by the program.

d. Other Expenses This grouping includes costs that do not fit into any other category, such as travel, inservice training, and workshops, as well as indirect costs associated with the administrative structure of the agency. For instance, if the agency director is responsible for four programs, then one-fourth the administrative costs for running the agency (e.g., salaries and fringe benefits for the director, the associate director, the executive secretary, the business manager, etc.) should also be included as costs.

STEP 3: COLLECT PROGRAM OUTCOME DATA

Before data are actually collected, a number of practical questions must be considered such as how many years to include or how much client data to acquire. When programs are relatively new, it may make sense to contact every graduate and dropout. On the other hand, well-established programs with large clientele may require the sampling of clients in the past 12 months.

STEP 4: COMPUTE PROGRAM OUTCOMES

In this step, the evaluator must document the program's successes. Examples of indicators of success for various programs are the number of clients who have not been hospitalized in the past 12 months; the number of clients employed; the number of new foster homes recruited; the number of clients who complete their GED; and the number of first-time DUI offenders who are not rearrested within 24 months. Keep in mind that a program may have more than one indicator of success.

STEP 5: COMPUTE THE COST-EFFECTIVENESS RATIO

The cost-effectiveness ratio is computed by dividing the total cost of the program by the effectiveness outcome indicator (e.g., the number of successes). This allows decision makers to see the relationship between costs and outcomes and to choose those programs that have the best cost-effectiveness ratio. Programs with

	SENSITIVITY ANALYSIS OF
BOX 10.1	THE COST-EFFECTIVENESS
	OF COUNSELING SMOKERS
	TO QUIT

Overview. Drawing on published reports of smoking cessation among patients given advice by a physician to quit smoking, this cost-effectiveness study used a hypothetical group of patients who were smokers. The authors estimated that a physician would use 4 minutes to promote nonsmoking during a routine office visit that cost $30 and would hand out a $2 booklet. Using four separate studies of patients who were given advice by a physician to quit smoking, an average cessation rate at one year was computed to be 2.7 percent.

Sensitivity Analyses. The authors assumed (1) a 50 percent increase in the cost of an office visit; (2) the cessation rate might drop to 1 percent or rise as high as 4 percent; and (3) although an annual rate of 5 percent was used to discount gains in life expectancy, discount rates of 3 percent and 7 percent were also used in the sensitivity analysis. The authors also examined the effect of a 50 percent relapse rate.

Source: Cummings, S. R., Rubin, S. M., & Oster, G. (1989). *Journal of the American Medical Association, 261* (1), 75–79.

substantial costs but that produce few positive effects can be discontinued and the resulting cost savings applied to more effective interventions.

STEP 6: PERFORM A SENSITIVITY ANALYSIS

The last step in a cost-effectiveness study is to conduct a sensitivity analysis. This means that recommendations based on the cost-effectiveness data are tested. (See Box 10.1.) This step is more important when extensive use of estimation was used in the cost-effectiveness study than when all costs and effects were real. When estimation is used liberally, the evaluator should go back and make high and low estimates in order to see if a different decision about the program might be justified. If the final decision is not affected by slightly different assumptions, then the evaluator will be more confident in the decision.

WHOSE POINT OF VIEW?

When doing any kind of economic analysis, it is important to keep in mind that the worth of a program can be viewed from a number of different accounting perspectives. For example, programs can be evaluated from the viewpoints of:

Society as a whole

The providers of the service

The consumers of the service

Payers (for example, third-party insurance carriers)

At times, different perspectives may clash. The costs associated with a needed intervention may be very important to one group but insignificant to another; one group of stakeholders may view success rates as acceptable but another group may be appalled by the same outcomes. Because the perspective can vary from study to study, cost-effectiveness analyses (CEAs) may not be comparable across interventions; this has resulted in the recommendation that CEAs be undertaken from a societal perspective (Allred et al., 1998). The societal perspective accounts for all costs and effects and ensures that the CEA does not represent the interests of only one group. (See Box 10.2 for one accounting of costs and effects.)

BOX 10.2 | **COST-EFFECTIVENESS OF TREATMENT FOR DRUG-ABUSING PREGNANT WOMEN**

Some studies have estimated that as many as one in four women may use illicit drugs during pregnancy. Those who are drug dependent have higher rates of spontaneous abortion and premature labor. Their infants are more likely to have medical problems and to require stays in neonatal intensive care units (NICU).

In this study, the first 100 women admitted to the Center for Addiction and Pregnancy were compared to a control group of pregnant drug-abusing women who were patients of a sister hospital serving the same catchment area in Baltimore but who did not receive drug abuse treatment. The two groups did not differ in race, marital status, or type of insurance coverage, but treatment subjects were approximately 3 years older and averaged 6 months more education than controls. Subjects were similar in age of onset with heroin and cocaine use, and there were no significant differences in months of regular heroin, alcohol, or marijuana use. Women admitted to the treatment program had greater involvement (longer regular use) with cocaine than the control subjects.

At the time of delivery, control subjects were 1.7 times more likely to be using illicit drugs as women in the treatment program (63 percent versus 37 percent). Their infants weighed approximately 400 grams less and had an estimated gestational age approximately 3 weeks shorter. Infants of controls were also more than twice as likely (26 percent) to require NICU hospitalization as infants of treatment subjects (10 percent). Infants requiring NICU admission had average stays six times longer (38.9 days) than infants of women from the treatment program (6.6 days).

At an average cost of $1,200 for each day in the NICU, the average stay for infants of women in the treatment program was $7,920. This compares to an average cost of $46,700 for infants of women who were not receiving treatment for their drug abuse. Even though the drug treatment program costs an estimated $6,639 per pregnancy, there was an estimated net savings of $4,644 in reduced NICU costs based on a conservative figure of $1,200 per day.

Source: Svikis, D. S., Golden, A. S., Huggins, G. R., Pickens, R. W., McCaul, M. E., Velez, M. L., Rosendale, C. T., Brooner, R. K., Gazaway, P. M., Stitzer, M. L., & Ball, C. E. (1997). Cost-effectiveness of treatment for drug-abusing pregnant women. *Drug and Alcohol Dependence, 45,* 105–113.

For instance, health care costs should include not only the costs of health care services but also the costs of patient time expended for an intervention, costs associated with caregiving (paid and unpaid), child care, travel expenses, and employer costs because of absenteeism and turnover, as well as other costs borne by employees and society as a whole (Allred et al., 1998).

COST-BENEFIT ANALYSIS

Cost-benefit analysis, also known as benefit-cost analysis, once was used only to assess such massive undertakings as large construction projects involving new highways or dams that would cause thousands of acres of land to be flooded and displace families, if not entire communities. The Tennessee Valley Authority and the Army Corps of Engineers are just two of many governmental agencies that have conducted cost-benefit analyses to help justify expensive projects. Today, the methodology has spread considerably beyond its early roots. For instance, Plotnick and Deppman (1999) have listed possible monetary benefits of funding programs that prevent and treat child abuse:

Reduced expenditures for health and mental health services

Reduced expenditures for child welfare services

Reduced expenditures for foster care and other out-of-home services

Reduced expenditures for other social services (e.g., drug and alcohol prevention)

Reduced expenditures for the criminal justice system

Reduced medical expenditures for victims of crime

Reduced administrative costs of income support programs

In cost-benefit analysis, effort is made to measure both costs and benefits in monetary units. Although it is theoretically possible to enumerate all of the benefits of a given social service program, it can be quite challenging to determine a monetary value for important but intangible benefits. For example, Plotnick and Deppman (1999) list these nonmonetary benefits of programs that prevent and treat child abuse:

Reduced personal and family stress

Better parenting and household management

Reduced family conflict

Improved social functioning of children

Fewer cognitive and language deficits

Improved mental health, fewer adjustment problems

Less fear of crime

Improved physical health, fewer injuries

Improved educational achievement

Although it is possible to determine whether an intervention group had fewer injuries or less medical expenses than some comparison group, the difficulty in estimating a monetary value associated with reduced stress or better household management is apparent.

Cartwright (1998) discusses the benefits of drug abuse treatment in terms of direct and indirect resource savings. Fewer drug addicts and drug abusers translates into direct savings in:

Court costs

Incarceration costs

Parole and probation costs

Physical injuries attributed to addicts during commission of crimes

Crime-related property damage

Private protection (e.g., security systems)

Treatment of illegal drug-related illnesses

Welfare caseloads

And fewer drug addicts and drug abusers in a society would result in savings in these indirect costs:

Loss of work related to crime-related losses or injuries

Victim fear and stress

Loss of work due to incarceration

To take another example, let's say that you work for an agency that has started a respite program for senior citizens. The program serves people 60 years old and older who live at home and who require constant care. The respite care program provides family members relief from the daily care of a disabled family member. Volunteers are recruited from within the community to provide primary caregivers with time off to take care of personal business, to go shopping, or just to have an afternoon to go to a movie or visit with friends.

The cost of the program can be computed easily enough. (There are the salary and fringe benefits associated with the volunteer coordinator's position, prorated expenses for the volunteer coordinator's share of the receptionist, as well as the prorated facility expenses—rent, insurance, utilities.) However, how do we measure the benefits of this program? How does one estimate the benefits that a care provider gets from respite services? What dollar figure do we place on the pleasure that the caregiver got from enjoying a movie or visiting with some friends? Should we measure a possible decrease in depression assessed by fewer dollars spent on counseling or prescription medications? Cost-benefit studies require that monetary value of these benefits be estimated or measured. Because of the difficulty in estimating the value of intangible benefits, it may not always make sense to do a cost-benefit analysis. (How does one appraise the value of a new playground for children located within the inner city?

How does one value the increase in self-esteem of a 55-year old migrant laborer who learns to read?) The most generally used conceptual measure of benefits is the "willingness to pay" for an outcome or action (Plotnick & Deppman, 1999).

There is very little agreement in the literature on how to define benefits. Some authors of cost-benefit analyses have defined benefits as cost savings or as return on investment, while others have used more abstract concepts such as "value-added" or secondary benefits such as institutional renewal (Cukier, 1997). Similarly, unit costs have been expressed in a wide variety of ways: total cost/number of participants; total cost/number of successful graduates; total cost/contact hour (Cukier, 1997). Further, economists use concepts such as shadow pricing and discounting that are somewhat foreign to most of us. A **shadow price** is an attempt to reflect the real cost of goods and services. For instance, a neighbor with a 5-acre field may rent it to an adjoining school to use for soccer fields for a fee of one dollar a year. However, the true value of that field is worth much more than the dollar, and the shadow price might be used to show what a comparable field would cost the athletic program to rent should the neighbor become unhappy and sell the parcel of land to a developer. **Discounting** involves reducing costs and benefits, or at least adjusting them, to reflect tapering-off effects that occur over a span of years. Thus, a drug court treatment intervention may see the biggest savings in incarceration expenditures the first year and substantially fewer savings in second and third years that clients were rehabilitated.

Because many benefits cannot be easily converted to a dollar figure, evaluators interested in examining a cost-benefit relationship may resort to employing pre- and post-standardized measurements of such outcome variables as satisfaction with life or satisfaction with services provided. Then, cost of a program or project can be understood relative to an increase in satisfaction. For instance, the creation of a micro city park on two lots where dilapidated and condemned houses previously existed might raise nearby residents' pride and satisfaction with their neighborhood from a low of 60 percent to 80 percent. If the park was constructed with volunteer help for approximately $250,000, then a cost-benefit analysis could report that the project cost $12,500 for each point of increased satisfaction ($250,000/20 = $12,500). When the benefits are nonmonetary, cost-benefit analyses will be virtually indistinguishable from cost-effectiveness studies.

Because the assessment of a given program's benefits may be somewhat arbitrary, cost-benefit analyses may use different perspectives to gauge the benefits. (See Table 10.2.) For example, McCaughrin et al. (1993) looked at the costs and benefits of supported employment for clients with developmental disabilities using the perspectives of the supported employee, the taxpayer, and society. They found from the supported employees' perspective that those with moderate or severe mental retardation increased their earnings by $1,027 during the first year, while those with mild mental retardation showed a $4,607 increase. From the taxpayers' perspective, break-even costs could be expected

TABLE 10.2 | EXAMPLES OF COST ANALYSES APPEARING IN THE LITERATURE

Author	Subject	Findings
Spoth et al. (2002)	Early interventions to prevent later alcohol use	The Iowa Strengthening Families Program provided a cost-benefit ratio of $9.60 per $1 invested.
French et al. (2002)	Modified Therapeutic Community Mentally Ill–Chemical Abusers	For a 12-month period, $13.34 in benefits were received for each $1 of investment in the program
Oss (1997)	CD Treatment: Evidence of Cost-Effectiveness	A 52-bed inpatient chemical dependency program for persons with multiple DUIs found a cost savings of $11,425 in reduced length of confinement compared to a control group in 3.5 years of follow-up.
Rosenheck et al. (1998)	Multiple Outcome Assessment Study of the Cost-Effectiveness of Clozapine in the Treatment of Refractory Schizophrenia	The authors found statistically significant differences favoring the effectiveness of clozapine, but these were of small magnitude. It was concluded that clozapine was a cost-neutral treatment for hospitalized patients.
Buescher et al. (1993)	Prenatal WIC Participation Can Reduce Low Birth Weight and Newborn Medical Costs: A Cost-Benefit Analysis of WIC Participation in North Carolina	For each dollar spent on the special supplemental food program for women, infants, and children (WIC), the savings to Medicaid was $2.91. Women with WIC were 1.45 times as likely to have a low-weight child with greater hospitalization costs.

in the fifth year. After 4 years, eliminated sheltered-employment costs were considered a savings from both the taxpayers' and society's perspective.

In traditional cost-benefit analysis, a ratio is computed by dividing the total benefits by the total costs. If the ratio is larger than 1, then the benefits exceed cost; if the ratio is less than 1, then the costs exceed the benefits. The Buescher et al. (1993) study showed that for each dollar spent on WIC, the benefit (savings to Medicaid) was $2.91. The benefit is clear. Most of us would like to get back almost $3.00 for each $1.00 we spend. Indeed, whenever the gains to society exceed the costs, a program is justified in a cost-benefit evaluation.

BOX 10.3	COST-BENEFITS OF DRUG COURTS

A cost-benefit analysis was recently conducted of three drug court programs in order to examine the economic benefits for their graduates. Drug courts combine substance abuse treatment with intensive judicial oversight and case management of offenders.

The authors of the study found that during a 12-month study period the average daily accounting costs (i.e., personnel, buildings and facilities, contractual services supporting the program) per client was $7.24. The economic benefits to the graduates in terms of annual earnings were 260 percent higher than predicted if he or she had not participated in the drug court program; child support payments were half the amount that would have been if the individual had not entered drug court; the total benefit for each drug court graduate was estimated to be $19,658. Graduates derived economic benefits from reduced incarceration and fewer convictions and charges. The benefit-cost ratio was $3.83. In other words, $3.83 in economic benefit was gained for every dollar spent on a drug court graduate. Further, the benefit-cost ratio for criminal justice outcomes was $1.76, which suggests that there was $1.76 in reduced criminal justice costs for every dollar invested in the drug court program. In contrast, the benefit-cost return for those who terminated from the program was $1.13. When both the graduates and the terminators were considered together, the net benefit was $2.71 for every dollar invested in the drug court.

Source: Logan, T. K., Hoyt, W. H., McCollister, K. E., French, M. T., Leukefeld, C., & Minton, L. (2004). Economic evaluation of drug court: Methodology, results, and policy implications. *Evaluation and Program Planning*, 27, 4, 381–396.

Note: When examining costs and program outcomes, call your analysis "cost-effectiveness" if the outcome variables are not measured monetarily.

CHAPTER RECAP

As Eddy (1992) has pointed out, the very notion underlying cost-effectiveness analysis is somewhat troubling to many practitioners. That is, helping professionals want to secure the *best* treatment possible for their clients. They do not want to have to worry about or haggle over costs. The lack of a strong tradition of, or even interest in, cost analytical studies at the direct service level means that many human service professionals remain distrustful and suspicious of these methodologies. Many tough questions are not easily resolved. For instance, how does one value the time of a person with disabilities? Indeed, can every success with clients be expressed in terms of a dollar? The lack of agreement in professional literature about how to define benefits and unit costs has contributed to the less than enthusiastic reception of cost analytical studies in many circles. At the same time, professions such as medicine are making great strides in this area, as seen in the formation of a national Panel on Cost-Effectiveness in Health and Medicine that has begun making recommendations

(Manning, 1999; Weinstein et al., 1996); In an essay on efficiency in the social services, Pruger and Miller (1991) observed: "Though efficiency never has been treated as a first order concept in the social services, it should be. No other idea on the table or on the horizon cuts so directly to the enterprise. No other has the same potential to revitalize the field as it moves into and through the twenty-first century" (p. 6).

Policy makers, agency directors, and managers want "efficient" programs. All too often, however, efficiency has meant serving the greatest number of clients with the least cost. Such decisions are based only on the up-front or immediate costs of a program and not on the overall reduction or amelioration of the problem. It is necessary to remember that assumptions about "least costly" must be stated relative to a time frame and a clear outcome objective. Least costly approaches may not always be the most effective.

Cost-effectiveness studies are important tools that can be used to help decision makers allocate scarce resources. Cost accounting is a concept familiar to those in the private sector and the corporate world. It is an approach that has not often been used to evaluate social and human services. Clearly, it is incumbent on evaluators to examine conventional and alternative ways of providing human services and to use that information to guide interventions tomorrow and thereafter. Examining a program's success or contributions to improving clients' lives while simultaneously looking at costs will become increasingly important. This is not a passing fad that will soon go away.

Despite certain medical ethicists (such as Williams, 1992, and Emery and Schneiderman, 1989) who argue that cost-effectiveness approaches may place some segments of the population at risk for not receiving expensive interventions (e.g., the very old with medical problems), professionals in the human services have the burden not only of implementing interventions but also of demonstrating that they are efficient. We have not done nearly enough of this. How many millions of dollars could be saved if we were to systematically examine each of our programs in terms of their cost and effectiveness and then make decisions about which programs to fund?

Important decisions should not be made without data to guide us. It is imperative that we develop the skills necessary to demonstrate the benefit and cost savings when one treatment is chosen over another. To the extent that we can successfully identify and adopt the most effective programs, a grateful and appreciative society will recognize our efforts in the human services and public health fields.

Questions for Class Discussion

1. Identify local, state, or national programs for which you would like to conduct cost-effectiveness evaluations. Discuss the program outcomes for these. Is there a choice of more than one outcome indicator per program? List all of the relevant indicators.

2. Discuss whether the following desired outcomes are likely to be monetary or nonmonetary. Would your evaluation be a cost-benefit analysis or a cost-effectiveness study?
    a. Increased employee morale in a social service agency
    b. Improved client satisfaction in an after-school tutoring program
    c. Reduced alcohol and drug use within a factory
    d. Improved employee health in a state agency
    e. Reduced stress for child protection workers
3. An outpatient counseling program has a long waiting list of potential clients. As a new manager, what actions could you take to reduce the waiting list? Make a list of these and discuss each relative to a cost-benefit analysis.
4. Discuss whether it is more important to know a program's cost or its effectiveness.
5. During periods of great flux, as when there is a dramatic increase in inflation, sensitivity analyses are important. What are some other situations or factors over which an evaluator has no control and which could change over a 2- or 3-year period that could significantly affect the value of "benefits" attributed to a project?
6. Discuss a proposal made to Congress to allow a $3,000 tax deduction for expenses incurred by parents who adopt a handicapped or older child. How would you evaluate such legislation using either a cost-effectiveness or a cost-benefit approach?

Mini-Projects: Experiencing Evaluation Firsthand

1. For a program of your choosing, outline a cost-benefit analysis. Identify the program, its major objective, monetary benefits and how these would be calculated, and relevant data collection procedures.
2. For a program of your choosing, outline a cost-effectiveness study. Identify the program, its major objective, outcome indicators, and relevant data collection procedures.
3. Defend an innovative or unorthodox approach to some social problem with which you are familiar. Justify your proposed program in terms of its relative costs and how it should be evaluated 5 years after it is implemented.
4. Before reading Shi's (1993) article examining the cost benefit of different health promotion interventions implemented in an industry, make a list of outcome variables you would use to show savings accruing from the provision of (1) a bimonthly health newsletter and health resource center; (2) classes on stress management, coping with high blood pressure, or smoking cessation; and (3) public health nurses case managing high-risk employees. Compare your choice of variables with those Shi used.

References and Resources

Allred, C. A., Arford, P. H., Mauldin, P. D., & Goodwin, L. K. (1998). Cost effectiveness analysis in the nursing literature, 1992–1996. *Image: Journal of Nursing Scholarship, 30*(3), 235–242.

Bandura, A., Blanchard, E. B., & Ritter, B. (1969). Relative efficacy of desensitization and modeling approaches for inducing behavioral, affective, and attitudinal changes. *Journal of Personality and Social Psychology, 13*, 173–199.

Buescher, P. A., Larson, L. C., Nelson, M. D., & Lenihan, A. J. (1993). Prenatal WIC participation can reduce low birth weight and newborn medical costs: A cost-benefit analysis of WIC participation in North Carolina. *Journal of the American Dietetic Association, 93*(2), 163–166.

Cartwright, W. S. (1998). Cost-benefit and cost-effectiveness analysis of drug abuse treatment services. *Evaluation Review, 22*(5), 609–636.

Cukier, J. (1997). Cost-benefit analysis of telelearning: Developing a methodology framework. *Distance Education, 18*(1), 137–152.

Eddy, D. M. (1992). Cost-effectiveness analysis: Is it up to the task? *Journal of the American Medical Association, 267,* 3342–3348.

Emery, D. D., & Schneiderman, L. J. (1989). Cost-effectiveness in health care. *Hastings Center Report, 19*(4), 8–12.

French, M., McCollister, K. Sacks, S., McKendrick, K., & De Leon, G. (2002). Benefit-cost analysis of a modified therapeutic community for mentally ill chemical abusers. *Evaluation and Program Planning, 25,* 137–148.

French, M. T., Sacks, S., DeLeon, G., Staines, G., & McKendrick, K. (1999). Modified therapeutic community for mentally ill chemical abusers: Outcomes and costs. *Evaluation and the Health Professions, 22,* 60–85.

French, M., Salome, H., Krupski, A., McKay, J., Donovan, D., McLellan, A. T.,

Durell, J. (2000). Benefit-cost analysis of residential and outpatient addiction treatment in the state of Washington. *Evaluation Review, 24*(6), 609–634.

Levin, H. M. (1983). *Cost-effectiveness: A primer.* Beverly Hills, CA: Sage.

Lombard, D., Haddock, C. K., Talcott, G.W., & Reynes, R. (1998). Cost effectiveness analysis: A primer for psychologists. *Applied & Preventive Psychology, 7,* 101–108.

Manning, W. G. (1999). Panel on cost effectiveness in health and medicine recommendations: Identifying costs. *Journal of Clinical Psychiatry, 60,* 54–56.

McCaughrin, W. B., Ellis, W. K., Rusch, F. R., & Heal, L. W. (1993). Cost-effectiveness of supported employment. *Mental Retardation, 31*(1), 41–48.

Oss, M. E. (1997). CD treatment: Evidence of cost-effectiveness. *Addiction and Recovery, 17, 34.*

Plotnick, R. D., & Deppman, L. (1999). Using benefit-cost analysis to assess child abuse prevention and intervention programs. *Child Welfare, 78*(3), 381–407.

Pruger, R., & Miller, L. (1991). Efficiency and the social services. *Administration in Social Work, 15*(1/2), 5–23.

Rosenheck, R., Cramer, J., Xu, W., Grabowski, J. H., Douyon, R., Thomas, J., Henderson, W., & Charney, D. (1998). Multiple outcome assessment in a study of the cost effectiveness of clozapine in the treatment of refractory schizrenia. *HSR: Health Services Research, 33,* 1237–1261.

Rossi, P. H., Freeman, H. E., & Lipsey, M. W. (1999). *Evaluation: A systematic approach.* Thousand Oaks, CA: Sage.

Schoenwald, S. K., Ward, D. M., Henggeler, S. W., Pickrel, S. G., & Patel, H. (1996). Multisystemic therapy treatment of substance abusing or dependent adolescent offenders: Costs of reducing incarceration, inpatient, and residential placement. *Journal of Child and Family Studies, 5*(4), 431–444.

Shi, L. (1993). Health promotion, medical care use, and costs in a sample of work site employees. *Evaluation Review, 17*(5), 475–487.

Spoth, R. L., Guyll, M., & Day, S. X. (2002). Universal family-focused interventions in alcohol-use disorder prevention: Cost effectiveness and cost-benefit analyses of two interventions. *Journal of Studies on Alcohol, 63,* 219–228.

Svikis, D. S., Golden, A. S., Huggins, G. R., Pickens, R. W., McCaul, M. E., Velez, M. L., Rosendale, C. T., Brooner, R. K., Gazaway, P. M., Stitzer, M. L., & Ball, C. E. (1997). Cost-effectiveness of treatment of drug-abusing pregnant women. *Drug and Alcohol Dependence, 45,* 105–113.

Weinstein, M. C., Siegel, J. E., Gold, M. R., Kamlet, M. S., & Russell, L. B. (1996). Recommendations of the panel on cost-effectiveness in health and medicine. *Journal of the American Medical Association, 276,* 1253–1258.

Williams, A. (1992). Cost-effectiveness analysis: Is it ethical? *Journal of Medical Ethics, 18*(1), 7–11.

Yates, B. T. (1994). Toward the incorporation of costs, cost-effectiveness analysis, and cost-benefit into clinical research. *Journal of Consulting and Clinical Psychology, 62*(4), 729–736.

Zarkin, G., Lindrooth, R., Demiralp, B., & Wechsberg, W. (2001). The cost and cost-effectiveness of an enhanced intervention for people with substance abuse problems at risk for HIV. *Health Services Research, 36*(2), 335–356.

11

MEASUREMENT TOOLS AND STRATEGIES

IMPORTANCE OF MEASUREMENT

There once was a primitive culture where counting followed this scheme: one, two, many. If you had more than two of something, you had many.

It is clear that our society is much more concerned with counting and measuring things. If we accept a new position paying a salary of $30,000 a year, we certainly do not want to be paid $19,000 or even $29,000. If we buy 2 pounds of steak at the supermarket, we do not want to be charged for 5 pounds. Measurement, if not accountability, is a fundamental aspect of our society.

We measure almost everything: the speed of computers, the horsepower of cars, the calories we burn jogging, the interest rate the bank or credit card company charges. We measure virtually every phenomenon because we want to know if things are changing or improving, because we are hungry for information about the world and our place in it. Progress and our ability to demonstrate and quantify it has become increasingly important to us—whether we are consumers, providers, or program evaluators.

In order to be accountable and show progress, precise measurements must be taken. Evaluators do not just rush out and start gathering data. As we learned earlier, outcome variables must be operationalized. On many occasions, evaluators use paper-and-pencil instruments to form the basis for measurements.

We may think of these instruments as questionnaires, although they do not always ask questions of respondents. Some instruments are composed of a number of statements (items) to which the respondent indicates levels of agreement or disagreement. Instruments can be complex and composed of many items or as simple as three or four items. Well-developed instruments help us understand why some clients benefitted from an intervention and others did not. They also allow us to examine more closely those whose progress was meager or moderate—interventions do not always have the same effect on every person.

Instruments allow us to use quantification to move beyond subjective opinions ("I think these clients have improved") into a domain where we can discuss the amount of change or improvement ("This group of clients is 37 percent more assertive than they were at the time of pretest" or "At the time of the posttest, 55 percent of the intervention group reported no clinically significant symptoms").

Objective instruments provide evaluators with a certain amount of precision in arriving at the magnitude or intensity of clients' problems and in determining any consequent change in those problems. We are afforded this precision because instruments allow us to quantify abstract or intangible concepts such as self-esteem or assertiveness. These instruments allow us to translate subjective perceptions of problems and concepts into numeric values.

Evaluation instruments are not just plucked from thin air. They must be selected with care. A hastily chosen instrument could provide unreliable or worthless information. It is important to select instruments that not only are psychometrically strong, but also are good indicators of what the programs are attempting to accomplish. Consider the following scenario:

> Jim Gradstudent was asked to evaluate a residential treatment center for youth who had experienced trouble with the juvenile justice system. He noticed that several of the most successful residents at the time of release seemed to have experienced an increase in self-esteem. One afternoon while in the university library, he found a self-esteem instrument that looked as if it could be used for program evaluation. After deciding on a one-group pretest–posttest design, Jim made a number of photocopies of the self-esteem instrument and, with the agency director's permission, began administering it to new admissions. Eleven months later he had collected 42 pre- and posttests from residents who had been discharged from the treatment center. He was surprised to learn that there was very little difference in the pre- and posttest scores. Does this mean that the residential treatment program was unsuccessful?

As you think about this scenario, the lack of information in several areas should cause you to raise questions. Is increasing the resident's self-esteem a clearly articulated goal of the residential treatment center? If it is not, would use of a self-esteem inventory to evaluate the whole program be a reasonable measure? Even if it is an important goal of the program, how likely is it that the youth in treatment will actually experience an increase in self-esteem? Is there evidence from the literature to suggest that residential treatment centers for this population commonly increase self-esteem? Could any other variable be used to gauge success of the program?

If it occurred to you that a fair measure of the treatment center's success might be recidivism—subsequent arrests or offenses that would bring these youths to the attention of the juvenile justice system again—you are right. It is not always necessary to use a paper-and-pencil instrument to measure program outcome. Furthermore, the use of an instrument of unknown psychometric qualities should be avoided. Evaluators need to know how "good" instruments are. Because we know nothing about the reliability and validity of the instrument that Jim selected, it is possible that it might not have detected changes in self-esteem even if they did occur. But more about that later. First, let us examine our alternatives.

DECIDING WHAT TO MEASURE

We start deciding what to measure when we ask how a program's "success" could best be demonstrated. What is a program trying to accomplish? If it fails, how would that failure be noted? As you can see in Table 11.1, for some programs the criteria are obvious.

Such programs as these do not always require paper-and-pencil instruments to evaluate their outcomes. In some cases, no instrument is required; programs can be evaluated with the data already collected. It is very likely, for instance, that a mental health center will know how many or what percent of its clients in the day treatment program became hospitalized during the course of a year. It should not be difficult for adoption workers to determine the

TABLE 11.1 | EXAMPLES OF BEHAVIORAL OUTCOMES FOR PROGRAMS

Program	Success	Failure
Alcohol and drug treatment programs	Days of sobriety	Days of drinking, public intoxication, DUIs
Day treatment for the severely mentally ill	Days of independent living in community	Rehospitalizations, number of days in hospital
Juvenile and adult criminal justice diversion programs	Days without arrest; employment or school attendance	Rearrests, days in jail, suspension from school
Employment and training programs	Wages and hours worked	Amount of entitlements received
Adoption programs	Number of permanent placements made	Number of children eligible for adoption still in foster care
Child protection programs	No further reports or evidence of abuse or neglect	Substantiated reports of abuse or neglect

number or percentage of children for whom a permanent placement was obtained. Forensic programs ought to be able to determine which of their clients are rearrested.

Schools know which students drop out and which ones graduate. Dropping out of school can be viewed as a behavior in much the same way as the logical consequences of substance abuse (such as arrest or DUI) reflect certain behaviors. Official records can be used to gauge the impact of interventions; programs can be evaluated in terms of *behavioral outcomes* without interviewing, observing, or distributing questionnaires to program recipients.

Many human service agencies are required to annually publish data on the number of clients they serve. Often these data are available on a county basis and may be useful to evaluators trying to determine the impact of broadly focused programs.

The use of official data to measure progress is nothing new. Florence Nightingale is said to have kept statistics on the mortality of British soldiers. She kept track of hospital deaths by diagnostic categories in order to show that improvements in sanitation reduced fatalities. Because of her efforts, the mortality rate dropped from 32 percent to 2 percent within 6 months (M. A. Nutting & L. L. Dock, 1907, cited in Meisenheimer, 1985).

Behavioral data can include such specific physiological measurements as those obtained from skinfold calipers, from measuring weight gained or lost, or from biochemical measures such as serum albumin, serum transferrin, and total lymphocyte count. Some drug treatment programs use urine analyses to detect which clients are staying "clean."

Behavioral data can also be obtained through the use of client self-monitoring and 7-day calendar recall methods. Rossiter et al. (1992) found that asking subjects to recall days on which they experienced binge episodes and the number of episodes on those days was more likely to illicit accurate information than asking subjects only to recall the number of binge-eating episodes.

Video- and audiotaping clients' interactions with others are additional sources of behavioral data. For instance, to determine if parents interact more appropriately with their young children after a nurturing program, videotaping sessions with parents and their children during meal times could be arranged. Although there might be some concerns with "staged" behavior, a benefit of videotaping is that facial expressions and general demeanor can be observed. Rating scales can be developed so that there is a quantitative count or rating on the presence or absence of desired behaviors. The tapes can also be used by clients for learning from self-observation, as well as for demonstrating progress.

However, behavioral outcomes are not always available to the evaluator. For instance, suppose you are the director of a program that provides drug prevention programming for elementary school children. The goal of your program is to prevent these children from becoming addicted as adolescents or adults. Most programs of this type will not have the ability to do any sort of follow-up study 3, 5, or 10 years later to see if the prevention programming resulted in fewer persons with drug dependency problems than in the control group. As a consequence, these and other programs without an ability to measure behavioral outcomes must consider success in terms of clients increasing their *knowledge* about a given problem or in terms of changing clients' *attitudes*.

Sometimes prevention programs measure whether the program recipients have increased their knowledge about a given problem. In AIDS prevention programs, for instance, the goal could be to provide sufficient information about how AIDS is transmitted so that program participants have an increased knowledge about its transmission. One could envision a pretest of 20 items and the typical respondent (before the intervention) getting four or five items correct. After the intervention (assuming that the educational presentation is effective), the typical respondent might answer correctly 18 or 19 items on the posttest. This would indicate that respondents' knowledge about AIDS had been increased.

For other programs, the main goal may be to change the participants' attitudes about some behavior or practice. For instance, if you were administering an intervention program for men who batter, the evaluator might use a behavioral measure (arrests, incidents of battering) as an outcome measure, but it would also be possible to determine if program participants had a change in attitudes about battering. The goal of the program might be to help batterers become more empathetic—to put themselves in the place of the victim—and to view battering as unacceptable behavior. In this instance, the evaluator may not want to measure batterers' knowledge about domestic violence but to change attitudes regarding its acceptability. The theory here would be that if attitudes change so will behavior.

Often, it is much easier to measure attitudes and knowledge than behavior. It is relatively easy to determine if adolescents have become more knowledgeable about drugs or if they have developed attitudes favorable to the use of illicit drugs. It is much more difficult to determine if program recipients sell, buy, or use illegal drugs once they are away from school. Using the men-who-batter example, even after a treatment program has been completed, battering may still occur in the home but go unreported. An evaluator might be tempted to conclude that an intervention program was successful because there were no rearrests among the program participants, when in reality battering was still occurring but less often or in a somewhat less severe form.

A major advantage of paper-and-pencil measures of knowledge and attitudes is that they can be administered easily in a classroom, waiting room, or office—and thus outcome data can usually be obtained more quickly than waiting for some future behavioral measure (such as clients being rearrested or hospitalized) that require weeks or months to pass.

A major disadvantage of focusing on knowledge and attitudes is that they may not be directly related to behavior. For example, clients may have knowledge that drug use is bad for them but continue with destructive drug use. (Think of how many persons smoke cigarettes even though the surgeon general's warning is printed on each pack.) Clients can increase their knowledge about alcoholism (or a number of other problems) and yet not change their behavior.

The connection between attitudes, knowledge, and behavior is tenuous at best. Probably the "best" measure in any situation would be one closest to the intent of the program intervention. When it is not possible to observe behavioral

| BOX 11.1 | SCALES, INDICES, TESTS |

A **scale** is generally considered to be an item that measures a solitary concept (like hostility or anxiety) and commonly attempts to assess intensity or amount of something. For instance, a scale might consistent of a single item (i.e., "Rate how anxious you are feeling today on a scale from 1 to 10.")

An **index** involves the creation of a new variable that is the sum of other items or variables that are thought to measure a single construct. Thus, a researcher might need 25 items to get an accurate measurement of clients' anxiety. The idea is that a composite score of these items is a stronger and more robust way to measure a slippery and often intangible construct. Don't be confused, however, when you begin looking at instruments and find out that most researchers use the terms *scale* and *index* interchangeably when multiple items are used to create a single score for an individual. (Just look at the Clinical Anxiety Scale in the next chapter and you'll see what we mean.) **Tests** are slang for just about any paper-and-pencil instruments that attempt to create some quantitative score.

One instrument may measure multiple dimensions of functioning and may include several **subscales**—each dedicated to evaluating a different construct. For instance, see the Smith, Arnold, Salston, Heindel, and Hudson (2002) article on the Brief Adult Assessment Scale which is composed of 16 different subscales that range in length from 10 to 15 items.

---

changes or to get reliable measures of specific behaviors from other sources, evaluators often use paper-and-pencil instruments to measure changes in attitudes, knowledge, or self-reported behavior.

Research instruments can be discussed and are evaluated along two primary psychometric dimensions: reliability and validity.

RELIABILITY

An instrument or questionnaire is said to be **reliable** when it consistently and dependably measures some concept or phenomenon with accuracy. If an instrument is reliable, then administering it to similar groups yields similar results. A reliable instrument is like a reliable watch—it should not be easily affected by external factors such as temperature, humidity, day of the week, cycle of the moon, and so forth.

The reliability of instruments is generally reported in a way that resembles a correlation coefficient—it will be a numerical value between 0 and 1. Nunnally (1994) says that in the early stages of research, one can work with instruments having modest reliability (by which he means .70 or higher), that .80 can be used for basic research, and that a reliability of .90 is the minimum where important decisions are going to be made with respect to specific test scores.

What does it mean when an instrument does not have even modest reliability? It means that the instrument cannot be counted on to be consistent. In other words, its accuracy varies in ways that might not be well understood. It might provide good measurement of some concept in one situation and be inaccurate in another situation. How could this happen? One way is when the items are vague and not interpreted the same way by various individuals. For instance, suppose I am interested in measuring knowledge about AIDS and I develop the following item: "It is possible to get AIDS from gay employees in restaurants or bars." Six out of ten individuals may interpret this item as asking whether food handlers can transmit AIDS presumably by handling plates, silverware, or breathing on food. However, if four out of every ten individuals read into the item the question of whether AIDS is transmitted by having sex with the employees of gay restaurants and bars, then this item would detract from rather than contribute to the making of a reliable instrument.

Reliable items provide a consistent frame of reference. If an item can be interpreted several different ways, then it should be tossed out. Pilot testing of questionnaires and data-gathering instruments on a small scale can often identify items that confuse respondents. Although a single item will seldom make a whole scale unreliable, several vague items can affect reliability. It is always in the evaluator's best interest to use as reliable a scale as is possible.

When a scale or instrument is used and reported in a professional journal article or evaluation effort, the author should include information about it. If there is no information on instrumentation, there can be no presumption of reliability or validity. This problem commonly arises when the author's instrument or questionnaire is "homemade." Whether you or a committee design a questionnaire, it cannot be assumed to be reliable until it has been tested.

Demonstrating Reliability

Although there are several ways to demonstrate reliability, most researchers start first with **internal consistency.** With this approach, each of the individual items that make up a scale is examined for how well it correlates with the scale as a whole. The Statistical Package for the Social Sciences (SPSS) is one of several computer software programs that can determine a scale's reliability. The reliability procedure provides an item analysis that helps the researcher know which items to drop.

To show you this process, we have incorporated data from a scale being developed to measure adolescents' attitudes about the value of work (see Box 11.2). Approximately 100 adolescents completed the "My Attitudes about Work" scale. When these data were entered into the computer, the printout in Table 11.2 was obtained.

Look at the column headed "Corrected Item—Total Correlation." Q5 and Q8 stand apart from the rest because they are negatively correlated to the scale as a whole. Including these items in the scale has the result of lowering the **alpha** (reliability coefficient). This outcome can be determined by looking at the column on the far right. Dropping Q5 would raise the scale's alpha to .82; deleting Q8 has about the same effect. Leaving them both in will produce a

---

BOX 11.2 | MY ATTITUDES ABOUT WORK

Instructions: For each of the statements below, indicate whether it is True (**T**), or False (**F**) for you. Use a question mark (**?**) if you cannot decide.

_____ 1. I would like to have a full-time job someday.
_____ 2. The idea of working for a living is exciting to me.
_____ 3. If I had a job, I would expect it to be boring.
_____ 4. Working 40 hours a week in a regular job is a waste of time.
_____ 5. I would rather have a job paying minimum wage than no job at all.
_____ 6. Earning a paycheck would make me feel important.
_____ 7. Holding down a job would give me a good feeling about myself.
_____ 8. There are plenty of ways to make money without working.
_____ 9. With a job, I would have more respect for myself.
_____ 10. Any job would probably pay less than I deserve.
_____ 11. Only stupid people work for a living.
_____ 12. It is possible to enjoy one's work.
_____ 13. I want to be employed when I grow up.
_____ 14. I would rather be unemployed than have a job that pays only minimum wage.
_____ 15. I would rather be unemployed than have a boss ordering me around.
_____ 16. Working people have more pride than people who do not work.

---

scale with an overall alpha of .77. Because we want the highest internal consistency possible, it would make sense to eliminate both of these items from the scale and use a shorter, revised scale.

However, let us assume that we went back over the scale, reading it closely and checking to see how the items were coded. You will note from reading Table 11.2 that the nine items (Q1, Q2, Q5, Q6, Q7, Q9, Q12, Q13, and Q16) should be coded positively because a "true" response would indicate a favorable view of work. "True" responses to items Q3, Q4, Q8, Q10, Q11, Q14, and Q15 should be coded differently (reverse coded) because a "true" response to these items would indicate an unfavorable view of work. In reviewing how the items were coded, we realized that we had reversed my instructions to the computer for items Q5 and Q8. Once they were coded correctly, the printout in Table 11.3 resulted.

The alpha obtained the second time is higher than the software program initially estimated. This is because even though Q5 and Q8 were coded erroneously the first time, the computer had no way of knowing this and simply followed instructions—considering them as valuable elements of the scale we wanted to develop. Coded correctly, these items add to, rather than detract from, the scale, resulting in the higher reliability coefficient.

A developer of a scale will probably compute its internal consistency on multiple occasions, revising the items and trying to find the best combinations of items and the highest alpha that can be obtained with the fewest items.

TABLE II.2 | RELIABILITY ANALYSIS—FIRST EFFORT

Item	Scale Mean If Item Deleted	Scale Variance If Item Deleted	Corrected Item— Total Correlation	Squared Multiple Correlation	Alpha If Item Deleted
Q1	36.8	28.3	.55	.60	.72
Q2	37.4	25.0	.61	.50	.70
Q3	37.2	26.2	.54	.51	.71
Q4	37.1	26.2	.59	.47	.71
Q5	38.3	37.9	−.71	.75	.82
Q6	37.0	28.2	.37	.41	.73
Q7	37.1	26.4	.57	.50	.71
Q8	38.0	35.9	−.46	.29	.81
Q9	37.1	25.8	.64	.56	.70
Q10	37.2	25.5	.61	.50	.70
Q11	36.8	30.3	.24	.42	.74
Q12	36.9	28.4	.47	.42	.73
Q13	36.9	28.6	.41	.50	.73
Q14	37.1	26.3	.55	.68	.71
Q15	37.2	25.3	.64	.59	.70
Q16	37.3	27.2	.42	.36	.73

ALPHA = .77

There are several other ways to determine whether an instrument has internal consistency. The **split-half** technique involves dividing a scale in half (using either top and bottom or even and odd items) and examining how well the two halves correlate with each other. Another approach is to devise **parallel** or **alternate** versions of the scale and administer the forms to similar groups. Reliability would be demonstrated when both versions correlate with each other—the higher the correlation coefficient, the stronger the reliability.

Still another form of reliability (**test–retest**) is demonstrated when the scale holds up well when administered to the same group of individuals on repeated occasions. Without the benefit of intervention, groups of individuals with any given problem (e.g., low self-esteem) should not experience major increases or decreases. Should an instrument show fluctuations in scores over a period of 2 weeks, for example, then one possible explanation may be that the instrument is not reliable.

Instruments with no or very low reliability are, for all practical purposes, worthless. This is not to say that you cannot obtain extremely valuable information from a questionnaire with nothing known about its reliability. The problem

TABLE I I . 3 | RELIABILITY ANALYSIS — SECOND EFFORT

Item	Scale Mean If Item Deleted	Scale Variance If Item Deleted	Corrected Item— Total Correlation	Squared Multiple Correlation	Alpha If Item Deleted
Q1	38.6	54.1	.52	.60	.89
Q2	39.2	48.8	.65	.50	.88
Q3	38.9	50.4	.60	.51	.88
Q4	38.9	51.1	.58	.47	.89
Q5	38.9	49.5	.72	.75	.88
Q6	38.8	53.4	.41	.41	.89
Q7	38.8	50.8	.61	.50	.88
Q8	39.2	51.0	.47	.29	.89
Q9	38.9	50.2	.66	.56	.88
Q10	39.0	49.9	.62	.50	.88
Q11	38.6	56.4	.25	.42	.89
Q12	38.7	53.9	.48	.42	.89
Q13	38.7	54.0	.44	.50	.89
Q14	38.8	50.0	.66	.68	.88
Q15	39.0	49.3	.68	.59	.88
Q16	39.0	52.0	.45	.36	.89
				ALPHA = .89	

is that without evidence that the items are reliable, there is no way to guarantee that the same results would be produced if they were administered again.

Survey questionnaires pose a special problem because the reliability of single items cannot be computed. However, what you can do is to examine the literature for items that have been used and refined by such survey-conducting organizations as the Roper, Harris, and Gallup polls.

As a rule, adding items to a scale increases its reliability. All else being equal, a longer scale, say 25 items, stands a better chance of having acceptable reliability than a scale of two or three items.

Novice evaluators are often tempted to develop scales of their own. However, Thyer (1992) has made this recommendation:

> Avoid this temptation like the plague! The design and validation of a scale or survey is a major project in and of itself, and a program evaluation is NO PLACE to try to develop such a measure. If you ignore this advice and prepare your own scale, your entire study's results may be called into question because the reader will have no evidence that your new measure is a reliable or valid one. As a social work journal editor, I can attest to the fact that this is a major reason why manuscripts get rejected: a well-meaning practitioner constructs his or her own idiosyncratic scale,

obtains interesting results, and tries to publish them. Invariably the reviewers note this fact, reject the study, and sadly suggest that next time the writer should use a previously published scale or outcome measure with well-established reliability and validity. (pp. 139–140)

Without doubt, instances arise when you will have to develop your own scale. There may not be an instrument available to measure the dimension you need to quantify. Or, the only instrument you find may have some problem associated with it, such as requiring a reading comprehension level that is too high, containing too many items for children or adolescents with short attention spans, or having weak or unknown reliability and validity. When you must create your own instrument, remember that it is your burden to demonstrate that it is reliable and valid.

The Reliability of Procedures

Reliability is a concern not only if you revise or devise an instrument to use in your evaluation, but also if you rely on secondary data like rearrests, suicides, and subsequent reports of abuse and neglect. The concern this time is not with the form or questionnaire used to create the data as much as it is with the reliability of the data-gathering and reporting procedures.

Siefert, Schwartz, and Ortega (1994), for example, investigated the infant mortality rates in Michigan's child welfare system and found a higher post-neonatal death rate among those infants in foster care placement than was occurring statewide. However, when the authors sought to verify information held by the Michigan Department of Social Services, they found that 5 of the 66 infants initially identified as having died during the study period were actually alive. The management information system used by the department was previously found to have a 30 percent error rate in recording entry and exit dates from specific types of placements (Lerman, 1990, cited in Siefert, Schwartz, & Ortega, 1994). Obviously, it is important to have accurate data that results from standardized procedures (e.g., everyone using the same definitions and forms, and reporting in the same way). Individuals who are not properly trained or supervised sufficiently do not provide data in a consistent and uniform manner. Incomplete and carelessly filled out forms almost always raise concerns about the reliability of the data being examined.

Most, if not all, social indicators vastly underestimate the true incidence of social problems in our country. (See Box 11.3.) We know, for example, that the incidence of domestic violence, child abuse, date rape, and so forth is much greater than the recorded arrests. Sometimes clients cross state lines and commit offenses that evaluators may not know about. And there can be indications of problems (e.g., suicide attempts) that never come to the attention of authorities.

This is *not* to suggest that you should refrain from using official reports to judge the success of the programs you are evaluating. In some agencies, hospitals and health care settings in particular, records may be excellent and very useful to the evaluator.

BOX 11.3

HOW RELIABLE ARE SELF-REPORTS OF DRUG USE, SEXUAL BEHAVIOR, AND USE OF TREATMENT SERVICES?

Clients ($n = 2,968$) in this study were participating in a large multi-site drug treatment study and were interviewed at 1 month and 3 months after intake. The sample was drawn from clients requiring residential, inpatient, outpatient, or methadone treatment. Over half of the sample was involved with the criminal justice system. Analysis focused on responses to 62 pairs of questions.

The investigators found a high level of consistency in clients' reports over a range of topics. The overall mean of inconsistent responses was less than 3 percent. Clients displayed remarkably high levels of internal consistency in their responding with less inconsistency regarding their drug use than with sexual behavior or use of treatment services.

This study found less inconsistency than Cox et al. (1992); however, that study relied on self-administered forms while this investigation employed trained interviewers who could verify and, in some instances, point out inconsistencies during the interview.

Source: Adair, E. B. G., Craddock, G., Miller, H., & Turner, C. F. (1996). Quality of treatment data: Reliability over time of self-reports given by clients in treatment for substance abuse. *Journal of Substance Abuse Treatment, 13*(2), 145–149.

If your measurement strategy is to use existing records for the evaluation, you need to be familiar with the procedures that generated the data. You may find problems of over- or underreporting, that the staff on one shift are more conscientious or more lax than those on another, that there were policy or procedural changes in reporting during the study period that no one remembered to tell you. Understand that any official records are somewhat limited in their ability to describe what is "really" going on, but they often constitute the best information available. In some instances, this type of data is superior to asking clients or their partners about subsequent acts of violence or participation in illegal activities. The literature in your field may indicate whether self-reported data from clients will provide more reliable estimates of the behavior than official records.

If the data you are collecting for your program evaluation comes from judgments, observations, or interviews of two or more persons who are rating the behavior independently, then you must be concerned with **inter-rater reliability**. Suppose you are screening persons with chronic mental illness for entry into a new program that will provide them with supervised employment and an apartment. The program is much in demand and there is a long waiting list. When you meet with Jill, you immediately notice that she does not make eye contact with you and seems to be staring into space a good deal of the time. Jill appears to be distracted, preoccupied with her own inner world, and you decide she would not be a good candidate for the program.

However, your colleague, Dr. Perceptive, is not troubled by Jill's lack of eye contact, viewing this as only shyness or fear of rejection. Based on Jill's responses, Dr. Perceptive gives Jill a high rating and recommends that she be selected for the program. If you and Dr. Perceptive do not agree at least 70 percent of the time or your scores do not correlate at least at .80 on a large sample, then you do not have adequate inter-rater reliability. The major way to improve inter-rater reliability is through training and role-playing so that the raters begin to adopt a more uniform perspective and recognize the same criteria.

VALIDITY

The second dimension important when evaluating instruments is validity. An instrument is said to be **valid** when it closely corresponds to the concept it was designed to measure. Let's say that you are developing a self-esteem inventory and in a sudden flash of inspiration it occurs to you that a high level of self-esteem would be indicated if respondents could identify the 27th president of the United States. If you incorporate a number of similar items into your self-esteem inventory, you probably would not create a self-esteem scale but rather a scale that measures knowledge of American history. This scale would very likely not be valid for measuring self-esteem.

There are various ways to go about demonstrating that an instrument has validity. Sometimes experts are asked to review it to see if the entire range of the concept is represented in the sample of items selected for the scale. This is known as **content validity**. For instance, if you were developing a scale to measure progress in the treatment of bulimia and did not include the behaviors of eating uncontrollably, binge eating, or intentionally vomiting, then you would not have covered the entire range of behaviors that ought to go into a scale designed to measure progress in treating bulimia. The term **face validity** is used when one's colleagues (or other knowledgeable persons) look over an instrument and agree that it appears to measure the concept. Neither content nor face validity is sufficient for establishing that the scale has "true" validity.

The developer of a new instrument must be concerned with more than face or content validity and must amass evidence that the scale really does measure what he or she intended. **Criterion validity** means that the instrument can be validated by an external criterion. If, for example, a new scale being developed is to measure social support, then one appropriate criterion might be the number of one's close friends. Logically, someone who scores on the high range of social support should self-report more friends than individuals scoring in the lower ranges. If the scale were being prepared for use with middle school or high school students, the criterion might be teachers' estimates of the number of friends that a sample of their students had. The criterion could also come from parents who could be asked to contribute data on the number of their children's friends.

This example shows that the creator of an instrument is not "locked" into using a specific criterion to measure the validity of an instrument. However, sometimes there may be only one appropriate criterion—for instance, academic success probably is better reflected by grades or grade point average than any other measure.

The best external criterion may not always be easy to select, as might be the case when attempting to select one to help validate a self-esteem scale. Sometimes no single behavior best characterizes the concept. In such situations, a researcher might use a scale from the literature or prior research that has been shown to be valid for the external criterion.

Criterion validity is generally categorized as either **predictive** (of future behavior or performance) or **concurrent,** which means the ability to predict current status. Concurrent validity might involve administering the new scale to the subjects, along with another scale that previous studies have shown to be a valid measure of the same concept. If scores from the two scales correlate well, then the new scale is said to have concurrent validity.

Another form of validity is known as **construct validity.** Construct validity is concerned with the theoretical relationship of the scale to other variables. It involves the testing of presumed relationships and hypotheses. Sometimes this involves the **known-groups technique** where the investigator administers the instrument to two very different kinds of groups expecting to find major differences in the way they respond. For instance, suppose you develop an instrument to measure attitudes about drug usage. (See Box 11.4.) You might administer it to persons recently arrested for possession of drugs, individuals in jail, or those awaiting to enter an outpatient drug treatment program. A contrast group could consist of persons of similar age and background who do not use drugs. If there are statistically significant differences in the means of these two groups along expected lines (e.g., the persons who admit to frequent drug use have a greater number of prodrug attitudes and those who don't use have antidrug attitudes), then evidence of construct validity is shown. Instruments that cannot make discriminations between two markedly different samples would be of no use to program evaluators.

For that reason, we were very interested in whether a sample of adolescents judged to have "good" attitudes about work would have higher scores than adolescents judged to have "poor" attitudes when tested on the "My Attitudes about Work" scale discussed earlier in the chapter. Fortunately, we found statistically significant differences. Those teens who were rated as having "good" attitudes about work had higher scores on the scale than teens who were rated, by persons who knew them, as having "poor" attitudes about work. Thus, the pilot study found some beginning evidence for the validity of the instrument.

Like reliability, there are many forms and approaches to establishing validity. Factor analysis may be used to understand or confirm the structure of a scaled construct. For example, Macdonald (1998) conducted factor analyses to provide corroborative evidence of a social support scale's two main factors (family and friends). In factor analysis, statistical procedures produce factor loadings not unlike correlations that identify items that relate and cluster around the major concept or concepts contained within the scale. For example, in the content area of emotional support, item # 1 ("I feel very close to my family") loaded .72 on the family factor but only .04 on the friends factor.

HOW VALID ARE SELF-REPORTS OF DRUG USE?

Although faulty memory may lead to inconsistencies in the reporting of past events, deliberate deception may also play a role when the behavior being investigated is illegal or socially unacceptable. How accurate, then, is the self-reported drug use of homeless persons with substance abuse disorders?

Research participants were being admitted to a demonstration project where they had a 50 percent chance of entering an enhanced day treatment program with an abstinent-contingent work therapy and housing program or to the usual care program. Subjects were assessed for drug use and then asked to submit a urine specimen for analysis. Any crack cocaine use within the last 30 days was operationally defined as "use." Assessments were made at four different points.

At baseline, 19 percent of those assigned to the usual care group and 5 percent of those assigned to the enhanced care group denied use of crack, but it was confirmed by urine toxicology results. Two months into the program, approximately 38 percent of both groups denied crack use in the last 30 days, but this denial was not supported by the lab results. Twelve months after admission, 56.5 percent of the usual care group and 40 percent of the enhanced care group could be classified as giving false-negatives. Overall, across four evaluation points, 32 percent of the clients appear to have misrepresented their crack drug use.

This rate was higher than reported among "substance abuse treatment admissions who were abusing alcohol (Brown et al., 1992), but lower than rates of inner-city public walk-in patients recruited for sexually transmitted disease testing (McNagny & Parker, 1992) and county jail arrestees (Mieczkowski et al., 1991)" (p. 337). In this study, denied but verified use was significantly less of a problem prior to treatment than at points during participation in treatment.

Source: Schumacher, J. E., Milby, J. B., & Raczynski, J. M. et al. (1995). Validity of self-reported crack cocaine use among homeless persons in treatment. *Journal of Substance Abuse Treatment,* 12(5), 335–339.

One problem with understanding validity as a concept is that there is no standardized taxonomy of terms. As Koeske (1994) has observed:

> After nearly four decades of methodological scholarship on measurement validation and its applications in research contexts, there exists no fully comprehensive language system for identifying and differentiating types of validity and procedures for their assessment. (p. 45)

Think of the problem of establishing validity as a gradual, ongoing, confirmatory process that builds on each study. However, if you are reviewing scales for potential use in a program evaluation, you can afford to be a little more critical. Choose those that have the most extensive evidence of validity—whether criterion, construct, convergent, predictive, or concurrent.

Although reliability and validity have been presented as separate concepts, they are interrelated in a complex fashion. If an instrument can be empirically demonstrated to have validity (and we are not talking about just face or content validity), then it can generally be assumed to have adequate reliability.

However, a reliable instrument may not be valid for the purpose we want to use it. That is, an instrument designed to assess depression in children may not provide valid measurements of depression in adults. An instrument created for respondents in one culture may not translate well in another language, which would raise concerns about the validity of any findings.

Both reliability and validity ought to be demonstrated as evidence that an instrument is psychometrically strong. This is not an either-or choice. The evaluator should try to obtain information about the instrument's reliability and validity before adopting it. If you know nothing about the reliability and validity of an instrument, it is important to realize that the results obtained from its use will have very little meaning. One obvious way of avoiding having to establish that your new scale has reliability and validity is to use instruments that already have been demonstrated to have reliability and validity.

Although our focus has been chiefly on reliability and validity, there are a number of other characteristics of instruments to consider when choosing among several for use in a program evaluation. These considerations have been summarized in Box 11.5.

| BOX 11.5 | CONSIDERATIONS FOR SELECTING OUTCOME MEASURES |

Instruments should be:

Relevant and appropriate to the client group. Instruments may be inappropriate in terms of clients' primary symptoms or problems, attention span, reading level, and may not correspond well with the purpose of intervention.

Easy to administer. Overly complex instruments or those with complicated instructions may not get administered uniformly across various sites—particularly if you are dependent on others to collect your data. Will it be a burden on clients and interfere with treatment?

Useful and easy to interpret. The scores you obtain should be clear and understandable—unambiguous for the majority of clients. Will the scores assist with diagnosis or treatment planning? Interpretation is often facilitated if there is a single outcome score and if norms are available on similar treatment groups and nonclients.

Reliable and valid. Additionally, is it easy to "fake" desirable scores?

Sensitive to change. If clients get better or worse, is the instrument capable of showing small gradations of improvement or deterioration? Scales with too few items may have a difficult time showing change in small increments. At the same time, you do not want a scale so sensitive that you are led to erroneous conclusions by a client having a single "bad" day.

Relatively inexpensive. Cost considerations include purchase of the instrument, scoring it, and training staff in its use.

LOCATING APPROPRIATE INSTRUMENTS

If you have a well-stocked library, *Measures for Clinical Practice* by Joel Fischer and Kevin Corcoran (2000)) contains examples and descriptive information of over 300 rapid assessment instruments. Another fine reference is *Outcomes Assessment in Clinical Practice* by Sederer and Dickey (1996). This source contains information on the Short-Form Health Survey (SF-36), the Behavior and Symptom Identification Scale (Basis 32), the Addiction Severity Index, the Global Assessment of Functioning Scale (GAF), the Life Skills Profiles, the Brief Symptoms Inventory, the Eating Disorder Inventory, the Child Behavior Checklist, the Beck Depression Inventory, the Brief Psychiatric Rating Scale, the Family Burden Interview Schedule, the Quality of Life Interview, and the CSQ-8, among other assessment instruments. Actual specimen copies are provided for a number of these measures.

A wide variety of dependable scales (usually about 25 items in length) can be purchased from Walmyr Publishing Company (www.walmyr.com). Many of these scales were developed by the late Walt Hudson, a prominent social work researcher, and can be purchased in blocks of 50 for approximately $20. A few examples of the scales available from Walmyr:

Clinical Anxiety Scale	Index of Homophobia
Global Screening Inventory	Child's Attitude Toward Mother
Generalized Contentment Scale	Child's Attitude Toward Father
Index of Self-Esteem	Index of Brother Relations
Index of Peer Relations	Index of Sister Relations
Index of Alcohol Involvement	Children's Behavior Rating Scale
Index of Marital Satisfaction	Client Satisfaction Inventory
Index of Sexual Satisfaction	Partner Abuse: Non-Physical
Index of Family Relations	Partner Abuse: Physical
Index of Parental Attitudes	Brief Adult Assessment Scale
Index of Managerial Effectiveness	Index of Job Satisfaction

A fourth useful reference is *Measures of Personality and Social Psychological Attitudes* (1991) by Robinson, Shaver, and Wrightsman. Their source book provides 150 examples of instruments organized in chapters on subjective well-being, self-esteem, social anxiety and shyness, depression and loneliness, alienation and anomie, interpersonal trust, locus of control, authoritarianism, sex roles, and values.

The advantage of browsing through these books is that they afford you an opportunity to visualize the scales. However, it is not always possible to see examples of instruments without purchasing them. Useful reference guides exist to help you locate instruments (see Box 11.6), but these generally do not contain test specimens. For instance, Touliatos, Perlmutter, and Straus (1990) have abstracted close to a thousand instruments. However, they do not provide examples of these scales. To see one you would have to write to the original author or track down the journal article that contained it.

INTERNET RESOURCES AND REFERENCES FOR FINDING INSTRUMENTS

An Internet search engine, Test Reviews Online, can be found at http://buros.unl. edu/buros/jsp/search.jsp. Test Reviews Online claims to have a database of 4,000 commercially available tests and about half of them have been reviewed by the Buros Institute of Mental Measurements. Reviews of specific tests can be purchased for $15 each or you could consult the last edition of the *Mental Mea-surements Yearbook* in your university library (see Plake, Impara, and Spies, 2003 below).

A third Internet resource is the Center for the Study and Prevention of Violence's database of evaluation instruments. It can be found at http://ibs.colorado.edu/cspv/infohouse/vioeval/. Entering the term *child abuse* returned a brief summary on 10 instruments, entering *parenting* returned 36 instruments, the search engine found 13 instruments for *depression*. Although the database doesn't provide a copy of the instrument for one to inspect, information is provided on how to obtain it and its cost. Abstracts are available on some instruments.

Internet Resources

Additional resources that may be of use to you are:

Fredman, N., & Sherman, R. (1987). *Handbook of measurements for marriage and family therapy.* New York: Brunner/Mazel.

Goldman, B. A., & Mitchell, D. (2002). *Directory of unpublished experimental mental measures.* Washington, DC: American Psychological Association.

Hamill, D. D. (1992). *A consumer's guide to tests in print.* Austin, TX: Pro-ED.

Jordan, C., & Franklin, C. (2003). *Clinical assessment for social workers.* Chicago: Lyceum.

Keyser, D. J., & Sweetland, R. C. (1992). *Test Critiques.* Austin, TX: Pro-ED.

Maddox, T., & Myles, B. (2002). *Tests: A comprehensive reference for assessments in psychology: education, and business.* Austin, TX: Pro ED.

McDowell, I., & Newell, C. (1987). *Measuring health: A guide to rating scales and questionnaires.* London: Oxford University Press.

Miller, D. C. (2002). *Handbook of research design and social measurement.* Newbury Park, CA: Sage.

Plake, B. S., Impara, J. C., & Spies, R. A. (2003). *The fifteenth mental measurements yearbook.* Lincoln, NE: Buros Institute of Mental Measurements.

Other references, although somewhat dated, may help you to locate a specific test or instrument:

Chun, K-T., Cobb, S., & French, J. R. Jr., (1975). *Measures for psychological assessment: A guide to 3,000 original sources and their applications.* Ann Arbor, MI: Institute for Social Research.

Educational Testing Service. (1989). *The ETS test collection catalog: Vol. 3. Tests for special populations.* New York: Oryx.

McCubbin, H., Thompson, C., & McCubbin, M. A. (1996). *Family assessment inventories for research and practice.* Madison, WI: University of Wisconsin.

If you do not find the instrument you need by looking through one of the reference books or searching online, do not despair. The next step is to conduct a thorough search of the literature. You have to do this anyway, even if you have an instrument, because you need to know what others have learned when they evaluated programs similar to the one you wish to evaluate. They may have discovered that the instrument did not provide the kind of information they had hoped for, or could report that a shorter or more reliable version has been developed.

Search such abstracting services as *Psychological Abstracts, Social Work Abstracts, Index Medicus (Medline),* and *ERIC* for the topic that is closest to the clients' problem or focus of the intervention. These may be searched manually or via a computer. Be prepared for hundreds or thousands of citations if you search on too broad of a topic. You may want to consult with a reference librarian before you begin your literature searches.

Those studies that have used an instrument to measure some dimension of interest to you (whether self-esteem, client satisfaction, or something else) may reproduce the scale in the journal article. Because of space limitations, few instruments are printed in journals. Commonly what is found are examples of items from the scale and information about the scale's reliability and validity. You may have to look up the article and consult its bibliography—perhaps searching through several other articles in order to find the instrument. In some instances, you will need to write to the author to obtain a copy of the instrument and permission to use it. This can be problematic when the article is not recent and the author cannot be located. When this obstacle is encountered, it may be possible to find more recent articles by the same author or even to identify others who have cited the original author in their bibliographies by looking in the *Social Sciences Citation Index*. Becoming familiar with the literature helps the evaluator ground the evaluation effort in terms of theoretical models and expectations for the program's potential success rate. This is particularly important in those instances where programs have been rapidly implemented with little prior planning or design.

Still another approach to locating instruments is to write publishing companies that specialize in selling research instruments. Fischer and Corcoran (2000) have listed over 30 such firms.

A final approach is to contact faculty members who are active researchers. They may have files of instruments or be able to refer you to sources or other researchers who will be able to help.

When every effort has been made to locate appropriate instruments and none have been found, *then* it may be time to consider developing your own instrument.

CONSTRUCTING "GOOD" EVALUATION INSTRUMENTS

Consider the following scenario:

A conscientious student conducted a thorough literature search and could find no instrument to measure the concept in which she was interested. She then talked with knowledgeable persons in the field but still came up empty-handed. With no other choice but to develop her own scale, she developed a pool of statements, had some "expert" graduate students select the best items from the pool, and then composed a new instrument. After she collected data with it, the internal consistency for her 10-item scale turned out to be a puny .35—not nearly good enough to use for the program evaluation she had in mind.

Developing good instruments requires much more explanation than an introductory evaluation textbook can provide. However, it is possible to point out some errors commonly made when constructing instruments or developing questionnaires. Please note, however, that the following illustrations do not constitute an exhaustive listing of all the ways it is possible to construct research tools that mystify and confuse. There must be thousands of ways to do that— including misspelled words ("piers" for "peers"), sloppy proofreading that does not catch omitted words ("Listed below are a number activities" instead of "Listed below are a number *of* activities"), as well as such incorrect grammar as the use of pronouns when the antecedent is not clear. There is no substitute for polishing and polishing and *polishing* any items you wish to use in data collection. Leave no stone unturned, and make sure that cover letters, instructions to research participants—any piece of written communication for which you are responsible—are as clearly written as possible.

Look at the examples of questions in Box 11.7. Can you identify anything wrong with these questions?

In the first question, notice that there are two positive evaluation choices ("excellent" and "good"), but only one negative possibility. Respondents have two opportunities to say something good about the program but only one to indicate dissatisfaction. This response scale is biased toward (more likely to get) positive feedback about the program than negative feedback. It is not balanced. A better way to handle this would be to provide the response categories of "excellent," "good," "undecided," "fair," and "poor."

The problem with the second question is that "often" is not defined. What does often mean to you? Once a week? Once a month? Daily? The same difficulty would exist if the term "regular" were used (e.g., "Do you attend AA meetings regularly?").

The third question does not get specific responses. One could be single because one had never married, because one was a widow or widower, or because one had been married and was in the process of legally dissolving it. On some occasions, it may be important to list as a separate response those who are "separated."

In the fourth question, there is a problem with the response set. Note that the response categories are not mutually exclusive. If one had been a client for exactly 6 months, both "a. 6 months or less" and "b. under a year" would be correct. There is also a problem with overlapping response categories in item 5. A client with a $20,000 income might select a. because it was the first category he or she read, or because it suggests the status of a higher income category. An additional problem with the income question is that "income" is a vague term. Is the intent of the question to identify the principal wage earner's annual salary? Or does the question seek to know the total family income from all sources?

| BOX 11.7 | EXAMPLES OF POORLY CONSTRUCTED QUESTIONS |

1. Please rate the quality of our services:
   a. excellent   b. good   c. poor

2. Do you come here often for help?
   a. yes   b. no   c. don't know

3. What is your marital status?
   a. single   b. married   c. divorced

4. How long have you been a client with us?
   a. 6 months or less
   b. under a year
   c. 1 year or longer

5. What is your income?
   a. $10,000 to $20,000
   b. $20,000 to $30,000
   c. $30,000 or more

6. Do you not make a practice of shopping only on weekends?
   a. yes   b. no   c. undecided

7. Do you have a male relative and a female relative over 55 years of age living at home with you?
   a. yes   b. no   c. undecided

8. Approximately how many minutes do you dream each evening?
   a. under 15   b. 16 to 30   c. more than 31 minutes

9. Wouldn't you agree that clients should keep their accounts current with the agency?
   a. yes   b. no   c. undecided

10. Are you an alcoholic?
    a. yes   b. no   c. undecided

Confusion about whether the question is asking for take-home (net) or gross pay is also likely.

Question 6 creates problems because the word "not" makes the question more complex than it needs to be. Many people will have to read the question a second time. Some individuals will inadvertently fail to see "not." Also, note that "shopping" is not defined. Does shopping refer to all shopping—shopping for essentials as well as nonessentials? What if one runs out of milk and stops to pick up a quart on the way home from work Thursday evening? Is stopping to buy a newspaper or a magazine considered to be shopping?

Item 7 is called a **"double-barreled" question.** It asks two things in one sentence. It is entirely possible to have a male relative over the age of 55 living at home without having a female relative over 55 residing there—and vice versa.

How would you respond to this question if you had only the male relative 55 or older but not the female living at home?

Item 8 asks for information that the respondent cannot be reasonably expected to have. Most of us do not know how long we dream each evening. This question asks for information that can only be conjecture. Absurd questions and those that ask for information that respondents do not have not only yield worthless data but on occasion may provoke angry responses resulting in respondents refusing to continue any further with the interview or the questionnaire.

When constructing questionnaires and developing items for instruments, be careful to use vocabulary that will be understood by the potential respondents. Avoid jargon and technical talk.

Item 9 is an example of a leading question. Few people tend to disagree with a question that suggests the answer. Further, there is an issue here of **social desirability.** Most people do not disagree with normal social conventions (e.g., cleanliness, being sober on the job). We all want to be liked by other people, and we tend to give responses that are "acceptable" even if that is not what we really believe or how we really act.

In regard to item 10, it may not be easy for clients whose behavior is excessive or outside of "normal" social behavior to admit the true extent of their problem. For example, few active alcoholics will admit to being an alcoholic—yet they might admit to "occasionally drinking more than they should." Terms such as "alcoholic," "junkie," "addict," and "delinquent" are stigmatizing to respondents, and most individuals will not deliberately choose a response that characterizes them as being flawed, deviant, or markedly different from the rest of humanity.

Additionally, the tenth question assumes that the respondent has knowledge that he or she may not have. When asking questions that have the potential for forcing negative labels on respondents, it is almost always better to rephrase and ask more neutrally about the behavior itself. In this case, improved questions might be:

> On how many days of the past 30 days have you had an alcoholic drink?
>
> On how many occasions have you tried to quit drinking but were unable to do so?
>
> Once you start drinking, do you find it difficult to stop before becoming completely intoxicated?
>
> In the past 30 days, how many times have you taken a drink the first thing in the morning?

Finally, there are important considerations in terms of what questions are asked first. As a general rule, it is better to ask sensitive questions (such as those about income, age, sexual practices, or illegal behaviors) toward the end of the questionnaire. The theory is that individuals are more likely to respond to these items once they have become involved in the process of completing the questionnaire (or in the case of interviews, established rapport with the interviewer).

Example 1: But It Is So Easy to Design a Questionnaire

Susie Caseworker was employed as a hospital social worker in a rural community. She was one of two social workers responsible for patients in the hospital. Although Susie liked her job, one annoying problem was that the emergency room staff could page her and she would have to drop what she was doing and race to the emergency room. She was constantly being interrupted and taken away from her patients in order to be of assistance in the emergency room. In her opinion, this happened with enough frequency to justify the hospital hiring another social worker solely for assignment in the emergency room. She discussed this with the hospital administrator, who said that he would make a decision once she had documented the need for an emergency room social worker. The five questions in Figure 11.1 are those that Susie prepared as part of that effort. Her intention was to give the survey to each nurse and physician who worked in the emergency room.

Figure 11.1 shows how difficult preparing an instrument can be. Consider the information that these five questions will produce. Will they provide the kind of evidence that will convince the hospital administrator of the need for an emergency room social worker? How can these questions be interpreted or misconstrued?

A potential problem with the first question is that it assumes that physicians and nurses know how often and on which occasions a social worker is needed. If physicians and nurses do not know exactly what it is that a social worker does, then it is entirely possible that they would under- or overestimate

---

FIGURE 11.1 | EMERGENCY ROOM SURVEY

Place an "x" by the answer that best corresponds to your thinking.

1. There are times when a social worker could be utilized in the emergency room.
   ( ) never   ( ) seldom   ( ) occasionally   ( ) frequently   ( ) always

2. When I worked with a social worker, he/she acted in a professional manner.
   ( ) never   ( ) seldom   ( ) occasionally   ( ) frequently   ( ) always

3. When I needed a social worker, one was readily available.
   ( ) never   ( ) seldom   ( ) occasionally   ( ) frequently   ( ) always

4. I see cases where family members are not coping well with a relative's illness or injury.
   ( ) never   ( ) seldom   ( ) occasionally   ( ) frequently   ( ) always

5. I have seen situations in the emergency room where social workers could have done counseling.
   ( ) never   ( ) seldom   ( ) occasionally   ( ) frequently   ( ) always

the number of occasions when a social worker could be appropriately employed. Do they think social workers are to be used to hold the hand of a person in pain? Are they to provide grief counseling only when the chaplain is not around? Are social workers to watch small children when there is no one else to supervise them? Better information might be obtained if the emergency room staff were asked to identify the needed activities to be performed by social workers or the occasions when a social worker could be used.

A related but missing question could be developed to identify times that a social worker was most needed. There may be shifts (such as between 11:00 P.M. and 7:00 A.M. on weekends when there are more emergencies requiring assistance from a social worker. It may be that the existing hospital social workers can adequately cover the emergency room during weekdays, but that the greatest need for a social worker is on the weekends and evenings.

It might also be helpful to ask the emergency room staff to enumerate the number of times during an average day, weekend, and evening shift when the services of a social worker would be beneficial. Here, too, the response set is important. Knowing that respondents indicated that a social worker could have been used an average of 25 times per shift is a lot more powerful information than knowing the most frequent response was "occasionally" or "frequently."

The second question inappropriately attempts to assess the professionalism of the existing social work staff. Professionalism is not the issue at hand. The inclusion of this question does not help to assess the need for a social worker in the emergency room.

The problem with the third question is that there is no way to know how many occasions the respondent might have had a need for a social worker. The emphasis appears to be on availability. Although it is not clear, perhaps the author of this question was trying to explore the time lag between the request for the social worker and the amount of time it took the social worker to disengage from other duties and to appear in the emergency room. If the social workers can always respond within a 5- or 10-minute period, perhaps there is no need to add another social worker just for the emergency room. If this is the case, the evaluator might want to ask the question, "What is the longest you have had to wait for the social worker to arrive in the emergency room?" This question could be followed by another: "About how often does this occur?"

Question 4 is vague and could be improved by asking how often (in terms of times per shift, week, or month) are cases observed where family members need brief counseling or referral from a social worker.

Question 5 seems to repeat the first question. It could be improved by listing a number of situations in which it is likely that emergency room staff would want to have a social worker available to assist. Once again, a frequency count of the times a social worker was needed (e.g., per shift or per week) would supply better information than the vague "occasionally" or "frequently."

See Box 11.8, which discusses the importance of phrasing when determining the questions to be asked.

| BOX 11.8 | THE IMPORTANCE OF PHRASING |

In their study of the reliability of self-reported drug use, sexual behavior, and treatment use, Adair, Craddock, Miller, and Turner (1996) identified three questions having high inconsistency rates because they contained poorly defined terms.

One of these questions asked, "Since your admission, have you had a checkup or have you received any scheduled individual services for medical problems other than those I have already asked about?"

The second question asked, "Since your admission, have you attended any other scheduled talks, lectures, or films as a part of your treatment?"

What is poorly defined in these items? Do you think everyone knows what constitutes "scheduled individual services"? Does a lab test or blood pressure screening qualify, for instance? Similarly, is it possible that some research subjects might not have known when they were participating in a "scheduled talk, lecture, or film"? Could that item be interpreted broadly enough to include lectures in college, or a talk at an art museum?

A third question asked, "Since your admission, how much would you say you have spent on drugs for your own nonmedical use, excluding alcohol?" At least two possibilities for inconsistencies exist here. One explanation could be that the information is unavailable (the respondent has no factual knowledge and is wildly guessing). This would be understandable, because being a drug addict probably precluded the keeping of accurate records. A second possibility is that the drug users were not always purchasing drugs but *shared* those purchased by someone else and/or *exchanged* goods and services (for example, sexual favors) for drugs. And what about over-the-counter drugs? Do they count as drug expenditures?

Source: Adair, E. B. G., Craddock, S. G., Miller, H. G., & Turner, C. F. (1996). Quality of treatment data: Reliability over time of self-reports given by clients in treatment for substance abuse. *Journal of Substance Abuse Treatment, 13*(2), 145–149.

Example 2: Evaluating Inservice Training

John Practitioner had responsibility for training social workers in a large state agency. John wanted to evaluate a major new training program for supervisors that he firmly believed would make them more effective managers. Knowing how participants at professional training sessions and workshops typically give positive feedback (remember our discussion about client satisfaction studies?), John was determined to go beyond asking, "Did the presenter do a good job?" "Was the presentation clear and well organized?" or "What is your overall rating of this workshop?" Instead, John wanted to know how the week-long workshop would impact trainees as they performed their jobs. He developed the instrument in Figure 11.2. Will this instrument help him to know the impact the workshop had on the trainees?

FIGURE 11.2 | EVALUATION OF THE SUPERVISION WORKSHOP

1. Will this training help you to reduce absenteeism among your staff?
   ( ) very little   ( ) moderately   ( ) very much

2. Will this training help you with the operating costs of your office?
   ( ) very little   ( ) moderately   ( ) very much

3. Will this training help you to deal with staff's documentation of records?
   ( ) very little   ( ) moderately   ( ) very much

4. Will this training help you to reduce accident rates among your staff?
   ( ) very little   ( ) moderately   ( ) very much

5. Will this training help you to increase the productivity of your employees?
   ( ) very little   ( ) moderately   ( ) very much

6. Will this training help you to get improved ratings from your district manager?
   ( ) very little   ( ) moderately   ( ) very much

These questions, drawn from a longer instrument, are straightforward and easy to understand. They do not seem to be vague, double-barreled, leading, and so forth—problems we discussed earlier. There is only one major problem with this collection of items—they measure the respondents' *attitudes* about whether the training has assisted them. John Practitioner has missed the mark if he is truly interested in the "effect" of the intervention. Despite his best intentions, John has prepared a questionnaire that essentially is just another version of other consumer satisfaction efforts.

There is nothing wrong with this if that is what the evaluator wanted to accomplish. But in John's case, he wanted to measure the effect or outcomes of the workshop—the transferability to solving problems on the job. What John really wanted to measure are such things as:

1. Absenteeism (Is there less absenteeism after the workshop than before?)
2. Operating costs (Are costs lower?)
3. Documentation of records (Are a greater percentage of records in compliance with quality assurance standards?)
4. Accident rates (Are there fewer accidents?)
5. Productivity (Does productivity increase?)
6. Performance ratings (Do performance ratings of supervisors improve?)

In devising his instrument, John opted for a quick measure that examined participants' opinions or attitudes about the workshop. Given his concerns and interests, John would have been better advised to obtain behavioral data such as absenteeism, operating costs, and accident, performance, and productivity rates for the preceding quarter or year for the departmental supervisors' use and to compare those rates with the data after training.

Conclusions from Examples 1 and 2

These two examples demonstrate how easy it is to go astray when designing a data collection instrument. Although this chapter furnishes a foundation for understanding what goes into "good" instrumentation, it cannot prepare the reader to anticipate every conceptual problem that may arise or provide the reader with everything he or she needs to know about scale construction. The evaluator who must, by necessity, construct an instrument is always well advised to have trusted colleagues review the newly drafted questionnaire or scale and then, after revising it, to pilot test the instrument on a small group of clients or consumers who represent the population to be studied. Such a process will often yield tremendous insights into the way others read and interpret your data collection tools.

LEVELS OF MEASUREMENT

Besides examining potential instruments for reliability and validity, the evaluator must also consider what kind of data the questionnaire or scale will produce for analysis. Evaluators do not want just a series of responses (e.g., 10 "Agrees" and 5 "Don't knows"); their aim is to measure, with some precision, the concepts being investigated. Measurement, for the quantitatively oriented evaluator, means that many of the responses are quantified and translated into numerical values that can be analyzed using statistical procedures. Evaluators usually have a great deal of latitude in deciding how variables are going to be operationalized and then, by extension, how the variables will be measured. The level of measurement associated with each variable has implications for what statistics can be used.

The **nominal level** of measurement is the lowest level of measurement because it is descriptive—meaning that names or terms are assigned to various categories that are sorted by a distinguishing characteristic. For example, clients might be grouped into those who are either male or female; veterans or not; employed or unemployed. Nominal data are categorical data. An agency's clientele might be grouped into those who are "active" or "inactive," insured or uninsured.

Nominal data do not have to be dichotomous (two categories only); a variable like marital status might have five categories associated with it (never married, married, divorced, separated, widowed). It may not be necessary to have that many distinctions—maybe all you need to know is whether a client is single or married. This is something you, the evaluator, must decide based on how you want to analyze the data for the final report. More categories will give you finer distinctions.

Nominal data restrict you to sorting the data into defined categories and reporting percentages. Evaluators typically do not compute averages for nominal data. For instance, think about a situation where you have the following data coded into your computer:

Variable #9	Gender	Frequency	Percent
Coded as 1	Female	12	60%
Coded as 2	Male	8	40%

Let's say that you ask the computer to compute the average of this data. The computer will report back to you that the answer is 1.4. However, this number has no real meaning because it does not make sense to average gender. It does, though, help us to understand the sample if we learn that 60% of the group is female. Nominal data lends itself quite well to bar graphs and pie charts.

Ordinal level of measurement uses rankings. A school social worker might rank the children most in need of psychological testing or those most in need of coats for the winter. If the same school social worker is conducting group therapy for children who have experienced major loss, he or she might rate the students in terms of those greatly improved, moderately improved, and slightly improved. (No improvement could also be a legitimate ranking.) Although ordinal measurement, like nominal, uses categories, the difference is that with ordinal data there is a clear direction, a hierarchy that represents gradations of amount. Ordinal data usually conforms well to a continuum, as shown in Figure 11.3.

In the example of ordinal data in Figure 11.3, it is apparent that a student with a "3" has much more depression than a student at a "1" level. Contrast this with the previous example when females were coded 1 for the computer and males were coded 2. With the nominal data, the "1" did not mean that the females had less of some trait than males.

It is reasonable to think of ordinal data as being much more like nominal data than the next higher level of measurement for this reason: as with nominal data, it is difficult to know the true distance between categories. Forget for the moment, about the numeric scale that shows a child with severe depression being a "3" and another child with moderate depression being a "2." What is the difference between a child with severe depression and one with moderate depression? Clinically, would a child with moderate depression resemble more the child with severe depression or the one with slight depression? If moderate

FIGURE 11.3 | RATING SCALE FOR DEPRESSION: CHILDREN WHO HAVE EXPERIENCED LOSS

0.....................1.....................2.....................3

No Depression   Slight   Moderate   Severe Depression

depression is more like severe depression than slight depression, then the distance between severe and moderate is less while the distance between moderate and slight is more. To switch examples, suppose these same children are ranked by their height. We have these categories: tall, average, and short. What is the distance between average and tall? Is it 3 inches or more like 7? How much shorter are those in the least tall category than those in the average category? We cannot tell with any precision because the ordinal data categories constrict our ability to make fine measurements.

Evaluators often use ordinal items and scales like the examples below:

#17 How would you rate the program?

1. Poor
2. Fair
3. Good
4. Excellent

#21 The program was everything I expected it would be.

1. Strongly Agree
2. Agree
3. Undecided
4. Disagree
5. Strongly Disagree

Do not mistake such categories as "good" and "poor" as nominal data. Variables #17 and #21 are measured at the ordinal level because the response set is directional—forming a continuum of increments. It is easy to see the *ranking* for those most and least satisfied with a program. Also, do not make the mistake of seeing the numbers 1, 2, 3, 4, and 5 and assuming that the presence of numbers means that you have continuous data or interval data. If you see categories (i.e., income brackets), then you are likely not dealing with interval data. Open-ended questions (i.e., "What is your yearly income?") will, however, furnish continuous or interval data when no response categories are provided.

The **interval level** of measurement allows more sophisticated statistical procedures to be used. Unlike the nominal and ordinal data, data measured at the interval level have known distances and equal intervals between the units. Interval data allow for the greatest level of precision and tell us how much more or how many more. For instance, scores on the ACT or the SAT, LSAT, and so forth report standard scores at the interval level. Evaluators create or employ instruments that combine many items that are summed to form an overall score, and that variable is usually considered to be interval level data.

The **ratio level** of measurement is very much like the interval. In fact, there is only one difference. With ratio data there is a true zero. The most common example given of this is a thermometer that could measure zero degrees Centigrade and then, if the weather turned colder, could drop even lower. A true zero means absolutely none, the real absence of something. Age and salary are good examples of variables commonly measured at the interval level. A salary of $36,000 is exactly three times a salary of $12,000; an individual who is 17 is exactly half the age of a 34-year-old. In conversation we often speak as if our comparisons have a real zero when in actuality they do not. Talking with a coworker we might attribute a zero quality to someone who just has low amounts of some characteristic (e.g., "Wanda has no money"). It might be possible to obtain low scores on certain variables (e.g., assertiveness or IQ), but even the lowest level would not mean that the individual had zero or negative levels of intelligence or assertiveness. It is good to keep in mind that even our best instruments are only crude approximations of the true levels of the characteristics that we are attempting to measure.

The reason statisticians make distinctions between the interval and ratio level of measurements is that a true zero means that comparisons of magnitude have a more precise meaning. In actuality, however, interval and ratio levels of measurement are more alike than they are different. For instance, the Clinical Anxiety Scale (illustrated later in the book) contains 25 items and produces a theoretical range of scores from 0 to 100. The distance between a client scoring 80 at pretest and 40 at posttest can be easily calculated and would represent the same amount of improvement as a client whose pretest was 90 and whose posttest was 50. This is because the intervals between scores are equal, predictable, and form a continuous variable. At some point most variables with many divisions or gradations become interval variables. Variables with as few as 15 or 20 graduations are often treated as interval variables. For all practical purposes, it would not matter to an evaluator if the theoretical range of the Clinical Anxiety Scale was 10 to 90, 20 to 100, or even 25 to 85. The analytical procedures used to analyze the scores will be the same.

For most purposes it is not necessary for evaluators to make distinctions between ratio and interval level of measurement when planning how data are to be analyzed. Either level allows for averages that have real meaning to be computed (unlike the first example that attempted to average males and females). Many of the data analytic procedures using ratio and interval level of data will be based on the computation of variable means.

Although the analysis of data will be addressed in more depth in Chapter 14, let us conclude this section with some key things to remember about level of measurement:

- For simple description (e.g., 15 percent of the clients were Vietnam vets), variables measured at the nominal level work fine.
- Ordinal variables also are appropriately used for describing samples ("Twenty percent of the clients slightly improved, 30 percent moderately improved, and 50 percent greatly improved").
- Both nominal and ordinal variables can be used to test whether similar proportions in two or more groups being compared.
- Data recorded at the nominal or ordinal level cannot usually be transformed into interval level data (e.g., if clients are given a form to complete that under "age" gives two response choices—"under 60" and "60 and older"—then these two categories will not allow the evaluator to compute the average age of the clients).

- Interval/ratio level of measurement is often desired for dependent variables. If one wants to know whether an intervention significantly reduced the level of depression in a treatment group compared to a control group, then an instrument providing scores on an interval/ratio level would be needed so that group averages could be computed.

Questions for Class Discussion

1. What is wrong with the following questionnaire items?
   a. Describe your mother's condition during her pregnancy with you.
   b. Yes or No: Have you ever been involved in any accidents?
   c. Have you been called names and had your life threatened?
2. Barbara Daydreamer designed a three-item questionnaire to be used as a pre- and posttest instrument to measure adolescents' knowledge of alcoholism as a disease. Later she was surprised to find that there were no significant differences between pre- and posttest scores. How would you explain this?
3. Discuss the following item taken from the evaluation instrument Barbara designed for adolescents:

   When you are an adult, what are the chances that you will be a drinker?
   _____ I am certain I will never drink
   _____ I don't think I will drink
   _____ I am not sure
   _____ I think I will drink
   _____ I am sure I will drink

4. If you were asked to evaluate an instrument measuring hyperactivity described in a journal, what information about the instrument would you want to find in the article?
5. For various client group, brainstorm what behaviors might be good indicators of treatment success or failure. Why might they work better than measurements of attitudes or knowledge?
6. Suggest one or more variables measured at the interval level that could be converted to nominal or ordinal level variables.

Mini-Projects: Experiencing Evaluation Firsthand

1. Skim one of the books containing rapid assessment instruments noted in this chapter. Make a list of at least five scales that you might be able to use in your future practice. Explain how each might be used.
2. Read one of the articles on the development and validation of a scale referenced at the end of this chapter. Summarize, in a short paper, all the steps the author went through.
3. Draft a set of 10 items for a potential scale you would like to see developed. Then, outline a plan to test the scale's reliability and validity. What would you need to do?

4. Develop a needs assessment questionnaire for a program with which you are familiar. Present it to the class for constructive criticism.

5. Group Project: Create a brief questionnaire using only nominal or ordinal variables to measure the sociodemographics of students in your class. Have another group construct a similar questionnaire using only variables measured at the interval level. Have a third group examine the data from the two questionnaires and conclude about what they learn from the exercise.

References and Resources

Fischer, J., & Corcoran, K. (2000). *Measures for clinical practice.* New York: Free Press.

Koeske, G.F. (1994). Some recommendations for improving measurement validation in social work research. *Journal of Social Service Research, 18*(3/4), 43–72.

Macdonald, G. (1998). Development of a social support scale: An evaluation of psychometric properties. *Research on Social Work Practice, 8,* 564–576.

Meisenheimer, C. G. (1985). *Quality assurance: A complete guide to effective programs.* Rockville, MD: Aspen Systems.

Nunnally, J. C., & Bernstein, I. H. P. (1994). *Psychometric theory.* New York: McGraw-Hill.

Robinson, J. P., Shaver, P., & Wrightsman, L. S. (1991). *Measures of personality and social psychological attitudes.* San Diego: Academic Press.

Rossiter, E. M., Agras, W. S., Telch, C. F., & Bruce, B. (1992). The eating patterns of non-purging bulimic subjects. *International Journal of Eating Disorders, 11*(2), 111–120.

Sederer, L. I., & Dickey, B. (Eds.). (1996). *Outcomes assessment in clinical practice.* Baltimore: Williams & Wilkins.

Siefert, K., Schwartz, I. M., & Ortega, R. M. (1994). Infant mortality in Michigan's child welfare system. *Social Work, 39*(5), 574–579.

Thyer, B. A. (1992). Promoting evaluation research in the field of family preservation. In E. S. Morton & R. K. Grigsby (Eds.), *Advancing family preservation practice* (pp. 131–149). Newbury Park, CA: Sage.

Touliatos, J., Perlmutter, B. F., & Straus, M. A. (1990). *Handbook of family measurement techniques.* Newbury Park, CA: Sage.

Readings on Instrument Construction

Comrey, A. L. (1988). Factor analytic methods in scale development in personality and clinical psychology. *Journal of Consulting and Clinical Psychology, 56,* 754–761.

Cummings, S. M., Kelly, T. B., Holland, T. P., & Peterson-Hazan, X. (1997). Development and validation of the Needs Inventory for Caregivers of the Hospitalized Elderly. *Research on Social Work Practice, 8,* 120–132.

Faul, A. C. (2002). Comprehensive assessment in occupational social work: The development and validation of the Corporate Behavioral Wellness Inventory. *Research on Social Work Practice, 12*(1), 47–70.

Glison, C., Hemmelgarn, A. L., & Post, J. A. (2002). The Shortform Assessment for Children: An assessment and outcome measure for child welfare and juvenile justice. *Research on Social Work Practice, 12*(1), 82–106.

Holden, G., Cuzzi, L., Rutter, S., Chernack, P., & Rosenberg, G. (1997). The Hospital Social Work Self-Efficacy Scale. *Research on Social Work Practice, 7,* 490–499.

Hudson, W. W., & McMurtry, S. L. (1997). Comprehensive assessment in social work practice. *Research on Social Work Practice, 7,* 78–98.

Koeske, G. F. (1994). Some recommendations for improving measurement validation in social work research. *Journal of Social Work Research, 18,* 43–72.

Krysik, J. & Lecroy, C. W. (2002). The empirical validation of an instrument to predict risk of recidivism among juvenile offenders. *Research on Social Work Practice, 12*(1), 71–81.

Lewis, S. J. & Abell, N. (2002). Development and evaluation of the Adherence Attitude Inventory. *Research on Social Work Practice, 12*(1), 107–123.

Mathiesen, S. G., Cash, S. J., & Hudson, W. W. (2002). The Multidimensional Adolescent Assessment Scale: A validation study. *Research on Social Work Practice, 12*(1), 9–28.

O'Hare, T., & Collins, P. (1997). Development and validation of a scale for measuring social work practice skills. *Research on Social Work Practice, 7,* 228–238.

Pike, C. K. (2002). Measuring racial climate in schools of social work: Instrument development and validation. *Research on Social Work Practice, 12*(1), 29–46.

Randall, E. J., & Thyer, B. A. (1994). A preliminary test of the validity of the LCSW examination. *Clinical Social Work Journal, 22*(2), 223–227.

Shields, J. J. (1992). Evaluating community organization projects: The development of an empirically based measure. *Social Work Research and Abstracts, 28*(2), 15–20.

Smith, M. A., Arnold, E. M., Salston, M. G., Heindel, D., & Hudson, W. W. (2002). The Brief Adult Assessment Scale: A validation study. *Research on Social Work Practice, 12*(1), 176–197.

Snyder, C. R., Hoza, B., Pelham, W. E., Rapoff, M., Ware, L., Danovsky, M., Highberger, L., Rubinstein, H., & Stahl, K. J. (1997). The development and validation of the Children's Hope Scale. *Journal of Pediatric Psychology, 22,* 399–421.

Springer, D. W., Abell, N., & Hudson, W. W. (2002). Creating and validating rapid assessment instruments for practice and research: Part One. *Research on Social Work Practice, 12*(3), 408–439.

Springer, D. W. Abell, N. & Nugent, W. R. (2002). Creating and validating rapid assessment instruments for practice and research: Part Two. *Research on Social Work Practice, 12*(6), 768–795.

Streiner, D. L., & Normal, G. R. (1995). *Health measurement scales: A practical guide to their development and use.* New York: Oxford University Press.

ILLUSTRATIONS OF INSTRUMENTS

It is one thing to talk about reliability and validity on a theoretical level, but theory takes on much more meaning when you have real instruments to apply. With some scales we get a sense of face validity immediately. Seeing the actual wording used by the scale developers assists us in thinking about how our clientele or study population might respond. Will it be over their heads? Will there be too many items for their level of attention? Are the questions too obvious or too subtle? For those who are not familiar with testing and what paper-and-pencil instruments actually look like, we have secured the permission of several authors to reproduce all or portions of their instruments.

As you review this small sampling of instruments, you will realize that when items are well chosen, internal consistency can be obtained with very few items. Some scales are elegant in their simplicity. You will probably also note that some scales look as if they could be improved. You may even wonder why some items were included and others left out. Measuring intangible concepts is not an easy task—it is a challenge even for the most experienced and capable researcher.

However, we also hope you come to a personal realization that a number of fine scales have been developed that you may want to use in your practice or agency—scales like the Child Abuse Potential Inventory that social workers and other practitioners *ought* to use much more often before placing children in foster care, adoptive care, or returning them to their parents.

There is nothing cryptic or obscure about the many wonderful instruments that are our tireless servants, constantly at our beck and call. They can be used to assess clients, to conduct basic research, and to evaluate programs. They perform their tasks dependably time and time again—or else they would not have the reliability they are reported to have.

Before adopting an instrument, pilot test it with an actual client or group. See if the instrument gives some new insight or provides you with objective data to help confirm your professional judgment.

Though a small sample, the following instruments demonstrate the great variety of those available. Because some of these instruments are protected by copyright, you should not reproduce them without permission. Read the section on "Availability" in order to know whether you must purchase the scale or request permission to use it.

As you review these instruments, ask yourself how they might be used in a program evaluation effort. What hypotheses or questions would they help you explore? What programs or special populations could they be used with?

CHILD ABUSE POTENTIAL INVENTORY

Description

The Child Abuse Potential (CAP) Inventory (see Figure 12.1) is a 160-item self-report questionnaire with a primary clinical scale, the physical child abuse scale, and six factor scales measuring distress, rigidity, unhappiness, problems with child and self, problems with family, and problems with others. Additionally, it contains three validity scales: the lie scale, the random response scale, and the inconsistency scale to check for "faking good," "faking bad," or randomly responding. An ego strength scale has recently been developed from items in the CAP Inventory. The CAP Inventory has been used successfully to evaluate a variety of secondary and tertiary prevention programs. The scale has been used worldwide by the U.S. Air Force to evaluate interventions with physical child abusers. (See, for example, Brewster et al.; Mollerstrom, Patchner, & Milner, 1995). Other studies have found that maternal abuse potential correlated with scores on the Neonatal Morbidity Index (Zelenko et al., 2001) and significantly related to developmental delays in children at ages 3 and 5 (Dukewich, Borkowski, & Whitman, 1999).

Psychometric Data

There is an extensive body of research on the CAP Inventory. Internal consistency estimates for the abuse scale range from .91 to .96. Test–retest reliabilities for the abuse scale are also strong. A number of cross-validation studies indicate the abuse scale has overall classification rates in the low 80 percent to low 90 percent range. Predictive validity has been demonstrated in a longitudinal study showing a significant relationship between elevated CAP abuse scores and subsequent confirmed physical child abuse. Construct validity has similarly been reported by a number of investigators.

FIGURE 12.1 | CHILD ABUSE POTENTIAL INVENTORY

CAP INVENTORY FORM VI

Joel S. Milner Ph D
Copyright 1977 1982 1984 Revised Edition 1986
Printed in the United States of America

Name:_____   Date:_____ ID #:_____

Age:____ Gender: Male____ Female____   Marital Status: Sin__ Mar__ Sep__ Div__ Wid__

Race: Black____ White____ Hispanic____   Number of children in home_____

Am. Indian ____ Other (specify)_____   Highest grade completed_____

INSTRUCTIONS: The following questionnaire includes a series of statements which may be applied to yourself. Read each of the statements and determine if you **AGREE** or **DISAGREE** with the statement. If you agree with a statement, circle **A** for agree. If you disagree with a statement, circle **DA** for disagree. Be honest when giving your answers. Remember to read each statement; it is important not to skip any statement.

●OOO

1. I never feel sorry for others ....A   DA
2. I enjoy having pets ....A   DA
3. I have always been strong and healthy ....A   DA
4. I like most people ....A   DA
5. I am a confused person ....A   DA
6. I do not trust most people ....A   DA
7. People expect too much from me ....A   DA
8. Children should never be bad ....A   DA
9. I am often mixed up ....A   DA
10. Spanking that only bruises a child is okay ....A   DA
11. I always try to check on my child when it's crying ....A   DA
12. I sometimes act without thinking ....A   DA
13. You cannot depend on others ....A   DA
14. I am a happy person ....A   DA
15. I like to do things with my family ....A   DA
16. Teenage girls need to be protected ....A   DA
17. I am often angry inside ....A   DA
18. Sometimes I feel all alone in the world ....A   DA
19. Everything in a home should always be in its place ....A   DA
20. I sometimes worry that I cannot meet the needs of a child ....A   DA
21. Knives are dangerous for children ....A   DA
22. I often feel rejected ....A   DA
23. I am often lonely inside ....A   DA
24. Little boys should never learn sissy games ....A   DA
25. I often feel very frustrated ....A   DA

●OOO

Availability

This instrument is copyrighted. You will need to purchase the manual and copies of the instrument from PSYTEC, Inc., P.O. Box 564, DeKalb, IL 60115 (815-758-1415).

Scoring

Scoring templates, scoring sheets, and computer scoring programs can be purchased along with the instrument from PSYTEC.

For Further Reference

Note: Dr. Milner says that as of March 2003 there were approximately 370 references on the CAPI. Only a sampling of those are shown below.

Baumann, B. L., & Kolko, D. J. (2002). A comparison of abusive and nonabusive mothers of abused children. *Child Maltreatment, 7,* 369–376.

Brewster, A. L., Milner, J. S., Mollerstrom, W. W., Saha, B. T., & Harris, N. (2002). Evaluation of spouse abuse treatment: Description and evaluation of the Air Force Family Advocacy Programs for spouse physical abuse. *Military Medicine, 167,* 464–469.

Cerny, J. E., & Inouye, J. (2001). Utilizing the Child Abuse Potential Inventory in a community nursing prevention program for child abuse. *Journal of Community Health Nursing, 18,* 199–211.

Combs-Orme, T., Martin, L., Fox, G. L., & Faver, C. A. (2000). Risk for child maltreatment: New mothers' concerns and screening test results. *Children and Youth Services Review, 22,* 517–537.

Dukewich, T. L., Borkowski, J. G., & Whitman, T. L. (1999). A longitudinal analysis of maternal abuse potential and developmental delays in children of adolescent mothers. *Child Abuse & Neglect, 23,* 405–420.

Merrill, L. L., Hervig, L. K., & Milner, J. S. (1996). Childhood parenting experiences, intimate partner conflict resolution, and adult risk for child physical abuse. *Child Abuse and Neglect, 20*(11), 1049–1065.

Milner, J. S. (1989). Additional cross-validation of the Child Abuse Potential Inventory. *Psychological Assessment: A Journal of Consulting and Clinical Psychology, 1,* 219–223.

Milner, J. S. (1990). An interpretive manual for the *Child Abuse Potential Inventory.* Webster, NC: Psytec, Inc.

Milner, J. S. (1994). Assessing physical child abuse risk: The Child Abuse Potential Inventory. *Clinical Psychology Review, 14*(6), 547–583.

Mollerstrom, W. W., Patchner, M. A., & Milner, J. S. (1995). Child maltreatment: The United States Air Force's response. *Child Abuse & Neglect, 19,* 325–334.

Zelenko, M. A., Huffman, L. C., Brown, B. W. Jr., Daniels, K., Lock, J., Kennedy, Q., & Steiner, H. (2001). The Child Abuse Potential Inventory and pregnancy outcome in expectant adolescent mothers. *Child Abuse & Neglect, 25,* 1481–1495.

CLINICAL ANXIETY SCALE

Description

The Clinical Anxiety Scale (see Figure 12.2) is a 25-item instrument designed to measure problems individuals have with anxiety and to have a clinical cutting score of 30. The scale can be used to measure a client's anxiety level before, during, or after a treatment program. The authors advocate its use as a self-report outcome measure for single system research designs (Westhuis & Thyer, 1989).

Psychometric Data

The Clinical Anxiety Scale has a coefficient alpha of .94 and 2-week test–retest correlations that range from .64 to .74. Validity has been demonstrated in the scale's ability to discriminate well between groups known to be suffering from anxiety and low-anxiety control groups. A discriminant validity coefficient of .77 and a phi coefficient of .81 have been reported when two criterion groups were dichotomized around the cutting score of 30.

Availability

The Clinical Anxiety Scale is available in pads of 50 or with other rapid assessment instruments on computer diskette from WALMYR Publishing Co., 3605 Green's Battery Court, Tallahassee, FL 32308. Or contact Bruce A. Thyer, School of Social Work, Florida State University, Tallahassee, FL 32306.

Scoring

Seven items on the CAS are first reverse scored (these are indicated on the bottom of the scale), then summed along with the remaining scores. The number of completed items are subtracted, the remainder is multiplied by 100, and that value is divided by the product of the number of items completed times 4. A range of scores from 0 to 100 is produced. Higher scores indicate more severe problems with anxiety. Computer software is available for scoring the scales.

For Further Reference

Courts, N. F. (2000). Psychosocial adjustment of patients on home hemodialysis and their dialysis partners. *Clinical Nursing Research, 9*(2), 177–190.

Lloyd-Cobb, P., & Dixon, D. R. (1995). A preliminary evaluation of the effects of a veterans' hospital domiciliary program for homeless persons. *Research on Social Work Practice, 5*(3), 309–316.

Thyer, B. A., & Westhuis, D. (1989). Test-retest reliability of the Clinical Anxiety Scale. *Phobia Practice and Research Journal, 2*(2), 113–115.

Valentine, P. V., & Smith, T. E. (2001). Evaluating traumatic incident reduction therapy with female inmates: A randomized controlled clinical trial. *Research on Social Work Practice, 11*(1), 40–52.

FIGURE 12.2 | THE CLINICAL ANXIETY SCALE

CLINICAL ANXIETY SCALE (CAS)

Name:_____   Today's Date:_____

This questionnaire is designed to measure how much anxiety you are currently feeling. It is not a test, so there are no right or wrong answers. Answer each item as carefully and as accurately as you can by placing a number beside each one as follows:

1   Rarely or none of the time
2   A little of the time
3   Some of the time
4   A good part of the time
5   Most or all of the time

1. _____ I feel calm.
2. _____ I feel tense.
3. _____ I feel suddenly scared for no reason.
4. _____ I feel nervous.
5. _____ I use tranquilizers or antidepressants to cope with my anxiety.
6. _____ I feel confident about the future.
7. _____ I am free from senseless or unpleasant thoughts.
8. _____ I feel afraid to go out of my house alone.
9. _____ I feel relaxed and in control of myself.
10. _____ I have spells of terror or panic.
11. _____ I feel afraid in open spaces or in the streets.
12. _____ I feel afraid I will faint in public.
13. _____ I am comfortable traveling on buses, subways of trains.
14. _____ I feel nervousness or shakiness inside.
15. _____ I feel comfortable in crowds, such as shopping or at a movie.
16. _____ I feel comfortable when I am left alone.
17. _____ I feel afraid without good reason.
18. _____ Due to my fears, I unreasonably avoid certain animals, objects or situations.
19. _____ I get upset easily or feel panicky unexpectedly.
20. _____ My hands, arms or legs shake or tremble.
21. _____ Due to my fears, I avoid social situations, whenever possible.
22. _____ I experience sudden attacks of panic which catch me by surprise.
23. _____ I feel generally anxious.
24. _____ I am bothered by dizzy spells.
25. _____ Due to my fears, I avoid being alone, whenever possible.

1,6,7,9,13,15,16

Westhuis, D., & Thyer, B. A. (1989). Development and validation of the Clinical Anxiety Scale: A rapid assessment instrument for clinical practice. *Educational and Psychological Measurement, 49,* 153–163.

CES-D SCALE

Description

Developed by the staff at the Center for Epidemiologic Studies, National Institute of Mental Health, the CES-D Scale (see Figure 12.3) is a brief self-report scale designed to measure depressive symptomatology in the general population (Radloff, 1977). It was developed from previously existing scales and was designed not to distinguish primary depressive disorders from secondary depression or subtypes of depression but to identify the presence and severity of depressive symptomatology for epidemiologic research, needs assessment, and screening (Radloff & Locke, 1986).

Psychometric Data

This depression scale has been found to have high internal consistency (.85 in the general population and .90 in the patient sample) and acceptable test–retest stability. The CES-D scores discriminate well between psychiatric inpatient and general population samples and moderately well among patient groups with varying levels of severity. The scale has excellent concurrent validity, and substantial evidence exists of its construct validity (Radloff, 1977).

Availability

The CES-D Scale is in the public domain and may be used without copyright permission. The Epidemiology and Psychopathology Research Branch is interested, however, in receiving copies of research reports that have utilized the instrument.

Scoring

Because the CES-D is a 20-item scale, it is easily scored. Responses are weighted 0 for "Rarely or none of the time" to 3 for "Most of the time." Items 4, 8, 12, and 16 are reverse scored (given a 3 for "Rarely" and 0 for "Most"). The range of possible scores is 0 to 60. High scores indicate the presence and persistence of depressive symptoms.

For Further Reference

Chapleski, E. E., Lamphere, J. K., Kaczynski, R., Lictenberg, P. A., & Dwyer, J. W. (1997). Structure of a depression measure among American Indian elders: Confirmatory factor analysis of the CES-D Scale. *Research on Aging, 19,* 462–485.

FIGURE 12.3 | CES-D SCALE

CES-D Scale

Circle the number for each statement which best describes how often you felt or behaved this way—during the past week

	Rarely or None of the Time (Less than 1 Day)	Some or a Little of the Time (1–2 Days)	Occasionally or a Moderate Amount of Time (3–4 Days)	Most or All of the Time (5–7 Days)
DURING THE PAST WEEK:				
1. I was bothered by things that usually don't bother me	____	____	____	____
2. I did not feel like eating; my appetite was poor	____	____	____	____
3. I felt that I could not shake off the blues even with help from my family or friends	____	____	____	____
4. I felt that I was just as good as other people	____	____	____	____
5. I had trouble keeping my mind on what I was doing	____	____	____	____
6. I felt depressed	____	____	____	____
7. I felt that everything I did was an effort	____	____	____	____
8. I felt hopeful about the future	____	____	____	____
9. I thought my life had been a failure	____	____	____	____
10. I felt fearful	____	____	____	____
11. My sleep was restless	____	____	____	____
12. I was happy	____	____	____	____
13. I talked less than usually	____	____	____	____
14. I felt lonely	____	____	____	____
15. People were unfriendly	____	____	____	____
16. I enjoyed life	____	____	____	____
17. I had crying spells	____	____	____	____
18. I felt sad	____	____	____	____
19. I felt that people disliked me	____	____	____	____
20. I could not get "going"	____	____	____	____

Source: Courtesy Department of Health and Human Services.

Chung, H., Teresi, J. H., Guarnaccia, P., Myers, B. S., Holmes, D., Bobrowitz, T., Eimicke, J. P., & Ferran, E. (2003). Depressive symptoms and psychiatric distress in low income Asian and Latino primary care patients: Prevalence and recognition. *Community Mental Health Journal, 39*(1), 33–46.

Kolomer, S. R., McCallion, P., & Janicki, M. P. (2002). African-American grandmother carers of children with disabilities: Predictors of depressive symptoms. *Journal of Gerontological Social Work, 37*(3/4), 45–63.

Lewis, R. J., Derlega, V. J., Berndt, A., Morris, L. M., & Rose, S. (2001). An empirical analysis of stressors for gay men and lesbians. *Journal of Homosexuality, 42*(1), 63–88.

Lyness, J. M., Noel, T. K., Cox, C., King, D. A., Conwell, Y., Caine, E. D. (1997). Screening for depression in elderly primary care patents: A comparison of the Center for Epidemiologic Studies Depression Scale and the Geriatric Depression Scale. *Archives of Internal Medicine, 157,* 449–454.

Prescott, C. A., McArdle, J. J., Hishinuma, E. S., Johnson, R. C., Miyamoto, R. H., Andrade, N. N., Edman, J. L., Makini, G. K., Nahulu, L. B., Yuen, N. Y., & Carlton, B. S. (1998). Prediction of major depression and dysthymia from CES-D scores among ethnic minority adolescents. *Journal of the American Academy of Child and Adolescent Psychiatry, 37,* 495–503.

Radloff, L. S. (1977). The CES-D Scale: A self-report depression scale for research in the general population. *Applied Psychological Measurement, 3*(1), 385–401.

Radloff, L. S., & Locke, B. Z. (1986). The Community Mental Health Assessment Survey and the CES-D Scale. In M. M. Weissman, J. K. Myers, & C. E. Ross (Eds.), *Community surveys of psychiatric disorders.* New Brunswick, NJ: Rutgers.

Simoni, J. M., & Oritz, M. Z. (2003). Mediational models of spirituality and depressive symptomatology among HIV-positive Puerto Rican women. *Cultural Diversity and Ethnic Minority Psychology, 9*(1), 3–15.

THE HOPE SCALE

Description

In the last 30 years, most scholars have conceptualized hope as a unidimensional construct that centers on an overall perception that goals can be met (Snyder et al., 1991). Many writers have used the concept of hope and its absence in individuals to explain diverse behavior, including physical health and psychopathology. The Hope Scale (see Figure 12.4) is based on the idea that hope is not dichotomous (present or absent). Rather, individuals should have varying degrees of hope. Snyder et al. view hope as composed of two goal–appraisal components—agency and pathways. The agency component is characterized by a willful sense of determination and energy to meet goals. The pathways component reflects an individual's perception of available routes by which a goal might be attained. Twelve items make up the Hope Scale; four items deal with the agency component, four with pathways, and four are constructed to be distractive—to make the overall intent of the scale less obvious.

FIGURE 12.4 | THE HOPE SCALE

The Hope Scale

Directions: Read each item carefully. Using the scale shown below, please select the number that best describes YOU and put that number in the blank provided.

1 = Definitely false   3 = Mostly true
2 = Mostly false   4 = Definitely true

_____ 1. I can think of many ways to get out of a jam.
_____ 2. I energetically pursue my goals.
_____ 3. I feel tired most of the time.
_____ 4. There are lots of ways around any problem.
_____ 5. I am easily downed in an argument.
_____ 6. I can think of many ways to get the things in life that are most important to me.
_____ 7. I worry about my health.
_____ 8. Even when others get discouraged, I know I can find a way to solve the problem.
_____ 9. My past experiences have prepared me well for my future.
_____ 10. I've been pretty successful in life.
_____ 11. I usually find myself worrying about something.
_____ 12. I meet the goals that I set for myself.

Source: From Journal of Personality and Social Psychology, 1991, 60, 570–585. Copyright © 1991 by the American Psychological Association. Reprinted with permission.

Psychometric Data

Cronbach's alphas ranged from .74 to .84 on the total scale. For the Agency subscale, alphas ranged from .71 to .76, and from .63 to .80 on the Pathways subscale. Test–retest reliability has been shown to be .73 over an 8-week interval and .76 and .82 over 10-week intervals in two samples. In terms of convergent validity, the Hope Scale correlated .60 and .50 with optimism as measured by the Life Orientation Test (LOT); .55 and .54 with the Generalized Expectancy for Success Scale; –.51 with the Hopelessness Scale; and –.42 with the Beck Depression Inventory. Factor analyses revealed that the theory-based components of agency and pathways were distinguishable. Persons in psychological treatment had lower scores than college students. Men and women tend to have virtually identical scores across various samples.

Availability

This instrument has been reproduced in Snyder et al. (1991) and Babyak, Snyder, and Yoshinobu (1993). Correspondence should be sent to C. R. Snyder, Department of Psychology, 305 Fraser Hall, University of Kansas, Lawrence, KS 66045.

Scoring

Responses to the distracter items 3, 5, 7, and 11 are ignored. Items 1, 4, 6, and 8 compose the Pathways subscale; the Agency subscale is composed of items 2, 9, 10, and 12. There are no reverse scored items on the two subscales.

For Further Reference

Hinton-Nelson, M. D., Roberts, M. C., & Snyder, C. R. (1996). Early adolescents exposed to violence: Hope and vulnerability to victimization. *American Journal of Orthopsychiatry, 66,* 346–353.

Horton, T. V., & Wallander, J. L. (2001). Hope and social support as resilience factors against psychological distress of mothers who care for children with chronic physical conditions. *Rehabilitation Psychology, 46*(4), 382–399.

Snyder, C. R., Harris, C., Anderson, J. R., Holleran, S. A., Irving, L. M., Sigmon, S. T., Yoshinobu, L., Gibb, J. U., Langelle, C., & Harney, P. (1991). The will and the ways: Development and validation of an individual-differences measure of hope. *Journal of Personality and Social Psychology, 60*(4), 570–585.

Snyder, C. R., Shorey, H. S., Cheavens, J., Pulvers, K. M., Adams, V. H., & Wiklund, C. (2002). Hope and academic success in college. *Journal of Educational Psychology, 94*(4), 820–826.

Snyder, C. R., Sympson, S. C., Ybasco, F. C., Borders, T. F., Babyak, M. A., & Higgins, R. L. (1996). Development and validation of the State Hope Scale. *Journal of Personality and Social Psychology, 70,* 321–335.

Steed, L. G. (2002). A psychometric comparison of four measures of hope and optimism. *Educational and Psychological Measurement, 62*(3), 466–482.

Tennen, H., Affleck, G., & Tennen, R. (2002). Clipped feathers: The theory and measurement of hope. *Psychological Inquiry, 13*(4), 311–317.

ROSENBERG SELF-ESTEEM SCALE

Description

The Rosenberg Self-Esteem Scale (see Figure 12.5) was originally developed on a sample of over 5,000 high school juniors and seniors from 10 randomly selected schools in New York state. A query in *Social Science Citation Index* produced close to 1,300 citations for Rosenberg's instrument—making it the most popular measure of global self-esteem and prompting Blascovich and Tomaka (1991) to observe that "it is the standard with which developers of other measures usually seek convergence" (p. 120).

Psychometric Data

Fleming and Courtney (1984) have reported a Cronbach alpha of .88 and test–retest correlations of .82 with a 1-week interval. Rosenberg (1965) presented a great deal of data on the construct validity of this measure.

FIGURE 12.5 | ROSENBERG SELF-ESTEEM SCALE

Rosenberg Self-Esteem Scale

Instructions:

BELOW IS A LIST OF STATEMENTS DEALING WITH YOUR GENERAL FEELINGS ABOUT YOURSELF. IF YOU <u>AGREE</u> WITH THE STATEMENT, CIRCLE <u>A</u>. IF YOU <u>STRONGLY AGREE</u>, CIRCLE <u>SA</u>. IF YOU <u>DISAGREE</u>, CIRCLE <u>D</u>. IF YOU <u>STRONGLY DISAGREE</u>, CIRCLE <u>SD</u>.

	Strongly Agree	Agree	Dis- agree	Strongly Disagree
(1) On the whole, I am satisfied with myself.	SA	A	D	SD
(2) At times I think I am no good at all.	SA	A	D	SD
(3) I feel that I have a number of good qualities.	SA	A	D	SD
(4) I am able to do things as well as most other people.	SA	A	D	SD
(5) I feel I do not have much to be proud of.	SA	A	D	SD
(6) I certainly feel useless at times.	SA	A	D	SD
(7) I feel that I'm a person of worth, at least on an equal plane with others.	SA	A	D	SD
(8) I wish I could have more respect for myself.	SA	A	D	SD
(9) All in all, I am inclined to feel that I am a failure.	SA	A	D	SD
(10) I take a positive attitude toward myself.	SA	A	D	SD

Source: Courtesy Morris Rosenberg.

Demo (1985) reported self-esteem scores correlating .55 with the Cooper-smith SEI.

Availability

This scale is in the public domain and may be used without securing permission.

Scoring

Using the Likert procedure, responses are assigned a score ranging from 1 to 4. Items 1, 3, 4, 7, and 10 are reverse scored. (For example, in item 1, "On the whole I am satisfied with myself," the "Strongly agree" response is assigned a score of 4 and "Strongly disagree" is assigned a score of 1.) This procedure yields possible total scores ranging from 10 to 40. The higher the score, the higher the self-esteem.

For Further Reference

Bedard, L. E., Pate, K. N., & Roe-Sepowitz, D. E. (2003). A program analysis of Esuba: Helping turn abuse around for inmates. *International Journal of Offender Therapy and Comparative Criminology, 47*(5), 597–607.

Blascovich, J., & Tomaka, J. (1991). Measures of self-esteem. In J. P. Robinson, P. Shaver, & L. Wrightsman (Eds.). *Measures of personality and social psychological attitudes*. New York: Academic Press.

Chen, E., Touyz, S. W., Beumont, P. J., Fairburn, C. G., Griffiths, R., Butow, P., Russell, J., Schotte, D. E., Gertler, R., & Basten, C. (2003). Comparison of group and individual cognitive-behavioral therapy for patients with bulimia nervosa. *International Journal of Eating Disorders, 33*(3), 241–254, discussion 155–156.

Dymek, M. P., Le Grange, D., Neven, K., & Alverdy, J. (2002). Quality of life after gastric bypass surgery: A cross-sectional study. *Obesity Research, 10*(11), 1135–1142.

Rosenberg, M. (1965). *Society and the adolescent self-image*. Princeton, NJ: Princeton University Press.

Schmitz, N. Kugler, J., & Rollnik, J. (2003). On the relation between neuroticism, self-esteem, and depression: Results from the National Comorbidity Survey. *Comprehensive Psychiatry, 44*(3), 169–176.

ADULT-ADOLESCENT PARENTING INVENTORY

Description

The Adult-Adolescent Parenting Inventory (AAPI; see Figure 12.6) is designed to provide professionals with a way to assess current parenting and child-rearing attitudes of adolescents, prospective parents, foster parents, and prospective employees of child caring staff (i.e., residential care staff and volunteers). It can also be used to determine if any changes have resulted from parenting education to high risk and abusive parents. The AAPI indicates degrees of agreement and disagreement with maladaptive parenting behaviors and can categorize respondents into those with low, medium, or high risk for abusive and neglecting behaviors. The constructs on which it is based are inappropriate parental expectations, lack of an empathic awareness of children's needs, beliefs in the use and value of corporal punishment, parent–child role reversal, and oppressing children's power and independence. The AAPI is composed of 40 items and its developer estimates that 12 to 17 minutes, on average, are taken to complete the form.

Psychometric Data

The AAPI-2 has been field-tested in 53 agencies from 23 different states in an effort to re-norm and validate it. The five constructs (identified above) have been confirmed by factor analysis and show Cronbach's alpha of .80 or higher. The AAPI has been found to have good discriminatory validity in being able to discriminate between the parenting attitudes of known child abusers and nonabusive adults and also between abused and nonabused adolescents within the general population.

FIGURE 12.6 | ADULT-ADOLESCENT PARENTING
INVENTORY AAPI

Form A

	Adult-Adolescent Parenting Inventory (AAPI)				
	Strongly Agree	Agree	Un-certain	Dis-agree	Strongly Disagree
1. Children should keep their feelings to themselves.	SA	A	U	D	SD
2. Children should do what they're told to, when they're told to do it. It's that simple.	SA	A	U	D	SD
3. Parents should be able to confide in their children.	SA	A	U	D	SD
4. Children need to be allowed freedom to explore their world in safety.	SA	A	U	D	SD
5. Spanking teaches children right from wrong.	SA	A	U	D	SD
6. The sooner children learn to feed and dress themselves and use the toilet, the better off they will be as adults.	SA	A	U	D	SD
7. Children who are one year old should be able to stay away from things that could harm them.	SA	A	U	D	SD
8. Children should be potty trained when they are ready and not before.	SA	A	U	D	SD
9. A certain amount of fear is necessary for children to respect their parents.	SA	A	U	D	SD
10. Good children always obey their parents.	SA	A	U	D	SD
11. Children should know what their parents need without being told.	SA	A	U	D	SD
12. Children should be taught to obey their parents at all times.	SA	A	U	D	SD
13. Children should be aware of ways to comfort their parents after a hard days work.	SA	A	U	D	SD
14. Parents who nurture them-selves make better parents.	SA	A	U	D	SD
15. It's OK to spank as a last resort.	SA	A	U	D	SD
16. "Because I said so!" is the only reason parents need to give.	SA	A	U	D	SD
17. Parents need to push their children to do better.	SA	A	U	D	SD
18. Time-out is an effective way to discipline children.	SA	A	U	D	SD
19. Children have a responsibility to please their parents.	SA	A	U	D	SD

1-99   AATA-2

Availability

The AAPI is protected by copyright. You will need to purchase instruments, the manual, profile and worksheets from Family Development Resources, P.O. Box 982350, Park City, Utah 84098, 1-800-688-5822 or fdr@nuturingparenting.com.

Scoring

The AAPI is available in two forms, A and B. Scoring stencils are used with the completed instruments to develop parenting profiles. The AAPI-2 is also available on CD-ROM so that clients or subjects can respond directly on a computer; worksheets and parenting profiles are then generated detailing the strengths and weaknesses of an individual's parenting practices.

For Further Reference

Bavolek, S. J. (1989). Assessing and teaching high-risk parenting attitudes. *Early Child Development and Care, 42*, 99–112.

Bavolek, S. J. (1984). An innovative program for reducing abusive parent–child interactions. *Child Resource World Review, 2*, 6–24.

Culp, A. M., Culp, R. E., Blankemeyer, M., & Passmark, L. (1998). Parent education home visitation program: Adolescent and nonadolescent mother comparison after six months of intervention. *Infant Mental Health Journal, 19*(2), 111–123.

Fox, R. A., Baisch, M. J., Goldberg, B. D., & Hochmuth, M. C. (1987). Parenting attitudes of pregnant adolescents. *Psychological Reports, 61*, 403–406.

Harm, N. J., Thompson, P. J., & Chambers, H. (1998). The effectiveness of parent education for substance abusing women offenders. *Alcoholism Treatment Quarterly, 16*(3), 63–77.

Harrison, K. (1997). Parental training for incarcerated fathers: Effects on attitudes, self-esteem, and children's self-perceptions. *Journal of Social Psychology, 137*(5), 588–593.

Marshall, E., Buckner, E., Perkins, J., Lowry, J., Hyatt, C., Campbell, C., & Helms, D. (1996). Effects of a child abuse prevention unit in health classes in four schools. *Journal of Community Health Nursing, 13*, 107–122.

Thompson, P. J., & Harm, N. J. (2000). Parenting from prison: Helping children and mothers. *Issues in Comprehensive Pediatric Nursing, 23*(2), 61–81.

Woods, E. R., Obeidallah-Davis, D., Sherry, M. K., Ettinger, S. L., Simms, E. U., Dixon, R. R., Missal, S. M., & Cox, J. E. (2003). The parenting project for teen mothers: The impact of a nurturing curriculum on adolescent parenting skills and life hassles. *Ambulatory Pediatrics, 3*(5), 240–205.

Questions For Class Discussion

1. Think about the instruments contained in this chapter. Brainstorm possible new uses for each of them. For example, could the Child Abuse Potential Inventory be used in conjunction with a parent education intervention geared toward teen mothers?

Could it be used as a screening mechanism when hiring new child care workers in residential agencies and group homes? What uses might the Clinical Anxiety Scale have?

2. Discuss the advantages and disadvantages of developing a new instrument versus spending effort to search for one that may not even exist. What would be the major determinants affecting your decision?

3. Choose an instrument from this chapter and brainstorm new ways to help document its validity.

Mini-Projects: Experiencing Evaluation Firsthand

1. Identify an instrument and read one or more articles on the instrument. Write a short paper on its development, as well as the reliability and validity that you would expect it to have if you were to use it in a program evaluation. (Be sure to identify the study's population and how you intend to utilize the instrument.)

2. With a partner, attempt to create a scale measuring some concept of your choice. Present the scale to the class for a discussion of its face and content validity.

3. Using either a scale that you have developed or one with known psychometrics, collect a small sample of data from your classmates or others. Enter the data into a computer with statistical analysis software so that you can compute the scale's internal consistency. Discuss what you found and possible explanations for the results.

4. Using a computer database or Internet search engine, search for a scale that you could use in a project of your choosing. Be sure to identify the concept the scale should measure and the population with which it would be used. List your search efforts: What key terms or concepts did you search under? What databases? What years?

DATA ANALYSIS

CHAPTER 13

WHAT DOES IT MEAN TO ANALYZE DATA?

Whether you are conducting a needs assessment, a process evaluation, or an outcome evaluation, once you have gathered all the information that you intend to collect, the next step is to examine it. This phase of the evaluation process is not unlike the experience of a paleontologist who walks along a dry riverbed and detects a small, oddly shaped fragment. As the loose sand is brushed away, more and more of the object is revealed until it is no longer a tiny fragment of fossil, but the fossilized femur of a dinosaur. A little more excavation and another piece is found and then another, until the whole skeleton is uncovered.

What evaluators seek is very similar—we want to be able to assemble bits of data into a logical structure, a meaningful pattern that gives us insight into the workings of a program that previously may never have been exposed to scientific scrutiny. Just as paleontologists do not usually find a complete skeleton, evaluators must often be content with data that are incomplete. Sometimes we must take surrogate and even tangential bits of data and construct information from them.

The purpose of data analysis is to answer the questions that were the catalyst for the investigation. If there were hypotheses to be tested, analysis of data informs as to whether the hypotheses are supported by the data. We condense information (sometimes massive amounts of data) hoping that meaningful patterns, trends, or relationships will emerge.

Whether you will be reporting on a needs assessment or a program evaluation, it is very likely that at some point you will need to use one or more statistical procedures. At times, for instance, you will want to conclude that there were statistically significant differences between pre- and posttests or between the control and intervention groups. If the differences between groups are markedly different (say 45 percent of those in the control group are successful compared to 83 percent of those in the intervention group), it may be possible to conclude that the intervention was an unqualified success, and perhaps no one will challenge it. However, what if the intervention group had only 20 participants and the control group was based on scores from 200 different individuals? Would you still feel secure about concluding that the intervention was an unqualified success? In computing a probability level, statistical procedures take into account the number of individuals and the variation in their scores. Most evaluators cannot determine whether observed differences between groups are statistically significant by visual observation and mental calculations alone.

The argument for using statistical procedures in analyzing data is that data coupled with the appropriate research design can provide objective evidence that the program was or was not successful—information not dependent on the evaluator's whims or judgment. Avoiding the use of statistical procedures when they are needed is not only amateurish but also suggests incompetence. Statistical procedures lend credibility and professionalism to your final report. Even though your audience may not understand what a t-test is or how to compute a chi-square, your usage of these statistical procedures helps to determine if differences are "real."

DATA ANALYSIS AND THE COMPUTER

Virtually all analysis of data these days is done on the computer. Almost no one uses a calculator and follows a formula like a secret recipe to calculate statistics of interest. Most of the software used for statistical procedures has become genuinely user friendly; and because so much of it is menu driven, even novice users do not find that it presents much of a problem. Universities usually have a great variety of statistical software programs available for students and faculty. You may find, however, that individual professors may have a particular preference for one, like the Statistical Package for the Social Sciences (SPSS), over another, like the Statistical Analysis System (SAS). Student versions of these programs are often available in university bookstores. The spreadsheet program Microsoft Excel can also produce an assortment of useful statistics and it is often already installed on most personal computers and laptops.

Even if your agency cannot afford to buy a statistical software program for program evaluation, help is available on the Internet. (See Box 13.1.) Professor John Pezullo at Georgetown University has constructed and is maintaining a web page of over 600 links and 380 calculating (interactive) statistical pages that allow you to perform a tremendous number of statistical procedures without even purchasing software. (See the first address in Box 13.1.) Some of the links

WEB LINKS FOR STATISTICAL COMPUTATIONS

http://members.aol.com/johnp71/javastat.html (A mother lode of sites)

http://www.statsoftinc.com/textbook/esc1.html (Electronic Statistics Textbook)

are instructional and present tutorials and demonstrations. Others guide and help you to select the right statistical test given the level of measurement of your variables. Still others allow you to graph your data and compute an extremely rich array of statistics—not only those discussed in this chapter but also those taught to students in intermediate and advanced statistics classes.

Before buying a statistical software program, you might want to at least browse through the websites listed in Box 13.1.

UNIVARIATE ANALYSIS

Univariate analysis looks at one variable at a time. There are several reasons for looking at variables individually. First, you might want to know how many respondents with a certain characteristic have been obtained. With the variable of marital status, you may want to know how many questionnaires divorced respondents completed. Examining variables one at a time can sometimes indicate that a certain group of individuals was inadvertently missed or that the range of responses was restricted (all of the possible responses were not represented). Univariate analysis helps the evaluator develop a "feel" for the data. Typically, the data are arranged in either ascending or descending order to facilitate finding "gaps" or missing values. Univariate analysis begins the process of making sense of data collected for a program evaluation.

All too frequently, evaluators who have only a cursory knowledge of analysis think they have analyzed the data when all they have done is to report what data were obtained. We once came across an "evaluation" of a program that consisted of more than *30 pages* of data that looked something like that in Table 13.1.

The pretest and posttest values were average scores on a 5-point scale where 1 = poor, 3 = fair, and 5 = great. Respondents had been asked to evaluate training that they had received at a series of workshops held around the state. The data were arranged by date and locality in which the training was provided. Although the "evaluator" had listed the questions used in the final evaluation report, there was no information on the reliability or validity of any scale(s) contained on the instrument.

Not only are 30 pages of such data tedious to wade through, it is also difficult to know what to conclude. For instance, are the increases shown in Table 13.1 (e.g., Q2 increases from 3.20 to 3.60 under the column headed

TABLE 13.1 | EVALUATION SUMMARY

	Parents		Professional Staff	
	Pretest $n = 62$	Posttest $n = 47$	Pretest $n = 32$	Posttest $n = 24$
Q1	3.24	4.54	3.50	4.30
Q2	3.20	3.60	3.80	4.50
Q3	3.70	3.90	3.50	4.20
Q4	2.80	3.10	2.00	2.30
Q5	2.50	2.22	2.00	3.30
Q6	2.30	2.80	2.22	2.45
Q7	2.60	4.70	3.40	4.00
Q8	3.40	4.00	4.40	5.00
Q9	2.10	1.75	4.50	2.60

Parents) statistically significant? If they are not statistically significant, then they are not really increases at all but represent scores that are essentially equivalent. What the "evaluator" did not realize is that it is the *overall* scores and not the item-by-item scores on an instrument that should be used for analysis. It is the *collection of items* that makes an instrument reliable. Any one item may or may not be useful for detecting significant change or improvement. In this instance, the evaluator concluded (apparently by visual inspection) that the training increased participants' knowledge "in all areas—indicating that the training sessions were effective." This conclusion could very well be unwarranted. The evaluator does not know (nor does the reader of the evaluation report) if participants' scores were significantly improved. This information can only be learned when a statistical test is employed. Further, unless we know more about the instrument, it is entirely possible that it was unreliable. Perhaps it would show improvement even when another more reliable instrument would not. Note, also, the loss of subjects at posttest. Could a loss of subjects have an effect on the findings?

Analysis is more than displaying the responses or data that were obtained. Look, for instance, at the example of data displayed in Figure 13.1. These data look as if they could be test results of some kind. However, until we know more about the data, it is extremely difficult to interpret what these numbers may indicate. Could these be the ages of persons in a nursing home? The weights of a class of fifth graders? The IQ scores of children enrolled in a remedial math class? Assume that they are the results of a final examination in an undergraduate research class. Knowing this much, we now may develop a strategy for trying to understand the data. We might, for instance, array the data in terms of the highest and lowest scores (Figure 13.2).

FIGURE 13.1 | DATA DISPLAY

88	94	66	73	81
77	78	65	97	69
73	90	90	94	82
75	87	79	99	74
86	91	75	85	91

FIGURE 13.2 | A DESCENDING ARRAY OF SCORES

99
97
94
94
91
91
90
90
88
87
86
85
82
81
79
78
77
75
75
74
73
73
69
66
65

TABLE 13.2 | FREQUENCY DISTRIBUTION OF CLIENT RATINGS OF QUALITY OF PROGRAM

(*"How would you rate the quality of our outpatient program?"*)

Rating	Frequency	Percent	Cumulative Percent
4 Excellent	173	33.0	33.0
3 Good	254	48.4	81.4
2 Fair	80	15.2	96.6
1 Poor	18	3.4	100.0
Total	525	100.0	

Frequency Distributions

Evaluators usually start analyzing their data by requesting ordered arrays of the data one variable at a time. These are called **frequency distributions** because for each value that appears, the computer counts how many times (or how frequently) it occurs. Note in the example in Table 13.2 that the data are *not* arrayed based on the largest frequencies but in terms of the highest (Excellent) to lowest (Poor) ratings. The data are shown in descending order. In this example, you can also see that the frequency distribution provides percentages and cumulative percentages.

From even a cursory glance, we can determine that very few respondents (about 3 percent) gave the program a poor rating. In fact, almost half of the respondents gave the program a good rating. By combining those who rated the program either "Good" or "Excellent," we could determine that 81 percent of respondents were pleased with the program. This statistic has already been computed for us under the cumulative percent column.

In Table 13.3, you can see how a frequency distribution (univariate analysis) can help you to understand who has been included and who may be missing from your sample. This example shows many more older than younger respondents. Note that there are no respondents between the ages of 22 and 30. In fact, about half of the subjects are older than 60. If the clients in your program are known to be much younger, a distribution like this may suggest that the sample is biased—that the younger clients were not included to the degree one might expect.

Besides wanting to understand who responded and who did not (the makeup of your sample), another reason for looking at each variable individually is to determine if any errors were made in preparing or recording the data. This would be immediately obvious, in Table 13.3, for instance, if you knew that there were no 15-year-olds in the outpatient program. The 15-year-old listed there may have been a 51-year-old for whom the digits were transposed. Before further analysis is done with this variable, the respondent's age should be verified.

TABLE 13.3	FREQUENCY DISTRIBUTION OF RESPONDENTS' AGES		
Age	Frequency	Percent	Cumulative Percent
15	1	1.8	1.8
22	2	3.6	5.5
30	1	1.8	7.3
32	1	1.8	9.1
34	2	3.6	12.7
38	1	1.8	14.5
39	1	1.8	16.4
42	1	5.5	18.2
43	1	1.8	20.0
44	3	5.5	25.5
48	2	3.6	29.1
52	3	5.5	34.5
57	2	3.6	38.2
58	4	7.3	45.5
61	3	5.5	50.9
64	2	3.6	54.5
65	5	5.5	63.6
66	2	3.6	67.3
67	2	3.6	70.9
68	2	3.6	74.5
70	5	9.0	83.6
71	2	3.6	87.3
72	3	5.5	92.7
75	3	5.5	98.2
81	1	1.8	100.0

Measures of Central Tendency

At times an evaluator is limited to univariate analysis. On these occasions, frequency distributions provide arrays for understanding the range of scores and the number of cases or respondents associated with each value.

Another advantage of having a computer produce frequency distributions is that the evaluator can request measures of central tendency such as the mean, median, or mode. The **mean** is the arithmetic average of scores. It is useful for understanding the "typical" case or client. However, the mean can easily be distorted when there are a few extreme scores.

By simply computing a frequency distribution of the data from Figure 13.1, we can easily identify that the highest score was 99 and that the lowest was 65. Further, if we knew that grades were awarded according to the following scheme,

$$A = 100 - 91$$
$$B = 90 - 81$$
$$C = 80 - 71$$
$$D = 70 - 61$$

then Figure 13.3 informs us that there are six As, eight Bs, eight Cs, and three Ds on this particular test.

FIGURE 13.3 | DISTRIBUTION OF GRADES

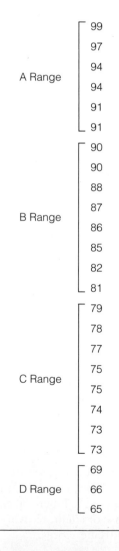

| TABLE 13.4 | SMALL SAMPLE DISTRIBUTION OF AGES |

Age	Frequency
17	1
18	1
19	1
20	1 < Median = 20
21	1
22	1
83	1 < Mean = 28.57

In Table 13.3, the mean is 56.96 years if the 15-year-old is a legitimate respondent, but 57.62 if the respondent is coded as a 51-year-old. However, the **median,** as the middle value in a frequency distribution, remains unchanged at 61. The median position is that value halfway between the top and the bottom. Because there are 55 respondents in Table 13.3, we can locate the median by counting down from the top to the 28th case or from the bottom up to the 28th case. The **mode** is the most common category or value. In Table 13.3, there are two modes, 65 and 70. The data would be described as being bimodal.

The mean is easily distorted in the presence of extreme values. In the next example (Table 13.4), note that the mean of 28.57 years is not representative of the bulk of the respondents. In fact, only one of them is older than 28, and that individual is considerably older. When data are obviously skewed in a small sample like that in Table 13.4, the median provides a more accurate portrait than the mean.

Standard Deviation and Range

In addition to the mean, median, and mode, another univariate statistic, the standard deviation, should be included when preparing tables and reporting data. The **standard deviation** is a measure of variability that provides information about how much scores tend to differ from each other and the mean.

In normally distributed data, where the mean and median are situated close together on a bell-shaped curve, 68 percent of the observations fall within one standard frequency of the mean—half of these (34 percent) fall above and half (34 percent) fall below the mean. Ninety-five percent of the observations fall within two standard deviations of the mean, and 99.7 percent fall within three standard deviations. The standard deviation is small when the deviations from the mean are small and larger when the observed values tend to be far from the mean.

TABLE 13.5 | SAMPLE OF CLIENTS' AGES

Age	Frequency	Percent
20	1	10
27	2	20
28	1	10
30	1	10
33	1	10
36	1	10
39	1	10
41	2	20
Total	10	100

In Table 13.5, the standard deviation is 7.0, and the mean is 32.2 whereas in Table 13.4 the standard deviation is 24. Do you understand why the standard deviation is greater in Table 13.4?

Means, medians, and standard deviations are not interpreted easily if you do not know the theoretical range of possible scores that could be obtained with the instrument you are using (another reason for becoming familiar with the literature before you begin an evaluation). The **range** is, of course, the distance between the lowest value and the highest value. The theoretical range is the distance between lowest and highest possible scores that an instrument is designed to measure.

BIVARIATE ANALYSIS

Once you have edited the data, corrected any mistakes, and learned what you can from the univariate analysis, you are ready to begin looking at variables two at a time. This process is called **bivariate analysis** of data. Evaluators look at variables two at a time to test hypotheses or to examine the strength of associations.

Before starting our discussion of bivariate analysis, however, the issue of sample size arises. If your samples are very small (i.e., fewer than 10 subjects), then it cannot be assumed that the population is normally distributed and thus you must use **nonparametric statistical procedures** (see the Box 13.2). With the exception of this brief mention, the balance of this chapter will focus on statistical techniques for analyzing larger data sets and which assume that the observations are independent and randomly selected.

We start our discussion of bivariate analysis with an independent variable measured at the *nominal* level and will use it to understand a dependent variable

NONPARAMETRIC STATISTICAL PROCEDURES

Nonparametric techniques are used not only when the research involves small samples but also when the data consist of ranks (instead of interval data), when positive and negative signs are used instead of numerical values, and when the data are gravely skewed. These techniques must be used when the data do not appear to be normally distributed—indications of this could be multiple outliers and when there is more than one mode.

Although this chapter primarily discusses parametric statistical procedures, note that for each of these techniques there are parallel methods for use with nonparametric data. For instance, the Mann-Whitney U Test and Wilcoxon Rank-Sum Test correspond to the *t*-test for independent samples. The Wilcoxon Matched Pairs Signed-Rank Test is similar to the paired samples *t*-test; the Spearman rank correlation coefficient is the equivalent of the Pearson correlation coefficient; and the Kruskal-Wallis Test is the nonparametric version of one-way analysis of variance. A classic reference on these statistical procedures is *Nonparametric Statistics for the Behavioral Sciences* by Sidney Siegel and N. J. Castellan (1988).

measured at the *interval* level. Specifically, in this section we discuss the *t*-test and analysis of variance procedures. This is only a quick overview, however; students who need more explanation may wish to consult an introductory statistics textbook.

Paired Samples *t*-test

Suppose that an AIDS educator has designed an instrument to evaluate the impact of her presentations to senior high students. Because her instrument produces interval data (with a theoretical range of 15 to 75) and she has one group with two administrations of the same instrument (pretest and posttest), the **paired samples *t*-test** is the appropriate statistical procedure. This form of the *t*-test matches Joe Student's score at pretest with his score at posttest. Simply looking at the scores arrayed in a frequency distribution would not help the evaluator to conclude that the program participants were more knowledgeable after the educational intervention. The nominal independent variable (pretest or posttest) represents the times when the students were assessed with the instrument.

In Figure 13.4, we can see that at pretest the average score was 50.67 for the class of 30 students. Six weeks later when the educator administered the instrument a second time, scores overall had improved by almost 5 points. The question for the evaluator is whether that increase in average scores was statistically significant.

FIGURE 13.4 | STATISTICS PRODUCED BY SPSS: THE PAIRED-SAMPLES *t*-TEST

	Mean	N	Std. Deviation	Std. Error Mean
Pair Pretest	50.6667	30	13.3115	2.4303
1 Posttest	55.4333	30	11.9732	2.1860

Paired Samples Correlations

	N	Correlation	Sig
Pair 1 VAR00003–VAR00004	30	−.016	.932

Paired Samples Test

	Paired Differences					
				95% Confidence Interval of the Difference		
	Mean	Std. Deviation	Std. Error Mean	Lower	Upper	t
Pair 1 VAR00003–VAR00004	−4.7667	18.0472	3.2950	−11.5056	1.9723	−1.447

Paired Samples Test

	df	Sig (2-tailed)
Pair 1 VAR00003–VAR00004	29	.159

Figure 13.4 also shows the actual *t*-value produced was −1.447 when a paired samples *t*-test was computed. This was, however, not statistically significant ($p = .159$). The AIDS educator now knows that although posttest scores were slightly higher (indicating somewhat more knowledge about the transmission of AIDS), no real or appreciable change in knowledge occurred for the group as a whole.

Note that the printout contains data reported to the nearest one-ten thousandth (e.g., 1/10,000) of a number. It is a good idea when working with these data to *round* these figures. For example, the mean of 50.6667 and the *SD* of 13.3115 can easily be rounded to 50.7 and 13.3. Reporting decimal points beyond a level that is genuinely informative to the reader conveys the pretense of scientific precision without any additional meaning.

See Box 13.3 for more information on statistical significance.

BOX 13.3

A BRIEF NOTE ABOUT STATISTICAL SIGNIFICANCE

How did the evaluator know that a significance level of .159 was not statistically significant? By general agreement in the scientific community, findings that could have occurred 5 or more times in 100 samples ($p > .05$) by chance alone are considered *not* significant. Differences between groups that could have occurred *less than 5 times per 100 samples* ($p < .05$) are regarded as significant because it is not likely that they were produced by chance—in other words, these differences are real and likely could be produced again and again.

When it is critical to reduce the role of chance even lower than 5 times in a 100, the evaluator may use $p < .01$ (1 time per 100) or $p < .001$ (1 time per 1,000) for the criterion by which to determine if findings are statistically significant.

It should be noted that evaluators must not be so focused on statistical significance that they lose sight of clinical significance. That is, regardless of whether clients score a few points better on an instrument at the end of an intervention, did the intervention make their problems more manageable or improve the quality of their lives? If neither clients nor therapists would agree that change was substantial and that improvement had occurred, then statistical significance could be meaningless. This topic is discussed in more detail in the latter part of the chapter.

The *t*-test for Independent Samples

Let's modify our example somewhat and assume that the health educator wanted to beef up the intervention and later compare the new intervention group with a control group that did not receive any information about AIDS. Assume that she wants to use the same instrument (which, you will remember, produces interval level data). For this statistical analysis, she will still use the *t*-test (because there are two groups and the dependent variable is measured at the interval level). However, the exact procedure she will need to use is the **t-test for independent** samples because the comparison draws on two different samples of individuals (the treatment group versus the control group). The type of group (control or intervention) is the nominal level independent variable.

Figure 13.5 shows the results when Holly, the AIDS educator, compared the means of the two groups at pretest to determine if they were equivalent in their knowledge about AIDS before the intervention. As you can see, although the group scheduled to get the intervention scored slightly more than 2 points better than the control group, the differences between the pretest mean scores were not statistically significant ($p = .54$).

You will note that with the independent samples *t*-test, the Levene's Test for Equality of Variances is also computed automatically (with the SPSS software) to determine if the difference in variances reached significant proportions. Because the variances in these two samples were similar ($p = .14$, rounded), that is, not significantly different ($p < .05$), the *t*-test formula for assuming equal variances can be used to derive the best estimate of statistical significance. In reporting

FIGURE 13.5

STATISTICS PRODUCED BY SPSS: THE
INDEPENDENT SAMPLES *t*-TEST

VAR00002	N	Mean	Std. Deviation	Std. Error Mean
Intervention	21	51.5238	10.5623	2.3049
Control Group	33	49.2727	14.5436	2.5317

Independent Samples Test

		Levene's Test for Equality of Variances	
		F	Sig
VAR00003	Equal variances assumed Equal variances not assumed	2.296	.136

		t-test for Equality of Means			
		t	df	Sig (2-tailed)	Mean Difference
VAR00003	Equal variances assumed	.613	52	.543	2.2511
	Equal variances not assumed	.657	50.987	.514	2.2511

		t-test for Equality of Means		
			95% Confidence Interval of the Difference	
		Std. Error Difference	Lower	Upper
VAR00003	Equal variances assumed	3.6724	–5.1180	9.6202
	Equal variances not assumed	3.4238	–4.6224	9.1246

the *t* value and significance level, Holly would use the correct one suggested by Levene's Test. In this case, t = .61 for equivalent variances.

The evaluator would also use the *t*-test for independent samples if she wanted to compare the average posttest scores of the intervention group with the posttest scores of the control group. What if the evaluator wanted to look for significant differences between the control group at pretest and posttest?

FIGURE 13.6 | STATISTICS PRODUCED BY SPSS: ANALYSIS OF VARIANCE

VAR00003

Group	N	Mean	Std. Deviation	Std. Error	95% Confidence Interval for Mean		Minimum	Maximum
					Lower Bound	Upper Bound		
1.00	21	51.5238	10.5623	2.3049	46.7159	56.3317	33.00	70.00
2.00	33	49.2727	14.5436	2.5317	44.1158	54.4297	20.00	73.00
3.00	26	54.8846	14.3926	2.8226	49.0713	60.6979	25.00	72.00
Total	80	51.6875	13.6118	1.5218	48.6583	54.7167	20.00	73.00

ANOVA

VAR00003

	Sum of Squares	df	Mean Squares	F	Sig.
Between Groups	458.750	2	229.375	1.246	.293
Within Groups	14178.437	77	184.136		
Total	14637.188	79			

Which would be the most appropriate: the paired samples or the independent samples t-test? (Hint: it *would not* be the independent samples.)

One-Way Analysis of Variance

If the AIDS educator had *three* groups instead of two *and* interval data, she would not have been able to use t-tests for analysis (t-tests can be used only with two groups). If data on three or more groups had been collected, the AIDS educator would likely have chosen **one-way analysis of variance (ANOVA)** as her statistical tool. One-way analysis of variance is, like the t-test, based on group means.

Suppose that Holly has now taken her intervention to two different schools and has a control group in a third school for three groups. All of the students are in the 11th grade. You can see from the tables in Figure 13.6 that the means of the first two groups (the original intervention group and the control group) have not changed. What is different about this table is the addition of the new intervention group at Willow Creek Independent High. Once again, the evaluator cannot tell if there are significant differences in the average scores by merely looking at group means. The F-test, however, reveals no significant differences ($p > .05$) in the pretests of the three groups even though the Willow

FIGURE 13.7 | CLASSIFICATION OF CLIENTS BY TREATMENT OUTCOME

VAR00001: Treatment Outcome

	Frequency	Percent	Valid Percent	Cumulative Percent
Successful	39	70.9	70.9	70.9
Unsuccessful	16	29.1	29.1	100.0
Total	55	100.0	100.0	

Creek group scored on average 5.5 points more than the control group and 3 points more than the original treatment group. The findings in this particular example tell us that although the mean scores from the three groups are different, they do not vary enough to be statistically significant.

Chi-Square

In the prior illustrations, the dependent variable was measured at the interval level. However, what would the evaluator do if her dependent variable was measured at the *nominal* level? You will remember from our discussion in Chapter 11 that nominal data are categorical variables that can be described by names (e.g., political affiliation, employment status, marital status, ethnic group). Think about how you might judge the success of an intervention measured at the nominal level. Suppose you can cut the data into two groupings: clients who have improved and clients who did not. In such a situation, **chi-square** would be a useful statistical procedure to use.

Assume that you are evaluating a program where numerical scores are not available. However, the staff have a well-established procedure for determining, at the point of closing a case, those clients for whom the intervention was successful and those for whom it was not successful. The director asks you to draw a random sample of clients in the outpatient program and to determine the proportion who have successful outcomes. Examining a sample of 55 cases closed in the past month, you find the information provided in Figure 13.7.

So far, there is only one variable and no bivariate analysis. However, say that you present these findings to the new executive director; and although she is happy that the program appears to be so successful with its clients, she asks if you can determine if the program is differentially effective—whether it is more successful with female clients than with male clients.

If you were to test such a hypothesis using this data, chi-square would be the appropriate statistic to use. The easiest way to compute this statistic is to enter the data into a computer and use the computer to make statistical computations. In the SPSS program, one would punch the "analyze" button and then choose "descriptive statistics" and then "crosstabs." Once the Crosstabs

FIGURE 13.8 | CROSS-TABULATION OF TREATMENT OUTCOME BY GENDER

		Treatment Outcome		
		Unsuccessful	Successful	Total
Gender	Females	5	25	30
	Males	11	14	25
Total		16	39	55

Chi-Square Tests

	Value	df	Asymp. Sig. (2-sided)	Exact Sig. (2-sided)	Exact Sig. (1-sided)	
Pearson Chi-Square	4.939	1	.026			⎤ null hypothesis
Continuity Correction	3.703	1	.054			
Likelihood Ratio	4.996	1	.025			
Fisher's Exact Test				.038	.027 ◄	directional hypothesis
N of Valid Cases	55					

Note: 0 cells (.0%) have expected count less than 5. The minimum expected count is 7.27.

screen pops up, it is then necessary to indicate which variables you want to be analyzed.

The tables shown in Figure 13.8 were produced with the SPSS crosstabs procedure, where the dependent variable (treatment outcome) was entered as the column variable and gender as the row variable. Although the males appeared to be a little less successful than the females, there were also fewer males—making it difficult to tell by visual inspection what is going on. The Pearson chi-square of 4.939 is, however, statistically significant ($p = .026$).

Note that the correct significance level to report depends on whether you are testing the null hypothesis or a directional hypothesis. If you were testing the null hypothesis (i.e., women are no more likely to have treatment success than men), the two-sided significance ($p = .038$) would be the correct one to report. If you were testing a directional hypothesis (i.e., women are more likely to have treatment success than men), the one-sided significance level would be reported ($p = .027$).

The table in Figure 13.9 is another presentation of the previous data, but this time the computer was asked to display the percentages going down the columns. This shows more clearly than the frequencies in each of the cells the pattern of females having more success than males. You can see that approximately two-thirds of the females were categorized as treatment successes and two-thirds of the males as treatment failures. The significance levels are not affected by the presentation of the percentages in each cell.

The chi-square statistical procedure can be used if you have three, four, five, or even more categories or groupings. It is possible, for instance, to construct

FIGURE 13.9 | CROSS-TABULATION OF TREATMENT OUTCOME BY GENDER (WITH PERCENTAGES)

| | | | Treatment Outcome | | Total |
			Unsuccessful	Successful	
Gender	Females	Count	5	25	30
		% within Treatment Outcome	31.3%	64.1%	54.5%
	Males	Count	11	14	25
		% within Treatment Outcome	68.8%	35.9%	45.5%
Total		Count	16	39	55
		% within Treatment Outcome	100.0%	100.0%	100.0%

Chi-Square Tests

	Value	df	Asymp. Sig. (2-sided)	Exact Sig. (2-sided)	Exact Sig. (2-sided)
Pearson Chi-Square	4.939[b]	1	.026		
Continuity Correction[a]	3.703	1	.054		
Likelihood Ratio	4.996	1	.025		
Fisher's Exact Test				.038	.027
N of Valid Cases	55				

Notes: a. Computed only for a 2 × 2 table.
b. 0 cells (.0%) have expected count less than 5. The minimum expected count is 7.27.

cross-tabulations where the independent variable has three categories and the dependent variable two categories (or vice versa). This would be known as a 2 by 3 contingency table. Such a table would contain six cells, whereas a 3 by 3 table would contain nine cells.

The only thing to watch for when the cross-tabulation contains many categories is that the chi-square statistic is not accurate when more than 20 percent of the cells have an expected frequency of 5 or less. The crosstabs procedure will automatically inform you if there is a problem with too many cells having expected counts of less than 5. When this does happen, one can choose to increase the sample size or to merge categories. For example, you might have four classifications of employment status (not employed, employed part time, employed full time, and retired). If the sample is small, it might make sense to combine the employed group with those employed part-time and have one employment category instead of two. Or, it may be possible to exclude the retired category if this is a very small cell. Chi-square can also be used with ordinal data. Consider the 5-point Likert scale frequently used in surveys and questionnaires. In some instances, it makes sense to merge the "agree" and "strongly agree" categories into one, and to aggregate the "disagree" and "strongly disagree" into another category, in order to better understand the patterns existing in the data.

Correlations

Sometimes students say that all they want to know about a program is whether the intervention correlated with successful outcomes. They anticipate that a moderate to strong correlation will convince the readers of their evaluation reports that the intervention was worthwhile. In fact, a **correlation** expresses only the amount or degree of linear relationship between two variables. For instance, suppose you conduct a study and find a correlation of .51 between clients' ages and the number of months of sobriety after leaving your program.

Correlations indicate whether two variables are moving in the same direction—if they tend to increase or decrease together. In this example, it is apparent that older clients have longer periods of sobriety and younger ones shorter periods—that's what the correlation means. But what do you do with that information? Refuse to treat younger clients? Is it the clients' maturity that made them successful? It is helpful to keep in mind that correlations do not establish "proof" that one variable caused another. Being older did not "cause" clients to have longer periods of sobriety. In fact, although .51 is a moderately strong correlation, only 26 percent of the **variance** in the dependent variable is explained by the independent variable.(The percentage of the variance explained is found by multiplying the correlation by itself.) Thus, 74 percent of the interaction between the two variables was not explained.

Correlations are the basis on which numerous procedures are based (e.g., calculating the reliability of a new scale). However, correlations are probably only going to be used in an incidental or auxiliary way by most program evaluators simply because they are so limited in what they can reveal. Here are a few examples of what they might show:

- The number of treatment sessions was associated with client satisfaction.
- The number of treatment sessions was associated with reduction in symptoms or symptom severity.
- Length of time in treatment was associated with fewer arrests.

Although correlations are not usually the goal or desired end of a data analysis process for the program evaluator, they can still be useful in understanding data. For example, if you will look back to Figure 13.4, you will find a correlation of .016 between the pretests and posttests. Because correlations run between 0 and 1, a .016 correlation is so close to 0 as to indicate almost no correlation between the average student's pretest score and his or her posttest scores. There was so much fluctuation in the two sets of scores that it is not possible to predict one from the other. This is another piece of information that could help the evaluator to understand why the posttest with a mean score almost five points higher than the pretest was not statistically significant. If, say, all the posttest scores were exactly five points higher than the individual pretest

TABLE 13.6 | SUCCESSFUL OUTCOMES BY GENDER AND LOCATION

	Area 1	Area 2	Area 3	Row Total
Male Clients	23	25	37	85
Successes—Male	20	16	15	51
Percent of Male Clients	(87%)	(64%)	(41%)	(60%)
Female Clients	39	45	31	115
Successes—Female	26	31	18	75
Percent of Female Clients	(67%)	(69%)	(58%)	(65%)
Total Clients	62	70	68	200
Successes—Total	46	47	33	126
Overall Success Rate	(74%)	(67%)	(49%)	(63%)

scores, there would have been a perfect correlation and it would be possible to predict a pretest score from knowing the posttest score—or vice versa. Perfect correlations like that do not occur very often in the social sciences.

MULTIVARIATE ANALYSIS

Multivariate analysis of data usually refers to the use of such procedures as multivariate analysis of variance, multiple regression, and discriminant analysis—subjects taught in intermediate level statistics courses. However, we can begin to understand the usefulness of a multivariate perspective by constructing a table that allows us to examine three variables at once.

Assume that you have conducted an evaluation and presented the findings to your executive director. At this point, another question is raised, perhaps because a client complained about services in one of the agency's three satellite offices. The executive director suspects problems with one of the offices, because complaints tend to come primarily from that geographical area and only rarely from the other two sites. She asks you to look at the success rate for men and women clients for each of the agency's three locations. Table 13.6 provides an illustration of a chi-square table that presents the three variables of gender, geographic area, and outcome at one time.

As shown in Table 13.6, 87 percent of the males receiving an intervention in Area 1 had a successful outcome—the best rate for either sex in any of the three areas. Males fared the poorest in Area 3, where only 41 percent had successful outcomes. Females did almost equally well in Areas 1 and 2 and, like males, did the poorest in Area 3. Overall, 60 percent of the male clients experienced a successful outcome compared to 65 percent of the females. Not only did the evaluator find that some locations seemed to be more successful with males than with females, it is also apparent that there are fewer successful clients produced at the Area 3 office than in the other two locations. Areas 1 and 2 were successful with a majority of their clients, but Area 3 was not.

Evaluators and researchers must be vigilant in their search for **extraneous variables** (variables that may be overlooked and not included in a study or evaluation but which influence the findings). Table 13.6 demonstrates how an evaluator concerned only with the dependent variable of a program's overall success rate could be missing an opportunity to provide additional and valuable information to the program director. By controlling for the variables of location and gender, the evaluator provides the program director with a better understanding of how and where the program succeeds. In order to further improve the agency's success rate, the director will need to focus on increasing the number of successes in Area 3. By anticipating that success may differ by location and client gender, the evaluator has improved the usefulness of the evaluation report. Armed with this information, the program director may want to test hypotheses or notions about why males have fewer successes than females or why the success rate is so low in Area 3 (e.g., poor morale, inadequate supervision, staff in need of training).

The evaluator can anticipate extraneous variables by keeping in mind that success with clients is seldom uniformly distributed across all clients. Evaluators need to speculate about the characteristics of clients who would be likely to show the least and the most progress. Programs may be differentially effective depending on clients' education, financial and social resources, and so on. Besides the clients' characteristics, the evaluator ought to consider any relevant factors that could interact with the intervention or have an influence on it. By identifying these variables and collecting information on them, the evaluator is able to comprehend the extent of their influence and produce an evaluation report containing real analysis.

Please note that even this example employing three variables is elementary. As suggested in the opening paragraph of this section, there is a large variety of sophisticated statistical procedures from which evaluators may choose.

MYTHS ABOUT STATISTICAL SIGNIFICANCE

As a general rule, most researchers or evaluators would love to find "statistically significant" differences when they push the raw data they have been collecting all those many months through their statistical software programs. We have gone to some lengths to explain levels of measurement and the associated statistical procedures so that you will be able to detect any statistically significant differences between or among the groups in your study. However, in the quest to find $p < .05$, we do well to keep in mind that slight differences may be statistically significant, but not *clinically significant*.

For example, imagine a group of 30 clients who are suffering from anxiety problems. They are administered the Clinical Anxiety Scale prior to the start of

TABLE 13.7 | COMPARISON OF PRE- AND POSTTEST ANXIETY SCORES (PAIRED SAMPLES t-TEST)

	Mean	Standard Deviation	t-value	df	Probability
Pretest	49.6	10.37			
$n = 30$			4.94	29	$p < .001$
Posttest	46.8	9.65			

an intervention and then again after 6 weeks. A paired samples t-test (because each individual's pretest is compared with his or her posttest) results in the data shown in Table 13.7.

The Clinical Anxiety Scale is designed so that a score of 30 is a clinical cutting score (indicative of a problem). From Table 13.7 we can observe that at pretest the group as a whole showed a high level of anxiety—well above the cutting score. And we can see that some time later, there is a statistically significant reduction in anxiety. Unfortunately, the data suggest that while a few clients may have shown major improvement, the group as a whole was still experiencing severe levels of anxiety at the point of the posttest. Clinically, if one were to observe this sample of clients in a formal treatment program, they would have many of the same symptoms and problems that they had at the pretest—practically speaking, there was no meaningful improvement.

So, although evaluators must look for statistical significance as a means of determining when a program is effective, they must also ask the important question regarding outcome: Are clients better off because of the intervention? Statistical significance is influenced by the size of the sample. Trivial differences in small groups can become statistically significant if the sample size is increased sufficiently. When we are working with very large samples, there is some risk that we could discover statistically significant relationships that are inconsequential in terms of whether real changes have occurred.

There are several ways to deal with this problem. One approach is to compute a **reliable change index** (Christensen & Mendoza, 1986; Jacobson et al., 1984; Jacobson & Truax, 1991), which subtracts clients' pretest scores from their posttest scores and divides that value by the standard error of difference between the two test scores. Any reliable change index larger than 1.96 would be unlikely to result ($p < .05$) without actual change taking place (Jacobson & Truax, 1991).

To compute this criterion for improvement, you need the standard deviation of the control group and pretreatment experimental group, the test–retest reliability of the instrument, the individual pretest (x_1) and posttest (x_2) scores, and this formula (Jacobson & Truax, 1991):

$$RC = \frac{x_2 - x_1}{S_{\text{diff}}}$$

TABLE 13.8	SATISFACTION WITH QUALITY OF LIFE, POSTTEST SCORES

| | Cases | Mean | Std. Dev. | Pooled Variance | | |
				t-value	df	Probability
Treatment Group	18	151	20.8	–2.64	25.25	.01
Control Group	20	117	53.0			

where

$$S_{\text{diff}} = \sqrt{2(S_E)^2}$$

$$S_E = \text{Std dev} \sqrt{1 - \text{reliability}}$$

Another method for weighing the importance of statistically significant findings is to examine the amount or proportion of variance in the dependent variable that is explained by one or more of the independent variables. This value can then be used to make judgments about substantive improvement or change.

With *t*-tests, the **proportion of variance (PVE)** explained can be computed with the following formula:

$$r^2 = \frac{t^2}{t^2 + df}$$

Using the data supplied in Table 13.8, take the *t*-value of –2.64, square it $(-2.64^2 = 6.97)$, divide that by 32.22 (6.97 + 25.25), and end up with .22. This value suggests, at most, 22 percent of the variance in CAS scores could be accounted for by the intervention. The intervention might account for less, but most likely would not be responsible for more than 22 percent. Given a study that you were not able to control perfectly, you could not usually claim that the intervention caused the change, but using the PVE statistic, you could calculate the maximum possible influence of the intervention *if* it were responsible for the observed changes.

Similar formulas for computing the proportion of variance explained are available for chi-square and the test statistic *F* (see Rubin & Conway, 1985). These statistics are equivalent to a squared Eta, a squared Pearson correlation, a squared Phi coefficient, or a squared multiple correlation coefficient in terms of assessing improvement due to intervention. (Further references that may be helpful to you include Cohen & Cohen, 1983; Freidman, 1968; Hudson, Thyer, & Stocks, 1986; Rosenthal, 1994; Snyder & Lawson, 1993; Thompson, 1999.)

UNDERSTANDING TRENDS

Assume that you are evaluating a community's intervention program for persons who have been arrested the first time for driving while under the influence (DUI). After some deliberation, you decide that the best measure of the effectiveness of the intervention is the number of persons who are rearrested for

TABLE 13.9 | DUIs AND REARRESTS, 1999–2003

	Number of DUIs	Program Participants Rearrested
1999	385	31 (8%)
2000	380	38 (10%)
2001	377	45 (12%)
2002	390	55 (14%)
2003	372	60 (15%)

DUI. Accordingly, you begin to gather your data. A pattern is revealed as you examine the data over a 5-year period.

In Table 13.9, we observe that while the number of DUIs remains about the same over the 5-year period, it appears that the intervention is less effective over time. However, a number of alternative explanations are possible. First, the police may have added staff or are making a greater effort to arrest drunken drivers. Second, because more drivers have cellular phones, it is possible that more citizens are calling the police when they spot an inebriated driver—resulting in more drinking drivers being arrested. Third, judges and magistrates may be less inclined to dismiss charges of DUI. Without a control group, it is difficult to understand the increasing number of those who are rearrested each year for DUI.

Add a control group to the example. By examining DUIs and rearrests in another similar-sized community, we might be able to better comprehend the trends in our own community (Table 13.10).

Although it is entirely possible that a greater proportion of DUIs in Community A are being rearrested than when the program first began, data from Community B reflect a similar pattern of a greater percentage of DUI drivers being rearrested. The conclusion that the program is becoming less effective

TABLE 13.10 | DUIs AND REARRESTS, 1999–2003

	Community A		Community B	
	Number of DUIs	Rearrested	Number of DUIs	Rearrested
1999	385	31 (8%)	340	48 (14%)
2000	380	38 (10%)	336	47 (14%)
2001	377	45 (12%)	351	53 (15%)
2002	390	55 (14%)	344	59 (17%)
2003	372	60 (15%)	360	70 (19%)

FIGURE 13.10

INDIVIDUAL COUNSELING PRODUCTIVITY:
ADVENT OF MANAGEMENT
INFORMATION SYSTEMS

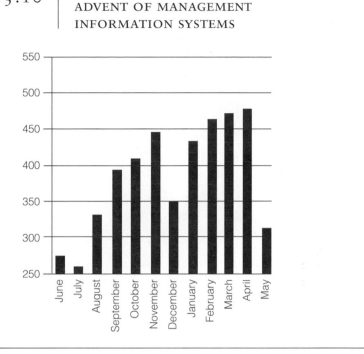

over time does not seem to be warranted. To understand why rearrests are increasing, the evaluator could look at whether the number of police cars or cell phones increased over the 5-year period or determine whether there were changes in legislation (such as lowering illegal blood alcohol levels from .10 to .08) that would affect the total number of DUI arrests.

In trying to make sense of trends, you must also be alert to seasonal trends or variations. We once examined the productivity of professional staff in a community mental health center after the installation of a new reporting system. We found that the amount of client counseling showed dramatic improvement almost immediately after the new system began in August and continued to rise, except during the month of December when a number of clients canceled appointments due to inclement weather and Christmas holidays. After December, staff productivity continued to climb until it dropped in the month of May.

As you look at these 12 months of data (see Figure 13.10), are you confident that the increase in productivity is due to the new reporting system? Or could Figure 13.10 be showing only a seasonal pattern of lower activity in the summer months due to staff taking vacations and fewer referrals being received from schools? Without additional data from prior years, it is hard to know.

If we think about the period of time necessary to observe an intervention or program change as a "window," the larger the window, the better chance we

TABLE 13.11 | ADULTS MAKING APPLICATION
                     AS A PERCENTAGE OF ALL INQUIRIES

Agency A	42.1%
Agency B	53.2%
Agency C	44.2%
Agency D	21.9%
Agency E	54.9%
Agency F	47.3%
Agency G	32.1%
Agency H	72.0%
Average	43.4%

have of accurately comprehending the effects of that intervention or program change. It is almost always better to look through a larger window (look at more data) than to try to assess a potential trend by looking through too small a window. We run the risk of erroneously concluding that we understand a phenomenon or a trend whenever we view too little of it. For instance, the data in Table 13.11 were obtained from eight different Big Brother/Big Sister agencies on the percentage of persons who followed through with an application after initially making an inquiry about the process (Roaf, Tierney, & Hunte, 1994). What might you conclude if your sample had included only data from Agency D? What conclusion might you reach using only the data from Agency H?

USING STATISTICS IN REPORTS

Just as it is possible to fail to use statistics when they are needed, it is also possible to inundate the readers of your evaluation report with too much data—too many tables—and to cite the results of too many statistical tests. It is vitally important that you consider the audience who read your evaluation report. You should not write over their heads and present statistical information that they are not likely to understand. With some audiences, you may want to note that statistically significant differences were found and not report the actual t or x_2 values. Usually it is not necessary to show any formulae used in the calculation of statistics. Present information that is important for understanding the major findings—not everything contained in the computer printout.

Evaluators can get carried away with all of the information available to them. We saw a good example of this when a student prepared a table of respondents' characteristics for a study she had completed. To select just one variable, she could have simply reported the information on marital status as it is reflected in Table 13.12. Instead, she unnecessarily complicated things by presenting all the information obtained from the computer printout. She included

TABLE 13.12 | MARITAL STATUS OF RESPONDENTS

	Number	Percent
Single	8	14.5
Married	28	50.9
Separated/Divorced	10	18.3
Widowed	9	16.3
Total	55	100.0

such information as the standard deviation (.911), the kurtosis (–.439), the skewness (.518), the variance (.830), the median (2.0), the mean (2.33), the standard error (.124), and so forth. Such information makes very little sense when we are talking about the variable of marital status. (These statistics would make much more sense when variables are not discrete categories but instead are interval level data such as test scores.)

At times you will want to provide such information as standard deviations or skewness to your readers, but most lay audiences are not going to easily digest technical information. One way to judge how much statistical detail to provide to your audience is to ask friends or colleagues to read your rough draft and give their opinion. If you are writing for academics or for a professional journal, look at what information tends to be presented in research reports carried in the journal you read most or are thinking about submitting to.

Remembering that evaluation is applied research, evaluators must keep in mind the pragmatic aspects of the findings. Even some findings that are not statistically significant may be important to report—especially those that result in recommendations or suggestions to the management. One way to display data so that audiences can easily digest it is with graphics like bar graphs and pie charts. Statistical software programs can produce a wide range of charts and graphs. (See Figure 13.11.) Even without a computer, you can still design charts that will help you to illustrate the numerical data.

Even though computer software can produce charts and graphs with a three-dimensional look like the example in Figure 13.12, this is not recommended when the three-dimensional effect makes it more difficult to clearly determine the intercepts.

TYPE I AND TYPE II ERRORS

Although it is more common for students of evaluation to fail to use statistical procedures when they are needed than to overuse them, readers are cautioned against computing a large number of correlations or other statistical tests just to hunt for "statistically significant" findings. If enough statistical tests are computed, some statistically significant differences will be produced.

FIGURE 13.11 | SAMPLE GRAPHICS GENERATED
BY A COMPUTER

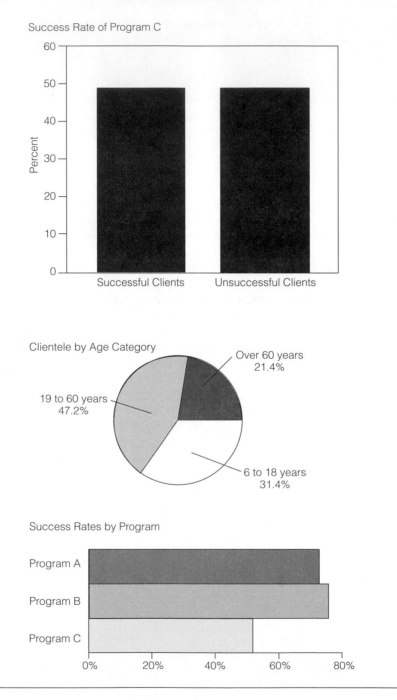

FIGURE 13.12   SUCCESS RATES BY PROGRAM

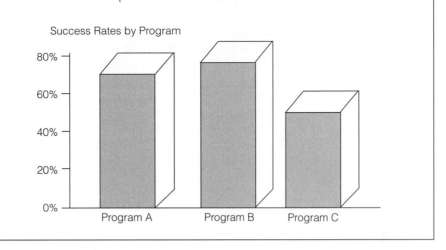

Suppose you had one dependent variable (e.g., recidivism) and you indiscriminately correlate 40 separate sociodemographic variables with this dependent variable. You could expect this "shotgun" approach would yield two statistically significant findings when significance is determined at the .05 level (i.e., .05 × 40 = 2). Even though these "significant" findings may not have been connected with the initial hypotheses or research questions, it sometimes is difficult to keep this in perspective when a bivariate test turns up something statistically significant. In your excitement over finding something significant, you may forget that its occurrence could be a fluke. The problem with conducting numerous bivariate tests is that a few significant results will occur if you conduct enough statistical tests, but such findings are likely to be related more to chance than to anything else. Avoid this problem by not computing correlations on all possible combinations of variables just to find something statistically significant. If you have many sociodemographic variables and you have no idea which of these will make the best predictors, use a more powerful statistical procedure (e.g., multiple regression analysis) to incorporate all of the variables simultaneously. However, even this method is no guarantee that all chance findings will be eliminated.

Finding significant differences just by chance is a **Type I error.** Type I errors lead you to conclude that a relationship exists between two variables (e.g., rejecting a null hypothesis) when there is no real relationship—merely a statistical fluke. Typically, we reduce the probability of making a Type I error by lowering the significance level. When it is terribly important to avoid making a Type I error, the traditional significance level of .05 can be lowered to .01 or less. However, by lowering the risk of a Type I error, the odds of making a Type II error are increased. In **Type II errors,** the null hypothesis is accepted when, in fact, there is a relationship between two variables.

In program evaluation and practice research, a Type II error is less problematic than a Type I because the Type II error claims that no difference exists between two groups (e.g., a treated one and an untreated one) when in reality a reliable difference (i.e., a statistically significant one) does exist. A Type I error is more problematic because it claims effective treatment when in reality the influence of the intervention could be negligible. Although social scientists seem to be more concerned with the risk of making Type I errors than Type II errors, it is possible to estimate the risk of committing a Type II error by using statistical power analysis. Tables have been prepared (Cohen, 1987) to enable evaluators to estimate the probability of committing a Type II error when using different statistical tests. Knowing that a few occurrences of statistical significance will be found when these findings have little value or meaning makes it easier for the evaluator to discard them and focus on the major findings.

Questions for Class Discussion

1. How much change do you and the others in the class have in pockets or purses? List all these amounts on the board. Manually prepare a frequency distribution. What is the mean? Is this nominal or interval data?

2. Using the data obtained in question 1 as the dependent variable, think of independent variables that could be used for bivariate analysis of the data. How might the data be grouped in several of these bivariate analyses? Would a *t*-test, one-way analysis of variance, or chi-square be the appropriate statistical test in each instance?

3. A student once conducted an evaluation and in a report began analyzing the data along this line: Client A showed the most improvement. This is understandable in that he and his spouse seem to have ironed out the domestic difficulties that have plagued them for the past 4 years. Client B progressed less than other clients. Whether a coincidence or not, this client has not had an intimate relationship in the last 5 years. Client C made minimal progress, possibly because her boyfriend violated his parole and was returned to prison. Client D made great strides after acknowledging her childhood trauma. Client E made minimal progress, possibly because of her surgery and time away from the group. What is wrong with analyzing data in this manner? If the report consisted of only this type of information, would you conclude that there had been an analysis of the data?

4. Bring in examples of data from the agencies where you have worked, interned, or volunteered. Look for trends in the data. Are there peak periods or times when fewer clients seek services? What other variables are needed to better understand apparent patterns in the data?

5. Discuss knowledge of and experience with statistical software programs. Which programs seem most user friendly? Which are more powerful?

6. Look through journals, magazines, and newspapers in order to bring in examples of ways that data are summarized and reported in tables, charts,

and graphs. Which examples are the easiest to read, and which are the most difficult?

Mini-Projects: Experiencing Evaluation Firsthand

1. Visit the university computer center to learn what statistical software is available. Are manuals for these programs in the library? Are consultants available to assist you in working with these programs? Summarize what you learned from this visit in a brief report.
2. Using either real or fictitious data, test a hypothesis using statistical software on a computer. Be sure to state your hypothesis, how your data were obtained (or if they were manufactured), and the statistical procedure used. Submit the corresponding printout along with your brief report.
3. Find a journal article evaluating an intervention and read it for the statistical procedures used. Write a brief paper summarizing: the outcome variable(s), the hypotheses tested, the statistical procedures used, and your reaction to the author's use of these tests. Were too many or not enough used? Were they appropriate? Did the report clearly benefit from the use of statistics? What could the author have concluded if no statistics had been used? Were the results clinically as well as statistically significant?
4. Locate a journal article that describes how a *t*-test was used to examine pretest-posttest differences in a group of clients and to obtain a "statistically significant difference." Calculate the PVE. Does the obtained PVE alter your interpretation of the phrase "statistically significant difference"?

References and Resources

American Psychological Association. (2001). *Publication Manual* (5th ed.). Washington, DC: Author.

Christensen, L., & Mendoza, J. L. (1986). A method of assessing change in a single subject: An alteration of the RC index. *Behavior Therapy, 17,* 305–308.

Cohen, J. (1987). *Statistical power analysis for the behavioral sciences.* New York: Academic Press.

Cohen, J., & Cohen, P. (1983). *Applied multiple regression/correlation analysis for the behavioral sciences* (2nd ed.). Hillsdale, NJ: Lawrence Erlbaum.

Freiman, J. A., Chalmers, T. C., Smith, H., & Kuebler, R. R. (1978). The importance of Beta, the Type II error, and sample size in the design and interpretation of the randomized control trial. *New England Journal of Medicine, 299,* 690–694.

Freidman, H. (1968). Magnitude of experimental effect and a table for its rapid estimation. *Psychological Bulletin, 70,* 245–251.

Hallahan, M., & Rosenthal, R. (1996). Statistical power: Concepts, procedures, and applications. *Behaviour Research and Therapy, 34,* 489–499.

Hudson, W. W., Thyer, B. A., & Stocks, J. T. (1986). Assessing the importance of experimental outcomes. *Journal of Social Service Research, 8*(4), 87–98.

Jacobson, N. S., Follette, W. C., & Revenstorf, D. (1984). Psychotherapy outcome research: Methods for reporting variability and evaluating clinical significance. *Behavior Therapy, 15,* 336–352.

Jacobson, N. S., & Truax, P. (1991) Clinical significance: A statistical approach to defining meaningful change in psychotherapy research. *Journal of Consulting and Clinical Psychology, 59,* 12–19.

Moncalm, D., & Royse, D. (2002). *Data analysis for social workers.* Boston: Allyn & Bacon.

Roaf, P. A., Tierney, J. P., & Hunte, D. E. I. (1994). *Big Brothers/Big Sisters: A study of volunteer recruitment and screening.* Philadelphia: Public/Private Ventures.

Rosenthal, R. (1994). Parametric measures of effect size. In H. Cooper & L. V. Hedges (Eds.), *The handbook of research synthesis* (pp. 231–244). New York: Russell Sage Foundation.

Rubin, A., & Conway, P. G. (1985). Standards for determining the magnitude of relationships in social work research. *Social Work Research and Abstracts, 21*(1), 34–39.

Snyder, P., & Lawson, S. (1993). Evaluating results using corrected and uncorrected effect size estimates. *Journal of Experimental Education, 61,* 334–349.

Thompson, B. (1999). Improving research clarity and usefulness with effect size indices as supplements to statistical significant tests. *Exceptional Children, 65,* 329–337.

Thyer, B. A. (1987). Statistics and research. *Social Work, 32*(6), 552.

Weinbach, R. W. (1989). When is statistical significance meaningful? A practice perspective. *Journal of Sociology and Social Welfare, 16*(1), 31–37.

PRAGMATIC ISSUES

CHAPTER 14

TREATMENT FIDELITY

Treatment fidelity has to do with how accurately or faithfully a program (or intervention) is reproduced from a manual, protocol, or model. You can imagine the problems that might arise in a multisite study if the staff in one location chose to implement only 30 percent of the program model while staff in other locations conformed on a continuum somewhere between 30 percent and 90 percent. In this situation, what would a program evaluator conclude if the program seemed effective in one location but not in another? Without some means for checking the extent of adherence to the designed model, it is almost impossible to assess whether lack of success with client outcomes is a failure of the model or a failure to implement the model as intended (Chen, 1990).

Lack of fidelity might lead an evaluator to conclude that a potentially effective program was ineffective, or a study might reveal significant results that were caused not by the intervention itself, but by activities or factors unknown to the evaluator. For the independent variable to have internal validity, fidelity is absolutely essential. Replication of a study (external validity) is also jeopardized when a treatment is poorly described or defined. It is easy to see that treatment fidelity is a vital and important concept for program evaluators. Unfortunately, it is one that is often overlooked.

From a statistical standpoint, lack of standardization inflates error variance and decreases statistical power. In other words, there is a greater chance of statistically significant behavioral change occurring when fidelity is high than when it is low (Moncher & Prinz, 1991). McGrew et al. (1994) found, with regard to an assertive community treatment program for persons needing mental health services, that program fidelity was positively correlated with effect size for reduction in days hospitalized. Those programs with the highest fidelity showed the greatest reduction in days of hospitalization.

Clients and service providers can unknowingly sabotage fidelity in many ways. For instance, clients can refuse to take their medications as prescribed. They may do this because they are trying to avoid unpleasant side effects, because they forget, or because they are trying to save money by not refilling expensive pre-scriptions. When John Client takes his medication once a day although the pre-scription calls for three doses a day, John gets a much smaller dosage than is actually needed. He has, in effect, diluted the treatment needed—perhaps to a level that he gets no benefit or shows no improvement. Similarly, another "dosage" problem is when clients cancel or do not show for needed individual therapy or choose not to participate in the required group therapy. They may not cooperate with directives from probation officers, do assigned "homework" given by thera-pists, or take good advice suggested by their AA sponsors.

Service providers, too, can undermine treatment fidelity by being inconsis-tent or deviating from procedures or treatment manuals. From an evaluation standpoint, interventions cannot and should not be vague, poorly defined, or operationalized—but occasionally they are. For instance, in a group session therapists might conversationally agree that they understand something we will call "culture-sensitive therapy" but then go back into their individual offices and practice it quite differently because of an underlying lack of information about the therapy and its key assumptions. If they have varying interpretations about how the therapy ought to be conducted, the therapy's fidelity is threatened.

To ensure fidelity, treatment providers must have instructions and guidelines about the necessary components of the intervention so that all clients receive essentially the same intervention despite variations in the therapist's age, gender, theoretical orientation, previous experience or training, educational degree, or other possible sources of deviation. In other words, service providers must be adequately trained in the use of the new intervention and given opportunity to practice it in role-plays or simulated sessions. They must clearly understand the intervention and know when and under what conditions it would be permissible to depart from it, and there must be agreement relative to the number and length of sessions. (See Box 14.1.) Fidelity consists of not only *doing* the planned inter-vention, but doing it well.

Someone (perhaps the director of the innovative program being evaluated) has the responsibility to see that adequate supervision is provided for the treat-ment providers. This may require weekly, or more frequent, meetings to discuss questions or problems with delivering the intervention. Evaluators might also want to view videotapes or listen to audiotapes of treatment sessions in order to try and determine the extent to which service providers are adhering to the treat-ment protocol. More formalized methods might involve interviewing or debrief-ing clients, preparing research instruments such as checklists or questionnaires

BOX 14.1	CHECKLIST FOR ENSURING TREATMENT FIDELITY

- All service providers are equipped with a treatment manual.
- All service providers are trained in the treatment protocol and are determined to be competent to perform the new technique.
- Periodic, ongoing training (booster sessions) designed to refresh and reinforce earlier training and to orient any new staff replacing those retiring, moving, or assuming new positions within the agency is provided.
- Supervisors meet regularly with their service provider supervisees to discuss progress and problems in implementing the intervention.
- Continuous monitoring of the new intervention includes routine efforts to verify that it is being implemented as planned.
- There is a mechanism to correct problems of treatment potency or content.
- No changes are made in the screening or selection of clients.

for service providers or clients to complete, observation (e.g., through one-way glass), and reading progress notes, therapists' logs, or other entries in the clients' files. Such procedures as these help to ensure internal validity. Other steps include identifying indicators or critical components of the model, describing sources of data for each indicator, collecting the necessary data, and analyzing the data. For a comprehensive review of over 20 studies that have developed, measured, validated, or used fidelity criteria and measures see Mowbray et al., 2003.

FIDELITY NIGHTMARES

Program evaluators commonly assume that other professionals understand the scientific process and such important principles as random selection, fair comparisons, standardization of procedures, and objective measures for gauging the performance of a program. However, agency directors, managers, and other employees may have strong motivations to present their programs or organizations more favorably than might otherwise occur in an unbiased program evaluation. The actions of these individuals can seriously affect treatment fidelity and make a complete mess of evaluation efforts.

Fidelity Nightmare 1

In an article entitled "The Family Preservation Evaluation from Hell: Implications for Program Evaluation Fidelity," Allen Rubin (1997) has described an agency administrator who (1) lengthened the treatment period for the experimental intervention group without informing the evaluation staff, (2) compromised the comparison group (30 percent of them were referred to an agency receiving an intensive 90-day treatment closely resembling the experimental intervention), and (3) informed the evaluator, after reading a preliminary analysis, that throughout the project she had not conformed to the case assignment protocol but had been assigning the tougher cases to the experimental intervention—and this was despite having collaborated from the very beginning on the evaluation design. When the first draft of the report revealed that the intensive program was no more effective than the customary form of service delivery, the administrator then began to try and explain the nonsignificant findings.

This is how Rubin (1997) concludes the account:

> The meaning of the essentially null outcome findings from the main component of this study, the overflow design, is unclear. One possibility is that the true effectiveness of the ADP program was masked by the Project Director's case assignment bias toward giving her unit the tougher cases. Skeptics might note that an at least equally plausible alternative is that the Project Director's ex post facto claim to have assigned her unit the tougher cases may not be accurate and may instead have resulted from a wishful memory. Less generous explanations for her claim are plausible, too, since she expressed great concern about what the null findings would do to the prospects for her program's future funding. A third possibility is that, regardless of the accuracy or motives concerning the Project Director's claim, the program simply was not effective. (p. 94)

It is obvious from this "nightmare," and the next, how important treatment fidelity is to program evaluation. We move from a covert violation of an evaluation design to something akin to benign neglect.

Fidelity Nightmare 2

A project was funded to test the efficacy of proactive crisis planning and peer (consumer) support volunteers in helping severely mentally ill people to better manage their illnesses and avoid psychiatric hospitalization. Proactive crisis planning involved a mental health professional working with a consumer to identify his or her personal symptoms that usually signaled a need for intervention. From those symptoms, a plan of action was developed, a contact or resource person specified, and so on. The peer support volunteers were conceptualized as being caring individuals who would engage with another person with severe mental illness. Volunteers were to be friendly supporters, helpful persons who could be expected to act as intermediaries if their assigned consumers began to deteriorate. This support might involve driving the consumer to the mental health office, sitting up with someone who was feeling depressed or lonely, arranging for groceries or meals if the consumer ran out of food, or just chatting occasionally to check up on the client of the mental health system. At least weekly contact was expected between a volunteer and his or her assigned consumer. The project was tested in three different implementation sites that involved rural community mental health centers in the eastern and western portions of the state as well as a center in a large urban location. Subjects were randomly assigned to one of three conditions where (1) proactive crisis plans were developed as an adjunct to usual clinical treatment, (2) proactive crisis plans were used in addition to peer support volunteers, or (3) the control condition was the customary clinical treatment.

Two different studies on the same population did not show that mental health consumers benefitted from proactive crisis plans and peer support volunteers. Guthrie (1992) found virtually no differences in psychosocial functioning one year after intervention when the experimental group was compared to non-participants in the control condition using a comprehensive battery including such instruments as the SCL-90-R, the Denver Community Mental Health Questionnaire–Revised, the Global Self-Esteem Inventory, the Quality of Life Inventory, and the Katz Adjustment Scale. Hasemann (1994) examined hospitalizations and arrests and found that consumers in the two treatment conditions did not differ significantly from the control group. As a result, a retrospective process evaluation was conducted to provide explanations for the lack of beneficial effects.

The process evaluation sought input from staff, consumers, and peer volunteers. What the evaluator found raises troubling concerns about the fidelity of the two interventions. Specifically,

- Only about half (52 percent) of the consumers had any memory of completing a crisis plan with their therapists. Of those who recalled making a crisis plan, only one-third thought that their crisis plan had ever been used.
- One-fifth of the therapists and case managers had not developed any crisis plans; 36 percent of those who said they had written crisis plans did so without any involvement from the consumer—a major departure from the way the intervention had been conceptualized.
- Only half (48 percent) of the consumers who should have been assigned a volunteer said that they had contact with a volunteer.
- Slightly more than one-third of the volunteers (who were consumers themselves) indicated that they were unable to function as a volunteer sometime during the period in which they were expected to be serving as a volunteer. One-third said that they had made more use of mental health services after taking on the volunteer assignment.
- One-fifth of the staff reported not spending any time in a typical week supervising or working with peer volunteers.
- Geographical differences were found. For instance, 75 percent of consumers in the western site remembered completing crisis plans, but only 53 percent of those in the urban site and 29 percent in the eastern site.
- The eastern site had the smallest percentage of consumers reporting volunteer contact and the fewest consumers reporting that their volunteers were helpful, available, and knowledgeable. None of the consumers from that location indicated that the volunteer's role had been explained to them. This result compares to 75 percent or more of the consumers in the other two locations.
- The median number of crisis plans completed per staff member over the project's 4 years was an average of only two plans per year.

- When an evaluation assistant went into one satellite location, the assistant found no crisis plans had been completed for clients assigned to the first condition. A staff member remarked that she knew she was "supposed" to develop crisis plans with consumers but that she had never received any instructions or training about them and so she did not bother. Another staff member commented that crisis plans "just sit in the charts."
- Volunteers were used in different capacities across the three sites. Some volunteers opted *not* to work with consumers but found jobs for themselves such as sweeping up at the end of the day or managing the clubhouse's petty cash fund. Although these activities were likely useful for the volunteers to perform, they deviated from the project's goal of using volunteers for peer counseling, outreach, and respite services.
- Not all of the volunteers were able to provide assistance to others. One was blind and hard of hearing; another was a person with both mental retardation and mental illness.

How could this project have been improved? First of all, the staff needed better training and supervision. The extent to which staff were writing and utilizing the proactive crisis plans needed to be monitored regularly. One part of this monitoring could have been as simple as having the medical records staff routinely check for the inclusion and completion of crisis plans. The other missing component was the establishment of procedures for training new staff and ensuring that ongoing staff are continuing to use crisis plans and peer support volunteers. In this project, staff were trained initially but there appeared to be little follow-up to see whether they were implementing the project as planned. Staff who were employed in the second, third, or fourth years of the project did not seem to have received any training. Normal staff turnover created a situation where a number of staff had received very little or no systematic orientation on the project.

Second, volunteers needed to be better screened and supervised. Ideally, volunteers should have been requested to make a commitment to spend at least 30 minutes a week with their assigned consumer, and it should have been perfectly clear what their roles entailed. Requiring volunteers to have their own phones and transportation would also have improved their impact.

The commitment to a project must flow from the top down. The enthusiasm of the grant writer or program evaluator (or even of a small group of staff) is not always sufficient to see that a project is implemented and maintained as originally planned over time. When interventions are not implemented fully or as intended, "dosage" issues—what and how much recipients received—can be problematic for the evaluator. In this case, the program implementation was so untidy and poorly supervised that it is impossible to know the value of the intervention. Could the two procedures truly help persons with severe mental illness to prevent psychiatric hospitalizations if they were implemented and supervised better? Or is the concept of using peer support volunteers and developing crisis action plans just a waste of time? Unfortunately, after more than 4 years of effort, these questions are still unanswerable.

PROGRAM DRIFT AND THE TRANSFER
OF PROGRAMS

What lessons are to be learned from these two disastrous examples? Treatment fidelity is not an all-or-nothing phenomenon but should be thought of as falling on a continuum (Moncher & Prinz, 1991). Just because a project is funded and staff are prepared for the new intervention, the evaluator cannot walk back to his or her office and assume that treatment fidelity will remain high. It may do so in the home office or in the locations with the most conscientious managers; then again, if the new intervention requires significant changes in the way staff do what they do, or if it increases their paperwork, staff may be resistant and overtly or covertly uncooperative. The further the distant offices are from the source of information about the new intervention, the more the evaluator should suspect and anticipate that treatment fidelity will suffer. It is reasonable to expect there will be less understanding and conformity to the model unless special effort is made to replicate procedures, provide training, and provide close supervision. The more complex the intervention, the more likely fidelity problems may arise.

High fidelity follows from conformity to the prescribed elements and an absence of nonprescribed elements (McGrew et al., 1994). McGrew et al. have suggested that, particularly with programs that extend over many years, programs "drift." That is, programs self-modify and, while preserving some of the elements or features of the original design, they become less than perfect replications. McGrew et al. conceptualized a generational variable that was a crude measure of departures from an original model. They found in their study of 18 assertive community treatment (mental health) programs that "third-generation" programs had poorer program fidelity as programs were developed over time and became distant from the initial model. The greater the number of treatment providers and the larger the number of settings in which a program is replicated, the more likely it is that the program will drift and modify over time (Lipsey et al., 1985).

Program change is inevitable during the transfer of programs from one setting to another (Bauman, Stein, & Ireys, 1991). Programs may change, for instance, if the sponsorship of the program is different in one setting than in the one where it was originally created. Bauman et al. (1991) raise the question, "Does it matter to workers if union or management sponsors an employee assistance program intended to help employees with personal problems?" (p. 627), and then suggest that a program may be successful in one setting because the organization's management has a good rapport with its employees, but not in another setting where the relations are more confrontational.

It should be expected that programs will change as their leadership changes and as they respond both indirectly and directly to pressures and forces exerted within specific locales. A program developed in Chicago and transplanted in Springfield, Missouri, will necessarily develop its own traditions, treatment successes, and failures. Despite efforts to keep it true to "the model," programs will be influenced and determined, to a large extent, by the personalities and experiences of the staff employed by the program—as well as by the clients who request and receive treatment. And this is to say nothing of the political forces that exert pressure not only on programs but also on the evaluation of the interventions.

POLITICAL NATURE OF EVALUATION

Ideally, program evaluations are conducted because of a commitment to providing the best possible services. But there can be other motives as well. For instance, an evaluation of an agency may be used to get rid of an administrator when the board of directors wants to hire a new person. Or, evaluation results from one program may be publicized to counter negative media attention given to another. Whether we like it or not, evaluations can be used as bludgeons to bring about changes in programs and personnel. The novice evaluator is well advised to remember that any evaluation may be perceived as a political activity by those being evaluated. Those not involved in the planning of the evaluation are often suspicious of some "hidden agenda." Furthermore, evaluation is intrinsically threatening to those being evaluated.

The political substructure to some evaluation activities can place the evaluator in an ethical dilemma. In Chapter 2 we examined ethical concerns at the front end of the evaluation process; we would do well to keep in mind that pressure can be applied at the end of the process to present the agency in the best possible light, to ignore unflattering findings, or to focus on strengths and not weaknesses. Additionally, as you will see in Box 14.2, there are many opportunities for ethical challenges to affect the evaluation process.

In agencies where staff morale is already poor, where there is a widespread feeling that the program is not working the way it should, or where there is inadequate supervision and incompetent leadership, evaluation is even more threatening than usual because staff may fear a "housecleaning" that will take away their jobs. On the other hand, an administrator may request a program evaluation to show that the criticism he or she has been receiving is unwarranted. And who knows how the results of a program evaluation will be used when a program is rumored to "have problems?"

Within any organization, there are likely to be as many opinions as to the "real" purpose and value of an evaluation as there are reasons for conducting the evaluation. As a result, some staff will be supportive and helpful, while others will be threatened because the evaluation was "imposed." Staff who feel under attack may attempt to undermine the evaluation effort. The evaluator may be seen as an investigative reporter, a critic, a "spy," a benevolent consultant, or some combination of these. Kennedy (1983) noted that:

> Evaluation is an inherently contradictory activity. . . . Evaluators are expected to help organizations achieve their goals, yet because organizations may consist of parts whose goals are incompatible, helping one group may entail hindering another. . . . Evaluators are often expected to observe organizational activities from an objective position, yet their credibility may depend on being perceived as sympathetic friends. Most of these tensions are inherent in the task of evaluation. (p. 519)

WHEN POLITICS
AND ETHICS COLLIDE

The Scenario

Imagine you are a program evaluator who has been asked to evaluate a new program and that you are unfamiliar with the programmatic context. You are asked to complete the evaluation in 6 months because although the program has been operating for about a year and a half, they have not conducted any evaluation activities and now realize that in order to extend funding they must have some results showing that their program works. The administrators assert that if you only collect information from program staff that you should be able to complete the evaluation within the time frame. Further, they want full access to all of the data you collect. You are just getting started in your evaluation career and want to do build a good reputation. What ethical challenges are present and how will you handle them? Let's begin by identifying the potential ethical problems and possible solutions.

Responding to Ethical Challenges

First, you should disclose to the administrators that you have not conducted an evaluation in this programming context before. This is important because, even though evaluation methods are fairly standard across a variety of program contexts, interpretations of findings or choice of approach may influence results. Because you aren't familiar with this type of program, you may have a steep learning curve that could impact the time it takes you to conduct the evaluation.

Second, evaluations should not be conducted within a context that is not scientifically sound. A time frame of 6 months to collect outcome data for a program you are not familiar with is probably unrealistic and not a good practice. This needs to be explained to the administrators and possibly a compromise developed in order to collect information that is accurate and valid but also meets their needs.

Third, it is critically important to include as many stakeholder perspectives as possible when conducting program evaluations. Focusing only on staff perceptions may severely bias the evaluation results and may render the evaluation invalid. Don't hesitate to advise the administrators that a stronger evaluation includes data obtained from consumers and others in the community.

Fourth, it is critically important in all data collection procedures that protection of human participants be maintained. Staff, clients, and other stakeholders should be given a promise of confidentiality and every effort should be incorporated to ensure confidentiality. If this is not possible for some reason, then all participants need to be told that the administration will have access to everything they say. This is likely to compromise the data collection findings and administrators should be aware of these trade-offs.

Fifth, given that the administrators have clearly given you the message that they need positive results to sustain funding, there may be a huge amount of pressure to "find positive results." This is very tricky. Several things can be done to combat the pressure to find positive outcomes. It is important to be careful to conduct a balanced evaluation—one that examines both positive and negative aspects of the program (even unintended effects of the program). It is also critical to recognize that many program outcomes are strongly influenced by methods (see Wilson & Lipsey, 2003). Thus, it is important to include a limitations section in your evaluation report that

(Continued)

WHEN POLITICS AND ETHICS
COLLIDE (CONTINUED)

carefully and fully articulates the methods and limitations of the study as they may have influenced the study results. This may be especially important when conducting a cost-benefit analysis of a program that includes a lot of cost and benefit "estimates" (see Pinkerton et al., 2002 for a discussion of ethical issues in cost-benefit analysis).

References

Pinkerton, S., Johnson-Masotti, A., Derse, A., & Layde, P. (2002). Ethical issues in cost-effectiveness analysis. *Evaluation and Program Planning, 25,* 71–83.

Wilson, D. & Lipsey, M. (2003). The role of method in treatment effectiveness research: Evidence from meta-analysis. In A. Kazdin (Ed.), *Methodological issues & strategies in clinical research* (3rd ed., pp. 589–616). Washington, DC: American Psychological Association.

The program evaluation literature contains many references to the political nature of program evaluation. Coffee (1989), in discussing opinions toward evaluators, noted that some individuals view evaluators as "mean-spirited, politically motivated, rewarded only for finding out what is wrong" (p. 59). Chelimsky (1987), in an article entitled "What Have We Learned about the Politics of Program Evaluation?" noted that "the choice of the program to evaluate emerges in *real terms* from the political process, with the determination of the types of policy questions to be asked being a function of the decision makers" (p. 10). Cronbach et al. (1980), in *Toward Reform of Program Evaluation,* summarized major points in a number of theses. Several of these speak to the political arena in which evaluators must operate. For instance, "the evaluator has political influence even when he does not aspire to it"; "evaluators' professional conclusions cannot substitute for the political process"; and "a theory of evaluation must be as much a theory of political interaction as it is a theory of how to determine facts" (p. 3).

Evaluators should not be naive in believing that program evaluation efforts are somehow immune to political processes and pressures. Muscatello (1989), in writing about his experience as manager of an evaluation team within a large public organization, observed that evaluators are sometimes asked by decision makers to develop data to verify or legitimize decisions that have already been made—an activity, he said, to which purists in the evaluation field may take exception. Other political implications for the evaluator are also apparent in that the "good evaluator" will work with the "good manager" to "ensure that the conclusions and recommendations reached during the study are overlaid first with relevant policy considerations, and then with the realities of organizational politics, organizational environment, and future business strategies" (p. 17). Muscatello further cautions:

> If this overlay process does not take place, implementation becomes far less practical and the effectiveness of the evaluation function is diminished, along with its

value to the organization. For any segment of his or her business, the chief executive officer has the right to ask, "Why do I need this function and/or these people?" Certainly it is a healthy company whose officers ask each segment of the business, "What have you done for me lately?" If the manager of a program evaluation unit cannot demonstrate impact for the evaluation function, then the logical business decision is to eliminate the unit itself. (p. 17)

This theme has also been discussed by Chelimsky (1987) who has written, "We must be useful to others if we are to be successful. That means understanding the political system in which evaluation operates, and understanding the information needs of those policy actors who use evaluation" (p. 17).

At the same time, the evaluator may be pressured by the administrator or administration to show that a program is successful—whether it is or not. Because of the potential for losing funds, administrators may be anxious that even negative findings be worded in such a way as to present the program in the best possible light. They may ask the evaluator to emphasize the positive points, or to include anecdotal accounts from satisfied clients or favorable remarks of influential persons in the community. Similarly, administrators may be concerned with the order in which the findings are presented. They may want the favorable points made early in the evaluation report and the negative points buried deep in the report. House (1986) has cautioned **internal evaluators** (staff evaluators employed full time by an organization) against confusing the interests of the organization with those of individual administrators with whom they identify personally.

The political realities are such that some administrators may want the "true findings" presented but may be looking for an evaluator to prepare an innocuous final report that will minimize any identified problems. Failing to get a "sugar-coated" version, these administrators may secretly hope that any document containing bad news will be so difficult to understand that even interested persons will not wade in very far. We may sound a bit cynical here, but objective information is not always desired by all parties. Sometimes it is the staff or the employees who want to prevent evaluation data from being aired publicly. When staff has strong anger and resentment toward an administration, employees may resort to devious and vicious means to frustrate evaluation efforts. In one recent situation, a staff member called the institutional review board with a manufactured complaint and held up the evaluation while an investigation was conducted. Months later, after a large expenditure of time and energy, the IRB concluded that there was no substance to the complaint. Because the IRB felt it was important to protect the identity of the complainant, it was not possible to reprimand the employee.

"THREAT" OF EVALUATION

Evaluation activities always pose a potential threat to someone or some group. Any time we are evaluated, whether as students or faculty or employees, we fear negative evaluation—being labeled or identified as inadequate or incompetent. Staying in touch with how we feel when we are evaluated can help us appreciate the feelings of others when we plan to evaluate their activities.

If the staff feel that *they* are being scrutinized in a situation where there is no examination of the administrative hierarchy, they will be angry and perhaps scared. On the other hand, if the staff feel that the problems lie not with their functioning but at the administrative level and the evaluation will detect this, they will be less threatened. Evaluators must be mindful that anyone fearing loss of job or other negative repercussions from an evaluation will feel threatened.

Even if staff do not fear loss of job but feel that the program has been unjustly singled out, they can be less cooperative than the evaluator might desire. Although they may not be as vicious as to slash the tires on the evaluator's car, they may quite pleasantly refuse to complete questionnaires or forms that are needed by the evaluator. They may be "too busy" to review their closed client records or to contact active clients for evaluation purposes. They may "forget" to return questionnaires on the date requested, or they may have "lost" the evaluator's instructions. If the evaluation requires ongoing data collection and the evaluator is not in the agency on a regular basis and has not designed adequate data collection mechanisms, the resulting data may be collected sporadically, only when it was convenient, or perhaps not at all. Passive-aggressive staff may argue, "We are here to help clients . . . not to use them as guinea pigs. We are too busy helping—we don't have the luxury of time to conduct research!"

Evaluators should not underestimate the amount of power that they are perceived to have by persons within the organization being evaluated. Thompson (1989) has described the evaluator as a "power broker." Part of the reasoning for this is that the evaluator can speak and act for others in positions of authority. Evaluators can stimulate action and change by speaking for and acting as agents for those who are reluctant to do so on their own. By gathering information and focusing on the important issues, the evaluator assists the decision makers in becoming more knowledgeable (and therefore more powerful).

Some agency staff will view the evaluator as a "hired gun" who has come into the agency to do away with certain staff by documenting their inefficiency or ineffectiveness. According to this line of thinking, the hired gun takes orders from those who did the hiring. The evaluator will not be seen as objective or even as interested in hearing the "truth" because of ties to those who are paying the consulting fees.

Regardless of whether you are an internal evaluator or an **external** (contract) **evaluator,** you will find that program evaluation is almost always conducted in a political arena. A finding that pleases one group may make another group unhappy. It can also be expected that political pressures will vary in strength, depending on what is at stake. The wise evaluator will be sensitive to any factors (political or otherwise) that can affect his or her judgment. Because it is not easy to know if you are being too accommodating or too intractable, you may find it useful to share your preliminary ideas or even a rough draft of a final report with a trusted friend or colleague who would be in a position to detect any lack of fairness or balance. When a program has serious problems, it is quite easy to focus on the negatives and fail to see the positives. Both need to be reported.

Agency directors often argue that anecdotal accounts of successes obtained by selected clients ought to be included. There is no harm in reporting such accounts, particularly when these anecdotal reports of individual cases are used to corroborate the findings of quantitative data. However, use of anecdotal data can quickly deteriorate into selective reporting if one is not careful, and by itself cannot constitute a credible evaluation.

Program evaluation *does not* consist of picking out anecdotal accounts to illustrate particular outcomes and conveying the impression that this material is somehow "representative" of program outcomes. Such a practice would be deceptive. On the other hand, employing anecdotal reports or selected quotes to illustrate various service outcomes, to "flesh out" the bare bones of reported quantitative outcomes, is a useful practice.

GUIDELINES FOR EVALUATION IN POLITICALLY CHARGED ARENAS

To help you stay as impartial and fair as possible, the following guidelines may be of use in managing political pressures.

1. Maintain Your Independence   There may be pressure from within the organization to present results in a favorable light. Prepare for such pressures. Suggest ahead of time that some of the findings may be positive and some may be negative. Let it be known that information from a variety of perspectives will be gathered and examined.

The evaluator's autonomy is less likely to be compromised when there is a clear notion of the purpose of the evaluation and what the evaluator's role will be. As an evaluator, will you be a consultant making suggestions to help a program grow and improve? Or will you be a "fact finder" who uncovers and diagnoses unhealthy programs so that the administration can perform "surgery"? Insist on a contract that states explicitly the evaluation sponsors' expectations of you and the evaluation product.

Your independence is safeguarded when, in the process of negotiating a contract, you insist on editorial authority in writing the evaluation report. Do not allow the evaluation sponsor to have final authority for writing or revising your evaluation report. (However, it is often a good idea to brief key personnel once you have a draft copy of the report ready. Sometimes such briefings can provide the evaluator with a different perspective or new way of interpreting the data. Briefings may also serve the useful purpose of keeping the administration from being totally surprised by negative findings. The little bit of additional time this may require is well worth its expenditure in a politically charged arena—a director will have time to prepare a response or implement corrective actions even before the report becomes "official.")

2. Negotiate a Contract   One way to reduce confusion about the evaluator's role and the purpose of the evaluation is to draft an agreement or contract. It might even be called "Memorandum of Understanding"—which is a little less formal and more friendly than a contract. These agreements can be complex or simple and will vary widely, depending on the amount of time and remuneration involved, the intricacy of the evaluation, and the amount of trust between the evaluation sponsor and the evaluator. Essentially, these agreements should cover:

a. The purpose or focus of the evaluation. (Incorporate a list of the questions that the evaluation sponsor wants answered or hypotheses that will be investigated.)

b. The beginning and ending dates of the evaluation. (At a minimum, it is important to specify deadlines when the evaluation products must be finished.) On some occasions, it may also be advisable to describe the sponsor's expectations of a final product—in terms of appearance, the amount of detail it will contain, and so forth.

c. The evaluation methodology: data, staff, and facilities needed. (Will the evaluation design necessitate the use of control groups? Will random assignment of clients be necessary? Will it be necessary to obtain sensitive information from clients? What other data will be necessary to access? How many and which employees will need to assist?)

d. The budget needed. (Not only is agreement important on the consultant's fee, but also there should be a definite budget for such items as travel, supplies, scales or instruments, printing, secretarial services, and so on. It is also important to specify the payment schedule—when the evaluator can be expected to be paid.)

e. Ownership of the data and editorial authority. (At the end of the evaluation, who keeps the completed questionnaires and other data? You may need the data, or at least access to it, should you decide to write an article for a professional journal. Further, it should be clear who will write and have editorial authority over the final evaluation report, and to whom it will and can be disseminated.)

In some instances, it is necessary for the evaluator to gather information about the program or agency before an evaluation design and data collection procedures can be recommended. This design phase (sometimes called a **feasibility study**) may be negotiated separately so that the evaluator can later submit a realistic estimate for conducting the actual evaluation.

3. Attempt to Obtain Evaluative Information from as Many Sources as You Can   Be inclusive rather than exclusive. Talk to clients, staff, board members, citizens in the community—in short, talk to anyone who may have an opinion about the program. Use more than one evaluation design if time and resources allow. Consider the worst case scenario—what would you be able to conclude if the evaluation model you have planned does not work as it was intended? What other sources of data would be valuable?

4. Explain and Communicate the Purpose of the Evaluation and Its Methodology to Staff and Other Interested Parties   Schedule a staff meeting and allow the staff to raise questions and interact with you. You may even want to develop an advisory committee. Even an ad hoc committee can provide you with feedback with regard to potential problems. They will know the educational level and abilities of the clients and may be able to point out ways to get around certain organizational obstacles or barriers. At a minimum, allowing staff to raise questions helps reduce the level of anxiety they have about the evaluation. Providing staff with information helps suppress rumors that may surface about the "real" purpose of the evaluation. The involvement of staff provides a richer and more comprehensive evaluation than can be obtained when they are not involved. Because they are likely to know the serious problems with the program, it is good evaluation practice to keep staff both informed and involved. Staff and administrators are also more likely to use the results of the evaluation if they participated in the process and their interest was kept at a high level.

Although it may seem like just common sense, it is vitally important that any instructions or directions be communicated clearly. Staff and clients will not be as familiar with the evaluation methodology or the instruments as the evaluator. They may require detailed instructions or training. (We once heard of an evaluation where the staff were given a rather lengthy questionnaire with practically no instructions at all. In the absence of guidelines, the staff improvised. Some requested additional instructions, while others "guessed" at what the evaluator wanted.) On the other hand, do not overdo the instructions. Do not make them too complex for busy people to quickly comprehend. If instructions are not readily understood, they are not likely to be followed. There should be virtually no confusion due to the complexity of evaluation procedures or feelings of frustration as a result of the "burden" that the evaluation imposes on clients, staff, or members of boards of directors.

Day-to-Day Pragmatic Problems

While navigating the shoals of agency politics, the evaluator must be alert to day-to-day problems that arise when he or she is not able to personally supervise the evaluation. An evaluator once told of her frustration when staff affiliated with a special project kept broadening the eligibility criteria in order to provide services to a greater number of needy persons. The evaluator discovered this much later when she followed up on service recipients and found out that they did not meet the criteria of persons for whom the project had been designed to help. Many of the service recipients could not be included in the evaluation. Too late to do anything about it, the evaluator had a much smaller group of service recipients to evaluate than had been planned. To make matters worse, somewhere along the line the staff had quit trying to randomly assign clients to the "regular" or the "intensive" intervention programs. They had begun using their own criteria to decide who could best benefit from the programs.

"War stories" of this type abound. Most evaluators have vivid memories of evaluations gone awry. Although it would be rare for an evaluation to experience no problems at all, the experienced evaluator learns to anticipate problems before they occur and plan for them. For instance, in planning for a large-scale survey to be mailed, the evaluator needs not only to calculate the amount of time required to word process the questionnaires, stuff and address the envelopes, and sort the mail by zip codes in time for the post office to deliver them but also to allow for an extra days for unexpected problems (i.e., computers and printers that break down). Things that have never happened before may occur at a critical time. For this reason, many evaluators estimate the amount of time taken for certain tasks beyond their control (e.g., the delivery of the mail) and then double their estimates to give themselves a comfortable "cushion" in case unanticipated problems arise. Even for those activities that are within your control, the unexpected can happen and can result in missing a deadline if planning does not allow for some "slippage."

Most nonpolitical problems that occur during a program evaluation are due to events beyond the evaluator's control. For instance, the director of data processing informs you that it will take 3 weeks longer than promised to get around to your request to pull 500 random client addresses. Or, questionnaires do not get administered because the evaluator depended on someone else in the agency to oversee the effort, and that individual got caught up in some more pressing problems. Clients' problems almost always have a higher priority than program evaluation.

Where possible, assume as much responsibility as you can handle. Do not rely on others to select the clients, design your forms, or collect your data. Control as much of the process as you can manage. For what you cannot do, hire your own staff to do it. If you have no other alternative but to rely on agency staff who have competing interests and responsibilities, stay in close contact with them. Do not call once at the beginning of the project and then again 6 months later when you need the data. Visit the agency or site often, let them know you, train and prepare those who will be collecting the data, and get them some reduction in their other responsibilities if possible. Involve staff in the process, and stay in touch with them.

CULTURALLY SENSITIVE EVALUATION PRACTICE

There is growing recognition that treatment programs in this country often have been designed for white, English speakers—thus making them potentially inappropriate and possibly ineffective for Hispanics, African Americans, Native Americans, as well as Asian and other ethnic minorities. For instance, Miller and Willoughby (1997) have noted that, with regard to treatment methods applied to alcohol problems, the vast majority of outcome studies have been conducted with urban, white, English-speaking populations of European heritage. Findings that result from treating white clients exclusively may not generalize to other groups.

That is not the only problem. Many, if not most, of the measurement tools currently in existence have been developed by European Americans and could contain substantial measurement bias when applied to another ethnic group. Further, these tests are often interpreted based on the scores (norms) obtained mostly from European American subjects (Malgady, 1996). And yet we know that even diagnoses can be affected by the sociocultural factors that cast the presentation of the symptoms of mental disorder (Rogler, 1993).

Foster and Martinez (1995) argue that even when ethnicity is not a major focus of a study, investigators should "attain a reasonable amount of cultural knowledge about the groups under investigation to ensure that measures, participant recruitment procedures, research stimuli, treatment procedures, and the like are equally applicable across groups" (p. 218). They also point out that socioeconomic status (SES) often confounds ethnic differences because many ethnic groups are over represented among the lower SES groups.

Historically, ethnic minorities have not been recruited for participation in research studies and are often considered as being less likely to consent to participate (Armstrong et al., 1999)—and for good reason. The Tuskegee syphilis study convinced many persons of color that white government-sponsored scientists viewed African Americans with such little respect that it was easy to believe in genocide conspiracy theories. As a result, many African Americans may distrust researchers and view investigators as taking more from their communities than giving back (Thompson et al., 1996). Thus, recruiting persons of color for studies when they could be randomly assigned to a control group has been described as presenting "numerous challenges" (Hauck et al., 2003).

Attitudes, however, may be improving. Armstrong et al. (1999) conducted a study of 119 undergraduates in a state university in the Southeast and found that although African Americans were more concerned than whites about the researcher being of the same race, no significant difference was found between whites and African Americans in terms of their likelihood of participation in a proposed (but fictitious) study supposedly involving the testing of a new vaccine for tuberculosis. There also were no differences between races when the willingness to participate was evaluated in terms of providing a series of incentives (from no incentive, to expenses only, to expenses plus $50, to expenses plus $500). The authors concluded:

> [I]n these samples of college students, we found no evidence that these negative attitudes necessarily make African Americans less likely to participate as subjects in clinical trials research. This apparent inconsistency between attitudes and reported likelihood of participation suggests that the decision to participate in a research study is a complex one that involves many factors besides attitudes of generalized mistrust, such as time availability, exposure to research opportunities, and trust in specific organizations that for this sample of college students may have "washed out" the effect of negative attitudes. (p. 567)

Thompson et al. (1996) used ethnically diverse psychiatric residents to approach both black and white inpatients in two Detroit psychiatric hospitals. They also found no differences between African American and white patients in the interview completion rate, the refusal rate, or the rate of early discharge. Matching African American patients with African American interviewers did not influence interview completion rates. However, in an 18-month long study that sought to collect data on childhood stresses and resources in women with and without alcoholic parents, the researchers were not able to obtain equal numbers African Americans and non-Hispanic whites. Of the goal of obtaining 150 African American women, only 132 could be recruited (Clay et al., 2003).

In a well-conceptualized study, Brown and Topcu (2003) learned that there were no statistically significant differences between older African Americans (72.5%) and whites (78%) when asked about willingness to take part in a clinical treatment trial if they had a serious medical illness such as cancer. And while older African Americans were significantly more likely than whites to indicate awareness of the Tuskegee syphilis experiment, knowledge of the Tuskegee experiment was not associated with willingness to participate in clinical cancer treatment trials.

How to Conduct Culturally Sensitive Evaluations

We all view the world through cultural lenses that have been shaped, to a large extent, by teachings that have been acquired from our families and close friends. We may never become fully aware of how much influential groups in our socialization—be it religious groups, peers, or social organizations—have contributed in the way of assumptions and misinformation about groups of people who look different from our own mirror image. Our "education" begins even before we start school.

In addition to these influences, we naturally tend to assume others think the way we do, know what we do. But this is an error that evaluators should not make. To provide a quick example: many clients of social service agencies would not have the same level of education as the evaluator with a master's degree or a Ph.D. And while the evaluator knows to use a vocabulary and reading level matched to that of the targeted client group on the informed consent and similar documents, other considerations are also worth keeping in mind.

Anyone who has been to college is familiar with the Likert scale and using questionnaires to register opinions and knowledge about things. We know that researchers can be trusted to protect our confidentiality or anonymity. However, individuals who have never gone to college may not think it necessary to answer every question, may chafe at having to relate to points on a continuum, and may *not* trust that they will *not* be identified or that their information about illegal behavior will *not* be given to the police. They may view completing questionnaires as a nuisance with less validity than orally "taking their word" for some event that they want to describe. In short, they may hold different assumptions about the value of research and the "right" way to conduct it. These concerns can be magnified if the client is from another ethnic or language group and has no knowledge of Western methods of survey research.

Involving others who do not share the evaluator's same cultural experiences in the evaluation process as well as pilot testing procedures and instructions with groups of clients who resemble the targeted group are the main ways to avoid the problem of being culturally insensitive and thus invalidating the findings of our studies. Relevant articles on minority recruitment can be found in Box 14.3. To maximize minority involvement, evaluators may wish to:

 | ARTICLES ON MINORITY
RECRUITMENT

The Gerontologist, Volume 43, (1) February 2003 is a special issue on minority recruitment. Within that issue are contained these articles:

- Arean, P. A., Alvidrez, J., Nery, R., Estes, C., & Linkins, K.. (2003). Recruitment and retention of older minorities in mental health services research. *Gerontologist, 43*(1), 36–44.
- Brown, D. R., & Topcu, M. (2003). Willingness to participate in clinical treatment research among older African Americans and Whites. *Gerontologist, 43*(1), 62–72.
- Curry, L., & Jackson, J. (2003). The science of including older ethnic and racial group participants in health-related research. *Gerontologist, 43*(1), 15–17.
- Ford, M. E., Havstad, S. L., & Tilley, B. C. (2003). Recruiting older African-American men to a cancer screening trial (the AAMEN) project. *Gerontologist, 43*(1), 27–35.
- Gallagher-Thompson, D., Solano, N., Coon, D., & Arean, P. (2003). Recruitment and retention of Latino dementia family caregivers in intervention research: Issues to face, lessons to learn. *Gerontologist, 43*(1), 45–51.
- Levkoff, S., & Sanchez, H. (2003). Lessons learned about minority recruitment and retention from the Centers on Minority Aging and Health Promotion. *Gerontologist, 43*(1), 18–26.
- Reed, P. S., Foley, K. L., Hatch, J., & Mutran, E. J. (2003). Recruitment of older African-Americans for survey research: A process research of the community and church-based strategy in the Durham Elders Project. *Gerontologist, 43*(1), 52–61.

Other articles worth reading include:

- Clay, C., Ellis, M. A., Amodeo, M., Fassler, I., & Griffin, M. L. (2003). Recruiting a community sample of African American subjects: The nuts and bolts of a successful effort. *Families in Society, 84*(3), 396–406.
- Napoles-Springer, A. M., Grumbach, K., Alexander, M., Moreno-John, G., Forte, D., Rangel-Lugo, M., & Perez-Stable, E. (2000). Clinical research with older African Americans and Latinos: Perspectives from the community. *Research on Aging, 22*(6), 668–691.

- Construct an ethnically diverse evaluation team so that all of the minority groups targeted for the study are represented.
- Be aware that the terms *race* and *ethnicity* are frequently confused. Hispanics, for instance, may identify their race as black. Persons who are biracial or bicultural are even more difficult to classify. You may want to ask individuals to identify themselves *culturally.*
- Allow the team to freely discuss and make recommendations for collecting data from targeted groups.

HOW ONE RESEARCH PROJECT MAXIMIZED PARTICIPATION BY AFRICAN AMERICANS

To reduce the problem of diabetes among African Americans by obtaining data on its behavioral, social, and environmental correlates, the Centers for Disease Control and Prevention awarded a contract to the Research Triangle Institute to conduct a community survey in Wake County, North Carolina.

One of the first things the research team did was to hire an African American health educator who was well known in the community. Another step involved the creation of a community advisory board (CAB) to educate the general public about the goals and objectives of the project and to increase the likelihood of achieving a high response rate. To identify appropriate individuals for the CAB, the local African American ministerial association, the general and African American medical associations, the health department, the media, and various organizations with a stake in diabetes care were contacted. From these interviews names of other persons were solicited, and persons whose names appeared three or more times were

---

- Examine tests and measurements being proposed for use in terms of their cultural bias and sensitivity. Attempt to choose those for which there is evidence of cross-cultural validity.
- Pilot test all procedures and information being presented about the project with a group of clients representing those to be contacted.
- Train interviewers with techniques on how to encourage clients to participate without coercing them.
- Require interviewers to role-play and practice interviewing with persons of a different race or ethnic group.
- Listen for any client concerns once the data collection phase begins.
- Be open to more than one interpretation of the data, and involve an ethnically diverse team in reviewing the findings. Abramowitz and Murray (1983) found that ethnic minority and white researchers examining the same data usually come up with conclusions drawn along ethnic lines.
- Realize that many normative samples needed for comparison will be composed primarily of the test scores of European Americans.

Box 14.4 provides a useful case example for improving the participation of minorities. Additionally, Hatchett et al. (2000) offer these suggestions:

- Offer a monetary incentive
- Visit African American community centers so as to allow word-of-mouth information sharing to increase awareness of the study
- Employ lay workers (people from the community) to advise and collect data.

In sum, evaluators should consider, at each step of the evaluation process, how their own cultural perspectives could affect the collection and interpretation

invited to serve. Each meeting of the CAB included education on diabetes and its management.

The CAB "continuously and diligently" reminded the research team of the importance of giving back to the community. Along this line, the project hired local members of the community to serve as survey staff and were employed for child care activities associated with the medical exam. In order to "give back," the project contacted participants who obtained non-normal results from the screenings along with a list of resources for those who needed medical care.

The community advisory board developed a promotional brochure and, to help establish its legitimacy, 25 CAB members agreed to have their names listed on the back of the brochure. The board also represented the project on local call-in talk shows and local television.

The project was able to screen 1,884 households or 89 percent of those contacted. Of all eligible black respondents, 81 percent completed the household exam, and 80 percent completed the long medical exam. A higher response rate was obtained for African Americans than for whites. The research team was particularly encouraged by the response rates, because one of the CAB members had reported that she had heard initially from some of her fellow community members that the project had been designed by the government to spread AIDS through the African American community.

Source: Burrus, B. B., Liburd, L. C., & Burroughs, A. (1998). Maximizing participation by Black Americans in population based diabetes research: The Project DIRECT pilot experience. *Journal of Community Health, 23*(1), 15–27.

of data from those who may come from different cultures. When necessary, evaluators should seek assistance from lay persons or professionals who reside in the minority community or who are familiar with the targeted population.

Questions for Class Discussion

1. Brainstorm ways that treatment fidelity could be compromised in a program with loose management.
2. From the class's knowledge of local agencies, discuss political pressures that might surface and influence (either positively or negatively) any evaluation effort in selected agencies.
3. Discuss ways in which the political pressures identified in question 2 might be neutralized or negated.
4. Is it possible to conceive of a situation in which program evaluation would *not* be threatening? Think about the characteristics of a program and its staff that would completely welcome and embrace evaluation activities.
5. Discuss the most common reactions to being evaluated and what an evaluator could do to make evaluation efforts less threatening.
6. Is program drift always bad? Could it serve to improve an intervention? From an evaluation perspective, is it always problematic?

Mini-Projects: Experiencing Evaluation Firsthand

1. Envision a scenario where an agency asks you to conduct a program evaluation. Prepare a contract that could result from the negotiations. Provide as many details as possible.
2. Interview a small sample of staff in the agency where you work, volunteer, or intern and try to discover whether they are or would be threatened by an evaluation of their work. Prepare a set of five to ten questions you would like to use in your interview, and discuss these with your instructor.
3. Read one of the articles found in the *Gerontologist* (see Box 14.3) and summarize your findings in a two-page paper.

References and Resources

Abramowitz, S. I., & Murray, J. (1983). Race effects in psychotherapy. In J. Murray & P. R. Abramson (Eds.), *Bias in psychotherapy* (pp. 215–255). New York: Praeger.

Armstrong, T. D., Crum, L. D., Rieger, R. H., Bennett, T. A., & Edwards, L. J. (1999). *Journal of Applied Social Psychology, 29*(3), 552–574.

Bauman, L. J., Stein, R. E. K., & Ireys, H. T. (1991). Reinventing fidelity: The transfer of social technology among settings. *American Journal of Community Psychology, 19*(4), 619–639.

Brown, D. R., & Topcu, M. (2003). Willingness to participate in clinical treatment research among older African Americans and Whites. *Gerontologist, 43*(1), 62–72.

Burrus, B. B., Liburd, L. C., & Burroughs, A. (1998). Maximizing participation by Black Americans in population based diabetes research: The Project DIRECT pilot experience. *Journal of Community Health, 23*(1), 15–27.

Chelimsky, E. (1987). What have we learned about the politics of program evaluation? *Evaluation Practice, 8*(1), 5–21.

Chen, H. (1990). *Theory-driven evaluations*. Thousand Oaks, CA: Sage.

Clay, C., Ellis, M. A., Amodeo, M., Fassler, I., & Griffin, M. L. (2003). Recruiting a community sample of African American subjects: The nuts and bolts of a successful effort. *Families in Society, 84*(3), 396–406.

Coffee, J. N. (1989). Advice for the evaluated. *Evaluation and the federal decision maker*. New Directions for Program Evaluation, No. 41. San Francisco: Jossey-Bass.

Cronbach, L. J., Ambron, S. R., Dornbusch, S. M., Hess, R. D., Hornik, R. C., Phillips, D. C., Walker, D. F., & Weiner, S. S. (1980). *Toward reform of program evaluation*. San Francisco: Jossey-Bass.

Foster, S. L., & Martinez, C. R. (1995). Ethnicity: Conceptual and methodological issues in child clinical research. *Journal of Clinical Child Psychology, 24*(2), 214–226.

Gil, E. F., & Bob, S. (1999). Culturally competent research: An ethical perspective. *Clinical Psychology Review, 19*(1), 45–55.

Guthrie, P. R. (1992). *The effects of proactive crisis planning services with and without peer support on the adjustment of severely mentally ill consumers: One year comparisons*. Unpublished doctoral dissertation, University of Kentucky.

Hasemann, D. M. (1994). *The effects of proactive crisis planning and peer support on arrests and hospitalizations of severely mentally ill adults.* Unpublished master's thesis, University of Kentucky.

Hatchett, B. F., Holmes, K., Duran, D. A., & Davis, C. (2000). African Americans and research participation: The recruitment process. *Journal of Black Studies, 30*(5), 664–675.

Hauck, F. R., Herman, S. M., Donovan, M., Iyasu, S., Moore, C. M., Donoghue, E., Kirschner, R. H., & Willinger, M. (2003). Sleep environment and the risk of sudden infant death syndrome in an urban population: The Chicago infant mortality study. *Pediatrics, 111*(5), 1207–1214 Suppl. S. (May).

House, E. R. (1986). Internal evaluation. *Evaluation Practice, 7*(1), 63–64.

Kennedy, M. M. (1983). The role of the in-house evaluator. *Evaluation Review, 7*(4), 519–541.

Krejcie, R. V., & Morgan, D .W. (1970). Determining sample size for research activities. *Educational and Psychological Measurement, 30*, 607–610.

Lipsey, M. W., Crosse, S., Dunkle, J., Pollard, J. U., & Stobart, G. (1985). Evaluation: The state of the art and the sorry state of the science. In D. S. Cordray (Ed.), *Utilizing prior research in evaluation planning* (pp. 7–28). San Francisco: Jossey-Bass.

Malgady, R. G. (1996). The question of cultural bias in assessment and diagnosis of ethnic minority clients: Let's reject the null hypothesis. *Professional Psychology, Research and Practice, 27*, 73–77.

McGrew, J. H., Bond, G. R., Dietzen, L., & Salyers, M. (1994). Measuring the fidelity of implementation of a mental health program model. *Journal of Consulting and Clinical Psychology, 62*(4), 670–678.

Miller, W. R., & Willoughby, K. V. (1997). Designing effective alcohol treatment systems for rural populations: Cross-cultural perspectives. In *Bringing excellence to substance abuse services in rural and frontier America* (Technical Assistance Publication Series, Vol. 20, pp. 83–92). Rockville, MD: Center for Substance Abuse Treatment.

Moncher, F. J., & Prinz, R. J. (1991). Treatment fidelity in outcome studies. *Clinical Psychology Review, 11*, 247–266.

Mowbray, C. T., Holter, M. C., Teague, G. B., & Bybee, D. (2003). Fidelity criteria: Development, measurement, and validation. *American Journal of Evaluation, 24*(3), 315–339.

Muscatello, D. B. (1989). Evaluation and the management process. *Evaluation Practice, 10*(3), 12–17.

Rogler, L. H. (1993). Culturally sensitizing psychiatric diagnosis: A framework for research. *Journal of Nervous and Mental Disease, 181*, 401–408.

Rubin, A. (1997). The family preservation evaluation from hell: Implications for program evaluation fidelity. *Children and Youth Services Review, 19*, 77–99.

Stufflebeam, D. L. (2000). Lessons in contracting for evaluations. *American Journal of Evaluation, 21* (3), 293–314.

Thompson, E. E., Neighbors, H. W., Munday, C., & Jackson, J. S. (1996). Recruitment and retention of African-American patients for clinical research: An exploration of response rates in an urban psychiatric hospital. *Journal of Consulting and Clinical Psychology, 64*(5), 861–867.

Thompson, R. J. (1989). Evaluator as power broker: Issues in the Maghreb. *International innovations in evaluation methodology* (New Directions for Program Evaluation). San Francisco: Jossey-Bass.

Wodarski, J. S., Feldman, R. A., & Pedi, S. J. (1974). Objective measurement of the independent variable: A neglected aspect in community-based research. *Journal of Abnormal Child Psychology, 2*, 239–244.

15

C H A P T E R

WRITING EVALUATION PROPOSALS, REPORTS, AND JOURNAL ARTICLES

An evaluation proposal is a written outline of a thoughtful and planned course of research. This description communicates the author's knowledge of the subject, intent, and ideas about how the question or topic should be explored. The term *proposal* suggests a tentativeness, a plan that might be modified or revised as needed. Even well-prepared and knowledgeable evaluators often encounter problems during the data collection that cause the project to deviate from what was originally proposed.

For instance, the evaluator may find several months into the project that the study sponsors were not specific enough in what they wanted. Unfortunately, the "true" purpose of the evaluation may only become clear to them only after they discover that the evaluator isn't going about the investigation as they had envisioned. Sometimes the evaluator simply misunderstands the correct emphasis—particularly if the evaluation has multiple goals—and may elevate a relatively minor goal and unknowingly discount one that is of major concern to an advisory board or the CEO.

Another factor that can change the proposal comes about because evaluation tools or procedures may not work as planned. Revisions may result because research participants have trouble completing an instrument or do not mail back their questionnaires. Then, too, there may be fewer actual clients (or fewer *cooperative* clients) in a particular group or program than the evaluator was led to believe. Many factors beyond the evaluator's immediate control impinge on the evaluation process and may result in modifications to the original proposal.

MAJOR CONTENT AREAS FOR EVALUATION REPORTS

BOX 15.1

1. Introduction
   a. Description of the problem
   b. Statement of the program and questions about it to be explored
   c. Purpose of the evaluation and rationale for it
2. Literature Review
   a. The context: theoretical/historical perspectives for understanding the program
   b. A survey of necessary and relevant literature
3. Methodology
   a. Evaluation design and data collection procedures
   b. Sampling design
   c. Description of subjects
   d. Description of instrumentation
   e. Procedures for analyzing the data
4. Results (Findings)
   a. Factual information presented (including tables, charts)
   b. Statistical and practical significance
5. Discussion
   a. Explanation of findings
   b. Application to agency, program or practice
   c. Limitations of the evaluation
6. References
7. Appendices

Fortunately, a well-developed proposal saves the evaluator time later on when he or she begins to write the evaluation report. Both the proposal and the report share many of the essential elements. (See Box 15.1.) These components are discussed next.

COMPONENTS OF THE EVALUATION PROPOSAL AND REPORT

Introduction

The purpose of the introduction is to describe why an evaluation is being planned (a proposal) or was conducted (the evaluation report). This is done by placing the program or problem within some context or frame of reference. For instance, Arnold et al. (1999) evaluated a statewide sex education program (Education Now and Babies Later) for middle school students, and this is how they explained the importance of the problem in their first paragraph:

> Although the birth rate for adolescents declined 8% between 1991 and 1995 (U.S. Department of Health and Human Services [HHS], 1997), adolescent pregnancy

> still looms as a social problem with a current annual national rate of 112 pregnancies per 1,000 female adolescents (Alan Guttmacher Institute, 1997). In Florida, the estimated number of pregnancies in 1994 for females ages 19 and younger was 52,639, with approximately 25% ending in abortion (Lopez, Westoff, Perrin, & Remmel, 1995). (pp. 10–11)

Right away, the reader gets a sense of the magnitude of the problem of teen pregnancy—particularly within Florida—and can understand why the authors were interested in examining the effects of an abstinence-based program designed to prevent teenage pregnancy.

In another example, the author leads off by discussing a problem for which a particular program was designed. In this case, the program is a group intervention for middle school youths with behavior problems (Dupper, 1998):

> Discipline is consistently ranked at or near the top of concerns facing educators today. A majority of teachers, in a recent survey, stated that student behavior had gotten worse during the past 5 years and more than one-third stated that they lose 2 hours or more of teaching time per week as a result of discipline problems (American Federation of Teachers, 1996). In response to these discipline problems, an increasing number of school districts are implementing zero tolerance discipline policies and practices (Brendtro & Long, 1995). A recent national survey, conducted by the National School Boards Association, found that suspension was the most frequent school response to student discipline problems (Amundson, 1993). The increasing use of suspension and other zero tolerance discipline practices as a response to student misbehavior is unjustified, ineffective, and contributes to the school failure of many students. . . .
>
> There is a critical need to implement alternatives to suspension, particularly for youths in middle school who are beginning to exhibit behavior problems that place them at risk of being suspended. Rather than being punished, removed, or both from school for their misbehavior, misbehaving youths need to learn school survival skills. This article describes and reports on the effectiveness of a large-scale study of a school survival group for middle school youths who are beginning to exhibit behaviors that place them at risk of suspension. (pp. 354–355)

In this brief excerpt from the article's introduction, the reader becomes aware of the need for a program to keep at-risk youths from becoming disciplinary problems and potential school dropouts.

Once the backdrop or context has been staged, then the rationale for the study needs to be made clear. The introduction ought to state the purpose of the study or evaluation as explicitly as possible. Here is a good example from a dissertation:

> The purpose of this study was to identify critical predictors of suicidality in adult male and female survivors of child sexual abuse. More specifically, selected factors from a review of the CSA trauma literature, associated with various long term effects, were investigated for their influence on suicidal behaviors. . . . The factors chosen to be investigated were related to: (a) the degree of exposure to CSA, (b) the degree of childhood maltreatment, (c) the degree of social support present in childhood, (d) the amount of revictimization in adulthood, (e) the degree of current self dysfunction, (f) the degree of current dysphoria, and (g) the degree of current traumatic stress. (Hughes, 1999, p. 2)

If the purpose cannot be stated succinctly (as in the first sentence of this quotation), then it follows that the rest of the evaluation proposal or report could become muddled.

Review of the Literature

Once the parameters of the social problem or concern have been described and the purpose or rationale of the evaluation stated, the evaluator is ready to begin reviewing the pertinent literature. The purpose of the literature review is to summarize for the reader the major studies and applications of the intervention that have been reported by other researchers and evaluators.

For instance, this is what Meezan and O'Keefe (1998) wrote in an article evaluating the effectiveness of multifamily group therapy (MFGT):

> During the past several decades, various forms of MFGT have been found to be useful with a variety of populations, including schizophrenics (Anderson, 1983; McFarlane, Link, Dushay, Marchal, & Crilly, 1995), battered women and their children (Rhodes & Zelman, 1986), inner city families (McKay et al., 1995), multi-problem families (Aponte, Zarski, Bixenstene, & Cigbik, 1991), African-American families (Boyd-Franklin, 1993), and adopted adolescents and their families (Lang, 1993). Furthermore, this modality has been described as useful with populations experiencing a variety of problems, including attention deficit disorders (Arnold, Sheridan, & Estreicher, 1986), depression (Robinson, Powers, Cleveland, & Thyer, 1990), drug abuse (Wermuth & Scheidt, 1986), chronic illness (Goldmuntz, 1990), and eating disorders (Eliot, 1990). Unfortunately, few studies have empirically demonstrated the effectiveness of MFGT (McFarlane et al., 1995; McKay et al., 1995), and no studies have examined its effectiveness in treating abusive and neglectful families. (p. 331)

In this instance, the authors show that MFGT has been used in a wide variety of settings. Note that this review, like most good ones, is like a funnel. That is, the reader is informed of the many applications and uses that have been made of MFGT, and yet all of that is drawn to a very narrow focus in the last sentence.

Reviews of the literature may identify major theoretical explanations of the social problem or theoretical models underlying different approaches to remedy the problem. The theoretical models on which an intervention is based are important. For instance, drug prevention programs might be based on a temperance model, a disease model, or developmental, sociocultural, or lifestyle risk reduction models. If the intervention is based on a model or theoretical approach that has been discredited or for which there is little empirical support, this information needs to be communicated to the reader.

When the intervention has been evaluated previously, the literature review should summarize the major findings of those studies and lead the reader to understand the limitations of those studies and the gaps in our knowledge concerning that intervention. This does not mean that you have to "trash" prior studies, but it does mean that you have a responsibility to share your knowledge with the reader if you know that other efforts have been made to show that a particular intervention is effective.

There may be very logical reasons why prior research could not show the superiority of a treatment. For instance, maybe an inappropriate instrument was used, the methodology was flawed in some way, or there were problems with the fidelity of the implementation (e.g., the staff were not properly trained). These and other defects in prior studies help form the rationale for the current evaluation.

Gaps in the Literature   It is not uncommon for new or innovative programs to be launched that do not build on prior evaluative or research studies. Evaluators of trail-blazing programs will not have an abundance of literature to draw on. In this situation, the evaluator will need to think about similar programs and related literature. For example, if there were no evaluative studies conducted on programs designed to teach safety in sheltered workshops to persons with mental retardation, the evaluator would have to think more creatively. Maybe an analogous problem would be teaching young children to use safety belts or teaching high school students safety in their "shop" classes. Even though these educational efforts are not on the same (MR) population, they may be the most relevant that can be obtained.

Guidelines for Literature Reviews   Begin your literature review with a thorough search of a comprehensive database such as MedLine, ERIC, or PsycINFO. If you do not find many studies, make sure that you are not searching with too narrow of a descriptor (key word). Try different synonyms and key words. You might want to go back 5, 10, or even more years—depending on the number of articles available and your familiarity with the topic. When you feel that you have a firm grasp of the literature on your topic, check to determine whether the following points are covered:

- Make sure that the early major or classical studies in the field are included. You will tend to see these studies cited time and time again. They establish the first efforts to explore or evaluate the problem. Subsequent studies have built on what was learned in those early studies. Including these studies in your literature review shows that you have done a thorough job of searching and that you are knowledgeable about your topic.
- Do not, however, focus so much on the earlier studies that the review of literature is "light" on current studies. Although it is interesting to know about studies in 1964 or 1985, your review will be considered dated if you do not include those that have been published in the last 5 years.
- Make minimal use of direct quotations from other sources and, by all means, avoid incorporating long passages from original sources. The review of related literature should be a survey, an overview. It is not necessary to try to convince the reader that you really did consult 25 different studies by citing something from each of them.
- Try to provide a balanced presentation; acknowledge theories or explanations that could be relevant—even if you do not subscribe to them.
- Construct the literature review so that the reader can easily follow your organizational scheme and will come away knowing the breadth of the prior

research, the gaps in the literature, and the purpose of your proposal or research initiative. Distinguish for the reader the uniqueness of your study or describe how it is similar to others.

Methodology

The methods section of the paper describes in detail how the evaluation will be done (proposal) or how it was conducted (report). In this section the reader is furnished with enough information to allow another investigator or evaluator to replicate the study. Commonly, subsections and subheadings are used to differentiate the various components of the methodology section.

The first information often presented in the methodology section usually pertains to the subjects. Your readers will want to know how many there were, how they were selected, and something about their characteristics—such as the male/female composition, average age, and other demographic information. Here is an example from a study involving a sample of adolescents attending pregnancy prevention programs:

DEMOGRAPHICS OF THE SAMPLE

This study surveyed 105 teenagers who were participating in statewide, mainly community-based, pregnancy prevention programs during 1995. Of the 105 participants in the study, 41% were pregnant, parenting, or both; and 59% were non-pregnant/nonparenting. Twenty-two percent were male and 78% were female. The breakdown according to race was 19% Anglo, 37% African American, and 40% Hispanic; by religion, 39% Catholic, 36% Protestant, and 25% other. The family structure in which teens identified as having spent the most time while growing up was represented as follows: 47% lived with both parents (including stepparents), 27% with a single parent, and the remainder (26%), classified as other, commonly resided with other relatives such as grandparents or aunts or uncles. The age range of the sample was from 11 to 22 with a mean age of 16. Income tended to be low: 45% of the sample had household incomes less than $9,999. (Corcoran, Franklin, & Bennett, 1998, p. 307)

Although in explaining the purpose of your evaluation you may have already mentioned the evaluation design used, it is appropriate to go into more depth in the procedure subsection of the methodology. You may want to discuss how the random assignment or recruitment process was conducted. See, for example how this was treated in the evaluation of a self-help manual for the female partners of heavy drinkers in Australia:

CLIENTS

Thirty-eight clients were recruited by placing advertisements in Adelaide's daily newspaper as well as a suburban newspaper in Victoria, capital city of Melbourne. Despite advertising for male and female clients, all those who were eligible for treatment were female. To be eligible, clients had to have been living in frequent contact with the drinker (not necessarily cohabiting). Additionally, the drinker had to be outside formal treatment and resistant to any suggestion of change or involvement in treatment. Finally, the drinker had to score above the threshold for dependence on the family form of the Short Michigan Alcoholism Screening Test (SMAST). . . .

Each eligible client was assigned to one of three groups: (a) Counseling, (b) Self-Help, or (c) A no-treatment waiting list control condition. Clients were randomly allocated to these conditions except for the requirement that all Melbourne-based clients be allocated to self-help to minimize the number of interstate trips required. This method of allocation resulted in $n = 12$ clients assigned to Group 1, $n = 15$ to Group 2, and $n = 11$ to the waiting list Group 3. (Barber & Gilbertson, 1998, pp. 144–145)

Besides the subjects and the recruitment method used to obtain them, the methods section ought to describe the research design, the data collection procedures, and the instrumentation used. This is how the authors of one study testing aggression replacement training (ART) on adolescents in a runaway shelter described their design:

An interrupted time series design was used in this study. Data on adolescents' antisocial behavior were obtained for a 310-day period prior to the implementation of the ART program and then for a 209-day period after the program was started. This design used the 310 pretreatment daily rates of antisocial behavior as a control against which to compare the subsequent 209 daily rates obtained during implementation of the ART program (Cook and Campbell, 1979). (Nugent, Bruley, & Allen, 1999, p. 469)

This is how the same authors described their measurement procedures:

OUTCOME MEASURES

The dependent variables in this study were the male daily rate of antisocial behavior and the female daily rate of antisocial behavior. Antisocial behavior was defined as any behavior that would be considered to be: (a) a violation of rules and/or behavioral guidelines of the shelter, (b) a violation of legal or social norms, (c) a violation of another person's personal property, or (d) would be considered as aggression toward another person's physical or emotional well-being. . . .

The case files of each adolescent residing in the shelter during the 519-day period were examined by two case file reviewers: reviewers A and B. Each reviewer examined different case files. (Nugent, Bruley, & Allen, 1999, p. 470)

In a quasi-experimental study of closed process sessions with survivors of childhood sexual abuse, this is how the authors described the instruments they used:

OUTCOME MEASURES

This study's dependent or outcome measures were selected for a number of reasons: (a) They have conceptual linkages to the research on consequences of childhood sexual abuse; (b) other practitioners in this field have successfully used them in their intervention efficacy research; (c) their psychometric properties have been substantively documented; and (d) they are relatively brief, unobtrusive, and easy to use in typical direct practice settings. The interrelated constructs of depression and self-esteem were measured with the Beck Depression Inventory (BDI, a 21-item scale with a theoretical score range of 0 to 63), the Generalized Contentment Scale (GCS, 25 items, range = 0–100), and the Index of Self-Esteem (ISE, 25 items, range = 0–100). . . .

After they gave their informed consent to participate, each client completed the three measures; typically, this took less than 15 minutes. Participants were then assigned to a group if one was available, that is, if one was beginning to be formed; otherwise, they waited for the next group to be offered (waiting list). When clients went from the waiting list to a group, they again completed the 71-item questionnaire that included the BDI, GCS, and the ISE. This assessment served simultaneously as their waiting-list posttest and group work pretest measurement. . . . (Richter, Snider, & Gorey, 1997, pp. 59–60)

In the methodology section authors commonly discuss how they plan to or did analyze their data. Data analysis should be planned at the time that the evaluation design is considered. This step is done so that evaluation does not produce data that cannot be analyzed as desired. This is an excerpt from an article examining a new scale to measure homesickness and contentment:

> The collected data were analyzed for the scale's reliability and validity tests using SPSS for Windows (Norusis, 1993). The alpha coefficient method was used for the reliability test, a factorial analysis was used to examine factor structure, and the Pearson product-moment bivariate correlation analysis was used for discriminant and convergent construct validity.
>
> A confirmatory factor analysis, rather than exploratory analysis, was used because the purpose was to verify the presence of factors designed as components of each subscale (Abell, McDonnell, & Winters, 1992). The multiple group centroid analysis, which places factors through proposed groupings (Nunnally & Bernstein, 1994), was conducted to see if the subscales could be confirmed as distinct factors. This method is known as oblique multi-group factor analysis and is used with unities on the main diagonal and correlations for part-whole correlations. (Shin & Abell, 1999, pp. 49–50)

Sometimes the data analysis description is quite brief, as in this passage:

> Statistically significant differences between subjects assigned to treatment (school survival) or comparison (attention-only) groups on the basis of posttests and follow-up scores from the Nowicki-Strickland Locus of Control Scale were determined through the use of *t* tests for independent samples. A secondary data analysis using analysis of covariance (ANOVA) was performed to examine possible differences in results attributable to race or gender. (Dupper, 1998, p. 361)

Once your methodology section has described the research design, the subjects that were (or are to be) recruited, the data collection procedures, and how the data were (or are to be) analyzed, then it is time to address the results section.

Results (Findings)

The results section of an evaluation report contains what you have learned from collecting and analyzing your data. This is where you provide the answers to the questions that were previously posed. Just the facts are presented in this section—statistically significant differences, results of pre- and posttesting, and so on. The implications of the findings (what the findings may mean practically) are handled in the discussion section of your report. In the evaluation proposal, the results section will, of course, contain no actual findings but could briefly discuss anticipated findings.

The mass of data that accumulates while evaluating a program can present something of a problem to those writing evaluation reports because they can be struck by a compulsion to "tell all." Wanting the sponsor to feel that the contract amount was truly earned, evaluators may compile such an awesome assemblage of tables, charts, and dry, boring paragraphs that only the boldest of academics would attempt to wade through that portion of the report.

Chelimsky (1987) acknowledged this problem: "To its author all of the evaluation's findings seem important. It is painfully difficult to trim surgically what is not relevant, to condense, to rank, to decide not only which finding is most important, but which is most important that is also manipulable by policy" (p. 15). Cronbach et al. (1980) referred to the problem of evaluators wanting to document everything as "self-defeating thoroughness."

Decide which of your findings are the most important or have the greatest implications. Do not fall into the trap of trying to report every statistically significant correlation or t-test.

Keep in mind that the most helpful of evaluation findings will contain standards for comparison. These may come from other studies found in the literature, your control group, other agencies in the area, and so on. Those who read the evaluation report will be able to interpret your findings with much more ease if they can compare and contrast the success of the program you have evaluated with similar data from other programs. For example, 35 percent recidivism is a "good" rate compared to a similar program experiencing a 65 percent re-offense rate.

If you have a lot of data, you probably will want to make use of tables, because they allow you to present a great deal of information in a small amount of space. Refer to the *Publication Manual* of the American Psychological Association (2001) for information and examples as to how tables should be prepared. It is good form to show the number of persons in each group as well as the mean and standard deviation of scores. When percentages are used, always show the number of persons on which the percentages are based. Refer also to the APA manual for ways to present the results of your statistical tests (e.g., t-tests, one-way analysis of variance). In addition to the probabilities obtained, you should include the t or F value and the degrees of freedom. To make sure that you are not ascribing greater importance than you should to a statistically significant finding, Thyer (1991) recommends reporting the PVE, the proportion of variance explained in the dependent variable by the independent variable(s).

It is unrealistic to expect that busy people will take the time to read tens of pages of detailed tables or reproductions of computer printouts. It is the evaluator's responsibility to write for the audience who read the evaluation report and to select the most important findings to highlight for that audience. Most evaluation reports probably should not contain more than six tables. If the program being evaluated was complex and there are numerous important findings, the evaluator may want to prepare a technical report in addition to a smaller executive summary designed to be given to the group of decision makers and other interested members of the public. Because it is easy to produce too many cross-tabulations and statistical tests, it is tempting to force into the results section much more of this information than most readers care to consume.

Discussion

In the discussion section, clearly explain which of the hypotheses were supported and which were not. State what was found relative to the purpose of the evaluation. Go on to interpret your findings for the reader. The focus in this section is on the implications the findings suggest for the agency and those who run similar programs.

For example, Mitchell (1999) compared medication alone with medication and cognitive-behavioral group therapy for persons being treated for panic disorder. He found that those who participated in the therapy group in addition to receiving medication experienced a greater reduction in anxiety than those who received medication alone. In the discussion section of his article, Mitchell states:

> The results of this study have important implications for social work practice and the treatment of anxiety, particularly in a managed care setting. The findings of this study clearly reveal that comprehensive treatment for anxiety includes therapy as well as medication. This corroborates other research that suggests a positive interaction effect when therapy and medication are combined (Mavissakalian, 1990). (p. 197)

If your findings run counter to what was predicted or expected, provide an explanation for why the results turned out the way they did. If you discover there was some source of bias that was not obvious at the time the study was planned, then identify it. If the study was not implemented in a way consistent with the treatment manual or as the intervention had been originally proposed, point out the major limitations of the study. Almost every study has some limitations, and these ought to be reported toward the end of the report.

This is the way Mitchell (1999) discussed the limitations associated with his study:

> These findings are not without limitations, however. When considering the findings of this study, it is important to recall that this sample of convenience was composed of people with panic disorder who voluntarily sought and followed through with treatment. These voluntary participants who actively sought treatment may have been more debilitated and/or more responsive than other people with panic disorder in the general public. Therefore some of the reduction in anxiety could be a result of nontreatment factors such as regression to the mean. In addition, because the participants volunteered for the therapy group, self-selection bias may have occurred. As a result, the external validity and generalizability of these findings to other populations may be limited.
>
> Another limitation of this study relates to the irregular use of medication by the participants. For ethical and other reasons, the study was unable to monitor and enforce compliance with the medication regimen. Participants were clearly advised how and when to take their medication, but it is unclear how many actually did comply with those recommendations. For greater validity, the study needs to be replicated with more rigorous controls. (Mitchell, 1999, pp. 197–198)

Some professional journals may require a separate section they call "Conclusion." Whether you use a separate conclusion section or place your concluding thoughts in the discussion section is a matter of individual taste or a journal's style. It is important, however, that you have conclusions. Did the program perform as it was designed? Should the program be continued? Are clients being helped? The answers to such questions as these make the evaluation relevant and interesting to those who read your evaluation report.

When discussing the benefits of a new program or intervention, do not become too exuberant and make claims that go beyond your findings. It is helpful to remember that evaluations rely on convenience samples of clients from a single agency and that it is rarely possible to generalize to the larger population of all clients with the same problem. For example, a stress reduction program that worked for long-distance truck drivers in Canada may not reduce stress in a sample of truck drivers in New York City. You are allowed to speculate, however. It is reasonable to assume that the stress reduction program designed for Canadian truck drivers *may* work for truck drivers in other *rural* areas.

References

If you cite studies in your evaluation report (and you probably should if you have done even a cursory review of the literature), then you owe it to your readers to provide a bibliography or a listing of these references. We find the APA style (the one used in this book) to be convenient, and it is widely used in professional journals. Insert the last name of the author and the year of the publication in the correct place in your report, and then list the full citation at the end of the document. The APA style does not use footnotes at the bottom of the page, and there is no danger of getting your notes in the wrong sequence or out of order, because the references are arranged alphabetically.

Appendices

Appendices are usually found in long evaluation reports and typically include such items as a copy of instruments that were employed during the course of the evaluation, a sample copy of the instructions that were read or given to the subjects, cover letters that went out to participants, and perhaps bulky tables that you feel are important to include but too lengthy to place in the results section. It is not always necessary to have an appendix.

MISTAKES TO AVOID IN PLANNING AND WRITING EVALUATION REPORTS

The following section describes several pitfalls to avoid when writing an evaluation report. Common mistakes are ignoring the fact that samples were not random, equivalent, or representative. Others include overgeneralizing, not defining concepts well, using instruments with poor reliability or validity, not recognizing major sources of bias, profound limitations, and use of inappropriate statistical tests. These are all problems that you should be able to recognize and attempt to avoid. However, just to make sure that your evaluation report does not contain any of these or other equally dreadful flaws, we discuss below some of the many ways an evaluator can go astray when writing proposals and reports.

Misunderstanding the Purpose of the Literature Review

One student who was assigned to critique an evaluation report wrote, "Although I did not verify the articles reported in the literature review section, I assume that they, as conscientious authors, left no stone unturned." The purpose of the literature review is to familiarize the reader with what is known about the problem under investigation and the intervention that has been applied. The literature review should provide the reader with enough information to understand the intervention, the theoretical model on which it was based, the ways these interventions have been evaluated in the past, and with what results. Normally, it is not your job to verify the existence of articles cited in the literature. (Unless, of course, you suspect that someone is making them up.)

Sample Too Small

An example of a program that is likely to impact only a small number of clients is an intensive in-home family intervention program. Such programs are designed so that each caseworker has responsibility for two to four families at a time. If only one or two caseworkers are employed in a program like this and if the evaluation period runs for one year, the resulting sample of clients served by this program is going to be meager at best.

Attrition is always a potential threat with very small samples; it is more likely to occur the longer the time between pretest and posttest. Clients move out of the area, families break up, children run away from home, and family members may be arrested or sent to prison, become hospitalized, or die. Even when former clients can be located, they may not agree to participate in the evaluation. Losing two or three clients from a small sample may still allow you to conclude something about the intervention—if it were clearly effective or clearly ineffective. Say, for instance, that 10 of 12 clients improved. However, imagine a scenario where 5 clients improved and 4 did not, and 3 clients cannot be located for the follow-up. Do you conclude that the program worked more times than not? How comfortable would you be in recommending that this program be expanded when 6 of 12 clients dropped out of the intervention?

In situations where the number of "graduates" is very small, it may be best *not* to present your report as a rigorous evaluation. If you are in a position to plan the evaluation effort, it would be better to conduct a formative evaluation at the end of the first year and a more thorough evaluation at such time when a sufficiently larger sample of families have been served.

In an intensive program like family preservation, another threat to the internal validity of the study would be the likelihood that these families were specially selected and not randomly assigned. Because only a small number of families can be served by this program, there is a greater probability that families who are believed to have the best chance of succeeding would be handpicked.

A small sample may also create problems when the evaluator assumes that clients entering a program at one time of the year (e.g., during the summer months) are representative of clients entering the program at other times during the year. If you think that the clientele varies by season or other predictable cycle (for example, requests for services at the end of the month might be different from those at the beginning of the month), your sample should not be restricted to clients entering or served during part of that cycle or season. This would result in an unrepresentative sample of the total clients served by the program.

Insufficient Information about Instruments

Students often think that a "good" evaluation is guaranteed if they are able to locate an already prepared instrument in the literature. The fact that an instrument has been photocopied or appears in print does not necessarily make it one that ought to be used in your evaluative study.

Occasionally, a student makes a statement in a paper to the effect that "two instruments were used to assess learning outcomes" but does not discuss who developed the instruments or for what purpose, whether the instruments are reliable, or if any studies have been done to show that they have validity. Neither is it sufficient to write, "This instrument has been researched for validity and reliability and proven to have both." The evaluator should provide sufficient information to enable the reader to determine that the instrument is psychometrically sound. An informed reader of an evaluation report will want to know about the instruments used. How many items did the instrument contain? How was it administered? How has the instrument been used in other studies?

Another mistake to avoid is taking selected items from an already prepared scale or instrument and combining these with several new items. The resulting scale or questionnaire may not have as much reliability or validity as the old scale or instrument. Any adjustment, revision, or substitution made to an already prepared scale has the potential for affecting its psychometric properties. The more extensive these changes, the greater the likelihood that the instrument's reliability and validity have been changed in some way. You will not know whether the change is for better or worse unless additional psychometric studies are conducted with the revised instrument. So, if you find a good instrument that you want to use, do not modify it unless it is absolutely necessary to make changes to fit a different population or age group.

Failure to Use a Comparison Group

Many individuals seem to not understand the value of or dislike the concept of control groups. We suspect this is because they believe that there is something unethical about their use. What they often do not realize is that control and comparison groups can be constructed without denying clients services. In many instances, it is impossible to make sense of evaluative data without a comparison. Two brief examples demonstrate the importance of comparison groups. A former student asked us to help interpret data he had prepared in conjunction with evaluating an inpatient mental health facility for emotionally disturbed adolescents. He was able to show that 75 percent did not return to the facility. We asked him if he knew what recidivism rates were reported in similar facilities in the area or in the literature, but he knew of none .We then asked if there could be legitimate reasons why some of the adolescents might not return to the facility. In fact, there were some very good reasons. They were not eligible to return if they had committed a felony, been arrested and sent to a detention facility, moved out of state, or if their 18th birthday was within 3 months. These and other reasons could easily explain why a large proportion of the adolescents did not return to the facility—and none of the reasons had anything to do with the effectiveness of the treatment they received.

Another student was doing a survey of social workers' attitudes about panhandlers. He spent quite a bit of time writing and refining a questionnaire. He collected his data, wrote his report, and just before the semester was over, came to talk to his advisor about his project. He realized, too late to do anything about it, that while he knew what social workers' attitudes were within his sample, he could not conclude much because he had no comparison group. He did not know whether social workers were more or less empathic than other professionals or lay citizens toward panhandlers. If he had used a comparison group of non–social workers, the data from the social workers would have been more meaningful.

Presenting Individual Scores

It is the evaluator's job to condense, summarize, and otherwise make sense of all the data that have been collected. It is *not* necessary to inform the reader of the pretest and posttest scores of every participant in the study. Instead, show the *average* pretest score for the control and intervention groups and the *average* posttest score. You may want to talk about the range of scores, or the standard deviation, but very seldom would it be necessary to document each and every score. Generally, when this occurs in an evaluation report, the reader can presume the author did not know how to go about analyzing the data and is trying to make up for this by presenting the reader with bulk rather than a perceptive grasp of the data.

Lack of Specificity

It seems that some writers of evaluation reports believe that others have the ability to read their minds. We make this assumption when we read a statement like the following: "Due to the controversial nature of the topic, every precaution was taken to ensure the anonymity of the persons taking part in the study." However, the reader is entitled to know exactly what precautions were taken. Perhaps the writer meant that no names, addresses, or phone numbers were gathered. Were social security numbers used in order to match subjects at pretest and posttest? If so, does this protect anonymity? Did the evaluator create a coding system to protect anonymity? Does protection of anonymity mean that the names were cut off or marked out by a student assistant before the questionnaires were given to the researcher?

Overgeneralizing

To understand this mistake, imagine an evaluation of a drug and alcohol prevention program for elementary school students. A study was completed of 250 fifth and sixth graders in one rural school district. Assume that the students are more knowledgeable about the harmful effects of drugs and alcohol after the educational intervention. The evaluator concludes the program is a success, and "the findings indicate that school counselors across the United States should encourage school administrators to adopt and expand this programs to all grades in their elementary schools."

The problem with this statement is, first of all, that because the population of students involved in this study came from only one rural school district, the author is overgeneralizing. There is no way of knowing, for instance, if the results would have been the same if students came from urban or suburban areas or even from different rural areas. Are students living in rural Montana different from those living in rural Mississippi or rural Vermont? Because the evaluation was limited to students in only one small school district, that is the only geographical area for which the intervention is known to have worked. It may be that the unique blend of sociodemographic characteristics found in the population receiving the intervention makes it quite unlike other populations of "typical" fifth and sixth graders.

Because no statement was made about a control group, there is always the possibility that the increase in knowledge about drugs and alcohol came from greater coverage of this topic on television or other media. Perhaps it came about because someone in the community died of a drug overdose and this became a popular topic of conversation—with a result that parents and other adults had more honest and candid discussions about substance abuse. Maturation is another threat to the internal validity of this study depending on the time interval between pretest and posttest.

Even if the program were a success with fifth and sixth graders, there is no evidence that the same program would work with younger children (second, third, or fourth graders). So, a statement that the program ought to be expanded to all grades is unfounded. It is a belief or value statement, not a finding the evaluation can make. A sampling of students from around the state or from other school districts would help to establish that other fifth and sixth graders could benefit from the intervention. This sample could also serve as a comparison or control group against which the "success" of the students receiving the educational intervention could be gauged. The more settings that are found where the intervention works, the greater the evaluator's ability to generalize.

Lack of Consistency

Periodically, we come across a report or a manuscript in which the following mistake has been made: analysis is conducted with variables without a priori foundation in the literature review. This problem seems to occur most often when evaluators or investigators are hunting for something statistically significant to report. Evaluators may be tempted to test for differences by gender, race, income, educational level, and so on until they find what is regarded as something of importance. However, if differences by sex, race, and so forth were not important enough to be included in the literature review or in the hypotheses, then the examination of these differences in the results section is not logical. The converse is also true—the evaluation would be incomplete if the literature review and hypotheses were concerned with differences by sex, race, and so on, but the analysis failed to report these comparisons.

CHECKLIST FOR WRITING AND ASSESSING EVALUATION REPORTS

Using the outline that appeared earlier in this chapter, a checklist can be constructed for ensuring that all the essential elements are contained within an evaluation report (see Figure 15.1). This checklist can also be used to help you evaluate reports or articles you may be reading.

Be concerned with reasonableness in all areas. Do the hypotheses or questions raised seem reasonable? Do they appear to follow what is known about the problem and gaps in the literature? If control groups are used, do they seem to be appropriate groups for comparison? Is the sample large enough for the conclusions that arc drawn? Do thc findings logically follow from thc proccdurcs that were used? Are there any major sources of bias or limitations that have not been recognized? Schalock and Thornton (1988) suggested a "test" where a program description or evaluation report would be considered against whether it would make sense to a skeptical, willing, careful, but generally reasonable audience.

Reasonableness also applies to the length of the evaluation report. If you write a report that is too long, few people will read it. If the report is too short, important details may be omitted. Our advice is to write for *your audience*. If you think none of them will read an 80-page report, then condense. Journal articles typically run 16 to 20 pages and manage to crowd an awful lot of information into that format. Instead of guessing what your audience will digest, pilot test a draft copy on someone representative of your audience who would be cooperative enough to give you needed feedback.

Although we have dealt with the evaluation report section by section, realize that the report should make a harmonious whole. The initial question should lead to the literature being reviewed, which should be followed by a discussion of the ways the problem has been studied in the past. These methods have a direct bearing on the procedures used in the study and the way the data are analyzed. And the conclusions should relate to the initial question(s) being asked.

FIGURE 15.1 | CHECKLIST FOR WRITING AND ASSESSING EVALUATION REPORTS

1. Introduction
    Does the introduction provide a clear notion of:
    ❑   a. the problem?
    ❑   b. the program?
    ❑   c. the purpose of the evaluation?
    ❑   d. the rationale for the evaluation?
2. Literature Review
    Does the literature review provide:
    ❑   a. a relevant context for understanding prior programs and evaluation efforts
            of these programs?
    ❑   b. a thorough survey of historical and current literature?
3. Methodology
    Does the methodology section describe:
    ❑   a. an evaluation design?
    ❑   b. sampling procedures?
    ❑   c. subjects?
    ❑   d. procedures for data collection?
    ❑   e. instruments used?
4. Results
    Does the results section contain:
    ❑   a. data relative to the stated problem(s) or purpose of the evaluation questions?
    ❑   b. appropriate statistical tests?
5. Discussion
    Does the discussion section address:
    ❑   a. an explanation of the data?
    ❑   b. practical implications for the agency, program, or practice?
    ❑   c. limitations of the study?
6. References
    Does the report present all the references referred to in the document?
    ❑   a. references provided
7. Appendices
    Does the report contain copies of instruments, important cover letters, survey forms?
    ❑   a. appendices provided

Finally, when writing your report, do not forget to proofread it closely. In fact, you should probably read and revise the manuscript three or four different times to make sure it communicates as clearly as possible. Do not forget to use the spell-check feature on your computer.

THE UTILIZATION OF EVALUATION REPORTS

One of the most disappointing things that can happen to an evaluator is that the evaluation report, after weeks of hard work, is placed on a bookshelf or filed away to be seldom noticed or referred to again. The ultimate goal of an evaluation should be to help the program improve service delivery. However, if the report is too wordy or too technical, or if stakeholders do not understand it, the potential users of the evaluation are not likely to draw on it to enhance the program. As a result, a lot of time, money, and effort could be wasted. Whenever you are responsible for planning an evaluation or writing up the findings of one just concluded, think about issues of dissemination and utilization of the data by others. Make it as accessible as possible.

There are four main issues involved with increasing the chances that an evaluation report will be used:

1. Presenting the report in a manner that gets and holds the attention of readers and stakeholders
2. Incorporating the needs and concerns of the program staff and policy makers
3. Dealing with negative findings
4. Using the evaluation as a building process

Each of these will be discussed in turn.

Presenting the report in a way that holds stakeholder attention is an important step in communicating the findings of your evaluation. If the evaluation is too long and complicated, most stakeholders will not read it. Write at the level of your audience. If the report is intended for a citizen advisory board of mostly persons without doctoral degrees, then do not write in an academic, dissertation style.

Further, it is important to be complete in your report without including unnecessary information. You may want to provide an executive summary that summarizes the purpose, methods, and main findings. Including tables and graphs to display data; making verbal presentations of your results to key stakeholders; and providing your results in a one-page news brief in addition to the report may also be important.

Incorporating the questions and concerns of program staff and other key stakeholders will also help to ensure your findings will be read, if not used. Be sure to address the specific questions of interest. It is sometimes easy to forget the original questions in trying to present all of the information on hand.

Sometimes evaluations produce unexpected findings or results contrary to what the stakeholders want to believe. Evaluations may show negative findings—that a program is not working or that clients are not better off. Negative or unexpected results are one reason a process evaluation is often useful in understanding the outcome findings. Also, it may be a good idea to present some positive information about the program along with the negative findings in order to keep the report from seeming too strongly critical and stakeholders from completely rejecting the report.

Finally, it is important to remember that it can take years to implement and refine a new program. Changing a program overnight is almost impossible. So, if you expect the evaluation that you conducted to have a profound impact right away, you are probably going to be disappointed. In addition, program change often has budget implications. Programs are often committed to a budget a year or two in advance. Thus, making major program changes would not be possible until the funding becomes available. Another way to view program change is as a gradual building process. Your evaluation may bring about some incremental changes—the first step toward making larger ones. What may be very useful to do is to identify the important lessons that have been learned. What would those who are considering developing or implementing a program benefit from knowing?

WRITING FOR PROFESSIONAL PUBLICATION

Although many human services professionals may never think of themselves as authors, many good evaluation reports have the potential to be slightly revised and submitted to a professional social work journal. Because of sensitive issues around ownership of the data and whether or not it may be proprietary, many, if not most, evaluation reports never get circulated to a wider audience. As a result, professionals outside of a particular agency or community may never learn of findings that could be applied in their geographical areas or agencies. Consequently, the transfer of technology is impeded, and much time is wasted in "reinventing the wheel." However, issues about publishing the findings and who would be the author and so forth can often be negotiated before the evaluation is contracted or finally assigned. Thus, these are not insurmountable barriers to writing articles for a professional audience.

Not only is writing for professional journals beneficial in terms of one's career, but the *Code of Ethics* also emphasizes its importance:

> 5.01(d) Social workers should contribute to the knowledge base of social work and share with colleagues their knowledge related to practice, research, and ethics. Social workers should seek to contribute to the profession's literature and to share their knowledge at professional meetings and conferences.

The main thing to keep in mind when writing a journal article is that publication of the paper is extremely competitive. Busy reviewers may not have much patience with papers containing misspelled words, and grammatical errors, or with papers that do not conform to the journal's citation and reference style requirements. Therefore, do not jeopardize your chances of getting a paper published by submitting one that has not been carefully proofread on several occasions. Also, make sure the topic is a "good fit" for the journal. Study the journal that you are considering; become familiar with it. Notice the length of the articles it normally publishes, the number of references in an "average" article, and the writing style. Write in simple declarative sentences. Make sure that the length of your manuscript is not longer than what the journal says that it accepts. Squeeze out all excessive verbiage. Thyer (2002) has prepared a useful article that directs interested persons in how to prepare a social work outcome study for publication.

Check the journal's instructions to authors to ensure that your manuscript would be of the type of interest to the journal. For instance, this is how *Research on Social Work Practice* defines its interest:

> *Research on Social Work Practice* is a disciplinary journal devoted to the publication of empirical research concerning the assessment methods and outcomes of social work practice. Social work practice is broadly interpreted to refer to the application of intentionally designed social work intervention programs to problems of societal or interpersonal importance. Interventions include behavior analysis and therapy; psychotherapy or counseling with individuals; case management; education; supervision; practice involving couples, families, or small groups; advocacy; community practice; organizational management; and the evaluation of social policies.

The journal will serve as an outlet for the publication of:

1. Original reports of evidence-based evaluation studies on the outcomes of social work practice.
2. Original reports of empirical studies on the development and validation of social work assessment methods.
3. Original evidence-based reviews of the practice-research literature that convey direct applications (not simply implications) to social work practice. The two types of review articles considered for publication are:
   A. reviews of the evidence-based status of a particular psychosocial intervention.
   B. reviews of evidence-based interventions applicable to a particular psychosocial problem.

Journals want original manuscripts that are clearly written, timely, appropriate to the journal's interest, of the right length, and in the correct style. Journal reviewers must decide whether your manuscript makes a contribution to the literature, but before they can get to that point, you have to present them with a product that is engaging and interesting to read. It is considered unethical to send your manuscript to more than one journal at a time. Because the review can take anywhere from 3 to 10 months, make sure that you have polished and revised and found all of the blemishes in your manuscript before putting it in the mail. Then, while you are waiting to hear something, start on a second manuscript.

If your paper is rejected by the first journal, do not take the criticism personally. Reviews are generally anonymous—most journals do not reveal who read your manuscript. Similarly, your identity will not be divulged to the reviewers. Reviewers do not always understand what you were trying to accomplish and may jump to conclusions about your data set or analysis. Weigh very carefully the accompanying feedback. Make the changes that make the most sense to you, and then resubmit it.

You can consult Mendelsohn's (1997) An *Author's Guide to Social Work Journals* to get ideas about other journals that might be interested in your manuscript. Thyer and Myers's (2003) article will give you information about what you can expect from a selection of journals in terms of the length of time between submitting a manuscript and receiving a decision letter, perceived quality of the review process, helpfulness of the reviewers' comments, and so forth.

After about three rejections, you might want to either significantly rewrite the paper or give up on it altogether. Consulting a colleague who has had more experience with publishing than you have can often be very useful.

Questions For Class Discussion

1. Which parts of the evaluation report appear to be the most difficult and the easiest to write? Give reasons for your beliefs.
2. Discuss the kinds of mistakes that you might easily make when writing an evaluation report.
3. How is writing a term paper different from writing an evaluation report? In what ways are they similar?

4. What would be more difficult to write, an evaluation report or a journal article? Why?
5. What section of an evaluation proposal would be most difficult to write?
6. Brainstorm all the ways that writing an evaluation proposal could differ from writing up the results of an evaluative study.

Mini-Projects: Experiencing Evaluation Firsthand

1. Show all that you have learned about program evaluation by drafting a small evaluation report of a fictitious program. Build in all manner of problems (e.g., threats to the internal validity). Exchange your "evaluation" with someone else in your class. Then, compare notes regarding the number of problems that were detected and what could have been done to strengthen the "evaluation."
2. Locate an actual program evaluation from an agency (or find a journal article reporting on one). Critique the report or article using the guidelines suggested in this chapter. Write a brief paper summarizing your points.

References and Resources

American Psychological Association. (2001). *Publication manual* (5th ed.). Washington, DC: Author.

Arnold, E. M., Smith, T. E., Harrison, D. F., & Springer, D. W. (1999). The effects of an abstinence-based sex education program on middle school students' knowledge and beliefs. *Research on Social Work Practice, 9*(1), 10–24.

Barber, J. G., & Gilbertson, R. (1998). Evaluation of a self-help manual for the female partners of heavy drinkers. *Research on Social Work Practice, 8*(2), 141–151.

Beebe, L. (1993). *Professional writing for the human services*. Washington, DC: NASW Press.

Chelimsky, E. (1987). What have we learned about the politics of program evaluation? *Evaluation Practice, 8*(1), 5–21.

Corcoran, J., Franklin, C., & Bennett, P. (1998). The use of the social support behaviors scale with adolescents. *Research on Social Work Practice, 8*(3), 302–314.

Cronbach, L. J., Ambron, S. R., Dornbusch, S. M., Hess, R. D., Hornik, R. C., Phillips, D. C., Walker, D. F., & Weiner, S. S. (1980).

Toward reform of program evaluation. San Francisco: Jossey-Bass.

Dupper, D. R. (1998). An alternative to suspension for middle school youths with behavior problems: Findings from a "school survival" group. *Research on Social Work Practice, 8*(3), 354–366.

Henson, K. T. (1995). *The art of writing for publication.* Needham Heights, MA: Allyn & Bacon.

Hughes, B. M. (1999). The prediction of suicidal behaviors in adults who were sexually abused as children. Doctoral dissertation, University of Kentucky.

Meezan, W., & O'Keefe, M. (1998). Evaluating the effectiveness of multifamily group therapy in child abuse and neglect. *Research on Social Work Practice, 8*(3), 330–353.

Mendelsohn, H. (1997). *An author's guide to social work journals.* Silver Spring, MD: National Association of Social Workers.

Mitchell, C. G. (1999). Treating anxiety in a managed care setting: A controlled comparison of medication alone versus medication plus cognitive-behavioral group therapy.

Research on Social Work Practice, 9(2), 188–200.

National Association of Social Workers. (1999). *Code of Ethics*. Washington, DC: Author.

Nugent, W. R., Bruley, C., & Allen, P. (1999). The effects of aggression replacement training on male and female antisocial behavior in a runaway shelter. *Research on Social Work Practice, 9*(4), 466–482.

Richter, N. L., Snider, E., & Gorey, K. M. (1997). Group work intervention with female survivors of childhood sexual abuse. *Research on Social Work Practice, 7*(1), 53–69.

Schalock, R. L., & Thornton, C. V. D. (1988). *Program evaluation: A field guide for administrators*. New York: Plenum.

Shin, H., & Abell, N. (1999). The Homesickness and Contentment Scale: Developing a culturally sensitive measure of adjustment for Asians. *Research on Social Work Practice, 9*(1), 45–60.

Thyer, B. (1991). Guidelines for evaluating outcome studies on social work practice. *Research on Social Work Practice, 1*(1), 76–91.

Thyer, B. (2002). How to write up a social work outcome study for publication. *Journal of Social Work Research and Evaluation, 3*(2), 215–224.

Thyer, B. (1994). *Successful publishing in scholarly journals*. Thousand Oaks, CA: Sage.

Thyer, B. A., & Myers, L. L. (2003). An empirical evaluation of the editorial practices of social work journals. *Journal of Social Work Education, 39*(1), 125–140.

INDEX

accreditation standards, 147
action evaluation, 93
Adult-Adolescent Parenting
    Inventory (AAPI), 335–337
African Americans, studies
    involving, 33, 34, 387, 391
aggression replacement therapy
    (ART), 170, 400
Alzheimer's disease patients, as
    research subjects, 44
American Counseling Association's
    ethical mandate for evaluation, 16
American Evaluation Association,
    48, 87
American Medical Accreditation
    Program (AMAP), 120
American Psychological Association
    (APA), 7, 402
American Psychologist Committee
    on Professional Standards ethical
    mandate for evaluation, 16
American Social Science Association
    (ASSA), 27
anecdotism, 22, 25
Annie E. Casey Foundation, 65
anonymity, 39

audit trail, 106
*Author's Guide to Social Work
    Journals,* 413

behavioral outcomes, 292, 293
Belmont Report, 34
benefits, defining, 283
bivariate analysis, 348
Brief Adult Assessment Scale, 295
Bruno, Frank, 27
budgets, 6
Buros Institute of Mental
    Measurements, 307

case studies, 103
causal inference, 177, 178, 182
census data, 63, 64
Center for the Study and Prevention
    of Violence, 307
Certified Nursing Assistants
    (CNAs), 172
CES-D Scale, 245, 329–331
Child Abuse Potential (CAP)
    Inventory, 324–326
children, as research subjects, 43
chi-square, 354, 355, 356, 361

chi-square (*continued*)
  Pearson, 355, 356
clergy survey, 79
Client Satisfaction Inventory, 216
Client Satisfaction Questionnaire, 209,
  210, 211, 212, 239
client satisfaction studies, 207–230
  annotations about, 212
  ballot box approach to, 219
  cognitive dissonance in, 216
  determining sample size in, 222, 224
  and focus groups, 219, 221
  four *Rs* of (relevance, response,
    relationship, results), 207
  frequency distribution in, 344
  importance of, 207
  mailed survey, 220, 226
  online, 219
  open-ended questions in, 217, 218
  problems with, 209
  psychometrics in, 216
  qualitative, 221
  ratings in, 215, 217
  recent sampling of, 212, 213, 214
  recommendations for, 216–221
  response rates in, 220, 226
  selection bias in, 216
client utilization survey, 80
Clinical Anxiety Scale, 295, 319,
  327–329, 359, 360, 361
clinical significance, 351, 359
Commission on the Accreditation of
  Rehabilitation Facilities, 147
community
  evaluation colliding with, 49
  readiness of, 80
  survey of, 79, 80
community advisory board (CAB), 391
comparison groups, 46, 47, 406
*Comprehensive Accreditation Manual
  for Behavioral Health Care*, 208
Comte, Auguste, 26, 28
Conference on Charities, 27
confidence interval, 223
confidence level, 223, 224, 225
confidentiality, 38, 39, 64
consent
  informed, 37
  passive, 43
consent forms, 35, 36, 37, 38

continuity correction, 355, 356
continuous quality improvement, 153
control groups, 45
  in multiple time series design, 253
  in nonequivalent control group
    design, 248
  in quasi-experimental designs, 46
  randomly assigned, 46
convergent analysis, in needs assessment,
  72, 73
correlation, 357
correlation coefficient, 295
  Pearson, 349
  Spearman rank, 349
cost, as evaluative criterion, 274
cost analysis
  designs for, 274–289
  examples in the literature, 284
cost-benefit analysis, 281
  of drug courts, 285
  traditional, 284
cost-effectiveness analysis, 280, 285
cost-effectiveness designs, 274–289
  example of, 276
  point of view in, 279
  sensitivity analysis in, 279
  steps in, 277, 278, 279
culturally sensitive evaluation practice,
  386, 388

DARE, 3, 4, 184
data
  behavioral outcome, 293
  census, 63
  client utilization, 65, 66, 140
  coding of, 103, 105, 152
  drug and alcohol statistics, 64
  emic and etic codes for, 103
  expressed need, 65
  independent, 185, 186
  interval, 318
  longitudinal, 252
  management of, 102, 103, 104
  meaning units in, 102
  nominal, 316, 354
  normally distributed, 185
  ordinal, 317, 356
  patterns of use, 65
  in process evaluation, 126, 127, 128
  in qualitative evaluation, 98

rates-under-treatment, 65
ratio, 318
saturation point of, 101
secondary, 63, 66
by state, 64
template approach to, 104
time-saving strategies for, 103
triangulation of, 105
trivial, 99
when to stop collecting, 101
data analysis, 102, 339–370
  bivariate analysis, 348
  chi-square in, 354, 355, 356
  classification of clients by treatment
    outcome, 354
  clinical significance in, 351
  by computer, 340
  correlations in, 357
  cross-tabulation in, 355, 356
  data display in, 343
  descending array of scores in, 343
  descriptive statistics in, 355
  directional hypothesis in, 355
  distributions in, 346, 347
  frequency distributions in, 344
  F-test, 353
  mean in, 345
  measures of central tendency in, 345
  median in, 347
  mode in, 347
  multivariate analysis, 358
  negative case analysis, 106
  null hypothesis in, 355
  one-way analysis of variance
    (ANOVA), 353
  planning for, 401
  range in, 348
  software for, 102
  standard deviation in, 347
  statistical significance in, 351, 359
  t-test for independent samples, 351
  understanding trends in, 361
  univariate, 341
  using case studies in, 103
  using in reports, 364
  Web links for, 341
  window in, 363
degrees of freedom, 185, 402
Delphi technique, 68
dementia patients, as research subjects, 44

Deming, William, 151
Deming cycle, 156
Denver Community Health
  Questionnaire–Revised, 375
Department of Veterans Affairs, 146
determinism, 22, 23
Diagnostic and Statistical Manual of
  Mental Disorders (DSM), 7
discounting, 283
documents, 98, 100, 101, 144
drift, 377
driving under the influence (DUI)
  statistics, 361, 362
drug control programs, 14, 15
drug court programs, 119
  cost-benefit analysis of, 285
  mission statement, goals, and objectives
    of, 136, 137
  monitoring monthly report of, 132
  needs assessment for, 58, 59, 60

ecological fallacy, 66
Education Now and Babies Later, 395
Educational Testing Service, 307
efficiency, 275
empiricism, 22, 24
epidemiologic surveys, 72
ERIC, 308, 398
ethical dilemma, 47
ethical guidelines, 40, 47
  potential problems with, 44
ethics
  and political nature of evaluations, 378,
    379, 380
  responding to challenges of, 379, 380
  of SSRDs, 188
  in writing for professional
    publication, 412
ethnography, 98
evaluation
  action, 93
  adjusting perspective in, 19
  comparisons in, 12
  culturally sensitive, 386
  day-to-day pragmatic problems of, 385
  defined, 11
  formative, 116–123
  fourth-generation, 88
  guidelines for, in politically charged
    arenas, 383, 384, 385

evaluation (*continued*)
  importance of, 1
  IRB ramifications of, 41
  mixed methods in, 92
  motivations for, 13, 14
  objective stance in, 20
  overcoming subjective perspective
    on, 17
  participatory, 93
  philosophical assumptions of, 21, 22
  political nature of, 378
  pragmatic issues in, 371–393
  process, 124–153
  qualitative methods in, 87–115
  reasons for, 12
  single system (SS), 91
  slippage in, 386
  summary in, 342
  "threat" of, 381
  triangulation of methods in, 92
  using case focus in, 18
  writing proposal for, 394–415
Evaluation Guidebook, 126
evaluator
  contract for, 383
  external, 382
  independence of, 383
  internal, 381
evidence-based practice, 8
exemption certificate, 40
  no granting of, 42
experiment, defined, 266
experimental designs
  $A_1 B_1 A_2 B_2$ design, 183
  A-B-A design, 179
  A-B-A-B design, 183
  causal inference in, 177, 178, 182
  in child-to-child aggression situation,
    182, 183
  contamination in, 181
  in measuring safety belt use by children,
    180, 181
  multiple baseline design, 182
  at senior citizen center, 179, 180
  SSRDs in, 177
  for staff completing psychiatric civil
    commitment forms, 182
experimental removal designs, 178
exposure therapy and response
  prevention (ETRP), 266

external evaluator, 382
external validity, 184, 185, 371

F test, 353, 361
F value, 402
face sheet, 144
factor analysis, 303
Family Few game, 79
family goal recording, 201
Family Privacy Act, 43
feasibility studies, 54
field notes, 98
fieldwork, 98
Fisher's Exact Test, 355, 356
Florida Healthy Kids Program, 152
focus groups, 69
  and client satisfaction studies, 219, 221
  interviews involving, 100
focused qualitative evaluation (FQE),
  92, 94
formative evaluation, 116–123
  conducting, 118
  at disabled adult halfway house, 171
  forming ad hoc committee for, 121
  getting expert consultation for, 121
  of Goodwill Industries, 169, 170
  in HIV prevention, 122
  for immunization program, 122
  inferential statistics in, 171
  locating model standards for, 118
  in nursing home, 171, 172
  in overall evaluation picture, 124
  of performance measurement of health
    care, 120
  of runaway shelter, 170
  SSRDs in, 169
  of Strengthening Families Program
    (SFP), 117
  uses of, 122
frame of reference, 296
frequency distributions, 344, 345
front-end analyses, 54
funding, stable, 6

gatekeepers, 37, 96
Gerontologist, The, 389
Global Self-Esteem Inventory, 375
goal attainment scaling (GAS), 194–206
  advantages of, 203
  for autistic child, 195

compared with other instruments, 196
description of, 195
examples in the literature, 200
family goal recording in, 201
follow-up guide with, 195, 199, 202
for home health care clients, 196
illustration of, 198
mean scores by stage of treatment in, 203
problems with, 202
and program evaluation, 199
steps in, 196, 197, 198
T-score in, 203
variations of, 201
"good," denotations of, 19
Goodwill Industries evaluation, 169, 170
graphs, 187, 188
group research designs (GRDs), 231–273
  classic experimental, 258
  for effectiveness studies, 265
  for efficacy studies, 265
  eliminating alternative explanations
    in, 254
  experimental, 258
  general principles of, 236
  interrupted time series design, 251
  longitudinal data in, 252
  multiple time series design, 253
  nonequivalent control group
    design, 248
  nonrandom assignment in, 243
  O phase of, 236
  one-group posttest-only design, 237
  one-group pretest-posttest design, 244
  one-shot case study, 239
  outcomes measured in, 231
  O-X-O design, 246, 247, 248
  posttest-only control group design, 261
  posttest-only design with nonequivalent
    groups, 242
  pre-experimental, 237
  protection against alternative
    explanations in, 257
  quasi-experimental, 248
  Solomon four-group design, 263
  threats to internal validity of, 254,
    255, 256
  time series analysis, 254
  time series design, 251
  t-test, 257
  X phase of, 236

Head Start, 122
Health Belief Model, 122
Health Insurance Portability and
  Accountability Act (HIPAA), 39
hidden agendas, 378
HIV screening program in Delhi, 155
Holmesburg Prison study, 45
Hope Scale, 331–333

index, defined, 295
Index Medicus, 308
inferential statistics
  graphs of, 186
  for inpatient psychiatric bed use, 186
  O-X-O design for, 185
  parametric and nonparametric, 187
  pretest-posttest design, 185
  specialized methods of, 186
  SSRDs in, 185
  time series analysis in, 186
  t-test, 185
  type 1 and type 2 errors in, 186
information
  archival, 47
  biased, 57
  sources of, 57, 60, 119
informed consent, 37, 43
Inpatient Consumer Survey, 217
institutional review boards (IRBs), 40
  history of, 33
  ramifications for evaluation and
    research, 41
instruments
  constructing, 308
  difficulty of designing, 312, 313
  double-barreled questions for, 310
  for evaluating in-service training, 315
  evaluation, 291
  illustrations of, 323–338
  insufficient information about, 406
  Internet resources for, 307, 308
  objective, 291
  phrasing of, 313, 314
  poorly constructed questions for, 310
  publishers of, 306
  reliability of, 295
  sources of, 306
  standardized, 163
integrators, 122
internal consistency, 296

internal evaluators, 381
Internal Revenue Service (IRS), 64
internal validity, 371
International Classification of Diseases codes, 152
International Standards Organization (ISO) 9000, 148, 149
International Standards Organization (ISO) 14000, 149
Internet
  abstracting services on, 308
  in data analysis, 340
  instruments available on, 307, 308
  sample size calculators available on, 226
  searches on, 119
interview
  coding of, 105
  focus group, 100
  guide for, 100
  in-depth, 98, 100
  in process evaluation, 129
  questions for, 100
  transcription of, 98, 104

Joint Commission on Accreditation of Healthcare Organizations (JCAHO), 120, 147, 208
journal articles, writing, 394–415

Katz Adjustment Scale, 375
Kentucky, needs assessment for drug court program in, 58, 59, 60
key informants, 67, 80, 96
Kids Count Data Book, 65
Kruskal-Wallis Test, 349

leadership styles, 104, 107
Levene's Test for Equality of Variances, 351
likelihood ratio, 355, 356
Likert scale, 356, 388
literature review, 397, 398
  misunderstanding purpose of, 405

management information systems, 144, 145, 363
mandatory safety belt use laws (MUL), 176, 177, 178
Mann-Whitney U Test, 349

March of Dimes, change in mission of, 134
margin of error, 223, 224, 225
Maternal and Child Health Programs, 148
matrices, 107
Mayo-Portland Adaptability Inventory, 204
mean, 345
measurement
  of attitudes, 294
  of attitudes about work, 297
  of behavioral outcomes, 292
  deciding what to measure, 292
  European instruments for, 386
  importance of, 290
  instruments for, 291
  interval level of, 318
  of knowledge, 294
  levels of, 316, 319
  nominal level of, 316
  ordinal level of, 317
  ratio level of, 318
  tools and strategies for, 290–322
  true zero in, 319
Measures for Clinical Practice, 306
measures of central tendency, 345
Measures of Personality and Social Psychological Attitudes, 306
median, 347
Medicaid, 148
medical patients and records, privacy of, 39
Medicare, 147, 148
MedLine, 308, 398
member checking, 106
Mental Health Statistics Improvement Program, 216
Mental Measurements Yearbook, 307
mental status examinations, 164
mentally retarded people, as research subjects, 44
Michigan Alcoholism Screening Test (MAST), 165
Microsoft Excel spreadsheet program, 340
Minnesota Multiphasic Personality Inventory (MMPI), 163
mission statements, 133, 135
mode, 347

Mozart effect, 10
multifamily group therapy (MFGT)
    study, 397
multimethod approaches to needs
    assessment, 73, 74, 75
multisystemic therapy (MST), 275
multivariate analysis, 358
  discriminant, 358
  extraneous variables in, 359
  multiple regression, 358
  of variance, 358

N of valid cases, 355, 356
National Association of Drug Court
    Professionals, 119
National Association of Social Workers
    (NASW), 189
  code of ethics, 47, 48, 49
  ethical mandate for evaluation, 16
National Commission for the Protection
    of Human Subjects in Biomedical and
    Behavioral Research, 34
National Committee for Quality
    Assurance (NCQA), 120, 150
National Conference of Charities and
    Corrections (NCCC), 27
National Conference on Social
    Welfare, 27
National Conference on Social Work, 27
National Homecaring Council, 147
National Institute of Mental Health
    CES-D Scale, 245, 329–331
National Institute on Drug Abuse, 118
National Institutes of Health, 41
National League for Nursing, 147
National Research Act, 34
Nazi atrocities, 33, 34
need
  comparative, 56
  definitions of, 55
  documenting, 60
  expressed, 55, 65
  felt, 55
  normative, 55
needs assessments, 53–86
  community forums in, 67
  community leaders in, 82
  community readiness model for, 80
  convergence of data in, 75
  convergent analysis in, 72

defined, 53
Delphi technique for, 68
experience of doing, 83
focus group technique for, 69
illustration of, 77
impressionistic approaches to, 67
multimethod approaches to, 58, 59, 60,
    73, 74, 75, 83
need for, 54, 55
nominal group technique for, 68
planning, 57
practice sampler for, 76
probability sample in, 70
public hearings in, 67
questionnaire in, 74
random sampling in, 71
representativeness in, 71
sampling in, 72
selecting approach to, 62
SSRDs for, 166
steps in, 60, 61, 62
surveys in, 69, 79, 80
target sampling in, 70
thinking creatively about, 75
negative case analysis, 106
neonatal intensive care unit (NICU)
    study, 280
Nightingale, Florence, 293
nihilism, 22, 25
nominal group technique, 68
nonparametric statistical procedures,
    348, 349
nonprofit organizations, 64
nursing home patients' care study, 171, 172

observation
  on-site, 98
  participant, 98
  skilled, 100
  unbiased, 99
Office of Juvenile Justice and
    Delinquency Prevention, 118
one-way analysis of variance (ANOVA),
    349, 353
open-ended questions, 215
operational definitions, 20
operationalism, 22
outcomes, 358
  distal, 137, 138
  evaluation of, 232, 234

outcomes (*continued*)
  GRD measurements of, 231–273
  indicators of, 232, 233, 234
  measures of, 163, 305, 400
  proximal, 137, 138
*Outcomes Assessment in Clinical
  Practice,* 306
outliers, 97

parametric analysis, 185, 186
parsimony, 22, 24
participant observers, 98
participatory evaluation, 93
Partnership for a Drug-Free America, 15
Pearson chi-square, 355, 356
Pearson correlation coefficient, 349
peer debriefing, 105
peer review, 148
persistent concomitant variation, 178
philosophical assumptions, 21, 22
Physician's Current Procedural
  Terminology codes, 152
pilot test, 46
placebo effect, 45, 251
political nature of evaluation, 378, 383,
  384, 385
positivism, 22, 26
practitioners, ethical responsibilities of, 47
pragmatism, 22, 24
privacy
  of medical patients and records, 39
  of research subjects, 38
problem, defined, 15
Problem Solving Scale, 259
process evaluation, 124–153
  becoming program monitor in, 131
  data sources in, 127, 128
  form for, 151
  goals and purposes of, 124, 125
  hierarchy of goals, objectives, and
    activities in, 140
  instruments for, 129
  interviews in, 129
  learning objectives in, 134, 135
  outcomes in, 137, 138
  in overall evaluation picture, 124
  program description in, 125
  program logic model in, 140, 141
  program monitoring in, 130
  quality assurance in, 147

reading goal statements in, 134, 135
reading mission statements in, 133, 135
steps in, 128, 129
through program monitoring, 135
total quality management, 150
useful data in, 126
useful questions in, 127, 128
what should be monitored, 141
writing program objectives in, 138
Professional Standards Review
  Organizations (PSROs), 148
program
  activities of, 141
  atheoretical, 10
  defined, 5
  drift of, 377
  "good," characteristics of, 5, 9
  inputs of, 141
  theoretical model for, 8
  transfer of, 377
program evaluation
  ethical issues in, 33–52
  GAS and, 199
  GRDs commonly used in, 269
  introduction to, 1–32
  literature addressing political nature
    of, 380
program logic model, 140, 141
  for college safe sex program, 142
program monitoring, 130, 135
  for large national agency, 146
  management information systems,
    144, 145
  outside evaluators in, 145
  questions for, 145
  steps in, 131, 132, 133
prolonged engagement, 105
prompts, 172
proportion of variance (PVE), 361, 402
proposals, 394, 395
Psychological Abstracts, 308
psychotic patients, as research
  subjects, 44
PsycINFO, 398

QS 9000, 149
Qualitative Data Analysis (QDA)
  software, 102
qualitative evaluation
  advocacy and, 108

data collection in, 98
defined, 88
designing, 95
dissemination of report on, 108
empirical, 88
examples of, 108
focused (FQE), 92
gaining access to site for, 96
managing and organizing data in, 102
methods of, 94
mixed methods study of AIDS
  prevention among women in sex
  industry, 111
mixed methods study of home-based
  family treatment, 110
on-site feedback in, 96
participatory research in, 109
payback in, 96
phenomenological research in, 109
of program for seriously mentally ill
  people, 109
quality control in, 105
reciprocity in, 96
reflexivity in, 100
sampling in, 97
self-monitoring in, 100
and single system (SS) evaluation, 91
strengths and liabilities of, 89, 90
systematic, 88
units of analysis in, 95
when useful, 89
writing of, 106, 107
qualitative methods in
  evaluation, 87–115
quality assurance
 accountability in, 150
 aspects of, 154
 for HIV screening program in
  Delhi, 155
 in hospital setting, 173
 medical model of, 148
 SSRDs in, 173
 statewide, 152
 at United Way, 173, 174
quality control strategies, 105
Quality of Life Inventory, 375
questions
 attitude, 100
 behavior, 100
 culturally sensitive, 388

feelings, 100
 knowledge, 100

rapid assessment procedures (RAPs), 92
rapid ethnographic assessments
  (REAs), 92
rationalism, 22, 24
realism, 22, 23
recidivism, 292
referrals, 17, 143
reflexivity, 100
reliability, 295, 342
 alpha (reliability coefficient) in, 296
 demonstrating, 296
 first-effort analysis of, 298
 internal consistency and, 296
 inter-rater, 301
 interrelated with validity, 304
 of procedures, 300
 second-effort analysis of, 299
 of self-reports, 301
 split-half technique for, 298
 test–retest, 298
reliable change index, 360
replication, 184, 185
report
 appendices in, 404
 avoiding mistakes in, 404
 checklist for writing and assessing,
  409, 410
 components of, 395
 discussion section of, 403
 lack of consistency in, 409
 lack of specificity in, 407
 major content areas of, 395
 methodology section of, 399
 overgeneralizing in, 408
 presenting individual scores in, 407
 references in, 404
 results section of, 401
 sample too small for, 405
 use of statistics in, 364
 use of tables and graphs in, 365,
  366, 402
 utilization of, 410
 writing, 394–415
representativeness, 71
research
 beneficence in, 34
 compensation for, 44

research (*continued*)
  deception in, 44
  denial of treatment in, 45
  distinguished from evaluation, 11
  ethical, 34, 44
  expedited category of, 42
  full review of, 43
  importance of, 3
  IRB ramifications of, 41
  justice in, 34
  respect in, 34
  sources for, 7
  with special populations, 43
  types of, 2, 3, 4
  undue inducement in, 45
  use of control groups in, 45
research designs
  idiographic, 162
  interrupted time series, 162
  longitudinal, 46
  posttest, 245
  pretest, 244
  qualitative design, 95
  single case experimental, 162
  single system, 161–193
  time series model for, 46
Research on Social Work Practice, 412
research subjects
  children as, 34, 43
  compensation for, 44, 45
  confidentiality of, 38
  ethical guidelines for using, 34
  exemptions from federal protections, 40
  information given to, 37
  labeling of, 43
  mandated reporting involving, 38
  minorities as, 389
  no harm principle for, 38
  people of diminished capacity as, 44
  privacy of, 38
  right to self-determination by, 35
  volunteer, 34
Research Triangle Institute, 391
researcher, as instrument, 98
Rosenberg Self-Esteem Scale, 333–335
runaway shelter evaluation, 170

sampling
  convenience, 98, 222, 227
  demographics of, 399

deviant case, 97
  maximum variation, 97
  in needs assessment, 70, 71, 72
  random, 227
  sample size calculators available on
    Internet, 226
  sample too small, 405
  snowball, 97
  typical case, 97
scales
  alternative, 298
  defined, 295
  parallel, 298
  self-developed, 299, 300
scientific skepticism, 22, 25
service philosophy, 6
service tickets, 144, 145
sex education study, 395
shadow price, 283
shotgun approach, 367
single system research designs (SSRDs),
    161–193
  A design, 168
  A-B design, 168
  A-B-A design, 168
  A-B-A-C design, 168
  of adolescent pregnancy, 169
  assessing measures over time, 165
  B-A-B design, 168
  baseline data in, 167, 168
  coding system of, 167
  data points in, 168
  ethics of, 188
  in experimental designs, 177
  in external validity, 184
  formative evaluations as, 169
  graphs for, 187
  in inferential statistics, 185
  for needs assessments, 166
  notation and general principles of, 167
  prerequisites for, 162
  pretest data in, 168
  in quality assurance studies, 173
  selecting outcome measures for, 163
  summative evaluation designs, 175
  time series analysis in, 168
single system (SS) evaluation, qualitative
    methods and, 91
social desirability, 251, 311
social indicators, 65, 79, 300

social physics, 26
Social Science Citation Index, 309
Social Security Act, 148
Social Work Abstracts, 308
social workers, ethical responsibilities
  of, 47
Society for Social Work and
  Research, 87
socioeconomic status (SES), 387
Spearman rank correlation
  coefficient, 349
squared Eta, 361
squared multiple correlation
  coefficient, 361
squared Pearson correlation, 361
squared Phi coefficient, 361
staffing, 5
stakeholders, 56
  observation of, 100
  in process evaluation, 128
Statistical Analysis System (SAS), 340
Statistical Package for the Social Sciences
  (SPSS), 296, 340, 349, 350, 351,
  352, 353
statistical significance, 351
  myths about, 359
statistics
  lack of standardization and, 371
  low statistical power, 185
  Type I and Type II errors in, 365,
  367, 368
  using in reports, 364
Strengthening Families Program
  (SFP), 117
Stuart, Richard, 161
subscale, defined, 295
summative evaluation, 175
  A-B design for, 176
  B design for, 175
surveys
  epidemiologic, 72
  in needs assessment, 69, 79, 80
  reliability of, 299
Symptom Checklist-90 (SCL-90), 246,
  250, 375

temporal arrangement, 178
temporal sequencing, 93
Tennessee Self-Concept Scale, 259
test, defined, 295

Test Link, 307
Test Locator, 307
Test Reviews Online, 307
theoretical model, 8
time series analysis, 168, 186
time series design, 46
total quality management, 150
*Toward Reform of Program
  Evaluation,* 380
treatment fidelity, 371
  checklist for, 373
  examples of nightmare situations in,
  373, 374
  and program drift, 377
  and transfer of programs, 377
treatment manuals, 8
triangulation of data, 105
triangulation of methods, 92
t-test, 360, 361, 402
  for independent samples, 351, 352
  paired samples, 349, 360
  statistics produced by SPSS, 349,
  350, 352
Tuskegee Institute studies, 33, 34, 387
typologies, 107

United Way quality assurance study,
  173, 174
univariate analysis, 341
U.S. Department of Health and Human
  Services, 126
U.S. General Accounting Agency
  (GAO), 235
U.S. Office of Consumer Affairs, 208
U.S. Public Health Service, and Tuskegee
  Institute studies, 34
utilization review, 147, 148

valid, defined, 302
validity, 302
  concurrent, 303
  construct, 303
  content, 302
  criterion, 302
  external, 371
  face, 302
  factor analysis in, 303
  internal, 371
  interrelated with reliability, 304
  known-groups technique for, 303

validity (*continued*)
  lack of taxonomy for, 304
  predictive, 303
  of self-reports, 304
variables, 367
  dependent, 253
  extraneous, 359
  independent, 267
variance
  equality of, 185
  proportion of (PVE), 361, 402

W. K. Kellogg Foundation Web-based
  Evaluation Handbook, 140

White House Office of National Drug
  Control Policy, 15
Wilcoxon Matched Pairs Signed-Rank
  Test, 349
Wilcoxon Rank-Sum Test, 349
writing proposals, reports, and articles,
  394–415

Youth in Congregate Care (YCC), 92,
  104, 108
Youth Services Survey, 217
Youth Services Survey for
  Families, 217

TO THE OWNER OF THIS BOOK:

I hope that you have found *Program Evaluation: An Introduction*, Fourth Edition useful. So that this book can be improved in a future edition, would you take the time to complete this sheet and return it? Thank you.

School and address:_____

_____

Department:_____

Instructor's name:_____

1. What I like most about this book is:_____

_____

_____

2. What I like least about this book is:_____

_____

_____

3. My general reaction to this book is:_____

_____

_____

4. The name of the course in which I used this book is:_____

_____

5. Were all of the chapters of the book assigned for you to read?_____

   If not, which ones weren't?_____

6. In the space below, or on a separate sheet of paper, please write specific suggestions for improving this book and anything else you'd care to share about your experience in using this book.

_____

_____

BROOKS/COLE
CENGAGE Learning

BUSINESS REPLY MAIL
FIRST-CLASS MAIL   PERMIT NO. 34   BELMONT CA

POSTAGE WILL BE PAID BY ADDRESSEE

Attn: Alma Dea Michelena, Social Work

Brooks/Cole
10 Davis Drive
Belmont, CA 94002-3098

OPTIONAL:

Your name:_____ Date:_____

May we quote you, either in promotion for *Program Evaluation: An Introduction*, Fourth Edition, or in future publishing ventures?

Yes: _____   No: _____

Sincerely yours,

David Royse, Bruce A. Thyer, Deborah K. Padgett, and TK Logan